# 2300 DAYS OF HELL

# 2300 DAYS OF HELL
## THE TWO WITNESSES, JOSEPHS 7 YEARS OF PLENTY AND 7 YEARS OF FAMINE

JOSEPH F. DUMOND

Copyright © 2014 by Joseph F. Dumond.

| | | |
|---|---|---|
| Library of Congress Control Number: | | 2014912768 |
| ISBN: | Hardcover | 978-1-4990-4962-6 |
| | Softcover | 978-1-4990-4963-3 |
| | eBook | 978-1-4990-4961-9 |

All rights reserved. No part of this book may be reproduced or transmitted in any form or by any means, electronic or mechanical, including photocopying, recording, or by any information storage and retrieval system, without permission in writing from the copyright owner.

Any people depicted in stock imagery provided by Thinkstock are models, and such images are being used for illustrative purposes only.
Certain stock imagery © Thinkstock.
**Front Cover:** Designed and created by Joshua Shallenberger
This book was printed in the United States of America.

Rev. date: 09/15/2014

**To order additional copies of this book, contact:**
Xlibris LLC
1-888-795-4274
www.Xlibris.com
Orders@Xlibris.com
635842

# Contents

Foreword ............................................................................. 13
Introduction ........................................................................ 23
Chapter 1 | Who Are Daniel's People? ........................................... 67
Chapter 2 | The Line of Phares, the Line of Zerah and
　　　　　　David's Throne ................................................... 130
Chapter 3 | Heraldry of the Tribes of Israel Then & Now ............. 228
Chapter 4 | The Christian 490-Year Prophecy—Where &
　　　　　　How It Developed .............................................. 281
Chapter 5 | What Does "Weeks" Mean? ..................................... 311
Chapter 6 | Why Daniel's Book Has Been Sealed Until the
　　　　　　Last Days & the Jubilee Cycle Explained ................. 339
Chapter 7 | The Apple of His Eye (Daniel 9:24) ........................... 367
Chapter 8 | The Burning Bush, the Moat & the Akra
　　　　　　(Daniel 9:25) ..................................................... 377
Chapter 9 | The Saints Destroyed (Daniel 9:26) ........................... 421
Chapter 10 | The 2,300 Days of Hell, Joseph's 7 Years of
　　　　　　 Plenty & 7 Years of Famine, & the Meal Offering
　　　　　　 (Daniel 9:27) ..................................................... 473
Chapter 11 | The Great Enlightenment of Mankind (Daniel 9:27) ..... 528
Chapter 12 | Conclusion ........................................................ 645
Epilogue ............................................................................ 707

# Disclaimer

I am using *The Scriptures* Bible translation throughout this book.

©Copyright 1998 by Institute for Scripture Research (Pty) Ltd.

This is a Sacred Name Bible that is true to the Paleo-Hebrew with regard to the names of Yehovah (God), and Yehshua Hamaschiach (Jesus)—as well as all other proper names for people and places described in Scripture. Therefore, if you are unfamiliar with the "who" or the "what" of that which is being referred to in this book, I strongly recommend you use your own Bible version as a point of reference or guide while you read the Scriptures put forth in this book.

# Dedication

It will become obvious, once you have read this book that all the glory for those things about to be revealed on the following pages is a result of Yehovah's mercy upon us. It is He who has revealed these things to us about Daniel 9:24-27 and Daniel 8, the Sabbatical and Jubilee year Cycles and the curses that go with disobedience to them. I have only shared what Yehovah has shown me from the pages of His bible; the patterns that are hidden there and throughout history. I thank Him for having allowed me the great privilege of sharing these truths to those who want them.

May He bless you in understanding the times in which we now find ourselves. May He bless you in understanding how these Sabbatical and Jubilee Cycles reveal the chronology of His prophecies for these, the very last days of this sixth millennial age.

I must also thank several women for their tireless help in putting this book together and the vast amount of research that was needed, which they cheerfully did for me. They also corrected my endless spelling mistakes and poor grammar and researched the Hebrew translations when needed. Moreover, in their modesty, have asked me not to publish their names this time. Nevertheless, without their help this book would still be just thoughts in my mind. Therefore, I thank them so much for the help and support they have provided.

Another person whose help has been awesome is Joli Darling who has been my editor of choice for all three of my books. "The Prophecies of Abraham," published in 2010, "Remembering the Sabbatical Years of 2016," published in 2013, and now this current one "The 2300 Days of Hell" published in 2014.

Joli is very thorough, methodical and accurate in the manner in which she edits books. She has done many other noteworthy projects which you can review on her web site. Even more important to me as a writer is the fact that she knows my subject matter and understands what I am trying to convey. She has an amazing grasp of the scriptures and a recollection of things I have written in previous books, which is very helpful. I cannot thank her enough for the wonderful help she has been in all of these projects, helping me to bring them to fruition.

Joli can be reached at LonelyMoonchild@comcast.net or through her web site www.wordforwordlineuponline.com

I must also thank my friend James Relf who has worked tirelessly to help me redesign my website in the fall of 2013. He has prepared the video and audio files, which highlight the subject of this book. His genius with the web site and our site on Google speaks for themselves. His professionalism has made my presentation of my material tops. I truly want to thank him for stepping up when I really needed his expertise and help.

I have at long last been able to video record those teachings, which make up the main parts of this book. In the fall of 2013 Joshua Shallenberger recorded all 12 presentations and then edited them and made them come to life. His expertise and professionalism have pleasantly surpassed my expectations. We all owe Joshua our sincere gratitude and thanks for what he has done to these teachings.

Finally, I have one more person I would like to thank. It is my wife of 36 years-Barbara had had to give up my time with her as I worked on this book, the website and the videos-all in an effort to be able to share this priceless message with you to the best of my ability. There were endless hours of writing, editing and preparation time for speaking and power point presentations. All of this time was given up by her. I hope one day you will understand these things. Until then know I love you more than words can say. Again, I love you and thank you.

# The 2300 Days of Hell

This book was originally titled The 70 Shavuot of Daniel but we combined this with what was to be our next book and used the title of the next book to cover both subjects.

Daniel 12:4 Shut up the words and seal the book until the time of the end

Brethren, I believe we are now in those last days and this Prophecy could not be understood until now, in this last Jubilee Cycle; until people began to once again obey Yehovah and keep his set apart times; the weekly Sabbath, the Annual Holy Days and the Sabbatical Years. This prophecy could not be understood until the Sabbatical and Jubilee Cycles were understood. You are about to learn exactly what they show us for this end time.

Get ready for the most terrifying Prophecy in the bible to now be revealed to you the reader for first time since it was given to Daniel over 2552 years ago; terrifying to those who do not and will not obey and exciting and thrilling to those who do obey the commandments of Yehovah.

Amos 3:7 For the Lord Yehovah will do nothing unless He reveals His secret to His servants the prophets.

It would be contrary to the promise of Yehovah to come to these last days and not have someone warn the people of what was about to happen.

You are about to learn exactly how close we are to the time when Satan is going to be locked away. But before that time all hell is going to be let loose. It begins in just a few short years from now in 2014 when we go to publish this book.

It is time to return to our Creator.

# Foreword

*5 See, I am sending you Ěliyahu the Prophet before the coming of the great and awesome day of יהוה. 6 And he shall turn the hearts of the fathers to the children, and the hearts of the children to their fathers, lest I come and smite the earth with utter destruction.* (Malachi 4:5-6)

*16 And he shall turn many of the children of Yisra'ěl to יהוה their Elohim. 17 And he shall go before Him in the spirit and power of Ěliyahu (Elijah), 'to turn the hearts of the fathers to the children,' and the disobedient to the insight of the righteous, to make ready a people prepared for יהוה.* (Luke 1:16-17)

*3 The voice of one crying in the wilderness, "Prepare the way of יהוה; make straight in the desert a highway for our Elohim. 4 Let every valley be raised, and every mountain and hill made low. And the steep ground shall become level, and the rough places smooth. 5 And the esteem of יהוה shall be revealed, and all flesh together shall see it. For the mouth of יהוה has spoken."* (Isaiah 40:3-5)

*19 Repent therefore and turn back, for the blotting out of your sins, in order that times of refreshing might come from the presence of the Master, 20 and that He sends יהושע Messiah, pre-appointed for you, 21 whom heaven needs to receive until the times of restoration of all matters, of which Elohim spoke through the mouth of all His set-apart prophets since of old. 22 For Mosheh (Moses) truly said to the fathers, יהוה your Elohim shall raise up for you a Prophet like me from your brothers. Him you shall hear according to all matters, whatever He says to you. 23 'And it shall be that every being who does not hear that Prophet shall be utterly destroyed from among the people.' 24 And likewise, all the prophets who have spoken, from Shemu'ěl (Samuel) and those following, have also announced these days.* -(Acts 3:19-24)

*25 "...and it speaks words against the Most High, and it wears out the set-apart ones of the Most High, and it intends to change appointed times[1] and law[2], and they are given into its hand for a time and times and half a time."* (Daniel 7:25 | Footnotes: [1]This is another word for festivals. [2]Changing the law amounts to lawlessness.)

I have begun this book, *"The 2300 Days of Hell"* with the same foreword as I had in my last book, *"Remembering the Sabbatical Year of 2016,"* which I published in 2013.

Looking back on all that has been accomplished since 2004 when I began this journey, I can now see how it has all been for a reason - and one reason in particular. The weekly newsletters[1] I started in 2006—of which you can sign up for, *as well as* the three websites—they have all proven to be instrumental in educating people about the Sabbatical Years and how they are related to the curses that are unfolding all around us right now. They have also been teaching those who come to these websites about keeping Torah and walking in obedience to Yehovah.

The speaking tours and the production of my DVD in March of 2008 of *"The Chronological Order of Prophecy in the Jubilee Cycles"*[2] was the direct result of my previous newsletters that went out each Shabbat regarding the very same subject matter. My newsletters have continued

---

[1] http://www.sightedmoon.com, http://www.sightedmoonnl.com, or http://www.sightedmoon.nl

[2] http://www.sightedmoon.com/?page_id=251

each week since 2006, and they produced *"The Prophecies of Abraham"*[3] in 2009, which was then published as a book in 2010, followed by being nominated for a Nobel Prize in 2011.[4] (How many other religious books get that distinction?) My second book, *"Remembering the Sabbatical Year 2016"* was written to answer the many questions and objections that keep coming up with regard to the Sabbatical Years and why they are so different today from what Yehovah originally intended. All of my speaking engagements, presentations, answering of emails and phone calls, as well as appearing on radio shows and the new TV series we have just begun and the new videos now hosted on our newest web site, have been done for this one reason and one reason only. To restore the keeping of the Sabbatical Years: remember since that is what Malachi 4:4[5] tells us we are to do - remember.

In October of 2012 we joined with a family in Israel to plant a vineyard of about ten dunam[6] of land with four varieties of grapes. We engaged in this undertaking to compare one section of the land that is going to use the Jewish Sabbatical Year in 2014-2015 Tishri to Tishri and every seven years thereafter—with the other section that will keep the Sabbatical Year in 2016-2017 Aviv to Aviv and for every seven years thereafter. Again I have done this as well for one reason and one reason alone.

---

[3] The Prophecies of Abraham can be ordered from the Authorhouse at: http://bookstore.authorhouse.com/Products/SKU-000366309/The-Prophecies-of-Abraham.aspx in North America & ousdide North America at: http://www.authorhouse.co.uk/Bookstore/BookDetail.aspx?Book=286642 or on Amazon at: http://tinyurl.com/a293j3d & on Barnes & Noble at: http://tinyurl.com/bjdhjcw

[4] Official letter shared in Appendix of Remembering the Sabbatical Year 2016

[5] Malachi 4:4 Remember the Law of Moses My servant, which I commanded to him in Horeb for all Israel, the statutes and judgments. 5 Behold, I *am* sending you Elijah the prophet before the coming of the great and dreadful day of Jehovah. 6 And he shall turn the heart of the fathers to the sons, and the heart of the sons to their fathers, that I not come and strike the earth *with* utter destruction.

[6] One hectare is also equivalent to: 2.4710439 US Acres or 10 Dunam as indicated on the Universal Hectare Conversion Table: http://www.conversiontable.org/universalhectareconversiontable.html

Everything I have produced and shared with the public has been for one reason and one reason only. To turn the hearts of the children back to the Father. Our Father Yehovah, to be specific. And in so doing that very thing—turning back to Yehovah, turning back to the Torah, to the Sabbath, to the Holy Days of Leviticus 23 and to the Sabbatical Years, this, in turn, will turn our Father's heart back to us—lest He smite us once again with yet another curse.

It has not been for fame or glory and it surely is not for the money. I still have to work at a full-time job to pay for all I do. No, the reason I do this is so that you, the brethren, can learn about the Sabbatical Years and the amazing prophecies they reveal to us in these last days. But if you do not keep the weekly seventh day Saturday Sabbath you cannot fully understand these prophecies. Again, if you do not keep the Holy Days that are told to you in Leviticus 23, then you will not understand the prophecies that are told to you in the Bible. If, in fact, you are keeping these two laws, but you are not keeping the Sabbatical Years, you will not and you simply cannot understand or fully grasp the prophecies that are specifically being told to us in these Last Days. You are, at best, just guessing at them.

Yes we are, beyond a shadow of a doubt, now in the Last Days as each of my two previous books and my DVD have clearly demonstrated to those who have ears to hear and eyes to see.

It is only by keeping the weekly Saturday Sabbath, the annual Holy Days that are shown to you in Leviticus 23, (and not adding to it nor taking away from it) and by keeping the Sabbatical Years as told to you in Leviticus 25, that you can fully understand and comprehend the meaning behind Daniel's 70 Weeks!

I am about to show you things that will truly stretch your mind as you grow to understand these things. It will make you angry with those who have been teaching you amiss all your life because they never showed you these things. Some of your teachers, in fact, have lied to you—either by their own ignorance, being deceived themselves or worse yet, willfully.

*Thus said יהוה[7], "For three transgressions of Yehuḏah, and for four, I do not turn it back, because they have rejected the Torah of יהוה, and did not guard His laws. And their lies after which their fathers walked lead them astray.* (Amos 2:4)

*For the leaders of this people lead them astray, and those who are guided by them are swallowed up.* (Isaiah 9:16)

*"...then you shall say to them, 'Because your fathers have forsaken Me,' declares יהוה, 'and have walked after other mighty ones and served them and bowed themselves to them, and have forsaken Me, and did not guard My Torah. 12 'And you have done more evil than your fathers, for look, each one walks according to the stubbornness of his own evil heart, without listening to Me."* (Jeremiah 16:11)

*O יהוה, my strength and my stronghold and my refuge, in the day of distress the gentiles shall come to You from the ends of the earth and say, "Our fathers have inherited only falsehood, futility, and there is no value in them."* (Jeremiah 16:19)

*Leave them alone. They are blind leaders of the blind. And if the blind leads the blind, both shall fall into a ditch.* (Matthew 15:14)

*"...knowing that you were redeemed from your futile way of life inherited from your fathers, not with what is corruptible, silver or gold."* (1 Peter 1:18)

Parents can and do lead their children astray and then their children grow up to lead their own children astray and so it goes. Yehovah bestows upon each one of us the not to be taken lightly responsibility of not only validating everything we are taught to make sure it is in alignment with the Word of Yehovah, but also to train up our children in the way they should go in accordance with all the things Yehovah has revealed to us through His Word.

---

[7]   יהוה is the Hebrew word for Yehovah, which is also the name of God.

> *21 Prove all things; hold fast that which is good.* (1 Thessalonians 5:21)

The spiritual wellbeing of all children (just like their physical well-being) will always be dependent upon the parents' faithfulness to Yehovah. Children, by teaching and by rote, will believe and practice the religious beliefs of their fathers. The very lives of your children, with regard to their eternal security, depend on you obeying Yehovah and teaching them truth from the Scriptures and not traditions which cannot be proven or have no spiritual merit or true spiritual substance.

> *16 And he shall turn many of the children of Yisra'ĕl to* יהוה *their Elohim. 17 And he shall go before Him in the spirit and power of Ĕliyahu (Elijah), to turn the hearts of the fathers to the children, and the disobedient to the insight of the righteous, to make ready a people prepared for* יהוה. (Luke 1:16-17)

In all of this, remember this one prayer that Moses wrote of in Leviticus 26, which is later repeated by Solomon in 1 Kings and then by Daniel in the book of Daniel. If we repent and turn 180° and turn back to keeping the Torah, then Yehovah will forgive us and remember the covenant He made with Abraham, with Isaac and with Jacob. He will remember us, protect us and take care us from that moment on if we just do our part. We are told in Exodus that if we do not obey Him, He will send the punishment on our children to the third and fourth generations. But, if we do repent and we do obey then He will show us mercy, which in the New Testament is called grace. It was always right there in Exodus all along—mercy and grace **"IF"** we obey and repent.

> *5 "... you do not bow down to them nor serve them. For I,* יהוה *your Elohim am a jealous Ĕl, visiting the crookedness of the fathers on the children to the third and fourth generations of those who hate Me, 6 but showing kindness to thousands, to those who love Me and guard My commands."* (Exodus 20:5-6)

*40 But if they confess their crookedness and the crookedness of their fathers, with their trespass in which they trespassed against Me, and that they also have walked contrary to Me, 41 and that I also have walked contrary to them and have brought them into the land of their enemies—if their uncircumcised heart is then humbled, and they accept the punishment of their crookedness, 42 then I shall remember My covenant with Ya'aqoḇ, and also My covenant with Yitsḥaq, and also remember My covenant with Aḇraham, and remember the land. 43 'For the land was abandoned by them, and enjoying its Sabbaths while lying waste without them, and they were paying for their crookedness, because they rejected My right-rulings and because their being loathed My laws. 44 And yet for all this, when they are in the land of their enemies, I shall not reject them, nor shall I loathe them so as to destroy them and break My covenant with them. For I am יהוה their Elohim. 45 Then I shall remember for their sake the covenant of the ancestors whom I brought out of the land of Mitsrayim before the eyes of the nations to be their Elohim. I am יהוה.' " 46 These are the laws and the right-rulings and the Torot¹ which יהוה made between Himself and the children of Yisra'ĕl on Mount Sinai by the hand of Mosheh.* (Leviticus 26:40-46 | Footnote: ¹Torot—plural of Torah, teaching)

*22 And Shelomoh stood before the altar of יהוה in front of all the assembly of Yisra'ĕl and spread out his hands toward the heavens, 23 and said, "יהוה Elohim of Yisra'ĕl, there is no Elohim in the heavens above or on earth below like You, guarding Your covenant and kindness with Your servants who walk before You with all their heart, 24 who has guarded that which You did promise Your servant Dawiḏ my father. Indeed, You have both spoken with Your mouth and have filled it with Your hand, as it is this day. 25 "And now, יהוה Elohim of Yisra'ĕl, guard what You promised Your servant Dawiḏ my father, saying, 'There is not to cease a man of yours before Me, sitting on the throne of Yisra'ĕl—only, if your sons guard their way, to walk before Me as you have walked before Me.'"* (1 Kings 8:22-25)

*26 "And now, O Elohim of Yisra'ĕl please let Your word come true which You have spoken to Your servant Dawiḏ my father. 27 For is it true: Elohim dwells on the earth? See, the heavens and the heavens of the heavens are unable to contain You, how much less this House which I have built! 28 Yet, shall You turn to the prayer of Your servant and his supplication, O יהוה my Elohim, and listen to the cry and the prayer which Your servant is praying before You today? 29 For Your eyes to be open toward this House night and day, toward the place of which You said, 'My Name is there,' to listen to the prayer which Your servant makes toward this place. 30 "Then, shall You hear the supplication of Your servant and of Your people Yisra'ĕl when they pray toward this place, when You hear in Your dwelling place, in the heavens? And shall You hear, and forgive? 31 If anyone sins against his neighbor, and he has lifted up an oath on him, to cause him to swear, and comes and swears before Your altar in this House, 32 then hear in the heavens, and act and rightly rule Your servants, declaring the wrongdoer wrong, bringing his way on his head, and declaring the righteous right by giving him according to his righteousness".* (1 Kings 8:26-32)

*33 "When Your people Yisra'ĕl are smitten before an enemy, because they have sinned against You, and they shall turn back to You and confess Your Name, and pray and make supplication to You in this House, 34 then hear in the heavens, and forgive the sin of Your people Yisra'ĕl, and bring them back to the land which You gave to their fathers. 35 When the heavens are shut up and there is no rain because they sin against You, when they pray toward this place and confess Your Name, and turn from their sin because You afflict them, 36 then hear in the heavens, and forgive the sin of Your servants, Your people Yisra'ĕl—for You teach them the good way in which they should walk—and shall give rain on Your land which You have given to Your people as an inheritance.* (1 Kings 8:33-36)

*37 "When there is scarcity of food in the land; when there is pestilence, blight, mildew, locusts, grasshoppers; when their enemy distresses them in the land of their cities; any plague, any sickness, 38 whatever prayer, whatever supplication made by anyone of all Your people Yisra'ěl, each knowing the plague of his own heart, and shall spread out his hands toward this House, 39 then hear in the heavens, Your dwelling place, and forgive, and act, and render unto everyone according to all his ways, whose heart You know. Because You—You alone—know the hearts of all the sons of men, 40 so that they fear You all the days that they live in the land which You gave to our fathers."* (1 Kings 8:37-40)

*41 "Also, concerning a foreigner, who is not of Your people Yisra'ěl, but has come from a far land for Your Name's sake— 42 since they hear of Your great Name and Your strong hand and Your outstretched arm—and he shall come and pray toward this House, 43 hear in the heavens Your dwelling place, and do according to all for which the foreigner calls to You, so that all peoples of the earth know Your Name and fear You, as do Your people Yisra'ěl, and know that this House which I have built is called by Your Name. 44 When Your people go out to battle against their enemy, in the way that You send them, and they shall pray to* יהוה *toward the city which You have chosen and toward the House which I have built for Your Name, 45 then shall You hear in the heavens their prayer and their supplication, and maintain their cause?"* (1 Kings 8:41-45)

*46 When they sin against You—for there is no one who does not sin—and You become enraged with them and give them to the enemy, and they take them captive to the land of the enemy, far or near; 47 and they shall turn back unto their heart in the land where they have been taken captive, and shall turn, and make supplication to You in the land of those who took them captive, saying, 'We have sinned and acted crookedly, we have committed wrong,' 48 and they shall turn back to You with all their heart and with all their being in the land of their enemies who led them away captive, and shall pray to You toward their land which You gave to their fathers, the city which You have chosen and the House which I have built for Your Name, 49 then shall You hear in the heavens Your dwelling place their prayer and their supplication, and maintain their cause, 50 and forgive Your people who have sinned against You, and all their transgressions which they have transgressed against You? And give them compassion before those who took them captive, and they shall have compassion on them. 51 'For they are Your people and Your inheritance, whom You brought out of Mitsrayim, out of the iron furnace.'"* (1 Kings 8:46-51)

*52 "Let Your eyes be open to the supplication of Your servant and the supplication of Your people Yisra'ĕl, to listen to them whenever they call to You. 53 For You have separated them unto Yourself for an inheritance, out of all the peoples of the earth, as You spoke by the hand of Your servant Mosheh, when You brought our fathers out of Mitsrayim, O Master* יהוה*." 54 And it came to be, when Shelomoh had ended praying all this prayer and supplication to* יהי*, that he rose up from before the altar of* יהוה*, from kneeling on his knees with his hands spread up to the heavens.* (1 Kings 8:52-54)

It is time to repent from disobeying Yehovah and refusing or failing to fully observe His Torah. All the indicators are in place that we are at the end of this age. I am confident you will be able to see and prove this to yourself by the time you reach the end of this book and matching up with the Scriptures provided. *"The 2300 Days of Hell"* will show you when these things are to take place year by year. Again, all of this is only possible when you understand the Sabbatical Cycles. May Yehovah bless you in your understanding and comprehension of the things I am about to share with you.

# Introduction

In this book, *The 2300 Days of Hell* formerly *The 70 Shavuot of Daniel*, we are going to be looking at one section of the book of Daniel—or, more specifically, his message that the angel gave to him which is preserved for us in these last days. This message is contained in Daniel 9:24-27.

How did Daniel come to find himself in the position he was in when this prophecy was given? Who is Daniel and why is this prophecy that Yehovah revealed to him something we need to heed?

To find the answers to these questions, one must begin by traveling back in time to the Assyrian Empire.

The Assyrian Empire was the first empire to come on the world scene early in 2000 B.C. There survives to this day, the remains of a ziggurat, (or temple tower) from that era that still stands near the site of its ancient capital called Asshur.

The city of Asshur was named after the person Asshur who was the second son of Shem, the son of Noah.

> *22 The sons of Shĕm: Ěylam, and Asshur, and Arpak̠shad̠shad and Lud, and Aram.* (Genesis 10:22)

History records Sargon as the first king of Asshur and Sargon was, in fact, Asshur himself.[8] They were one and the same person. Sargon was the first to forge, by military campaigns, the Assyrian Empire. Asshur was also the leading general in Nimrod's service. At some point, Asshur and Nimrod parted ways and became rulers of two separate kingdoms. These two *would* however, for all of history, be tied together.

> *9 He was a mighty hunter before* יהוה, *therefore it is said, "Like Nimroḏ the mighty hunter before* יהוה*." 10 And the beginning of his reign was Baḇel, and Ereḵ, and Akkaḏ, and Kalnĕh, in the land of Shin'ar. 11 From that land he went to Ashshur and built Ninewĕh, and Reḥoḇoth Ir, and Kelaḥ, 12 and Resen between Ninewĕh and Kelaḥ, the great city.* (Genesis 10:9-12)

All of this took place over a period of 391 years between the Flood of Noah, which took place in 2181 B.C., and the execution of Nimrod by Shem in 1790 B.C.[9]

In the 9th century B.C., Assyria developed into an aggressive and powerful empire and was expanding. It was also during this time period that the Kingdom of Israel split apart to form two separate and distinct kingdoms.

We read in the Old Testament how King David became king over Judah in 1010 B.C. and later had united the Twelve Tribes of Israel under his kingship in 1017 B.C. King Solomon succeeded King David in 970 B.C and reigned for forty years. Upon his death in 930 B.C., the United Kingdoms of Israel split into two distinct kingdoms—Israel and Judah. We read of this event in 1 Kings.

> *16 And all Yisra'ĕl saw that the sovereign did not listen to them. Then the people answered the sovereign, saying, "What portion do we have in Dawiḏ? And there is no inheritance*

---

[8] http://www.originofnations.org/HRP_Papers/Ancient%20roots%20of%20kingofnorth%20&%20kingofsouth.pdf

[9] *The Prophecies of Abraham* by Joseph F. Dumond; Charts

*in the son of Yishai. To your mighty ones, O Yisra'ĕl! Now, see to your own house, O Dawiḏ!" So Yisra'ĕl went to their tents. 17 But as for the children of Yisra'ĕl who dwelt in the cities of Yehuḏah, Reḥaḇ'am reigned over them. 18 And when Sovereign Reḥaḇ'am sent Aḏoram, who was over the compulsory labour, all Yisra'ĕl stoned him with stones, and he died. And Sovereign Reḥaḇ'am hastily mounted his chariot to flee to Yerushalayim. 19 Thus Yisra'ĕl revolted against the house of Dawiḏ to this day.* (1Kings 12:16-19)

*20 And it came to be when all Yisra'ĕl heard that Yaroḇ'am had come back, they sent for him and called him to the congregation, and set him up to reign over all Yisra'ĕl. There was none who followed the house of Dawiḏ, except the tribe of Yehuḏah only. 21 And Reḥaḇ'am came to Yerushalayim, and he assembled all the house of Yehuḏah with the tribe of Binyamin, one hundred and eighty thousand chosen brave men, to fight against the house of Yisra'ĕl, to bring back the reign to Reḥaḇ'am son of Shelomoh. 22 But the word of Elohim came to Shemayah the man of Elohim, saying, 23 "Speak to Reḥaḇ'am son of Shelomoh, sovereign of Yehuḏah, and to all the house of Yehuḏah and Binyamin, and to the rest of the people, saying, 24 'Thus said* יהוה*, Do not go up or fight against your brothers the children of Yisra'ĕl. Let every man return to his house, for this matter is from Me'". So they obeyed the word of* יהוה*, and turned back, according to the word of* יהוה*.* (1 Kings 12:20-24).

As I stated earlier, this split resulted in the rearrangement of the United Kingdom of the Twelve Tribes of Israel into two separate kingdoms as follows:

The Ten Tribes of "Israel" under King Jeroboam with Samaria as their capital made up of Reuben, Gad, Manasseh, Dan, Asher, Issachar, Simeon, Zebulon, Ephraim, and Naphtali.

In addition, the remaining tribes of Judah and Benjamin and a sizeable portion of Levites formed the kingdom of "Judah" under King

Rehoboam in Jerusalem. (The Levites were distributed amongst all of the tribes, but Jerusalem was one of their main cities.)

From that time onward, Israel and Judah were two completely separate, distinct and independent nations. While they were allies when faced with a common enemy, the historical accounts of them being at war with one another are recorded many times in the Bible.

One of the most important keys to understanding Bible prophecy is recognizing that although all Jews are Israelites, not all Israelites are Jews. This is an *absolutely vital* point because many of the end-time prophecies that speak of "Israel" are not referring solely to the modern-day Jewish people in the State of Israel or anywhere else.

Here are some examples of Israel warring with Judah and Benjamin.

> *21 And Reḥab'am came to Yerushalayim, and he assembled all the house of Yehudah with the tribe of Binyamin, one hundred and eighty thousand chosen brave men, to fight against the house of Yisra'ĕl, to bring back the reign to Reḥab'am son of Shelomoh.* (1 Kings 12:21)

> *24 Thus said יהוה, "Do not go up or fight against your brothers the children of Yisra'ĕl. Let every man return to his house, for this matter is from Me." So they obeyed the word of יהוה, and turned back, according to the word of יהוה.* (1 Kings 12:24)

Not to mention this occasion:

> *16 And there was fighting between Asa and Ba'asha sovereign of Yisra'ĕl all their days. 17 And Ba'asha sovereign of Yisra'ĕl came up against Yehudah, and built Ramah, to keep anyone from going out or coming in to Asa sovereign of Yehudah.* (1 Kings 15:16-17)

We also read in Judges of the time when Israel fought against their brother Benjamin:

> *30 And the children of Yisra'ĕl went up against the children of Binyamin on the third day, and put themselves in battle array against Giḇ'ah as at the other times.* (Judges 20:30)

It was during this time when Israel and Judah were divided and at war with each other that the Assyrians began to menace and conquer their neighbors and eventually subjugated the entire Fertile Crescent from Mesopotamia to Egypt.

The first encounter of Israel fighting against Assyria took place at the infamous battle of Qarqar in 853 B.C. in which Ahab, King of Israel made an alliance with Ben Hadad II of Damascus. This battle is recorded on the Kurth Monolith[10] and was erected by Shalmaneser V. Consequently, Ahab died in this battle. For further reading, read 1 Kings 22. This is the first of only two occasions where we are provided with any kind of record or account of a king of Israel referenced in another nation's chronology—a chronology that has been proven to be extremely accurate. These records are called the Limmu Lists of the Assyrian kings found in Nineveh.[11]

Just over a hundred years later, we see *once again* where Israel was at war with Judah.

In 732 B.C., Pekah, the King of Israel, allied himself with Rezin, the King of Aram. Together they threatened to attack Jerusalem. Ahaz, the King of Judah appealed to Tiglath-Pileser III (also known as Pul in 1 Chronicles 5:26), the King of Assyria, for help. After Ahaz paid tribute to Tiglath-Pileser, Tiglath-Pileser sacked Damascus and annexed Aram. According to 2 Kings 16:9, the population of Aram was deported and Rezin was executed.

---

[10] http://www.sacred-texts.com/ane/rp/rp204/rp20412.htm
[11] *The Mysterious Number of the Hebrew King*s by Edwin R. Thiele; p. 68

We also read in 2 Kings of the first time Israel was attacked and defeated by the Assyrians and how those who were defeated were transported to another land.

> *29 In the days of Peqaḥ sovereign of Yisra'ĕl, Tig̅lath-Pileser sovereign of Ashshur came and took Iyon, and Abĕl Bĕyth Ma'aḵah, and Yanowaḥ, and Qedesh, and Ḥatsor, and Gil'ad, and Galil, all the land of Naphtali, and took them into exile to Ashshur.* (2 Kings 15:29)

These captivities began in 732 B.C., when the first successful Assyrian invasions began. But they only began because of the invitation of Assyria *by Judah* to fight against the Ten Northern Tribes of Israel.

> *26 So the Elohim of Yisra'el stirred up the spirit of Pul sovereign of Ashshur, even the spirit of Tiglath-Pileser sovereign of Ashshur. And he took the Re'ubenites, and the Gadites, and the half-tribe of Menashsheh into exile, and brought them to Halah, and Habor, and Hara, and the river of Gozan, unto this day.* (1 Chronicles 5:26)

It is interesting to note the account in Scripture when Joseph was taken prisoner by his brothers and sold into captivity by Judah. For here we see again how it is Judah who has invited a foreign power to take Joseph captive upon whom the birthright name of Israel had been passed on to. The Ten Northern Tribes are referred to as Joseph in prophecy. It is my belief that we will see Judah, the State of Israel turn on the USA in the future. But this is just my position.

Tiglath-Pileser III died in 727 B.C. and was succeeded by his son Shalmaneser V who continued the assault on Israel until his death in 722 B.C.

> *10 "... and they captured it at the end of three years. In the sixth year... Shomeron was captured. 11 And the sovereign of Ashshur exiled Yisra'ĕl* to Ashshur and placed them in Halah and Habor, the River of Gozan, and in the cities of the Medes." (2 Kings 18:10-11)

The Quartz Hill School of Theology has this to say on the matter:

> Shalmaneser V himself never took the city, since it was actually taken by his successor.
>
> In the Khorsabad annals of his reign, the monarch, Sargon II, lists the fall of Samaria as the outstanding event of the first year of his reign:
>
>> At the beginning of my rule, in my first year of reign... the people of Samaria... 27,290... who lived therein, I carried away...
>
> In Sargon's so-called "Display Inscription" at Khorsabad, which summarizes the principal events of the first 15 years of his reign, he says:
>
>> I besieged and captured Samaria, carrying off 27,290 of its inhabitants. I gathered 50 chariots from among them. I replaced the deported inhabitants with new immigrants. Finally, I set my officers over them and imposed upon them the tribute of the former king.[12]

From the first request for aid by Judah in 732 B.C. until the final capitulation of Israel in 723 B.C., it took just nine years for Assyria to wipe out the Northern Ten Tribes of Israel. Israel would never recover from this in the context of returning back to the Promised Land, but they would recover in all other respects, and change their names as you are soon going to learn. There are also no records of the Assyrians having exiled people from Dan, Asher, Issachar, Zebulon or Western Manasseh. It is my belief, based on a great deal of research I have done, that they escaped before the onslaught came from Assyria and settled in far off communities or outposts built by King David. These are believed to be the Sea Peoples in ancient history, also known as the Phoenicians.[13]

---

[12] http://www.theology.edu/lec20.htm
[13] *The Missing Simeonites* by Stephen M. Collins, http://stevenmcollins.com/html/simeon.html

But they too were defeated by Assyria, only we did not know them as Israelites.

> At its height Assyria conquered the 25th dynasty of Egypt (and expelled its Nubian/Kushite dynasty) as well as Babylon, Chaldea, Elam, Media, Persia, Ararat (Armenia), Phoenicia, Aramea/Syria, Phrygia, the Neo-Hittites, Hurrians, Northern Arabia, Gutium, Israel, Judah, Moab, Edom, Corduene, Cilicia, Mannea, and parts of Ancient Greece (such as Cyprus) and defeated and/or exacted tribute from Scythia, Cimmeria, Lydia, Nubia, Ethiopia and others.
>
> The Assyrian Empire at its height encompassed the whole of the modern nations of Iraq, Syria, Egypt, Lebanon, Israel, Jordan, Kuwait, Bahrain, Palestine, and Cyprus, together with swaths of Iran, Saudi Arabia, Turkey, Sudan, Libya, Armenia, Georgia, and Azerbaijan.[14]

Roughly one hundred years after the destruction of the Northern Ten Tribes of Israel, all the wars and the ongoing cost of empire expansion had begun to take a huge toll on Assyria as they expanded into Egypt. There were constant rebellions by Egyptian princes and in the East; one of the peoples that Assyria had formerly captured and moved was now rising up and becoming a threat. These were the Cimmerians whom we will be reading about in the next chapter. The expense of maintaining the armies and horses along with the moving of siege engines from one rebellious city to the next was draining them dry.

A new empire began to flex its muscle and began to attack the mighty Assyrian Empire from The South.

> Egypt was able to break away from Assyrian rule. The Assyrians were then weakened by conflicts over succession, by coups and civil war. During these conflicts, cities in Canaan broke away from Assyrian control and Phoenicia began ignoring Assyrian directives. Other petty kingdoms joined the rebellion against Assyria, and in 623 B.C. the

---

[14] http://en.wikipedia.org/wiki/Old_Assyrian_period

well-led Chaldean army drove north from around Sumer and expelled the Assyrians from Babylon.

With the independence of Egypt and Babylon, and a weakened Assyria, the new king of Judah, Josiah—the grandson of Manasseh—declared Judah independent.

Between Mesopotamia and the Caspian Sea, tribes of an Indo-European people called Medes had become united under a single king. A later king of the Medes, Cyaxares, reorganized his army and attempted to expand westward against the Assyrians. He allied his army with the Chaldeans, who were now in control of Babylon and Sumer. The Medes and Chaldeans attacked, and together they defeated the Assyrians, overrunning Assyria's capital, Nineveh, in 612 B.C. Ninevah's walls were broken by the siege engines that Assyria had introduced centuries before.[15]

After four years of bitter fighting, Nineveh was finally sacked in 612 B.C., after a prolonged siege followed by house to house fighting. Sin-shar-ishkun was killed defending his capital.

Despite the loss of its major cities and in the face of overwhelming odds, Assyrian resistance continued. Ashur-uballit II (612 B.C.–605? B.C.) took the throne, won a few battles, and occupied and held out at Harran (where he founded a new capital) from 612 B.C. until 608 B.C. when he was overrun by the Babylonians and Medes.[16]

When the Babylonians overran the Assyrian capital of Nineveh in 612 B.C., the Assyrians moved their capital to Harran on the southern border of modern Turkey and Syria. The Babylonians then captured Harran in 610 B.C. and the Assyrians once again moved their capital to Carchemish, on the Euphrates River. Egypt was allied with the Assyrian king

---

[15] http://www.fsmitha.com/h1/ch08.htm
[16] http://en.wikipedia.org/wiki/Ancient_Assyria

Ashur-uballit II, and marched in 609 B.C. to his aid against the Babylonians.

The Egyptian army of Pharaoh Necho II was delayed at Megiddo by the forces of King Josiah of Judah. Josiah was killed and his army was defeated. The Egyptians and Assyrians together crossed the Euphrates and laid siege to Harran in 608 B.C., which they failed to re-take. They then retreated to northern Syria.[17]

We read of this event in 2 Kings:

*29 In his days Pharaoh Neko sovereign of Mitsrayim went up against the sovereign of Ashshur to the river Euphrates. And Sovereign Yoshiyahu went out to him, and he killed him at Megiddo, when he saw him. 30 And his servants conveyed his body in a chariot from Megiddo, and brought him to Yerushalayim, and buried him in his own tomb. And the people of the land took Yeho'ahaz the son of Yoshiyahu, and anointed him, and set him up to reign in his father's place.* (2 Kings 23:29-30)

With the death of Josiah, Jehoiakim's younger brother Jehoahaz (or Shallum) was proclaimed king, but after three months, Pharaoh Necho II deposed him and replaced him with the eldest son, Eliakim, who adopted the name Jehoiakim and became king at the age of twenty-five.

*34 Pharaoh Necho made Eliakim son of Josiah king in place of his father Josiah and changed Eliakim's name to Jehoiakim. But he took Jehoahaz and carried him off to Egypt, and there he died.* (2 Kings 23:34)

The next three years were witness to the Egyptians and the existing remnants of the Assyrian army vainly attempting to eject the invaders from Babylon. In 605 B.C., the Babylonians and Medes defeated the Egyptians and Assyrians at Carchemish, bringing an end to Assyria

---

[17] http://en.wikipedia.org/wiki/Battle_of_Carchemish

as an independent political entity, also utterly destroying the Egyptian army at this time.

Both Israel and now Judah suffered the misfortune of living on a relatively narrow bridge of land between great, imperial powers—Assyria and Egypt and now, the Babylonians. The Chaldeans, under King Nebuchadnezzar II, won the battle of Carchemish and then wiped out the remaining Egyptian army at Hamath. The Babylonians were now the new rulers over Judah, who had been a vassal of Egypt the past three years, but Babylon had, in fact, taken charge of Judah once they defeated the Assyrians in 609 B.C. at the battle of Harran. This is why Josiah went to fight Pharaoh Necho II of Egypt and there died. This is an important date, as you will soon see.

Jeremiah also spoke to all of Judah during this fourth year of Jehoiakim's reign.

> *1 The word that came to Yirmeyahu concerning all the people of Yehudah, in the fourth year of Yehoyaqim son of Yoshiyahu, the sovereign of Yehudah, which was the first year of Nebukadretstsar sovereign of Babel, 2 which Yirmeyahu the prophet spoke to all the people of Yehudah and to all the inhabitants of Yerushalayim, saying, 3 "From the thirteenth year of Yoshiyahu son of Amon, sovereign of Yehudah, even to this day, this is the twenty-third year in which the word of* יהוה *has come to me. And I have spoken to you, rising early and speaking, but you have not listened." (Jeremiah 25:1-3)*
>
> *9 "... see, I am sending and taking all the tribes of the north," declares* יהוה, *"and Nebukadretstsar the sovereign of Babel, My servant, and shall bring them against this land and against its inhabitants, and against these nations all around, and shall put them under the ban, and make them an astonishment, and a hissing, and everlasting ruins. 10 And I shall banish from them the voice of rejoicing and the voice of gladness, the voice of the bridegroom and the voice of the bride, the sound of the millstones and the light of the lamp. 11 And all this land shall be a ruin and a waste, and these*

> nations shall serve the sovereign of Baḇel seventy years. 12 And it shall be, when seventy years are completed, that I shall punish the sovereign of Baḇel and that nation, the land of the Chaldeans, for their crookedness," declares יהוה, "and shall make it everlasting ruins. 13 And I shall bring on that land all My words which I have pronounced against it, all that is written in this book, which Yirmeyahu has prophesied concerning all the nations." (Jeremiah 25:9-13)

Nebuchadnezzar's father, Nabopolassar, died, and Nebuchadnezzar went back to Babylon, where he was crowned king. When Nebuchadnezzar left Jerusalem, he took with him hostages in order to keep Judah in line. These hostages were taken from the families of the aristocrats or leaders of Judah, and Daniel was one of them.

> 1 In the third year of the reign of Yehoyaqim, sovereign of Yehuḏah, Neḇuḵaḏnetstsar, sovereign of Baḇel came to Yerushalayim and besieged it. 2 And יהוה gave Yehoyaqim sovereign of Yehuḏah into his hand, with some of the utensils of the House of Elohim, which he brought to the land of Shinʻar to the house of his mighty one. And he brought the utensils into the treasure house of his mighty one. 3 And the sovereign said to Ashpenaz, the chief of his eunuchs, to bring some of the children of Yisra'ěl and some of the sovereign's descendants and some of the nobles, 4 young men in whom there was no blemish, but good-looking, having insight in all wisdom, having knowledge and understanding learning, capable to stand in the sovereign's palace, and to teach them the writing and speech of the Chaldeans. 5 And the sovereign appointed for them a daily ration of the sovereign's food and of the wine which he drank, and three years of training for them, so that at the end thereof they should stand before the sovereign. 6 Now among them were from the sons of Yehuḏah: Dani'ěl, Ḥananyah, Misha'ěl, and Azaryah. 7 And the chief of the eunuchs gave them names. For he called Dani'ěl, Bělteshatstsar; and Ḥananyah, Shaḏraḵ; and Misha'ěl, Měyshaḵ; and Azaryah, Aḇěḏ-Negō. (Daniel 1:1-7)

Daniel had been caught up in the major world events of that time. A time when the great Assyrian Empire had been so thoroughly destroyed, they disappeared completely from history after that. Egypt, another great nation, was also destroyed at the same time and Babylon became the world ruling authority.

Daniel, who in Hebrew means, "God is my Judge," was a young man when he was taken into Babylonian captivity, in the fourth year of the reign of Jehoiakim. Jehoiakim became king in 609 B.C.[18] over Judah, so his fourth year was 605 B.C. when Daniel was taken along with his friends, Hananiah, Mishael and Azariah into the Babylonian captivity.[19]

In 601 B.C. the Egyptians successfully launched a major defeat upon the Babylonians.[20] This defeat was so bad that in 600 B.C., Nebuchadnezzar II did not go out to war. Jehoiakim switched back to the Egyptians and ceased paying the tribute to Babylon. In 599 B.C., Nebuchadnezzar II invaded Judah and laid siege to Jerusalem. In 598 B.C., Jehoiakim died and his body was thrown out of the walls just as Jeremiah 22:19 had predicted.

We are also told why this was about to happen to Judah.

> *8 And many gentiles shall pass by this city, and they shall say to one another, "Why has* יהוה *done so to this great city?" 9 Then they shall say, "Because they have forsaken the covenant of* יהוה *their Elohim, and bowed themselves to other mighty ones and served them."* (Jeremiah 22:8-9)

This is a stern warning for those of us today who will not keep the covenant of Yehovah.

Jehoiakim was then succeeded by his son Jeconiah, (also known as Jehoiachin). Jeconiah was then taken captive and led away to Babylon.

---

[18] *The Mysterious Numbers of the Hebrew Kings* by Edwin R. Thiele; p. 181
[19] *The Mysterious Numbers of the Hebrew Kings* by Edwin R. Thiele; p. 185
[20] *The Mysterious Numbers of the Hebrew Kings* by Edwin R. Thiele; p.186

*10 At that time the servants of Neḇuḵaḏnetstsar sovereign of Baḇel came up against Yerushalayim, and the city was besieged. 11 And Neḇuḵaḏnetstsar sovereign of Baḇel came against the city, as his servants were besieging it. 12 And Yehoyaḵin sovereign of Yehuḏah, and his mother, and his servants, and his heads, and his eunuchs went out to the sovereign of Baḇel. And the sovereign of Baḇel, in the eighth year of his reign, took him prisoner. 13 And he took from there all the treasures of the House of יהוה and the treasures of the sovereign's house, and he cut in pieces all the objects of gold which Shelomoh sovereign of Yisra'ěl had made in the Hěḵal of יהוה, as יהוה had said. 14 And he exiled all Yerushalayim, and all the officers and all the mighty brave men—ten thousand exiles—and all the craftsmen and smiths. None remained except the poorest people of the land. 15 And he exiled Yehoyaḵin to Baḇel. And the sovereign's mother, and the sovereign's wives, and his eunuchs, and the leading men of the land he exiled from Yerushalayim to Baḇel. 16 And all the mighty brave men, seven thousand, and craftsmen and smiths, one thousand, all who were strong and fit for battle, these the sovereign of Baḇel brought to Baḇel into exile. (2 Kings 24:10-16)*

Jehoiachin was released from prison in the year 561 B.C. by Evil-Merodach[21] and allowed to live out the rest of his days in Babylon.

*27 And it came to be in the thirty-seventh year of the exile of Yehoyaḵin sovereign of Yehuḏah, in the twelfth month, on the twenty-seventh of the month, that Ewil-Meroḏaḵ sovereign of Baḇel, in the year that he began to reign, released Yehoyaḵin sovereign of Yehuḏah from prison, 28 and spoke kindly to him, and set his throne above the throne of the sovereigns who were with him in Baḇel, 29 and changed his prison garments. And he ate bread continually before the sovereign all the days of his life. 30 And as his allowance, a continual allowance was given to him from the sovereign, a quota for each day, all the days of his life. (2 Kings 25:27-30)*

---

[21] http://en.wikipedia.org/wiki/Amel-Marduk

With the capture of Jerusalem and the death of King Jehoiakim in 597 B.C. Jehoiachin became king and this lasted three months until King Nebuchadnezzar II took him captive and replaced him with his uncle, Zedekiah.

> *17 And the king of Babylon made Mattaniah his father's brother king in his stead, and changed his name to Zedekiah.* (2 Kings 24:17)

King Zedekiah would reign in Jerusalem for eleven years until the destruction of the Temple in 586 B.C. by Nebuchadnezzar II.

Ezekiel, at the age of twenty-five[22], was part of the 3,000 elite of Judah who were taken to Babylon along with Jehoiachin in 597 B.C.

However, while in captivity, the deported Jews still regarded Jeconiah as their legitimate king. Even Ezekiel refers to Jeconiah as king and dates certain events from when Jehoiachin went into exile. Ezekiel never mentions, by name, Zedekiah, the successor to the Kingdom of Judah.

Ezekiel started his prophetic ministry in the fifth year of the captivity, which is the year 593 B.C.

> *1 And it came to be in the thirtieth year, in the fourth month, on the fifth of the month, as I was among the exiles by the River Kebar, the heavens were opened and I saw visions of Elohim. 2 On the fifth of the month, in the fifth year of Sovereign Yehoyakin's exile, 3 the word of יהוה came expressly to Yeḥezqěl the priest, the son of Buzi, in the land of the Chaldeans by the River Kebar. And the hand of יהוה came upon him there.* (Ezekiel 1:1-3)

---

[22] Based on Ezekiel 1:1-3 that the thirtieth year was his age. Since a man entered into priestly service at the age of thirty (Numbers 4:3, 23, 30, 39, 43; 1 Chronicles 23:3), Yehovah may have elected to start using him as a prophet at this critical age, perhaps highlighting the priestly aspect of Ezekiel's commission.

At that time Daniel, whom Ezekiel probably knew, had already been a prisoner for twelve years in the palace of the king of Babylon. Ezekiel mentions Daniel's name in Ezekiel 14:14, 20 and Ezekiel 28:3.

The last dated message of Ezekiel was given in the twenty-seventh year of the captivity—that is, the year 571 B.C. (Ezekiel 29:17) Ezekiel therefore prophesied in Babylon for at least twenty-two years but we do not know exactly when he died.

Jeremiah began his warning messages in the thirteenth year of King Josiah's reign, which was the year 627 B.C. and was still active even after the death of Zedekiah in 586 B.C. as you will see in chapter two of this book.

> *1 The words of Yirmeyahu the son of Ḥilqiyahu, of the priests who were in Anathoth in the land of Binyamin, 2 to whom the word of יהוה came in the days of Yoshiyahu son of Amon, sovereign of Yehuḏah, in the thirteenth year of his reign. 3 And it came in the days of Yehoyaqim, son of Yoshiyahu, sovereign of Yehuḏah, until the end of the eleventh year of Tsiḏqiyahu, son of Yoshiyahu, sovereign of Yehuḏah, until the exile of Yerushalayim in the fifth month.* (Jeremiah 1:1-3)

Jeremiah at this time was warning the people of Jerusalem of the coming danger, but they would not listen to him.

> *9 "... see, I am sending and taking all the tribes of the north," declares יהוה, "and Nebukaḏretstsar the sovereign of Baḇel, My servant, and shall bring them against this land and against its inhabitants, and against these nations all around, and shall put them under the ban, and make them an astonishment, and a hissing, and everlasting ruins."* (Jeremiah 25:9)

> *11 "And all this land shall be a ruin and a waste, and these nations shall serve the sovereign of Baḇel seventy years. 12 And it shall be, when seventy years are completed, that I shall punish the sovereign of Baḇel and that nation, the land*

of the Chaldeans, for their crookedness," declares יהוה, *"and shall make it everlasting ruins."* (Jeremiah 25:11-12)

Along with Jeremiah and Ezekiel, Joel is thought to have been a contemporary, but there is not enough hard evidence to know this for a fact. Obadiah, Habakkuk and Zephaniah were all prophesying just before and during the Babylonian captivity. In all of this we have the young boy, Daniel, being set apart by Yehovah for a specific purpose. Toward the end of Daniel's life Zechariah begins his prophecies.

In the book Book of Daniel, chapter two, it is the second year of Nebuchadnezzar II's reign. It is the year 604 B.C. and Daniel's second year in captivity. Right here in the second year of his captivity Yehovah, is showing Daniel, through Nebuchadnezzar II's dream, of the statute of this huge man and of the four world ruling empires that were going to come on the world scene, with Babylon being the first one and the head of gold.

> *1 And in the second year of the reign of Nebukadnetstsar, Nebukadnetstsar had dreams. And his spirit was so troubled that his sleep left him. 2 And the sovereign gave orders to call the magicians, and the astrologers, and the practicers of witchcraft, and the Chaldeans to declare to the sovereign his dreams. So they came and stood before the sovereign. 3 And the sovereign said to them, "I have had a dream, and my spirit is troubled to know the dream." 4 And the Chaldeans spoke to the sovereign in Aramaic, "O sovereign, live forever! Relate the dream to your servants, and we shall reveal the interpretation." 5 The sovereign answered and said to the Chaldeans, "My decision is firm: if you do not make known the dream and its interpretation to me, your limbs shall be taken from you, and your houses made dunghills. 6 But if you reveal the dream and its interpretation, you shall receive gifts, and rewards, and great esteem from me. So reveal to me the dream and its interpretation."* (Daniel 2:1-6)

> *7 They answered again and said, "Let the sovereign relate to his servants the dream, and we shall reveal its*

*interpretation." 8 The sovereign answered and said, "I know for certain that you would gain time, because you see that my decision is firm: 9 If you do not make known the dream to me, there is only one decree for you! For you have agreed to speak lying and corrupt words before me till the time has changed. So relate the dream to me, then I shall know that you shall reveal its interpretation for me." 10 The Chaldeans answered the sovereign, and said, "There is no one on earth who is able to reveal the matter of the sovereign. Because no sovereign, master, or ruler has ever asked a matter like this of any magician, or astrologer, or Chaldean. 11 And the matter that the sovereign is asking is difficult, and there is no other who is able to reveal it to the sovereign except the elahin, whose dwelling is not with flesh."* (Daniel 2:7-11)

*12 Because of this the sovereign was enraged and very wroth, and gave orders to destroy all the wise ones of Baḇel. 13 So the decree went out, and they began killing the wise ones. And they sought Dani'ěl and his companions, to kill them. 14 Then with counsel and wisdom Dani'ěl answered Aryoḵ, the chief of the sovereign's guard, who had gone out to kill the wise ones of Babel—15 he answered and said to Aryoḵ the sovereign's officer, "Why is the decree from the sovereign so urgent?" So Aryoḵ made the decision known to Dani'ěl.* (Daniel 2:12-15)

*16 And Dani'ěl went in and asked the sovereign to give him time, and he would show the sovereign the interpretation. 17 Then Dani'ěl went to his house, and made the decision known to Ḥananyah, Misha'ěl, and Azaryah, his companions, 18 to seek compassion from the Elah of the heavens concerning this secret, so that Dani'ěl and his companions should not perish with the rest of the wise ones of Baḇel. 19 Then the secret was revealed to Dani'ěl in a night vision, and Dani'ěl blessed the Elah of the heavens. 20 Dani'ěl responded and said, "Blessed be the Name of Elah forever and ever, for wisdom and might are His. 21 And He changes the times and the seasons. He removes sovereigns and raises up sovereigns. He gives wisdom to the wise and knowledge to those who possess understanding. 22 He reveals deep and secret matters. He knows what is in the darkness, and light dwells with Him. 23 I thank You and praise You, O Elah of my fathers. You have given me wisdom and might, and have now made known to me what we asked of You, for You have made known to us the sovereign's matter."* (Daniel 2:16-23)

*24 So Dani'ĕl went to Aryok̄, whom the sovereign had appointed to destroy the wise ones of Baḇel. He went and said this to him, "Do not destroy the wise ones of Baḇel. Bring me in before the sovereign, and I shall show the interpretation to the sovereign." 25 Then Aryok̄ brought Dani'ĕl in a hurry before the sovereign, and said thus to him, "I have found a man among the sons of the exile of Yehuḏah, who does make known to the sovereign the interpretation." 26 The sovereign answered and said to Dani'ĕl, whose name was Bĕlteshatstsar, "Are you able to make known to me the dream which I have seen, and its interpretation?"* (Daniel 2:24-26)

*27 Dani'ĕl answered before the sovereign, and said, "The secret which the sovereign is asking—the wise ones, the astrologers, the magicians, and the diviners are unable to show it to the sovereign. 28 But there is an Elah in the heavens who reveals secrets, and He has made known to Sovereign Nebuk̄aḏnetstsar what is to be in the latter days. Your dream, and the visions of your head upon your bed, were these: 29 As for you, O sovereign, on your bed your thoughts came up: What is going to take place after this. And He who reveals secrets has made known to you what shall be after this. 30 As for me, this secret has not been revealed to me because I have more wisdom than anyone living, but for our sakes who make known the interpretation to the sovereign, and that you should know the thoughts of your heart. 31 You, O sovereign, were looking on, and saw a great image! This great image, and its brightness excellent, was standing before you, and its form was awesome. 32 This image's head was of fine gold, its chest and arms of silver, its belly and thighs of bronze, 33 its legs of iron, its feet partly of iron and partly of clay. 34 You were looking on, until a stone was cut out without hands, and it smote the image on its feet of iron and clay, and broke them in pieces. 35 Then the iron, the clay, the bronze, the silver, and the gold were crushed together, and became like chaff from the summer threshing-floors. And the wind took them away so that no trace of them was found. And the stone that smote the image became a great mountain and filled all the earth."* (Daniel 2:27-35)

*36 "This is the dream, and its interpretation we declare before the sovereign. 37 You, O sovereign, are a sovereign of sovereigns. For the Elah of the heavens has given you a reign, power, and strength, and preciousness, 38 and wherever the children of men dwell, or the beasts of the field and the birds of the heavens, He has given them into your hand, and has made you ruler over them all. You are the head of gold. 39 And after you rises up another reign lower than yours, and another third reign of bronze that rules over all the earth. 40 And the fourth reign is as strong as iron, because iron crushes and shatters all. So, like iron that breaks in pieces, it crushes and breaks all these."* (Daniel 2:36-40)

*41 "Yet, as you saw the feet and toes, partly of potter's clay and partly of iron, the reign is to be divided. But some of the strength of the iron is to be in it, because you saw the iron mixed with muddy clay. 42 And as the toes of the feet were partly of iron and partly of clay, so the reign is partly strong and partly brittle. 43 And as you saw iron mixed with muddy clay, they are mixing themselves with the seed of men, but they are not clinging to each other, even as iron does not mix with clay. 44 And in the days of these sovereigns the Elah of the heavens shall set up a reign which shall never be destroyed, nor the reign pass on to other people—it crushes and puts to an end all these reigns, and it shall stand forever[1]. (Daniel 2:41-44 | Footnote:[1] Daniel 7; Psalms 22:28;*

*Jeremiah 30:11; Joel 3:16; Obadiah 15-17; Habbukuk 3:12-13; Zephaniah 3:8; Haggai 2:22; Revelation 11:15)*

*45 "Because you saw that the stone was cut out of the mountain without hands, and that it crushed the iron, the bronze, the clay, the silver, and the gold, the great Elah has made known to the sovereign what shall be after this. And the dream is true, and its interpretation is trustworthy." 46 Then Sovereign Nebukadnetstsar fell on his face, and did obeisance before Dani'ĕl, and gave orders to present to him an offering and incense. 47 The sovereign answered Dani'ĕl, and said, "Truly your Elah is the Elah of elahin, the Master of sovereigns, and a revealer of secrets, since you were able to reveal this secret." 48 Then the sovereign made Dani'ĕl great and gave him many great gifts, and made him ruler over all the province of Babel, and chief of the nobles, over all the wise ones of Babel. 49 And Dani'ĕl asked of the sovereign, and he set Shadrak, Mĕyshak, and Abĕd-Nego over the work of the province of Babel, and Dani'ĕl in the gate of the sovereign.* (Daniel 2:45-49)

This is the account then of how Daniel was promoted from just being one of the Jewish captives to one who ruled over the province of Babylon and was given the status Chief of the Governors over all the wise men of Babylon. This was a huge promotion.

We then read of Daniel's three friends being thrown into the fiery furnace for not bowing down to the golden image Nebuchadnezzar II had made. And when they came out, they too, were raised in rank over the Provinces of Babylon. This proved to be of great encouragement for the Jewish captives during that time to hear of these great events with regard to both Daniel and his three friends and how they were both promoted and rose in rank within the Babylonian government system.

After a little time, there arose false prophets in Babylon who were telling the people things that were not true and we find Jeremiah speaking out against them. I am sharing this with you so that you can better understand the exceedingly great turmoil and stress Daniel and the Jewish people were under at this time as they tried to understand what had happened to them—both in the context of why Yehovah let this happen to them and by way of the people Yehovah was working through—one of those people being Daniel.

Jeremiah wrote a letter to the captives of Babylon warning against placing their belief in these two false prophets and admonishing them to build and settle in the land of Babylon.

> *1 And these are the words of the letter which Yirmeyahu the prophet sent from Yerushalayim to the rest of the elders of the exile, and to the priests, and to the prophets and to all the people whom Nebukadnetstsar had exiled from Yerushalayim to Babel—2 after Yekonyah the sovereign, and the sovereigness mother, and the eunuchs, and the heads of Yehudah and Yerushalayim, and the craftsmen, and the smiths had gone into exile from Yerushalayim—3 by the hand of El'asah son of Shaphan, and Gemaryah the son of Hilqiyah, whom Tsidqiyah sovereign of Yehudah sent to Babel, to Nebukadnetstsar the sovereign of Babel, saying, 4 "Thus said יהוה of hosts, Elohim of Yisra'ěl, to all the exiles whom I exiled from Yerushalayim to Babel, 5 'Build houses and dwell in them, plant gardens and eat their fruit. 6 Take wives and bring forth sons and daughters. And take wives for your sons and give your daughters to husbands, and let them bear sons and daughters, and be increased there, and not diminished. 7 And seek the peace of the city where I have exiled you, and pray to יהוה for it, for in its peace you have peace.'"* (Jeremiah 29:1-7)

> *8 For thus said יהוה of hosts, Elohim of Yisra'ěl, "Let not your prophets and your diviners who are in your midst deceive you, neither listen to the dreams which you are dreaming. 9 For they are prophesying falsely to you in My Name. I have not sent them," declares יהוה. 10 For thus said יהוה, "When seventy years are completed, at Babel I shall visit you and establish My good word toward you, to bring you back to this place. 11 For I know the plans I am planning for you,"*

declares יהוה, *"plans of peace and not of evil, to give you a future and an expectancy. 12 Then you shall call on Me, and shall come and pray to Me, and I shall listen to you. 13 And you shall seek Me, and shall find Me, when you search for Me with all your heart.¹"* (Jeremiah 29:8-13 | Footnote: ¹Deuteronomy 4:29; Joel 2:12)

*14 "And I shall be found by you," declares* יהוה, *"and I shall turn back your captivity, and shall gather you from all the gentiles and from all the places where I have driven you," declares* יהוה. *"And I shall bring you back to the place from which I have exiled you. 15 Because you have said, '*יהוה* has raised up prophets for us in Babel' 16 thus said* יהוה *concerning the sovereign who sits on the throne of Dawiḏ, concerning all the people who dwell in this city, and concerning your brothers who have not gone out with you into exile, 17 thus said* יהוה *of hosts, 'See, I am sending on them the sword, the scarcity of food, and the pestilence. And I shall make them like spoilt figs, so spoilt as to be uneatable. 18 And I shall pursue them with the sword, with scarcity of food, and with pestilence. And I shall make them a horror among all the reigns of the earth, to be a curse, and an astonishment, and a hissing, and a reproach among all the gentiles where I have driven them. 19 For they did not heed My words,' declares* יהוה, *'which I sent to them by My servants the prophets, rising up early and sending them, yet you did not listen,'" declares* יהוה. (Jeremiah 29:14-19)

*20 "You, therefore, hear the word of* יהוה, *all you exiles whom I have sent from Yerushalayim to Baḇel. 21 Thus said* יהוה *of hosts, the Elohim of Yisra'ěl, concerning Aḥaḇ son of Qolayah, and Tsiḏqiyahu son of Ma'asěyah, who are prophesying falsely to you in My Name, 'See, I am giving them into the hand of Neḇuḵaḏretstsar sovereign of Baḇel, and he shall smite them before your eyes. 22 And because of them all the exiles of Yehuḏah who are in Baḇel shall use a curse, saying,* יהוה *make you like Tsiḏqiyahu and Aḥaḇ, whom the sovereign of Baḇel roasted in the fire, 23 because they have done wickedness in Yisra'ĕl, and committed adultery with their neighbours' wives, and have spoken a word in My Name falsely which I have not commanded them. And I am He who knows, and a witness,'" declares יהוה.* (Jeremiah 29:20-23)

*24 And speak to Shemayahu the Neḥelamite, saying, 25 "Thus speaks יהוה of hosts, the Elohim of Yisra'ĕl, saying, 'Because you have sent letters in your name to all the people who are at Yerushalayim, to Tsephanyah son of Ma'asĕyah the priest, and to all the priests, saying, 26 יהוה has made you priest instead of Yehoyaḏa the priest,' so that there are overseers in the House of יהוה over everyone who is mad and makes himself a prophet, that you should put him in the stocks and in the iron collar. 27 So why have you not reproved Yirmeyahu of Anathoth who makes himself a prophet to you? 28 For he has sent to us in Baḇel, saying, 'This captivity is long—build houses and dwell in them, and plant gardens and eat their fruit.'" 29 And Tsephanyah the priest read this letter in the hearing of Yirmeyahu the prophet.* (Jeremiah 29:24-29)

*30 Then the word of יהוה came to Yirmeyahu, saying, 31 "Send to all those in exile, saying, Thus said יהוה concerning Shemayah the Neḥelamite, 'Because Shemayah has prophesied to you, and I have not sent him, and he has made you to trust on falsehood,' 32 therefore thus said יהוה, 'See, I am bringing punishment upon Shemayah the Neḥelamite and his seed: he shall have no one to dwell among this people, nor is he to see the good that I am about to do for My people,' declares יהוה, 'because he has spoken apostasy against יהוה.'"* (Jeremiah 29:30-32)

Take special note of verse ten of the above Bible passage.

*10 For thus said יהוה, "When seventy years are completed, at Baḇel I shall visit you and establish My good word toward you, to bring you back to this place."* (Jeremiah 29:10)

The above passage makes two things clear: 1) Babylon's domination of Judah would include a captivity during which Jews would be taken as captives to Babylon. 2) That the captivity would end when the "seventy years" ended. But Jeremiah never said that the captivity *itself* would last seventy years. He only said that the Babylonian rule would last seventy years. Babylon's rule lasted seventy years, from 609 B.C. when the last Assyrian king, Ashur-uballit II, was defeated in Harran, until 539 B.C. when the Medo-Persians conquered Babylon.[23]

Yehovah informed Ezekiel that Jerusalem was under siege and would surely fall. We said previously that Ezekiel's and Jehoiachin's fifth year was 593 B.C. so the ninth year was 588 B.C. Ezekiel dated his writings according to the years of captivity he shared with Jeconiah, and he mentions several events related to the fall of Jerusalem in those writings.[24] Ezekiel does not relate his writings according to the Sabbatical and Jubilee years, as some today would have us believe.

> *1 And in the ninth year, in the tenth month, on the tenth of the month, the word of* יהוה *came to me, saying, 2 "Son of man, write down the name of the day, for on this same day the sovereign of Babel has thrown himself against Yerushalayim. 3 And speak a parable to the rebellious house, and you shall say to them, Thus said the Master* יהוה, *'Put on a pot, put it on, and also pour water into it. 4 Gather pieces of meat in it, every good piece, the thigh and the shoulder, fill it with choice bones. 5 Take the choice of the flock, also pile bones under it, cook it thoroughly, also let the bones cook in it." 6 Therefore thus said the Master* יהוה, *'Woe to the city of blood, to the pot in which there is rust, and whose rust has not gone out of it! Bring it out piece by piece, on which no lot has fallen. 7 For her blood is in her midst. She has set it on a shining rock. She did not pour it on the ground, to cover it with dust.'"*
>
> *8 "To stir up wrath and take vengeance, I have set her blood on a shining rock, so that it would not be covered."*

---

[23] http://www.aboutbibleprophecy.com/years.htm
[24] http://en.wikipedia.org/wiki/יְכָנְיָה

> *9 Therefore thus said the Master יהוה, "Woe to the city of blood! Let Me also make the pile great. 10 Heap on the wood, kindle the fire, cook the meat well, mixing in the spices, and let the bones be burned up. 11 And set it on the coals, empty, so that it gets hot, and its bronze glows. And its filthiness shall be melted in it, and its rust be consumed. 12 She has wearied herself with sorrows, and her great rust has not gone from her. Into the fire with her rust! 13 In your filthiness is wickedness. Because I have cleansed you, but you are not clean. You shall not be cleansed of your filthiness any more, till I have caused My wrath to rest upon you. 14 I, יהוה, have spoken. It shall come, and I shall do it. I do not hold back, nor do I pardon, nor do I relent. According to your ways and according to your deeds they shall judge you," declares the Master יהוה."* (Ezekiel 24:1-14)

Ezekiel was told that his beloved wife would soon die. The delight of his eyes would be taken from him just as the temple, the delight of Israel's eyes, would be taken from her. He was not to mourn openly for his wife, as a sign to his people not to mourn openly for Jerusalem.

> *15 And the word of יהוה came to me, saying, 16 "Son of man, see, I am taking away from you the desire of your eyes with one stroke. But do not mourn, nor weep, nor let your tears run down. 17 Groan silently, make no mourning for the dead. Bind your turban on your head, and put your sandals on your feet. Do not cover your upper lip, and do not eat man's bread of sorrow." 18 And I spoke to the people in the morning, and in the evening my wife died. And the next morning I did as I was commanded. 19 And the people said to me, "Would you not explain to us what these matters you are doing mean to us?" 20 And I said to them, The word of יהוה came to me, saying, 21 "Speak to the house of Yisra'ěl, Thus said the Master יהוה, 'See, I am profaning My set-apart place—the pride of your strength, the desire of your eyes, and the delight of your being. And your sons and daughters whom you left behind shall fall by the sword.'"* (Ezekiel 24:15-21)

*22 "And you shall do as I have done, do not cover your upper lip nor eat man's bread of sorrow, 23 and let your turbans remain on your heads and your sandals on your feet. Do not mourn, nor weep, but you shall pine away in your crookednesses and groan with one another. 24 'And Yeḥezqěl shall be a sign to you. Do according to all that he has done. When this comes, you shall know that I am the Master יהוה.' 25 'And you, son of man, on the day when I take from them their stronghold, the joy of their adorning, the desire of their eyes, and the lifting up of their being, their sons and their daughters, 26 on that day one that has escaped shall come to you to let you hear it with your ears. 27 On that day your mouth shall be opened to him who has escaped, and you shall speak and no longer be silent. And you shall be a sign to them. And they shall know that I am יהוה.'"* (Ezekiel 24:22-27)

Nebuchadnezzar II had instated Zedekiah as tributary King of Judah when he took Jehoiachin prisoner in 597 B.C. Zedekiah later revolted against Babylon and entered into an alliance with Pharaoh Hophra of Egypt who had given Babylon a severe defeat two years before.

Nebuchadnezzar II responded by invading Judah and began a siege of Jerusalem in January 589 B.C. During this siege, which lasted about thirty months, "every worst woe befell the city, which drank the cup of God's fury to the dregs."

*1 And it came to be in the ninth year of his reign, in the tenth month, on the tenth of the month, that Neḇuḵaḏnetstsar sovereign of Baḇel and all his army came against Yerushalayim and encamped against it, and they built a siege wall against it all around. 2 And the city was besieged until the eleventh year of Sovereign Tsiḏqiyahu. 3 By the ninth of the month the scarcity of food had become so severe in the city that there was no food for the people of the land.* (2 Kings 25:1-3)

*2 The precious sons of Tsiyon who were weighed against fine gold, how they have been reckoned as clay pots, the work of the hands of the potter! 3 Even jackals have presented their breasts, they have nursed their young. The daughter of my people has become as cruel, as ostriches in the wilderness. 4 The tongue of the infant has clung to the roof of its mouth for thirst; children asked for bread, no one breaks it for them.* (Lamentations 4:2-4)

*5 Those who ate delicacies have have been laid waste in the streets; Those who were brought up in scarlet have have embraced dunghills. 6 And the crookedness of the daughter of my people is greater than the punishment of the sin of Sedom, which was overthrown in a moment, and no hands were wrung over her! 7 Her Nazirites were brighter than snow and whiter than milk; more ruddy in body than rubies, their cut like sapphire. 8 Their appearance has become blacker than soot; they have become unrecognized in the streets; their skin has shriveled on their bones, it has become dry, it has become as wood. 9 Better off were those pierced by the sword than those pierced by hunger; for these pine away, pierced through for lack of the fruits of the field. 10 The hands of the compassionate women have boiled their own children; they became food for them in the destruction of the daughter of my people. 11 יהוה has completed His wrath, He has poured out His burning displeasure. And He kindled a fire in Tsiyon, and it consumed her foundations.* (Lamentations 4:2-11) 4:5-11)

In 586 B.C., the eleventh year of Zedekiah's reign, Nebuchadnezzar II broke through Jerusalem's walls, conquering the city. Zedekiah and his followers attempted to escape, but were captured on the plains of Jericho and taken to Riblah. There, after seeing his sons killed, Zedekiah was blinded, bound, and taken captive to Babylon, where he remained a prisoner until his death.

*4 Then the city wall was breached, and all the men of battle fled at night by way of the gate between two walls, which*

> *was by the sovereign's garden, even though the Chaldeans were still encamped all around against the city. And the sovereign went by way of the desert plain. 5 And the army of the Chaldeans pursued the sovereign, and overtook him in the desert plains of Yeriḥo, and all his army was scattered from him. 6 And they seized the sovereign and brought him up to the sovereign of Baḇel at Riblah, and they pronounced sentence on him. 7 And they slaughtered the sons of Tsiḏqiyahu before his eyes, and put out the eyes of Tsiḏqiyahu, and bound him with bronze shackles, and took him to Baḇel.* (2 Kings 25:4-7)

> *11 Tsiḏqiyahu was twenty-one years old when he began to reign, and he reigned eleven years in Yerushalayim. 12 And he did evil in the eyes of יהוה his Elohim. He did not humble himself before Yirmeyahu the prophet, who spoke from the mouth of יהוה. 13 And he also rebelled against Sovereign Neḇuḵaḏnetstsar, who had made him swear by Elohim, but he stiffened his neck and hardened his heart against turning to יהוה Elohim of Yisra'ěl.* (2 Chronicles 36:11-13)

You can read more about this time in the accounts of Jeremiah 32:4-5, 34:2-3, 39:1-7, and 52:4-11.

The Babylonians laid siege to Jerusalem in 588 B.C., and in July 586 B.C., the walls were breached and the city plundered. On August 14th, 586 B.C., the city and temple were burned. This is also known as the tenth of Av.

> *18 Tsiḏqiyahu was twenty-one years old when he began to reign, and he reigned eleven years in Yerushalayim. And his mother's name was Ḥamutal the daughter of Yirmeyahu of Liḇnah. 19 And he did evil in the eyes of יהוה, according to all that Yehoyaqim did. 20 For this took place in Yerushalayim and Yehuḏah because of the displeasure of יהוה, until He had cast them out from His presence. And Tsiḏqiyahu rebelled against the sovereign of Baḇel.* (2 Kings 24:18-20)

## The Temple was destroyed on Av 10, 586 B.C.

> *12 And on the tenth of the fifth month, which was the nineteenth year of sovereign Nebukadretstsar sovereign of Babel, Nebuzaradan, chief of the guard, who served the sovereign of Babel, came to Yerushalayim, 13 and he burned the House of* יהוה, *and the sovereign's house, and all the houses of Yerushalayim, and all the houses of the great men, he burned with fire.* (Jeremiah 52:12-13)

> *2 And the city was besieged until the eleventh year of Sovereign Tsidqiyahu. 3 By the ninth of the month the scarcity of food had become so severe in the city that there was no food for the people of the land. 4 Then the city wall was breached, and all the men of battle fled at night by way of the gate between two walls, which was by the sovereign's garden, even though the Chaldeans were still encamped all around against the city. And the sovereign went by way of the desert plain. 5 And the army of the Chaldeans pursued the sovereign, and overtook him in the desert plains of Yeriho, and all his army was scattered from him. 6 And they seized the sovereign and brought him up to the sovereign of Babel at Riblah, and they pronounced sentence on him. 7 And they slaughtered the sons of Tsidqiyahu before his eyes, and put out the eyes of Tsidqiyahu, and bound him with bronze shackles, and took him to Babel.* (2 Kings 25:2-7)

> *8 And in the fifth month, on the seventh of the month, which was the nineteenth year of Sovereign Nebukadnetstsar sovereign of Babel, Nebuzaradan the chief of the guard, a servant of the sovereign of Babel, came to Yerushalayim. 9 And he burned the House of* יהוה *and the house of the sovereign, and all the houses of Yerushalayim—even every great house he burned with fire. 10 And all the army of the Chaldeans who were with the chief of the guard broke down the walls of Yerushalayim all around. 11 And Nebuzaradan the chief of the guard took into exile the rest of the people who were left in the city and the deserters who deserted to*

*the sovereign of Baḇel, with the rest of the multitude. 12 But the chief of the guard left some of the poor of the land as vinedressers and farmers.* (2 Kings 25:8-12)

*13 And the bronze columns that were in the House of* יהוה, *and the stands and the bronze Sea that were in the House of* יהוה, *the Chaldeans broke in pieces, and took their bronze away to Baḇel. 14 And they took the pots, and the shovels, and the snuffers, and the ladles, and all the bronze utensils the priests used in the service. 15 And the chief of the guard took the fire holders and the basins which were of solid gold and solid silver. 16 The bronze of all these utensils was beyond measure—the two columns, the one Sea, and the stands, which Shelomoh had made for the House of* יהוה. *17 The height of one column was eighteen cubits, and the capital on it was of bronze. And the height of the capital was three cubits, and the network and pomegranates all around the capital were all of bronze. And the second column was the same, with a network.* (2 Kings 25:13-17)

*18 And the chief of the guard took Serayah the chief priest, and Tsephanyahu the second priest, and the three doorkeepers. 19 And out of the city he took a certain eunuch who was appointed over the men of battle, and five men of those who saw the sovereign's face, who were found in the city, and the chief scribe of the army who mustered the people of the land, and sixty men of the people of the land who were found in the city. 20 And Neḇuzaradan, chief of the guard, took them and made them go to the sovereign of Baḇel at Riblah. 21 And the sovereign of Baḇel smote them and put them to death at Riblah in the land of Ḥamath. So he exiled Yehuḏah from its own land. 22 And he appointed Geḏalyahu son of Aḥiqam, son of Shaphan, over the people who were left in the land of Yehuḏah, whom Neḇukaḏnetstsar sovereign of Baḇel had left.* (2 Kings 25:18-22)

*23 And all the commanders of the armies, they and their men, heard that the sovereign of Baḇel had appointed Geḏalyahu.*

> *And they came to Gedalyahu at Mitspah, even Yishmaĕl son of Nethanyah, and Yoḥanan son of Qarĕaḥ, and Serayah son of Tanḥumeth the Netophathite, and Yaʿazanyahu the son of a Maʿaḵathite, they and their men. 24 And Gedalyahu swore to them and their men, and said to them, "Do not be afraid of the servants of the Chaldeans. Dwell in the land and serve the sovereign of Baḇel, and let it be well with you." 25 And in the seventh month it came to be that Yishmaĕl son of Nethanyah, son of Elishama, of the seed of the reign, came with ten men and smote Gedalyahu that he died, and the Yehudim, and the Chaldeans who were with him at Mitspah. 26 And all the people rose up, small and great, and the commanders of the armies, and went to Mitsrayim, for they were afraid of the Chaldeans.* (2 Kings 25:23-26)

> *21 And it came to be in the twelfth year of our exile, in the tenth month, on the fifth of the month, that one who had escaped from Yerushalayim came to me and said, "The city has been smitten!"* (Ezekiel 33:21)

The tenth month is in December 586 B.C.

In 586 B.C., twelve years after Nebuchadnezzar II's first attack on Jerusalem, the people of Jerusalem rebelled against Chaldean rule, and the Chaldeans responded by burning Jerusalem and tearing down its walls. They also looted the Temple and burned it down. The Chaldeans procured roughly 40,000 from Judah as captives—including political leaders and high priests, and took them to their capital, Babylon, while some people from Judah fled into Egypt or Arabia, and still others fled north into Chaldean-controlled Mesopotamia.

We will pick back up with Jeremiah later on, but for now know and understand the horrendous stress Daniel and his countrymen of this era were forced to operate under as they were beaten in war and then watched as they were taken in captivity and then made to watch while the Temple was being destroyed. The Northern Tribes of Israel were also watching these events unfold from far off while still in their respective places of captivity.

In Daniel, chapter four, we read of the tree that was cut down and Daniel's interpretation of that dream.

> 24 "... this is the interpretation, O sovereign, and this is the decree of the Most High, which has come upon my master the sovereign: 25 'That you are going to be driven away from men, and your dwelling be with the beasts of the field, and you be given grass to eat like oxen, and you be wetted with the dew of the heavens, and seven times pass over you, till you know that the Most High is ruler in the reign of men, and that He gives it to whomever He wishes. 26 And they that gave the command to leave the stump of its roots of the tree: your reign remains yours, from the time you come to know that the heavens are ruling. 27 Therefore, O sovereign, let my counsel be acceptable to you, and break off your sins by righteousness, and your crookednesses by showing favour to the poor—your prosperity might be extended." 28 All this came upon Sovereign Nebukadnetstsar. 29 At the end of the twelve months he was walking about the palace of the reign of Babel. 30 The sovereign spoke and said, "Is not this great Babel, which I myself have built, for the house of the reign, by the might of my power and for the esteem of my splendour?" 31 The word was still in the sovereign's mouth, when a voice fell from the heavens, "Sovereign Nebukadnetstsar, to you it is spoken: the reign has been taken away from you, 32 and you are driven away from men, and your dwelling is to be with the beasts of the field. You are given grass to eat like oxen, and seven seasons shall pass over you, until you know that the Most High is ruler in the reign of men, and He gives it to whomever He wishes." (Daniel 4:24-32)

> 33 In that hour the word was executed on Nebukadnetstsar, and he was driven from men and he ate grass like oxen, and his body was wet with the dew of the heavens till his hair had grown like eagles' feathers and his nails like birds' claws. 34 "And at the end of the days I, Nebukadnetstsar, lifted my eyes to the heavens, and my understanding returned to me. And I blessed the Most High and praised and made Him

*great who lives forever, whose rule is an everlasting rule, and His reign is from generation to generation. 35 And all the inhabitants of the earth are of no account, and He does as He wishes with the host of the heavens and among the inhabitants of the earth. And there is none to strike against His hand or say to Him, 'What have You done?' 36 At the same time my understanding returned to me, and for the preciousness of my reign, my esteem and splendour were returning to me. And my counselours and nobles sought me out, and I was re-established to my reign, and excellent greatness was added to me. 37 Now I, Nebukadnetstsar, am praising and exalting and esteeming the Sovereign of the heavens, for all His works are truth, and His ways right. And those who walk in pride He is able to humble."* (Daniel 4:33-37)

The years in which the seven years of insanity took place are not known. However, I would strongly suspect it to be after Nebuchadnezzar II was king for some time in order to accomplish many of the things he did and in order for him to speak the words he does in Daniel chapter four. But there is a prophecy in this chapter that reveals something of utmost importance to us.

The tree in this dream of chapter four represents not only Nebuchadnezzar II but the Babylonian Empire as a whole as well. Babylon fell in 539 B.C., but we know from the Book of Revelation that it is to experience an end-time revival as a powerful European empire dominated by a great false Christian system referred to in Revelation 17 as *"Babylon the Great."* All things considered, it is believed that the seven times are as seven 360-day prophetic periods of years. The prophetic "day-for-year" principle (Numbers 14:34; Ezekiel 4:6) yields 2,520 years (i.e. 360 x 7)—stretching from the fall of ancient Babylon to the beginnings of its revival in modern times. There even exists a potential parallel to this figure of 2,520 in the mysterious inscription of Daniel 5, as we will examine later, more closely.

2,520 years forward in time from 539 B.C. brought us to 1982 when Pope John Paul, strongly urged his followers to get back to their roots.

The stump of Babylon, therefore, began to sprout once again in 1982. Here is Pope Benedict's speech and his reference to Pope John Paul's speech in 1982:

> Speaking before yesterday's Angelus prayer to a group of some 8,000 pilgrims in Les Combes, in Italy's Valle d'Aosta, where he is vacationing, the Holy Father recalled **Europe's deeply Christian roots and challenged the continent to return to them.** Pope Benedict noted today's feast of the Apostle James, "whose relics are venerated in the famous shrine of Santiago de Compostela in Spain, the destination of countless pilgrims from all over Europe." He also recalled Friday's feast day of St. Bridget of Sweden, patroness of Europe, and the July 11th feast of St. Benedict, who he called "another great patron of the 'old continent.'"
>
> "Contemplating these saints," he said, "it is natural to pause and reflect on the contribution that Christianity has made, and continues to make, to the building of Europe."
>
> Benedict then turned to the pilgrimage made by "Servant of God John Paul II in 1982 to Santiago de Compostela, where he performed a solemn 'European act' during which he pronounced these memorable words: "I, bishop of Rome and pastor of the Universal Church, from Santiago, address to you, old Europe, a cry full of love: Return to yourself! Be yourself! Discover your origins. Revive your roots. Experience again those authentic values that made your history glorious and your presence in other continents beneficial.'"
>
> The Pope pointed out that during the 1982 visit, John Paul II launched "the project of a Europe aware of its own spiritual unity, based on the foundation of Christian values."
>
> "He returned to this theme on the occasion of World Youth Day 1989," the Pope continued, "held at Santiago de Compostela, expressing his hope for a Europe without frontiers, a Europe

that does not deny the Christian roots from which it grew and that does not renounce the true humanism of Christ's Gospel. How appropriate this call remains today in the light of recent events on the European continent."[25]

Pope John Pauls said to "get back to your roots" in 1982. Then, seven years later, the Berlin Wall came down[26] in 1989 uniting East and West Germany. The Germans are the ones who would go on to lead a United Europe in the latest and final most revival of Babylonian super power that has been coming together even to this present hour, as I write.

Getting back to the Book of Daniel, we have no more information about his life until we read in Daniel chapter five of the banquet of Belshazzar. Daniel, who was taken in the raid of Jerusalem in 605 B.C. as one of the children, is now over eighty years of age. This is assuming he was at least ten when the seventy years ended in 539 B.C., as I have already shown you.

In the book of Daniel we read about King Belshazzar of Babylon who held a great feast for all his nobles followed by him using the sacred vessels taken from the Temple. Suddenly, the fingers of a man's hand appear and write on the wall in front of the king at this banquet and all the guests see it. When none of his wise men are able to interpret the message, Daniel is called in at the suggestion of the Queen Mother. Daniel rebukes the king for his lack of respect for those things from the Temple of Yehovah. Daniel then tells the king what the handwriting on the wall means. Daniel told Belshazzar that he is about to lose his kingdom to the Medes and the Persians. For successfully reading the cryptic handwriting, Daniel is rewarded with a purple robe and elevated to the rank of "third ruler" of the kingdom. The very same night as this was going on, we are told, "Belshazzar, king of the Babylonians, was slain" and his successor was King Darius the Mede who had captured the city.

---

[25] http://tinyurl.com/b3af3tk
[26] http://news.bbc.co.uk/onthisday/hi/witness/november/9/newsid_3241000/3241641.stm

The writing on the wall was: Mene, Mene, Tekel, Upharsin.

These words were units of weight, much like the ounce and pound or the gram and kilogram.

The base unit in Babylon was the gold Shekel or "Tekel." Twenty-five shekels equaled one "Upharsin" and fifty shekels equaled a "Mena."

The phrase was also telling us the sum, as follows:

**MENA (50) + MENA (50) + TEKEL (1) + UPHARSIN (25) = 126**

In the Book of Ezekiel we discover that each shekel was divided into twenty gerahs:

*12 And the shekel shall be twenty gerahs.* (Ezekiel 45:12)

Therefore, the above total of 126 shekels also equals 2,520 gerahs.

*25 And this is the writing that was inscribed: MENĚ, MENĚ, TEQĚL, UPHARSIN. 26 This is the interpretation of each word: MENĚ—Elah has numbered your reign, and put an end to it. 27 TEQĚL—You have been weighed on the scales, and found lacking. 28 PERES—Your reign has been divided, and given to the Medes and Persians."* (Daniel 5:25-28)

I have just explained to you how Daniel told King Nebuchadnezzar II that the dream he had concerning the tree being cut down and how it was going to be for 2,520 years. This prophecy is also confirming that Babylon was going to be punished for 2,520 years. This was now the second time this was shown to Daniel.

King Nebuchadnezzar II had been told that his kingdom would suffer punishment of "seven times." In the Bible, a "time" is equal to a year of 360 days, as indicated in Revelation 12:6, 14 and 13:5. Each verse is talking about the *same* period of time—or 1,260 days, 3 ½ "times" or forty-two months, respectively. Therefore, seven times is the equivalent of 2,520 days. However, as is the case in many prophecies, a day represents a year (Number 14:34; Ezekiel 4:6), so this "seven times" actually indicates 7 x 360, which, in turn, equals 2,520 years.

The very night Daniel read this to the king was when this prophecy began in the year 539 B.C. 2,520 years later brings you to 1982 C.E.—after which this Babylonian monster came to power again, one final time, as the Holy Roman Empire in Europe. Each of the empires in Daniel's visions held the land that the previous empire occupied and then expanded on it so that its territory was enlarged.

Chapter six of the Book of Daniel is about Daniel being thrown in the lion's den under the reign of Darius the Mede shortly after he had conquered Babylon.

Chapters seven and eight of the Book of Daniel go back to the first year of Belshazzar and then the third year of Belshazzar as king respectively.

Now keep in mind what Daniel has seen already. In chapter two—the dream of the image with the head of gold, arms of silver, belly of brass, legs of iron and toes of iron and clay. The head of gold was Babylon, the arms were the Medes and Persians, the belly of brass was Greece and the legs of iron represented Rome.

All of this is part of the same body or same government system.

Then, in Daniel chapter four, Daniel is shown the tree that is Babylon, which was to be cut down for 2,520 years. It was then confirmed many years later when Belshazzar was king in chapter five right up to the "Mene, Mene, Tekel, and Upharsin" pronouncement. Again, adding up to the 2,520 years from that very night brings us to 1982 C.E.

In chapter seven, Daniel is told that the four beasts he sees are four kings and four kingdoms. The first one (like a lion) was Babylon; the second one (like a bear) was the Medo-Persian Empire; the third one (like a leopard) was the Grecian Empire; and the fourth and last beast that is the worst of all was and is the Roman Empire which is coming back to life again now.

In chapter eight Daniel has yet another dream, this one about the ram goats. The Angel Gabriel comes and tells Daniel what this means. The one ram with two horns was Media and Persia and the other male goat was Greece. Out of this Grecian Empire would rise up four other kingdoms.

Many are trying to rewrite the Bible, and yet we are told what these symbols mean in the Bible itself by an angel sent to explain it.

This brings us to Daniel, chapter nine.

We are now told that this dream comes to Daniel in the first year of Darius the Mede's reign. This is 539 B.C.

Daniel is contemplating the prophecy that Jeremiah had written and trying to come to a complete understanding of it.

> 2 "... in the first year of his reign I, Dani'ěl, observed from the Scriptures the number of the years, according to the word of יהוה given to Yirmeyahu the prophet, for the completion of the wastes of Yerushalayim would be seventy years." (Daniel 9:2)

What Daniel was reading was Jeremiah 25.

> 8 "Therefore thus said יהוה of hosts, 'Because you did not obey My words, 9 see, I am sending and taking all the tribes of the north,' declares יהוה, 'and Nebukadretstsar the sovereign of Babel, My servant, and shall bring them against this land and against its inhabitants, and against these nations all around, and shall put them under the ban, and make them an astonishment, and a hissing, and everlasting ruins. 10 And I shall banish from them the voice of rejoicing and the voice of gladness, the voice of the bridegroom and the voice of the bride, the sound of the millstones and the light of the lamp. 11 And all this land shall be a ruin and a

*waste, and these nations shall serve the sovereign of Baḇel seventy years."* (Jeremiah 25:8-11)

*10 "For thus said יהוה, 'When seventy years are completed, at Baḇel I shall visit you and establish My good word toward you, to bring you back to this place.'"* (Jeremiah 29:10)

Daniel understood the words of Jeremiah. He understood that the seventy years were over in 539 B.C. having begun with the defeat of the Assyrian King, Ashur-uballit in 609 B.C. Now that Daniel understands this prophecy as having already come true, the first thing he does is pray to Yehovah and make confessions on behalf of the Nation of Israel.

*3 So I set my face toward יהוה the Elohim to seek by prayer and supplications, with fasting, and sackcloth, and ashes. 4 And I prayed to יהוה my Elohim, and made confession, and said, "O יהוה, great and awesome Ěl, guarding the covenant and the kindness to those who love Him, and to those who guard His commands. 5 We have sinned and did crookedness, and did wrong and rebelled, to turn aside from Your commands and from Your right-rulings. 6 And we have not listened to Your servants the prophets, who spoke in Your Name to our sovereigns, our heads, and our fathers, and to all the people of the land. 7 O יהוה, to You is the righteousness, and to us the shame of face, as it is this day—to the men of Yehuḏah, to the inhabitants of Yerushalayim and all Yisra'ěl, those near and those far off in all the lands to which You have driven them, because of their trespass which they have trespassed against You."* (Daniel 9:3-7)

*8 "O Master, to us is the shame of face, to our sovereigns, to our heads, and to our fathers, because we have sinned against You. 9 To יהוה our Elohim are the compassions and forgivenesses, for we have rebelled against Him. 10 And we have not obeyed the voice of יהוה our Elohim, to walk in His Torot, which He set before us through His servants the prophets. 11 And all Yisra'ěl have transgressed Your Torah, and turned aside, so as not to obey Your voice. So the curse and the oath written in the Torah of Mosheh the servant of Elohim have been poured out on us, for we have sinned against Him."* (Daniel 9:8-11)

*12 "And He has confirmed His words, which He spoke against us and against our rulers who judged us, by bringing upon us great evil. For under all the heavens there has not been done like what was done to Yerushalayim. 13 As it is written in the Torah of Mosheh, all this evil has come upon us, and we have not entreated the face of* יהוה *our Elohim, to turn back from our crookednesses, and to study Your truth. 14 Hence* יהוה *has watched over the evil and has brought it upon us. For* יהוה *our Elohim is righteous in all the works which He has done, but we have not obeyed His voice. 15 And now, O* יהוה *our Elohim, who brought Your people out of the land of Mitsrayim with a strong hand, and made Yourself a Name, as it is this day—we have sinned, we have done wrong!"* (Daniel 9:12-15)

*16 "O* יהוה*, according to all Your righteousness, I pray, let Your displeasure and Your wrath be turned away from Your city Yerushalayim, Your set-apart mountain. For, because of our sins, and because of the crookednesses of our fathers, Yerushalayim and Your people have become a reproach to all those around us. 17 And now, our Elohim, hear the prayer of Your servant, and his supplications, and for the sake of* יהוה *cause Your face to shine on Your set-apart place, which is laid waste. 18 O my Elohim, incline Your ear and hear. Open Your eyes and see our wastes, and the city which is called by Your Name. For we do not present our supplications before You because of our righteous deeds, but because of Your great compassions. 19 O* יהוה*, hear! O* יהוה*, forgive! O* יהוה*, listen and act! Do not delay for Your own sake, my Elohim, for Your city and Your people are called by Your Name."* (Daniel 9:16-19)

Take special note that Daniel is praying on behalf of all of the Twelve Tribes of Israel.

> *7 O Lord, righteousness belongeth unto thee, but unto us confusion of faces, as at this day; to the men of Judah, and to the inhabitants of Jerusalem, and **unto all Israel, that are near, and that are far off,** through all the countries whither thou hast driven them, because of their trespass that they have trespassed against thee.* (Daniel 9:7)

Daniel is praying the exact same prayer we are told to pray in Leviticus 26 which I shared with you at the beginning of this Introduction. Daniel is praying the exact prayer King Solomon prayed when he dedicated the Temple in 1 Kings. Now Daniel has realized all that has happened has come to pass, has gone full circle and is completed just as Yehovah prophesied it would be in the very same year King Darius of the Medes took control over Babylon. Daniel then repents and prays for mercy from Yehovah on behalf of all of Israel.

> *20 And while I was speaking, and praying, and confessing my sin and the sin of my people Yisra'ěl, and presenting my supplication before יהוה my Elohim for the set-apart mountain of my Elohim, 21 while I was still speaking in prayer, the man Gaḇri'ěl, whom I had seen in the vision at the beginning, came close to me, in swift flight about the time of the evening offering. 22 And he made me understand, and talked with me, and said, "O Dani'ěl, I have now come forth to make you wise concerning understanding. 23 At the beginning of your supplications a word went out, and I have come to make it known, for you are greatly appreciated. So consider the word and understand the vision:"* (Daniel 9:20-23)

I share this because it is important for each of you to know and understand.

In 2005, I was stagnating spiritually and no longer growing in my understanding of Scripture. I was also beset by sin and kept going back to it and justifying it while telling myself it really was not all that bad.

I wrote down all my sins and the things that kept coming between Yehovah and me. I then went and confessed all my sins to my pastor at the time so that it would no longer be a secret I felt compelled to hide.

Immediately after that, Yehovah was gracious and quickened my understanding with regard to the Sighted Moon versus the Conjunction Moon to start the month by. And then I was shown how to prove which one was right by a couple of key passages in Scripture Yehovah led me to (Isaiah 7:14 and Revelation 12:1-4). Once I was shown this, I had to prove to Yehovah whether or not I would act on the information I had been shown. I did act and as soon as I had done what was right by the Word of Yehovah in choosing the Sighted Moon method by which to keep Passover at the right time, it was then revealed to me the secrets of the Sabbatical Years and how to not only prove them, but to be made aware of all the curses for not keeping them.

Ever since then, all the information I have been sharing with my readership about the Sabbatical cycles, as well as the information put forth in my book *"The Prophecies of Abraham"* and *"Remembering the Sabbatical Years of 2016"* and now this book, *"The 2300 Days of Hell"*—all of these things have come about and come to pass as a result of my asking Yehovah, in all sincerity, for forgiveness of my sins and after having done so, repenting from my sins and not only turning from them, but choosing to walk in the way of Torah instead.

This was the very thing that Daniel did and as soon as he had done it—in fact, even as he had only just begun to do it, Yehovah had already sent the Angel Gabriel to answer his prayers. This is *how fast* Yehovah wants to answer us and help us. But first, we must repent and really mean it and then begin to walk in Torah.

But as to the end of Daniel's days, we do not know the age of Daniel when he died. We do know that he was still alive in the third year of Cyrus, the King of Persia's reign as described in Daniel, chapter ten. He would have been almost 100 years old at that point, having been brought to Babylon in his teens—a little over eighty years previously.

Tradition holds that his tomb is located in Susa, in Iran at a site known as Shush-e Daniyal.[27]

History can and does have a way of repeating itself.

All that you have now been made aware of in the Book of Daniel will come to pass once again. Assyria is going to attack Israel again in the near future. In fact, it is one of my primary objectives to prove this very thing to you in this book, the same as I proved it to you in my DVD, *"The Chronological Order of Prophecies In the Jubilees"*[28] and in my book, *"The Prophecies of Abraham."*[29] Babylon is tied in with Assyria. The Medes and Persians *will* attack Babylon. But this is not the case just yet and we are getting ahead of ourselves.

I now have, in sufficient detail, fully covered with you the tumultuous and exciting days leading up to the beginning of Daniel's life, on through to the end of his life, as well as all the visions that were shown to Daniel along the way. That being said, I would now like to have you concentrate on the next four verses in Daniel (Daniel 9:24-27). This will take some doing, however, especially when it comes to fully grasping the manifold meaning they hold.

---

[27] http://www.biblediscovered.com/biblical-prophets/daniel-the-prophet/
[28] http://www.sightedmoonnl.com
[29] http://www.sightedmoonnl.com/?page_id=601

# Chapter 1 | Who Are Daniel's People?

> *24 Seventy weeks are decreed for your people and for your set-apart city, to put an end to the transgression, and to seal up sins, and to cover crookedness, and to bring in everlasting righteousness, and to seal up vision and prophet, and to anoint the Most Set-apart. 25 Know, then, and understand: from the going forth of the command to restore and build Yerushalayim until Messiah the Prince is seven weeks and sixty-two weeks. It shall be built again, with streets and a trench, but in times of affliction. 26 And after the sixty-two weeks Messiah shall be cut off and have naught. And the people of a coming prince shall destroy the city and the set-apart place. And the end of it is with a flood. And wastes are decreed, and fighting until the end. 27 And he shall confirm a covenant with many for one week. And in the middle of the week he shall put an end to slaughtering and meal offering. And on the wing of abominations he shall lay waste, even until the complete end and that which is decreed is poured out on the one who lays waste.[1] (Daniel 9:24-27 | Footnote: [1] Matthew 24:15)*

One of the things I have learned over the years when talking to other people, is to know or come to know how ignorant they are of *who* the Bible is talking about in the context of passages in Scripture like the above passage and especially when it comes to prophetic messages.

Most of them assume the Bible is talking strictly about the Jews, and we all know what assume means (making an "ass" out of "u" and "me").

It is only when you dig deeper and learn who is who, that then *and only then* does the Bible become alive and real.

> *24 Seventy weeks are decreed for your people and for your set-apart city, to put an end to the transgression, and to seal up sins, and to cover crookedness, and to bring in everlasting righteousness, and to seal up vision and prophet, and to anoint the Most Set-apart.* (Daniel 9:24)

That is what the Angel Gabriel was saying to Daniel.

We are about to examine this verse in greater detail, but I first have to explain who exactly Daniel's people are so that you can then understand to whom these four verses apply. Once you know what the Scripture is actually saying, what it really means and to whom it actually applies to, then you will be far more compelled to get out of your comfort zone and begin telling everyone you can about this warning.

Everyone who looks at this verse and this prophecy sees Daniel as one of the Jewish captives and that he was. Far too many read the Bible, however, from a strictly New Covenant perspective—that is, one that does not keep or want to keep The Commandments found in the first five books of the Bible or see the need to understand the events that took place in what is commonly referred to as the OLD Testament. They perceive the Old Testament to be all about the Jews. Yet nothing could be further from the truth. I am about to prove to you who Daniel's people were and who they are today and I will use three chapters to do so using three different witnesses.

> *6 At the mouth of two or three witnesses shall he that is to die be put to death. He is not put to death by the mouth of one witness.* (Deuteronomy 17:6)

> *15 One witness does not rise up against a man concerning any crookedness or any sin that he sins. At the mouth of*

*two witnesses or at the mouth of three witnesses a matter is established.* (Deuteronomy 19:15)

*16 But if he does not hear, take with you one or two more, that 'by the mouth of two or three witnesses every word might be established.'* (Matthew 18:16)

*1 This is the third time I am coming to you. "By the mouth of two or three witnesses every word shall be established."* (2 Corinthians 13:1)

Despite the fact we live in the Information Age, there are still too many of us 'ever learning but never able to come to the knowledge of the truth.'(2 Timothy 3:7). Just like the Bible says. Too many of us who profess to believe, do not read the Bible to the extent we ought to. When people do not know *whom* the Bible is talking about and by what names they are known by today, they cut themselves off from understanding history and many of its prophecies. It is like they are reading the New Testament having no knowledge of the Old Testament or starting to read a book from the middle of it.

You cannot read and understand the New Testament unless you are walking in The Commandments of the Old Testament. You cannot understand the New Testament unless you know *who* it is that is being spoken of in the Old Testament.

When you do this, and *only* when you do this, will the Bible then become alive to you and be the living, breathing book Yehovah created it to be, speaking to you today about real people. It is not just about those Jews who lived a long time ago or the Jews who are now a part of the State of Israel. For almost all of those who will be reading this book, the Bible is written about you and what is about to happen to you, as I will set out to prove to you in the following chapters.

Before Daniel 9:24, we find Daniel praying—not just on behalf of the Jewish people, although he does pray for them too—but for ***ALL*** of Israel.

*3 So I set my face toward* יהוה *the Elohim to seek by prayer and supplications, with fasting, and sackcloth, and ashes. 4 And I prayed to* יהוה *my Elohim, and made confession, and said, "O* יהוה*, great and awesome Ěl, guarding the covenant and the kindness to those who love Him, and to those who guard His commands. 5 We have sinned and did crookedness, and did wrong and rebelled, to turn aside from Your commands and from Your right-rulings. 6 And we have not listened to Your servants the prophets, who spoke in Your Name to our sovereigns, our heads, and our fathers, and to all the people of the land. 7 O* יהוה*, to You is the righteousness, and to us the shame of face, as it is this day—**to the men of Yehudah, to the inhabitants of Yerushalayim and all Yisra'ěl, those near and those far off in all the lands to which You have driven them**, because of their trespass which they have trespassed against You.* (Daniel 9:3-7)

*8 O Master, to us is the shame of face, to our sovereigns, to our heads, and to our fathers, because we have sinned against You. 9 To* יהוה *our Elohim are the compassions and forgivenesses, for we have rebelled against Him. 10 And we have not obeyed the voice of* יהוה *our Elohim, to walk in His Torot, which He set before us through His servants the prophets. 11 And **all Yisra'ěl have transgressed** Your Torah, and turned aside, so as not to obey Your voice. So the curse and the oath written in the Torah of Mosheh the servant of Elohim have been poured out on us, for we have sinned against Him."* (Daniel 9:8-11)

7 "... **all Yisra'ěl, those near and those far off in all the lands to which You have driven them** ..." (Daniel 9:7)

This is referring to the Ten Northern Tribes of Israel who were taken into captivity beginning in 732 B.C. and with the final capitulation and the remaining people taken captive in 723 B.C. as I shared with you in the Introduction to Daniel.

11 "... **all Yisra'ěl have transgressed** ..." (Daniel 9:11)

Again, Daniel is praying for *all* of Israel (not just Judah but also the Ten Northern Tribes). I simply cannot stress this enough. Daniel is praying for **ALL** of Israel *as well as* **ALL** of Judah.

Here, in 539 B.C., the first year of Cyrus's reign, [the same year that Babylon fell], Daniel, who was residing in Babylon himself, is telling us in his prayer that Israel was in other countries "near and still others far off." Even 193 years *after* the first wave of captives were taken in 732 B.C., Daniel is very aware of the places Israel had been taken to or moved to after their captivity. Daniel was living in "modern day Iran" and yet 193 years after Israel had been taken into captivity, Daniel still knew where the northern ten tribes had been taken.

Those of you in the USA should, at this point, research the population of the USA 193 years ago and compare it to today's U.S. population. In a similar fashion, the Ten Northern Tribes would have grown in population to become a real concern to those around them, as you will shortly see.

Let us now learn the identity of the Ten Northern Tribes, where they went and where they are now.

In order to do this, we must begin at the time of the captivity of the Kingdom of Israel. We will then, from that point on, chronologically follow them through time and read accounts of what they were called by other nations. The records are all there if we know where to look. All we have to do is search them out.

> *25 But they trespassed against the Elohim of their fathers, and whored after the mighty ones of the peoples of the land, whom Elohim had destroyed before them. 26 So the Elohim of Yisra'ĕl stirred up the spirit of Pul sovereign of Ashshur, even the spirit of Tiḡlath-Pileser sovereign of Ashshur. And he took the Re'uḇĕnites, and the Gaḏites, and the half-tribe of Menashsheh into exile, and brought them to Ḥalaḥ, and Ḥaḇor, and Hara, and the river of Gozan, unto this day.* (1 Chronicles 5:25-26)

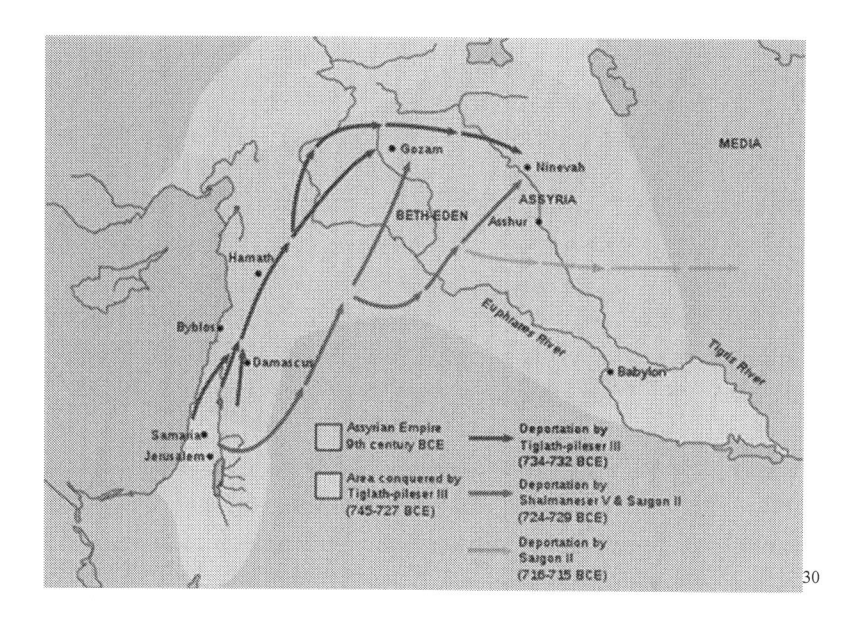

*29 In the days of Peqaḥ sovereign of Yisra'ĕl, Tiglath-Pileser sovereign of Ashshur came and took Iyon, and Aḇĕl Bĕyth Ma'aḵah, and Yanowaḥ, and Qeḏesh, and Ḥatsor, and Gil'āḏ, and Galil, all the land of Naphtali, and took them into exile to Ashshur. (2 Kings 15:29)*

We read of the cities that Tiglath-Pileser III built—cities such as: Sakka, Danium, Elisansa, Abrania and Evasa.[31] It is in these cities that he placed the newly captured Israelites spoken of in 2 Kings 15:29.

The names are distinctly Israeli in origin.[32]

We then read of the next invasions by Shalmaneser V and then again by Sargon II who actually took the captives to Halah, Habor and Gozan and to the cities of the Medes.

---

[30] Permission is granted to copy, distribute and/or modify this document under the terms of the GNU Free Documentation License, Version 1.2 or any later version published by the Free Software Foundation; with no Invariant Sections, no Front-Cover Texts, and no Back-Cover Texts. A copy of the license is included in the section entitled GNU Free Documentation License.

[31] *Assyrian Discoveries* by George Smith; p. 253; http://tinyurl.com/b9hdxxl

[32] *Missing Links Discovered In Assyrian Tablets* by E. R. Capt; p. 67

*6 In the ninth year of Hoshea, the sovereign of Ashshur captured Shomeron and exiled Yisra'ĕl to Ashshur, and settled them in Halah and Habor, the Rivr of Gozan, and in the cities of the Medes.* (2 Kings 17:6)

*11 And the sovereign of Ashshur exiled Yisra'ĕl to Ashshur, and placed them in Halah and Habor, the River of Gozan, and in the cities of the Medes:* (2 Kings 18:11)

When we look at the artifacts from the Assyrian period we are able to learn of some of the names the ancient Israelites were called.

[33]

The late Henry Layard discovered the Black Obelisk of Shalmaneser III in 1845. The seven-foot black limestone monument was found in the ruins of the palace of Shalmaneser III at ancient Calah, near Nineveh. It contains many panels displaying the exploits of the Assyrian kings. The Black Obelisk is one of the most important discoveries in Biblical

---

[33] Material: Black Limestone Obelisk; Neo Assyrian; Date: 858-824 B.C.; Height: 197.85 cm (77.8937008 inches); Width: 45.08 cm (17.7480315 inches); Depth: Nimrud (ancient Calah), northern Iraq; Excavated by: Henry Layard; 1845-1849; Location: British Museum, London

Archaeology because one of the panels depicts the Hebrew King Jehu, or possibly one of his servants, bringing gifts to Shalmaneser III and kneeling at his feet. The inscription above it reads:

> *The tribute of Jehu, son of Omri, silver, gold, bowls of gold, chalices of gold, cups of gold, vases of gold, lead, a sceptre for the king, and spear-shafts, I have received.*

You will notice that the Assyrians call Jehu the son of Omri. Omri was one of the kings of Israel prior to Jehu.

> The Hebrew name "Omri" begins with the consonant "Y," called "Ayin," which is pronounced with a guttural "H" and is represented in Assyrian transliteration as "Gh" or "Kh." The Israelites would naturally pronounce "Omri" as "Ghomri" which became "Khumri" in Assyrian. Thus, the Assyrians, even before the Israelites were taken into captivity, called the Israelites "Beth Khumri," meaning "House of Omri." Similar pronunciations are found in the names "Gomorrah" and "Gaza," both of which begin with consonant "Y."
>
> The Assyrian name "Khumri," used to denote the Israelites is also found in the annals (records) of the King Tiglath-Pileser III concerning his invasion of Israel when he removed the first Israelites to Assyria: "The cities of Gilead and Abel-beth-maacah on the borders of the land of **Khumri**, and the widespread land of Hazael to its whole extent, I brought with the territory of Assyria."
>
> Sargon II (722 B.C.-704 B.C.) also makes mention of the "khumri" in his records of the capture of Samaria. He refers to himself as the conqueror of "Bit-Khumri" (Omri). Apparently this is the last mention of the Israelites by the name "Khumri."[34]

---

[34] *Missing Links Discovered In Assyrian Tablets* by E. R. Capt; p. 99

Today, when we search out the name "Khumri" we find it still in use as a district of the Baglan Province in Afghanistan and it is called Puli Khumri.[35]

Of all the royal letters found in the ruins of Nineveh, there are many written by one King Esarhaddon who reigned from 681 B.C. until 669 B.C. He writes many times of the Land of Gamir and calls the inhabitants "Gamera" and in still yet other letters identifies them as "Cimmerians" (ga-me-ra-a-ans).[36]

Prior to the captivity, the Assyrians called the Israelites "Bet-Khumri," and during this captivity the Assyrians called them "Gimira" and "Gamera" and finally "Cimmerians."

King Esarhaddon wrote of being in a battle against the Cimmerians in 679 B.C. In other prayer letters, King Esarhaddon wrote of the Gamir and also of a new group of people called the "Ishkuza." They are spoken of as if they are the *same as* the Gamira.

We are told something very interesting in Genesis when Yehovah told Abraham, *"In Isaac shall your seed be called."* You can take this to mean that his descendants would be called after the name of Isaac.

> *12 But Elohim said to Aḇraham, "Let it not be evil in your eyes because of the boy and because of your female servant. Whatever Sarah has said to you, listen to her voice, for in Yitsḥaq your seed is called."* (Genesis 21:12)

We read in Amos of Israel being called the house of Isaac as prophesied back in Genesis.

> *9 "And the high places of Yitsḥaq shall be laid waste, and the set-apart places of Yisra'ěl shall be destroyed. And I shall rise with the sword against the house of Yaroḇ'am." 10 Then Amatsyah the priest of Běyth Ěl sent to Yaroḇ'am sovereign*

---

[35] http://en.wikipedia.org/wiki/Puli_Khumri_District & http://en.wikipedia.org/wiki/Baghlan_Province
[36] *Missing Links Discovered In Assyrian Tablets* by E. R. Capt; p. 115

> *of Yisra'ĕl, saying, "Amos has conspired against you in the midst of the house of Yisra'ĕl. The land is not able to endure all his words... 16 And now, hear the word of יהוה. You are saying, 'Do not prophesy against Yisra'ĕl, and do not drop words against the house of Yitsḥaq.'"* (Amos 7:9-10, 16)

Israel was also known as the house of Isaac. Isaac could be known as "Isaaca," which the Assyrians would call "Ishkuza."[37]

> It is universally accepted by modern historians that the Iskuza were called "Shuthae" by the Greeks and "Sacae" (also "Saka" and "Sakka") by the Persians. Herodotus further tells us the Persians called the Sacae "Scythians."
>
> The name "Gimira" was strictly an Assyrian name—not one the Israelites would have used.
>
> To summarize, we have observed from Assyrian documents (tablets and inscriptions) that the Israelites were called "Khumri" or "Khormri" (after the House of Omri) before their captivity. However, after the reign of Sargon II (721 B.C.-705 B.C.) that name is never mentioned again. Then around 707 B.C. a people known as "Gimira" and "Gamera" are recorded as living among the Mannai. Their territory was only a few miles from the Medes, in the very areas where the Scriptures state the Ten Northern Tribes (of the) Kingdom of Israel had been placed just a few years previously. We have noted that the names "Gimir," "Gimira," and "Gamera" could easily be corruptions of "Khumri" or "Khormri," the Assyrian name for the Israelites. The names "Sacae" or "Sakka" (Scythians) are probably derived from "Isaaca" or "House of "Isaac." It is further noted that the Assyrian name of "Ga-me-ra-a-an" is translated into "Cimmerian."[38]

---

[37] *Missing Links Discovered In Assyrian Tablets* by E. R Capt; p. 121
[38] Translation by Professor Leroy Waterman-Royal Correspondence of the Assyrian Empire-published by University of Michigan, 1930; *Missing Links Discovered In Assyrian Tablets* E. R, Capt; p. 123

From the 700's B.C. to the mid-500's B.C. we can now read of the exploits of the Gamirians—also known as the Cimmerians, which the Greeks called "Kimmeriori" as they moved into Phrygia, which is now called Turkey.

We read in Esdras an interesting account of the Ten Tribes as they were migrating into what was then called Arsareth on the Northwest Coast of the Black Sea in what is today called Bulgaria and Romania. This took place circa 525 B.C.

> *39 And whereas thou sawest that he (the Son of God) gathered another peaceable multitude unto him; 40 Those are the ten tribes, which were carried away prisoners out of their own land in the time of Osea the king, whom Salmanasar the king of Assyria led away captive, and he carried them over the waters, and so came they into another land. 41 But they took this counsel among themselves, that they would leave the multitude of the heathen, and go forth into a further country, where never mankind dwelt, 42 That they might there keep their statutes, which they never kept in their own land. 43 And they entered into Euphrates by the narrow places of the river. 44 For the most High then shewed signs for them, and held still the flood, till they were passed over. 45 For through that country there was a great way to go, namely, of a year and a half: and the same region is called Arsareth. (2 Esdras 13:39-45)*

The Greeks now called the Cimmerians the Kimmeriori. The "c" being a hard "c" as in the word "cat."

The reign of Cyrus the Great lasted from 539 B.C. when he defeated the Babylonians until he himself died in battle, fighting the Massagetae along the Syr Darya—also known as the Jaxartes or Yaxartes in December 530 B.C.

His son, Cambyses II, succeeded him and according to Herodotus, he reigned seven years and five months—from 530 B.C.E. to the summer of 523 B.C. King Darius would take the throne in the year of 522 B.C.

This is King Darius, the son of Ahasuerus of Daniel 9:1. Ahasuerus is also the same king referred to in Esther 1:1.

I am just trying to demonstrate to you how many of the books of the Bible are related to world events during this time. I have shown you, in my Introduction to Daniel, the captivity of the Ten Northern Tribes, followed by the time of Jeremiah through the captivity of Daniel and down to the time of at least the first year of King Darius, which is mentioned in Daniel 9:1. Let us now turn our attention to the next two reigns after Darius as they also come into play as I explain in the 70 Shavuot (Weeks)[39] prophecy of Daniel.

Darius was succeeded in 486 B.C. when he died at the hand of Xerxes the Great who reigned from 486 B.C., until his death in 465 B.C. He was the fourth king of the Achaemenid Empire. Artaxerxes I was the fifth king of the Achaemenid Empire from 465 B.C.E. to 424 B.C.E.

It is from one of these five kings that the various decrees are to rebuild Jerusalem in Daniel 9:24 comes from, presumably. There were several different decrees permitting rebuilding of various parts of Jerusalem; one by Cyrus in 538 B.C. or 537 B.C., another by Darius in 519 B.C., a third one by Artaxerxes in 458 B.C., and the last one again by Artaxerxes in 445 B.C.

But I am getting ahead of myself. Let us go back to when Cyrus is killed, as this too will help us to identify the alleged "Lost" Ten Tribes of Israel.

Cyrus was fighting the Massagetae along the Syr Darya—also known as the Jaxartes or Yaxartes in December 530 B.C., and it was at this time that he was killed. Syr Darya, also spelled Syrdarya, Kazak Syrdarīya, Tajik Daryoi Sir, and Uzbek Sirdaryo, has the ancient name Jaxartes River in the Central Asian Republics of Uzbekistan, Tajikistan, and Kazakhstan. The Syr Darya flows northwest until it empties into the Aral Sea.

---

[39] http://biblesuite.com/hebrew/7620.htm

In 329 B.C., Alexander the Great had set this same river as the northeastern border of his empire when he *also* found himself in a fight with the Massagetae.

The classical and modern authorities say that the word "Massagetae" means "great" Getae.[40] The 9th-century work entitled, *De Universo* of Rabanus Maurus states, "The Massagetae are in origin from the tribe of the Scythians, and are called Massagetae, as if heavy, that is, strong Getae."[41]

Weer Rajendra Rishi, wrote, "In Pahlavi language the word 'massa' means great. In Avesta, massa is also used in the sense of greatness."[42]

Herodotus wrote that the Massagetae were the same as the Scythians. It is the Massagetae that Cyrus is seeking to conquer. Cyrus learned that one Tomyris led them and he sought to marry her and expand his empire through marriage. She said "no" and then Cyrus led his armies to attack her.

> According to the accounts of Greek historians, Cyrus was victorious in his initial assault on the Massagetai. His advisers suggested laying a trap for the pursuing Scythians: the Persians left behind them an apparently abandoned camp, containing a rich supply of wine. The pastoral Scythians were not used to drinking wine—"their favored intoxicants were hashish and fermented mare's milk"—and they drank themselves into a stupor. The Persians attacked while their opponents were incapacitated, defeating the Massagetai forces, and capturing Tomyris's son, Spargapises, the general of her army. Of the one third of the Massagetai forces that fought, there were more captured than killed. According

---

[40] Dhillon, Balbir Singh (1994). *History and Study of the Jats: With Reference to Sikhs, Scythians, Alans, Sarmatians, Goths and Jutes* (illustrated ed.). Canada: Beta Publishers. p. 8.
http://books.google.ca/books?id=U9KpAAAACAAJ&redir_esc=y

[41] Maurus Rabanus(1864). Migne, Jacques Paul. ed. De universo. Paris.

[42] Rishi, Weer Rajendra (1982). India & Russia: Linguistic & Cultural Affinity. Roma. p.95. http://books.google.co.in/books?id=Vns_AAAAMAAJ&q=Getae#search_anchor

to Herodotus, Spargapises coaxed Cyrus into removing his bonds, thus allowing him to commit suicide while in Persian captivity.[43]

Tomyris sent a message to Cyrus denouncing his treachery, and with all her forces, challenged him to a second battle. In the fight that ensued, the Massagetai got the upper hand, and the Persians were defeated with high casualties. Cyrus was killed and Tomyris had his corpse beheaded and then crucified, and shoved his head into a wineskin filled with human blood. She was reportedly quoted as saying, "I warned you that I would quench your thirst for blood, and so I shall."[44]

This gruesome end at the hands of Tomyris befell Cyrus in 530 B.C. His son Cambyses II succeeded him and died in 523 B.C. It was at this time that Darius the Great began to reign and in roughly 515 B.C. he commissioned the engraving of what is today called the Behistun Rock detailing his exploits in three separate languages. The amazing thing about this is that he identifies the Israelites in three different languages so that we can know today what they were known as back then.

> The inscription not only fixes the date of his reign but provides some interesting references to the so-called "Lost Tribes of Israel." The memorial measures about 150 feet long by 100 feet high.
>
> The inscriptions were in three languages, Babylonian (Accadian), Elamite (Susian) and Persian. They were chiefly in the cuneiform or wedge-like characters. While many scholars should be recognized for their efforts toward solving the puzzle of the wedge-shaped script, a young English

---

[43] *Internet Ancient History Sourcebook | Herodotus: Queen Tomyris of the Massagetai and the Defeat of the Persians under Cyrus."* Retrieved 2010-05-14.
http://www.fordham.edu/halsall/ancient/tomyris.asp; ©Paul Halsall (August 1998)

[44] *Herodotus, The History* by George Rawlinson; 1.204.

officer in the Persian army, Henry C. Rawlinson, is given credit for successfully deciphering the Old Persian signs. The trilingual inscription on what today is known as the "Behistun Rock" provided the 'key.' Once it was determined that the texts of the three languages were identical it was only a matter of time (until) scholars were able to read the Elamite and Accadian writings.

The dominant feature of the Behistun Rock inscriptions is King Darius, in royal attire and surrounded by captives. Around the captives are five main panels, twenty in all. The first panel contains 19 paragraphs and 96 lines. Each paragraph commences with the words: "I am Darius, the

---

[45] *The Behistun Inscription* (also Bistun or Bisutun, meaning "the place of god") is a multi-lingual inscription located on Mount Behistun in the Kermanshah Province of Iran, near the city of Kermanshah in western Iran.
Permission is granted to copy, distribute and/or modify this document under the terms of the GNU Free Documentation License, Version 1.2 or any later version published by the Free Software Foundation; with no Invariant Sections, no Front-Cover Texts, and no Back-Cover Texts. A copy of the license is included in the section entitled GNU Free Documentation License.

king of kings, the king of Persia." The second panel has 16 paragraphs and 96 lines; over each figure is a brief history of the man and the tribe he represents. The tenth panel is most interesting to a Bible student because it speaks of "Sarocus," the Sacan, who has the Hebrew form of head-dress.

Most noteworthy is King Darius majestically standing before nine persons united by a rope around their necks and their hands fastened behind their backs. A tenth man is prostrate on his back; the right foot of the king is upon his body. No two of the prisoners are dressed alike. Some of them have short tunics, others have long flowing robes. They are evidently the head chiefs of the Ten Tribes of Israel. The word "Kana" occurs 28 times in the inscription and the word "Armenia" also occurs frequently. This is the area from which the prisoners were taken—the very area where the Ten Tribes of Israel had been placed by the Assyrians.

The inscriptions include a list of 23 nations over whom Darius ruled and named among these are the "Sakkas." In both the Persian and Elamite versions the original word is "Sakka," but in the Babylonian version the same people are called "Gimiri." (verified on behalf of the British Museum by L. W. King and R. C. Thomson—Sculptures and Inscriptions of Behistun—p. 161) This proves that the Assyrians and the Babylonians called the Israelite exiles "Gimiri" regardless of where they lived. It also indicates that by this time (about 517 B.C.) a branch of the Gimiri (called "Sakka" by the Persians) had already migrated a long way beyond Bactria and dwelt on the eastern extremity of the Persian Empire.

In another inscription, written on a gold tablet about a foot square, Darius wrote: "This kingdom that I hold is from Sakka which is beyond Sogdiana to Kush (Ethiopia) and from India to Sardis." (Translation published by Sidney Smith of the British– Museum—1926) This provides added evidence that by 500 B.C. some of the Sakkas were far to the east near the upper Jaxartes Basin. Additional evidence that the Sakka were a branch of the Gimiri (Israelites) is provided by another trilingual inscription found in the tomb of Darius, in southwestern Persia. The tomb is cut into the face of a cliff in the valley of Naksh-i-Rustam, near the ancient city of Persepolis. The inscription again included a list of the nations over which Darius ruled. On this occasion, Darius listed three separate groups of "Sakkas:" the "Amyrgian Sakkas," the "Sakkas with the pointed caps," and the "Sakkas who are beyond the sea." In each case the name "Gimri" in the Babylonian text, is translated "Sakka" in the Persian.

These inscriptions have been known for many years but the publications dealing with them have generally passed over the translation often with scarcely a comment.

Perhaps it seemed quite inexplicable to the historians. And yet, the only conclusion that can be drawn from the inscriptions (also the writings of Josephus) is that the Iskuza were called "Sakka" by the Persians. Therefore, the logical conclusion is that the "Iskuza," the "Sakka," and the "Gimiri" are the same people. Then in reviewing the Royal Correspondence of the Assyrian Empire it is evident that the "Iskuza," the "Sakka," the "Scythians," the "Cimmerians," and the "Gimiri" are all Israelites.[46]

Scholars confirm that the people known to the Persians as SAKA, to the Babylonians as GIMIRRI, and to the Assyrians as KHUMRI, were but different names for the Lost Ten Tribes in captivity. "Saka" or "Sacae" meant "House of Isaac," while the terms "Khumri" and "Gimirri" translate as "House of Omri." (The Assyrians later also adopted the Babylonian variant of Khumri, *Gimirr.)* From this word Khumri or Gimirri developed the tribal name, "Cimmerian," as well. The famed ancient writer, Herodotus, visited these tribes about 450 B.C. Sir Henry Rawlinson, decipherer of the Behistun Rock, informs us that, *"We have reasonable grounds for regarding the GIMIRRI, or CIMMERIANS,*

---

[46] http://www.keithhunt.com/Arch8.html

*who first appeared on the confines of Assyria and Media in the seventh century B.C., and the SACAE of the Behistun Rock, nearly two centuries later, as identical with the BETH-KHUMREE of Samaria, or the Ten Tribes of the House of Israel ..."* George Rawlinson, translator of the *History Of Herodotus*, stated, *"The SACAE or Scythians, who were termed GIMIRRI by their Semitic neighbors, first appear in the cuneiform inscriptions as a substantive people under Esar-Haddon in about B.C. 684."* By this date the Ten Tribes, Israel-Gimirri, were entirely resident in Assyria, for a great deportation of the whole seed of Ephraim (Jeremiah 7:15) had removed them from Palestine. We read *"... there was none left but the tribe of Judah only... so was Israel carried away out of their own land to Assyria unto this day."* (2 Kings 17:18, 23)

### ISRAEL→ SAKA → GIMIRRI → KHUMRI

The famed Roman-Jewish historian, Flavius Josephus, said in the 1st-century, A.D: *"Therefore there are but two* (Israel) *tribes In Europe and Asia subject to the Romans, while the ten tribes are beyond the Euphrates (until) now, and are an immense multitude, and not to be estimated by numbers."* The "Lost" Ten Tribes were dwelling beyond the Euphrates Valley, traveling northward, so our next step is to trace their migrations through the Caucasus Mountains.

The *Jewish Encyclopedia* says: **"If the Ten Tribes have disappeared, the literal fulfillment of the prophecies would be impossible; if they have not disappeared, obviously they must exist under a different name."** This is the only real choice! If the Bible's prophecies are to be literally fulfilled, the Lost Tribes must be known today by a name other than "Israel," but what other name?

**"... the Sacae, or Scythians, who, again, were the Lost Ten Tribes."**

*The Jewish Encyclopedia; vol.* 12, p.250

Historian Sharon Turner, author of the scholarly three-volume *History of the Anglo-Saxons,* tells us this: "... *Of the various Scythian nations which have been recorded, the* **SAKAI, or SACAE**, *are the people from whom the descent of the* **SAXONS** *may be inferred with the least violation of probability.* **Sakai-suna**, *or the* **sons of the Sakai**, *abbreviated into* **Saksun**, *which is the same sound as Saxon, seems a reasonable etymology of the word,* **Saxon**. *Strabo places them east of the Caspian... this important fact of a part of Armenia having been named* **Saka-sina** *is mentioned by Strabo in another place (lib. xi pp. 776, 778); and seems to give a geographical locality to our primeval ancestors, and to account for the Persian words that occur in the Saxon language as they must have come into Armenia from the northern regions of Persia. It is also important to remark that* **Ptolemy** *(a celebrated scholar of about A.D. 150) mentions a Scythian people, sprung from the* **SAKAI**, *by the name of* **SAXONES**. *If the Sakai, who reached Armenia were called Sacassani, they may have traversed Europe with the same appellation; which, being pronounced by the Romans from them, and then reduced to writing from their pronunciation, may have been spelled with the x instead of the ks, and thus* **Saxones** *would not be a greater variation from* **Sacassani or Saxsuna**, *than we find between French, Francois, Franci, and their Greek name Phrange; or between Spain, Espagne, and Hispania.*"

"THE IDENTIFICATION OF THE SACAE, OR SCYTHIANS, WITH THE TEN TRIBES BECAUSE THEY APPEAR IN HISTORY AT THE SAME TIME, AND VERY NEARLY IN THE SAME PLACE, AS THE ISRAELITES REMOVED BY SHALMANESER, IS ONE OF THE CHIEF SUPPORTS OF THE THEORY WHICH IDENTIFIES THE ENGLISH PEOPLE, AND INDEED THE WHOLE TEUTONIC RACE, WITH THE TEN TRIBES."

**WORD ORIGINS**

**(House of) OMRI→ KHUMRI** *(Assyrian)*→ **GIMIRRI** *(Babylonian)*→ **CIMMERIAN** *(Greek)* → **KYMRY** → **Cimbri** → **CELT**

**(House of) ISAAC** → **SAKA** *(Persian)* →**SACA-SUNA,** or *"Sons of the Saka"*→ **SAXONS**

The origin of the Caucasian race is shrouded in antiquity, but this much is certain: The name itself indicates that many of these people streamed into Europe through the **Caucasus Mountain** region of Eastern Europe, just north of Assyria and Palestine. Historians still debate whether these tribes originated in northern Europe and later traveled south to the Caucasus region, or conversely, originated down in Mesopotamia and migrated north through the Caucasus into Europe. The Encyclopedia Britannica, while professing no final opinion on this, makes the revealing admission, *"It has been observed with truth that so many populous nations can hardly have sprung from the Scandinavian Peninsula."*

The same source also points out that these tribes spoke a language akin to ancient "Iranian" (i.e., an early Mesopotamian dialect. This was no accident, for the Israelites descended from Abraham who originated in Chaldea in Mesopotamia.) It would therefore seem obvious that these newly discovered peoples originated in Mesopotamia, at the same time and place that the Ten Tribes of Israel were *"lost"* and disappeared from history. God's people disappeared under the name of Israel by the early 7th-century B.C., and immediately reappeared in the same region under other names by which they played an important part in the early history of Asia Minor and Eastern Europe.

Many history books show an area marked, **"Iberia,"** or **HEBREW'S LAND**, in the Caucasus Mountain region between the Caspian and Black Seas, north of the Euphrates River. The word, Hebrew, means a descendant of Eber, the great-grandson of Noah. Even to this day, Spain is known as the **Iberian Peninsula,** and Ireland by the slight variation, **Hibernia,** both indicating their Hebrew origins in antiquity.[47]

The whites of North America and the U.K. are called Caucasian because our ancestry came through the Caucasus Mountains. This is exactly what the Ten Tribes did when they were being attacked by the Medes. This was also the area that our ancestry used to dwell in which is today called Armenia.

> **CIMMERII:** *"An ancient people... one body of whom is called in Assyrian sources Gimirrai and is represented as coming through the Caucasus. They were probably Iranian speakers... Later writers identified them with the Cimbri of Jutland, who were probably Teutonized Celts."*[48]

Much evidence has been presented documenting that Hebrew tribes passed through the Caucasus Mountain Region into Europe throughout the early pre-Christian centuries. This account of a visit to the region is reprinted from the article, *The Pass of Israel* by Colonel R.G. Pearse, *The National Message*, October 23rd, 1937, p. 676. Here is a transcript of this interesting article:

> Colonel Pearse spent a number of years himself in the very district described in this article. At that time he had no knowledge of our Israel identity or of the migrations of our forefathers, and the significance of the names and legends were not apparent to him. Recently he found the long-forgotten photographs, which were reproduced, and as a result, he wrote the following article:
>
> It has been my good fortune, upon several occasions, to travel through the Caucasus Mountains, taking the route of the Georgian Road. This is one of the two highways through

---

[47] http://www.ensignmessage.com/archives/diaspora.html
[48] *Encyclopedia Britannica*, 14th ed., 1957, 5:70

the mountains from south to north—the other being but a mule-track—and, although now a wonderfully engineered road, is known in native legendary and song as "The Pass of Israel." It was constructed as a modern highway in about 1856, but still shows traces of its former characteristics as a wagon track.

When Israel of the Ten Tribes were faced with their journey from Guta, in Media, to Arsareth, they had to travel through the mighty Caucasus Range by this, the only, way for a large concourse of people. It must be realized that these mountains extend for hundreds of miles, and average, throughout their whole length, over 10,000 feet in height.

When undertaking this part of their migrations, after having traversed the smaller mountain ranges lying between Media and the Caucasus, they approached this great obstacle to their march near where Tiflis, the capital of Georgia now stands.

From there they passed through the foothills which contain nowadays many monasteries and ruins dating back even to A.D. 100; for the people of Georgia were one of the first Christian communities.

Still traversing such foothills, the Israel migration approached and finally entered, as the track narrowed, the real Pass through the mountains. For many miles they traveled through a great ravine marching between towering heights and along the banks of a swift river, the waters of which had come from the great mountain range and which finally emptied into the southern portion of the Caspian Sea. It is this river, which has formed the mighty gorge extending to the heart of the Caucasus.

They continued along this ravine, rising some thousands of feet on the way, until they came towards the centre of The Pass. Here, at a place now designated Mlete, they were faced with their most difficult task. For at this point The Pass rises abruptly by some thousands of feet until a final height of 11,000 feet is reached.

On surmounting this—and who can say now how long it took for the multitude of people to transport themselves, their wagons and their other belongings?—they reached the highest plateau, which is some miles in extent and where, although the weather is at times very severe, the travelers were probably afforded a respite from the hardships of continual climbing. Actually, during the winter this plateau lies under many feet of snow and at times is impassable, but during the remainder of the year it can be traversed with reasonable facility. When the snow melts in such a district there is revealed a wonderful sight of mountain peaks, snow-clad upon their summits but of many vivid colors below due to the rich mineral deposits in the rocks.

Having passed successfully over this, the real ridge of The Pass, Israel (was) faced with the descent into Europe. Although not so precipitous as the ascent from Mlete, it took them through some very stark and rocky ravines, from end to end of which ran another great river emptying itself in the northern portion of the Caspian Sea.

On the way down they would leave behind them the mountain named "Zion"—a mountain which has always been known as such, and which has given its name to a village now situated in The Pass. It is interesting to speculate about this mountain and its name, for perhaps the latter goes back to the time of the passing of our forefathers. Personally, I came across no trace of its actual history, and, therefore, can only speculate.

At a later stage in their journey Israel obtained (its) first sight of the great mountain peak of Kazbek, which, rising to over 16,000 feet, seems to be watching over the European side of The Pass. Afterwards they entered a series of precipitous and intensely rugged and rocky gorges, on their way passing through the "Dariel Gorge," or the Gorge of Darius. It was in this gorge that, as contemporary history and the current legendary of the natives inform us, Darius the Persian brought, some time after Israel's migrations, an army to avenge the death of Cyrus and the rout of his forces by Israel in Arsareth. Coming to such a gorge as this, the army of Darius encountered the forces of Israel under the leadership of Queen Tamara (the Queen Thomyris of early history), and in turn his army was defeated and routed. The ruins of the castle of Queen Tamara still remain as a watchtower in the center of the gorge.

Still traveling through these ravines went Israel until, passing over the foothills; they finally emerged upon the European plains at the Gate of the Caucasus, the place known as Vladikavkas before the present Russian regime.

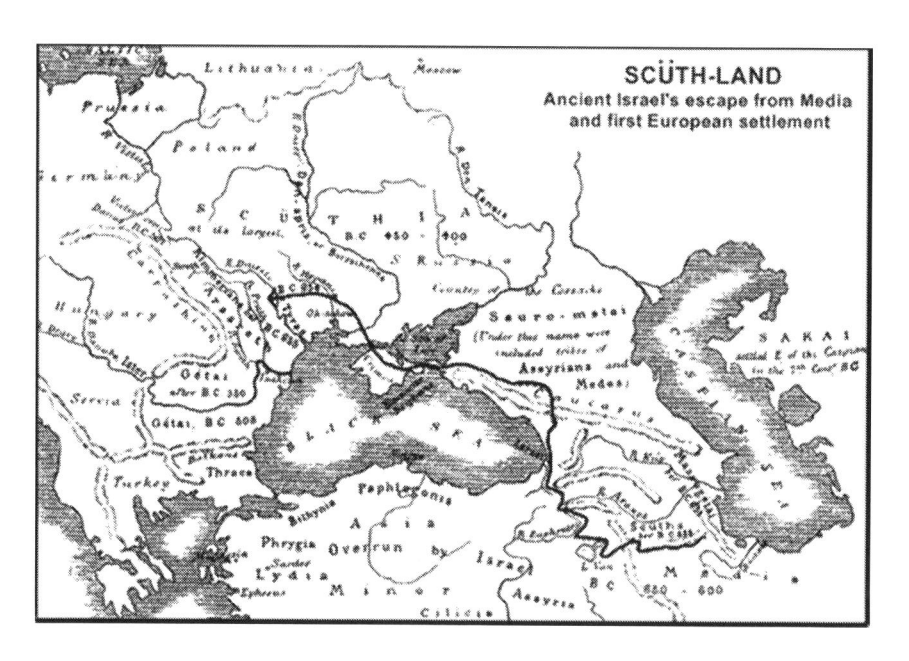

SCÜTH-LAND
Ancient Israel's escape from Media and first European settlement

Here we find the tale of the migration taken up by Herodotus, and we realize that Israel had traversed the greatest obstacle in the course of (its) migration in this march of a year and a half, as the Book of Esdras informs us:

> *40 Those are the ten tribes, which were carried away prisoners out of their own land in the time of Osea the king, whom Salmanasar the King of Assyria led away captive, and he carried them over the waters, and so came they into another land. 41 But they took this counsel among themselves, that they would leave the multitude of the heathen, and go forth into a further country, where never mankind dwelt. 42 That they might there keep their statutes, which they never kept in their own land. 43 And they entered into Euphrates by the narrow passages of the river. 44 For the Most High then shewed signs for them, and held still the flood, till they were passed over. 45 For through that country there was a great way to go, namely of a year and a half: and the same region is called Arsareth. (2 Esdras 13:40-45)*[49]

I have now called attention to two different routes traversed by two different peoples to the area of Arsareth. One group known as the Scythians, who went through the Caucasus Mountains and over the north side of the Black Sea as we just read; the other group known as the Cimmerians, who came south of the Black Sea and up to the Crimea area and Southern Ukraine.

I would now like to show you some of the tombstones from this area. It is things like this that cause me to be in total awe and wonderment and yet also put me at a severe loss as to why so few seem to know these things. Yet the information is there to be found by all of us. All one has to do is look. For Yehovah promises to show us the treasures, which are, hidden in darkness—the thick darkness that surrounds His incredible light.

> The imprint of the Lost Israelites living in the Crimean Region above the Black Sea was discovered in the ancient cemeteries in which numerous tombstones with Hebrew-Phoenician inscriptions engraved were found. Seven hundred of these inscriptions were deciphered by a Professor Chwolson[50] of

---

[49] http://www.israelite.info/research/sourcedocumentsfiles/dariel-pass.html
[50] http://www.jewishencyclopedia.com/articles/4383-chwolson-daniel-abramovich

Petrograd and recorded in the archeological records. These striking tombstones that gave their Hebrew names and dates today reside in the Museum of St. Petersburg. The script as noted by Haberman was "not square Hebrew but marks a transition from the Phoenician characters to the later Hebrew." These tombstone engravings include:

1. "This is the tombstone of Buki, the son of Izchak, the priest. May his rest be in Eden at the time of the salvation of Israel. In the year 702 of our –exile."

If the date of The Exile began in the year of 717 B.C.E., then this tombstone was created in the year of 15 B.C.E. (Using 723 B.C. as the date of The Exile then the year would be 21 B.C. Noted by Joseph Dumond)

2. "To one of the faithful in Israel, Abraham ben Mar-Sinchah of Kertch, in the year of our exile 1682, when the envoys of the Prince of Rosh Meschek came from Kiou to our Master Chazar Prince David, Halmah, Habor and Gozan, to which place Tiglath-Pileser had exiled the sons of Reuben and Gad, and the half tribe of Manasseh, and permitted to settle there, and from which they have been scattered through the entire coast, even as far as China."

Here again we have archeological confirmations of the "wanderings" of the Lost Tribes of Israel, except the date would have to have been from the date of the Exodus (1486 B.C.E.) of which would give us a date of the tombstone in the year of 197 C.E. (Again, if we use the date of the Exodus as shown to us in *The Prophecies of Abraham* as 1379 B.C. then this date would be 303 C.E. Noted by Joseph Dumond)

3. "Rabbi Moses Levi died in the year 726 of our exile." (Using 723 B.C. as the date of the exile then this year is 3 C.E. Noted by Joseph Dumond)

"Zadok, the Levite, son of Moses, died 4,000 years after the creation, 785 years of our exile."[51]

These tombstones were not from the descendants of the Russian Jews who were driven out of Spain in the 5th-century C.E., but were descendants of the Lost Israelites who were known by a multitude of names: Sakasuni, Saki, Guti, Getai, Sak-Geloths, Skuthai, Skoloti, and the Scythians. These names were also confirmed by Herodotus who identified that the Scythians rose from the loins of the Sakai, or the Saxones, who "came from the country of the Medes." It was Aeschylus, the Greek poet and the Greek Platonist philosopher[52] and poet, Albinus who wrote:

Aeschylus:"The Sacae were noted for good laws, and were predominantly a righteous people."

Albinus: "The Saxons were descended from the ancient Sacae of Asia, and that in process of time they came to be called Saxons."[53]

In the region of Southern Russia, there were discovered many tumuli or kurgans that archeologists have now excavated and are now known to be the burial places of the Royal Scythians. In many of them, the interiors were lined with white marble. Frederick Haberman wrote about these excavations and the exquisite reliefs, furnishings, golden jewelry as reported (in) the American Journal of Archeology of 1914, Vol, XVIII and the Illustrated London News in January 3rd and February 14th, 1914. As reported:

Frederick Haberman: "In these (tumuli) were found chariots, pottery, jewelry, bracelets, gold, and precious stones of the finest workmanship of greatest abundance. The finest of those tumuli is that of the Solokha in the Crimea, which

---

[51] *Tracing Our Ancestors* by Frederick Haberman; 1930's; p. 130
[52] http://en.wikipedia.org/wiki/Albinus_%28philosopher%29
[53] *Tracing Our Ancestors* by Frederick Haberman; 1930's; p. 130

served as a mausoleum for the Scythian kings for several centuries. This tomb contained magnificent furnishing of silver and gold.

One of the royal skeletons found in it wore a heavy golden necklace with lion headed ends. Couching lions are also very prominent on the exquisite repoussé relief work of solid gold, adorning the walls and on the various gold and silver ornaments found, as well as on the handles and sheaths of the swords, which themselves were made of fine steel. The repoussé relief work pictured mostly battle and hunting scenes, on which the warriors appear in chain mail coats. It is also noteworthy that they are not bare-legged like the Greeks of that period were, but are wearing trousers. All the ornamental design is of most unusual excellence."[54]

It was Professor Hebert Hannay, who wrote in his 1915 book titled, *European and other Race Origins* about a Hebrew manuscript that was excavated from one of these tumuli in the Crimean region above the Black Sea, which stated:

Professor Hebert Hannay: "I am Jehudi the son of Moses, the son of Jehudi the Mighty, a man of the Tribe of Naphtali, which was carried captive with the other tribes of Israel, by the Prince Shalmaneser, from Samaria during the reign of Hoshea, King of Israel. They were carried to Halah, to Habor–which is Cabul–to Gozan and to the Chersonesus–which is the Crimea." [55]

Why are these things not part of the history taught in our schools? Why is this information not common knowledge even amongst those who study the Bible regularly?

---

[54] *Tracing Our Ancestors* by Frederick Haberman; 1930's; p. 130
[55] *European and Other Race Origins* by Herbert B. Hannay; London: 1915 cited by Frederick Haberman in *Tracing Our Ancestors*; 1930's; p. 129 http://www.biblesearchers.com/hebrewchurch/primitive/losttribesisrael12.shtml#TombstoneImprint

Here are some other historians who made notes on different peoples and have passed them down to us to consider and evaluate. We are now getting into names that hopefully at least some of us will recognize from our history books.

> Ammianus Marcellinus was a 4th-century Roman historian who considered the Alans to be the former Massagetae.[56] At the close of the 4th-century C.E., Claudian (the court poet of Emperor Honorius and Stilicho) wrote of (the) Alans and (the) Massagetae in the same breath: "the Massagetes who cruelly wound their horses that they may drink their blood, the Alans who break the ice and drink the waters of Maeotis' lake." (In Rufinem.)

> Procopius[57] writes in *History of the Wars Book III: The Vandalic War*: "the Massagetae whom they now call Huns" (XI. 37.), "there was a certain man among the Massagetae, well gifted with courage and strength of body, the leader of a few men; this man had the privilege handed down from his fathers and ancestors to be the first in all the Hunnic armies to attack the enemy." (XVIII. 54.).

> Now while Honorius was holding the imperial power in the West, barbarians took possession of his land; and I shall tell who they were and in what manner they did so. (A.D. 395-423) There were many Gothic nations in earlier times, just as also (in) the present, but the greatest and most important of all are the Goths, Vandals, Visigoths, and Gepaedes. In ancient times, however, they were named Sauromatae and Melanchlaeni; and there were some too who called these

---

[56] Ammianus Marcellinus: "Iuxtaque Massagetae Halani et Sargetae;" "Albanos et Massagetas, quos Alanos nunc appellamus;" "Halanos pervenit, veteres Massagetas."

[57] Procopius of Caesarea (Latin: Procopius Caesarensis, c. A.D. 500–c. A.D. 565) was a prominent Byzantine scholar from Palaestina Prima. Accompanying the general Belisarius in the wars of the Emperor, Justinian I became the principal historian of the 6th-century, writing *The Wars of Justinian*, *The Buildings of Justinian* and the celebrated *Secret History*. He is commonly held to be the last major historian of the ancient world.

nations Getic. All these, while they are distinguished from one another by their names, as has been said, do not differ in anything else at all. For they all have white bodies and fair hair, and are tall and handsome to look upon, and they use the same laws and practice a common religion. For they are all of the Arian faith, and have one language called Gothic; and, as it seems to me, they all came originally from one tribe, and were distinguished later by the names of those who led each group. This people used to dwell above the Ister River from of old. Later on, the Gepaedes got possession of the country about Singidunum (Belgrade) and Sirmium (Mitrovitz) on both sides of the Ister River, where they have remained settled even down to my time (II).[58]

*Evagrius Scholasticus*, (*Ecclesiastical History*. Book 3. Ch. 2.): "... and in Thrace, by the inroads of the Huns, formerly known by the name of Massagetae, who crossed the Ister without opposition."[59]

The Asian Jats have been identified directly with the Massagetaeans ("great" Getae/Jat) by Professor Tadeusz Sulimirski.[60 & 61]

"The Jats... trace their descent to the land of Ghazni and Kandahar, watered by the mother-river of the Kushika race, the sacred Haetuman or Helmand. Their name connects them

---

[58] *History of the Wars* by Procopius; http://en.wikisource.org/wiki/History_of_the_Wars/Book_III

[59] *Evagrius Scholasticus, Ecclesiastical History* (A.D. 431-A.D. 594), translated by E. Walford (1846). Book 3 http://www.tertullian.org/fathers/evagrius_3_book3.htm

[60] *The Sarmatians* by Tadeusz Sulimirski (1970); *Ancient Peoples and Places*; Vol. 73, pp. 113-114; New York: Praeger. "The evidence of both the ancient authors and the archaeological remains point to a massive migration of Sacian (Sakas)/Massagetan ("great" Jat) tribes from the Syr Darya Delta (Central Asia) by the middle of the 2nd-century B.C. Some of the Syr Daryan tribes; they also invaded North India." http://books.google.co.in/books?id=gdjhuAAACAAJ

[61] http://en.wikipedia.org/wiki/Tadeusz_Sulimirski

with the Getae of Thrace, and thence with the Gattons, said by Pytheas to live on the southern shores of the Baltic, the Gaettones placed by Ptolemy and Tacitus on the Visula in the country of the Lithuanians, and the Goths of Gothland, which is Sweden. The Getae of the Balkans are said by Herodotus to be the bravest and most just of the Thracians."[62]

This, once again shows us that the Scandinavian ancestors were The Goths. What I am doing here is showing you as many different authoritative sources that can be found, that I deem to be the most reliable, who have written about the groups of people we are following. They used different names at different times. All you have to do is connect the names as if you were connecting the dots of human history, and at the same time, know what group lived where and when.

> When describing the Sacae Scythian tribes who migrated from the Caspian Sea region in the 2nd-century B.C., to settle within the Parthian Empire, historian George Rawlinson notes that the greatest tribe, the Massagetae, was also named the "great Jits, or Jats."[63] These migrating Sacae or Saka gave their name to the Parthian province of Sacastan and to the Saka kingdoms of Northwest India. The term "Jat" has survived as a caste-name in Northwest India into modern times, attesting to the ancient dominance of the Jats in that region. The *Encyclopedia Britannica* states the following about the ancient "Jats."

> "The early Mohammedans wrote of the Jats' country as lying between Kirman and Mansura… Speculation has identified them with the Getae of Herodotus… (or the) Scythians or Indo-Scythians."[64] (*Emphasis added.*)

---

[62] The *Ruling Races of Prehistoric Times in India, South-Western Asia and Southern Europe* by James Francis Hewitt (1894). London: Archibald Constable & Co.; pp. 481-482
[63] *The Sixth Oriental Monarchy* by George Rawlinson, p. 118
[64] "Jat." *Encyclopedia Britannica*, Vol. 12, p. 970

The Asian Jats lived near the land of Kirman (i.e. the Kerman or German region of Parthia). If they were Asian "Getae," their later European name was the "Getes" or "Goths." If they were Scythians (Sacae), they became known as Germans or Saxons as they entered Europe. *Collier's Encyclopedia* states of the Jats:

"They are believed to be descended from the Saka or Scythians, who moved into India in a series of migrations between the 2nd-century B.C. and A.D. 500.[65] (*Emphasis added*.)

Since the Jats were a branch of the "Sacae" called "Saxones" by Ptolemy, it is not surprising that they were still allied to the Saxons and called "Jutes" by the time they reached Europe and the British Isles. Note that the consonants of the words "Jats" and "Jutes" are identical.

Many Sacae moved into Parthia in the 2nd-century B.C., but some did stay in Asia centuries after the fall of Parthia as we will document in the next chapter.

In Asia, the Sacae and Jats lived next to the Kermans (Germanii); in Europe they were called the Saxons and Jutes, and were part of the migrating Germans. Their names changed very little as they moved from Parthian Asia into Europe as part of the great Caucasus Mountain migrations. The names "Kerman" and "Jats" also remained in the regions of Asia where they once lived. Some Jats stayed in India and intermarried with other tribes in the region. Today, the Indian Jats "in general have a fair complexion,"[66] supporting the conclusion that they had Saka ancestors. As discussed in books two and three of this series, the Massagetae, a leading tribe of the Sacae, were most likely the descendants of the Israelite tribe of Manasseh, and the suffix "-getae" indicates a common origin with the "Getae" ("Goths") of

---

[65] "Jats." *Collier's Encyclopedia*, Vol. 11, p. 356
[66] "Jats." *Collier's Encyclopedia*, Vol. 11, p. 357

the Black Sea region. Historian Herbert Hannay wrote about this connection:

> "The Goths, too, it will be remembered, when in Asia as the Massagetae, had been worshippers of the Sun ..."[67] (*Emphasis added.*)

When I begin to explain the different banners for each tribe, keep in mind what I am about to share with you next with regard to the Anglos as in "Anglo-Saxons:"

> Many Saxon tribes migrated to the British Isles, along with the Angles and Jutes. Angle, or Engle, is likely based on the Hebrew word "egel" for "bull" or "calf," an identifying sign historically attached to the tribe of Ephraim. "Jutes" may simply be a variation of the name, Judah or Jats.[68]

I have to include the part below about Germany that others and Mr. Collins (who I have cited earlier) will now explain. In the Introduction portion, I showed you how in 612 B.C. the Babylonians routed the Assyrians and destroyed their capital of Ninevah and then delivered the final deathblow in 609 B.C. But what became of the Assyrian people themselves?

> Medieval Arab authors say that the Assyrians are from the same source as the Germans ... Barhebraeus, a Syria Bishop living during the 12th-century wrote that 'The Germanikah are a people in Mosel (Nineveh) who came from Persia'... Arab traditions have the Germanikah as Assyrians.[69]

> After the fall of the Assyrian Empire, the Roman historian Pliny mentioned a tribe of the "Assyriani" among the Scythian peoples in the Crimea north of the Black Sea.[70]

---

[67] *European and other Race Origins* by Herbert Hannay, p. 233
[68] http://stevenmcollins.com/html/Bk4_excerpt.htm
[69] *Israelites un Hyksos* by Gemol M. Leipzig, 1913, pp.88-90, as shown translated in White, p. 92
[70] *Natural History*, Book IV. XII. p. 81

Researcher Leon Poliakov notes the ancient Bavarian account that the people of Bavaria came into Central Europe from the region of Armenia by the Black Sea.[71]

Considering this information, it is not surprising to find medieval Arab writers describing the Germans as "Assyrians."[72]

The ancient city of Germanicopolis was located in Cilicia, in southeastern Asia Minor according to Ammianus Marellinus, Book 1, § 27. It belonged of old to the Hatti. Cilicia is mentioned several places in the Bible. Paul was born in Cilicia (Acts 21:39 and 22:3). Now look at a map of Europe. We find that one of the eastern provinces of pre-World War II Germany is called SILESIA!—spelled slightly different, but pronounced the same! The name of Cilicia in Asia Minor was simply transplanted to Eastern Germany by the Hatti who migrated from Cilicia to Silesia, then to the Rhine. Silesia is only a modern spelling! [73]

Asia's "Germanii" Become Europe's "Germans"

Other names from the Parthian Empire were brought to Europe as well. One Parthian province was named Carmania, the home of the Kermans or Germanii. The Sassanian Persians attacked these people along with the Parthians, so the Kermans also had to flee Persian persecution. Indeed, since the Kermans were one of the first nations attacked by the anti-Semitic Persians, it is logical that the Kermans were Semites. Where did these people get their name? Historian Herbert Hannay answered that question in his 1915 book, *European and Other Race Origins*. Hannay wrote:

"It was the Romans, then, about 58 B.C., who, by applying the name of a particular Persian tribe in a loose way to

---

[71] *The Aryan Myth*, p. 76
[72] *Israelites und Hyksos* by Germol M., pp. 89–90
[73] *Germany In Prophecy* by Hoeh H. *Plain Truth*, January 1963, p. 17

other tribes inhabiting the same country, originated, or rather appropriated and established the name Germanii, "Germans," as a generic appellation for the collection of tribes who eventually became so called."[74] (*Emphasis added.*)

It was the Romans who gave this name to a variety of tribes living in Persia in 58 B.C! Of course, at that time, all of Persia was in the Parthian Empire! So at the time the name "Germans" was placed on a group of tribes in Asia, they were all living in the Parthian Empire! By the time Parthian fell, large tribes of Germanii, or Germans, had been living in the Parthian Empire for almost three centuries! (58 B.C–A.D. 226) In 58 B.C., the Parthians were called "Persians" by many writers because they lived in and ruled the entire territory of the former Persian Empire.

Herbert Hannay also wrote the following about the Germans when they left Asia:

"... the original ancient Persians—amongst whom the Germans were included—took advantage of the occasion to abandon Asia and to migrate bodily into Europe."[75]

The many German tribes came to Europe from the Parthian Empire. Yet the Germans, or "Kermans" came from but one province in Parthia. If the very numerous Germans coming into Europe came from but one of Parthia's provinces, it gives us an insight into just how huge and heavily-populated the entire empire of Parthia was!

As the "Kermans" or "Germanii" migrated into Europe with the rest of Parthia's refugees, they were still called "Germans." The name "Carmania" was transplanted into Europe as "Germania" a general name used by the Romans to describe many different, but similar, tribes. However, we

---

[74] *European and other Race Origins* by Herbert Hannay, p. 232
[75] *European and other Race Origins* by Herbert Hannay, p. 232

have evidence that the name "German" was applied to tribes in the Persian region long before the Roman Empire existed!

Herodotus recorded that the "Germanii" were a subject people in the Old Persian Empire of the Achaemenids, before either the Roman or Parthian Empires existed.[76] The Encyclopedia Britannica, in commenting on this passage of Herodotus, indicates that the "Germanii" and the "Carmanians" were two names for the same people.[77] Obviously, these people kept that same name for centuries and were still called the "Germanii" in the Parthian Empire. Clearly, the term "German" originated in the Iranian-Mesopotamian region, and later spread to Europe. We have already seen that the Sacae Scythians of Asia had colonial outposts in Europe long before the main body of Sacae and Parthians migrated to Europe to seek refuge. Perhaps the Germans did as well. As the reader can see, the ancient Asian tribal name, "Germanii," was virtually unchanged over the centuries, as it became "Germany" in Europe.

It is this book's opinion that the original people called "Germanii" by Herodotus were not the only people later called "Germans" by the Romans. As noted above, the Romans came to "loosely" attach that same name to other tribes who happened to live in the same region as the Germanii during Parthian times. This fact indicates that the name "German" was eventually applied to many other Semitic people by the time these commonly named tribes were attacked by the Sassanian Persians and driven from Asia. As the Germans migrated from their old Parthian homelands into Europe, they kept the name "German" which had been applied by the Romans to a much larger grouping of tribes.

Readers can confirm for themselves the region of ancient Persia in which the ancient Kermans (or "Germanii") formerly lived. The region of ancient Persia is now called

---

[76] *Herodotus, The History*, 1, 125
[77] *Encyclopedia Britannica*, Vol. 17, Heading entitled p. 611

"Iran" and a modern city in Southern Iran is still named "Kerman," after the ancient Semitic tribes, which formerly inhabited that region before they migrated to Europe.

The ancient writer, Strabo, records that the Carmanians (Germanii or Kermans) were a warlike people.[78] Also interesting is the fact that Strabo records that an area of Asia Minor was named "Prusa."[79] When Hannibal, Carthage's greatest general, fled in the 2nd-century B.C., after being defeated by the Romans, he fled to Armenia and was given refuge in Asia Minor by a King "Prusias."[80] Were the residents of Prusa called "Prusians?" The resemblance between the ancient names "Prusa" and "Prusias" with the modern term "Prussia" is obvious, and both the ancient "Prusa" and the modern "Prussians" were known for their warlike traits. The region of Armenia/Asia Minor where the Prusa (and King Prusias) lived was often within Parthia's empire but always within Parthia's sphere of influence. Given the very large migration of people from the region of Parthia into Europe after Parthia fell, it is possible that the ancient Prusa were the namesake or ancestors of the modern Prussians.

The term "German" also came to include many of the Scythian tribes who migrated into Europe. In A.D. 100, the Roman historian and writer Pliny wrote concerning the Scythians in Europe:

"...the name of the Scythians has altogether been transferred to the Sarmatae and the Germans."[81]

This is a very important historical observation. It confirms that many Scythians, as they migrated out of Asia into Europe, also became known as "Germans." The *Encyclopedia Britannica* notes that the Greek writers Herodotus and

---

[78] *Strabo, The Geography of Strabo*, Vol. 7, 15. 2. 14
[79] *Strabo, The Geography of Strabo*, Vol. 5, 12. 4. 3
[80] *Carthage* by Alfred Church, p. 269
[81] *Greek and Roman Maps* by O.A.W. Dilke p. 46 (citing Pliny, iv. 81)

**Israelite Migration Routes**

→

**Circa 230-500 A.D.**

Hippocrates regarded the Sarmatae, or Sarmatians, as a Scythian tribe.[82] The above sources confirm that the Scythians were not in history, but simply became known as "Germans" when they migrated into Europe. We also have seen that many Sacae Scythians came to be known as "Saxons" when they entered Europe, and the Saxons are viewed as a branch of the Germanic tribes. Since many Israelite tribes were known as "Scythians" in Asia, this confirms that many of them were called "Germans" or "Saxons" as they entered Europe.[83]

As you study the map above, you can see the area that the Juts and Massagetae Scythians lived in and their relationship to the Kermans and Parthia.

---

[82] *Encyclopedia Britannica*, Vol. 19, Heading entitled "Sarmartae," p. 1,001
[83] http://stevenmcollins.com/html/Bk4_excerpt.htm

In my book, *The Prophecies of Abraham*[84] I show you how biblical prophecy clearly indicates that Assyria (modern day Germany) is going to attack and defeat Israel in the end-times. I am showing you, once again, the migrations of Israel, where they went, what historians and other cultures/nations called them along the way, and finally—where they ended up. Prophecy *does* repeat itself. Although this chapter has many historical quotes, I have had to lay this groundwork because so many deny the obvious and refuse to acknowledge proven historical facts. That being said, knowing who Assyria and the tribes of Israel are at the end of this age makes it very easy to understand whom prophecy is talking about and that which is about to befall these nations.

Continuing with Steven Collins comments about the Massagetae:

> The second book in this series discussed the Massagetae in detail, acknowledging that they were sun-worshippers. After crushing the army of the Persian King, Cyrus the Great, in the 6$^{th}$-century B.C., they migrated into Parthia in the 2$^{nd}$-century B.C. They lived in the Parthian province of Sakastan, named for their Sacae origins. It must be acknowledged that while Christianity had significant numbers of converts in the Parthian Empire, many Parthians and Scythians remained Zoroastrians or sun-worshippers. Hannay's quote identifies the Massagetae with the "Goths" who migrated into Europe. However, this author thinks most of the Massagetae (a "Sacae" tribe) merged into the Saxon tribes who migrated into northern Europe after Parthia fell.
>
> Another Asian tribe that moved from Asia into Europe was the Alans (or Alani). Historian George Rawlinson notes that bands of Alani lived from the Black Sea region to the east of the Caspian Sea.[85] They have been called "half-caste Scyths," and many Alani followed the Vandals into Europe.[86] *Collier's Encyclopedia* asserts the Alans were a

---

[84] http://bookstore.authorhouse.com/Products/SKU-000366309/The-Prophecies-of-Abraham.aspx & http://tinyurl.com/ac5bjkq
[85] *The Sixth Oriental Monarchy* by George Rawlinson, p.291 (see also, footnote 2)
[86] *Encyclopedia Britannica*, Vol. 1, Heading entitled "Alani," p. 496

tribe of "Iranian-speaking nomads" who moved from Asia into Europe in A.D. 500 and established a kingdom of their own in Portugal.[87] Even as the numerous Goths by the Black Sea exhibited "Iranian" (i.e., Parthian) traits, the Alans had an "Iranian" language. This confirms they had a common origin with the Parthians and Scythians, whose "Iranian" language and culture is well documented.

The Indo-Europeans who migrated from Asia into Europe in the aftermath of Parthia's fall included many different nations and tribes. As tribes intermingled, became allied or split up as they poured into Europe, there came to be considerable overlap in terms such as "Germans," "Goths," and "Saxons." The term "Caucasian" became an overall term to describe all these tribes migrating into Europe through the Caucasus Mountain/Black Sea region.[88]

We now come to the juncture in history of the Roman Empire where the Cimmerians are now being called by other names. As they move westward they come to be called "Celts" by the Greeks and "Gauls" by the Romans. Modern historians know them as "Celto-Scythiae," however. Cimmerians moved up into what is now called Belgium Holland and Northwest Germany and onto what was then called "Cimbric Chersonesus" and is now called "Jutland" or Denmark. The Romans called them the Cimbri.[89]

Roman Historian Sallust[90] records that the Cimbri were Gauls. Other Roman historians called the Cimbri Celts. The Igaevones, who moved into the Jutland area and Holland along with the Frisians, Chauci and Cimbri were all of one stock from the Cimmerian tribes according to Tacitus and Pliny.

---

[87] *Collier's Encyclopedia*, Vol. 1, Heading entitled "Alani," p. 310
[88] http://www.israelite.info/bookexcerpts/israelstribestoday.html
[89] Plutarch in his *Life of Marius* says "they were called at first Cimmerians and then, not inappropriately Cimbri."
[90] http://en.wikipedia.org/wiki/Sallust

The Gauls in 280 B.C. invaded the western region of Asia Minor (Western Turkey) from Central Europe and maintained a presence in Phrygia and gave their name to the area. It became known as Galatia, which is the same area mentioned in Acts 16:6 and is the same area Paul wrote his epistle to the Galatians. These "Caucasians" used to be known over 500 years earlier as the Israelites.

> *6 And having passed through Phrygia and the Galatian country, they were forbidden by the Set-apart Spirit to speak the word in Asia.* (Acts 16:6)

We can also read in Acts of another event on the day of Pentecost.

> *5 Now in Yerushalayim there were dwelling Yehudim, dedicated men from every nation under the heaven. 6 And when this sound came to be, the crowd came together, and were confused, because everyone heard them speak in his own language. 7 And they were all amazed and marveled, saying to each other, "Look, are not all these who speak Galileans? 8 And how do we hear, each one in our own language in which we were born? 9 Parthians and Medes and Ěylamites, and those dwelling in Aram Naharayim, both Yehudah and Kappadokia, Pontos and Asia, 10 both Phrygia and Pamphulia, Mitsrayim and the parts of Libya around Cyrene, visitors from Rome, both Yehudim and converts, 11 Cretans and Arabs, we hear them speaking in our own tongues the great deeds of Elohim."* (Acts 2:5-11)

Notice the word "dedicated men." These are the men from each of these far off countries who had come to Jerusalem to keep the Feast of Shavuot or Pentecost. These are the Israelites.

We are commanded to come up to Jerusalem three times a year for the Feast Days.

> *14 "Three[1] times in the year you are to observe a festival to Me: (Footnote: [1]The Festivals of יהוה are grouped in three, for three different times of the year.) 15 Guard the Festival*

*of Unleavened Bread. Seven days you eat unleavened bread, as I commanded you, at the time appointed in the month of Abib—for in it you came out of Mitsrayim—and do not appear before Me empty-handed; 16 and the Festival of the Harvest, the first-fruits of your labors which you have sown in the field; and the Festival of the Ingathering at the outgoing of the year, when you have gathered in the fruit of your labors from the field. 17 Three times in the year all your males are to appear before the Master יהוה."* (Exodus 23:14-17)

*16 "Three times a year all your males appear before יהוה your Elohim in the place which He chooses: at the Festival of Unleavened Bread, and at the Festival of Weeks, and at the Festival of Booths. And none should appear before יהוה empty-handed ..."* (Deuteronomy 16:16)

*4 Where the tribes have come up, The tribes of Yah, A witness to Yisra'ěl, To give thanks to the Name of יהוה.* (Psalm 122:4)

Only those from the tribes of Israel who were keeping the Feast Days would have made the trip to Jerusalem to keep them. Peter is addressing the people hailing from the Ten Tribes who have not returned to the Land of Israel permanently. They came for the feasts from the places they had migrated to or were exiled to and were currently living at. The Ten Tribes were known and not "lost" as we are told.

I would now like to go back and touch upon some things more in depth that I have already mentioned, but not provided you with any of the supporting details regarding.

The Amyrgians were called *Saka haumavarga* ("Haoma-drinking Scythians") in Old Persian, which is a reinterpretation of the personal names *Amorges* and *(H)omarges*.[91] The Greek form of their name was *Amyrgioi*. They have been known from the days of Cyrus and are recorded by Herodotus as having fought against Cyrus and joined forces

---

[91] http://en.wikipedia.org/wiki/Amyrgians

with him. They are amongst the Scythian and as we have shown you the descendants of the Israelites.

There is a wealth of information, believe it or not, in what many call the boring and wearisome genealogies of the Bible. Below, in 1 Chronicles and in Numbers, the descendants of Manasseh are identified for us:

> *14 The sons of Manashsheh: his Aramean concubine bore him Makir the father of Gil'ad, the father of Asriel.* (1 Chronicles 7:14)

> *29 sons of Manashsheh: of Makir, the clan of the Makirites. And Makir brought forth Gil'ad, of Gil'ad, the clan of the Gil'adites.* (Numbers 26:29)

> *39 And the sons of Mikir son of Menashsheh went to Gil'ad and took it, and dispossessed the Amorites who were in it. 40 So Mosheh gave Gil'ad to Mikir, son of Menashsheh, and he dwelt in it. 41 And Ya'ir son of Menashsheh went and took its small towns, and called them Hawoth Ya'ir. 42 And Nobah went and took Qenath and its villages, and called it Nobah, after his own name.* (Numbers 32:39-42)

In his book, *A Jewish Princedom In Feudal France*, Arthur Zuckerman notes that Machir (Ha-Machiri) to ("belonging to Machir") was referred to as Al Makhiri, "AYMERI," "Maghario" (p.180) or "Magharius," as "Aymeri," p.121, n.16, and as "Aimerico," and "Aimericus." Zuckerman p.131, n.38[92]

> In Biblical Hebrew "HaMachiri" literally denotes "The Sons of Machir" (Numbers 26:29), but it could also connote "That which Comes of Machir" and in this case it was applied as a nickname to Machir himself and then Latinized to sound something like "America!" The Hebrew version is difficult

---

[92] *A Jewish Princedom In Feudal France* by Arthur Zuckerman Jr., pp. 768-900" New York, 1972. http://www.amazon.com/Jewish-Princedom-Feudal-768-900-History/dp/0231032986

for untrained westerners to pronounce (or even remember) and so was rendered in Early Medieval Latin as "Americo" or "Amerigo" and this name was later given to Amerigo Vespucci who gave his name to the land of America. It follows that the name AMERICA may well be understood to mean "Land of Machir" (or "Land of the Sons of Machir") son of Menasseh.[93]

Zuckerman describes how Machir ("Aimericus") became a legend whose name was celebrated in the ballads of Southern France and neighboring regions.[94]

From Yair Davidiy we have the following research on the name of Machir, his descendants, where they went and what they became known as there.

> Menasseh = Mannus (legendary ancestor of tribes in Germany who moved to Gaul and Britain).
>
> Clans of Menasseh:
>
> Machir: Maracanda, Maruka, Amyrgioi (all east of Caspian Sea), Makran (southern Iran), Skati Marika (name given to Mercians, means east of the Caspian Sea), Mercia known on the continent as "Myringas", important element amongst Goths and Anglo-Saxons. Marcomanni in Germany.
>
> The name of MACHIR son of Menasseh became (after a simple letter permutation) the name "AMERICA" which therefore may be understood as meaning "Land of Machir."
>
> Gilead: Galatae (in Gaul), Galadi (name of Galatae), Giladon (in Wales), Caledonians (in Scotland).

---

[93] http://britam.org/america.html
[94] *A Jewish Princedom In Feudal France* by Arthur Zuckerman Jr., pp. 768-900" New York, 1972. http://www.amazon.com/Jewish-Princedom-Feudal-768-900-History/dp/0231032986

Helek: = Heleucones (Germany to Britain), Calucones, (Germany to the west).

> Asriel: = Isari (Emodian mountains in Scythia, legendary place of sojourn of the Angles, Saxons, and Frisians). Aorsi (from western Scythia to Scandinavia), Surrey (Saxon England).
>
> Schechem (Secem): = Scymbi (east Scythia),
>
> Sigambri-Sicambri (Afghanistan, Bactria, from Germany to Gaul).
>
> Shemida: = Soumboi Aggiloi (branch of Angles),
>
> Soumboi-Laggobardi (branch of Lombards), Samides (legendary ancestor of Gauls), Saemdag (Scandinavian Ancestral hero).
>
> Hepher: = Hefr (nickname for Gothic warrior).
>
> Haeferingas (Middle Saxons in England).
>
> Jeezer (in Hebrew is pronounced like) Aiezer (Ai-g-azar): = Agathyrsi (became Khazars who converted to Judaism and Picts of Scotland).
>
> Daughters of Zelophahad: Tirtsah (Thirtsah) = Thyrsagettae (name for Thysagettae of Scythia, migrated to Scandinavia).
>
> Milcah: = Melicertii in Scythian Caucasus - Basiloi (Royal =MLC root in name Milcah) of Khazars, Scandinavia, and Royal Scyths.
>
> Hoglah
>
> Noah: = Neuri of Scythia to Scandinavia, Nervi of Celtic Gaul

Mahlah

Additional Clan Names of Menasseh based on the Book of Chronicles:

Sheresh (Seres): = Seres in Serica (East Scythia).

Peresh (Peres): = Parissi (of Gaul and Britain), Frissi (of Holland and England), Phiressi (Scandinavia), Parsi (Parthians from east of the Caspian and in Iran). The name "Peresh" means "separated, sanctified" (cf. Pharisee) which is the same meaning as "Nemed" an ancestor in Irish mythology). When pronounced with a slightly different intonation the name also connotes horseman= SUS (susmeans horsein Hebrew) = SUESSIONS, (Gaul), Sassi. There was a prince of the Tribe of Manasseh Gaddi, the son of Susi (Numbers 13:11).

Epher: = Heartho-Raemes (Scandinavia).

Jeremiah: = Heartho-Raemes (Scandinavia), Raumar (Norway).

Ishi: = Hossi (Scythia, maybe part of Picts and Khazars).

Azriel (Gazriel): = Gazaria (name of "Khazaria").

Eliel: = Hilleviones (Scandinavia), Elvaones (Vandals, Anglo-Saxons).

Hovadiah (pronounceable as Howadiah): = Eadwine (amongst Mercians of England and Lombards).

Mercia in Anglo-Saxon England comprised the largest realm. Mercia derives from Machir. Mercian clans in England included Magonsaete, Nox, Oht gaga, Henrica, Unecinga, Hwicce, Gifel, Spale, and Grywe (Thundy p.105). The Magonsaete have a name that in Hebrew could mean armor-bearers (Magon-Saeti).

Other clans of Machir (1-Chronicles 7; 14-17) included Likhi and Aniam (=Unecinga of Mercia). Shupim =Spale of Mercia, Chupim =Gifel of Mercia.[95]

The map below shows you the routes the various tribes took over time from the captivity and how their names were changed and where they ended up.

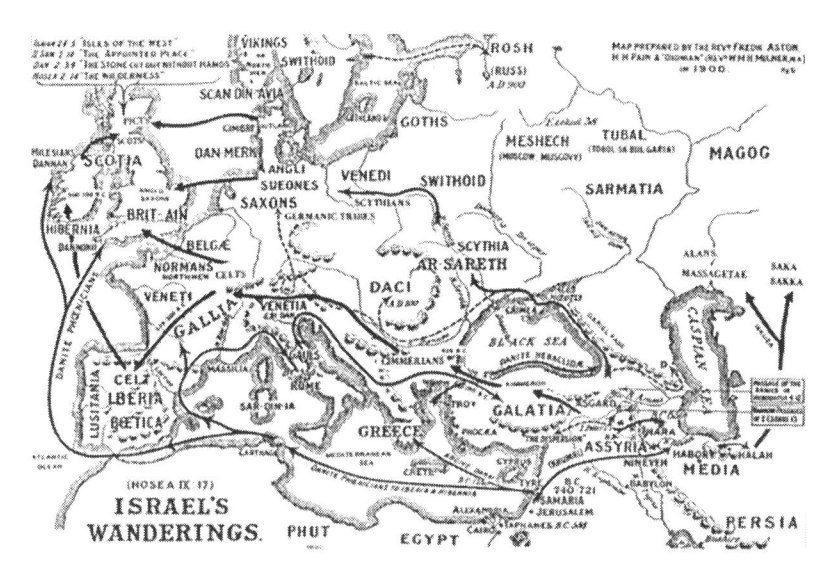

*ISRAEL'S WANDERINGS.*

We can also read that Yehshua knew the locations of the Ten Northern Tribes because of what He says to the Apostles.

> *And He answering, said, "I was not sent except to the lost sheep of the house of Yisra'el."* (Matthew 15:24)

> יהשוע *sent these twelve out, having commanded them, saying, "Do not go into the way of the gentiles, and do not enter a city of the Shomeronites, 6 but rather go to the lost sheep of the house of Yisra'ël. 7 "And as you go, proclaim, saying, 'The reign of the heavens has drawn near.'* (Matthew 10:5-7)

---

95   http://britam.org/now/now337.html

And this was 763 years after the first captivity in 732 B.C. The Apostles were to go to the tribes of Israel and tell them of the good news. But where did they go? We read in our very own Bible the following:

> *1 Kĕpha, an emissary of יהושע Messiah, to the chosen, strangers of the dispersion in Pontos, Galatia, Kappadokia, Asia, and Bithunia ..."* (1 Peter 1:1).

Let me now quote an article from *Hope of Israel* as they show you where the Twelve Apostles went to.

> These were not Gentiles. Peter was not the Apostle to the Gentiles (Galatians 2:8). Paul was. Peter was Chief Apostle to the Lost Sheep of the House of Israel.
>
> Notice the word "strangers." It does not mean Gentiles. The original Greek (term) is parepidemos. It means "a resident foreigner," literally, "an alien alongside." It refers not to Gentiles, but to non-Gentiles who dwelt among Gentiles, as foreigners and aliens. Abraham, for example, was a stranger, (and) an alien, when he lived among the Canaanite Gentiles in Palestine.
>
> Peter was addressing part of the Lost Ten Tribes who dwelt among the Gentiles as aliens or strangers. He was not writing primarily to Jews. He would not have addressed them as "strangers," for he himself was a Jew.
>
> Now notice the regions to which Peter addressed his letter. You may have to look at a Bible map to locate them. They are all located in the northern half of Asia Minor, modern Turkey. These lands lay immediately west of the Parthian Empire!
>
> Greek writers, in the time of the Messiah, recognized that the regions of northern Asia Minor were non-Greek (except for a few Greek trading colonies in the port cities). New peoples, the Greeks tell us, were living in northern Asia Minor in New

Testament times. Here is the surprising account of Diodorus of Sicily:

"... many conquered peoples were removed to other homes, and two of these became very great colonies: the one was composed of Assyrians and was removed to the land between Paphlagonia and Pontus, and the other was drawn from Media and planted along the Tanais (the River Don in ancient Scythia—the modern Ukraine, north of the Black Sea, in southern Russia." (See book II, s. 43.)

> Notice the areas from which these colonies came—Assyria and Media. The very areas to which the House of Israel was taken captive! "So was Israel carried away out of their own land to Assyria unto this day." (2 Kings 17:23) "The king of Assyria took Samaria, and carried Israel away into Assyria and placed them in Halah and in Habor by the River of Gozan, and in the cities of the Medes" (verse 6).
>
> The House of Israel dwelt in captivity as aliens or strangers among the Assyrians. When the Assyrians were later removed from their homeland to northern Asia Minor, part of the House of Israel migrated *with* them!
>
> Here's the proof from Strabo, the geographer. Strabo named the colonists in northern Asia Minor "White Syrians" (12, 3, 9), instead of Assyrians. There were therefore, two peoples—Assyrians and White Syrians. Who were these so-called "White Syrians?" None other than the House of Israel, which had been carried into Assyrian captivity.
>
> "Syria" was the Greek name for the whole eastern Mediterranean coastal strip north of Judea. Because the House of Israel lived in Palestine—southern Syria in Greek terminology—the Greeks called them "White Syrians." By contrast, the dark-complexioned Arameans remained in Syria and (have) dwelt there to this day.

When the Assyrians were compelled to migrate to Northern Asia Minor, their former slaves—the "White Syrians" or Ten-Tribed House of Israel—migrated with them! We find them still there in New Testament times. To these people—the Lost Sheep of the House of Israel—the strangers among the Assyrians (1 Peter 1:1)—the Apostle Peter addresses his first letter! Could anything be plainer? The Chief Apostle to the House of Israel writing to a part of the Ten Lost Tribes dwelling among the Assyrians who originally carried them captive![96]

Who the Parthians were has long remained a mystery. They suddenly appear near the Caspian Sea around 700 B.C. as slaves of the Assyrians. "According to Diodorus, who probably followed Ctesias, they passed from the dominion of the Assyrians to that of the Medes, and from dependence upon the Medes to a similar position under the Persians." (Rawlinson's, *Monarchies*, vol. IV, p. 26, quoted from Diod. Sic., ii 2, 3; 34, 1 and 6.)

The Parthians rose to power around 250 B.C. in the lands along the southern shores of the Caspian Sea. That was the very land into which Israel was exiled! What puzzles historians is that the Parthians were neither Persians, nor Medes, nor Assyrians or any other known people. Even their name breathes mystery—until you understand the Bible.

The word Parthian means exile! (See Rawlinson's *The Sixth Monarchy*, p, 19.) The only exiles in this land were the Ten Tribes of Israel! The Parthians included none other than the exiled Lost Ten Tribes who remained in the land of their captivity until A.D. 226. That's when the Persians drove them into Europe. Josephus, the Jewish historian, was familiar with Parthia as a major dwelling place of the Ten Tribes. He declares: "But then the entire body of the people of Israel (the Ten Tribes) remained in that country (they did not return to Palestine); wherefore there are but two tribes

---

[96] http://www.hope-of-israel.org/12apost.htm

in Asia and Europe subject to the Romans, while the Ten Tribes are beyond Euphrates (until) now, and are an immense multitude, and not to be estimated by numbers" *(Antiquities of the Jews*, bk. xi, ch. v. 2).

There it is! The very area to which Thomas (The Apostle) sojourned was, reports Josephus, filled with uncounted multitudes of the Ten Tribes! Josephus was, apparently, unaware of those who had already migrated westward. But he does make it plain that only the House of Judah ever returned to Palestine. The House of Israel was "beyond Euphrates (until) now!"

Thomas also journeyed into Northwest India, east of Persia, where the "White Indians" dwelt. These "White Indians"—that is, whites living in India—were also known as Nephthalite Huns, in later Greek records. Any connection with the tribe of Naphtali? They were overthrown in the 6th-century and migrated into Scandinavia. The archaeology of Scandinavia confirms this event.

Scythia and Upper Asia (meaning Asia Minor) were the regions assigned to Philip. (See William Cave's *Antiquities Apostolicae*, p. 168.) Scythia was the name of the vast plain north of the Black and the Caspian Seas. To this region a great colony of Israelites migrated after the fall of the Persian Empire in 331 B.C. From Scythia migrated the Scots. The word Scot is derived from the word Scyth. It means an inhabitant of Scythia. The Scots are part of the House of Israel.

Interestingly, the word Scythia, in Celtic, has the same meaning that Hebrew does in the Semitic language—a migrant or wanderer![97]

Given the fact I have not yet spoken to you of another great nation that grew out of the captivity of the Israelites I shall now do so. Once

---

[97] http://www.hope-of-israel.org/12apost.htm

again, one can glean a great deal from the genealogies of the various clans found in the Bible. In the Book of Numbers, it is said of the sons of Ephraim:

> 35 *These are the sons of Ephrayim according to their clans: of Shuthelah, the clan of the Shuthalhites; of Beker, the clan of the Bakrites; of Tahan, the clan of the Tahanites. 36 And these are the sons of Shuthelah: of Eran, the clan of the Eranites. 37 These are the clans of the sons of Ephrayim according to their registered ones: thirty-two thousand five hundred. These are the sons of Yoseph after their clans.* (Numbers 26:35-37)

In the region where Parthia was to become the great nation that it did before the birth of Yehshua, and in the pockets where portions of the Ten Tribes were taken in the captivity, is a province known as Bactria. It was a Seleucid Province and the language they spoke was related to the Saka Scythians.

Henry Rawlinson states in his book *Bactria*, "… there seems to be very little doubt that the population of Bactria was largely Scythian …" (and he cites Justine, a classical author, who wrote "… the Bactrian Empire was founded by the Scythians …")[98]

Notice the clan of Eranites mentioned in Numbers 26. This one is easy to see even today as the country in which Eran was transplanted is today called by his name in the form of Iran and its capital, is Teheran.[99] These Ephraimites would be chased out of there in the years to come by the Medes and the Persians, but their name would remain.

Another clan from Numbers 26 is also mentioned. It too was located in what would become Parthia and they were the Tahanites whose name would become the Dahanites. (The "D" and the "T" being interchangeable linguistically).

---

[98] *Parthia* by Steven Collins, p. 15, Footnote: Bactria by Henry Rawlinson, p. 12
[99] *Media Babylon and Persia* by Zenaide A. Ragozin, pp. 57-60 and map before page p. 1

Here is what Steven Collins has to say on this same subject.

> When the capital of ancient Israel, Samaria, fell to the Assyrians, 2 Kings 17:5-6 records that the last Israelite defenders were transplanted to the region of the Medes (now northern Iran). Samaria was in the territory of the Israelite tribe of Ephraim, and one would expect many of the last wave of Israelite captives to be from the tribe of Ephraim. Numbers 26:35-37 also records that the tribe of Ephraim was subdivided into four clans, three of which were named the Bachrites, the Eranites and the Tahanites. In later centuries, three powerful tribes of the Scythian-Parthian alliance were the Bactrians, the Eranians and the Dahanites. Notice the striking similarity in the names of the Ephraimite clans and the Scythian-Parthian tribes. These tribes were all clans of the same Israelite tribe of Ephraim grown into exceedingly great numbers. The term "Eran" is an archaic one from which is derived the name of the modern nation of "Iran." Interestingly, the nation of Iran (although it is now Persian, not Israelite) is still known by the name of a clan of the Israelite tribe of Ephraim, which used to live in that region. "D" and "T" are related (and often interchangeable) consonants even as "P" and "B" were often interchangeable consonants in the ancient world, making the Dahanites and the Tahanites the same Ephraimite clan. Bactria was derived from the Ephraimite clan name of the "Bachrites." I doubt you will ever see the Israelite origin of all these names in any history book.
>
> In the post-Parthian period, Afghanistan was also ruled for a time by the "White Huns," a name given to them to differentiate this "Caucasian" tribe from the other Mongoloid Huns of Asia. The *Encyclopedia Britannica* **(1943 Ed., Vol. 8, p. 646) records the White Huns were also called "Ephthalites" or "Nephthalites" by ancient historians. Either name preserves the distinctively-Israelite name of the tribe of Naphtali, which was taken captive by Assyria and relocated in one single mass into**

Asia years before the fall of Samaria. The White Huns who ruled Afghanistan for a time were the Israelite tribe of Naphtali. The Scythians and Parthians did not forget their Israelite origins. During the time of the Parthian Empire (circa 250 B.C.—A.D. 227), one Parthian city located southeast of the Caspian Sea was named "Samariane" (*Ancient History* by George Rawlinson, p. 475), preserving the exact name of the capital city of Samaria in the Israelite ancestral homeland in the old Promised Land.[100]

The second story of the Parthians I am about to share comes from Eusebius about the Messiah. You can read this for yourself.

Chapter 13. Narrative concerning the Prince of the Edessenes.

1. The divinity of our Lord and Savior Jesus Christ being noised abroad among all men on account of his wonder-working power, he attracted countless numbers from foreign countries lying far away from Judea, who had the hope of being cured of their diseases and of all kinds of sufferings.

2. For instance, the King Abgarus, who ruled with great glory the nations beyond the Euphrates, being afflicted with a terrible disease which it was beyond the power of human skill to cure, when he heard of the name of Jesus, and of his miracles, which were attested by all with one accord, sent a message to him by a courier and begged him to heal his disease.

3. But he did not at that time comply with his request; yet he deemed him worthy of a personal letter in which he said that he would send one of his disciples to cure his disease, and at the same time promised salvation to himself and all his house.

4. Not long afterward, his promise was fulfilled. For after his resurrection from the dead and his ascent into heaven,

---

[100] http://stevenmcollins.com/WordPress/?p=242

Thomas, one of the twelve apostles, under divine impulse, sent Thaddeus, who was also numbered among the seventy disciples of Christ, to Edessa, as a preacher and evangelist of the teaching of Christ.

5. And all that our Savior had promised received through him its fulfillment. You have written evidence of these things taken from the archives of Edessa, which was, at that time, a royal city. For in the public registers there, which contain accounts of ancient times and the acts of Abgarus, these things have been found preserved down to the present time. But there is no better way than to hear the epistles themselves which we have taken from the archives and have literally translated from the Syriac language in the following manner:

Copy of an epistle written by Abgarus, the ruler to Jesus, and sent to him at Jerusalem by Ananias the swift courier.

6. Abgarus, ruler of Edessa, to Jesus the excellent Savior who has appeared in the country of Jerusalem, greetings. I have heard the reports of you and of your cures as performed by you without medicines or herbs. For it is said that you make the blind to see and the lame to walk, that you cleanse lepers and cast out impure spirits and demons, and that you heal those afflicted with lingering disease, and raise the dead.

7. And having heard all these things concerning you, I have concluded that one of two things must be true: either you *are* God, and having come down from heaven you do these things, or else you, who does these things, are the *Son of* God.

8. I have therefore written to you to ask you if you would take the trouble to come to me and heal the disease, which I have. For I have heard that the Jews are murmuring against you and are plotting to injure you. But I have a very small yet noble city, which is great enough for us both.

The answer of Jesus to the ruler Abgarus by the courier Ananias:

9. "Blessed are you who hast believed in me without having seen me. For it is written concerning me, that they who have seen me will not believe in me, and that they who have not seen me will believe and be saved. But in regard to what you have written me, that I should come to you, it is necessary for me to fulfill all things here for which I have been sent, and after I have fulfilled them, thus to be taken up again to him that sent me. But after I have been taken up I will send to you one of my disciples, that he may heal your disease and give life to you and yours."

Further accounts:

10. To these epistles there was added the following account in the Syriac language. After the ascension of Jesus, Judas, who was also called Thomas, sent to him Thaddeus, an apostle, one of the seventy. When he had come, he lodged with Tobias, the son of Tobias. When the report of him got abroad, it was told (to) Abgarus that an apostle of Jesus had come, as he had written him.

11. Thaddeus began then, in the power of God, to heal every disease and infirmity, insomuch that all wondered. And when Abgarus heard of the great and wonderful things which he did and of the cures which he performed, he began to suspect that he was the one of whom Jesus had written him, saying, 'After I have been taken up. I will send to you one of my disciples who will heal you.'

12. Therefore, summoning Tobias, with whom Thaddeus lodged, he said, I have heard that a certain man of power has come and is lodging in your house. Bring him to me. And Tobias coming to Thaddeus said to him, "The ruler Abgarus summoned me and told me to bring you to him that you might heal him." And Thaddeus said, "I will go, for I have been sent to him with power."

13. Tobias therefore arose early on the following day, and taking Thaddeus, came to Abgarus. And when he came, the nobles were present and stood about Abgarus. And immediately upon his entrance a great vision appeared to Abgarus in the countenance of the Apostle Thaddeus. When Abgarus saw it, he prostrated himself before Thaddeus, while all those who stood about were astonished; for they did not see the vision, which appeared to Abgarus alone.

14. He then asked Thaddeus if he were, in truth, a disciple of Jesus the Son of God, who had said to him, 'I will send you one of my disciples, who shall heal you and give you life.' And Thaddeus said, "Because you have mightily believed in him that sent me, therefore have I been sent unto you. And still further, if you believe in him, the petitions of your heart shall be granted you as you believe."

15. And Abgarus said to him, "So much have I believed in him that I wished to take an army and destroy those Jews who crucified him, had I not been deterred from it by reason of the dominion of the Romans." And Thaddeus said, "Our Lord has fulfilled the will of his Father, and having fulfilled it, has been taken up to his Father." And Abgarus said to him, "I too have believed in him and in his Father."

16. And Thaddeus said to him, "Therefore, I place my hand upon you in his name." And when he had done it, immediately Abgarus was cured of the disease and of the suffering, which he had.

17. And Abgarus marveled, that as he had heard concerning Jesus, so he had received in very deed through his disciple Thaddeus, who healed him without medicines and herbs, and not only him, but also Abdus the son of Abdus, who was afflicted with the gout; for he too came to him and fell at his feet, and having received a benediction by the imposition of his hands, he was healed. The same Thaddeus cured also

many other inhabitants of the city, and did wonders and marvelous works, and preached the word of God.

18. And afterward Abgarus said, "You, O Thaddeus, do these things with the power of God, and we marvel. But, in addition to these things, I pray you to inform me in regard to the coming of Jesus, how he was born; and in regard to his power, by what power he performed those deeds of which I have heard."

19. And Thaddeus said, "Now indeed will I keep silence, since I have been sent to proclaim the word publicly. But tomorrow assemble for me all your citizens, and I will preach in their presence and sow among them the word of God, concerning the coming of Jesus, how he was born; and concerning his mission, for what purpose he was sent by the Father; and concerning the power of his works, and the mysteries which he proclaimed in the world, and by what power he did these things; and concerning his new preaching, and his abasement and humiliation, and how he humbled himself, and died and debased his divinity and was crucified, and descended into Hades, and burst the bars which from eternity had not been broken, and raised the dead; for he descended alone, but rose with many, and thus ascended to his Father."

20. Abgarus therefore commanded the citizens to assemble early in the morning to hear the preaching of Thaddeus, and afterward he ordered gold and silver to be given him. But he refused to take it, saying, "If we have forsaken that which was our own, how shall we take that which is another's?" These things were done in the three hundred and fortieth year.

I have inserted them here in their proper place, translated from the Syriac literally, and I hope to good purpose.[101]

---

[101] Fathers of the Church: Church History by Eusebius
http://www.newadvent.org/fathers/250101.htm

There is a wealth of information available now at one's fingertips that fills in the necessary gaps historically and opens up a whole new world of understanding of the people groups now coming to be known in the world that have been written exhaustively about by many ancient historians. I have now shown you the names with which the Israelites have been called from the captivity up to the Common Era (C.E.). You can now locate the Ten Tribes of Israel from the time of their captivity in 723 B.C. right down to our present era and, in some cases you can do this tribe by tribe once you know the names of all the Celtic tribes.

I have so many other books I could have used with information that is simply amazing but it is not the purpose of this book to examine this subject exhaustively—for as essential as this information is for laying the foundation for this book, it is not the main thrust of this book. I have shown you how the Ten Tribes of Israel and also some of the tribes of Judah after their captivity migrated north and west and finally settled down where the Celtic peoples are recorded to have settled.

We all know who the Celtic people are today. Britain and her Commonwealth Nations are one of the sons of Joseph (Ephraim—Britain, Canada, Australia, New Zealand). The USA is another (Manasseh). It is upon *these two* that the name of Israel has been passed down to and it is upon these two and the other tribes of Israel (Norway, Sweden, Finland, Denmark, Holland, South Africa, parts of France, Belgium, Scotland, Ireland, Wales and the State of Israel—which represents Judah) that the punishments of Leviticus 26 and the prophecy contained within this book about Daniel 9, are going to come and are already coming.

Read the Scottish Declaration of Independence written in 1320 C.E. and sent to the Pope by Robert the Bruce and sealed by twenty-five of his nobles. These are not religious people but they did know their history. Do you? Search this out below and think about your ancestry.

> "We know Most Holy Father and Lord, and from the chronicles and books of the ancients gather, that among other illustrious nations, ours, to wit, the nation of the Scots, has been distinguished by many honours; which passing from the greater Scythia through the Mediterranean Sea

and **Pillars of Hercules** *(Rock of Gibraltar)* and sojourning in Spain *(Iberia—Heberia—the Hebrew's Land)* among most savage tribes through a long course of time, could nowhere be subjugated by any people however barbarous; and **coming thence one thousand two hundred years after the outgoing of the People of Israel** *(the Exodus)*, they by many victories and infinite toil, acquired for themselves the possessions in the West which they now hold... In their kingdom one hundred and thirteen kings of their own royal stock, no stranger intervening, have reigned ..." For so long as a hundred of us are left alive we will yield in no least way to English domination. We fight not for glory, nor for wealth nor honour, but only and alone for freedom, which no man surrenders but with his life."[102]

If we are not Israel then who is and where are they, exactly? Where are those people whom Yehovah promised countless blessings to? Where are they who would control the gates of their enemies? Where are those who would be so great in number you could not count them—the ones prophesied to be as the sand of the seashore or the stars in the heavens? Has any other nation fulfilled the promises of Yehovah?

No brethren, they are not scattered and lost amongst the nations of the world as some would have you believe. The promises have gone to Britain who has controlled the gates of her enemies since the 1700's and upon her Empire the sun has never set. After World War II, Britain faded a little while the USA then took center stage on the world scene. No country has been able to compare, however, to these two mighty nations that have been blessed by Yehovah and in and through whom the world has been blessed as well. You cannot name one country in the world that has been blessed as much as these two nations and their respective Commonwealth Nations have.

But...these two nations, unfortunately, have not returned to the Torah and do not keep The Commandments and it is because of this that the punishments have begun to come *and will continue to come* until

---

[102] http://www.bbc.co.uk/history/scottishhistory/independence/features_independence_arbroath.shtml

these people repent and return to Yehovah. Until then, more and more tribulation, heartaches, and judgments are coming.

> *1 I say then, has Elohim rejected His people? Let it not be! For I also am a Yisra'ĕlite, of the seed of Aḇraham, of the tribe of Binyamin. 2 Elohim has not rejected His people whom He knew beforehand.1 Or do you not know what the Scripture says of Ěliyahu, how he pleads with Elohim against Yisra'ĕl, saying, (Footnote: [1]Psalm 94:14.) 3 "יהוה, they have killed Your prophets and overthrown Your altars, and I alone am left, and they seek my life?" 4 But what does the answer of Elohim say to him? "I have left for Myself seven thousand men who have not bowed the knee to Baʿal." 6 And if by favor, it is no longer of works, otherwise favor is no longer favor. And if it is of works, it is no longer favor, otherwise work is no longer work. 7 What then? Yisra'ĕl has not obtained what it seeks, but the chosen did obtain it, and the rest were hardened. 8 As it has been written, "יהוה has given them a spirit of deep sleep, eyes not to see and ears not to hear, unto this day."* (Romans 11:1-8)

> *9 Dawiḏ also says, "Let their table become for a snare, and for a trap, and for a stumbling-block and a recompense to them, 10 let their eyes be darkened, not to see, and bow down their back always." 11 I say then, have they stumbled that they should fall? Let it not be! But by their fall deliverance has come to the gentiles, to provoke them to jealousy. 12 And if their fall is riches for the world, and their failure riches for the gentiles, how much more their completeness! 13 For I speak to you, the gentiles, inasmuch as I am an emissary to the gentiles, I esteem my service, 14 if somehow I might provoke to jealousy those who are my flesh and save some of them. 15 For if their casting away is the restoration to favor of the world, what is their acceptance but life from the dead? 16 Now if the first-fruit is set-apart, the lump is also. And if the root is set-apart, so are the branches. 17 And if some of the branches were broken off, and you, being a wild olive tree, have been grafted in among them, and came to*

*share the root and fatness of the olive tree, 18 do not boast against the branches. And if you boast, remember: you do not bear the root, but the root bears you! 19 You shall say then, "The branches were broken off that I might be grafted in." 20 Good! By unbelief they were broken off, and you stand by belief. Do not be arrogant, but fear. 21 For if Elohim did not spare the natural branches, He might not spare you either. 22 See then the kindness and sharpness of Elohim: on those who fell sharpness, but toward you kindness, if you continue in His kindness, otherwise you also shall be cut off. 23 And they also, if they do not continue in unbelief, shall be grafted in, for Elohim is able to graft them in again. 24 For if you were cut out of the olive tree which is wild by nature, and were grafted contrary to nature into a good olive tree, how much more shall these who are the natural branches, be grafted into their own olive tree? 25 For I do not wish you to be ignorant of this secret, brothers, lest you should be wise in your own estimation, that hardening in part has come over Yisra'ĕl, until the completeness of the gentiles[1] has come in. (Footnote: [1] Genesis 48:19).* Romans 11:9-25)

*26 And so all Yisra'ĕl shall be saved, as it has been written, "The Deliverer shall come out of Tsiyon, and He shall turn away wickedness from Ya'aqoḇ, 27 and this is My covenant with them, when I take away their sins."[1] (Footnote: Isaiah 59:20-21). 28 Truly, as regards the Good News they are enemies for your sake, but concerning the choice they are beloved for the sake of the fathers. 29 For the gifts and the calling of Elohim are not to be repented of. 30 For as you also at one time disobeyed Elohim, but now have obtained compassion through their disobedience, 31 so also these have now disobeyed, that through the compassion shown you they also might obtain compassion. 32 For Elohim has shut them all up to disobedience, in order to have compassion on all. 33 Oh, the depth of riches, and wisdom and knowledge of Elohim! How unsearchable His judgments and untraceable*

*His ways! 34 "For who has known the mind of* יהוה*? Or who has become His counselor?" 35 Or who first gave to Him, and it shall be given back to him?" 36 Because of Him, and through Him, and to Him, are all, to whom be esteem forever. Amĕn.* (Romans 11:26-36)

# Chapter 2 | The Line of Phares, the Line of Zerah and David's Throne

I have now shown you the lineage of the Israelites after the captivity, where they went, what people of other nations called them and how history records them, yet never connects the one with the other. The exciting part being, they have now been connected in an unbroken line!

I would now like to show you another lineage to add to the one I have just covered in Chapter One. Chapter One began with the captivity of Israel in 723 B.C. This chapter will predate Chapter One by about 1,100 years to begin with, and then ties into Chapter One with the arrival of the Celtic clans. Finally, when all is said and done, it will also connect back to the Introduction I shared with you and, as Paul Harvey used to say, "Now you know the rest of the story." We are going to be looking once again at ancient history and it will seem very complicated. However it really is not once you understand it. So take your time in studying this subject. We are doing this exhaustive study in order to know who Daniel's people are so that we can understand to whom that prophecy in Daniel 9 is talking about.

This story[103] begins with Abraham, who, in 1814 B.C.,[104] left Haran in Mesopotamia and came to Canaan, which is now the land of Israel. In reward for his faithful obedience, Yehovah promised fantastic national blessings for his posterity.

> *1 And יהוה said to Abram, "Go yourself out of your land, from your relatives and from your father's house, to a land which I show you. 2 And I shall make you a great nation, and bless you and make your name great, and you shall be a blessing! 3 And I shall bless those who bless you, and curse him who curses you. And in you all the clans of the earth shall be blessed."* (Genesis 12:1-3)

> *16 And said, "By Myself I have sworn, declares יהוה, because you have done this, and have not withheld your son, your only son, 17 that I shall certainly bless you, and I shall certainly increase your seed as the stars of the heavens and as the sand which is on the seashore, and let your seed possess the gate of their enemies. 18 And in your seed all the nations of the earth shall be blessed, because you have obeyed My voice."* (Genesis 22:16-18)

Yehovah also promised that kings would come from him and his wife Sarah.

> *6 "And I shall make you bear fruit exceedingly, and make nations of you, and sovereigns shall come from you."* (Genesis 17:6)

> *16 And I shall bless her and also give you a son by her. And I shall bless her, and she shall become nations—sovereigns of peoples are to be from her.* (Genesis 17:16)

---

[103] http://www.sightedmoonnl.com/?page_id=575 adapted on my website from a series of articles by Tom Robinson http://www.ucg.org/ebooklet/throne-britain-its-biblical-origin-and-future/introduction-throne-britain/ with some editing.

[104] All chronology is based on the reckoning of the Sabbatical & Jubilee Cycles. See charts in my book, *The Prophecies of Abraham*

This means that a line of kings would spring from them, culminating in the Messiah who would bring salvation for the whole world. We get this from the word spoken to Isaac that said, *"...in thy seed shall all the nations of the earth be blessed."* These promises were confirmed to Abraham's son Isaac.

> *3 "Sojourn in this land. And I shall be with you and bless you, for I give all these lands to you and your seed. And I shall establish the oath which I swore to Aḇraham your father. 4 And I shall increase your seed like the stars of the heavens, and I shall give all these lands to your seed. And in your seed all the nations of the earth shall be blessed."* (Genesis 26:3-4)

Later, around 1650 B.C., Yehovah promised essentially the same thing to Isaac's son Jacob.

> *10 And Yaʻaqoḇ went out from Beʼĕrsheḇa and went toward Ḥaran. 11 And he came upon a place and stopped over for the night, for the sun had set. And he took one of the stones of that place and put it at his head, and he lay down in that place to sleep. 12 And he dreamed and saw a ladder set up on the earth, and its top reached to the heavens, and saw messengers of Elohim going up and coming down on it. 13 And see, יהוה stood above it and said, "I am יהוה Elohim of Aḇraham your father and the Elohim of Yitsḥaq. The land on which you are lying, I give it to you and your seed; 14 And your seed shall be as the dust of the earth, and you shall break forth to the west and to the east, to the north and the south. And all the clans of the earth shall be blessed in you and in your seed. 15 And see, I am with you and shall guard you wherever you go, and shall bring you back to this land. For I am not going to leave you until I have done what I have spoken to you."* (Genesis 28:10-15)

> *16 And Yaʻaqoḇ awoke from his sleep and said, "Truly, יהוה is in this place, and I did not know it." 17 And he was afraid and said, "How awesome is this place! This is none other than*

> *the house of Elohim, and this is the gate of the heavens!"*
> *18 And Ya'aqoḇ rose early in the morning, and took the stone that he had put at his head, set it up as a standing column, and poured oil on top of it. 19 And he called the name of that place Bĕyth Ĕl, however, the name of that city had been Luz previously.* (Genesis 28:16-19)

Later on, Yehovah addressed Jacob in the following manner: *"And Elohim said to him, 'I am Ĕl Shaddai. Bear fruit and increase, a nation and a company of nations shall be from you, and sovereigns come from your body.'"* (Genesis 35:11)

In this verse you are being told that both a nation and a company of nations are to come from him. A company of nations would be a *commonwealth*.

Between 1645 B.C.[105] and 1638 B.C. Jacob, who was now renamed Israel, had fathered eleven sons, with Benjamin being the twelfth and last one being born in 1628 B.C. Each one was to be the progenitor of one of the 12 Tribes of Israel. Through his son Joseph, born in 1638 B.C., and Joseph's two sons Ephraim and Manasseh born sometime after 1608 B.C.—would continue the birthright promise of national greatness.

> *1 And after these events it came to be that it was said to Yosĕph, "See, your father is sick." And he took with him his two sons, Menashsheh and Ephrayim. 2 And Ya'aqoḇ was told, "See, your son Yosĕph is coming to you." And Yisra'ĕl strengthened himself and sat up on the bed. 3 And Ya'aqoḇ said to Yosĕph, "Ĕl Shaddai appeared to me at Luz in the land of Kena'an and blessed me, 4 and said to me, 'See, I am making you bear fruit and shall increase you and make of you an assembly of peoples, and give this land to your seed after you as an everlasting possession. 5 And now, your two sons, Ephrayim and Menashsheh, who were born to you in the land of Mitsrayim before I came to you in Mitsrayim, are*

---

[105] All dates are according to the Sabbatical and Jubilee Cycles as can be seen in my book *The Prophecies of Abraham*.

mine—as Re'uḇĕn and Shim'on, they are mine.'" (Genesis 48:1-5)

*6 "'Your offspring whom you shall bring forth after them are yours, and let them be called by the name of their brothers in their inheritance. 7 And I, when I came from Paddan, Raḥĕl died beside me in the land of Kena'an on the way, when there was but a little distance to go to Ephrath. And I buried her there on the way to Ephrath, that is Bĕyth Leḥem.'" 8 And Yisra'ĕl saw Yosĕph's sons, and said, "Who are these?" 9 And Yosĕph said to his father, "They are my sons, whom Elohim has given me in this place. And he said, 'Please bring them to me, and let me bless them. 10 And the eyes of Yisra'ĕl were dim with age, and he was unable to see. And he drew them near him, and he kissed them and embraced them. 11 And Yisra'ĕl said to Yosĕph, I had not thought to see your face. But see, Elohim has also shown me your seed!'"* (Genesis 48:6-11)

*12 So Yosĕph brought them from between his knees, and he bowed down with his face to the earth. 13 And Yosĕph took them both, Ephrayim with his right hand toward Yisra'ĕl's left hand, and Menashsheh with his left hand toward Yisra'ĕl's right hand, and brought them near him. 14 And Yisra'ĕl stretched out his right hand and laid it on Ephrayim's head, who was the younger, and his left hand on Menashsheh's head, consciously directing his hands, for Menashsheh was the first-born. 15 And he blessed Yosĕph, and said, "The Elohim before whom my fathers, Aḇraham and Yitsḥaq walked, the Elohim who has fed me all my life long to this day, 16 the Messenger who has redeemed me from all evil— bless the youths! And let my name be called upon them, and the name of my fathers, Aḇraham and Yitsḥaq. And let them increase to a multitude in the midst of the earth."* (Genesis 48:12-16)

*17 And when Yosĕph saw that his father laid his right hand on the head of Ephrayim, it was evil in his eyes; and he took hold of his father's hand to remove it from the head of Ephrayim to the head of Menashsheh. 18 And Yosĕph said to his father, "Not so, my father, for this one is the first-born, put your right hand on his head." 19 But his father refused and said, "I know, my son, I know. He also becomes a people, and he also is great. And yet, his younger brother is greater than he, and his seed is to become the completeness of the nations." 20 And he blessed them on that day, saying, "In you Yisra'ĕl shall bless, saying, 'Elohim make you as Ephrayim and as Menashsheh!' Thus he put Ephrayim before Menashsheh. 21 And Yisra'ĕl said to Yosĕph, "See, I am dying, but Elohim shall be with you and bring you back to the land of your fathers. 22 And I, I have given to you one portion above your brothers, which I took from the hand of the Amorite with my sword and with my bow."* (Genesis 48:17-22)

*22 Yosĕph is an offshoot of a fruit-bearing tree, an offshoot of a fruit-bearing tree by a fountain, his branches run over a wall. 23 And the archers have bitterly grieved him, shot at him and hated him. 24 But his bow remained in strength, and the arms of his hands were made strong by the hands of the Mighty One of Ya'aqob—from there is the Shepherd, the Stone of Yisra'ĕl: 25 from the Ĕl of your father who helps you, and by the Almighty who blesses you with blessings of the heavens above, blessings of the deep that lies beneath, blessings of the breasts and of the womb. 26 The blessings of your father have excelled the blessings of my ancestors, up to the limit of the everlasting hills. They are on the head of Yosĕph, and on the crown of the head of him who was separated from his brothers.* (Genesis 49:22-26)

These blessings are those that went to Manasseh and Ephraim—of whom I have demonstrated to you in Chapter One became the USA and United Kingdom. These blessings have come down to our time and explain why the United Kingdom and her commonwealth countries of Canada and Australia and New Zealand and United States of America have been so blessed above all the other nations of the world.

We also see this in 1 Chronicles:

> *1 As for the sons of Re'ŭbĕn the first-born of Yisra'ĕl—he was the first-born, but because he profaned his father's bed, his birthright was given to the sons of Yosĕph, son of Yisra'ĕl, so that the genealogy* (Reuben—father of the French) *is not listed according to the birthright, 2 for Yehudah prevailed over his brothers, and from him came a ruler,* ("the chief ruler," KJV) *although the birthright was Yosĕph's* (Father of the British and American people)." (1 Chronicles 5:1-2)

Thus, while Joseph received the birthright, to Jacob's son Judah, father of the Jews, went the promise of a kingly line leading to the Messiah. Just before Jacob died in 1582 B.C., he prophesied: *"Yehudah is a lion's cub... The scepter* (ruler's staff) *shall not turn aside from Yehudah, nor a Lawgiver from between his feet, until Shiloh comes* [Shiloh meaning "Peaceable One," "Peacemaker" or "To Whom It (the Scepter) Belongs"—thus a reference to the Messiah]; *and to Him is the obedience of peoples."* (Genesis 49:9-10) You will notice the "Him" here is referring to the Messiah and *not* to Judah. It is probably because of this prophecy that the lion, the "king of beasts," became the heraldic emblem of Judah. Lion is mentioned three times in verse nine and is going to be very important in the next chapter—a chapter in which I will provide you with a close look at the concept of Heraldry in an effort to show you how the 12 Tribes of Israel kept record of their ancestral lines for posterity's sake.

Some thirty years before this prophecy was given concerning Judah, around 1612 B.C., a strange event had occurred in the family of Judah, when Tamar bore him twin sons. During the delivery, a hand of one of the twins came out first, around which the midwife tied a scarlet thread to identify the firstborn—who was customarily preeminent when it came to inheritance or birthrights (Genesis 38:27-28). But the baby pulled his hand back in and his brother came out first. The midwife exclaimed: "How did you break through? This breach (or breaking out) be upon you!" (v. 29) In other words, "You are to be identified with this from now on." And to ensure it the child was named Perez (or Pharez), meaning "Breach."

Then the baby with the scarlet thread on his hand was born—and he was named Zerah (or Zarah), meaning "Rising" or "Appearing," perhaps because his hand had appeared first (v. 30). This surely seems a rather odd occurrence to record in the Bible if it were to have no further significance. The implication is perhaps that Perez, who forced himself into the firstborn position, would need to eventually be reconciled with Zerah. And we will later see that this appears to have actually happened. In any event, since Perez was the firstborn, the right of inheritance went to him—although Zerah, with the scarlet thread, would seem to have some claim in this.

Neither Perez (Pharez), Zerah (Zarah) nor Judah ever received the scepter. Even in the time of Moses and the Exodus, in 1379 B.C., when Israel became a nation, there was no king.

The king at the time of the Exodus and for the next 330 years was the Rock of Israel, the Eternal Yehovah Himself (compare Deuteronomy 32:4; 1 Corinthians 10:4; John 1:1-3, 14; 17:5). Though ruling through His chosen "judges"—from Moses and Joshua all the way to Samuel—Yehovah sat on the throne of Israel.

> *22 So the men of Yisra'ĕl said to Gid'on, "Rule over us, both you and your son, also your son's son, for you have saved us from the hand of Midyan." 23 But Gid'on said to them, "I do not rule over you, nor does my son rule over you. יהוה does rule over you."* (Judges 8:22-23)

Samuel described this period as the time

> *12 "...when יהוה your Elohim was your sovereign."* (1 Samuel 12:12)

That's why, when the Israelites told Samuel around 1050 B.C. that they wanted a human king like the nations around them, Yehovah told him:

> *6 But the word was evil in the eyes of Shemu'ĕl when they said, "Give us a sovereign to rule us." So Shemu'ĕl prayed to יהוה. 7 And יהוה said to Shemu'ĕl, "Listen to the voice of the*

> *people in all that they say to you, for they have not rejected you, but they have rejected Me from reigning over them. 8 According to all the works which they have done since the day that I brought them up out of Mitsrayim, even to this day—forsaking Me and serving other mighty ones—so they are doing to you too. 9 And now, listen to their voice, but you shall certainly warn them, and shall make known to them the ruling of the sovereign who does reign over them."* (1 Samuel 8:6-9)

The very first king Yehovah gave Israel was not of the tribe of Judah but rather, he was from the tribe of Benjamin and his name was King Saul. It is interesting to note that unlike other ancient rulers, the king of Israel was not an absolute despot. Yehovah had Samuel anoint Saul "commander" or "captain" (KJV) over His people.

> *16 At this time tomorrow I shall send you a man from the land of Binyamin, and you shall anoint him leader over My people Yisra'ĕl, and he shall save My people from the hand of the Philistines. For I have seen My people, because their cry has come to me.* (1 Samuel 9:16)

> *1 And Shemu'ĕl took a flask of oil and poured it on his head, and kissed him and said, "Is it not because יהוה has anointed you leader over His inheritance?"* (1 Samuel 10:1)

This Hebrew term "nagiyd" used here could be rendered in English as viceroy or governor-general—the stand-in for the real monarch.

> H5057. נָגִיד nagiyd: A masculine noun meaning a leader, a ruler, a prince. This term has a broad range of applications. At the top, it could allude to the king of Israel (1 Samuel 9:16, 13:14; 1 Kings 1:35).

We will come back to this "nagiyd" when we get to Daniel 9.

The very act of anointing a ruler in the ancient world implied a vassal relationship. It is later explained that Israel's king "sat on the throne of Yehovah," essentially reigning as king for Him.

> *23 And Shelomoh sat on the throne of יהוה as sovereign instead of Dawiḏ his father, and prospered; and all Yisra'ĕl obeyed him.* (1 Chronicles 29:23)

> *8 Blessed be יהוה your Elohim, who delighted in you, to put you on His throne to be sovereign for יהוה your Elohim! Because your Elohim has loved Yisra'ĕl, to establish them forever, therefore He made you sovereign over them, to do right-ruling and righteousness.* (2 Chronicles 9:8)

Did you notice that in 1 Samuel it says over HIS inheritance? That is over Yehovah's inheritance. In the above verses it states they sat on the throne of Yehovah. Now consider the fact that we are called to be kings, a royal priesthood and a holy nation unto Yehovah. Look at what the Scripture passages below are telling us.

> *6 "...and you shall be to Me a reign of priests and a set-apart nation. Those are the words which you are to speak to the children of Yisra'ĕl."* (Exodus 19:6)

> *6 "But you shall be called, 'Priests of יהוה,' 'Servants of our Elohim' shall be said of you. You shall consume the strength of the gentiles, and boast in their esteem."* (Isaiah 61:6)

> *5 "...you also, as living stones, are being built up, a spiritual house, a set-apart priesthood, to offer up spiritual slaughter offerings acceptable to Elohim through* **יהושע** *Messiah.* (1 Peter 2:5)

> *6 And has made us sovereigns and priests to His Elohim and Father, to Him be esteem and rule forever and ever. Amĕn.* (Revelation 1:6)

> *10 "...and made us sovereigns and priests to our Elohim, and we shall reign upon the earth."[1]* [Footnote: [1]Dan. 7:18-27 | (Revelation 5:10)]

Paul says in Romans 5:17 that we will reign in life through Yehshua, the Greek word for "REIGN" is derived from the word for "KING" and means to be a king.

G936 βασιλεύω basileuō *bas-il-yoo'-o*

From G935; to *rule* (literally or figuratively): king, reign.

This is quite different than with the other kingdoms of the earth. In other countries the kings made the laws and were thus above them. But in Israel, Yehovah's prophet explained "the rights and duties of the kingship" (1 Samuel 10:22). The ruler was subject to the law as we are told in Deuteronomy.

> *14 "When you come to the land which* יהוה *your Elohim is giving you, and shall possess it and shall dwell in it, and you shall say, 'Let me set a sovereign over me like all the gentiles that are around me,' 15 you shall certainly set a sovereign over you whom* יהוה *your Elohim shall choose. Set a sovereign over you from among your brothers, you are not allowed to set a foreigner over you, who is not your brother. 16 Only, he is not to increase horses for himself, nor cause the people to return to Mitsrayim to increase horses, for* יהוה *has said to you, 'Do not return that way again.' 17 And he is not to increase wives for himself, lest his heart turn away, nor is he to greatly increase silver and gold for himself. 18 And it shall be, when he sits on the throne of his reign, that he shall write for himself a copy of this Torah in a book, from the one before the priests, the Lĕwites. 19 And it shall be with him, and he shall read it all the days of his life, so that he learns to fear* יהוה *his Elohim and guard all the Words of this Torah and these laws, to do them, 20 so that his heart is not lifted up above his brothers, and so as not to turn aside from the command, right or left, so that he prolongs his days in his reign, he and his children, in the midst of Yisra'ĕl."* (Deuteronomy 17:14-20)

Essentially, Yehovah set up a constitutionally limited monarchy—in which He would send prophets as His representatives to the king to give him his "report card." Tragically, Saul failed in the end and Yehovah removed him from office by bringing about his death. Then, in 1010 B.C., more than 571 years after the scepter prophecy had been given to Judah, Yehovah at last raised up a man from that tribe, of the preeminent branch of Perez, to be king. Speaking to King Saul, Samuel said:

> *14 But now, your reign is not going to stand. יהוה shall seek for Himself a man after His own heart, and יהוה shall command him to be leader over His people, because you have not guarded what יהוה commanded you.* (1 Samuel 13:14)

> *21 But then they asked for a sovereign, and Elohim gave them Sha'ul the son of Qish, a man of the tribe of Binyamin, for forty years. 22 And having removed him, He raised up for them Dawid as sovereign, to whom also He gave witness and said, "I have found Dawid the son of Yishai, a man after My own heart, who shall do all My desires."* (Acts 13:21-22)

Yehovah told David he would make him a "house"—that is, a royal dynasty. It was to be an enduring dynasty through his son Solomon:

> *11 "...even from the day I appointed rulers over My people Yisra'ĕl, and have caused you to rest from all your enemies. And יהוה has declared to you that He would make you a house. 12 When your days are filled and you rest with your fathers, I shall raise up your seed after you, who comes from your inward parts, and shall establish his reign. 13 He does build a house for My Name, and I shall establish the throne of his reign forever. 14 I am to be his Father, and he is My son. If he does perversely, I shall reprove him with the rod of men and with the blows of the sons of men. 15 But My kindness does not turn aside from him, as I turned it aside from Sha'ul, whom I removed from before you. 16 And your house and your reign are to be steadfast forever before you— your throne is established forever." 17 According to all these*

*words and according to all this vision, so Nathan spoke to Dawiḏ.* (2 Samuel 7:11)

*1 And these are the last words of Dawiḏ, the saying of Dawiḏ son of Yishai, the saying of the man raised up on high, the anointed of the Elohim of Yaʽaqoḇ, and the sweet singer of Yisraʼěl: 2 "The Spirit of* יהוה *has spoken through me, and His word is on my tongue. 3 The Elohim of Yisraʼěl said, The Rock of Yisraʼěl spoke to me, 'One who rules over man righteously, 4 who rules in the fear of Elohim, is like the light of the morning when the sun rises, a morning without clouds, tender grass from the earth from sunshine, from rain.' 5 For is not my house so with Ěl? For He has made an everlasting covenant with me, ordered in all matters, and guarded. For all my deliverance and all desire, shall He not make it send forth a Branch?"* (2 Samuel 23:1- 5)

*9 "See, a son is to be born to you, who is a man of rest. And I shall give him rest from all his enemies all around, for Shelomoh is his name, and peace and rest I give to Yisraʼěl in his days. 10 He does build a house for My Name, and he is to be My son, and I am to be his Father. And I shall establish the throne of his reign over Yisraʼěl forever."* (1 Chronicles 22:9-10)

*4 "Yet* יהוה *Elohim of Yisraʼěl chose me above all the house of my father to be sovereign over Yisraʼěl forever, for He has chosen Yehuḏah to be the ruler. And of the house of Yehuḏah, the house of my father, and among the sons of my father, He was pleased with me to make me reign over all Yisraʼěl. 5 And of all my sons—for* יהוה *has given me many sons—He has chosen my son Shelomoh to sit on the throne of the reign of* יהוה *over Yisraʼěl."* (1 Chronicles 28:4-5)

It would seem that this promise from Yehovah is not true. If we look on the world scene, where is that King of Israel today?

This requires some clarification, particularly the statement about Solomon's dynasty enduring forever. The Hebrew word translated "forever" here is "olam" and does not always mean forever. Occasionally it means unending as long as certain conditions apply. Recorded elsewhere, there were definite conditions attached to the endurance of Solomon's throne.

> *"And I shall establish his reign forever, if he is strong to do My commands and My right-rulings, as it is this day."* (1 Chronicles 28:7)

Yehovah would again state these conditions in 2 Chronicles. Take special notice of the word "if."

> *17 "And you, if you walk before Me as your father Dawid walked, and do according to all that I have commanded you, and if you guard My laws and My right-rulings, 18 then I shall establish the throne of your reign, as I covenanted with Dawid your father, saying, 'There is not to cease a man of yours as ruler in Yisra'ěl.' 19 But if you turn away and forsake My laws and My commands which I have set before you, and shall go and serve other mighty ones, and bow yourself to them, 20 then I shall pluck them from My land, which I have given them, and this house which I have set apart for My Name I shall cast out of My sight and make it to be a proverb and a mockery among all peoples. 21 And this house, which has been exalted, everyone who passes by it is shall be astonished and say, 'Why has יהוה done thus to this land and this house?' 22 Then they shall say, 'Because they forsook יהוה Elohim of their fathers, who brought them out of the land of Mitsrayim, and embraced other mighty ones, and bowed themselves to them and served them, therefore He has brought all this evil on them.'"* (2 Chronicles 7:17-22)

If Solomon lived in disobedience to Yehovah, the promise of an unending Solomonic Dynasty would be rendered null and void. Sadly, this would come to pass, as Solomon's heart was eventually turned toward following after other gods.

> *4 And it came to be, when Shelomoh was old, that his wives turned away his heart after other mighty ones. And his heart was not perfect with יהוה his Elohim, as was the heart of his father Dawiḏ.* (1 Kings 11:4)

What are we to make of the promise Yehovah made to King David in 2 Samuel 7:15, *"But My kindness does not turn aside from him, as I turned it aside from Sha'ul, whom I removed from before you?"*

It must simply have meant that, in the event of Solomon's disobedience, Yehovah would not bring about his death to end his reign, as happened with Saul. Instead, Solomon would be allowed to live out his days with his kingdom intact for the sake of David—and indeed this is what happened.

> *11 And יהוה said to Shelomoh, "Because you have done this, and have not guarded My covenant and My laws, which I have commanded you, I shall certainly tear the reign away from you and give it to your servant. 12 Only, I do not do it in your days, for the sake of your father Dawiḏ. Out of the hand of your son I shall tear it. 13 Only, I shall not tear away all the reign but give one tribe to your son for the sake of my servant Dawiḏ, and for the sake of Yerushalayim which I have chosen."* (1 Kings 11:11-13)

Nevertheless, Solomon violated the conditions that would have guaranteed him a perpetual dynasty. So while nothing forbade his descendants from reigning until well into the future, Yehovah was not obligated to ensure their continuance upon the throne. On the other hand, Yehovah's promise to David in 2 Samuel 7:15-16—that David's own kingdom and throne would be established forever—still stands. Yehovah did obligate Himself to this course no matter what Solomon did. Notice His confirmation of this tremendous pledge in the book of Psalms:

> *3 You said, "I have made a covenant with My chosen, I have sworn to My servant Dawiḏ: 4 'I establish your seed forever, and shall build up your throne to all generations.'" Selah.* (Psalms 89:3-4)

So from then on, David would have a descendant sitting on a continuing throne in every generation! Yehovah further proclaimed:

> *27 "I also appoint him first-born, highest of the sovereigns of the earth. 28 I guard My kindness for him forever, and My covenant is steadfast with him. 29 And I shall establish his seed forever, and his throne as the days of the heavens."*
>
> *34 "I shall not profane My covenant, neither would I change what has gone out from My lips. 35 Once I have sworn by My set-apartness, I do not lie to Dawiḏ: 36 His seed shall be forever, and his throne as the sun before Me; 37 like the moon, it is established forever, and the witness in the heavens is steadfast." Selah.* (Psalm 89:27-29, 34-37).

We also read in Jeremiah:

> *19 And the word of יהוה came to Yirmeyahu, saying, 20 "Thus said יהוה, 'If you could break My covenant with the day and My covenant with the night, so that there be not day and night in their season, 21 then My covenant could also be broken with Dawiḏ My servant—so that he shall not have a son to reign upon his throne* (that is, a descendant)*—and with the Lĕwites, the priests, My attendants.'"* (Jeremiah 33:19-21)

Here, then, was an unbreakable promise of an unbreakable dynasty—a dynasty preeminent above all others! But what happened to that dynasty? Again we ask you, where is it today?

Because of Solomon's disobedience, Yehovah split the nation into two kingdoms following his death in 930 B.C. as you have already read in 1 Kings:

> *12 Only, I do not do it in your days, for the sake of your father Dawiḏ. Out of the hand of your son I shall tear it.* (1 Kings 11:12)

The tribes of Judah and Benjamin in the south (with many from Levi)—as the kingdom of Judah—continued under the throne of David, beginning with Solomon's son Rehoboam. The 10 Northern Tribes, however—as the kingdom of Israel—went through a number of different dynasties. And because of the Northern Kingdom's continual idolatry, Yehovah finally had its people taken into captivity beginning in 733 B.C. until it fell in 723 B.C. by the Assyrians, who exiled the 10 Tribes to what is now northern Iraq and Iran (2 Kings 15, 17). This is what I went over with you in the introduction as I explained the times in which Daniel was growing up and in chapter one as I had you follow the migration route of the 10 Tribes of Israel after their captivity.

Subsequently, as the centuries passed, the 10 Tribes were seemingly lost according to today's generation but I have shown you where they went in Chapter One of this book. Roughly twenty years after Israel's final fall, the nation of Judah, following repeated cycles of idolatry and reformation, was invaded by Assyria as well, reducing Judah "to a shadow of its former self; at least two thirds of the population perishing or being carried away captive."[106]

Thus, a great number of Jews, Benjamites and Levites were also taken away to join the Israelite captivity. Yehovah gave the remnant of Judah another century to prove its loyalty and devotion to Him. Yet sadly, despite witnessing Israel's captivity and experiencing its own bitter taste of it, Judah lapsed into idolatrous rebellion once again.

> 8 "And I saw that for all the causes for which backsliding Yisra'ĕl had committed adultery, I had put her away and given her a certificate of divorce; yet her treacherous sister Yehuḏah did not fear, but went and committed whoring too. 9 And it came to be, through her frivolous whoring, that she defiled the land and committed adultery with stones and wood. 10 And yet for all this her treacherous sister Yehuḏah has not turned to Me with all her heart, but falsely," declares יהוה. 11 And יהוה said to me, "Backsliding Yisra'ĕl has shown herself more righteous than treacherous Yehuḏah." (Jeremiah 3:8-11)

---

[106] *Judah, The Illustrated Bible Dictionary*, 1980, Vol. 2, p. 825

The rest of the nation of Judah went into captivity as well—this time by the hands of the Babylonians under Nebuchadnezzar II (ca. 604 B.C. to 586 B.C.) as I already shared with you in my introduction to the life and times of Daniel. The Davidic line had continued all the way to this point, with King Zedekiah now reigning over Judah. But according to Jeremiah, the Babylonian forces took the Jewish king to Nebuchadnezzar, who—after killing Zedekiah's sons in front of his face and slaying "all the nobles of Judah" to ensure that no heir to the throne remained—put out Zedekiah's eyes and threw him in a dungeon in Babylon, where he eventually died.

> *1 In the ninth year of Tsiḏqiyahu sovereign of Yehuḏah, in the tenth month, Neḇuḵaḏretstsar sovereign of Baḇel and all his army came against Yerushalayim, and besieged it. 2 In the eleventh year of Tsiḏqiyahu, in the fourth month, on the ninth day of the month, the city was broken into. 3 And all the heads of the sovereign of Baḇel came in and sat in the Middle Gate: Nĕrḡal-Shar'etser, Samgar-Neḇo, Sarseḵim, Raḇsaris, Nĕrḡal-Sarezer, Raḇmaḡ, and all the rest of the heads of the sovereign of Baḇel. 4 And it came to be, when Tsiḏqiyahu the sovereign of Yehuḏah and all the men of battle saw them, they fled and left the city by night, by way of the sovereign's garden, by the gate between the two walls. And he went out toward the desert plain. 5 But the army of the Chaldeans pursued them and overtook Tsiḏqiyahu in the desert plains of Yeriḥo. And they captured him, and brought him up to Neḇuḵaḏnetstsar sovereign of Baḇel, to Riḇlah in the land of Ḥamath, where he spoke judgment on him. 6 And the sovereign of Baḇel slew the sons of Tsiḏqiyahu before his eyes in Riḇlah. The sovereign of Baḇel also slew all the nobles of Yehuḏah. 7 And he put out the eyes of Tsiḏqiyahu, and bound him with bronze shackles to bring him to Baḇel.* (Jeremiah 39:1-7)

> *1 Tsiḏqiyahu was twenty-one years old when he began to reign, and he reigned eleven years in Yerushalayim. And his mother's name was Ḥamutal the daughter of Yirmeyahu of Liḇnah. 2 And he did evil in the eyes of* יהוה, *according to all*

> *that Yehoyaqim had done. 3 For through the displeasure of יהוה this came to be against Yerushalayim and Yehudah, until He had cast them out from His presence. And Tsidqiyahu rebelled against the sovereign of Babel. 4 And it came to be in the ninth year of his reign, in the tenth month, on the tenth of the month, that Nebukadretstsar sovereign of Babel and all his army came against Yerushalayim and encamped against it. And they built a siege wall against it all around. 5 And the city was under siege until the eleventh year of Sovereign Tsidqiyahu. 6 On the ninth of the fourth month the scarcity of food was so severe in the city that there was no food for the people of the land.* (Jeremiah 52:1-6)

> *7 Then the city wall was breached, and all the men of battle fled and went out of the city at night by way of the gate between the two walls, which was by the sovereign's garden, while the Chaldeans were near the city all around. And they went by way of the desert plain. 8 But the army of the Chaldeans pursued the sovereign, and they overtook Tsidqiyahu in the desert plains of Yeriḥo, and his entire army was scattered from him. 9 Then they captured the sovereign and brought him up to the sovereign of Babel at Riblah in the land of Ḥamath, and he pronounced judgments on him. 10 And the sovereign of Babel slew the sons of Tsidqiyahu before his eyes, and he also slew all the heads of Yehudah in Riblah. 11 And he put out the eyes of Tsidqiyahu. And the sovereign of Babel bound him in bronze shackles, and took him to Babel, and put him in prison till the day of his death.* (Jeremiah 52:7-11)

As I shared with you in the Introduction, there was a former king of the Solomonic line still alive in the dungeons of Babylon. In fact this man, Jeconiah—also called Coniah or Jehoiachin—was restored to honor thirty-seven years into the Jewish captivity.

> *27 And it came to be in the thirty-seventh year of the exile of Yehoyakin sovereign of Yehudah, in the twelfth month, on the twenty-seventh of the month, that Ewil-Merodak sovereign*

> *of Baḇel, in the year that he began to reign, released Yehoyaḵin sovereign of Yehuḏah from prison, 28 and spoke kindly to him, and set his throne above the throne of the sovereigns who were with him in Baḇel, 29 and changed his prison garments. And he ate bread continually before the sovereign all the days of his life. 30 And as his allowance, a continual allowance was given to him from the sovereign, a quota for each day, all the days of his life.* (2 Kings 25:27-30)

He was even given the title "king" along with numerous other captive, vassal rulers. When the Persian conquerors of Babylon later permitted a contingent of Jews to return to their homeland, Jeconiah's grandson Zerubbabel was made governor—but not king—of Judea. To dispel any notion that this line could have been the means whereby Yehovah preserved the Davidic dynasty, it must be pointed out that Yehovah had earlier decreed that no descendant of Jeconiah would ever sit on the throne of David, ruling over Judah.

> *24 "As I live," declares יהוה, "though Konyahu son of Yehoyaqim, sovereign of Yehuḏah, were the signet on My right hand, I would still pull you off from there..." 30 Thus said יהוה, "Write this man down as childless, a strong man who is not to prosper in his days, for none of his descendants shall prosper, sitting on the throne of Dawiḏ, or rule any more in Yehuḏah."* (Jeremiah 22:24, 30)

None of Jeconiah's seed ever did sit on David's throne. In fact, while a minority of the Jewish captives did return to the Holy Land following the Babylonian captivity, the Jewish throne was never reestablished there at all. What are we to make of Yehovah's promises then that David's Dynasty would never end?

David's throne was supposed to be occupied in "all generations." From the time of Zedekiah's death until our time now, does that mean more than 2,500 years have gone by without a descendant of David reigning as king? Has Yehovah broken His word after all?

One important factor often overlooked about the scepter prophecy in Genesis 49:10 is that it shows Judah still having a ruling monarch, waiting for the Messiah to take over, "in the last days" (v. 1).

> *1 And Ya'aqob called his sons and said, "Gather together, so that I declare to you what is to befall you in the last days:"* (Genesis 49:1)

> *10 The sceptre shall not turn aside from Yehudah, nor a Lawgiver from between his feet, until Shiloh comes, and to Him is the obedience of peoples.* (Genesis 49:10)

Therefore, since Yehshua has not yet returned in power and glory, there must be a monarch of Jewish descent reigning somewhere on the earth during this generation. In fact, that monarch must be of the line of David, occupying a throne that has continued throughout all generations since David. Otherwise, the Bible is unreliable.

The obvious question to be asking yourself now is: Did the Davidic Dynasty come to an end with the death of Zedekiah and his sons—or did it somehow survive? In searching for an answer, we begin with the prophet Jeremiah, who was warning the nation of Judah while Daniel was still yet a child and to whom Yehovah had given a mysterious commission:

> *10 "See, I have this day set you over the nations and over the reigns, to root out and to pull down, to destroy and to overthrow, to build and to plant."* (Jeremiah 1:10)

Even though Judah was the only nation or kingdom in the Promised Land at this time, notice that Jeremiah was set over "nations" and "kingdoms"—plural. Setting that fact aside for now, and based on Jeremiah's life after the prophecy was given, it is easy to ascertain what Yehovah meant by plucking up, pulling down, destroying and overthrowing. This great prophet repeatedly warned the Jews to repent of their disobedience—but they scorned him. So Yehovah used him to pronounce judgment on the nation: the people and the kings of David's line would be overthrown in the Babylonian conquest and uprooted—to

Babylon. But did *all* of them go there? The latter part of the prophet's commission yet remained: "to build and to plant." But what did this entail, exactly?

From Jeremiah 45:4 we can see that building and planting in this context originally entailed God's planting His people in the land and building a kingdom of them there—now to be supplanted and destroyed. So the commission would seem to involve planting people in another place in order to establish a kingdom elsewhere. But did this have anything to do with the house of David? Intriguingly, Jeremiah did prophesy regarding David's Dynasty. And a prophecy from Ezekiel will answer the question of *who* was to be planted—and *where*. Yet first, I would ask you take note of this next amazing fact: Following the carrying away of Judah's people, a remnant that was left in the land included the "king's daughters."

> *10 Then Yishmaʿěl took captive all the rest of the people who were in Mitspah, the sovereign's daughters and all the people who were left in Mitspah, whom Neḇuzaraḏan, chief of the guard, had entrusted to Geḏalyahu son of Aḥiqam. And Yishmaʿěl son of Nethanyahu took them captive and went to go over to the Ammonites.* (Jeremiah 41:10)

These daughters were evidently young girls since their father Zedekiah was only thirty-two when he died. But could the royal line continue through a daughter? According to Israel's Law of Inheritance, the answer would certainly appear to be "yes."

> *1 Then came the daughters of Tselophḥaḏ, son of Ḥěpher, son of Gilʿaḏ, son of Maḵir, son of Menashsheh, from the clans of Menashsheh, son of Yosěph. And these were the names of his daughters: Maḥlah, Noʿah, and Hoḡlah, and Milkah, and Tirtsah. 2 And they stood before Mosheh, and before Elʿazar the priest, and before the leaders and all the congregation, by the doorway of the Tent of Meeting, saying, 3 "Our father died in the wilderness, yet he was not in the company of those who were met together against* יהוה, *in company with Qoraḥ, but he died in his own sin. And he had*

*no sons. 4 Why should the name of our father be removed from among his clan because he had no son? Give us a possession among the brothers of our father." 5 Mosheh then brought their case before יהוה. 6 And יהוה spoke to Mosheh, saying, 7 "The daughters of Tselophḥad speak what is right. You should certainly give them a possession of inheritance among their father's brothers, and cause the inheritance of their father to pass to them. 8 And speak to the children of Yisra'ĕl, saying, 'When a man dies and has no son, then you shall cause his inheritance to pass to his daughter. 9 And if he has no daughter, then you shall give his inheritance to his brothers. 10 And if he has no brothers, then you shall give his inheritance to his father's brothers. 11 And if his father has no brothers, then you shall give his inheritance to the nearest relative in his clan, and he shall possess it.'" And it shall be to the children of Yisra'ĕl a law of right-ruling, as יהוה commanded Mosheh.* (Numbers 27:1-11)

(In fact, if kingship could not pass through a woman then it could not have passed through Mary to Yehshua.)

What happened then to the king's daughters and that remnant? In Jeremiah 42:1-19, we are told they went against Yehovah's commands and they fled from the Babylonian invaders to Egypt to seek the protection of Pharaoh Hophra.

The *Encyclopedia Britannica* explains:

> Apries... Hebrew Hophra (d. 567 B.C.), fourth king (reigned 589 B.C.-570 B.C.) of the 26th dynasty of Egypt; he succeeded his father Psamtik II. Apries failed to help his ally King Zedekiah of Judah against Babylon, but after the fall of Jerusalem he received many Jewish refugees into Egypt."[107]

This Jewish remnant took with them some very distinct people.

---
[107] *Apries, Encyclopedia Britannica, Micropaedia*, 1985, Vol. 1, p. 496 http://www.britannica.com/EBchecked/topic/30809/Apries

> 6 "...the men, and the women, and the children, and the sovereign's daughters, and every being whom Nebuzaradan, chief of the guard, had left with Gedalyahu son of Aḥiqam, son of Shaphan, and Yirmeyahu the prophet, and Baruk son of Něriyahu." (Jeremiah 43:6)

The last name Baruch being Jeremiah's secretary or scribe. The majority of these, according to Yehovah, would die by sword or famine.

> 15 "...then hear the word of יהוה, O remnant of Yehudah! Thus said יהוה of hosts, the Elohim of Yisra'ěl, 'If you indeed set your faces to enter Mitsrayim, and shall go to sojourn there, 16 then it shall be that the sword which you feared overtakes you there in the land of Mitsrayim, and the scarcity of food of which you were afraid clings to you there in Mitsrayim, and you die there.'" (Jeremiah 42:15-16)

But a few would escape and some would return:

> 12 "And I shall take the remnant of Yehudah who have set their faces to go into the land of Mitsrayim to sojourn there. And they shall all be consumed in the land of Mitsrayim—fall by the sword, consumed by scarcity of food. From the least to the greatest they shall die, by the sword and by scarcity of food. And they shall be an oath and an astonishment and a curse and a reproach! 13 And I shall punish those dwelling in the land of Mitsrayim, as I have punished Yerushalayim, by the sword, by scarcity of food, and by pestilence. 14 And none of the remnant of Yehudah who have gone into the land of Mitsrayim to sojourn there shall escape or survive, lest they return to the land of Yehudah, to which they are longing to return to dwell there. For they shall not return, except those who escape." (Jeremiah 44:12-14)

> 28 "And those who escape the sword, few in number, shall return from the land of Mitsrayim to the land of Yehudah. And all the remnant of Yehudah, who came into the land

*of Mitsrayim to sojourn there, shall know whose word is established, Mine or theirs."* (Jeremiah 44:28)

We know that Baruch and Jeremiah, who did not go to Egypt by choice, survived and, as we will see, so did at least *one* of the king's daughters.

> *2 Thus said* יהוה, *the Elohim of Yisra'ěl, concerning you, Baruk: 3 "You have said, 'Woe to me now! For* יהוה *has added grief to my pain. I have been wearied with my sighing, and I have found no rest.' 4 Say this to him, Thus said* יהוה, *"See, what I have built I am breaking down, and what I have planted I am plucking up, that is, the entire land. 5 And do you seek great matters for yourself? Do not seek them, for look, I am bringing evil on all flesh," declares* יהוה. *"But I shall give your life to you as a prize in all places, wherever you go."* (Jeremiah 45:2-5)

Those who had escaped the sword in the Land of Israel had taken Jeremiah, Baruch, the King's daughters and others as they set out upon their journey into Egypt.

> *7 So they went to the land of Mitsrayim, for they disobeyed the voice of* יהוה. *And they went as far as Tahpanhes. 8 And the word of* יהוה *came to Yirmeyahu in Tahpanhes, saying, 9 "Take large stones in your hand, and you shall hide them before the eyes of the men of Yehudah, in the clay in the brick courtyard which is at the entrance to Pharaoh's house in Tahpanhes."* (Jeremiah 43:7-9)

Notice this account from the famous British pioneer Archaeologist and Egyptologist, Flinders Petrie, who discovered the site of Tahpanhes in 1886:

> Tahpanhes was an important garrison, and as the Jews fled there it must have been close to the frontier. It is thus clear that it was the Greek Daphnae, the modern Tell Defneh, which is on the road to Palestine... Of this," he continues,

> "an echo comes across the long ages; the fortress mound is known as Qasr Bint el Yehudi, the palace of the Jew's daughter. It is named Qasr, as a palace, not Qala, a fortress. It is not named Tell Bint el Yehudi, as it would be if it were called so after it were a ruinous heap. Qasr is a name, which shows its descent from the time of… habitation for nobility and not merely for troops. So through the long ages of Greek and Roman and Arab there has come down the memory of the royal residence for the king's daughters from the wreck of Jerusalem."[108]

Yet there certainly were many troops there as well. Petrie states:

> Psamtik (Pharaoh Psammetichus I, founder of Egypt's 26th dynasty of which Hophra was the fourth king) guarded the frontiers of Egypt with three strong garrisons, placing the Ionian and Carian mercenaries especially at the Pelusian Daphnae… in the northeast, from which quarter the most formidable enemies were likely to appear." (p. 40) These were Greek forces primarily from the west coast of Asia Minor (modern Turkey). "Ionian" and "Carian" primarily designated the Greek city of Miletus there: "Within Egypt itself, normally hostile to any foreign settlement, the Greeks gained a foothold… About 650 (B.C.) the Milesians (from Miletus) opened a 'factory,' or trading post, at Naucratis on the Canopic branch of the Nile. Pharaoh Psamtik I tolerated them because they made good mercenaries, while their commerce provided rich prey for his collectors of customs revenues."[109]

Miletus will factor in greatly in pursuing this whole subject to its conclusion. Suffice it to say that, for now, many of these "Greek" forces in Egypt were not so unrelated to the Jews taking refuge with them. There was evidently a kinship going way back. The ancient Greeks had

---

[108] *Egypt and Israel*, 1911, pp. 85-86; see also *Daphne, Encyclopedia Britannica*, 14th ed., Vol. 7, p. 48

[109] *The Story of Civilization* by Will Durant, Vol. 2: *The Life of Greece*, 1966, p. 173

often referred to themselves as Danaans—a name evidently derived from the Israelite tribe of Dan.

Indeed, a number of the Greek mercenaries employed in Egyptian service were probably Israelites whose ancestors had earlier settled in Greece and neighboring lands. And here they were—guarding the remnant of the Davidic royal family under orders of the Egyptian pharaoh! Yet this arrangement was not to last.

> The Greeks continued to play a prominent role during the reigns of Psammeticus II and Apries (the Pharaoh Hophra of Jeremiah). Under the latter, however, a national movement among the Egyptians led to a revolt (ca. 570 B.C.) against the (Egyptian) king and the Greek element, with the result that the throne passed to the general Amasis (Ahmosis II), who withdrew the Greeks from Daphnai.[110]

Evidently, he expelled many of them whom he considered loyal to Hophra.

Adding to the need for expulsion was the fact that although Amasis (Ahmosis II) confined the remaining Greek mercenaries near his capital, making many of them part of a royal guard, "an element within Egyptian culture... resisted this; and the presence of foreigners in Egypt, both as invaders and settlers, led to the rise of a nationalism" that wanted the foreigners out.[111]

It was now roughly sixteen years after the fall of Jerusalem, and up to this point, things had apparently gone rather well in Egypt for those who had fled there. But Yehovah had warned of the calamity to befall Hophra.

> *30 Thus said יהוה, "See, I am giving Pharaoh Ḥophra sovereign of Mitsrayim into the hand of his enemies and into the hand of those who seek his life, as I gave Tsiḏqiyahu*

---

[110] *Chamber's Encyclopedia*, 1959, Vol. 5
[111] *Egypt, Encyclopaedia Britannica, Macropaedia*, Vol. 18, 1985, p. 165; *Ahmose II, Micropaedia*, Vol. 1, p. 168

*sovereign of Yehudah into the hand of Nebukadretstsar sovereign of Babel, his enemy who sought life."* (Jeremiah 44:30)

And He had warned the Jewish remnant seeking refuge in Egypt that they would be consumed there:

> 27 *"See, I am watching over them for evil and not for good. And all the men of Yehudah who are in the land of Mitsrayim shall be consumed by the sword and by scarcity of food, until they come to an end. 28 And those who escape the sword, few in number, shall return from the land of Mitsrayim to the land of Yehudah. And all the remnant of Yehudah, who came into the land of Mitsrayim to sojourn there, shall know whose word is established, Mine or theirs."* (Jeremiah 44:27-28).

Clearly, then, Yehovah authored this turn of events. The Egyptians drove many of the Greco-Israelite mercenaries from the country. And most of the Jewish remnant was probably slaughtered around this time, if not in the uprising, then probably in Nebuchadnezzar's invasion of Egypt two years later in 568 B.C., which laid waste to most of the Nile valley.

But what about Jeremiah, Baruch and the king's daughters? Where did they go? The book of Jeremiah doesn't actually tell us, although it contains some hints.

## The Line of Calcol

I would like to stop at this point and go back 811 years to the Exodus *and earlier*. We have now followed the line of Phares and the promises made to David of that line down to this point in time—to the point where Zedekiah's sons are all killed and there are no other heirs except the King's daughters in Jeremiah's care. But this is not the conclusion.

As you will recall, Tamar had twin sons—one who put forth his hand and drew it back into the womb named Zerah, while the other one, Phares, came out first. Phares has now had his day in the sun, in a manner of speaking, and Zerah is about to shine forth. Actually, Zerah was also leaving his mark on the world scene but is not well known by us today in this modern world in which we now live.

Let me first share with you what little the Bible *does say* about Zerah and his descendants.

> *6 And sons of Zerah: Zimri, and Ethan, and Heman, and Calcol, and Dara; all of them five.* (1 Chronicles 2:6 | NKJV)

> *6 And the sons of Zeraḥ*: Zimri, and Ěythan, and Hěman, and Kalkol, and Dara, five of them in all. (1 Chronicles 2:6 | NIV)

> *30 And Shelomoh's wisdom excelled the wisdom of all the men of the East and all the wisdom of Mitsrayim. 31 For he was wiser than all men, than Ěythan the Ezrahite, and Hěman, and Kalkol, and Darda, the sons of Maḥol. And his name was in all the nations round about.* (1 Kings 4:30-31)

Judah was born in 1642 B.C. and was twenty-one years of age when Joseph was sold to the Midians at age seventeen, which was the year 1621 B.C. Immediately after Joseph was sold, we read in Genesis 38 about Judah going into Tamar. Time must pass in order for Judah to have three sons, for them to grow and for the first one to marry Tamar and then die.

It was also twenty-two years after Joseph was sold that he then revealed himself to his brothers in the year 1599 B.C., the second year of the famine. With this being said, then we must conclude that the birth of Phares and Zerah was very close to this time of the famine, as Judah met Tamar while still in Palestine. That took place around 1601 B.C.

I am showing you this because, by the time of the Exodus, about 221 years would have had to have passed from the approximate birth of Phares and Zerah.

Joseph is recorded as dying in the year 1528 B.C. at the age of 110. This then means that there were 149 years until the Exodus. And it was during this time that the sons of Zerah would have reached their fame amongst the Israelites.

> These five are here stated to be the sons of Zerah, that is, of Ezra, whence they were called Ezrahites (1 Kings 4:31). In that passage they are called "the sons of Mahol," which, however, is to be taken not as a proper name, but appellatively for "sons of music, dancing," etc. The traditional fame of their great sagacity and acquirements had descended to the time of Solomon and formed a standard of comparison for showing the superior wisdom of that monarch. Jewish writers say that they were looked up to as prophets by their countrymen during the abode in Egypt.[112]

His descendants were called Zarhites, Ezrahites and Izrahites. (Numbers 26:20; 1 Kings 4:31; 1 Chronicles 27:8, 11)

It was also during these 149 years that we are told in Exodus of another Pharaoh who knew not Joseph.

> *8 Then a new sovereign arose over Mitsrayim, who did not know Yosĕph, 9 and he said to his people, "See, the people of the children of Yisra'ĕl are more and stronger than we, 10 come, let us act wisely towards them, lest they increase, and it shall be when fighting befalls us, that they shall join our enemies and fight against us, and shall go up out of the land."* (Exodus 1:8-10)

This would have been the beginning of the affliction upon the Israelites increasing over the years all the way up to the Exodus in 1379 B.C. There are a number of things that took place before the Exodus that most people are unaware of.

Rambam[113] comments on Ephraim before the Exodus.

---

[112] *Jamieson, Fausset and Brown's Commentary On the Whole Bible* http://www.amazon.com/Jamieson-Fausset-Browns-Commentary-Whole/dp/0310265703

[113] *The Chumash* concerning the 430 years of the Exodus 12:40, p. 359

The tribe of Ephraim believed that the 400 years of time that they would be in Egypt was started with the time when Yahweh made the covenant with Abraham. Based on this understanding they set out for the land of Canaan 30 years before the Exodus by the northern route. The Egyptians slaughtered them. It is partly for this reason that 30 years later when Moses left with them they took the southern route away from the Garrisons along the northern highway.

Rab said:[10] They were the Ephraimites, who counted (the years) to the end (of the Egyptian bondage), but erred therein, [11] as it is written, And the sons of Ephraim; Shuthelah, and Bared his son, and Tahath his son, and Eladah his son, and Tahath his son. And Zabad his son, and Shuthelah his son, and Ezzer, and Elead, whom the men of Gath that were born in that land slew.[12] And it is written, 'And Ephraim their father mourned many days, and his brethren came to comfort him.'[13] (Sanhedrin 92b: 10-13)

1. They counted the four hundred years foretold by God to Abraham (Genesis 15:13) as commencing from the covenant, whereas, in reality, they should have started from Isaac's birth,[114] which according to tradition took place thirty years later. As a result, they left Egypt thirty years *before* the rest of Israel.

2. 20 And the sons of Ephrayim: Shuthelah, and Bered his son, and Tahath his son, and Eladah his son, and Tahath his son, 21 and Zabad his son, and Shuthelah his son, and Ezer and El'ad. But the men of Gath who were born in that land slew them because they came down to take their livestock. 22 And Ephrayim their father mourned many days, and his brothers came to comfort him. 23 And when he went in to his wife, she conceived and bore a son. And he called his name Beri'ah, because evil had come upon his house. (I Chronicles 7:20-23)

---

[114] Actually the 400 years start when Isaac would have been ten as we show you our book "Remembering the Sabbatical Year of 2016"

> 3. Ibid. 22. One of the most tragic disappointments experienced by the Israelites in Egypt, the premature emigration of the Tribe of Ephraim, actually preceded the Exodus.
>
> According to our sages, members of the Tribe of Ephraim attempted to calculate the end of the Egyptian Exile and erroneously fixed the date 30 years early. So certain were they of their conclusion and so eager for redemption that 200,000 armed tribesman of Ephraim left Egypt by force 30 years before the Exodus, only to be slaughtered by the Philistines at Gat, where their corpses were left to rot.[115]

One can well imagine the skepticism aroused by the memory of that catastrophe when the true redemption got underway with the miracles of Moses, which may account for the Hebrews' recurrent suspicion that Moses had taken them out of Egypt only to have them die in the desert. In fact, the sages inform us that Yehovah did not lead the Hebrews on the direct route from Egypt to Israel, which passed through the Land of the Philistines, precisely to avoid arousing their deep-seated fears by exposing them to the traumatic sight of the bleached bones of the Ephraimites along the way.

Imagine this for yourself. Thirty years prior, a great disaster takes place and many of those from your area are killed. Then this man that few if any know tells you to follow him out of Egypt. You see the great miracles but you are not sure what you are seeing or if it is just nature or your mind playing tricks on you.

It is in hindsight that we see the greatness of the events that Yehovah did through Moses. At the actual time you and everyone else are in doubt about what to do next.

Years before Moses came on the scene, the people of Israel could see the evil coming; much in the same way one could see the evil coming in Europe before WWII actually began and the holocaust. Many of

---

[115] *Shemot* 13:17 by Mechilta and Targum Yehonatan, Sanhedrin 92b

the Jewish people saw what was coming and left. Others denied it and stayed, only to be caught up in it when it did come.

One of those who left Egypt early was the son of Zerah, the son of Judah. His name was Calchol, who became known as Cecrops.

> *6 And the sons of Zeraḥ: Zimri, and Ĕythan, and Hĕman, and Kalkol, and Dara, five of them in all.* (1 Chronicles 2:6)

The migrations out of Egypt led by the Ephraimites and also, the Exodus, led by Moses, are not the only ones recorded in ancient history. Another important GRECIAN COLONY was founded by CECROPS who became the FIRST "LEGENDARY" KING OF ATTICA. Cecrops, as we shall see, was an Israelite! Author E. Raymond Capt notes:

> According to "The Harmsworth Encyclopedia," CECROPS ("CALCOL" of I Chronicles 2:6 and "CHACOL" of I Kings 4:31—and BROTHER OF DARDA) was the 'mythical' founder of ATHENS and its FIRST KING. He was thought to have been the LEADER OF A BAND OF HEBREW COLONISTS FROM EGYPT.[116]

> CALCOL, or CECROPS, as the Greeks called him, evidently left Egypt BEFORE the Exodus of the Bible. Hermon L. Hoeh, states that "ATHENIAN history commences with the founding of the city by Cecrops in 1556 (B.C.)."[117]

> The Encyclopedia Britannica states that Cecrops was "traditionally the FIRST KING OF ATTICA (Pausanias ix. 33). He was said to have divided the inhabitants into 12 COMMUNITIES, to have instituted the LAWS OF MARRIAGE and PROPERTY and a NEW FORM OF WORSHIP. The introduction of BLOODLESS SACRIFICE,

---

[116] *Missing Links Discovered In Assyrian Tablets* by E. Raymond Capt, Artisan Sales, Thousand Oaks, CA. 1985, p. 65
[117] *Compendium of World History* by Herman L. Hoeh, Vol. I, p. 390

the BURIAL OF THE DEAD and the invention of WRITING were also attributed to him."[118]

One of the reasons noted as to why Cecrops would have left Egypt and his countrymen so early was that, after the death of Joseph in 1528 B.C., the children of Joseph may have sought revenge for what his brothers had done to him. If in fact this rumor was going around the camp, this could explain why Cecrops left twenty-eight years before the death of Joseph. It also explains why Joseph is recorded as saying to his brothers to 'fear not.' This was after Jacob died in the year 1582 B.C. So the founding of Athens by Cecrops in 1556 B.C. fits perfectly with what was going on in Egypt at this time—fear and distrust.

> *14 And after he had buried his father, Yosĕph returned to Mitsrayim, he and his brothers and all who went up with him to bury his father. 15 And when Yosĕph's brothers saw that their father was dead, they said, "What if Yosĕph hates us, and pays us back all the evil which we did to him?" 16 And they sent word to Yosĕph, saying, "Before your father died he commanded, saying, 17 This is what you are to say to Yosĕph, 'I beg you, please forgive the transgression of your brothers and their sin, for they did evil to you. And now, please forgive the transgression of the servants of the Elohim of your father.' And Yosĕph wept when they spoke to him. 18 And his brothers also went and fell down before his face, and they said, "See, we are your servants." 19 And Yosĕph said to them, "Do not fear, for am I in the place of Elohim. 20 And you, you intended evil against me, but Elohim intended it for good, in order to do it as it is this day, to keep a great many people alive. 21 And now, do not fear, I provide for you and your little ones." So he comforted them and spoke kindly to them. 22 And Yosĕph dwelt in Mitsrayim, he and his father's household. And Yosĕph lived one hundred and ten years.* (Genesis 50:14-22)

---

[118] *The Encyclopedia Britannica*, 1943 edition. Vol. 5, p. 85

Although Calcol died in Greece in the year 1506 B.C., he directed his son GATHELUS to plant the royal line of Judah (through Zarah) in distant lands to the west![119] Raymond Capt also says that:

> The Danaan were not the first Hebrews into Ireland. CALCOL (1 Chronicles 2:6—Chalcol of 1 Kings 4:31) FOUNDER OF THE ANCIENT IRISH LINE OF KINGS (through his son Gathelus) planted a royal Dynasty in ULSTER (as well as other royal dynasties in Europe). He and his brother DARDA (DARDANUS) the founder of TROY had both migrated from Egypt BEFORE the Exodus. They are SONS OF ZARAH, one of the twin sons of Judah. The Hebrew name "Zarah" signifies "to scatter," and the subsequent history of Zarah and his descendants fully justifies the claim that he was named with prophetic intention, even as was Jacob, the supplanter.[120]

The movements of Gathelus are noted by Capt:

> Historical records tell of the WESTWARD MIGRATION of the descendants of CALCOL along the shores of the Mediterranean Sea, establishing "IBERIAN" (HEBREW) trading settlements. One settlement, now called "SARAGOSSA,"[121] in the EBRO valley in Spain, was originally known as "ZARAH-GASSA," meaning the "STRONGHOLD OF ZARAH." From Spain they continued westward as far as Ireland. The Iberians gave their name to Ireland, calling the island "Iberne" which was later abbreviated to "Erne," and subsequently Latinized to "Hibernia," a name that still adheres to Ireland.[122]

> For, as the old chronicles reveal, there was a Greek, called GATHELUS, SON OF CECROPS (CALCOL) OF ATHENS,

---

[119] http://www.hope-of-israel.org/moreexodus.html
[120] *Missing Links Discovered In Assyrian Tablets* by E. Raymond Capt. Artisan Sales, Thousand Oaks, CA. 1985, p. 64
[121] Zaragosa in Spanish. http://en.wikipedia.org/wiki/Zaragoza
[122] *Missing Links Discovered In Assyrian Tablets* by E. Raymond Capt. Artisan Sales, Thousand Oaks, CA. 1985, p. 65

> otherwise of Argus, King of the Argives, who... left his native country of Greece and CAME TO EGYPT with a strong company of goodly young men... At this time there reigned in Egypt Pharaoh, THE SCOURGE OF THE PEOPLE OF ISRAEL: whose SON, following in his father's iniquities, was DROWNED IN THE RED SEA, with all his army... The King Pharaoh received Gathelus openly because he (Gathelus) appeared to support the Pharaoh against the Ethiopians and the people of Midian... The Pharaoh, with the support of Gathelus, won a fierce battle against the Ethiopians, and brought them so close to defeat that Gathelus took their principal city called MEROE. Gathelus, after this great victory, returned to Egypt; and... was made general lieutenant over all of the Pharaoh's army. Soon after, because he was... of the ROYAL BLOOD LINE OF GREECE... King Pharaoh gave him his DAUGHTER, CALLED SCOTA, in marriage...[123]

Another version of the story goes like this:

> One of the most memorable chapters in the history of the Celtic race deals with Niul, youngest son of Fenius Farsa, King of Scythia. Niul was reputed to have mastered all of the languages of the then-known world. The fame of his learning and wisdom spread worldwide, and King Forond (probably a corruption of Pharaoh), the first-styled 'Pharaoh Cingris' of Egypt, invited him to Egypt to instruct Egyptian youth in the sciences. The King gave Niul a large fiefdom on the Red Sea, and gave him, also, his daughter, Scota, in marriage.[124]

This story of Scota in Irish folklore often gets mixed in with Jeremiah, which is about 900 years later.

> But, according to the account related by Keating, Miledh, again seemingly the same as Gathelus befriended Moses and

---

[123] *The Chronicles of Scotland* by Hector Boece translated into Scottish by John Bellenden in 1531 C.E.
[124] *The MacGeoghegan Family Society Newsletter*, May 3rd, 1990

the Israelites. Pharaoh Intur (supposed son of Nectonibus) and the Egyptians, in time, remembered their old grudge to the descendants of Niul and the family of Gaedal (Gathelus), namely their resentment for the friendship the latter had formed with the children of Israel. They, then, made war upon the Gaels, who were thereby compelled to exile themselves from Egypt.

The Chronicles of Scotland next relate the return of Moses:

A few years after this, the Pharaoh died, and his son Bochoris Pharaoh received the crown of Egypt, and he oppressed the people of Israel with a worse slavery than did his father. Therefore, no hope of liberty appeared to the people of Israel, until MOSES returned from Midian, where he was banished, to show the commands of God to this Bochoris Pharaoh, in order to deliver the Israelites out of bondage. Following this, Egypt was punished with strange plagues, because they held the prophecy of Moses in contempt... Gathelus... concerned by the present plague that was the terrible response of God, resolved TO LEAVE EGYPT FOR ANOTHER ABODE... A short time afterwards he provisioned a ship and SAILED OUT OF THE MOUTH OF THE RIVER NILE with his wife, friends and servants—Greeks and Egyptians—for fear of the plagues of God... After a dangerous voyage ON THE MEDITERRANEAN SEA, Gathelus... LANDED IN A PART OF SPAIN CALLED LUSITANIA, which was afterwards called PORTUGAL, that is, THE PORT OF GATHELE (GATHELUS).[125]

This Port of Gathelus would later become known as Port of Gael and then Port-u-gal to what it is now called the country of Portugal.

---

[125] *The Chronicles of Scotland* by Hector Boece translated into Scottish by John Bellenden in 1531 C.E.

According to an Irish and Scottish medieval tradition, Goídel Glas (Latinized as Gathelus) is the creator of the Goidelic languages and the eponymous ancestor of the Gaels.[126]

It may surprise some of you to know that the Gaelic language and the Hebrew language have many very similar words.[127]

To add more weight to the fact that the two languages, Welsh and Hebrew, are very similar even today, is the 2012 event of the Welsh Journalist arrested in Libya simply because the Libyans thought the Welsh language was Hebrew and the journalists were Israeli spies. Here is that account:

> A Welsh journalist arrested in Libya said that the militia held him after they confused the Welsh language on his supplies for Hebrew, and decided he was an Israeli spy.[128]

Continuing with Gathelus and the Milesians;

> In Irish origin legends, Míl Espáine or Míl Espáne (later pseudo-Latinized as Milesius; also Miled/Miledh) is the ancestor of the final inhabitants of Ireland, the "sons of Míl" or Milesians, who represent the vast majority of the Irish Gaels. His father was Bile, son of Breogan.
>
> Míl is very much the product of Latin Christian scholarship. His name is an Irish version of Latin Miles Hispaniae, meaning "Soldier of Hispania," which is attested in a passage (§ 13) in the 9th-century pseudo-history Historia Brittonum ("The History of the Britons"). The work offers an account of how Ireland was successively taken by settlers from Iberia, among them Partholom, Nimeth and the "three sons of a

---

[126] http://en.wikipedia.org/wiki/Gathelus
[127] http://www.britam.org/language.html
[128] http://www.walesonline.co.uk/news/wales-news/2012/03/20/libyans-confused-welsh-for-hebrew-claims-arrested-welsh-journalist-gareth-montgomery-johnson-91466-30581290/

Hispanic soldier" (tres filii militis Hispaniae).[129] As A.G. Van Hamel has suggested, the status of Iberia as the land of origin can be traced back to Isidore of Seville, who in the introduction to his history of the Goths, Vandals and Suebi had elevated Iberia to the "mother of all races."[130] A further explanation may lie in the mistake made by some classical geographers in locating Ireland closely opposite Iberia. For instance, the Lebar Gabála (§ 100) recounts that from Bregon's Tower, the Milesian Íth was able to see right across the sea to Ireland.[131]

He served as a soldier in Scythia and Egypt, before remembering a prophecy that his descendants would rule Ireland. He set off to the west, getting as far as Iberia where he fought several battles before dying, never seeing Ireland himself.

His wife Scota and his uncle Íth, who had spied Ireland from a tower, sailed to Ireland where Íth was killed by the Tuatha Dé Danann. When his body was brought back to Iberia, Míl's eight sons and Íth's nine brothers invaded Ireland and defeated the Tuatha Dé Danann.

He figures prominently in the mythological genealogies of John O'Hart, being the common ancestor of all the Irish.

Milesius died in Iberia before he could reach the Isle of Destiny. His wife Scota went to Ireland with their eight sons. Due to some terrible storms (attributed to the magic of the

---

[129] *Irish National Origin Legend* by Dr. John Carey (1994), pp. 5-6. *The Sources of Mediaeval Gaelic History* by Edmund Crosby Quiggin, Quiggin Pamphlets, 1. Cambridge.

[130] *On Lebor Gabála* by A.G. Van Hamel, (1914-1915). Zeitschrift fur celtische Philologie 10:97–197, p. 173.

[131] *Míl Espáine and the Milesians* by Petra S. Hellmuth, (2006). In John T. Koch's *Celtic Culture. A Historical Encyclopedia.* 5 volumes. Santa Barbara, Denver and Oxford: ABC Clio. p. 1298

Tuatha Dé Danann who already lived in Ireland) most of Milesius' sons died when they tried to land.[132]

Gathelus' settlement of Spain is described next:[133]

> Soon afterwards he built a town UPON THE RIVER OF MUNDE, then called BRACHARA—NOW BARSALE… (After a major battle with the Spaniards) they (the Spaniards) therefore asked Gathelus for a peace conference and quickly gave him… part of their land in the NORTH PART OF SPAIN, NOW CALLED GALYCIA, because they had a prophecy that said a strange people would sometime come to dwell there… with the close collaboration of the inhabitants, (he) built the TOWN OF BRYGANCE—now called COMPESTELLA… Following this Gathelus NAMED ALL HIS SUBJECTS SCOTS, IN HONOR AND AFFECTION FOR HIS WIFE, WHO WAS CALLED SCOTA, with whom he had two sons—HIBER AND HEMECUS…[134]

Notice WHERE the Scots went from Spain:

> Gathelus, seeing the number of his people increasing in Brigance, thought it more fitting to take his people to SOME OTHER PLACE where they may live in peace… Gathelus… assembled all the SHIPS he could find in a nearby port, in which he placed his sons HIBER and HEMECUS—with sailors, warriors and all the other things necessary for the expedition. He commanded Hiber, as Admiral, to go to the ISLAND… with favorable winds, (they) arrived five days later… HIBER sacrificed to the honor of his God… then returned to Spain… Hemecus, who was left behind on the island by his brother, NAMED THE ISLAND HIBERNIA after Hiber—that is to say, IRELAND. And since this island was inhabited by two peoples, the SCOTS and the

---

[132] http://en.wikipedia.org/wiki/M%C3%ADl_Espáine
[133] http://www.hope-of-israel.org/moreexodus.html
[134] William Blackwood & Sons, Vol. I., pp. 21-24

> old inhabitants... Hemecus governed both those peoples in great justice.[135]

Eventually the SCOTS moved on once more and invaded the land TO THE NORTH OF ENGLAND! Notice!

> The Scots historically are intruders—THEY CAME FROM IRELAND AND BUILT THE KINGDOM OF DALRIADA on land which had once been Pictish, IN THE WEST OF SCOTLAND, IN ARGYLL and the ISLES. By the mid-sixth century they held a sizable kingdom lying north of the Britons of Strathclyde and stretching up beyond the Great Glen, and they named it AFTER THE DISTRICT IN ULSTER (Northern Ireland) FROM WHICH THEY TOOK THEIR ROYAL HOUSE...[136]

> The oldest Irish chronicles reveal that Abbot Tighernac, a descendant of the SCOTIC KINGS OF ULSTER, led a colony of MILESIAN SCOTS from Antrim in Northern Ireland to the northernmost parts of England. After defeating the PICTS in a number of battles, they gained complete control of this area and also named it in honor of SCOTA—SCOTLAND, "THE LAND OF THE SCOTS!"

(As a personal side note with regard to my family: Antrim is the place from where our Irish ancestry left Ireland to come to Canada in the early 1800's. Their name was McGowan, which is understood to be Mc, as Son of, and Gowan is from the Hebrew word Kohane, Kohen and Cohen)

> The LAST MAJOR MOVEMENT of these descendants of ZARAH occurred in recent centuries when waves of emigration from SCOTLAND traveled across the Atlantic to NOVA SCOTIA in Canada! Once again, probably

---

[135] William Blackwood & Sons, Vol. I., pp. 24-27
[136] *A History of Scotland* by Rosalind Mitchison. Methuen & Co., Ltd. London, 1970, p. 6

unconsciously, they named their new home in Canada after SCOTA—the wife of Gathelus![137]

Before we close this section on Cecrops—also known as Chalcol from the Bible, I also want you to understand what historians called these people. You have now read that Cecrops was the first King of Attica and then he laid out twelve other city-states. Keep this in mind as you read the following:

> The Mycenaean civilization flourished during the period roughly between 1600 B.C., when Helladic culture in mainland Greece was transformed under influences from Minoan Crete, and 1100 B.C., when it perished with the collapse of (the) Bronze Age Civilization in the eastern Mediterranean. The collapse is commonly attributed to the Dorian[138] invasion, although other theories describing natural disasters and climate change have been advanced as well. The major Mycenaean cities were Mycenae and Tiryns in Argolis, Pylos in Messenia, Athens in Attica, Thebes and Orchomenus in Boeotia, and Iolkos in Thessaly. In Crete, the Mycenaeans occupied Knossos. Mycenaean settlement sites

---

[137] http://www.hope-of-israel.org/moreexodus.html

[138] The Dorian Invasion is a concept devised by historians of Ancient Greece to explain the replacement of pre-classical dialects and traditions in southern Greece by the ones that prevailed in Classical Greece. The latter were named Dorian by the ancient Greek writers after the historical population that owned them, the Dorians. Greek legend asserted that the Dorians took possession of the Peloponnesus in an event called the Return of the Heracleidae.

Classical scholars saw in the legend a hypothetically real event they termed the *Dorian Invasion*. The meaning of the concept has changed several times, as historians, philologists and archaeologists used it in attempts to explain the cultural discontinuities expressed in the data of their fields. The pattern of arrival of Dorian culture on certain islands in the Mediterranean, such as Crete, is also not well elucidated. The Dorians colonized a number of sites on Crete such as Lato. (Hogan, C. Michael, January 10th, 2008). *Lato Hillfort. The Modern Antiquarian* by Julian Cope.) As you will see, the Dorians are another group of Israelites. It is my strong opinion they were Danites.

also appeared in Epirus,[139 & 140] Macedonia,[141] on islands in the Aegean Sea, on the coast of Asia Minor, the Levant,[142] Cyprus[143] and Italy[144 & 145] and Mycenaean artifacts have been found well outside the limits of the Mycenaean world: namely Mycenaean swords are known from as far away as Georgia in the Caucasus,[146] an amber object inscribed with Linear B symbols has been found in Bavaria, Germany[147] and Mycenaean bronze double axes and other objects dating from 13th-century B.C. have been found in Ireland and in Wessex and Cornwall in England.[148]

Quite unlike the Minoans, whose society benefited from trade, the Mycenaeans advanced through conquest. Mycenaean civilization was dominated by a warrior aristocracy. Around

---

[139] *Migrations and Invasion In Greece and Adjacent Areas* by N.G.L. Hammond (1976). Park Ridge, N.J.: Noyes P., p. 139.

[140] Figure 1: Map of Epirus Showing the Locations of Known Sites with Mycenaean Remains by Tandy, p. xii. Figure 2-A: The strongest evidence for Mycenaean presence in Epirus is found in the coastal zone of the lower Acheron River, which in antiquity emptied into a bay on the Ionian coast known from ancient sources as *Glykys Limin by* Tandy, p. 2.

[141] *In the Shadow of Olympus: The Emergence of Macedon* by Eugene N. Borza (1990). (Nachdr. ed.), Princeton, NJ: Princeton University Press, p. 64.

[142] *The Synchronization of Civilizations In the Eastern Mediterranean in the Second Millennium B.C.* III, Proceedings of the SCIEM 2000—2nd EuroConference, Vienna, 28th of May—1st of June 2003

[143] *Use and Appreciation of Mycenaean Pottery: In the Levant, Cyprus and Italy* by Gert Jan Van Wijngaarden

[144] *The Mycenaeans and Italy: the Archaeological and Archaeometric Ceramic Evidence*, University of Glasgow, Department of Archaeology.

[145] *Mycenaeans In Early Latium* by Emilio Peruzzi, (Incunabula Graeca 75), Edizioni dell'Ateneo & Bizzarri, Roma, 1980.

[146] http://www.bu.edu/historic/hs/september02.html

[147] Amber object bearing Linear B symbols, from the Freising District, Germany, excavations in the years 1994-1997

[148] *The Ancient Greeks: An Introduction*, Stephanie Lynn Budin, Oxford University Press
[46] *The Celtic Encyclopedia*
[46] *The Encyclopedia Americana*, Vol. 13
[46] *Mycenaean Civilization: An Annotated Bibliography Through 2002* by Bryan Avery Feuer, McFarland & Co. Inc., 2004

1400 B.C., the Mycenaeans extended their control to Crete, center of the Minoan civilization, and adopted a form of the Minoan script (called Linear A) to write their early form of Greek in Linear B.[149]

# **The Line of Dara**

Now let us go back and follow the migrations of one of the other sons of Zerah. You have already looked at Calcol who was also known as Cecrops. He was the first to leave from Egypt before Joseph died. He also left long before the Exodus. But his son Gathelus was in Egypt just before the Exodus with Moses, which was before 1379 B.C. the year of the Exodus.

But there were other sons of Zerah and other tribes from the Israelites, who migrated together after Calcol.

> *6 And the sons of Zeraḥ: Zimri, and Ĕythan, and Hĕman, and Kalkol, and Dara, five of them in all.* (1 Chronicles 2:6)

Dara's descendants did not leave Egypt at the same time as Calcol did. It would be years later as we will soon see. Dara has been recorded in history as Dardanus. It is this Dara that the Bible says King Solomon was even wiser than he was. This is quite the honor.

> Dardanus left Egypt BEFORE the Exodus: "Dardanus is said to have BUILT TROY about THIRTY-FOUR YEARS BEFORE THE EXODUS."[150]

I shared with you earlier how just thirty years before the Exodus that many from the Tribe of Ephraim tried to leave by the Road of the Philistines heading back into the Promised Land and were wiped out. But Dara first settled another area before going to what would be Troy which means he left much earlier than just 34 years. The Ephraimites were encouraged to leave upon learning of the success of Cecrops and

---

[149] http://en.wikipedia.org/wiki/Mycenaean_Greece#cite_note-6
[150] *British History Traced From Egypt and Palestine* by L.G.A. Roberts, p. 27

also of Dara. There were also groups from the tribe of Dan and they were known as Danaus.

> Now the Egyptians say that also AFTER these events (the plagues of Exodus) a GREAT NUMBER of colonies were SPREAD FROM EGYPT all over the inhabited world... They say also that those who set forth with DANAUS, likewise from Egypt, settled what is practically the OLDEST CITY OF GREECE, ARGOS, and that the nations of the COLCHI IN PONTUS and that of the JEWS, which lies between ARABIA and SYRIA, were founded as colonies by certain emigrants from their country (EGYPT); and this is the reason why it is a long-established institution among these peoples to CIRCUMCISE THEIR MALE CHILDREN, the custom having been BROUGHT OVER FROM EGYPT. Even the ATHENIANS, they say, are COLONISTS FROM SAIS IN EGYPT.[151]

> Hecateus therefore, tells us that the EGYPTIANS, formerly being troubled by calamities (referring to the TEN PLAGUES AT THE TIME OF THE EXODUS), in order that the divine wrath might be averted, EXPELED ALL THE ALIENS GATHERED TOGETHER IN EGYPT. Of these, SOME, under their leaders DANUS and CADMUS, MIGRATED INTO GREECE; others into OTHER REGIONS, THE GREATER PART INTO SYRIA (meaning Palestine). THEIR LEADER IS SAID TO HAVE BEEN MOSES, a man renowned for wisdom and courage, founder and legislator of the state. Afterward, many Mosaic institutions followed.[152]

> "In short, the most celebrated leaders of the Grecian colonies such as Danaus, Erectheus, Cecrops, Cadmus, and Phoenix, all came from Egypt. Hence it is evident that the Greeks were,

---

[151] *Diodorus of Sicily* by G. H. Oldfather. Vol. I, Books I-II, pp. 1-34. 1933, p. 91
[152] *Fragmenta Historicorum Graecorum* by Karl and Theodor Müller, Vol. II, p. 385 http://archive.org/search.php?query=Fragmenta%20Graecorum%20Historicorum

strictly speaking, an Egyptian nation, and consequently *not* the descendants of Japheth."[153]

What you are reading here is the summation of many of these historians. Keep in mind they are blending the migrations of a number of tribes over 149 years and directly linking it to the Exodus.

The "calamities" referred to here are obviously the PLAGUES, which YEHOVAH God brought down on the Egyptians, and the "ALIENS" are clearly the Israelites, some of whom migrated into GREECE with DANUS AND CADMUS. Others, under the leadership of Moses, made their escape to Palestine.

The legends of ancient Greece are unanimous in claiming that the people who founded their nation CAME FROM EGYPT. Furthermore, the time of the arrival of these groups in Greece is also the TIME OF THE BONDAGE OF THE ISRAELITES IN EGYPT. The ancient writers all agree that these founders of the Greek nation were, without doubt, ISRAELITISH REFUGEES from the Egyptian bondage.[154]

Although there seems to be some confusion, there are in fact, from what I have been able to discern, three groups. One group of Danites which I will talk to you more of in a moment and another group which fled Egypt under the leadership of DARDA—brother to Calcol and son of Zarah who fled earlier.

...let us now turn to that other part of ZARAH'S DESCENDANTS which FLED OUT OF EGYPT under the leadership of... DARDA. In the Authorized Version of the Bible this name is spelled DARA, but in the margin the alternate spelling is DARDA and the Jewish historian Josephus calls him DARDANUS. This is significant because the group, which he led, went NORTHWARD across the

---

[153] http://stonekingdom.org/articles/Cecrops_Danaus.pdf
[154] http://www.hope-of-israel.org/moreexodus.html

Mediterranean Sea to the northwest corner of what we now call ASIA MINOR. There, under the rule of DARDA (DARDANUS) they established a Kingdom, later called TROY, on the southern shore of that narrow body of water, which bears his name to this day—DARDANELLES.[155]

Again, Dardanus is said to have built Troy about thirty-four years after the Exodus. Today the land that straddles the waterway between the Black Sea and the Aegean Sea is known as the Dardanelles named after Dardanus. But he left Egypt many years before the Exodus building the cities of ancient Crete.

Actually, the FIRST stopover for Dardanus, on his way to the Troad (Modern western Turkey), was CRETE! Notice what Herman L. Hoeh says in his discussion of the Early Bronze Age: "'Early Bronze I'—ends in 1382 (B.C.) with VIOLENT DESTRUCTION everywhere in WESTERN ANATOLIA and AT TROY; 1382 (B.C.) marks the conquest of the Troad by DARDANUS AND THE TEUCRIANS FROM CRETE..."[156]

The flood or deluge mentioned by the *Encyclopedia Britannica* and others is prominent in the Greek legends of Dardanus. At the time of the Exodus, tremendous events of a cataclysmic nature occurred in the Mediterranean area. Caius Julius Solinus, in his work, *Polyhistor*, notes that "following the DELUGE which is reported to have occurred in the days of Ogyges, a heavy night spread over the globe."[157]

Heavy DELUGES of rain are reported in the works of early Arab historians—all the result of massive upheavals in earth and sky. The great volcanic explosion of the island of Thera in the Aegean Sea occurred around this time and would

---

[155] W. H. Bennett, *Symbols of Our Celto-Saxon Heritage*. Canadian British-Israel Assn., Windsor, Ontario. 1985, pp. 119-121
[156] *Compendium of World History*, Vol. I. Ambassador College, Pasadena, CA; 1962, p. 470
[157] *Beyond Star Wars* by William F. Dankenbring, p. 13

have caused huge tidal waves or tsunamis throughout the Mediterranean.

It seems apparent, therefore, that Dardanus left Egypt before the Exodus, spending some time in CRETE before voyaging on to Samothrace. After leaving the island of Samothrace, his ship was probably disabled by the deluge or flood that occurred at the time of the Exodus, and drifted helplessly across the sea to the Troad.[158]

You can read more about this huge event known as the Minoan eruption of Thera, and also referred to as the Thera eruption or Santorini eruption.[159] The exact time in which this cataclysmic event took place is still being debated.

I would now like to direct your focus on another group that emigrated and settled an area of Greece who were called the Danaus. It is this author's belief that they are from the tribe of Dan based on the things they first did.

According to Euripides and the Greek geographer and historian STRABO (63? B.C.-A.D. 24?): DANAUS having arrived in ARGOS made a law that those who had borne the name of PELASGIOTAE throughout GREECE should be called DANAI.[160]

If you compare this with Judges 18:29 in the Bible you will find that this act of Danaus was one employed by the TRIBE of DAN throughout their history!

*29 And they called the name of the city Dan, after the name of Dan their father, who was born to Yisra'ël. (Judges 18:29)*

Writes E. Raymond Capt:

---

[158] http://hope-of-israel.org/i000109a.htm
[159] http://en.wikipedia.org/wiki/Minoan_eruption
[160] *Strabo V*, ii. 4

We further learn from STRABO and others that this ARGOS soon spread its name to the PELOPONNESUS and afterwards to all Greece, for he says, "Homer calls the WHOLE of Greece ARGOS, for he calls all ARGIVES, as he calls them DANAI and ACHAEI."[161]

What the historians are revealing to us is that there was a group of Danites and another group under Dara known as the Dardanites. These are in addition to the earlier migration of the Cecrops.

Consider now the populations of each of the tribes of Israel that were taken shortly after the Exodus and then later on during the wandering in the wilderness.

> *37 And the children of Yisra'ĕl set out from Ra'meses to Sukkoth, about six hundred thousand men on foot, besides the little ones. 38 And a mixed multitude went up with them too, also flocks and herds, very much livestock.* (Exodus 12:37-38)

In Numbers, Chapter One, we get the head counts of each of the tribes just after the Exodus. Then, in Numbers 26—right after Phineas kills the Simeon Prince in Numbers 25 roughly forty years later[162]—another census was taken. When we look at how much each tribe has grown we have to conclude that something else was going on during this time.

You can see that there are four tribes—Issachar, Manasseh, Benjamin and Asher—that have all increased over those years between about 10,000 and 20,000. And keep in mind; this was *in spite of* those over the age of twenty all dying off during the forty years of wandering in the Wilderness. When we look at Simeon, Gad, Ephraim, and Naphtali—all of whom decreased between 5,000 and 37,000—we must ask "Why?" Did Yehovah not *bless* these tribes? Nothing is written about this. The other tribes, Reuben, Judah, Zebulon, and Dan are simply in a 'holding

---

[161] *Missing Links Discovered In Assyrian Tablets* by Raymond Capt, p. 62
[162] http://stevenmcollins.com/html/simeon.html

pattern.' Again, *why*? And all of those over twenty would have been dying off at the same rate in each tribe during this time.

| | | | |
|---|---|---|---|
| **REUBEN** | 46,500 | 43,730 | -2,770 |
| **SIMEON** | 59,300 | 22,200 | -37,100 |
| **GAD** | 45,650 | 40,500 | -5,150 |
| **JUDAH** | 74,600 | 76,500 | +1,900 |
| **ISSACHAR** | 54,400 | 64,300 | +9,900 |
| **ZEBULON** | 57,400 | 60,500 | +3,100 |
| **EPHRAIM** | 40,500 | 32,500 | -8,000 |
| **MANASSEH** | 32,200 | 52,700 | +20,500 |
| **BENJAMIN** | 35,400 | 45,600 | +10,200 |
| **DAN** | 62,700 | 64,400 | +1,700 |
| **ASHER** | 41,500 | 53,400 | +11,900 |
| **NAPHTALI** | 53,400 | 45,400 | -8,000 |
| **TOTAL** | 603,550 | 601,730 | -1,820 |

I would propose that at various times, groups of people would get up and leave and go to one of the places that Cecrops and Darda had already founded in which the Israelites were flourishing.

Historians would call them: The Minoans, the Mycenae, the Milesians, the Spartans, the Trojans and the Dorians—all of them members of the same group of tribes, arriving at different times. They were the Israelites who were in Egypt.

> Petavius' *History of the World* says: Danaus was the son of Bela a sojourner in Egypt; he fled from his brother Egyptus and came into Greece three years after the death of Joseph. Sir Walter Raleigh places the flight of Danaus 148 years before the Exodus, and the death of Joseph 145 years before the Exodus. This gives the flight of Danaus three years before the death of Joseph. (Exodus 1379 B.C. + 148 years = 1527 B.C. Joseph died in 1528 B.C. This is according to the Sabbatical and Jubilee Chronology)
>
> There seems to have been three migrations of Danai into Greece.
>
> 1st—circa 1528 B.C. About the time of Joseph's death.
>
> 2nd—circa 1356 B.C. Whilst Israel was in the Wilderness.
>
> 3rd—circa 1296 B.C. When Jabin, King of Canaan, afflicted Israel.
>
> Clinton (Fasti Hellenici) places the landing of Danaus in Greece, 1466 B.C. according to Eratosthenes; or 1410 B.C., if we regard Callimachis to be right.

(These dates are based on the traditional dates for the Exodus, which we do not agree with. According to the Jubilee cycles, which we have proven in "The Prophecies of Abraham," the Exodus took place in the year 1379 B.C.[163])

> There seems to be very cogent reasons why some Israelites left Egypt before the main body. It will be remembered that the sons of Bilhah (Genesis 37:2) (is this the original of Bela, the ancestor of Danaus?) were among Joseph's earliest

---

[163] *The Prophecies of Abraham* by Joseph F. Dumond; Charts at the back of the book.

remembrances, and their evil report was taken by Joseph to his father. These may have taken a very prominent part in the affliction of Joseph, and, when arrived in Egypt, must have been terribly abashed (Genesis 42:21-23), when they found out before whom they had spoken so freely. When Jacob had been gathered to his fathers, their misdoings must have caused them serious anxieties (Genesis 1:15-18) and the most guilty would probably have sought safety in flight. What if this is the origin of the story of the two brothers Danaus and Egyptus? Is Joseph Egyptus? And are these fugitives Danai? If so, the flight of Danaus about the time of the death of Joseph can be very well accounted for. Antagonism would have sprung up between Joseph's children and these persecutors of their father, which, although under restraint during Joseph's lifetime, would have found vent as the old man was passing away.[164]

I would like to point out something here before we move on. Steven Collins has a very interesting article on the consequences of Phineas' killing of the Simeonite prince who was having sex with the Moabite woman.

> The book, *Sparta,* by A.H.M. Jones, a Professor of Ancient History at Cambridge University, noted several things about Sparta. He states the Spartans worshipped a "great lawgiver" who had given them their laws in the "dim past" (p. 5 of his book). This lawgiver may have been Moses.
>
> Professor Jones also noted the Spartans celebrated "the new moons" and the "seventh day of the month" (p. 13). Observing new moons was an Israelite calendar custom, and their observance of "a seventh day" could originate with the Sabbath celebration. Professor Jones also notes, as do other authorities, that the Spartans were known for being "ruthless" in war and times of crisis. This sounds exactly like the Simeonite nature, which was given to impulsive cruelty, as the Bible confirms.

---

[164] http://stonekingdom.org/articles/Cecrops_Danaus.pdf p. 4

Interestingly, Professor Jones writes that the Spartans were themselves divided into several "tribes" which constituted distinct military formations within the Spartan army (pp. 31-32). If the Spartans were descended from Simeonites and several other Israelite tribes who left the rest of their tribesmen just prior to the census of Numbers 26, it would make sense that they would be allied together as distinct tribes even in a new homeland like Sparta. The Spartans also founded a colony in Italy called "Tara" (pp. 11 and 33). The name "Terah" is a Semitic/Israelite name as Terah was the father of Abraham (Genesis 11).

Also, I make the case in my book, *The "Lost" Ten Tribes of Israel... Found!*, that Carthage was founded by Semites from Israel, Tyre and Sidon who continued the Semitic/Hebrew language of the Israelites, as well as the Baal worship that Israel, Tyre and Sidon shared. Carthage and the Greeks were historically enemies, but Sparta exhibited a community of interest with Carthage. When Carthage's army was not fighting well against the Roman legions, it was a Spartan named Xanthippus who traveled to Carthage to reorganize and drill the Carthaginian army to fight Rome. Who better than a Spartan to teach military tactics? This event is recorded on p. 14 of a book, *Hannibal's War With Rome*, by Terrence Wise and Mark Healy.

I have saved the greatest proof to the last, however. The Spartans themselves declared that they were a fellow tribe of the Jews and corresponded with an ancient Jewish High Priest about their relationship. The book of I Maccabees 14:16-23 records this correspondence, which includes this statement:

And this is the copy of the letter which the Spartans sent: The Chief magistrates and the city of the Spartans send greeting to Simon, the chief priest, and to the elders and the priests and the rest of the Jewish people, *our kinsmen. (Emphasis added.)*

Notice the Spartans called the Jews "our kinsmen." The Spartans did not proclaim *themselves* to be Jews, but rather that they were "kinsmen" *to* the Jews (i.e. members of one of the other tribes of Israel). That the Spartans acknowledged a common ancestry with the Jews of the tribe of Judah gives powerful weight to the assertion that they were Israelites who migrated to Greece instead of the Promised Land. The Spartan culture is most like that of the tribe of Simeon, most of which apparently left the Israelite encampment in the Wilderness after a Simeon prince was executed by a Levite.[165]

We will now take a look at Darda and see when and where he and his people traveled to.

**The Cretan Connection!**[166]

There are numerous links between Troy and Crete. Dardanus built a city at the foot of MOUNT IDA in the Troad; there is also a MOUNT IDA near the Cretan city of MYCENAE! *The Link,* published by the Christian Israel Foundation, notes that "...perhaps the most striking evidence of an ISRAELITISH MIGRATORY SETTLEMENT IN CRETAN MYCENAE is to be found in Sir Arthur Evans' monumental work, 'Mycenaean Tree and Pillar Cult,' in which it is established that HEBREW RITUALS were observed there...This culture MOVED TO ASIA MINOR, where, behind TROY, we again find a MOUNT IDA (JUDAH), and where, as in MILETUS, survived the belief in the CRETAN ROYAL DESCENT." (June, 1989, p. 261).

Crete had early contacts with Greece and Asia Minor, where many archaeological finds testify to the fact. The civilization of Cretan Mycenae bore a STRIKING RESEMBLANCE to that of the Hebrews and, according to the Roman historian TACITUS, the "Jews" were "natives of the ISLE OF CRETE,"

---

[165] http://stevenmcollins.com/html/simeon.html
[166] http://hope-of-israel.org/i000109a.htm

who derived their name from that of Mt. Ida (JUDAH), well known in ancient history and mythology. This account in the works of Tacitus might well be considered fantastic were it not for the fact that a MOST INTIMATE cultural link existed BETWEEN THE MYCENAEANS AND THE ISRAELITES!

Later Greek myths indicate that they (the TROJANS) CAME FROM THE SAME SOURCE as THE MYCENAEANS, but moved farther north to cross into Asia Minor at the Bosporus, the strait between the Sea of Marmara and the Black Sea in Russia.

They then migrated into what is now TURKEY. Finally, a branch under ILUS founded TROY under the name 'Ilium.'[167]

Tacitus, Josephus, and others point to the establishment of a JUDAHITE ROYAL LINE IN CRETAN MYCENAE— established by EXILES FROM EGYPT who practiced CIRCUMCISION and were considered "ALIENS" by the Egyptians!

Dardanus was clearly the Darda of the Bible—the son of Zarah and grandson of Judah—and a prince of Judah in his own right![168]

The legends claim that the oldest town in the land of Troy (the Troad) was founded by Teucer, who was a son of the Scamander (a stream of Crete, according to John Tzetzes, the 12th-century Byzantine poet and grammarian) and the nymph Idaea. During the reign of Teucer, DARDANUS— son of Zeus and the nymph Electra –drifted from the island of Samothrace in the Aegean to the Troad, following a great deluge in the Mediterranean area. After he arrived in the Troad, Dardanus received a grant of land from Teucer and

---

[167] *The Mysteries of Homer's Greeks* by I. G. Edmonds. Elsevier/Nelson Books, N.Y. 1981, pp. 71-72
[168] http://hope-of-israel.org/i000109a.htm

married his daughter Batea, shortly thereafter founding the city of DARDANIA at the foot of MOUNT IDA. On the death of Teucer, Dardanus succeeded him as king, and called the whole land DARDANIA.

He sired Erichthonius, who begat TROS by Astyoche, daughter of Simois. Tros named the country TROY (after himself) and the people TROES (TROJANS). By Callirrhoe, daughter of Scamander, Tros had three sons—Ilus, Assaracus and Ganymede. From two of Tros' sons—Ilus and Assaracus—sprang TWO SEPARATE LINES; Ilus, Laomedon, Priam, Hector; and Assaracus, Capys, Anchises, Aeneas.[169]

According to the *Encyclopedia Britannica*:

Ilus went to Phrygia, where he received, as a wrestling prize from the king of Phrygia, a spotted cow, with an injunction to found a city where she lay down. The cow lay down on the hill of the Phrygian Ate; here Ilus founded Ilion; and Dardania, Troy and Ilion became one city. Desiring a sign from Zeus, Ilus prayed and found lying before his tent the Palladium, a wooden statue of Pallas, for which he built a temple. By Eurydice, daughter of Adrastus, he had a son, Laomedon, who married Strymo, a daughter of Scamander (or Placia, daughter of ATREUS or of Leucippus). In his reign, Poseidon and Apollo (or Poseidon alone), built the walls of Troy, but Laomedon withheld their reward. In his reign also, HERACLES besieged and took the city, slaying Laomedon and his children, except one daughter, Hesione, and one son, Podarces.[170]

According to the legends, the life of this Podarces was spared at the request of Hesione—on condition that Podarces first be a slave and then be redeemed by Hesione. Hesione gave her veil for him; hence his name of PRIAM (Greek for

---

[169] http://hope-of-israel.org/i000109a.htm
[170] *Encyclopedia Britannica,* 1943 Ed., Vol. 22, p. 503

"to buy"). After gaining his freedom, Priam first married Arisbe and then Hecuba, fathering 50 sons and 12 daughters! Among these sons were HECTOR and PARIS, and among the daughters Polyxena and Cassandra.

Paris became betrothed to Oenone, and awarded the golden "apple of strife" to Aphrodite (who promised him the love of the fairest of women) and brought upon Troy the resentment of Hera and Athena.

Following this Paris, visiting Sparta, found favor with HELEN, heiress of Tyndareus and wife of MENELAUS, SON OF ATREUS, and carried her to Troy. To recover Helen, the ACHAEANS under AGAMEMNON, brother of Menelaus, besieged Troy for ten years.[171]

This is the Helen that launched a thousand ships. In the tenth year of the siege, Hector was killed by Achilles, and he, by Paris. The war began in 1194 B.C.–1184 B.C. Hector was killed by Achilles and then dragged around in front of the Trojan walls.

After building the city of Dardanus in the Troad, DARDA established his ROYAL LINE in the land. Aeneas (meaning "to praise") was a Trojan hero, the son of the prince Anchises and the goddess Aphrodite. His father was the second cousin of King Priam of Troy, making Aeneas Priam's second cousin, once removed.

Priam's reign ended in 1184 B.C.—the year the Trojans were crushed in the First Trojan War by their brethren the Greeks. AENEAS, of the royal line, escaped the destruction of Troy and made his way to ITALY. The story of his migration is found in the *Aeneid*, written by the Roman historian Virgil. *Funk and Wagnall's New Encyclopedia* outlines the story:

The AENEID is a mythical (according to the "experts") work in twelve books, describing the wanderings of the

---

[171] http://hope-of-israel.org/i000109a.htm

hero AENEAS and a small band of TROJANS after the fall of Troy. Aeneas escaped from Troy with the images of his ancestral gods, carrying his aged father on his shoulders, and leading his young son ASCANIUS by the hand, but in the confusion of his hasty flight he lost his wife, Creusa.

He collected a FLEET OF TWENTY VESSELS, and sailed with the surviving Trojans to THRACE, where they began building a city. Aeneas subsequently abandoned his plan of a settlement there and went to CRETE, but was driven from that island by a pestilence. After visiting EPIRUS and SICILY (where his father died), Aeneas was shipwrecked on THE COAST OF AFRICA and welcomed by DIDO, Queen of CARTHAGE. After a time he again set sail; Dido, who had fallen in love with him, was heartbroken by his departure and committed suicide. After visiting SICILY again and stopping at CUMAE, ON THE BAY OF NAPLES, he landed at the MOUTH OF THE TIBER RIVER, SEVEN YEARS after the fall of Troy. Aeneas was welcomed by LATINUS, KING OF LATIUM. Lavinia, the daughter of Latinus, was destined to marry a stranger, but her mother Amata had promised to give her in marriage to TURNUS, King of the Rutulians. A war ensued, which terminated with the defeat and death of Turnus, thus making possible the marriage of Aeneas and Lavinia. Aeneas died three years later, and his son ASCANIUS FOUNDED ALBA LONGA, the mother city of Rome.[172]

The *Compendium of World History* records that "the refugees of the First Trojan War settled... in Italy. They founded Lavinium two years after the First Trojan War—that is, in 1179 B.C.—and later the city of Alba (the site of the Pope's summer palace today) at the time of the Second Trojan War in 1149 B.C. The TROJAN ROYAL HOUSE founded in Italy a line of kings that reigned in Alba from 1178 B.C. until 753 B.C., when the center of government passed to Rome."

---

[172] *Funk and Wagnalls New Encyclopedia* Vol. I. MCMLXXV, p. 196.

Latinus, king of Latium, was himself descended from JUDAH! Notice:

The famous woman ELECTRA or ROMA was daughter of Atlas Kittim. Josephus reveals ATLAS to have been Epher, ABRAHAM'S GRANDSON. His daughter, the concubine of JUPITER or JUDAH (see Icelandic history...), could be no other than the biblical TAMAR. From Electra, who later married Cambon, came a LINE OF RULERS who were later accounted gods or divine heroes. The list carries us down to the coming of AENEAS OF TROY... All these royal lines were related to the family of... JUDAH.[173]

1. JUPITER (JUDAH)
2. ROMA (TAMAR)
3. ROMANESSUS
4. PICUS I
5. FAUNUS
6. ANNUS
7. VULCAN
8. MARTE (MARS)
9. SATURN
10. PICUS II
11. LATINUS
12. AENEAS
13. ASCANIUS

The 35th year of Latinus' reign was 1181 B.C.-1180 B.C.—the year of AENEAS OF TROY'S arrival in Italy.[174]

In his 38th year Latinus died and Aeneas succeeded him, thus ensuring the line from Judah would continue.

Latinus, the king of Latium who preceded the Trojans, died in 1178 B.C.—three years after the fall of Troy in 1181 B.C. Aeneas the Trojan, son-in-law of Latinus, succeeded him and

---

[173] *Compendium of World History*, Vol. II, pp. 137-138
[174] See *Dionysius of Halicarnassus*, Vol. I, p. 44

reigned for three years (1178 B.C.-1175 B.C.). He, in turn, was succeeded by his son ASCANIUS—who reigned for 38 years (1175 B.C.-1137 B.C.).

The *Annals of the Romans* relate that after Aeneas founded Alba, he married a woman who bore him a son named SILVIUS. Silvius, in turn, married; and when his new wife became pregnant, Aeneas sent word to him that he was sending a wizard to examine the wife and try and determine whether the baby was male or female. After examining Silvius' wife, the wizard returned to his home, but was killed by ASCANIUS because of his prophecy foretelling that the woman had a male in her womb who would be the child of death—for, as the story goes, the male-child would eventually kill his father and mother and be a scourge to all mankind.

During the birth of the child, Silvius' wife died, and the boy was reared by the father and named BRITTO (BRUTUS). Many years later, fulfilling the wizard's prophesy, the young man BRITTO killed his father by accident while practicing archery with some friends.

Geoffrey of Monmouth's account tells much the same story, but in greater detail.[175] In this version, Brutus is explicitly the grandson, rather than son, of Ascanius; his father is Ascanius' son Silvius. The magician who predicts great things for the unborn Brutus also foretells he will kill both his parents. He does so, in the same manner described in the *Historia Britonum*, and is banished. Traveling to Greece, he discovers a group of Trojans enslaved there. He becomes their leader, and after a series of battles, they defeat the Greek king Pandrasus by attacking his camp at night after capturing the guards. He takes him hostage and forces him to let his people go. He is given Pandrasus's daughter Ignoge

---

[175] *Historia Regum Britanniae* by Geoffrey of Monmouth, Vol.1, pp. 3-18, Vol.2 p. 1 http://en.wikisource.org/wiki/History_of_the_Kings_of_Britain/Book_1#3

in marriage, and ships and provisions for the voyage, and sets sail.

The Trojans land on a deserted island and discover an abandoned temple to Diana. After performing the appropriate ritual, Brutus falls asleep in front of the goddess's statue and is given a vision of the land where he is destined to settle, an island in the western ocean inhabited only by a few giants.[176]

After leaving the Aegean area Brutus "MIGRATED TO MALTA, and there was advised to re-establish his people in 'the Great White Island' (an early name for BRITAIN due to its chalk cliffs). This advice is recorded in an archaic Greek form on the Temple of Diana in CAER TROIA (New Troy)."[177]

Where BRUTUS and his people traveled to next is preserved by the British historian Nennius, who states that "Aeneas... arrived in GAUL (modern FRANCE), WHERE HE FOUNDED THE CITY OF TOURS, which is called Turnis..."[178]

Tradition says that on the way to the "White Island" Brutus came across FOUR OTHER TROJAN COLONIES UPON THE COAST OF SPAIN and persuaded them to join him.

After some adventures in North Africa and a close encounter with the Sirens, Brutus discovers another group of exiled Trojans living on the shores of the Tyrrhenian Sea, led by the prodigious warrior Corineus. In Gaul, Corineus provokes a war with Goffarius Pictus, king of Aquitaine, after hunting in the king's forests without permission. Brutus's nephew Turonus dies in the fighting, and the city of Tours is founded where he is buried. The Trojans win most of their battles but

---

[176] http://en.wikipedia.org/wiki/Brutus_of_Britain#cite_note-5
[177] *Jacob's Pillar*, p. 26
[178] *Nennius: British History and the Welsh Annals*, translated by John Morris. Phillimore, London and Chichester. 1980. p. 19

are conscious that the Gauls have the advantage of numbers, so go back to their ships and sail for Britain, then called Albion. They meet the giant descendants of Albion and defeat them.

The Historia Britonum states that "The island of Britain derives its name from Brutus, a Roman consul" who conquered Spain. A more detailed story, set before the foundation of Rome, follows, in which Brutus is the grandson or great grandson of Aeneas.

Following Roman sources such as Livy and Virgil, the Historia tells how Aeneas settled in Italy after the Trojan War, and how his son Ascanius founded Alba Longa, one of the precursors of Rome. Ascanius married, and his wife became pregnant. In a variant version, the father is Silvius, who is identified as either the second son of Aeneas, previously mentioned in the Historia, or as the son of Ascanius. A magician, asked to predict the child's future, said it would be a boy and that he would be the bravest and most beloved in Italy. Enraged, Ascanius had the magician put to death. The mother died in childbirth.

The boy, named Brutus, later accidentally killed his father with an arrow and was banished from Italy. After wandering among the islands of the Tyrrhenian Sea and through Gaul, where he founded the city of Tours, Brutus eventually came to Britain, named it after himself, and filled it with his descendants. His reign is synchronized to the time the High Priest Eli was judge in Israel, and the Ark of the Covenant was taken by the Philistines.[179]

Brutus renames the island after himself and becomes its first king. Brutus then founds a city on the banks of the River Thames, which he calls Troia Nova, or New Troy, siting his palace where is now Guildhall and a temple to Diana on what is now St. Paul's (with the London Stone being a part

---

[179] 1 *Historia Britonum, Vol.* 7, pp. 10-11

of the altar at the latter). The name is in time corrupted to Trinovantum, and is later called London. He creates laws for his people and rules for twenty-four years. He is buried at a temple at Tower Hill. After his death, the island is divided between his three sons, Locrinus (England), Albanactus (Scotland) and Kamber (Wales).

Geoffrey said that King Brutus (who gave his name to Britain), was guided by the goddess Diana to lead Britain's first inhabitants to the island, arriving around 1100 B.C. Thus, it is worth speculating whether Brutus (Brwth) himself was connected with the Pagan site which once stood on St. Paul's Cathedral.

The site is also connected with the King Lud, who gave his name to the present day Ludgate Circus and Ludgate Hill, on which St. Paul's Cathedral stands. Heli (Beli Mawr in the Welsh) in about the year 113 B.C. Lud, the son of Heli (Beli Mawr), became King in 73 B.C. Lud rebuilt the city of London that King Brutus had founded and had named New Troy, and renamed it Caerlud, the city of Lud, after his own name. The name of the city was later corrupted to Caerlundein, which the Romans took up as Londinium, hence London.

In the manuscript section of the British Library lies an old document—MS43968—that used to be kept in Windsor Castle. This particular chart gives the descent of the British Royal Family from ADAM THROUGH BRUTUS. Also, charts published by the Covenant Publishing Co., Ltd., by W. M. H. Milner entitled, *The Royal House of Britain* and by M. H. Gayer entitled, *The Heritage of the Anglo-Saxon Race* both trace the ancestry of the Royal House THROUGH SEVERAL LINES OF DESCENT FROM THE PATRIARCH JUDAH—INCLUDING BRUTUS who is shown as a descendant of Judah's son Zarah.

Every British schoolboy knew by heart the letter British king Caractacus sent to Claudius Caesar. But not many know about the letter, written about a century earlier, from King Cassibellaunus to Julius Caesar. This letter is quoted in full by Geoffrey of Monmouth, who possessed an ancient manuscript from BRITTANY that evidently contained the letter. Geoffrey quotes widely from this manuscript in his historical work. The letter reads as follows:

Cassibelaun, King of the Britains, to Caius Julius Caesar. We cannot but wonder, Caesar, at the avarice of the Roman people, since their insatiable thirst after money cannot let us alone, whom the dangers of the ocean have placed in a manner out of the world; but they must have the presumption to covet our substance, which we have hitherto enjoy'd in quiet. Neither is this indeed sufficient: we must also prefer subjection and slavery to them, before the enjoyment of our native liberty.[180]

Your demand therefore, Caesar, is scandalous, since the SAME VEIN OF NOBILITY, FLOWS FROM AENEAS, IN BRITONS AND ROMANS, and ONE AND THE SAME CHAIN OF CONSANGUINITY SHINES IN BOTH: which ought to be a band of firm union and friendship. That was what you should have demanded of us, and not slavery: we have learned to admit of the one, but never to bear the other. And so much have we been accustomed to liberty, that we are perfectly ignorant what it is to submit to slavery. And if even the gods themselves should attempt to deprive us of our liberty, we would to the utmost of our power resist them in defense of it.

Know then, Caesar, that we are ready to fight for that and our kingdom if, as you threaten, you shall attempt to invade Britain.

---

[180] http://hope-of-israel.org/i000109a.htm

The reference in this letter to AENEAS provides support for the fact that the ancient British royal line STEMMED FROM TROY, as did, traditionally, the descent of certain of the EARLY RULERS OF ROME. And, as we have already seen, the tradition that the TROJAN LEADERS WERE JUDAHITES is upheld by testimony from many quarters.[181]

Cassibellaunus was not the only king of Britain who knew of his Trojan bloodline. Edward I, who removed the Stone of Destiny from Scone in Scotland to London, used to BOAST about his descent from the Trojans: "The Irish and Scottish kings, Fergus and EDWARD HIMSELF were all DESCENDANTS OF JUDAH: in fact it is said that EDWARD used to boast of his DESCENT FROM THE TROJANS!"[182]

Edward I (17$^{th}$ June 1239 C.E.—7$^{th}$ July 1307 C.E.), also known as Edward Longshanks and the Hammer of the Scots (from Latin: *Malleus Scottorum*), was King of England from 1272 C.E. to 1307 C.E. [183]

We will stop here with this line of Trojans coming to England to now follow another line that also escaped the fall of Troy.

**The Migration to Illyria**

On the eastern shores of the Adriatic Sea, approximately halfway between the ruins of the Acropolis in Athens and those of the Colosseum in Rome, lie the ruins of a string of colonies the HELLENES established on Illyrian soil—in what is now the country of Albania. These HELLENES founded colonies not only on the Adriatic Coast, but also on the BLACK SEA, SICILY, NORTH AFRICA and other parts of the Mediterranean.

---

[181] http://familytreemaker.genealogy.com/users/m/i/n/Colleen-Miner/WEBSITE-0001/UHP-0692.html

[182] *Co-Incidences? Pointers to Our Heritage* by Brigadier G. Wilson

[183] From whom my Grandmother's line (the Crockers) in Newfoundland are said to have hailed.

The ancient ruins, hardly known to the general public today are, according to the experts, CLOSELY CONNECTED to the Classical Greek civilization. These colonies were organized in the typical Greek fashion and ran as autonomous political entities—enacting their own laws, organizing their own defense, and contracting accords with other city-states and foreign powers.

WHO founded these colonies, and WHERE did the colonizers come from?

The Roman poet, VIRGIL, tells us in his *Aeneid (Book III)* that this area of the Adriatic Coast was founded by A GROUP OF TROJAN EXILES who fled Troy after the Greek victory. The exiles were under the leadership of HELENUS who, in Greek legend, was a son of PRIAM and Hecuba, and twin brother of Cassandra. This HELENUS was, therefore, of the royal line of DARDANUS and a JUDAHITE!

The *Encyclopedia Britannica* notes that "after the capture of Troy, he (HELENUS), and his sister-in-law, Andromache, accompanied Neoptolemus (Pyrrhus) as captives to EPIRUS, where HELENUS persuaded him to settle. After the death of Neoptolemus, Helenus married Andromache and became ruler of the country. He was the reputed FOUNDER OF the cities of BUTHROTUM AND CHAONIA, named after a brother or a companion, who he had accidentally slain while hunting."[184]

Buthrotum (now known as BUTRINT) was established on a headland on the shores of a fine bay only 9 miles from the island of CORFU. This location fell within the land of the Caeones, an Illyrian tribe already settled there when Helenus arrived. The name BUTHROTUM means, "place abounding with cattle and grazing land" and was a perfect place for the new city.

---

[184] The *Encyclopedia Britannica,* 1943 ed. Vol. II, p. 393

Norman Hammond, in an article "Dashing Through Albania"[185] expresses the following: "Butrint (ancient BUTHROTUM) lies just south of Saranda on a rocky peninsula. Its legendary founding as a NEW TROY (was) by (according to Vergil) the TROJAN PRINCE HELENOS and Andromache, widow of HECTOR..."

Eventually the city of EPIDAMNUS was founded by the Hellenes (also known as DYRRAHION) and it is from this word that DURRES, as the city is known today, derives its name.

Encouraged by their expanding trade with the Illyrians, the Hellenes established a NEW COLONY to the south of Epidamnus, which they named APOLLONIA (now Pojan) in honor of the god Apollo. This new colony was built on a hill a mile or so from the coast and on the banks of the Vjosa River. Since the river was navigable from that point westward, Apollonia had an indirect outlet to the Adriatic Sea—thus keeping it within the trade routes.[186]

The old Trojan Royal House—of the line of DARDANUS—was restored to power after the Greek defeat at Troy in 1149 B.C. As noted by Herman L. Hoeh:

The full story of the royal Trojan House that returned to power in Troy has been preserved—of all places—in the records of the SPANISH HAPSBURGS! The reason? The Hapsburgs were, in fact, LINEAL DESCENDANTS OF THE HOUSE OF TROY![187]

---

[185] *Archaeology Magazine*, Jan./Feb., 1993 p. 76
[186] http://hope-of-israel.org/i000109a.htm
[187] A complete list of TROJAN RULERS after the fall of Troy in 1181 B.C. may be found in the original Spanish work by Bartholome Gutierrez entitled: *Historia del Estado Presente y Antiguo, de la mui Noble y mui Leal Ciudad de Xerez de la Frontera.* It was published in Xerez, Spain in 1886. *Compendium of World History*, Vol. II.

As we have already seen HELENUS, the son of Priam and Hecuba, fled Troy after the first Trojan War and settled in Illyria or Epirus. There Helenus and his followers founded the cities of Buthrotum and Chaonia. Through him the royal blood of Judah was preserved in the Near East.

During the Second Trojan War in 1149 B.C., the descendants of Helenus REGAINED CONTROL of Troy from the Greeks and restored the Royal House of DARDANUS to the city. The Spanish history by Gutierrez records the names of Helenus' descendants who controlled Troy and the surrounding region until the Third Trojan War in 677 B.C.:

At the fall of Troy in 677 B.C., members of the Trojan Royal Family, and most of the population of the city, fled to the NORTHERN SHORES OF THE BLACK SEA in Eastern Europe. For the next 234 years, in this region, the JEWISH TROJAN HOUSE provided eleven rulers over the people who fled Troy:

In 442 B.C. MARCOMIR, Antenor's son, ascended the throne; and in 441 B.C. he migrated out of Scythia and settled the people on the DANUBE. In 431 B.C. the Goths forced him, along with over 175,000 men, out of the area and into the country now called West Friesland, Gelders and Holland. Then, nine years later, Marcomir crossed the Rhine and conquered part of Gaul—MODERN FRANCE! He made his brother governor, and continued the gradual conquest of the entirety of Gaul.

Eventually this people became known as FRANKS or Franconians after a king called FRANCUS who reigned from 39 B.C.—11 B.C. The last King of the Franks—Marcomir V—won a great victory over the Romans at Cologne in A.D. 382 C.E. and recovered all the lands in the possession of the Romans, except Armoria or Little Brittany, in 390 C.E. However, he was slain in battle three years later and the Romans conquered the FRANKS—commanding them to refrain from electing kings over themselves. Instead, the Franks elected dukes to reign over them, starting with Genebald I in 328 C.E.

The fifth Duke of the East Franks, Pharamund (404 C.E.- 419 C.E.) is recognized by early historians as being the FIRST TRUE KING OF FRANCE. In 427 C.E. the succession passed to Clodion who founded the MEROVINGIAN DYNASTY.[188]

There is something VERY INTERESTING about this dynasty that bears explanation:

Its kings all wore LONG HAIR. They kept their kingly office until the Pope suggested to the East Franks (Germans) that they could gain the power over the Merovingians by cutting the king's hair. The last Merovingian was accordingly tonsured. The government thereafter passed to Pippin, father of the German king Charlemagne, who RESTORED the Roman Empire to The West in 800 C.E. The history of the Merovingians, WHO DESCENDED FROM THE TROJAN LINE AND THE HOUSE OF JUDAH, is made especially interesting in a book entitled *The Long-haired Kings* by J. M. Wallace-Hadrill. (See especially ch. 7.) The Merovingians recognized that though they came from Judah, THEY WERE NOT OF THE THRONE OF DAVID and would hold their power only so long as they kept a NAZARITE TRADITION—long hair—symbolizing their subjection to a Higher Power—God who rules supreme among men. (See Numbers 6.)[189]

---

[188] http://hope-of-israel.org/i000109a.htm
[189] *Compendium of World History*, Vol. II, p. 183

## Conclusion of the House of David

I have laid out before you the line of Israelite Kings from Saul down to the last king of the line of David—King Zedekiah. I left off with that chapter where we find Jeremiah still in the company of the king's daughters and the armed guards of the Milesian's forces in Egypt.

I have shown you the kingdoms of the line of Calcol and then of Dara, as well as both of the lines of Zerah, and his brother Phares, the sons of Judah. I have also shown you how these two lines of Calcol and Dara both migrated through time and the Trojan Royal Line to all the royal houses of Europe—especially the royal line in Ireland, Scotland and then England.

There is a wealth of information that you can explore on this subject even more in depth should you decide to. I have tried to be as brief as possible. Now, let me wrap this chapter up and show you how Jeremiah ties in with all of this.

> Lands of Iberia: The land of Spain and Portugal, it should be mentioned, is also known as the Iberian Peninsula. Notes Microsoft Encarta: "Iberia, ancient name for both the Iberian Peninsula and the country lying between the Greater Caucasus and Armenia, approximately co-extensive with present-day Georgia (which is south of Russia)"[190]
>
> *Faiths of Man: Encyclopedia of Religions*[191] states: "The Iberes of the Caucasus were Georgians... In Sicily, the Iberes were on the west... Spain was Iberia... (And the Roman historian) Tacitus speaks of Iberes in the west of England (in Cornwall), who may have come from Spain."[192]

---

[190] *Iberia, Microsoft Encarta,* 1994
[191] http://books.google.com/books/about/Faiths_of_Man.html?id=XQbXAAAAMAAJ
[192] *Faiths of Man: Encyclopedia of Religions,* 1964, Vol. 2, p. 259

Why would Iberia be the name of places and people so far removed from each other? As I have demonstrated to you in Chapter One and now in this chapter, it is because the Israelites—the Hebrews—migrated through both Spain and the Caucasus and also went to Britain! Iber is nearly identical to the name of Abraham's ancestor Eber or Heber, father of the Hebrews.

> *14 And Shelaḥ lived thirty years, and brought forth Ěḇer. 15 And after he brought forth Ěḇer, Shelaḥ lived four hundred and three years, and brought forth sons and daughters. 16 And Ěḇer lived thirty-four years, and brought forth Pelegˉ.* (Genesis 11:14-16)

Furthermore, the name Hebrew appears to have taken on an added meaning. McClintock & Strong's *Cyclopaedia of Biblical, Theological and Ecclesiastical Literature* adds that the word came to mean: "one of the other side, i.e… immigrant."[193]

Bible Translator, Ferrar Fenton, noted that in 1 Samuel 4:6:

> Eberim, if translated, means 'Colonists'—a fit term to be used by the Philistines of the Israelites, who were really colonists in Palestine.

And it would be a fit term for Israelite colonists in other lands to apply to themselves. Considering the Hebrew migration through Spain, the name of the River Ebro situated there appears to be of the same origin. And the same may go for Ireland—or at least one of its earlier names. The word Ireland originates from Eire-land—Eire being the nation's Gaelic name. Traditionally, Ireland has also been called Erin. The Romans called it Hibernia or Ivernia. Harvard Professor, Barry Fell wrote:

> One of the ancient names of Ireland is Ibheriu, pronounced as Iveriu, a fact that suggests the word is derived from a still-earlier pronunciation, Iberiu. Now this is very interesting,

---

[193] *Cyclopaedia of Biblical, Theological and Ecclesiastical Literature* by James Strong & John McClintock, Vol. 4, p. 128

for the Gaelic histories assert that the ancestors of the Gaels came to Ireland from Iberia, the old name of Spain. Could Iberiu be the same as Iberia, the name of the older homeland having been transferred to the younger? Many people, including some linguists, think this may well be the case.[194]

The connection between Iveriu and Hebrew is even stronger when we realize that the Hebrew word for "Hebrew" is actually pronounced Ivri. However, it should be noted that while Iber is a likely root for Iberiu and the Roman names Hibernia and Ivernia, it is possible that the particular names Erin and Eire originated from another source.

Let us then consider the influx into Ireland of people from the Iberian Peninsula. Northwest Spain is called Galicia, apparently after the Gaels. Likewise, Portugal, as I explained earlier, is "Port of the Gaels."

Thomas Moore, in *The History of Ireland*, states:

> In process of time, the Tuatha-de-Danaan (in Ireland) were themselves dispossessed of their sway; a successful invasion from the coast of Spain having put an end to the Danaanian Dynasty, and transferred the scepter into the hands of that Milesian or Scotic race, which through so long a series of succeeding ages, supplied Ireland with her kings. This celebrated colony, though coming directly from Spain, was originally; we are told, of Scythic race.[195]

The Gaels (or Celts) and Scythians were, by and large, Israelites— just like the Danaans. Who then were the Milesians? Note that the Scythians from Spain were also known as Milesians—a recurrent name throughout the Irish annals.

---

[194] *America B.C.: Ancient Settlers In the New World* by Barry Fell, 1976, p. 43
[195] *The History of Ireland* by Thomas Moore, 1837, Vol. 1, p. 61

Peter Berresford Ellis, one of the foremost Celtic scholars now writing, states in his 2002 book, *Erin's Blood Royal: The Gaelic Noble Dynasties of Ireland*:

> The indigenous Gaelic aristocracy of Ireland is, without doubt, the most ancient in Europe... The Irish royal houses have genealogies... tracing their descent, generation by generation, from the sons of Golamh, otherwise known as Milesius or Mile Easpain (soldier of Spain), who, according to tradition, invaded Ireland at the end of the second millennium B.C. (a timeframe which is problematic, as we will see). He is regarded as the progenitor of the Gaels.[196]

Ellis thus sees the name Milesius as deriving from a root that means, "soldier," as the Latin word 'miles," the origin of our word military. Yet, as you saw earlier, the term 'Milesian' is normally used to designate the people of Miletus in Western Asia Minor (now Western Turkey).

According to the *Encyclopaedia Britannica*:

> The Greek city traced its foundation to Neleus and his followers from Pylos.[197]

> The Mycenaean kingdom of Pylos was conquered by Neleus, and thereafter was ruled by his youngest son, Nestor.[198]

The city of Pylos was located on the Southwest Coast of Greece on the Ionian Sea. Ionian Greeks from this area colonized throughout the Mediterranean.

Historian, Will Durant explains in his acclaimed work, *The Story of Civilization*:

---

[196] *Erin's Blood Royal-The Gaelic Noble Dynasties of Ireland* by Peter Berresford Ellis, 2002, p. 3
[197] *Miletus, Encyclopaedia Britannica*, 1985, Vol. 8, p. 125
[198] *Pylos, Baedeker's Greece*, 1995, p. 417

> There is nothing more vital in the history of the Greeks than their rapid spread throughout the Mediterranean… The migration followed five main lines—Aeolian, Ionian, Dorian, Euxine, Italian… The second line (the Ionian line) took its start in the Peloponnesus (Southern Greece), whence thousands of Mycenaeans and Achaeans (whom Homer identified with the Danaans) fled… "Some of them settled in Attica (the region of Athens), some in Euboea (the large island northeast of Athens); many of them moved out into the Cyclades (islands of the Aegean Sea between Greece and Turkey), ventured across the Aegean, and established in Western Asia Minor (Turkey) the twelve cities of the Ionian Dodecapolis (including Miletus)… The fifth line moved westward to what the Greeks called the Ionian Isles, thence across to Italy and Sicily, and finally to Gaul (France) and Spain…One by one these colonies took form, until Greece was no longer the narrow peninsula of Homeric days, but a strangely loose association of independent cities scattered from Africa to Thrace (in northern Greece) and from Gibraltar (in Southern Spain) to the eastern end of the Black Sea.[199]

And this is exactly what I have shown you with regard to tracing the lines of Calchol, Dara and the tribe of Dan at Peloponnesian where the city of Pylos is found.

It should not come as a surprise then that one would find the name 'Milesians' in *both* ancient Turkey and Spain since these were undoubtedly related peoples. This becomes even more likely when we realize the scope of influence of Miletus itself.

Durant reports:

> Miletus, southernmost of the Ionian Twelve, was, in the sixth century (B.C.), the richest city in the Greek world. The site had been inhabited by Carians from Minoan days and when, about 1000 B.C., the Ionians came there from Attica (the region of Athens), they found the old Aegean culture (of

---

[199] *The Story of Civilization* by Will Durant, Vol. 2, pp. 127-129

nearby ancient Troy)… waiting to serve as the advanced starting point of their civilization…:"Taking a lesson from the Phoenicians and gradually bettering their instruction, Ionian merchants established colonies as trading posts in Egypt, Italy, the Propontis (Sea of Marmara between Istanbul and the site of ancient Troy), and the Euxine (Black Sea). Miletus *alone* had eighty such colonies, sixty of them in the north.[200]

Surely, then, the Milesians of Spain were from Miletus or any of its many colonies. But who were these people? They hailed from Mycenaean Greece, which was predominantly Danite. Yet Danites, it should be realized, were not the only Israelites in Southern Greece. Indeed, as I have been showing you, many inhabitants of Mycenaean Greece—and of ancient Troy—were of the Tribe of Judah, which seems to have migrated through Crete. Indeed, it appears that kings descended from Judah's son Zerah, ruled them. Zerah, the infant who had the scarlet thread placed on his wrist when he stuck his hand out of the womb before Phares was born. From this descent emerged two main royal Zarhite lines—the Trojan Royal House, from which most of European royalty is surprisingly descended, and the Athenian Royal House, which became the royal line of Miletus. Milesius or Miledh, the father of Ireland's Milesian Dynasty from Spain—also called Golamh or Gathelus—is referred to as either the son of Nel (also Niul or Neolus) or the son of Cecrops, the founder of Athens in Greek Mythology.

This is; in fact, *proof positive* that Ireland's traditional histories link its Milesians to those of the Aegean. For besides the mention of Cecrops, we have already seen that the Milesians of Asia Minor traced their descent from Neleus, the ruler of Mycenaean Pylos on the Ionian Sea (who, as with other Mycenaean rulers, was likely of Jewish descent). Therefore, Milesius was probably not the actual name of the founder of the Milesian Dynasty in Ireland. Rather, the name Milesius or Miledh itself meant Milesian (one from Miletus). Thus, it most likely did not *just* mean "soldier." Likewise, the name Golamh and its variants are not personal names. Rather, they simply denote nationality, coming from

---

[200] *The Story of Civilization* by Will Durant, Vol. 2, pp. 134-135

the same origin as Gaul and Gael. These names denote "wandering Israelites"—as did the term Scythian.[201]

Interestingly, as noted elsewhere, Milesius was said to descend from the king of Scythia—namely one Feinius Farsaidh. But this may not be an actual personal name either.

> Feinius appears to be the same word as Feni, a name for Ireland's earliest Celtic inhabitants.[202]

These were probably the Phoenicians—many of whom were Israelites. Continuing on, the high kings of Ireland:

> "…claimed their descent from the two sons of Milesius, Eremon and Eber Fionn, who were progenitors of the Gaels in Ireland and who divided Ireland between them—Eremon ruling in the north and Eber Fionn in the south."[203]

Again, these may not have been personal names. The meaning of Eremon or Heremon, may have been a real name or at least a title. However, Eber Fionn or Eber Finn may simply denote "Hebrew Phoenician." Whatever the case may be, the most likely conclusion regarding the identity of the Milesian invaders of Ireland is that they were Israelites—yet not just any Israelites, but Zarhite Jewish Royalty from Miletus.

I last talked to you about Jeremiah being in the company of Ionian and Carian forces at Tahpanhes and I quoted Durant who said these Grecians were also called Milesians. Let me remind you of this quote:

> Psamtik (Pharaoh Psammetichus I, founder of Egypt's 26th dynasty of which Hophra was the fourth king) guarded the

---

[201] *Linguistic Links: What's In A Name?*, p. 30 http://www.ucg.org/booklet/united-states-and-britain-bible-prophecy/mysterious-scythians-burst-history/linguistic-links/

[202] *Erin's Blood Royal-The Gaelic Noble Dynasties of Ireland* by Peter Berresford Ellis, 2002, p. 228

[203] *Erin's Blood Royal-The Gaelic Noble Dynasties of Ireland* by Peter Berresford Ellis, 2002, p. 5

frontiers of Egypt with three strong garrisons, placing the Ionian and Carian mercenaries especially at the Pelusian Daphnae... in the northeast, from which quarter the most formidable enemies were likely to appear." (p. 40) These were Greek forces primarily from the west coast of Asia Minor (modern Turkey). "Ionian" and "Carian" primarily designated the Greek city of Miletus there: "Within Egypt itself, normally hostile to any foreign settlement, the Greeks gained a foothold"... About 650 (B.C.) the Milesians (from Miletus) opened a 'factory,' or trading post, at Naucratis on the Canopic branch of the Nile. Pharaoh Psamtik I tolerated them because they made good mercenaries, while their commerce provided rich prey for his collectors of customs revenues.[204]

Now that you know who the Milesians were, where they went and the lands they settled, we can now pick up with Jeremiah in the year 570 B.C. where we left off before I explained to you who all these people are.

May I remind you once again about the clue that is given us of where Jeremiah was to go? He had earlier prophesied that, from his time forward, David would *always* have an heir on the throne.

> 17 *"For thus said יהוה, 'For Dawiḏ there is not to cease a man to sit on the throne of the house of Yisra'ěl.'"* (Jeremiah 33:17)

This verse is *crucial* to understanding the whole of the matter. Read it again. Notice—it does *not* say Judah, but rather the House of Israel, which had gone into captivity around 150 years before. So from Jeremiah's time on, David would never lack a descendant to reign over Israel—which again, is *not synonymous* with Judah.

Through Ezekiel the Prophet, Yehovah fills us in with more details. (As I showed you in the Introduction to Daniel, Ezekiel began his prophecies *after* going into captivity, which was *before* Jeremiah had finished his prophesying in Jerusalem). Prior to Jerusalem's fall, he posed

---

[204] *The Story of Civilization* by Will Durant, Vol. 2: *The Life of Greece*, 1966, p. 173

a riddle to the House of Israel (Ezekiel 17:2)—again, not Judah—which He explained afterward. If you stop and think about it, the prophecies Yehovah gave to Ezekiel and to Jeremiah would not have been known by everyone at that time nor understood and most likely not by each of them. Those things shared with and spoken through them to those who had ears to hear were for us today to come to grips with and understand.

> *3 And you shall say, "Thus said the Master יהוה, 'The great eagle with large wings of long pinions, covered with feathers of various colors, came to Leḇanon and took the top of the cedar. 4 He plucked off the topmost of its young twigs and brought it to a land of traders. In a city of merchants he placed it. 5 He also took some of the seed of the land and planted it in a field for seed. He took it by many waters, set it like a willow tree. 6 So it grew and became a low, spreading vine. Its branches turned toward him, and its roots were under it. And it became a vine, and brought forth branches, and sent out shoots. 7 And there was another great eagle with large wings and many feathers. And see, this vine bent its roots toward him, and stretched its branches toward him, to water it, away from the beds where it was planted. 8 It was planted in a good field by many waters, to bring forth branches, and to bear fruit, to be a splendid vine.'"*
> *9 "Say, Thus said the Master יהוה, 'Is it going to thrive? Is he not going to pull up its roots, and cut off its fruit, and let it wither? All of its sprouting leaves wither, without great power or many people, to pluck it up by its roots. 10 See, it is planted, is it going to thrive? Would it not utterly wither when the east wind touches it—wither in the beds where it grows?'"* (Ezekiel 17:3-10)

> *11 And the word of יהוה came to me, saying, 12 "Please say to the rebellious house, 'Do you not know what these mean?' Say, 'See, the sovereign of Baḇel went to Yerushalayim and took its sovereign and heads, and brought them with him to Baḇel. 13 And he took one of the royal seed, and made a covenant with him, and put him under oath. And he took away the mighty of the land, 14 so that the reign would be*

*brought low and not lift itself up, but guard his covenant, that it might stand. 15 But he rebelled against him by sending his messengers to Mitsrayim, to give him horses and many people. Shall he thrive? Shall he escape who is doing these? And shall he break a covenant and still escape?" 16 "As I live," declares the Master יהוה, "in the place where the sovereign dwells who set him up to reign, whose oath he despised and whose covenant he broke, with him in the midst of Baḇel he shall die! 17 And Pharaoh with his great army and great company is not going to help him in battle, when they heap up a siege mound and build a wall to cut off many beings. 18 And he despised the oath by breaking the covenant. And see, he has given his hand and he has done all this, he is not going to escape." 19 Therefore, thus said the Master יהוה, "As I live, My oath which he has despised, and My covenant which he has broken, shall I not put it on his own head? 20 And I shall spread My net over him, and he shall be taken in My snare. And I shall bring him to Baḇel and enter into judgment with him there for the trespass which he committed against Me, 21 and all his fugitives with all his bands fall by the sword, and those who are left be scattered to every wind. And you shall know that I, יהוה, have spoken." 22 Thus said the Master יהוה, "And I shall take of the top of the highest cedar and set it out. And I Myself shall pluck off a tender one from the topmost of its young twigs, and plant it on a high and lofty mountain. 23 On the mountain height of Yisra'ěl I plant it. And it shall bring forth branches, and bear fruit, and become a big cedar. And under it shall dwell birds of every sort, in the shadow of its branches they shall dwell. 24 And all the trees of the field shall know that I, יהוה, have brought down the high tree and exalted the low tree, dried up the green tree and made the dry tree flourish. I, יהוה, have spoken and shall do it."* (Ezekiel 17:11-24)

"A great eagle... came to Lebanon and took from the cedar the highest branch" (v. 3). Meaning: "The king of Babylon went to Jerusalem and took its kings and princes" (v. 12). Then: "He cropped off the top of his young twigs" (v. 4, KJV). Meaning: "And he took of the king's offspring" (v. 13). Having explained these symbols, Yehovah, through Ezekiel, gave the following clear parable: "I will take also (a sprig, NRSV) of the highest branches (Zedekiah and princes) of the high cedar (Judah) and set it out. I will crop off from the topmost of its young twigs (Zedekiah's children) a tender one (female), and will plant it on a high and prominent mountain (a great kingdom). On the mountain height (top of the kingdom—the throne) of Israel (not Judah!) I will plant it; and it will bring forth boughs, and bear fruit, and be a majestic cedar. Under it will dwell birds of every sort (all manner of peoples)... And all the trees of the field (nations of the earth) shall know that I, Yehovah, have brought down the high tree (Judah) and exalted the low tree (Israel)" (vv. 22-24). Here, then, is what the latter part of Jeremiah's commission was all about. Remarkably, he must have been responsible for transplanting the throne of David to Israel by taking a daughter of King Zedekiah to the 10 Lost Tribes. Yet where did the Israelites live at this time?

In my Introduction and in Chapter One, I showed you that of those who were captured, the Tribe of Dan was *not* one of them. Once the tribes had settled in the land, the Tribe of Dan became known as Mariners and had been sailing the seas with the Phoenicians. Moreover, as you have just read, some of them also left Egypt before the Exodus and had settled in parts of what is now called Greece.

As sailors they had been setting up colonies around the world. In the days of King David it is said they would take up to three years to make one of their voyages and finally return home.[205] King David even employed them to supply his kingdom with the wealth of the world of which Solomon *also* was blessed. The Davidic Kingdom had colonies around the world and the Phoenicians and the Tribe of Dan were the sailors.[206]

It is then no surprise to realize that the Tribe of Dan and some Israelites migrated prior to the Assyrian captivity. The Danites, Mariners in their own right and later, more so with the Phoenicians, sailed far

---

[205] http://stevenmcollins.com/html/Bk1%20ch6%20Phoenician%20Maritime%20Skills%20pp206-232-1.html
[206] http://www.giveshare.org/israel/steve-collins-books.html

and wide over the seas. As you have seen, some settled in Greece and became known as the Danaans. Interestingly, all early histories of Ireland mention the arrival there of people from Greece called the Tuatha de Danaan. While some today equate them with ancient demigods or mythical fairy folk, they were definitely an authentic and genuinely historical people. The word "tuath" simply means "tribe." Notice: "Old Irish 'tuath,' Welsh 'tud' (people, country), Breton 'tud' (people) and Gaulish 'teuta' (tribe) all come from common Celtic 'towta,' from the Indo-European word 'teuta' (tribe)."[207]

Tuatha de Danaan is thus the tribe of Danaan. The *Annals of Ireland* report:

> The Dan'ans were a highly civilized people, well skilled in architecture and other arts from their long residence in Greece, and their intercourse with the Phoenicians. Their first appearance in Ireland was 1200 B.C., or 85 years after the great victory of Deborah.

The Tuatha de Danaan, then, must be synonymous with the Danaans of Greece and thus, the Israelite Tribe of Dan. This is not at all farfetched. Indeed, it is widely accepted that the Phoenicians established trading outposts or colonies as far away as the British Isles:

> The Phoenicians are believed to have played an important part in spreading the early bronze culture by their trade in tin, which their ships brought to the Eastern Mediterranean from Great Britain and Spain at least as early as 1100 B.C.[208]

Yet what many often fail to realize is that the ancient maritime power designated as "Phoenicia" was actually an alliance between the city-states of Tyre and Sidon and the nation of Israel—in which Israel was the senior partner. The *Universal Jewish Encyclopedia* says:

---

[207] *Focal an Lae: The Word of the Day In Irish* by Dennis King, online at: www.lincolnu.edu/~focal/backinst/focal114.htm

[208] *Industries, Extraction and Processing, Encyclopaedia Britannica, Macropaedia*, Vol. 21, 1985, p. 424

> In the time of Solomon, Phoenicians, accompanied by Hebrews, reached as far as England... England was therefore known to the Israelites and they may have sought a refuge there after the fall of their kingdom.[209]

> King Solomon, we are told in Scripture, "had a fleet of ships of Tarshish at sea with the fleet of Hiram (the Phoenician King of Tyre)."

> *22 For the sovereign had ships of Tarshish at sea with the fleet of Ḥiram. Once every three years the ships of Tarshish came bringing gold, and silver, ivory, and apes, and baboons. 23 And Sovereign Shelomoh was greater than any of the sovereigns of the earth in riches and wisdom.* (1 Kings 10:22-23)

Tarshish was an ancient port of Southern Spain, also known as Tartessus. It was evidently named after Tarshish, the son of Javan (Genesis 10:4)—Javan (or Yavan) being the name for Greece in the Old Testament. As an early Ionian Greek settlement, it was actually an Israelite-Phoenician colony.

The Trojans were forced out of the Aegean region through a series of national conflicts—one of which is presented to us in the famous Trojan War of Homer's *Iliad*, which occurred around 1200 B.C. Some refugees seem to have migrated north into Europe via the Black Sea. Others from Troy migrated south to the area of Miletus.[210]

And still other Trojans appear to have traveled west—even all the way to Spain and France, some of them eventually migrating to Britain as I have shown you by following Brutus. And we know that the Milesians also migrated to Spain from the Eastern Mediterranean at a later time—ending up in Ireland. It is amazing that two royal lines from Zerah—the Trojan Dynasty and the Athenian-Milesian Dynasty—both passed through the Iberian Peninsula. Arriving here, these settlers sailed up the Ebro River and, upon its banks, founded the

---

[209] *The Universal Jewish Encyclopedia*, Vol. 1, p. 316
[210] *The World of the Bible* by Roberta Harris, 1995, Map on p. 63

city of Saragossa—which some have identified as Hebrew Zerah-gaza, meaning "stronghold of Zerah."

Strengthening the identification with Zerah is the fact that the Milesian rulers who assumed the Irish throne were known as the people of the "Red Hand." In fact, the Red Hand appears even today on the official flag of Northern Ireland and on the coat-of-arms of many an Irish and Scottish clan.

This "ancient regional emblem (is known as) the Blood-red Right Hand of Ulster."[211] Ulster, being the Northern Province of Ireland through which the high kingship was later transferred to Scotland.

It is reported that Ulster's emblem prior to the division of Ireland in 1920, when most of Ulster became the British state of Northern Ireland, was a blood-red hand encircled by a scarlet cord. Consider: A hand, red with blood—perhaps the blood of birth—encircled by a scarlet cord. Surely this is no mere coincidence! According to a Northern Irish newspaper, "…one tradition has it… that the Red Hand goes back to biblical times; when the twin sons were being born to Judah."[212]

Indeed, the scarlet thread tied around Zerah's hand would seem rather likely to be the origin of this emblem. Scholar Peter Ellis, however, sees hints for the origins of the Ulster emblem in various Indo-European words for king. "The terminology is related—the Irish Ri(gh) compared to the Gaelish Celtic Rix, the Latin Rex and the Sanskrit Rajan (Hindi = raj). Certainly the English king from the Gothic Kunnings has no relationship, but a surprising harking back to the concept appears in the English words 'rich' and 'reach.' The ancient Indo-European concept was that a king reached forth his hand to protect his people. Also in Old Irish, for example, rige was not only the concept for kingship but also the word for the act of reaching… The Ui Neill's ancient symbol of the Red Hand doubtless stems from this concept" (p. 25). Yet could it not be that the very idea of one reaching forth for kingship came from the story of Zerah reaching forth from the womb—especially considering that

---

[211] *The Observer's Book of Flags* by Idrisyn Evans, 1959, 1975, p. 28
[212] *Did A Lost Tribe of Israel Land At Carrickfergus?* by David Hume, *Larne Times*, Dec. 24th, 1986

the Israelites, under Zarhite leadership, were scattered across, and had a major influence over, the entire Indo-European geographical region?

Regarding the story of Zerah, the *Larne Times* article[213] continues: "The Red Hand of Ulster is thus claimed in some circles to be symbolic of this event, and also considered symbolic is the fact that the ancient Knights of Ulster were the most distinguished in the history of the island. They were known as the Knights of the Red Branch." Ellis says: "There are several orders of elite warrior corps mentioned in the sagas and chronicles of ancient Ireland. Perhaps the best known were the Ulster Red Branch Knights, or the Craobh Radh. They emerge in the Ulster Cycle of Myths, especially in the famous epic, *Tain Bo Cualigne* (Cattle Raid of Cooley), which has been compared with the Greek *Iliad*. Its date of origin is uncertain. Scholars have identified it as having been handed down in oral form probably from the La Tene period, from about 500 B.C." (p. 338). Indeed, when viewed in conjunction with the Red Hand, might not the Red Branch represent the Zerah branch of Judah's family? This, then, provides us with even more reason to believe that the Milesian royal line of Ireland originated with Judah's son Zerah."

I have now provided you with a plausible explanation as to how Yehovah's promise of the scepter being retained by Judah was fulfilled—through the line of Zerah. Judah's Zarhite heirs, through Trojan and Milesian descent, would reign over the nations of Europe—particularly over Israel in the British Isles, as the high kingly line of Ireland would eventually be transferred to Scotland and later, to England.

The heyday of Ephraim's national greatness came during the British Empire—as mentioned earlier, the largest empire in the history of the world. David's descendants, as we've seen, were to rule over Israel and become the "highest of the kings of the earth."

> 25 *"And I shall set his hand on the sea, and his right hand on the rivers... 27 I also appoint him first-born, Highest of the sovereigns of the earth."* (Psalm 89:25, 27)

---

[213] The *"Larne Times"* of N. Ireland, Dec. 24th, 1986

Yehovah further said of David's Dynasty, "I will set his hand (or authority) also in the sea" (v. 25). This is very much like the unofficial anthem of the British people:

> When Britain first, at Heaven's command,
> Arose from out the azure main,
> This was the charter of her land,
> And guardian angels sung the strain:
> Rule, Britannia! Britannia rules the waves!
> Britons never shall be slaves.[214]

Indeed, no nation has ruled the sea—nor the land for that matter—as has Great Britain. Clearly, the Monarchy of David must be one and the same with the Monarchy of Britain. Following the primary line of descent of the British throne back to the time of Jeremiah leads us to Ireland. Yehovah, of course, knew that the Irish royal line of Jeremiah's day would eventually become the British Monarchy. Logically, then, that is where He would have directed the steps of Jeremiah with at least *one of* Zedekiah's daughters in tow—to marry her into the royal line of Zerah and thereby perpetuate the throne of David.

> 26 "...thus said the Master יהוה, 'Remove the turban, and take off the crown! This shall not remain! Exalt the humble, and humble the exalted. 27 Overthrown, overthrown, I make it overthrown! It shall be no longer, until He comes to whom it rightly belongs—and I shall give it!'" (Ezekiel 21:26-27)

Yehovah declared that Zedekiah was to "remove the turban and take off the crown: This shall not be the same (a change or transfer was occurring); exalt him that is low (the Zarhite ruler in Israel) and abase him that is high (Zedekiah of the line of Perez). I will overturn, overturn, overturn it (the crown, that is, the throne); and it shall be no more (overturned) until HE come whose right it is; and I will give it to HIM (Yehshua)" (KJV). Notice that the final

---

[214] James Thomson (1700–1748), British poet, and David Mallet (1705?-1765). *A Masque: Rule Brittania* (Vol. 1. pp. 1–6) http://www.amazon.com/The-Masque-Alfred-David-Mallet/dp/B00000E6WE

"overturned" was added in parentheses for the sake of clarity. Some see this verse as a prophecy of the overthrow of the crown—that it would "be no more" (meaning 'no longer exist') until Yehshua came to claim it. Yet, this cannot be the meaning of this prophecy or Yehovah would be breaking His unbreakable promise to David of an unbreakable dynasty. So the overturning must refer to removing the throne from one nation and raising it up in another. And the mentioning of overturn three times would certainly seem to be saying that such overturning would occur three times—that three times the throne would be transferred to another nation and that it wouldn't be transferred again until Messiah's coming in power and glory to take it over.

When was the last time a reference was given to another country's monarchy being transplanted into the throne's present location in England? The answer is 1603 C.E., when King James VI of Scotland became King James I of Great Britain (the one who commissioned the King James Bible).[215] This is obviously the last overturn to have taken place. Because of it, today's British monarchs are of royal Scottish descent.

Prior to that, was another country's throne ever transplanted into Scotland's? Yes. The throne of the Scoti (as the Irish were anciently called) was moved from Ireland into Southwest Scotland in the late 5th-century—their kingdom of Dalriada in that area, centered at Iona (a name perhaps related to Ionia of Greece), eventually growing to envelop what is now Scotland. This was clearly the previous overturn—which is why Scotland's Monarchy, which became Britain's Monarchy, was actually *Irish*.

Now, since these were the *last* two overturns of three, there can only have been one other—*the first*. And that first overturn had to have been the transfer of the throne from

---

[215] Footnote for my own Family. The Crocker Family comes from this line. Sophie Crocker was my Grandmother on my Mom's side.

Judah. Thus it should be clear that this transfer must have been from Judah to Ireland. Had the throne been transferred from Judah to some other country before later being reestablished in Ireland, that would add a fourth overturn—when Scripture appears to allow for only three. By simple deduction, the three overturns must have been: 1) Judah to Ireland, 2) Ireland to Scotland, 3) Scotland to England.

It should be mentioned, however, that in the first overturn it is possible that the daughter of Zedekiah married into the Milesian Zerah line in Spain or elsewhere around the time it was in the process of assuming control over Ireland. This would not be adding another overturn from Spain to Ireland, as it would all be part of the *same* overturn. Whether or not this happened, however, is wholly dependent on exactly when the Milesians from Spain took over Ireland, which is not entirely clear. They may have already become established in Ireland before Jeremiah's journey—though perhaps still maintaining control over part of Spain when he arrived. Again, however, it is possible that Zedekiah's daughter and Jeremiah actually accompanied the Milesians in their invasion of Ireland from Spain.

Irish tradition lends support to what happened. Let's continue further in the *Larne Times* article quoted earlier:

Many centuries ago three people arrived on the shore at what is today Carrickfergus (Northern Ireland). It was around 582 B.C. (no doubt a rough date, but essentially after Babylon destroyed Jerusalem), and the three were an aged man called Ollam Fodhla (the Lawgiver), his secretary, and a beautiful princess called Tamar. With them they brought a large, rough stone.[216]

Jerusalem fell in 586 B.C., so 582 B.C. would be four years later and entirely consistent with the possibility of when they arrived.

---

[216] The "*Larne Times*" of N. Ireland, Dec. 24th, 1986 (You can also search online for the Stone of Scone)

According to Charles O'Conor:

> "Ollam Fola is celebrated in ancient history as a sage and legislator, eminent for learning, wisdom and excellent institutions; and his historic fame has been recognized by placing his medallion in basso relievo (bass relief) with those of Moses, and other great legislators, in the interior of the Dome of the Four Courts in Dublin."[217]

Irish Historian, Thomas Moore says that of the storied figures of the early

> "dim period of Irish history... the Royal Sage, Ollamh Fodhla, is almost the only one who, from the strong light of tradition thrown round him, stands out as being of historical substance and truth. It would serve to illustrate the nature and extent of the evidence with which the world is sometimes satisfied, to collect together the various celebrated names which are received as authentic, on the strength of tradition alone; and few, perhaps, could claim a more virtual title to this privilege than the great legislator of the Irish, Ollamh Fodhla."[218]

Ollam Fodhla's laws bear a striking resemblance to the Ten Commandments and other Hebrew statutes.

Interestingly, Ollam can be read in the Hebrew language as "ancient" or "secret"[219] —perhaps indicating a possessor of secret knowledge (Milner, p. 12). Fodhla or Fola can be understood in Hebrew to mean

---

[217] *The Annals of the Kingdom of Ireland* by Charles O'Conor of Belanagare's notes (1826) on *The Annals of the Kingdom of Ireland* by the Four Masters p. 227

[218] *The History of Ireland from the Earliest Kings of That Realm Down to Its Last Chief: Part One* by Thomas Moore, p. 86

[219] *Hebrew and Chaldee Dictionary* by James Strong; *Strong's Exhaustive Concordance of the Bible* by Abingdon, Strong's Hebrew No. 5769; *Enhanced Strong's Lexicon*, Logos Software, Strong's Hebrew No.'s 5769, 5956

"wonderful"[220] or in Celtic as "revealer" (Milner, p. 12). All of these meanings considered together seem to indicate a Hebrew prophet.

In Old Gaelic, ollamh designated "the highest qualification of learning and (is) now the modern Irish word for professor" (Ellis, p. 4). It appears that Ollam Fodhla founded a royal school or university within the national palace—referred to in the Chronicles of Eri as Mur Olamain, perhaps translatable as "House of the Prophets."

The individual mentioned above as Ollam's secretary is sometimes referred to as Simon Breck, Brach or Berach[221]—though there is dispute over his being a contemporary of Ollam. And Tamar is also a biblical name (denoting three women in Scripture, all in the lineage of David), which means, "palm"[222] in Hebrew. The Tamar of Ireland is also at times, it appears, referred to in Irish histories and poems as Tea (Hebrew "wanderer"[223]) and Tephi (Hebrew "timbrel"[224]—or a Hebrew variant meaning "a diminutive of affection, or... the beauty and fragrance of fruit" Milner, p. 19).

The *Larne Times* article states, "According to some religious scholars, the aged man who landed at Carrick many centuries ago was the Prophet Jeremiah."[225]

There is a strong tradition in Ireland to support this notion. That would seem to make Simon Breck out to be Jeremiah's scribe, Baruch (Berekh in Palaeo-Hebrew), who perhaps was also named Simeon. In any case, both names are certainly Hebrew. Tamar or Tea-Tephi would be Zedekiah's daughter. As the same article further reports, the tradition also states:

---

[220] *Enhanced Strong's Lexicon*, Strong's Hebrew No. 6381
[221] A biblical name meaning "bless" or "kneel," Strong's Hebrew No.'s 1263, 1288
[222] *Hebrew and Chaldee Dictionary* by James Strong; *Strong's Exhaustive Concordance of the Bible* by Abingdon, Strong's Hebrew No.'s 8558, 8559
[223] *Hebrew and Chaldee Dictionary* by James Strong; *Strong's Exhaustive Concordance of the Bible* by Abingdon, Strong's Hebrew No. 8582
[224] *Hebrew and Chaldee Dictionary* by James Strong; *Strong's Exhaustive Concordance of the Bible* by Abingdon, Strong's Hebrew No. 8596
[225] The "*Larne Times*" of N. Ireland, Dec. 24th, 1986

Princess Tamar married the High King of Ireland and... all the kings of Ireland and Scotland are descended from their royal line.[226]

The name of the ancient seat of the high kings of Ireland just northwest of Dublin is Tara. Yet it should be mentioned that some believe the name Tara is derived from the Hebrew Torah, or "law"—Tara being the seat of the Law perhaps brought about by Jeremiah. Says Gerber:

> Teamhair is the Irish for her name—mutated, through usage, to 'Tara.'[227]

Notice this from one of the Irish chronicles:

> Soon after this conquest made by the sons of Miletus their kinsmen and friends, they divided the whole kingdom among themselves in manner as followeth. But first, before they landed on this land, Tea, the... wife of Heremon, desired one request of her said husband and kinsmen, which they accordingly granted, which was, that the place she should most like of in the kingdom, should be, for ever after, the principal seat of her posterity to dwell in; and upon their landing she chose Leitrim, which is since that time called Tara, and which she caused to be called Tea-mur—the house, palace, or town of Tephi.[228]

The name of the high king she married is sometimes given as Heremon, Eremon, Erimionn or something similar and sometimes as Eochaidh—the latter being not a name but simply the word for "prince."

If Ollam Fodhla was indeed Jeremiah, his identification as a king is fairly easy to reconcile. It could have resulted from his appearing to be the father or grandfather of the eastern princess he brought with him—or, even more likely, confusion over his being a great lawgiver.

---

[226] The *"Larne Times"* of N. Ireland, Dec. 24th, 1986
[227] *Stone of Destiny* by Pat Gerber, p. 49
[228] *Annals of Clonmacnoise* by Conell MacGeoghegan (a translation), 1627, p. 27

Says Gerber in *Stone of Destiny*:

> Ollam Fodhla was the first king to hold the Fes, or Parliament of Tara, and the first to ordain district chiefs in Ireland.[229]

Remember that in Israel the prophet was Yehovah's representative to the king. And in ancient Ireland:

> "an ollamh was treated as of princely rank. An ollamh of law and poetry was even considered the equal of a king at the court; he, or she, for both were equal under the law, could speak even before the king at a council and give advice."[230]

If Jeremiah wielded this kind of authority in Ireland, the general populace may well have thought him a king. Notice again Jeremiah's commission from Yehovah:

> *10 "See, I have this day set you over the nations and over the reigns, to root out and to pull down, to destroy and to overthrow, to build and to plant."* (Jeremiah 1:10)

"See, I have this day set you over the nations and over the reigns..." It appears, then, that he was to exercise considerable authority. An interesting consideration in this regard is that *The History of Ancient Caledonia*—an 1897 C.E. Scottish publication that is reputedly the transcribing by author John MacLaren of a much older source—repeatedly refers to Ireland as "Jeremy's Land." Consider also that the king himself may have referred to the prophet as "my father" simply out of sheer respect, just as was the custom in ancient Israel.

> *12 And Elisha saw it, and he cried out, "My father, my father, the chariot of Yisra'ĕl and its horsemen!" And he saw him no more. Then he took hold of his own garments and tore them into two pieces.* (2 Kings 2:12)

---

[229] *Stone of Destiny* by Pat Gerber, p. 50
[230] *Erin's Blood Royal-The Gaelic Noble Dynasties of Ireland* by Peter Berresford Ellis, 2002, p. 337

*21 And when the sovereign of Yisra'ĕl saw them, he said to Elisha, "My father, should I smite? Should I smite?"* (2 Kings 6:21)

This, too, could have made Jeremiah appear a king. In fact, Gede, one name given for the king at the time, is referred to in an old poem as the son of Ollam Fodhla. And there may be yet another reason for the confusion, which you will soon see in just a moment. It also appears that Simon Brach could be chronologically aligned with Ollam Fodhla—if they are listed in sections that should actually overlap. The reckoning of Brach as a king, it should be noted, may have been a mistake. In the Bible, Baruch is called the son of Neriah. Yet, consider what a linguistics textbook says: "Sound changes... (such as) 'r becomes l'... are 'natural' sound changes often found in the world's languages."[231]

Perhaps Neriah was read as Nelia. So Baruch may have inadvertently been reckoned as the son or descendant of Neleus, forefather of the Milesian Dynasty. Simon Breck was also said to be a descendant of Gathelus. As this name is an eponym for the Goidels or Gaels, it really means that Breck was a Gael (an Israelite). But because Gathelus, or Gede, was considered as an actual name of the founder of the Milesian Dynasty, Simon Breck was made to be his descendant, even though he probably wasn't—and most definitely wasn't if he were Baruch.

There is further confusion over the identity of Heremon or Eremon. He is often said to be the son of Milesius, but is sometimes identified as Milesius himself. Furthermore, there is, as mentioned, a Gede or Ghede who seems to be synonymous with Heremon. It is sometimes stated that Heremon had a son named Heremon. This name, a Hebrew derivative that may have meant something like "highest" (see Milner, p. 11 footnote), could have become a title for the Irish high king—similar to Eochaidh being a general term for 'prince.' Thus, no matter what the actual name of the king at the time of Jeremiah, he may have been referred to both as Eochaidh *and* Heremon. Tea is reputed to have married Gede "the Heremon" in some accounts. There is another possibility regarding the name Heremon that is rather astounding to

---

[231] *An Introduction To Language* by Victoria Fromkin and Robert Rodman, Fourth Ed., 1988, p. 318

contemplate. For the Hebrew derivation just mentioned is reckoned from the root 'ruwm,' meaning "high... lofty... exalted."[232] And this root forms the name of a well-known Hebrew name—Jeremiah! His name, broken down as Yerem-Yah, is understood to mean, "Exalted by the Eternal" or "Appointed by the Eternal."[233]

In Greek his name is Ieremias. In Spanish his name is pronounced Heremias. With the Celtic augmentative suffix, this would become Heremion or Heremon. So it just may be that Jeremiah's name appears in the Irish annals after all—and that his name became confused with his contemporaries. If so, then Heremon was not actually the name of the husband of Zedekiah's daughter—although it could have been the name of their son. For as important as Jeremiah was, it would not be at all surprising to find that others, particularly in the royal family, were named after him. In any event, it is interesting to consider that, as one source has put it, "Heremon and Ollam Fola are mingled together in hopeless confusion."[234]

If Heremon or Eremion is the Irish form of Jeremiah, this could give us another possible origin of the name Eire or Ire-land. Indeed, it could explain why Ireland has been called Jeremy's Land. For Ireland would actually mean "Jeremiah's Land"—the land of Jeremiah! Yet it must still be kept in mind that the name Heremon became attached to the first Milesian king of Ireland, whether or not that was his actual name.

Concerning the names Tea, Tephi and Tamar, one of the primary Irish chronicles, *The Annals of the Kings* of Ireland by the Four Masters, mentions:

> Tea, daughter of Lughaidh, son of Itha, whom Eremhon married in Spain.[235]

---

[232] *Enhanced Strong's Lexicon*, No. 7311
[233] *Enhanced Strong's Lexicon*, No. 3414
[234] Matthew Kelly, 1848, translation notes accompanying John Lynch's *Cambrensis Eversus*, 1662
[235] *The Annals of the Kings of Ireland* by the Four Masters, 1636, Vol. 1, p. 31

At first glance, this would seem to rule out her being the daughter of Zedekiah. However, Lughaidh may not refer to an actual person. The Irish are referred to as the "race of Lughaidh" and Ireland as "the Land of Lughaidh"—"one of the many arbitrary bardic names for Ireland."[236]

Lughaidh in old Gaelic could mean "House of God"—broken down as Logh, "God," and aidhe, "house, habitation, fortress."[237]

"House of God" (Hebrew Beth-El) may have been a designation for David's Dynasty or even for the "large, rough stone" reportedly brought by Jeremiah.[238]

The word Lughaidh may also come from "lugha" or "lughadh," meaning "oath"—apparently because it invokes Yehovah—and could be related to Yehovah's oath to David.[239] The name Itha or "ith" may mean "crown," as does the related Welsh "yd" (O'Reilly). Ith, coming from Spain, is said to be the son of Breoghan in some accounts, but this may simply be because the Milesian line of kings came to Ireland from Brigantium (modern Corunna near Santiago de Compostella) on the Northwest Coast of Spain. Indeed, Tea is in at least one old poem called *Temor of Bregia*. "Brega" or "Breagh," it should be noted, was the immediate territory of Tara in ancient Ireland, named after the Celtic tribe known as the Brigantes (or vice versa). The Brigantes were located in Southeast Ireland by the Roman geographer Ptolemy around A.D. 150. He also mentioned them as being one of the Celtic tribes in Britain at that time, as other sources also attest.[240]

Some now believe that they derived their name from the Celtic goddess Brigid. Indeed, it could be that she is simply a later deification of Tea, combined with features of other pagan goddesses. According to some scholars, the name Brigid "comes from the Old Irish brigante, meaning 'the exalted one.'"[241] This title could conceivably correspond

---

[236] *The Annals of the Kings of Ireland* by the Four Masters, Vol. 6, Appendix
[237] *An Irish-English Dictionary* by Edward O'Reilly, 1821, 1864
[238] *Stone of Destiny* by Pat Gerber
[239] *O'Reilly*, note by editor John O'Donovan, p. 671; *A Dictionary of the Gaelic Language by N. MacLeod and D. Dewar*, 1831, 1909
[240] http://www.roman-britain.org/tribes/brigantes.htm
[241] *Saints, In Search of Ancient Ireland, Program 2*: PBS Home Video, 2002

to the modern "highness" for a royal personage. In any event, it is certainly possible that the name Brigantes or Brega originally came from Brigantium in Northwest Spain—all perhaps relating to a royal title. Thus, "Tea, daughter of Lughaidh, son of Itha, son of Breoghan" could conceivably be read as "Tea, daughter of the House of God (or oath), child of the crown, child of Brigantium (or child of royalty)." This would well describe a Jewish princess of David's line who came to Ireland by way of the Iberian Peninsula.

I must now repeat the words of F.R.A. Glover, who wrote at length about this subject in the 19th-century:

> I have... no desire to encumber my hypothesis, with any argument, as to whether the Ollam Fodhla of Irish tradition is, or is not a mistake for Jeremiah the Prophet. I feel that the case of the presence of the illustrious Seer in Ireland is made out on other grounds; that, indeed, he must have been the transporter of the Stone (of Destiny), the conductor of 'the King's Daughters' and the planter of the Standard of Judah, in Ireland. I was satisfied of this, long before I heard a word of the Legend, of his having been Instructor to the great warrior Finn McCoyle, or even of the existence of this Ollam Fola.[242]

Glover makes a strong case for the identification of Ollam Fodhla as Jeremiah. His work is available online[243] as are many other articles and publications on this whole subject of the transfer of the throne of David to the British Isles.

Another is *Judah's Sceptre and Joseph's Birthright* by J.H. Allen.[244]

One major source, already cited, is *The Royal House of Britain: An Enduring Dynasty* by W.M.H. Milner. First published in 1902, this book

---

[242] *England, the Remnant of Judah, and the Israel of Ephraim*, 1861
[243] http://www.churchofgodtwincities.org/lit/booklets/throne-britain-its-biblical-origin-and-future/other-sources-and-caution.htm
[244] http://www.churchofgodtwincities.org/lit/booklets/throne-britain-its-biblical-origin-and-future/other-sources-and-caution.htm

has gone through numerous reprintings. It is available to order from The Covenant Publishing Co., Ltd., in London.[245]

For a more recent work, see *The Throne of David* by Peter Salemi.[246] Please bear in mind that the recommendation of outside sources for further study is not an endorsement of everything contained within those sources.

For those interested in the Irish king lists and annals, many of them are now available over the Internet.[247] However, it should be noted up front that, as already mentioned, these records are rather confusing and contradictory. And they do not contain all the information available on the various characters that have been mentioned. Some material is derived from the various clan pedigrees of Ireland and Scotland—as well as traditional rhymes, poems, songs and stories—some of which have been passed down by word of mouth.

Besides what you've already seen, there are other corroborating factors connecting the Davidic line with Ireland. Three miles north of Tara is an area known as Dowd's Town. Dowd is a Hebrew name. In English we write it as David, but the Hebrew pronunciation of David is "Duwd" or "Dowd." That being said, right next to ancient Tara, where the line of David was established, is a town designated as the Settlement of David. Furthermore, going back to the *Larne Times* article: "When Jeremiah's party arrived at Carrick that day many centuries ago they found themselves among kith and kin of the scattered people of Israel… Those who believe the Tribes of Israel traveled to the British Isles also cite the use in Ulster of a six-pointed star… being a symbol of the royal

---

[245] http://ukbookworld.com/book-for-sale/leckey/13383/milner-rev-the-royal-house-britain-enduring-dynasty &… http://www.churchofgodtwincities.org/lit/booklets/throne-britain-its-biblical-origin-and-future/other-sources-and-caution.htm

[246] http://www.british-israel.ca/David.pdf &… http://www.churchofgodtwincities.org/lit/booklets/throne-britain-its-biblical-origin-and-future/other-sources-and-caution.htm

[247] http://www.magoo.com/hugh/irishkings/html Also, see related links: http://www.british-israel.ca/CDRom.htm & http://www.churchofgodtwincities.org/lit/booklets/throne-britain-its-biblical-origin-and-future/other-sources-and-caution.htm

line of David." This truly is remarkable. Earlier, it was mentioned that the flag of Northern Ireland had the "blood-red right hand of Ulster" upon it.

What was not mentioned is that this red hand appears in the center of a six-pointed star. The star is said to represent the six counties of Ulster. Yet it is the very "Star of David"—the symbol of the Jews. Is it mere coincidence that the Red Hand of Zerah is symbolically fused with the Star of David? And atop that star on the flag is the royal crown. This seems too uncanny to be just a mere coincidence. Indeed, it appears to be further evidence that the royal line of David married into the Milesian royal line of Zerah. Furthermore, the *Larne Times* article says, "Jeremiah may have brought King David's harp with him." The harp has long since been the national emblem of Ireland. David himself, the "sweet psalmist of Israel" (2 Samuel 23:1), was a "skillful player on the harp" (1 Samuel 16:16-17)—and it is entirely possible that the harp became a symbol of his dynasty.

In 1581 C.E., Vencenzo Galilei, musician and father of the famous Astronomer Galileo, published a book in which he stated regarding the harp: "This most ancient instrument was brought to us from Ireland where such are most excellently worked and in great number; the inhabitants of the said island have made this their art during the many centuries they have lived there and, moreover, it is a special undertaking of the kingdom; and they paint and engrave it in their public and private buildings and on their hill; stating as their reason for doing so that they have descended from the royal prophet David."[248]

Of course, this would apply more to the royal family than to the Irish as a whole—who, of primarily Danaan heritage, are mostly Danite. Today, the harp of Ireland—the harp of David—appears on the flag of the Irish Republic and on the British Royal Coat-of-Arms. Surprisingly, British royal heraldry seems to have much to tell us regarding the identity of Britain and its enduring dynasty (I will provide you with a closer look at this in the following chapter).

---

[248] *Dialogo della Musica Antica* by Vencenzo Galilei, 1581

With all the evidence now at our disposal, I think you will agree we may confidently assert that Jeremiah came to Ireland. Traveling with him was at least *one of* Zedekiah's daughters. She, of the line of David, married into the Irish royal line of Zerah. Finally, at long last, the breach between the Perez and Zerah branches of Judah was healed! And from their union would spring an enduring dynasty that would persevere throughout the reigns of the kings of Ireland, later of Scotland, and later still of all Great Britain. Curiously, it appears that almost all of these kings were crowned upon the same "large, rough stone" as mentioned earlier—which again, may well have been brought to Ireland by Jeremiah, as tradition maintains. Indeed, of that stone alone there is quite a tale to tell. In any case, from the time that Jeremiah arrived, the succession of Irish, Scottish and British monarchs were all members of the *same* dynasty—the Davidic Dynasty.

# Chapter 3 | Heraldry of the Tribes of Israel Then & Now

I have now provided you with a reliable account of not only the migratory route of the Israelites, but also, what names they were known by from the time of their captivity in 723 B.C.—starting with Khoumri and Gameri, followed by Gamera and Cimera, and ending with what we now know as Celtic. I also brought the Ishaka Saca and Scythians to your attention and followed them through time for your benefit until they too were known as Celtic.

In order to completely understand the prophecy of Daniel 9:24-27, however, and in my sincere desire to prove to you exactly *who* Daniel's people were and are today, I continued to probe deeper in my search with regard to the lines of royalty and followed the line of Judah through both the line of Phares and the line of Zerah from antiquity to the present. I began from the time of Abraham and the blessings promised to the children of Abraham and specifically to the one child—that child being Judah. Then I jumped ahead to those days leading up to and right before the Exodus as the Israelites left Egypt and sought out new lands and a new life. I traced the royal line of Phares down through King David until the end of that line with the death of King Zedekiah. I also traced the line of Zerah throughout Trojan history and how it came to each of the royal houses of Europe and also, to Ireland, Scotland and England. I then followed Zerah's lineage throughout the ages until this line merged with King Zedekiah's line and found its way to Ireland,

Scotland and finally, to England where it still presides and is represented by Queen Elizabeth II the current Monarch as of 2014.

I have now provided you with multiple proofs as to just *who* Israel is today in the 21st-century.

But I also know there are still those among you who will not believe the evidence I have now presented you with in chapters one and two, so I am now going to share with you another set of proofs to give additional support for the information I have shared with you already.

> *6 At the mouth of two or three witnesses shall he that is to die be put to death. He is not put to death by the mouth of one witness.* (Deuteronomy 17:6)

> *15 One witness does not rise up against a man concerning any crookedness or any sin that he commits. At the mouth of two witnesses or at the mouth of three witnesses a matter is established.* (Deuteronomy 19:15)

> *16 But if he does not hear, take with you one or two more, that "by the mouth of two or three witnesses every word might be established."* (Matthew 18:16)

> *1 This is the third time I am coming to you. "By the mouth of two or three witnesses every word shall be established."*[1]
> [Footnote: [1]Deuteronomy 19:15 (2 Corinthians 13:1)]

Once I have provided you with this additional set of proofs, there should be no more denying *where* the Ten Lost Tribes of Israel went and *who* they are today. And then, once I have established this matter, by the multiple number of witnesses we have from history and from the current facts I am about to show you, we will then go on to read the *rest of* the prophecy of Daniel 9:24-27. This prophecy is a death sentence to those who refuse to repent. This is the real reason I am sharing all of this with you. It is because you have this death sentence looming in front of you. And not just you, but in front of and over: your spouse, your children, your parents, your town, your state, your county or province, and last but not least, your entire country and all the countries of the various tribes of Israel. It can be rescinded of course by Yehovah, but *only if* you repent and begin to walk the walk (and not just talk the talk) of keeping Torah.

In Chapter 2 I talked about the Red Hand of Zerah and how this royal line came to be in Ireland. I showed you the story of Tamar and Judah in Genesis 38 and how Zerah stuck out his hand and then pulled it back into the womb. Below is the Crest of Northern Ireland. It has the Red Hand inside the Star of David and it is crowned with a royal Crown.

**Figure**[249]

You should also note that the banner the Lion is holding features the Harp of David as I explained to you in Chapter 2.

In this chapter, I am going to explain some heraldry to you. Almost everyone has a family crest with some strange things on it and very few know what those strange things symbolize or exemplify. Go and get your family crest out, if you have one, and have it within arm's reach as I proceed to dig deeper into where Israel is today and exactly where you and your family tree fit into all of this.

---

[249] http://commons.wikimedia.org/wiki/File:Northern_Ireland_coat_of_arms.png

If you do not know your family crest, then you can go look it up or you can use the one for your city, state or country and see just how many of the symbols I am about to explain to you appear on your crest.

We are going to begin our search in Ezekiel where we read of something that is very different from anything we have read up to this point in the Bible. I know this is an odd place to begin our heraldry search, but bear with me for a bit.

> *1 And it came to be in the thirtieth year, in the fourth month, on the fifth of the month, as I was among the exiles by the River Kebar, the heavens were opened and I saw visions of Elohim. 2 On the fifth of the month, in the fifth year of Sovereign Yehoyakin's exile, 3 the word of* יהוה *came expressly to Yeḥezqěl the priest, the son of Buzi, in the land of the Chaldeans by the River Kebar. And the hand of* יהוה *came upon him there. 4 And I looked and saw a whirlwind coming out of the north, a great cloud with fire flashing itself. And brightness was all around it, and out of its midst like glowing metal, out of the midst of the fire, 5 and out of the midst of it came what looked like four living creatures. And this was their appearance: they had the likeness of a man. 6 And each one had four faces, and each one had four wings.*
>
> *7 And their feet were straight feet, and the soles of their feet were like the sole of a calves' foot. And they sparkled like the appearance of polished bronze, 8 and under their wings on their four sides were the hands of a man. And each of the four had faces and wings—9 their wings touched one another. They did not turn when they went, but each one went straight forward. 10 And the likeness of their faces: the face of a man, and each of the four had the*

**Figure**[250]

---

[250] http://www.bible-history.com/tabernacle/TAB4The_Cherubim.htm

> *face of a lion on the right side, and each of the four had the face of an ox on the left side, and each of the four had the face of an eagle. 11 Such were their faces. Their wings were spread upward, two of each touched one another, and two covered their bodies.* (Ezekiel 1:1-11)

Throughout the Bible there are many references to Cherubim and Angels, but it is in Ezekiel that we are told what they actually look like. The image I am using here is not 100% right. The Lion and the Bull need to be on the *opposite* sides of where they are depicted here. But I still find it to be a great image nonetheless.

Cherubim (plural of Cherub) are celestial angelic beings in the spiritual realm who have always been associated with the holiness of Yehovah. When Adam sinned, Cherubim, wielding a flaming sword that turned every direction, were stationed at the entrance to the Garden of Eden to guard the way to the Tree of Life. Cherubim represent the righteous government of Yehovah and are the executors of Yehovah's righteous and holy judgments.

> *22 And יהוה Elohim said, "See, the man has become like one of Us, to know good and evil. And now, lest he put out his hand and take also of the tree of life, and eat, and live forever..." 23 so יהוה Elohim sent him out of the garden of Ěden to till the ground from which he was taken, 24 and He drove the man out. And He placed kerubim at the east of the garden of Ěden, and a flaming sword which turned every way, to guard the way to the tree of life.* (Genesis 3:22-24)

The Cherubim were represented on the curtains around and above the Holy Place and as part of the Mercy Seat in the Holy Of Holies as explained to us in Exodus 25 and 26. This stresses their prominence, importance and their righteousness of those who serve Yehovah in His perfect holiness. This is extremely important to understand. In addition, as we continue along this vein, you are going to be amazed to discover what Yehovah is showing us.

In Revelation, John sees a vision of the Cherubim, which is as follows:

> *5 And out of the throne came lightnings, and thunders, and voices. And seven lamps of fire were burning before the throne, which are the seven Spirits of Elohim. 6 And before the throne there was a sea of glass, like crystal. And in the midst of the throne, and around the throne, were four living creatures, covered with eyes in front and in back. 7 And the first living creature was like a lion, and the second living creature like a calf, and the third living creature had a face like a man, and the fourth living creature was like a flying eagle. 8 And the four living creatures, each having six wings, were covered with eyes around and within. And they do not cease, day or night, saying, "Set-apart, set-apart, set-apart, יהוה Ĕl Shaddai, who was, and who is, and who is coming!"* (Revelation 4:5-8)

The Cherubim are described to us by Ezekiel as Four Living Creatures—each one having four different faces—the face of a Man, Lion, Ox, and Eagle.

- Face of a Man—Man's face represents intellect (the mind, the ability to reason, the soul), emotions, and all things that constitute and pertain to being human.
- Face of a Lion—The Lion has always been recognized as being strong, fierce, and majestic. He is considered to be the most royal of animals or the "King of the Beasts."
- Face of an Ox—The Ox has always been depicted as the animal that patiently labours for his owner. He is strong, able to bear a heavy burden, and is well acquainted with his owner.
- Face of an Eagle—The majestic bird that flies above life's tempests and storms, while below there are only sorrows, dangers, turmoil and distress. A swift bird of prey—strong and powerful, that unlike human beings, never becomes weary.

*30 A lion, which is mighty among beasts and does not turn away from facing all.* (Proverbs 30:30)

*2 The dread of a sovereign is like the roaring of a lion; whoever provokes him sins against his own life.* (Proverbs 20:2)

*4 Where there are no oxen, the crib is clean; but from the strength of an ox comes much increase.* (Proverbs 14:4)

*14 Our cattle well-laden; no breaking in, no going out; and no crying in our streets.* (Psalms 144:14)

*3 An ox knows its owner and a donkey its master's crib— Yisra'ĕl does not know, My people have not understood.* (Isaiah 1:3)

*18 Three matters are too marvelous for me, and four which I do not understand: 19 The way of an eagle in the heavens, the way of a snake on a rock, the way of a ship in the heart of the sea, and the way of a man with a girl.* (Proverbs 30:18-19)

*31 "... but those who wait on יהוה renew their strength, they raise up the wing like eagles, they run and are not weary, they walk and do not faint."* (Isaiah 40:31)

*5 Who satisfies your desire with the good, your youth is renewed like the eagle's.* (Psalms 103:5)

*4 "You have seen what I did to the Mitsrites, and how I bore you on eagles' wings and brought you to Myself."* (Exodus 19:4)

*3 And you shall say, "Thus said the Master יהוה, 'The great eagle with large wings of long pinions, covered with feathers of various colors, came to Leḇanon and took the top of the cedar.'"* (Ezekiel 17:3)

*1 "Put the ram's horn to your mouth, like an eagle against the House of יהוה, because they have transgressed My covenant, and they have rebelled against My Torah.* (Hosea 8:1)

When you read Numbers, Chapter 2, you are given the description as to how the camp of Israel was to be set up in the Wilderness. It is very specific:

*1 And יהוה spoke to Mosheh and to Aharon, saying, 2 "The children of Yisra'ěl are to camp, each one by his own banner, beside the sign of his father's house. Let them camp around the Tent of Meeting at a distance." 3 And on the east side, towards sunrise: those of the banner of the camp of Yehuḏah camp according to their divisions. And the leader of the children of Yehuḏah: Naḥshon, son of Amminaḏaḇ. 4 And his army with their registered ones: seventy-four thousand six-hundred. 5 And those camping next to him is the tribe of Yissaskar, and the leader of the children of Yissaskar: Nethaně'l, son of Tsu'ar. 6 And his army with its registered ones: fifty-four thousand four-hundred. 7 Then the tribe of Zeḇulun, and the leader of the children of Zeḇulun: Eliyaḇ, son of Ḥělon. 8 And his army with its registered ones: fifty-seven thousand four-hundred. 9 All the registered ones of the camp of Yehuḏah, according to their divisions: one-hundred and eighty-six thousand four-hundred. These depart first. 10 On the south side: the banner of the camp of Re'uḇěn according to their divisions, and the leader of the children of Re'uḇěn: Elitsur, son of Sheḏěy'ur. 11 And his army with its registered ones: forty-six thousand five-hundred.* (Numbers 2:1-11)

*12 And those who camp next to him: the tribe of Shim'on, and the leader of the children of Shim'on: Shelumi'ěl, son of Tsurishaddai. 13 And his army with their registered ones: fifty-nine thousand three-hundred. 14 Then the tribe of Gaḏ, and the leader of the children of Gaḏ: Elyasaph, son of Re'uw'ěl. 15 And his army with their registered ones: forty-five thousand six-hundred and fifty. 16 All the registered ones of the camp of Re'uḇěn, according to their divisions:*

one-hundred and fifty-one thousand four-hundred and fifty. And they are the second to depart. 17 And the Tent of Meeting, the camp of the Lĕwites, shall move out in the middle of the camps. As they camp, so they move out, everyone in his place, by their banners. 18 On the west side: the banner of the camp of Ephrayim according to their divisions, and the leader of the children of Ephrayim: Elishama, son of Ammihuḏ. 19 And his army with their registered ones: forty-thousand five-hundred. (Numbers 2:12-19)

20 And next to him the tribe of Menashsheh, and the leader of the children of Menashsheh: Gamli'ĕl, son of Peḏahtsur. 21 And his army with their registered ones: thirty-two thousand two-hundred. 22 Then the tribe of Binyamin, and the leader of the children of Binyamin: Aḇiḏan, son of Giḏ'oni. 23 And his army with their registered ones: thirty-five thousand four-hundred. 24 All the registered ones of the camp of Ephrayim, according to their divisions: one-hundred and eight-thousand one-hundred. And they are the third to depart. 25 On the north side: the banner of the camp of Dan, according to their divisions, and the leader of the children of Dan: Aḥi'ezer, son of Ammishaddai. 26 And his army with their registered ones: sixty-two thousand seven-hundred. 27 And those who camp next to him: the tribe of Ashĕr, and the leader of the children of Ashĕr: Paḡ'i'ĕl, son of Oḵran. 28 And his army with their registered ones: forty-one thousand five-hundred. 29 Then the tribe of Naphtali, and the leader of the children of Naphtali: Aḥira, son of Ĕnan. 30 And his army with their registered ones: fifty-three thousand four-hundred. 31 All the registered ones of the camp of Dan: one-hundred and fifty-seven thousand six-hundred. They depart last, with their banners. 32 These were registered ones of the children of Yisra'ĕl by their fathers' houses. All who were registered according to their divisions of the camps: six-hundred and three-thousand five-hundred and fifty. 33 But the Lĕwites were not registered among the children of Yisra'ĕl, as יהוה commanded Mosheh. 34 And the children of Yisra'ĕl did according to all that יהוה commanded Mosheh.

*So they camped by their banners and so they departed, each one by his clan, according to their fathers' houses.* (Numbers 2:20-34)

**The Tabernacle In The Wilderness**
Order of Camp: Levites  Other Tribes

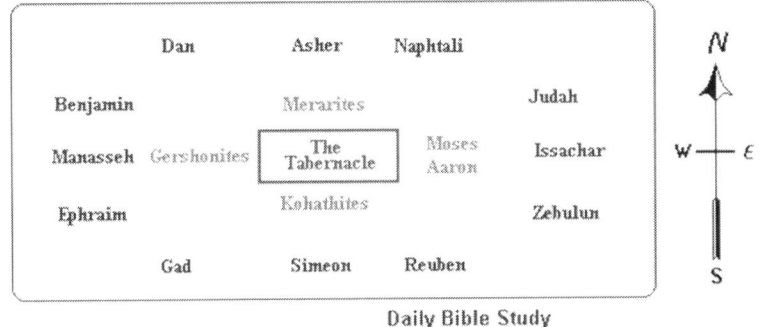

|  | Dan | Asher | Naphtali |  |
|---|---|---|---|---|
| Benjamin |  | Merarites |  | Judah |
| Manasseh | Gershonites | The Tabernacle | Moses Aaron | Issachar |
| Ephraim |  | Kohathites |  | Zebulun |
|  | Gad | Simeon | Reuben |  |

Daily Bible Study

**Figure**[251]

As you have just read, the Levites held a very different position around the camp. We first read of this in Numbers, Chapter 1.

*49 "Only the tribe of Lĕwi you do not register, nor take a census of them among the children of Yisra'ĕl. 50 Instead, appoint the Lĕwites over the Dwelling Place of the Witness, over all its furnishings, and over all that belongs to it. They bear the Dwelling Place and all its furnishings, and they attend to it, and camp around the Dwelling Place. 51 And when the Dwelling Place is to go forward, the Lĕwites take it down. And when the Dwelling Place is to be set up, the Lĕwites set it up. And the stranger who comes near is put to death. 52 And the children of Yisra'ĕl shall pitch their tents, everyone by his own camp, everyone by his own banner, according to their divisions, 53 but let the Lĕwites camp around the Dwelling Place of the Witness, so that there be no wrath on the congregation of the children of Yisra'ĕl. And the Lĕwites shall guard the duty of the Dwelling Place of the Witness." 54 And the children of Yisra'ĕl did according*

---

[251] http://www.keyway.ca/htm2000/20001016.htm

*to all that* יהוה *commanded Mosheh, so they did.* (Numbers 1:49-54)

# The Levite Camp

Camped just outside the Tabernacle were the Levite tents. The Levites performed the priestly duties and therefore were mediators between God and the people. The Tribe of Levi was divided into four families. Their tents were pitched between the Tabernacle and the people—one family on each side. The Kohathites on the south numbering 8,600. The Gershonites on the west numbering 7,500. The Merarites on the north numbering 6,200. On the east side were the tents of *Moses, Aaron the high priest, and Aaron's sons the priests.* Camped in the center was God.

Moses divided the Levites into three sections by their descent from the sons of Levi, namely, Gershon, Kohath, and Merari. They were under the general supervision of Eleazar, the son of Aaron.

### Gershonites

The Gershonites had a leader named Eliasaph (Numbers 3:24). They numbered 7,500 men, with 2,630 qualified for active service (Numbers 3:22, 4:40). They camped on the west side of the Tabernacle (Numbers 3:23). Their duty was to have charge of taking down and setting up the curtains, the tent, the coverings and the hanging for the door of the Tabernacle, the hangings of the court and the court entrance, their cords and instruments of service (Numbers 3:25-26, 4:22-28).

### Kohathites

The leader of the Kohathites was Elizaphan (Numbers 3:30). At the building of the Tabernacle they numbered 8,600 men (Numbers 3:28), with 2,750 qualified for active service (Numbers 4:36). They camped on the south side of the

Tabernacle (Numbers 3:29). Their duty was to have charge of the Ark, the table of the Bread of the Presence, the Lampstands, the Altars of Burnt Offering and of Incense, the Sacred Vessels used in the service, and the Veil (Numbers 3:31, 4:4-15).

**Merarites**

The leader of Merarites was Zuriel (Numbers 3:35). They numbered 6,200 men, with 3,200 qualified for active service (Numbers 3:34, 4:44). They camped on the north side of the Tabernacle (Numbers 3:35) Their duty was to have charge of the frames, bars, pillars, and sockets of the Tabernacle; also the pillars of the court, their sockets, pegs, cords, and tools pertaining thereto (Numbers 3:36-37, 4:29-32). Owing to the heavy nature of the materials they had to carry, four wagons and eight oxen were assigned to them; and in the march, both they and the Gershonites followed immediately after the standard of Judah, and before that of Reuben, that they might set up the Tabernacle before the arrival of the Kohathites (Numbers 7:8).[252]

I want to now bring to your attention a certain word I have already made reference to and zero in on what that word signifies. The word is "Banner" or "Standard."

> *17 And the Tent of Meeting, the camp of the Lĕwites, shall move out in the middle of the camps. As they camp, so they move out, everyone in his place, by their **banners**.* (Numbers 2:17 | *The Scriptures* 1998)

> *17 Then the Tent of Meeting shall set out, with the camp of the Levites in the midst of the camps. As they encamp, so shall they set out, every man in his place, by their **standards**.* (Numbers 2:17 | NKJV)

Below are all the biblical versions that employ the use of the word "Standard." (WEB, KJV, JPS, ASV, DBY, WBS, YLT, NAS)

---

[252] http://www.bible-history.com/tabernacle/TAB4The_Encampment.htm

> *31 All who were numbered of the camp of Dan were one-hundred fifty-seven thousand six-hundred. They shall set out last by their **standards**.* (Numbers 2:31)

> *34 And the children of Yisra'ĕl did according to all that* יהוה *commanded Mosheh. So they camped by their **banners** and so they departed, each one by his clan, according to their fathers' houses.* (Numbers 2:34)

We are commanded to set up our Banners or our Standards in the name of Yehovah and we are told that our enemies will also set up their Banners or Standards against us.

> *5 We will triumph in thy salvation, and in the name of our God we will set up our **banners**: Jehovah fulfil all thy petitions.* (Psalm 20:5 | See JPS)

> *4 Your adversaries have roared in the midst of your assembly. They have set up their **standards** as signs.* (Psalms 74:4 | WEB, NAS, NIV)

Psalm 74:4 is very revealing when we consider the ensigns of the Romans. We are told that they set up these ensigns at the East Gate of the Temple in 70 C.E. and paid idolatrous honors to them.

Almost the entire religion of the Roman camp consisted of worshiping the ensign, swearing by the ensign, and preferring the ensign over all other gods. These Roman ensigns were an "abomination" to the Jews, or the "abomination of desolation."[253]

> *15 Moses built an altar, and called its name Yahweh our **Banner**.* (Exodus 17:15)

> *4 You have given a **banner** to those who fear you, that it may be displayed because of the truth. Selah.* (Psalms 60:4 | WEB, KJV, JPS, ASV, DBY, WBS, NAS, RSV, NIV)

---

[253] http://www.christiananswers.net/dictionary/abomination.html

*4 He brought me to the banquet hall. His **banner** over me is love.* (Song Of Songs 2:4 | WEB, KJV, JPS, ASV, DBY, WBS, YLT, NAS, RSV, NIV)

*26 He will lift up a **banner** to the nations from far, and he will whistle for them from the ends of the earth. Behold, they will come speedily and swiftly.* (Isaiah 5:26 | WEB, DBY, NIV)

*10 It will happen in that day that the nations will seek the root of Jesse, who stands as a **banner** of the peoples; and his resting place will be glorious.* (Isaiah 11:10 | WEB, DBY, NIV)

*12 He will set up a **banner** for the nations, and will assemble the outcasts of Israel, and gather together the dispersed of Judah from the four corners of the earth.* (Isaiah 11:12 | WEB, DBY, NIV)

*2 Set up a **banner** on the bare mountain! Lift up your voice to them! Wave your hand, that they may go into the gates of the nobles.* (Isaiah 13:2 | WEB, KJV, DBY, WBS, NIV)

*3 All you inhabitants of the world, and you dwellers on the earth, when a **banner** is lifted up on the mountains, look! When the trumpet is blown, listen!* (Isaiah 18:3 | WEB, DBY, NIV)

*17 One thousand will flee at the threat of one. At the threat of five, you will flee until you are left like a beacon on the top of a mountain, and like a **banner** on a hill.* (Isaiah 30:17 | WEB, DBY, NIV)

Is this not what we do now? Do you not see soldiers valiantly hoisting the flag at the top of a hill to inspire the troops or to claim a victory? Once you have come to the place (i.e., your campsite) where you are going to set up your tent, you plant your flag or banner so people know who you are, where you are from and whether you are friend or foe.

*9 "His rock will pass away by reason of terror, and his princes will be afraid of the **banner**," says Yahweh, whose* *fire is in Zion, and his furnace in Jerusalem.* (Isaiah 31:9 | WEB, DBY)

*22 Thus says the Lord Yahweh, "Behold, I will lift up my hand to the nations, and set up my **banner** to the peoples; and they shall bring your sons in their bosom, and your daughters shall be carried on their shoulders."* (Isaiah 49:22 | WEB, DBY, NIV)

*19 And they shall fear the name of Jehovah from the west, and from the rising of the sun, his glory. When the adversary shall come in like a flood, the Spirit of Jehovah will lift up a **banner** against him.* (Isaiah 59:19 | DBY)

*10 Go through, go through the gates! Prepare the way of the people! Cast up, cast up the highway! Gather out the stones! Lift up a **banner** for the peoples.* (Isaiah 62:10 | WEB, DBY, NIV)

*6 "Set up a **banner** toward Zion; take to flight, stay not! For I am bringing evil from the north, and a great destruction."* (Jeremiah 4:6 | DBY)

*2 Declare ye among the nations, and publish, and lift up a **banner**; publish, conceal not! Say, Babylon is taken, Bel is put to shame, Merodach is dismayed: her images are put to shame, her idols are dismayed.* (Jeremiah 50:2 | DBY, RSV, NIV)

*12 Lift up a **banner** toward the walls of Babylon, make the watch strong, set the watchmen, prepare the ambushes; for Jehovah hath both devised and done that which he spoke against the inhabitants of Babylon.* (Jeremiah 51:12 | DBY, NIV)

*27 Lift up a **banner** in the land, blow the trumpet among the nations, prepare nations against her; call together against her the kingdoms of Ararat, Minni, and Ashkenaz; appoint a captain against her; cause the horses to come up as the bristly caterpillars.* (Jeremiah 51:27 | DBY, NIV)

> *7 Of fine linen with embroidered work from Egypt was your sail, that it might be to you for a **banner**; blue and purple from the islands of Elishah was your awning.* (Ezekiel 27:7 | WEB, DBY, NIV)

Another word for "Banner" is the word "Ensign." I have already provided you with quite a few examples of where the word "Banner" is found in various Bible translations and will now do the same for "Ensign"—the more archaic term for what we now refer to as a "Flag." Today in the U.S.A. they pledge an Oath of Allegiance to the American flag. Interestingly, the word "**Oth**" is the Hebrew word for "Banner."

**Ensign**[254]

> (*nes,* in the Authorized Version generally "ensign," sometimes "standard"; *degel,* "standard," with the exception of (Solomon 2:4) "banner"; *oth,* "ensign"). This distinction between these three Hebrew terms is sufficiently marked by their respective uses. *Nes* is a *signal,* and *not* a military standard. It is an occasional signal, which was exhibited on the top of a pole from a bare mountaintop (Isaiah 13:2, 18:3). *Degel* a military *standard* for a *large* division of an army; and *oth* the same for a *small* one. Neither of them, however, expresses the idea which "standard" conveys to our minds, viz. a flag. The standards in use among the Hebrews probably resembled those of the Egyptians and Assyrians—a figure or device of some kind elevated on a pole; usually a sacred emblem, such as an animal, a boat, or the king's name.

Each camp of Israel, each group within the camp of Israel and potentially every leader of each one of those groups had their own flags and their own banners which represented who they are and which tribe they belonged to. This is amazing to understand as you are soon going to see.

> The Hebrew word "oth," denotes a military standard, especially of a single tribe (Numbers 2:2). Each separate tribe had its own "sign" or "ensign."

---

[254] *Smith Bible Dictionary,* http://topicalbible.org/e/ensign.htm

The Hebrew word "nes," denotes a "lofty signal," as a "column" or "high pole" (Numbers 21:8-9); a "standard"... "signal" or "flag" placed on high mountains to point out to the people a "place of rendezvous" on the irruption of an enemy (Isaiah 5:26, 11:12, 18:3, 62:10; Jeremiah 4:6, 4:21; Psalm 60:4). This was an occasional signal, and *not* a military standard. "Elevation" and "conspicuity" are implied in the word.

The Hebrew word "degel" denotes the "standard" given to each of the four divisions of the host of the Israelites at the Exodus (Numbers 1:52, 2:2, 10:14).

In Cant. 2:4 it is rendered "banner." We have no definite information as to the nature of these military standards. (See "Banner.")[255]

*11 And after three months we sailed in a ship which had wintered in the island, an Alexandrian, with the Dioscuri for its* **ensign**. *(Acts 28:11 | DBY)*

*2 Every man of the children of Israel shall pitch by his own standard, with the* **ensign** *of their father's house: far off about the tabernacle of the congregation shall they pitch.* (Numbers 2:2 | KJV, JPS, ASV, DBY, WBS, YLT, RSV)

*8 And Jehovah saith unto Moses, "Make for thee a burning 'serpent,' and set it on an* **ensign**; *and it hath been, everyone who is bitten and hath seen it—he hath lived."* (Numbers 21:8 | YLT)

*9 And Moses maketh a serpent of brass, and setteth it on the* **ensign**, *and it hath been, if the serpent hath bitten any man, and he hath looked expectingly unto the serpent of brass—he hath lived.* (Numbers 21:9 | YLT)

---

[255] *Easton's Bible Dictionary*, http://topicalbible.org/e/ensign.htm

*4 Thou hast given to those fearing thee an **ensign**. To be lifted up as an ensign because of truth. Selah.* (Psalm 60:4 | YLT)

*26 And he will lift up an **ensign** to the nations from far, and will hiss unto them from the end of the earth: and, behold, they shall come with speed swiftly.* (Isaiah 5:26 | KJV, JPS, ASV, WBS, YLT)

*10 And in that day there shall be a root of Jesse, which shall stand for an **ensign** of the people; to it shall the Gentiles seek: and his rest shall be glorious.* (Isaiah 11:10 | KJV, JPS, ASV, WBS, YLT, RSV)

*12 And he shall set up an **ensign** for the nations, and shall assemble the outcasts of Israel, and gather together the dispersed of Judah from the four corners of the earth.* (Isaiah 11:12 | KJV, JPS, ASV, WBS, YLT, RSV)

*2 Set ye up an **ensign** upon the bare mountain, lift up the voice unto them, wave the hand that they may go into the gates of the nobles.* (Isaiah 13:2 | ASV, JPS, YLT)

*3 All ye inhabitants of the world, and dwellers on the earth, see ye, when he lifteth up an **ensign** on the mountains; and when he bloweth a trumpet, hear ye.* (Isaiah 18:3 | KJV, JPS, ASV, WBS, YLT)

*17 One thousand shall flee at the rebuke of one; at the rebuke of five shall ye flee: until ye be left as a beacon upon the top of a mountain, and as an **ensign** on an hill.* (Isaiah 30:17 | KJV, JPS, ASV, WBS, YLT)

*9 "And he shall pass over to his strong hold for fear, and his princes shall be afraid of the **ensign**," saith the LORD, whose fire is in Zion, and his furnace in Jerusalem.* (Isaiah 31:9 | KJV, JPS, ASV, WBS, YLT)

*19 And they fear from the west the name of Jehovah, and from the rising of the sun—His honor, when come in as a flood doth an adversary, the Spirit of Jehovah hath raised an **ensign** against him.* (Isaiah 59:19 | YLT)

*10 Go through, go through the gates; prepare ye the way of the people; cast up, cast up the highway; gather out the stones; lift up an **ensign** for the peoples.* (Isaiah 62:10 | ASV, JPS, YLT, RSV)

*6 Lift up an **ensign** Zionward, strengthen yourselves, stand not still, for evil I am bringing in from the north, and a great destruction.* (Jeremiah 4:6 | YLT)

*21 Until when do I see an **ensign**? Do I hear the voice of a trumpet?* (Jeremiah 4:21 | YLT)

*2 Declare ye among nations, and sound, and lift up an **ensign**, sound, do not hide, Say ye: "Captured hath been Babylon, put to shame hath been Bel, broken hath been Merodach, put to shame have been her grievous things, broken have been her idols."* (Jeremiah 50:2 | YLT)

*12 Unto the walls of Babylon lift up an **ensign**, strengthen the watch, establish the watchers, prepare the ambush, for Jehovah hath both devised and done that which He spake concerning the inhabitants of Babylon.* (Jeremiah 51:12 | YLT)

*27 Lift ye up an **ensign** in the land, blow a trumpet among nations, sanctify against it nations, summon against it the kingdoms of Ararat, Minni, and Ashkenaz; appoint against it an infant head, cause the horse to ascend as the rough cankerworm.* (Jeremiah 51:27 | YLT)

*7 Of fine linen with broidered work from Egypt was thy sail, that it might be to thee for an **ensign**; blue and purple from* *the isles of Elishah was thine awning.* (Ezekiel 27:7 | ASV, JPS, YLT, RSV)

*16 And the LORD their God shall save them in that day as the flock of his people: for they shall be as the stones of a crown, lifted up as an **ensign** upon his land.* (Zechariah 9:16 | KJV, WBS)

According to Jewish tradition, it was believed that the banners of the tribes were as follows:

- Judah—East (Lion of gold with a scarlet background).
- Ephraim—West (Ox of black on gold background).
- Reuben—South (Man on gold background).
- Dan—North (Eagle of gold on a blue background).[256]

If you haven't already, are you starting to see a pattern now with the Cherubim we talked about in Ezekiel? The question then is, what did the flags (aka. banners and ensigns) over each one of the Twelve Tribes look like? We can find that answer easy enough just by reading what Jacob had to say concerning each of his sons at the end of his life.

In Genesis 49, we read about Jacob who is nearing the end of his days and wants to tell his twelve sons what is to happen to them in the Last Days. He is speaking to them of things, which pertain to the end of this age and *not just* in specific reference to them in their lifetime.

*1 And Ya'aqoḇ called his sons and said, "Gather together, so that I declare to you what is to befall you in the last days: 2 Gather together and hear, you sons of Ya'aqoḇ, and listen to Yisra'ěl your father."* (Genesis 49:1-2)

---

[256] http://www.bible-history.com/tabernacle/TAB4The_Encampment.htm

# Reuben

**Figure**[257]

> *3 Re'uḇĕn, you are my first-born, my power and the beginning of my strength, the excellency of exaltation and the excellency of power.* (Genesis 49:3)

> *4 Boiling like water, you do not excel, because you went up to your father's bed, then you defiled it—he went up to my couch.* (Genesis 49:4)

## Reuben's Two Symbols: A Man & Water

Reuben's primary emblem was a "man," representing the "excellency of power." His secondary emblem is recorded as being "wavy lines," representing "unstable waters."

I would strongly urge you to read each one of the links from the Brit-Am website, as they go into far greater detail explaining how different tribes from each of the clans migrated and ended up where they are now. Different groupings of various tribes would migrate to different areas and were not always found co-existing in the same area. In some cases, you can research your own family all the way back to Israel.[258] In order to help you in this search, see footnote below.

---

[257] *Symbols of Our Celto-Saxon Heritage* by W.H. Bennet, 1976
[258] http://britam.org/tribes.html

**Figure**[259]        **Figure**[260]

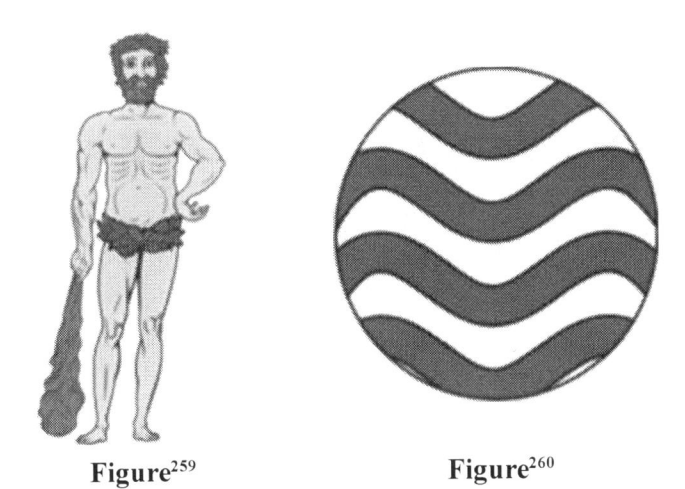

In v. 3, Jacob referred to Reuben as "my might" and "the excellency of dignity." France has portrayed these characteristics to the world. In the past, she was the greatest colonial power behind Britain and called the "Queen of Culture."

The *Encyclopedia Americana* notes that:

> "... during the 70 years of the third republic [1875-1945]... more than a hundred cabinets succeeded one another, in France, with an average tenure in office of less than eight months. The main cause of this ministerial instability was the lack of disciplined parties..."

This "unstable" and fickle French political system has also produced eleven constitutions since 1791!

> Jacob also goes on to say of Reuben that, "... you shall not excel; because you went up to your father's bed; then defiled you [it]: he went up to my couch" (Genesis 49:4).

---

[259] http://christianliving101.org/Site/pdf_files/Heraldry_of_the_lost_tribes.pdf
[260] http://christianliving101.org/Site/pdf_files/Heraldry_of_the_lost_tribes.pdf

It is interesting to note that kings and leaders of France usually have their own mistress—"concubine"—a hedonistic pattern that has become an all too pervasive part of their national worldview.

## Simeon & Levi

The next blessing Jacob bestows is with regard to Simeon and Levi:

> 5 *"Shim'on and Lĕwi are brothers, their weapons are implements of violence. 6 Let my being not enter their council, let my esteem not be united to their assembly; because they slew a man in their displeasure, and they lamed an ox in pleasure. 7 Cursed be their displeasure for it is fierce, and their wrath for it is cruel! I divide them in Ya'aqob̠ and scatter them in Yisra'ĕl."* (Genesis 49:5-7)

Simeon and Levi have the Sword and the Castle as their crest:

Levi was scattered among the tribes, with some serving within the Levitical priesthood. However, Simeon's primary emblem was a Sword—an "instrument of cruelty."

**Figure**[261]

Simeon and Levi were brothers—destined to be divided in Jacob and scattered in Israel (Genesis 49:7). Consequently, they were *not*

---

[261] *Symbols of Our Celto-Saxon Heritage* by W.H. Bennet, 1976

meant to be concentrated in one specific area. The name LEVI seems to recur in family appellations such as Levison, and Lewis. They were the priestly tribe to which Moses and Aaron belonged. From Aaron came the priests or COHANS. (McGowan is an Anglicized form of Cohan as I have pointed out in previous chapters).

You will notice in the crest of Milano the capital of Lombardy, that there is a Castle on the top. The Castle is the symbol of *both* Levi and Simeon. If you go to Brit-Am's site, you can learn how some of the Tribe of Simeon ended up in Milano.

Another symbol for Levi and Simeon is the Sword. You can see an example of this in the crests that are to follow. As I have also indicated previously, Simeon and Levi were mixed amongst the tribes.

## Judah

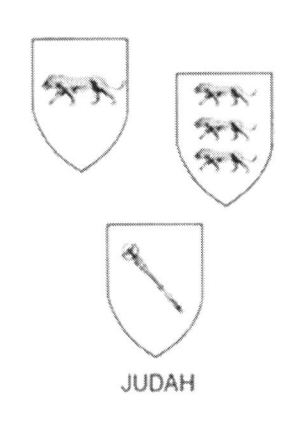

**Figure**[262]  **Figure**[263]

Jacob bestows his blessing upon Judah next. The things said here are pivotal to our discussion, so read on carefully:

---

[262] http://en.wikipedia.org/wiki/Royal_arms_of_England
[263] *Symbols of Our Celto-Saxon Heritage* by W.H. Bennet, 1976

> *8 You, Yehudah, your brothers praise you; your hand is on the neck of your enemies; your father's children bow down before you. 9 Yehudah is a lion's cub; from the prey you have gone up, my son! He bowed down, he crouched like a lion. And like a lion, who does rouse him? 10 The sceptre shall not turn aside from Yehudah, nor a Lawgiver from between his feet, until Shiloh comes, and to Him is the obedience of peoples. 11 Binding his donkey to the vine, and his donkey's colt to the choice vine, he washed his garments in wine, and his robes in the blood of grapes. 12 His eyes are darker than wine, and his teeth whiter than milk.* (Genesis 49:8-12

You will notice how the Lion is mentioned three times here in this blessing. One of the symbols of Judah is represented by three Lions; another by the single Lion and another by the Scepter.

Judah's emblem was and still is a Lion, with two secondary emblems:

1. Three Lions (since he is described as a Lion three times.)

2. A Scepter: A Lion with a Crown represented the House of David, the royal line of kings.

But the line of Zerah, which was also of Judah, was represented by both the Red Hand and the Red Lion.

> Recall that the Zerah Line of Judah originally settled in Ireland. It is also interesting that "the official flag of Northern Ireland has a Magen David Star in its center which symbol is traditionally associated with Judah and the Jewish people."[264]

The Scarlet Hand, which typified the line of Zerah, is in the very center of the flag of Northern Ireland.

---

[264] *The Tribes* by Yair Davidy, p. 221

Of course, the Tribe of Judah is the most widely recognized tribe today. Despite having endured much persecution throughout the centuries from counterfeit religions and various despots, they are the only ones to have fulfilled Zephaniah 2 and Zechariah 12 in the prophetic context of returning to their ancient homeland, Israel. Only a fraction of Judah, however, lives in the actual nation of Israel. New York City's Jews *alone* outnumber those currently residing in Israel.

Today, the State of Israel and Judah share the Blue Lion in common as one of their national symbols.

Jacob's prophecy foretells how Judah will be a "lion's whelp." A whelp is another name for a young lion cub. Jacob prophesied that Judah would be a very young nation in the latter-day period of time. This describes the modern Israeli nation to a 'T', which was "born" in 1948 and is still a "young nation" by today's standards.

Based on everything I have revealed to you in previous chapters, it should therefore come as no surprise to you to see the three Golden Lions featured on the flag paying tribute to the Queen of England.

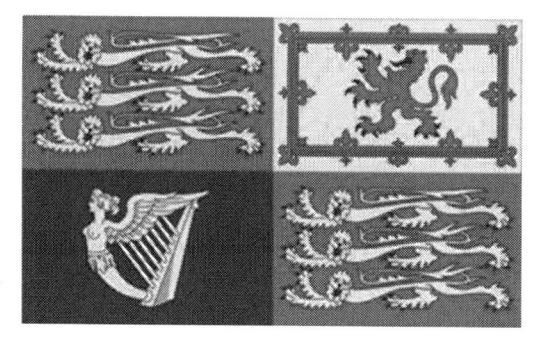

Here, on the HRH (Her Royal Highness) Queen's Royal Standard, we have the three Golden Lions as you just read about in the blessing to Judah. We also have the Harp, which is the flag of Ireland and represents the Davidic line. In addition, we have the Scottish flag or banner of the Red Lion. This Red Lion represents the Red Hand and the line of Zerah that I discussed with you in the last chapter.

Featured on this particular banner we have the line of Phares, the three Golden Lions and the line of Zerah—the Red Lion representing Scotland and the royal line that was once in Ireland.

> 27 "I will overturn, overturn, overturn, it: and it shall be (overturned) no more, until he come whose right it is; and I will give it him." (Ezekiel 21:27)

Again, the Lion is a symbol of the Tribe of Judah and is the banner of Judah. You will encounter quite a few more instances of this as we continue.

Here is the national emblem of Scotland. It again features the Red Lion symbolizing the line of Zerah. It does not have the Crown, however, as that belongs to England.

## Zebulun

*13 Zebulun dwells at the seashore, he is for a haven for ships, and his border is unto Tsidon.* (Genesis 49:13)

Zebulun took on the emblem of a Ship in a harbor.

Yair Davidy states:

**ZEBULUN Figure**[266]

"The Netherlands (Holland) features lions on its coat of arms. Lions symbolize all of Israel, especially as united under the House of David from Judah, whose special sign is a lion...The Dutch come mainly from Zebulon though other tribal groups (such as those from Naphtali) are also present."[265]

Prophesied to be a "haven of the sea,"[267] Holland is composed primarily of an abundance of rich farmland reclaimed from the ocean. In addition, Amsterdam (at the mouth of the mighty Rhine River, with a vast flotilla of barges arriving daily) and Rotterdam (world-renowned as a Europort and vital shipping link for the European Union) were two of the world's greatest ports in the early 1960's.

---

[265] *The Tribes* by Yair Davidy, p. 318
[266] *Symbols of Our Celto-Saxon Heritage* by W.H. Bennet, 1976
[267] http://britam.org/zebulon.html

Below on the left is a shield from Blason, France, showing the symbolism of Zebulon on a modern day crest.

**Figure**[268]    **Figure**[269]

Another prophecy in Deuteronomy shows that Zebulun was exhorted to:

> *18 Rejoice... in your going out.* (Deuteronomy 33:18)

Notice what author Luigi Barzini says about the Dutch peoples in his book, *The Europeans*:

> "This passion for the sea drove them [the Dutch] to conquer not neighboring provinces... but to set up distant trading points all over the world... They settled in New Amsterdam [which became New York City], a vast natural port, cluttered with flat, sandy islands large and small, at the mouth of a big river, which evidently reminded them of home; in South Africa, Japan, Formosa, Brazil, Ceylon, Indonesia, the West Indies, and many other profitable places."[270]

The prophecy continues by explaining that Zebulun would:

---

[268] http://commons.wikimedia.org/wiki/File:Blason_paris.png
[269] http://commons.wikimedia.org/wiki/File:Coat_of_arms_of_the_Netherlands.svg
[270] *The Europeans* by Luigi Barzini, p. 208

*19 "...suck [of] the abundance of the seas, and [of] treasures hid in the sand."* (Deuteronomy 33:19)

The Netherlands has always been able to do this in several ways, of which I will mention a couple. One is through international commerce by the use of her shipping fleet. Another is through the reclamation of land from the sea. Historically and to this day, the Dutch are well known for building dykes and reclaiming land[271] for the use of farming.

Here are the official flags of Holland. The one Lion is holding a Bunch of Arrows, which are a symbol of Joseph and the Sword is also a symbol of Simeon and Levi showing you how the different clans had their own symbols added to the dominant Tribe.

**Figure**[272]

## Issachar

*14 Yissaskar is a strong donkey lying down between two burdens.* (Genesis 49:14)

*15 "... and he saw that a resting place was good, and that the land was pleasant, and he inclined his shoulder to bear a burden, and became a subject to slave labor."* (Genesis 49:15)

ISSACHAR

---

[271] http://britam.org/zebulon.html
[272] http://en.wikipedia.org/wiki/File:Gouda_Arms_of_Dutch_republic_County_Holland_Kingdom_The_Netherlands.JPG

"Issachar's coat of arms was a Donkey or Ass carrying a heavy load."[273]

Several sources state that the Tribe of Issachar is primarily found in Finland.

**Figure**[274]

Yair Davidy writes:

> "Finland has been identified in this work as belonging mainly to the Tribes of Gad, Simeon and especially Issachar. For many years, Finland was ruled by Sweden... and many Swedes remained in Finland... Both the Sword (Simeon) and the Lion (Gad) are prominent on the Finnish coat of arms."[275]

From the 12th-century to the 19th-century, Finland had been a battleground between Russia and Sweden. It was initially under Swedish rule until 1809. It then became a Russian grand duchy until 1917, when it officially declared its independence. Finland has had to balance careful neutrality, because of its close proximity to Russia in the east, and its ethnic ties to Scandinavia in the West. It could be considered the "Switzerland of Scandinavia."

---

[273] *Symbols of Our Celto-Saxon Heritage* by W.H. Bennet, 1976
[274] http://en.wikipedia.org/wiki/File:Coat_of_arms_of_Finland.svg
[275] *The Tribes* by Yair Davidy, p. 217

## Dan

*16 Dan rightly rules his people as one of the tribes of Yisra'ĕl. 17 Dan is a serpent by the way, an adder by the path, that bites the horse's heels so that its rider falls backward. 18 I have waited for your deliverance, O יהוה.* (Genesis 49:16-18)

**Figure**[276]

Dan's primary emblem was an Eagle carrying a Serpent. This symbol would then become a winged serpent with eagles wings and claws as we see in the Welsh Flag.

**Figure**[277]

From *Dan, the Pioneer of Israel* by Colonel Gawler, we find that Dan settled in Ireland and Denmark.[278] Although Yair Davidy places Dan primarily in Ireland and Denmark as well, Dan is also strongly represented in Wales and in *all* Scandinavian countries. The flag of Wales depicts a Dragon, which is one of the symbols of Dan.

The symbol of Dan was originally a Serpent, which would have *easily* become a Dragon over the centuries.

---

[276] *Symbols of Our Celto-Saxon Heritage* by W.H. Bennet, 1976
[277] http://en.wikipedia.org/wiki/File:Flag_of_Wales_2.svg
[278] http://www.nordiskisrael.dk/artikler/jcgawler_dan_the_pioneer_of_israel_chap1.html

## Asher

*20 Bread from Ashĕr is rich, and he gives delicacies of a sovereign.* (Genesis 49:20)

*20 Out of Asher his bread shall be fat, and he shall yield royal dainties.* (Genesis 49:20)

**Figure**[279]

**Figure**[280]

While this description is brief, Asher's ensign was a covered Cup or Goblet.

There is an abundance of evidence to suggest Belgium is where the Tribe of Asher settled. It is famous for its use of hot vegetable oils and the creation of french fries (chips, or "frites"). Belgium is also famous for high-quality chocolates (the ultimate "royal dainty") and pralines. Since the 15th-century, Belgium has been renowned for its lacework and tapestries, which decorate many castles and palaces throughout Europe.

## Naphtali

*21 Naphtali is a hind let loose: he gives goodly words.* (Genesis 49:21)

Naphtali's emblem was a leaping Hind, or female Deer. This female Deer "let loose" denotes sexual immorality and promiscuity. This best describes modern day Sweden.

Movement toward "equality" of the sexes in Sweden took hold *long before* many other countries

**Figure**[281]

---
[279] http://en.wikipedia.org/wiki/File:Greater_Coat_of_Arms_of_Belgium.svg
[280] *Symbols of Our Celto-Saxon Heritage* by W.H. Bennet, 1976

experienced this same trend. The incidence of premarital sex exceeds 90% and divorce is granted on almost *any* grounds. Many pornographic materials, by other countries' standards, are widespread in Sweden due to their liberal legislation.

W.H. Bennet claims the Naphtalites were to become part of Sweden. Yair Davidy says they are mostly of Norway:

- Naphtalite-Huns - Thyssagetae of east Scythia, - Sian Yueh-chi (i.e., Little Goths).
- Thule (Norway).

**Clans of Nephtali**:

- Jahzeel - Zeeland (Holland), Zealand (Denmark), Yssel (Scandinavia).
- Guni - Egan (Norway), Gugerni (Holland), Chouni (Huni, Huns of Scandinavia etc.,)
- Jezer - Jassar (Alans); Vraesi (Denmark, emigrated en-masse to Britain).[282]
- Shillem -Sillingae (amongst the Vandals, Holland, and Scandinavia).

**Figure**[282]

---

[281] http://en.wikipedia.org/wiki/File:Greater_coat_of_arms_of_Sweden.svg
[282] *Symbols of Our Celto-Saxon Heritage* by W.H. Bennet, 1976

## Benjamin

*27 Binyamin is a wolf that tears, in the morning he eats prey, and at night he divides the spoil.* (Genesis 49:27)

Benjamin's ensign was a Wolf.

*Symbols of Our Celto-Saxon Heritage* states:

"Many of these [Benjamites] settled in Scandinavia, giving their name to Norway and later, to Normandy in France."

**BENJAMIN**
**Figure**[283]

Similar to the Levites, Benjamin (Jacob's youngest son) was dispersed in Judah and remains so today. However, higher concentrations of Benjamites inhabit Norway and Iceland.

Both of these countries were heavily influenced by Viking exploration, which always involved plundering, pillaging and "dividing the spoil." During the Viking Age, family was considered the most important, integral unit of society and blood feuds were not only legal but all too common. Consider how this coincides with the highly structured family unit of a wolf pack.

**Figure**[284]

BENJAMIN was also represented amongst the BELGAE and the NORMANS.

The important features to notice with regard to the coat of arms for Iceland are: the Man, the Bull, the Eagle, and the Dragon—all of which are symbols from the Tribes of Israel.

---

[283] http://commons.wikimedia.org/wiki/File:Coat_of_arms_of_Iceland.svg
[284] *Symbols of Our Celto-Saxon Heritage* by W.H. Bennet, 1976

## Joseph

*22 Yosĕph is an offshoot of a fruit-bearing tree, an offshoot of a fruit-bearing tree by a fountain, his branches run over a wall. 23 And the archers have bitterly grieved him, shot at him and hated him. 24 But his bow remained in strength, and the arms of his hands were made strong by the hands of the Mighty One of Ya'aqob̲—from there is the Shepherd, the Stone of Yisra'ĕl—25 from the Ĕl of your father who helps you, and by the Almighty who blesses you with blessings of the heavens above, blessings of the deep that lies beneath, blessings of the breasts and of the womb. 26 The blessings of your father have excelled the blessings of my ancestors, up to the limit of the everlasting hills. They are on the head of Yosĕph, and on the crown of the head of him who was separated from his brothers.* (Genesis 49:22-26)

MANASSEH

**Figure**[285]

We have a wealth of symbols here that are used as symbols of Joseph and his tribes.

A fruit-bearing tree is often represented as an Olive Branch. A quiver full of Arrows is another symbol often used. In fact, the number Thirteen, in this context, is commonly used to depict the number of Arrows, the number of Leaves and the number of Berries on the Olive Branch. But we must not forget that Joseph had two sons who were blessed *separately* by Jacob *as well*.

In this Scripture, Joseph—the father of Ephraim and Manasseh—is likened to a fruitful Bough or Branch, most likely an Olive Branch. Joseph is also described as being shot by archers.

England means, "Land of the Angles" (Angle-land) Consequently, "Angle" is a form of "Aegel" meaning bull-calf and a nickname for Ephraim (Hosea10:11).

---

[285] *Symbols of Our Celto-Saxon Heritage* by W.H. Bennet, 1976

*11 "And Ephrayim is a trained heifer, loving to thresh grain. But I Myself shall pass over her comely neck—I put Ephrayim to the yoke, Yehuḏah ploughs, Ya'aqoḇ harrows for him." (Hosea10:11)*

The Tribe of Ephraim is very predominant in England. The Anglo-Saxons possessed biblical Hebrew characteristics.

"In old Ashkenazic (European) Hebrew the "ayin" letter could have an "an" sound instead of the usual "a," thus Yankel was a nickname for someone called Yakov, with the Ya- in Yacov being pronounced as "Yan."[286]

This is where we get the term Yank. The other nickname for England is Johnny Bull—again coming from the meaning of "Aegel."

Later, Joseph's descendants are further described:

**EPHRAIM**
**Figure**[287]

*17 His splendor is like a first-born bull, and his horns are like the horns of the wild ox. With them he pushes the peoples to the ends of the earth. And they are the ten thousands of Ephrayim, and they are the thousands of Menashsheh. (Deuteronomy 33:17)*

The King James notes that the word for "***wild ox***" is a "***Unicorn.***"

*His glory is like the firstling of his bullocke, & his hornes are like the hornes of Unicornes: with them he shall push the people together, to the ends of the earth: and they are the ten thousands of Ephraim, and they are the thousands of Manasseh. (Deuteronomy 33:17)*

---

[286] http://www.britam.org/Proof/Joseph/joBull.html
[287] *Symbols of Our Celto-Saxon Heritage* by W.H. Bennet, 1976

With these descriptions divided between both sons, Manasseh's primary emblem was that of an Olive Branch, and his secondary emblem a Cache of Arrows. Also attached to Manasseh's ensign was the number Thirteen, since he was the thirteenth tribe. Ephraim's primary emblem was an Ox, with his secondary emblem being a Unicorn.

Another symbol of Joseph that shows up in heraldry is the Wheat Sheaves, which is the story of Joseph in Genesis 37.

**Figure[288]**

Space does not permit the inclusion of the countless historical records showing the usage of these emblems by early Celto-Saxon peoples for centuries following their migrations throughout Northwestern Europe. Nor is there any room for the symbols found on the Trojan, Argos and Spartan shields, which are very similar to those I have already described to you.

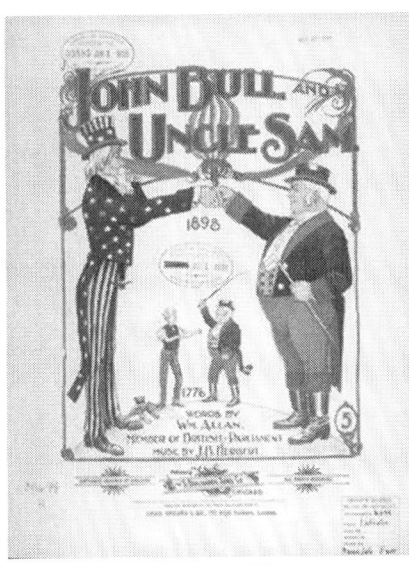

**Figure[289]**

Two of the major identifying attributes of the birthright Tribe of Joseph, of which the son who was given the greater of the blessings, are illustrated on the U.S.A. Great Shield. On the left is the Olive Plant, with its abundance of olives. The Olive Plant is a symbol of richness of oil, and is an emblem of Peace.

---

[288] http://commons.wikimedia.org/wiki/File:William_de_Braose,_4th_Lord_Bramber.svg

[289] http://www.loc.gov/exhibits/british/britintr.html

Interestingly enough, the Olive Branch, the Arrows of Joseph-Manasseh, the Eagle of the Tribe of Dan, and the Shield of Thirteen Stars and Stripes comprise the emblem of the United States of America.

**Figure**[290]

The Great Seal of the United States has many key elements showing its connection with the Tribe of Manasseh: Note in particular the Olive Branch with Thirteen Leaves, the Thirteen Arrows, the Thirteen Stripes on the flag/shield, the thirteen letters in "E Pluribus Unum," and the Thirteen Stars above the Eagle. Manasseh was the youngest "son" of Jacob and therefore, the thirteenth and final tribe. The number "13" does not mean bad luck at all and is a good number according to the Jewish authorities—for it denotes super-abundance. The cloud above the Eagle is symbolic of the Shekinah, or the Cloud of Glory that hovered above Israel over the Tabernacle.

Recall that Manasseh's two emblems incorporated an Olive Branch and a Cache of Arrows. While the American Seal depicts Thirteen Stars to reflect the original Thirteen Colonies, Manasseh was in fact, the thirteenth Tribe of Israel. This is clear evidence linking America with the symbols described in the Bible for Manasseh. The duality is inherently obvious! All these significant, yet little known facts serve as additional proofs of the identity of the British and American peoples today.

It is interesting that one major identifying sign, showing the correlation between the royal family of Britain and Judah's royal line, is found in Britain's national crest.

First notice Balaam's ancient prophecy:

---

[290] http://commons.wikimedia.org/wiki/File:Great_Seal_of_the_United_States_(obverse).svg

*19 Ĕl is not a man, to lie; nor a son of man, to repent! Has He said, and would He not do it; or spoken, and would not confirm it? 20 See, I have received, to bless. And He has blessed, and I do not reverse it. 21 He has not looked upon wickedness in Ya'aqoḇ, nor has He seen trouble in Yisra'ĕl. יהוה his Elohim is with him, and the shout of a Sovereign is in him. 22 Ĕl who brought them out of Mitsrayim, is for them like the horns of a wild ox. 23 For there is no sorcery against Ya'aqoḇ, nor is there any divination against Yisra'ĕl. Now it is said to Ya'aqoḇ and to Yisra'ĕl, 'What has Ĕl done?!' 24 Look, a people rises like a lioness, and lifts itself up like a lion; it lies not down until it devours the prey, and drinks the blood of the slain.* (Numbers 23:19-24)

Recall that Joseph's coat of arms was the Unicorn and that Judah's was the Lion. In addition to this, the ensign for David's royal lineage was a Lion wearing a Crown. After the kingdoms divided, the Kingdom of Israel was represented in prophetic scriptures as a "*wild ox*" and or a "*Unicorn.*" The Lion represented the Kingdom of Judah. Also take note of the Unicorn, which represents Israel. It has a chain around its neck fastened to the ground. This is to show the captivity they went into. The Lion of Judah does *not* have a chain. They returned from their captivity, whereas Israel never did.

In modern times, these emblems have carried over onto Britain's coat of arms—which features a Lion wearing a Crown—and a Unicorn! The union of the national emblems of Israel and Judah represent the connection of the royal Pharez line, or the bloodline of King David, to the Zerah line of kings in Britain.

Notice Scotland's royal coat of arms as shown here. The Unicorn represents Israel, the Northern Ten Tribes who went into captivity. The captivity is represented by the chain around the neck and anchored to the ground. The Lion, represents the royal line of Judah. You can see the three Lions, the Red Lion of Zerah and the Harp of King David from Ireland in the crest. The Unicorn represents the Tribe of Joseph (Deuteronomy 33:17). The Unicorn itself is an ancient symbol of the Tribe of Manasseh, as is shown by the Midrash of Numbers 2:7.

There is also another message for us in the royal coat of arms of the United Kingdom still in use in Scotland. In the Book of Revelation, in referring to Himself, Yehshua says: "I am the Alpha and Omega, the Beginning and the End, the First and the Last."

> *I am the Alpha and Omega, the Beginning and the Ending, says the Lord, who is and who was and who is to come, the Almighty. I, John, who also am your brother and companion in the affliction, and in the kingdom and patience of Jesus Christ, was in the island that is called Patmos, for the Word of God and for the testimony of Jesus Christ. I came to be in the Spirit in the Lord's day and heard behind me a great voice, as of a trumpet, saying, I am the Alpha and Omega, the First and the Last. Also, What you see, write in a book and send it to the seven churches which are in Asia: to Ephesus, and to Smyrna, and to Pergamos, and to Thyatira, and to Sardis, and to Philadelphia, and to Laodicea.* (Revelation 1:8-11)

The significance of this is that "alpha" and "omega" are the first and the last letters in the alphabet of the Greek language in which the New Covenant/Testament is most commonly written. By using them as a name for Himself, the Lord is emphasizing His identity with the eternal One—the everlasting Yehovah, the first and the last of all things. We read in Isaiah something of interest as well in three verses.

*Who has planned and done it, calling forth the generations from the beginning? I, Jehovah, am the first and the last; I am He.* (Isaiah 41:4)

*So says Jehovah, the King of Israel, and His redeemer Jehovah of Hosts; I am the first, and I am the last; and besides Me there is no God.* (Isaiah 44:6)

*Listen to me, O Jacob and Israel, My called; I am He; I am the first, I also am the last.* (Isaiah 48:12)

# The Aleph and Tav את

We read more of the Alpha and Omega in Revelation.

*He said to me, "It is done! I am the Alpha and the Omega, the Beginning and the End. I will give of the fountain of the water of life freely to him who thirsts.* (Revelation 21:6) (The **Aleph** and **Tav** את)

*"I am the Alpha and the Omega, the Beginning and the End, the First and the Last."* (Revelation 22:13) (The **Aleph** and **Tav** את)

Yehovah is the Aleph and Tav את found within the Torah. By seeing the Aleph and the Tav we know that these are Yehovah's words. Yeshua said in John

*"For if you believed Moses, you would believe Me; for he wrote about Me.* (John 5:46)

We see the Aleph and Tav את also validating this as Yeshua's words found within Torah

Here is a very telling use of the Aleph and the Tav found in Deuteronomy 6:5. The Aleph and the Tav את are pointing to יהוה YHWH Yehovah.

ואהבת **את יהוה** אלהיך בכל־לבבך ובכל־נפשך ובכל־מאדך:

> And you shall love (H157 **אהב** aw-hab', aw-habe') יהוה (Jehovah) your God with all your heart and with all your soul and with all your might. (Deuteronomy 6:5)

When you read of the Aleph and Tav את in Zechariah it should become very apparent what we have done.

> And I will pour on the house of David, and on the people of Jerusalem, the spirit of grace and of prayers. And they shall look on **Me** (**H853** את ayth) *whom they have pierced, and they shall mourn for Him, as one mourns for his only son, and shall be bitter over Him, as the bitterness over the firstborn.* (Zechariah 12:10)

**Zec 12:10 דויד ועל יושב ירושלם רוח חן ותחנונים והביטו אלי את אשר־דקרו וספדו לעיו ושפכתי על־בית**

> "and they shall look upon (see what the Aleph and Tav is pointing at את) me whom they have pierced"

This is a picture of the Messiah of Israel who is pierced for our transgressions, the Aleph and the Tav את points to the Messiah of Israel.

In Revelation we read Yeshua is calling Himself, **"the pierced one"**; the aleph and the tav; the alpha and omega.

> *Behold, He comes with the clouds, and every eye will see Him, and those who pierced Him will see Him, and all the kindreds of the earth will wail because of Him. Even so, Amen.* (Revelation 1:7)

Is this speaking of Yehshua or is it speaking of Yehovah? Whom are we talking about? Yehshua said to Phillip that He was the Father.

> *Philip said to Him, Lord, show us the Father, and it is enough for us. 9 Jesus said to him, Have I been with you such a long*

*time and yet you have not known Me, Philip? He who has seen Me has seen the Father. And how do you say, Show us the Father? 10 Do you not believe that I am in the Father and the Father in Me? The Words that I speak to you I do not speak of Myself, but the Father who dwells in Me, He does the works. (John 14:8)*

Yehshua is telling Philip that He, Yehshua was also the Father. They are the same, not two and not three, but one and the same person.

*"Behold, this is our God; We have waited for Him, and He will save us. This is Yehovah; We have waited for Him; We will be glad and rejoice in His salvation." (Isaiah 25:9)*

The word for Salvation is H3444 ישועה yesh-oo'-aw Feminine passive participle of H3467; something saved, that is, (abstractly) deliverance; hence aid, victory, prosperity: – deliverance, health, help (-ing), salvation, save, saving (health), welfare.

Yesh-oo'-aw is where we get the name Yehshua for the Messiah but in fact it is Yehovah Himself.

*For I am Yehovah your God, The Holy One of Israel, your Savior...(Isaiah 43:3)*

*"You are My witnesses," says Yehovah, "And My servant whom I have chosen, That you may know and believe Me, And understand that I am He. Before Me there was no God formed, Nor shall there be after Me. I, even I, am Yehovah, And besides Me there is no Savior. (Isaiah 43:10-11)*

The word Savior here is H3467 ישע yaw-shah' A primitive root; properly to be open, wide or free, that is, (by implication) to be safe; causatively to free or succor: – X at all, avenging, defend, deliver (-er), help, preserve, rescue, be safe, bring (having) salvation, save (-iour), get victory.

Read these verses again. Besides Yehovah THERE IS NO SAVIOR. So who is Yehshua?

> *Thus says Yehovah: "...They will plead with you, saying: 'Surely God is in you, and there is no other, no god besides Him.'" Truly, you are a God who hides Himself, O God of Israel, the Savior. All of them are put to shame and confounded; the makers of idols go in confusion together. But Israel is saved by Yehovah with everlasting salvation; you shall not be put to shame or confounded to all eternity. For thus says Yehovah, who created the heavens (he is God!), who formed the earth and made it (he established it; He did not create it empty, He formed it to be inhabited!): "I am Yehovah, and there is no other. I did not speak in secret, in a land of darkness; I did not say to the offspring of Jacob, 'Seek me in vain.' I Yehovah speak the truth; I declare what is right. "Assemble yourselves and come; draw near together, you survivors of the nations! They have no knowledge who carry about their wooden idols, and keep on praying to a god that cannot save. Declare and present your case; let them take counsel together! Who told this long ago? Who declared it of old? Was it not I, Yehovah? And there is no other god besides Me, a righteous God and a Savior; there is none besides Me. "Turn to Me and be saved, all the ends of the earth! For I am God, and there is no other. By Myself I have sworn; from My mouth has gone out in righteousness a word that shall not return: 'To Me every knee shall bow, every tongue shall swear allegiance.'* (Isaiah 45:14-23)

> *"Yet I am Yehovah your God ever since the land of Egypt, And you shall know no God but Me; For there is no Savior besides Me."* (Hosea 13:4)

> *To whom will you liken Me and make Me equal, and compare Me, that we may be alike? ...for I am God, and there is no other; I am God, and there is none like Me, ...I bring near My righteousness; it is not far off, and My salvation will*

*not delay; I will put salvation in Zion, for Israel My glory."* (Isaiah 46:5,9,13)

*For My own sake, for My own sake, I do it, for how should My Name be profaned? My glory I will not give to another. "Listen to Me, O Jacob, and Israel, whom I called! I am He; I am the first, and I am the last.* (Isaiah 48:11-12)

*I came to be in the Spirit in the Lord's day and heard behind me a great voice, as of a trumpet, 11 saying, I am the Alpha and Omega, the First and the Last. Also, What you see, write in a book and send it to the seven churches which are in Asia: to Ephesus, and to Smyrna, and to Pergamos, and to Thyatira, and to Sardis, and to Philadelphia, and to Laodicea. 12 And I turned to see the voice that spoke with me. 13 And having turned, I saw seven golden lampstands. And in the midst of the seven lampstands I saw One like the Son of man, clothed with a garment down to the feet, and tied around the breast with a golden band. 14 His head and hair were white like wool, as white as snow. And His eyes were like a flame of fire. 15 And His feet were like burnished brass having been fired in a furnace. And His voice was like the sound of many waters. 16 And He had seven stars in His right hand, and out of His mouth went a sharp two-edged sword. And His face was like the sun shining in its strength. 17 And when I saw Him, I fell at His feet as dead. And He laid His right hand upon me, saying to me, Do not fear, I am the First and the Last, 18 and the Living One, and I became dead, and behold, I am alive for ever and ever, Amen. And I have the keys of hell and of death.* (Revelation 1:10-18)

It is Yehovah who is the FIRST AND THE LAST. Yehovah is the Aleph and the Tav. Yehovah is the Alpha and Omega. Yehovah is the one we have pierced.

*And behold, I am coming quickly, and My reward is with Me, to give to each according as his work is. 13 I am the Alpha and the Omega, the Beginning and the Ending, the First and the Last. 14 Blessed are they who do His commandments, that their authority will be over the Tree of Life, and they may enter in by the gates into the city.* (Revelation 22:12)

*Hear, O, Israel. Jehovah our God is one Jehovah.* (Deuteronomy 6:4)

Yeshua is the only prophet of God who claimed to be the Aleph and the Tav, the beginning and the end, the alpha and the omega. Again the question was just asked, "Who was Yehshua?

*In the beginning was the Word, and the Word was with God, and the Word was God. 2 He was in the beginning with God. 3 All things came into being through Him, and without Him not even one thing came into being that has come into being.* (John 1:1-3)

*And the Word became flesh, and tabernacled among us. And we beheld His glory, the glory as of the only begotten of the Father, full of grace and of truth.* (John 1:14)

In other words, in the beginning was the Word and the Word was Yehovah and the Word, Yehovah, became flesh and was known as Yehshua, the Aleph Tav, the Alpha Omega and the את in the Hebrew alphabet.

These two letters in the Hebrew Alphabet are "aleph" and "tau," and in the original Hebrew alphabet, the "aleph" appears as a diagonal cross or "X" and the "tau" as an upright cross "+." Thus, when combined as a symbol to express the idea of the Eternal Yehovah, they would appear like the diagonally crisscrossed cross of Britannia's shield; the flags of the Celtic/Israelites in Northern Spain and the British Flag known as the Union Jack.

In his book, *Or Torah*, author and Rabbi, Dov Ber, the Maggid of Mezritch, explains the very first words of Torah; Bereshit Bara Elohim Et (Genesis 1:1) below:

> "Note that et is an untranslatable word used to indicate that 'a definite direct object is next' (thus there needs to be an et before the heavens and the earth)."

But Dov Ber points out that "et" is spelled—Aleph-Tav, an abbreviation for the Aleph-Bet. Aleph is the first letter of the Hebrew alphabet. Since God did this *before* creating the Heavens and the Earth, the letters are considered to be the primordial building blocks of *all* of creation (Genesis 1:1).

The "Aleph" is the "X" being held by the Unicorn of Israel and the "Tav" is the Cross being held by the Lion of Judah. Again, this is the *same* Cross you encounter on the flag of Northern Ireland that I showed you at the beginning of this chapter with the Red Hand in it. Again, these are the symbols of the Union Jack flag of Great Britain.

I began this chapter showing you about the Cherubim and what they looked like. I then went on to show you the camp of Israel as it was in the Wilderness. As a recap, I will go over it with you again:

- The Cherubim had a face like a Lion, which is representative of Judah the leading tribe on the east side of the camp of Israel.
- The Cherubim had the face of Man, which is represented by Reuben on the south side of the camp of Israel.
- The Cherubim had a third face like that of an Ox, which represented Ephraim on the west side of the camp of Israel.
- The Cherubim had a face like that of an Eagle, which represented the Tribe of Dan on the north side of the camp of Israel.

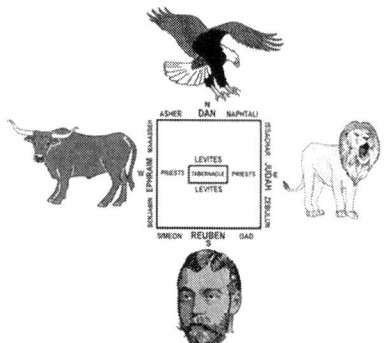

The facts and national characteristics I have listed and described to you in this chapter are only a thumbnail sketch of what I could have presented you with. But I wanted to include just enough information to strengthen the body of evidence and historical record left behind by Yehovah for all those who have "eyes to see." I will let you draw your own conclusions regarding what I have just presented, but we have an awesome responsibility and are to be held all the more accountable by Yehovah once we know *who* we really are and where we come from.

If you have Unicorns, Lions, Bulls, Sheaves of Wheat, Eagles, Wolves or Boats/Ships in your heraldry—or any of the other symbols I have shown you here, then it is highly likely your family, or parts of your family, have come from the Tribes of Israel as they migrated to where you are now.

Here are some other examples of the symbols of Israel's heritage for you to consider:

COAT of ARMS AZORES

Notice how the Bulls, which represent Ephraim, are chained as if in captivity.

**Figure**[291]

---

[291] http://en.wikipedia.org/wiki/File:Azr.png

## DEVON COUNTY COUNCIL

Devon is one of the places of my ancestry on my Mother's side. They have the Red Lion of Zerah, the Ship of Zebulun, the Gold Lion of the Royal Crown and the Bull of Ephraim. The Horse is yet another symbol of Ireland.

**Figure**[292]

## SOMERSET COUNTY COUNCIL

Somerset is another place on my Mother's side. Here we have the Stag of Naphtali, the Serpent of Dan with the wings of the Eagle holding the Scepter. Also, we have the Bull of Ephraim.

In this crest, we have the Castle of either Levi or Simeon and the Serpent of Daniel. In the crest is the Red Lion of Zerah, and the fleur-de-lys, which is symbol of Reuben who picked mandrakes for his Mother Leah.

**Figure**[293]

## DORSET COUNTY COUNCIL HAMPSHIRE COUNTY COUNCIL

On this crest we find the Stag of Naphtali and the Lion of Judah with the Castle of Simeon or Levi. But in the middle of the shield is the Tudor Rose. I will explain this more in a moment.

---

[292] http://www.civicheraldry.co.uk/cornwall_wessex.html
[293] http://www.civicheraldry.co.uk/cornwall_wessex.html

## MID-DEVON DISTRICT COUNCIL

In this crest you can see the Sheaves of wheat that are a symbol of Joseph and the Castle of Simeon or Levi. Water is also depicted on this crest, which is representative of Reuben.

## FAREHAM BOROUGH COUNCIL (HANTS)

In Jewish liturgy the expression "Shoshana Ya'acov" (Rose of Jacob) represents all of Israel. In the Bible, Israel is likened to a rose: [Hosea 14:5] I will be as the dew unto Israel: he shall grow as the lily [Hebrew "shoshana," (i.e. "rose")], and cast forth his roots as Lebanon. "Lily" in Hebrew is "shoshana" and actually means "rose." The rose (in a rosette shape based on the rose) was a symbol of royalty in ancient Israel and in other nations. In the beginning of the "*Zohar*" it says: "As the rose among the thorns, so is my love among the maidens." (Song of Solomon 2:2). What is the rose? What does it symbolize? It represents the Assemblage of Israel or the Community of Israel. For there is a rose (above) and a rose (below). Just as the rose, which is found among the thorns, is both red and white, so does the Assemblage of Israel represent justice and mercy. Just as a rose has Thirteen Petals, so does the Assemblage [Hebrew: "Knesset"] of Israel have Thirteen Measures of Compassion encompassing it on all sides. "…five strong leaves surround the rose…"

In ENGLAND BETWEEN THE YEARS 1450–1485 there was a series of civil wars known as "Wars of the Roses" occurring between the rival houses of York and Lancaster. Each side was represented by a rose, York by a White Rose, and Lancaster by a Red Rose. At the end of the struggle, a partly Welsh noble named Henry Tudor became king. Henry claimed to unify in his person the two rival sides. He chose as his symbol, a rose with *both* red and white petals (i.e. a large white rose with a smaller red rose overlaid on it) and with five green leaves around it. Dr. Clifford Smyth of Ulster supplied Yair Davidiy with color photographs of pictures from the Tudor Period depicting the Tudor Rose. These paintings show that there then existed in England a real breed of rose that looked like Tudor Rose. This rose, unbeknown to Henry, was (says the above quoted Zohar) the symbol of Israel. Henceforth, the red and white petal "Tudor Rose" became the symbol of the English monarchs and therefore of England itself. It still is an official symbol of Britain. The Tudor Rose admittedly has only ten petals, whereas the "Rose of Israel" described in the Zohar has thirteen, but then England, being dominated by the Tribe of Ephraim, represents only ten out of the original thirteen Israelite Tribes. Henry Tudor was a great man. He came from a ruling house legendarily connected with King Arthur and he may have… descended (as some believe) from King David. "He has been called the Solomon of England." He asserted the independence of England from Europe. The history of modern England as an outwardly looking, independently minded great nation begins with Henry. His reign marks the beginning of that period in which the blessings promised to the seed of Israel would be realized in the British and British descended peoples![294]

---

[294] http://britam.org/Roses.html

The Tudor Rose is the same as the Israeli flower, the Shoshanna.

# Chapter 4 | The Christian 490-Year Prophecy—Where & How It Developed

> *24 Seventy weeks are decreed for your people and for your set-apart city, to put an end to the transgression, and to seal up sins, and to cover crookedness, and to bring in everlasting righteousness, and to seal up vision and prophet, and to anoint the Most Set-apart. 25 Know, then, and understand: from the going forth of the command to restore and build Yerushalayim until Messiah the Prince is seven weeks and sixty-two weeks. It shall be built again, with streets and a trench, but in times of affliction. 26 And after the sixty-two weeks, Messiah shall be cut off and have naught. And the people of a coming prince shall destroy the city and the set-apart place. And the end of it is with a flood. And wastes are decreed, and fighting until the end. 27 And he shall confirm a covenant with many for one week. And in the middle of the week he shall put an end to slaughtering and meal offering. And on the wing of abominations he shall lay waste, even until the complete end and that which is decreed is poured out on the one who lays waste."[1]* [Footnote: [1]Mt. 24:15. (Daniel 9:24-27)]

I will now begin to explain these four verses in Daniel.

## "Seventy Weeks Are Decreed"

When the average individual in our modern society reads this, they all do the exact same thing when trying to understand this prophecy. They multiply 70 x 7 believing that the "7" represents the seven day week and arrive at 490. They then use the concept of a year to represent a day, as the Bible states, and in keeping with what I already explained to you in the Introduction. So this 490 then becomes 490 years. But what does this really *mean*, exactly?

Most will then erroneously jump to what is said (in v. 25) "...from the going forth of the command" and begin to search for the answer to what this means. They then take this from the time of Artaxerxes' decree[295] in either 447 B.C., 445 B.C. or 444 B.C. and mistakenly tack 483 years on to this to get the time in which the Messiah began His ministry. With the belief that the remaining 7 years represents those 3 ½ years of his ministry which began in the fall of 27 C.E. until He was killed on the tree at Passover in 31 C.E. The last 3 ½ years being assumed to be the Great Tribulation that is yet to come at some point in the future. I urge you all to just do the math and check this for yourselves.

It may surprise many of you to know that while Yehshua was here on Earth, the disciples *never* asked Him about this prophecy. It is not recorded in any of the Gospels and especially not in the context of Yehshua showing them how He had fulfilled it as many today claim He did. But did Yehshua, in truth, actually fulfill this prophecy? Had He actually done so, one would think He surely would have made it known to the disciples. They, in turn, would have used it to better persuade the Jews. But none of this actually happened. Could it be that this actually does not apply to the Messiah's first coming after all?

---

[295] Ezra 7:21 And I, Artaxerxes the king, make a decree to all the treasurers who *are* Beyond the River, that whatever Ezra the priest, the scribe of the Law of the God of Heaven, shall ask of you, it shall be done exactly, 22 to a hundred talents of silver, and to a hundred measures of wheat, and to a hundred baths of wine, and to a hundred baths of oil, and salt without saying. 23 Whatever is commanded by the God of Heaven, let it be carefully done for the house of the God of Heaven, for why should there be wrath against the realm of the king and his sons?

As I prepared to write this chapter of the book, I was, in all honesty, quite surprised to read the comments that many have made about these four verses in Daniel. There is an army of scholars who have written volumes and volumes of papers on the meaning of these four verses. To know, for sure, that I have been given a revelation that none of these other scholars have been able to figure out is extremely humbling, to put it mildly. It is humbling because I know I did not figure it out using my "superior" intelligence. It is humbling because I know I am not wiser than or better than any of these men—or more righteous, for that matter. In fact, quite the opposite would be true. Nevertheless, I was shown something by Yehovah back in 2005 and I've been faithful to tell others about it as to the best of my ability since then and to obey Him and keep this special time. It was that understanding of the Sabbatical and Jubilee years, that enabled me to understand this revelation when it came later on. I will get to that shortly.

But first, let me quote to you a few of the many perspectives others have given on Daniel 9.

> The 70 Weeks Prophecy in Daniel 9:24-27 has been one of the most notorious interpretive problem passages in Old Testament studies. As (James) Montgomery put it, "The history of the exegesis of the 70 Weeks is the dismal swamp of O.T. criticism."[296] Early church fathers commonly embraced a messianic interpretation of the passage and sought to prove a chronological computation for the time of Messiah's coming based on this prophecy. This approach has been favored by many conservatives—both premillennial and amillennial—down through the centuries. Advocates of the messianic view differ over the details of interpretation (e.g., the number of times Messiah is referred to in the passage, the termini of the calculations, or how the final 70th week relates to the first 69), but they agree that this passage is one of the most astounding references to the Lord Jesus Christ and the time of His first advent.[297]

---

[296] *Commentary on the Book of Daniel* by James Montgomery, (Edinburgh: T. & T. Clark, 1927), pp. 400–-01.
[297] *Is Daniel's Seventy-Weeks Prophecy Messianic, Part I?* by J. Paul Tanner.

J. Paul Tanner goes on to say in the Introduction of his work, *The Messianic Interpretation in the Development of Daniel's 70 Week Prophecy*:

> The most prevalent interpretations of Daniel's 70 Weeks in modern days is that it is a messianic prophecy climaxing in Messiah Yehshua's crucifixion and His subsequent return. However, this belief is not consistent with early church writings. In fact, according to James Montgomery, "The specifically 'Christian' interpretation, which found the terminus of the Weeks in the advent of Jesus Christ, only slowly made its way; it is not found at all in the New Testament, it is not made use of at all in Justin Martyr's [103 C.E.–165 C.E.] *Apologies*, and outside of a passing allusion in [the Epistle of] Barnabas… we have to come to the Fathers at the end of the 2nd-century, to obtain this exegesis."[298]

Did you catch that? No one associated this prophecy with the advent of the Messiah until the second century C.E., no one!

I will now have you take a look at some of the interpretations of this prophecy before the birth of Yehshua and provide you with a glimpse of how some have interpreted it. I will begin with another quote from J. Paul Tanner.

> Beckwith[299] has concluded, "The Essenes began Daniel's 70 Weeks at the return from the Exile, which they dated in Anno Mundi 3430, and that they therefore expected the period

---

http://www.dts.edu/download/publications/bibliotheca/DTS-Is%20Daniel%27s%20Seventy-Weeks%20Prophecy%20Messianic.pdf, J. Paul Tanner is Middle East Director, BEE World, Bullard, Texas. (You will have to enter *"Daniel's Seventy-Weeks Prophecy Messianic"* in the search engine when you arrive at this link)

[298] *A Critical and Exegetical Commentary On THE BOOK OF DANIEL* by James Montgomery, New York: C. Scribner, 1927, p. 398, Print.

[299] For a more complete discussion of the evidence see: *Daniel 9 and the Date of Messiah's Coming In Essene, Hellenistic, Pharisaic, Zealot and Early Christian Computation* by Roger Beckwith, *Revue de Qumran* 10 (December 1981): pp. 521–42.

of 70 Weeks or 490 years to expire in A.M. 3920, which meant, for them, between 3 B.C. and A.D. 2. Consequently, their hopes of the coming of the Messiah of Israel (the Son of David) were concentrated on the preceding 7 years, the last week, after the 69 weeks. Their interpretation of the 70 Weeks is first found in the *Testament of Levi* and the *Pseudo-Ezekiel Document (4 Q 384–390)*, which probably means that it was worked out before 146 B.C."[300]

From a very early time, a non-messianic perspective also existed. Perhaps this was due in part to the old Greek rendering of Daniel 9:26: καὶ μετὰ τὰς ἑβδομάδας τὰς ἑξήκοντα δύο ἐξολεθρευθήσεται χρῖσμα, καὶ κρίμα οὐκ ἔστιν ἐν αὐτῷ· καὶ τὴν πόλιν καὶ τὸ ἅγιον διαφθερεῖ σὺν τῷ ἡγουμένῳ τῷ ἐρχομένῳ, καὶ ἐκκοπήσονται ἐν κατακλυσμῷ, καὶ ἕως τέλους πολέμου συντετμημένου τάξει ἀφανισμοῖς. ["and after 7 and 70 and 62, the anointing (or 'unction,' χρῖσμα) will be taken away and will not be, and the Kingdom of the Gentiles will destroy the city and the Temple with the Anointed One."] It seems that the Septuagint translators were straining to make the text say what they wanted it to say. Once the sum of the figures (i.e., 139) is subtracted from the beginning of the Seleucid Era (311 B.C.–310 B.C.), the result conveniently falls at 172 B.C.–71 B.C., that is, the approximate year of the murder of the high priest Onias III during the troublesome times of Antiochus IV Epiphanes.[301] Yet this was not the only attempt to connect the 70 Weeks Prophecy to the Maccabean Era, for another piece of evidence to this effect comes from the Hellenistic Jewish Historian Demetrius, preserved by Clement of Alexandria (in his *Stromata* I, XXI, p. 141).[302]

---

[300] Ibid., pp. 523, 525. See also, *The Significance of the Calendar for Interpreting Essene Chronology and Eschatology* by Roger Beckwith, *Revue de Qumran* 10 (May 1980): pp. 167–202.

[301] On the beginning of the Seleucid Era according to the Babylonian Calendar. See also, *Handbook of Biblical Chronology* by Jack Finegan, rev. ed. (Peabody, MA: Hendrickson, 1998), p. 103.

[302] *Daniel 9 and the Date of Messiah's Coming* by Roger Beckwith, pp. 528–29.

Therefore, although there is evidence for both a messianic and non-messianic interpretation of the 70 Weeks Prophecy well before the Christian Era, the destruction of Jerusalem and the Temple in A.D. 70 (along with the failed Bar Kokhba Revolt shortly thereafter in A.D. 132–A.D. 35) decisively altered the Jewish interpretations of Daniel 9:24–27. From several statements made by Josephus, it seems clear that he viewed the fulfillment of the prophecy in the events leading up to A.D. 70 rather than in the Maccabean Era.[303] He seems to have drawn a connection between the "cutting off" of the anointed high priest (Ananus, who was murdered by the Idumaeans in the Temple around A.D. 66–A.D. 68) and the destruction of the "city" and "sanctuary" by the Romans. As Beckwith concludes, "Up to A.D. 70, the different Pharisaic dates for the coming of the Messiah and the different reckonings of the 70 Weeks which they implied, must have existed among the rabbis as three rival interpretations. After A.D. 70, however, when the Messiah had not come as expected, but the desolation foretold in Daniel 9 (vv. 26–27) had, it was natural to tie the end of the 70 Weeks to A.D. 70 and also to adopt a non-messianic interpretation of the prophecy."[304]

This tendency in Jewish circles to see the 70 Weeks fulfilled in Jerusalem's destruction in A.D. 70 is even more strongly affirmed in the Jewish chronological work, *Seder Olam*

---

[303] Although Josephus's comments are somewhat vague, this seems to be the most sensible interpretation of his remarks. See especially *The Jewish Wars* 4.5.2 (pp. 318, 323) and 6.2.1 (pp. 109–10), in *The Works of Josephus*, trans. by William Whiston (Peabody, MA: Hendrickson, 1987). For further discussion see: *The Apocalyptic Survey of History Adapted by Christians: Daniel's Prophecy of Seventy Weeks* by William Adler, in *The Jewish Apocalyptic Heritage in Early Christianity* by James C. VanderKam and William Adler, ed., (Minneapolis: Fortress, 1996), pp. 210–16; *Daniel 9 and the Date of Messiah's Coming* by Roger Beckwith, pp. 532–36; *Josephus and Daniel, Annual of the Swedish Theological Institute* by F.F. Bruce, 4 (1965): pp. 148–62; and *Josephus' Treatment of the Book of Daniel, Journal of Jewish Studies* by Geza Vermes, 42 (1991): pp. 149–66.

[304] *Daniel 9 and the Date of Messiah's Coming* by Roger Beckwith, p. 536.

*Rabbah*, which, according to tradition, was composed about A.D. 160 (though it may have been supplemented and edited at a later period). This work provides a chronological record that extends from Adam to the Bar Kokhba Revolt of A.D. 132–A.D. 135. The significance of *Seder Olam Rabbah* is that the chronology espoused therein became commonly accepted in subsequent Jewish writings, including the Talmud and the consensus of Jewish rabbinical scholars (e.g., Rashi, A.D. 1040–A.D. 1105). *Seder Olam Rabbah* says that the 70 Weeks were 70 years of exile in Babylon followed by another 420 years until the destruction of the second Temple in A.D. 70.[305] The latter figure of 420 is achieved by assigning 34 years for the domination of the Persians, 180 years (for) the Greeks, 103 years for the Maccabees, and 103 years for the Herods. The problem, of course, is that these figures are simply unacceptable to modern historians, especially the significantly low figure of 34 years for the Persians. Nevertheless this became the basis for Jewish calculations of the prophecy, though Jewish commentators differed on the details.[306]

In my last book, *Remembering the Sabbatical Years 2016*, I devoted all of Chapter 22 to explaining the erroneous teaching of the Seder Olam and how it is now the basis for what much of Judaic chronology is based upon. Once this error is unraveled, the truth leads you to a chronology that is found both in the pages of your Bible and in history.[307]

---

[305] *Seder Olam Rabbah*, Ch. 28, See: *Seder Olam: The Rabbinic View of Biblical Chronology* by Heinrich Guggenheimer, (Lanham, MD: Jason Aronson, 1998), pp. 240–46.

[306] For a survey of classical rabbinic interpretations of Daniel 9:24–27 see: *Daniel: A New Translation With A Commentary Anthologized From Talmudic, Midrashic and Rabbinic Sources* by Hersh Goldwurm, 2nd ed. (Brooklyn, NY: Mesorah, 1980), pp. 259–67. Jewish commentators tended to interpret the cutting off of the j" yvim; in Daniel 9:26 in one of three ways: (1) the cessation of the sacrifices offered by the *anointed* priesthood; (2) the death of King Agrippa II, who ruled Judah at the time of the Temple's destruction; and (3) the death of the high priest, Ananus, at the time of the Jewish revolt leading up to A.D. 70.

[307] *Remembering the Sabbatical Years 2016* by Joseph F. Dumond, Ch.22 http://bookstore.xlibris.com/Products/SKU-0125561049/

In *Remembering the Sabbatical year of 2016* I explain how Rabbi Jose, author of the Seder Olam, changed the historical dates in an effort to prove that Simon bar Kochba was the expected messiah. Although the Sages agreed that Simon was not the long awaited Messiah, they still accepted the false chronology as true, even though history proves those dates that Rabbi Yossi claims the two temples were destroyed, to be false dates.

There are some other factors to keep in mind as well about this time I am speaking of. Everyone was expecting the fulfillment of Daniel's 70 Week's Prophecy. They first expected it during the Maccabean times and that of Antiochus IV Epiphanes. They then expected it around the time of Augustus Caesar[308] and around the time of the Messiah's birth in 3 B.C. They thought this prophecy applied to the time when the Temple was destroyed and expected the Messiah then. Finally, they anticipated the Messiah's death at the time of the Bar Kochba Revolt. Daniel's 70 Weeks kept being reinvented each time to try and answer the question "are we there yet?" in order to bring some solace to those who were suffering, so that they could endure—all the while believing, "yes, we are at the end," when the Messianic Kingdom will be ushered in—when, in fact, they were not. All of this is before the church fathers begin to write about this prophecy.

We have seen the same thing in our day with those who claimed the rapture was in May and then again in October of 2011.[309] People want it all to be over with and this is what this prophecy is all about and what it still means to people. It is a chronology of when it finally is going to be all over.

> As the Book of Daniel was well-known during the time that the New Testament was written, if Messiah Yahshua fulfilled

---

Remembering-The-Sabbatical-Years-of-2016.aspx

[308] He was born Gaus Julius Caesar Octavian. He was the grandnephew of Julius Caesar, the founder of the Roman Empire who turned the empire over to Octavian whom the people of Rome called Augustus Caesar, that is, "Exalted Caesar." The name Augustus means exalted. He ruled the Roman Empire from 27 B.C. to 14 A.D.

[309] http://abcnews.go.com/blogs/business/2011/10/harold-camping-doomsday-prophet-wrong-again/

Daniel's 70 Weeks, it should be mentioned somewhere in the text. But, it isn't. There are references to certain passages within Daniel, such as the Abomination of Desolation in Matthew 24:15 and Mark 13:14, but nowhere do we find any statement where Daniel's 70 Weeks were fulfilled. In fact, as Yahshua told the Apostles which scriptures spoke of Him (Luke 24:27), if He did indeed fulfill this prophecy, He certainly would have mentioned it and the New Testament writers would have recorded it.

In fact, there is very little evidence to show that there was very much interest in Daniel's vision of the 70 Weeks during the first two centuries of the early church. However, as they were expecting the imminent return of Messiah, they believed that the prophecies contained in the Book of Daniel were to occur in their immediate future. Their writings show that "a deeply held belief in early Christian apocalypticism understood the eschatological 70th Week as the 70 years of the church between Christ's ascension and his expected return. This expectation, which evidently influenced the dating of the close of the apostolic period in around the year (A.D.) 100, did receive partial confirmation from the events occurring in Judea in the year (A.D.) 70."[310]

Up until this point I have only shown you what Jewish thought was on this prophecy of Daniel 9:24-27 and how they had interpreted it against the events of their day and how each one was, in turn, proven to be not true. Now we are about to begin to see where Christian thought developed about this same prophesy and builds on the views of the previous writers.

---

[310] *The Apocalyptic Survey of History Adapted by Christians: Daniel's Prophecy of 70 Weeks* by William Adler, *The Jewish Apocalyptic Heritage In Early History* by James C. VanderKam and William Adler, ed., Assen: Van Gorcum & Comp. B.V., 1996, p. 219, Print.

## IRENAEUS (WRITING CA. A.D. 180)[311]

Early Christian writers often used the 70 Weeks Prophecy for polemical purposes against Jewish unbelief in Jesus as the promised Messiah. For that reason it is strange that Justin Martyr made no reference to Daniel 9 in his apologetic work, *Dialogue With Trypho the Jew* (ca. A.D. 153–A.D 165), though he made 14 other references to Daniel. The earliest clear Christian reference to Daniel 9:24–27 is by Irenaeus in his, *Against Heresies* (ca. A.D. 180). In Book 5.25.3, Irenaeus clearly linked the Prophecy of the Little Horn in Daniel 7 to 2 Thessalonians 2, and he indicated that the Antichrist will be in power 3½ years. In 5.25.2, he quoted Matthew 24:15 and stated that this will be fulfilled with the Antichrist literally going into the Jewish Temple for the purpose of presenting himself as Christ. In 5.25.4, Irenaeus has an extended discussion about the Antichrist, which culminates in his linking this with Daniel 9:27. "And then he [Daniel] points out the time that his [Antichrist's] tyranny shall last, during which the saints shall be put to flight, they who offer a pure sacrifice unto God: 'And in the midst of the week,' he says, 'the sacrifice and the libation shall be taken away, and the abomination of desolation [shall be brought] into the temple: even unto the consummation of the time shall the desolation be complete.' Now 3 years and 6 months constitute the ½ week."[312]

Like many early church fathers, Irenaeus held to the 6,000 year view of history (corresponding to the 6 days of Creation with each day representing 1,000 years), at the end of which the Lord will return to defeat the Antichrist and establish His kingdom (5.28.3). According to this theory, the 7th

---

[311] http://www.dts.edu/download/publications/bibliotheca/DTS-Is%20Daniel%27s%20Seventy-Weeks%20Prophecy%20Messianic.pdf, J. Paul Tanner, p. 185 (You will have to enter *"Daniel's Seventy-Weeks Prophecy Messianic"* in the search engine when you arrive at this link)

[312] *Against Heresies* by Irenaeus, *The Ante-Nicene Fathers* by Alexander Roberts and James Donaldson, 1:554.

day of Creation—the Sabbath, will be fulfilled in Christ's millennial kingdom, the true Sabbath). Although Irenaeus did not give any calculation of the 70 Weeks, it is clear from his writings that the 70 Weeks were not completely fulfilled in the first coming of Jesus Christ, for Irenaeus said that the ½ a week in verse 27 is the 3½ years when the Antichrist will reign (5.25.4).

Let us now look at what the early Christian Fathers had to say about this subject and how what they said was developed and added to with each new generation.

### CLEMENT OF ALEXANDRIA (WRITING CA. A.D. 200)[313]

Clement of Alexandria (A.D. 150—A.D. 211-216) succeeded Pantaenus as head of Alexandria's Catechetical School. He is one of the first Christian writers to record a computation of the 70 Weeks Prophecy, though in only vague detail. In his *Stromata* ("Miscellanies"), Book 1, Chapter 21, he cited the Theodotionic version of Daniel 9:24–27 and then linked this to Jesus Christ (whom he regards as the "most holy" one, v. 24, NKJV). The completion of the first 7 weeks is apparently related to the temple, for Clement stated, "That the temple accordingly was built in 7 weeks, is evident; for it is written in Esdras."[314] The 62 weeks then lead up to the first advent of Christ, but for Clement, the final week encompasses both Nero's erection of an "abomination" in Jerusalem as well as the destruction of the city and Temple in Vespasian's reign. Although Clement's interpretation is essentially messianic-historical, his associating the final

---

[313] http://www.dts.edu/download/publications/bibliotheca/DTS-Is%20Daniel%27s%20Seventy-Weeks%20Prophecy%20Messianic.pdf, J. Paul Tanner, p. 186 (You will have to enter *"Daniel's Seventy-Weeks Prophecy Messianic"* in the search engine when you arrive at this link)

[314] *Stromata* by Clement, *The Ante-Nicene Fathers* by Alexander Roberts and James Donaldson, Vol. 2, ed., (Edinburgh, 1867; reprint, Grand Rapids: Eerdman's, 1981), p. 329. *Esdras, The Septuagint* (a Greco-Latin variation of the name Ezra), refers to the Books of Ezra and Nehemiah.

week with the events of A.D. 70 is significant. As Adler has noted, "Moreover, by establishing a chronology of the 70 Weeks that comprehended both Christ's advent as well as the destruction of the temple, he is the first to posit what becomes conventional in later interpretations: a presumed hiatus between the first 69 weeks, and the final week."[315]

Jerome, writing some 200 years later, referred to the interpretation of Clement (indicating that his view must have held some significance for the early church), but Jerome chided Clement for the obvious discrepancy of the numbers stretching from Cyrus to Vespasian.[316] Yet Clement is the first patristic writer to view the 70 Weeks as referring to Israel's existence *as a nation*.

This is very interesting to me as we work through this history. The whole reason we have gone through the first three chapters of this book was to detail exactly who are Daniels People. Clement also considered that the Nation of Israel is to whom this prophecy was to be applied and not just to the Jews, as many today now believe. But did you also notice that here was the first mention of the so-called Hiatus between the 69th and the 70th week of Daniels prophesies. Today it is called the Gap Theory, which now extends about 2,000 years. I will explain this shortly.

## TERTULLIAN (WRITING CA. A.D. 203)[317]

Tertullian, the famous Latin theologian of Carthage, wrote many works, including *Contra Judaeos* ("Against the Jews"). In Chapter 8 of that work he used the 70 Weeks Prophecy to

---

[315] *The Apocalyptic Survey of History* by William Adler, p. 225. Irenaeus, writing earlier than Clement, did link Daniel's seventieth week to the time of Antichrist, but he did not fix the terminus ad quem of the 70 Weeks with the A.D. 70 events.

[316] *St. Jerome's Commentary On Daniel* trans. by Gleason L. Archer Jr. (Grand Rapids: Baker, 1958), p. 105.

[317] http://www.dts.edu/download/publications/bibliotheca/DTS-Is%20 Daniel%27s%20Seventy-Weeks%20Prophecy%20Messianic.pdf, J. Paul Tanner, p. 187 (You will have to enter *"Daniel's Seventy-Weeks Prophecy Messianic"* in the search engine when you arrive at this link)

argue against the Jews that Jesus fulfilled this prophecy in His first advent (including the Roman capture of Jerusalem in A.D. 70) and that the Old Covenant had been replaced by the New.[318]

After quoting Daniel 9:24–27, Tertullian presented an explanation of the time periods that differs significantly from almost all other commentators.[319] Instead of three periods for the 70 "Weeks" (7+ 62 + 1), he has only two: one of 62 ½ and another of 7½.[320] These are translated as "hebdomads," but from the context he clearly meant units of 7 years.[321] Tertullian attempted to show how the 1st period of 62½ hebdomads (i.e., 437½ years) was fulfilled from the time of Darius (when Daniel received the vision) until the birth of Christ. He listed all the rulers from Darius onward as well as the length of their rule, which he tabulated as being 437½ years. Yet Tertullian mistakenly assumed that the Darius mentioned in Daniel 9:1 (i.e., Darius the Mede) is the same as the Darius under whom the Temple was rebuilt; he left out some rulers altogether (e.g., Xerxes); and he gave inaccurate figures for the length of the reigns of some of them. Thus, there are far more than 437½ years from Darius until the birth of Christ. He assumed that the "anointing" of the "most holy" refers to Christ, and that with His first coming "vision

---

[318] *Tertullian, Against the Jews* by A. Cleveland Coxe, *The Ante-Nicene Fathers* by Alexander Roberts and James Donaldson, Vol. 3, ed. (Edinburgh, 1867; reprint, Grand Rapids: Eerdman's, *Handbook To the Bible* 1981).

[319] For further analysis of Tertullian, see: *Tertullian and Daniel 9:24–27: A Patristic Interpretation of a Prophetic Timeframe* by Geoffrey D. Dunn, *Zeitschrift für antikes Christentum* 6 (2002): pp. 330–44; *Tertullian* by Geoffrey D. Dunn, (New York: Routledge, 2004).

[320] It is not known if this view was original with Tertullian or if others suggested this to him. It could have possibly come from Jewish sources, for a similar view is expressed among some Jewish commentators, including Rashi himself (*Daniel* by Goldwurm, pp. 262–63).

[321] The term "hebdomad" is taken from the Greek term used by Theodotion, namely, "eJbdomavde" from the root "eJbdomav" ("week"). This term was used in the *Septuagint* of Leviticus 25:8 to indicate a 7 year period. The Hebrew has "seven sabbaths of years," meaning 49 years.

and prophecy" were "sealed" (i.e., there is no longer a vision or a prophet to announce His coming).

Tertullian suggested that the final 7½ hebdomads (i.e., 52½ years) refer to the time from the birth of Christ until the 1st year of Vespasian when Herod's temple was destroyed, and again he includes a list of rulers and the length of each one's rule. Yet even here his data and calculations are in error, for 52½ years before A.D. 70 gives not the year of Christ's birth but the year A.D. 17. Furthermore, Tertullian omitted the reign of Claudius. Nevertheless, Tertullian said the ceasing of sacrifices (v. 27) was fulfilled with the destruction of the Temple in A.D. 70.

## HIPPOLYTUS (WRITING CA. A.D. 202–A.D. 230)[322]

Hippolytus (ca. A.D. 170–ca. A.D. 236), a disciple of Irenaeus, who served as a presbyter of the church at Rome in the early A.D. 300, wrote his *Commentary on the Prophet Daniel* in which he clearly espoused a pre-millennial prophetic outlook (as did Irenaeus), anticipating the millennial kingdom about the year A.D. 500 (in accord with the 6,000 year theory of history).[323] This is the first known extant commentary on Daniel. Hippolytus's view of Daniel 9:24–27 is also quoted later by Jerome. Hippolytus equated the beast of Revelation

---

[322] http://www.dts.edu/download/publications/bibliotheca/DTS-Is%20Daniel%27s%20Seventy-Weeks%20Prophecy%20Messianic.pdf, J. Paul Tanner, p. 188 (You will have to enter *"Daniel's Seventy-Weeks Prophecy Messianic" in the search engine when you arrive at this link*)

[323] The dating of Hippolytus *of Rome's Commentary* is uncertain. L. E. Knowles believes it was written about A.D. 202 [*The Interpretations of the Seventy Weeks of Daniel In the Early Fathers, Westminster Theological Journal* 7 (May 1945), p. 139], though Wilbur M. Smith dates it around A.D. 230 *(Introduction* in *Jerome's Commentary On Daniel* by St. Jerome, 5). Since Christ was believed to have been born in the year 5500 A.C. from Adam, there remained five hundred years until the end of the age, the appearance of the Antichrist, and the establishment of Jesus' kingdom. The idea of 5,500 years from Creation until Christ was an allegorical interpretation, this figure being the sum of the dimensions of the Ark of the Covenant (i.e., 5½ cubits), with Christ being the "true Ark."

13 and the "Little Horn" of Daniel 7 with the future Antichrist, who will rule for 3½ years, while he expected the "Ten Horns" of Daniel 7 to arise out of the Roman Empire of his day.

Hippolytus saw the 70 Weeks Prophecy as taking place in three periods.[324] The first 7 weeks were the 49 years before Joshua, the high priest.[325] This was followed by 62 weeks (434 years) from Joshua/Zerubbabel/Ezra until Jesus Christ. (This is a puzzling assertion, since Joshua and Ezra were separated by quite a few years). This 62 weeks would then be followed by a "gap" of time before the final "week."[326] During this final week (a future period of 7 years in which the Antichrist will come to power), Elijah and Enoch will appear as the two witnesses (Revelation 11). The "anointing" of "the most holy" in Daniel 9:24 refers to the anointing of Christ in His first coming (a view common among the early church fathers). The halting of sacrifice (mentioned in v. 27) is taken in a spiritual sense rather than in reference to literal sacrifices. Hippolytus wrote, "But when he [the Antichrist] comes, the sacrifice and oblation will be removed, which now are offered to God in every place by the nations."[327] Although Hippolytus said the occurrence of יהושוע; (in v. 25) refers to Joshua, the high priest, at the time of the return from the Babylonian Captivity, he said the second reference to יהושוע; is to Jesus Christ. Hippolytus followed a messianic-eschatological interpretation (which he probably obtained

---

[324] *Exegetical On Daniel, Part 2* by Hippolytus; in *The Extant Works and Fragments of Hippolytus* by A. Cleveland Coxe, in *The Ante-Nicene Fathers* by Alexander Roberts and James Donaldson, Vol. 5, ed. (Edinburgh, 1867; reprint, Grand Rapids: *Eerdman's,* 1981). See also *Hippolytus' Commentary To Daniel* by Georg N. Bonwetsch and Hans Achelis, eds., (Leipzig: Hinrichs, 1897); and *Hippolytus' Commentaire sur Daniel* trans. by M. Lefèvrre and G. Bardy, ed. (Paris: Cerf, 1947).›

[325] According to Hippolytus, Daniel prophesied in the 21st year of the captivity, and there were "7 Weeks" (i.e., 49 years) remaining in the captivity. The 21 plus 49 added up to the 70 years of captivity.

[326] *Commentary On the Prophet Daniel* by Hippolytus, 2.22.

[327] *Commentary On the Prophet Daniel* by Hippolytus, 2.22.

from Irenaeus), in contrast to the messianic-historical view of Clement, who saw the entire 70 Weeks fulfilled in the A.D. 100. As time moved on, the latter view tended to dominate.

## JULIUS AFRICANUS (WRITING AFTER A.D. 232)[328]

Julius Africanus (b. ca. A.D. 170; d. after A.D. 240), a native of Aelia Capitolina (Jerusalem), wrote his five-volume *Chronographia* ("Chronology") in which he attempted to synchronize sacred and secular history. Like others, he held to the 6,000 year theory of history and believed that Christ had been born 5500 A.C. Hence, he was expecting the return of Christ about A.D. 500. In his *Chronographia* he devoted an entire treatise to the 70 Weeks passage in Daniel entitled, *On the Weeks and This Prophecy*. Only portions of this work are extant today.[329] Yet, in addition to this, Julius explained the 70 Weeks Prophecy in other writings that are preserved in Volume 6 of *The Ante-Nicene Fathers*.

His views are cited by both Eusebius and Jerome, which indicates the esteem with which he was regarded.[330]

---

[328] http://www.dts.edu/download/publications/bibliotheca/DTS-Is%20Daniel%27s%20Seventy-Weeks%20Prophecy%20Messianic.pdf, J. Paul Tanner, p. 189 (You will have to enter *"Daniel's Seventy-Weeks Prophecy Messianic"* in the search engine when you arrive at this link)

[329] *Georgii Syncelli Ecloga Chronographica by A. A. Mosshammer, ed.*, (Leipzig: Tübner, 1984), 393.23–24. Portions of Africanus's views are also preserved in *Eusebius, Demonstratio Evangelica* trans. by W. J. Ferar (London: SPCK, 1920), Book 8, Ch. 2; and *Jerome's Commentary On Daniel*.

[330] William Adler and Paul Tuffin suggest the possibility that Africanus may have abandoned his theory about the "lunar years" of Daniel's prophecy [*The Chronography of George Synkellos: A Byzantine Chronicle of Universal History from the Creation* (Oxford: Oxford University Press, 2002)]. They state, "See e.g., the *Chronicon Paschale* 307.15–308.9, which ascribes to Africanus a completely different analysis of the 70 year-weeks. According to this interpretation, the first 69 years of the prophecy extended from Ol. 81.4 (A.M. 5048) up to 14 Tiberius (Ol. 202.1 = A.M. 5530). The final year-week of the prophecy extended from 15 to 22 Tiberius" (ibid., p. 470 n. 3). *Chronicon Paschale* was a 7th-century Byzantine universal chronicle of the world. For a partial English translation see *Chronicon Paschale A.D. 284–A.D. 628* trans.

Julius held to the view that the entire 70 Weeks would be completely fulfilled by the time of the first advent of Christ. Of significance is the fact that he rejected the decree of Cyrus as the terminus a quo in favor of the decree of Artaxerxes in the 20th year of his reign (since the city and its walls were never built in the era following Cyrus's decree). He stated:

*It [the city] remained in this position, accordingly, until Nehemiah and the reign of Artaxerxes, and the 115th year of the sovereignty of the Persians... And reckoning from that point, we make up 70 Weeks to the time of Christ. For if we begin to reckon from any other point, and not from this, the periods will not correspond, and very many odd results will meet us. For if we begin the calculation of the 70 Weeks from Cyrus and the first restoration, there will be upwards of one hundred years too many, and there will be a larger number if we begin from the day on which the angel gave the prophecy to Daniel, and a much larger number still if we begin from the commencement of the captivity.*[331]

In ancient history, dating was often done on the basis of Olympiads. An Olympiad was a 4 year period between the Olympic Games. Julius indicates that the 20th year of Artaxerxes was in the 4th year of the 83rd Olympiad. According to Finegan, this would be Nisan of 444 B.C.[332] From this year (the same year in which Artaxerxes permitted the rebuilding of the Jerusalem walls; Nehemiah 2:1–5) Julius calculated

---

by Michael and Mary Whitby (Liverpool: Liverpool University Press, 1989).

[331] *The Extant Fragments of the Five Books of the Chronography of Julius Africanus* by Julius Africanus, in *The Ante-Nicene Fathers* by Alexander Roberts and James Donaldson, Vol. 6, ed. (Edinburgh, 1867; reprint, Grand Rapids: Eerdman's, 1989), 16.2.

[332] *Handbook of Biblical Chronology* by Finegan, pp. 92–98. Xerxes, the father of Artaxerxes, died shortly after December 17th, 465 B.C. [*The Fifth-Century Jewish Calendar at Elephantine* by S.H. Horn and L. H. Wood, *Journal of Near Eastern Studies* 13 (January 1954): p. 9]. Hence, the accession year of Artaxerxes would be December 465 B.C. to Nisan 464 B.C. His 1st regnal year as king (according to the Persian system) would be Nisan 464 B.C. to Nisan 463 B.C., and his 20th regnal year would then have begun in Nisan 444 B.C.

the 70 Weeks. Apparently, he saw the terminus ad quem as being the time when Christ was baptized and entered into His public ministry, because he based his calculations on Luke 3:1—which mentions the 15th year of the reign of Tiberius Caesar. Thus, Julius argued that there are 70 Weeks of years from the decree of Artaxerxes (in his 20th year) to the beginning of Christ's public ministry in Tiberius Caesar's 15th year.[333] One must keep in mind, however, that Julius was not basing his dates on the modern Gregorian Calendar but rather on Olympiads. Hence, he took the 20th year of Artaxerxes as the 4th year of the 83rd Olympiad, and the 15th year of Tiberius Caesar as the 2nd year of the 202nd Olympiad.[334] According to Julius, this results in a span of 475 years. He argued, however, that 490 years (70 Weeks) is equivalent to 475 years when viewed according to Hebrew numeration. The Jews, he said, reckoned a year as 354 days rather than 365¼ days. The former represents 12 months according to the moon's course, while the latter is based on the solar year. This amounts to a difference of 11¼ days per year, but is eventually made up by the insertion of extra months at 8 year intervals. "Hence the Greeks and the Jews insert 3 intercalary months every 8 years. For 8 x 11¼ days

---

[333] The 15th year of Tiberius Caesar would be approximately A.D. 28–A.D. 29, but there is some debate over this. See *Commentary On Luke* by I. Howard Marshall, *New International Greek Testament Commentary* (Grand Rapids: Eerdman's, 1978), p. 133. Most modern scholars reckon that Tiberius's reign began after the death of Augustus on August 19th, A.D. 14 (Chris Scarre, *Chronicle of the Roman Emperors* (London: Thames and Hudson, 1995, p. 27).

[334] In *The Ante-Nicene Fathers* edition (based on a fragment found in *Eusebius*), Julius refers to the date of Tiberius's 16th year, which he gives as the 2nd year of the 202nd Olympiad, but Jerome (in his quotation of Julius) gave it as Tiberius's 15th year (*Jerome's Commentary On Daniel*, p. 97). Jerome claimed to have been quoting Julius Africanus "verbatim" (ibid., p. 95). So there is some confusion on whether Julius's calculations were reckoned to Tiberius's 15th or 16th year. In any case, according to Finegan, the second year of the 202nd Olympiad would be from July 1st, A.D. 30, until June 30th, A.D. 31 (*Handbook of Biblical Chronology*, p. 47). This does not correspond to the year commonly given for Tiberius's 15th year according to modern reckoning (see: footnote 31). Finegan concludes that Jesus was baptized and began His public ministry in the fall of A.D. 29 (ibid., p. 342).

makes up 3 months."[335] Thus, over a 475-year period, there would be over 59 eight-year periods in which 3 months would be added, or close to 15 years in all, and by this means, Julius explains how 490 years by Hebrew numeration would be equivalent to nearly 475 solar years.

Elsewhere, Julius wrote more precisely that his calculations began with the 20th year of Artaxerxes. "And the beginning of the numbers, that is, of the 70 Weeks which make up 490 years, the angel instructs us to take from the going forth of the commandment to answer and to build Jerusalem. And this happened in the 20th year of the reign of Artaxerxes, King of Persia."[336]

This explanation of the 70 Weeks Prophecy offered by Julius is unique among the church fathers. First, he was the first one to take the terminus a quo as the 20th year of Artaxerxes.[337] Second, he viewed the terminus ad quem as the 15th year of Tiberius, the beginning of Jesus' public ministry. His view, then, is clearly messianic-historical, and he does not attempt to relate the prophecy to the destruction of Jerusalem in

---

[335] *The Extant Fragments of the Five Books of the Chronology of Julius Africanus* by Julius Africanus, 6:135.

[336] *The Extant Fragments of the Five Books of the Chronography of Julius Africanus* by Julius Africanus, in *The Ante-Nicene Fathers* by Alexander Roberts and James Donaldson, Vol. 6, ed. (Edinburgh, 1867; reprint, Grand Rapids: *Eerdman's*, 1989), 16.1.

[337] One cannot know for sure how many followed Julius's view of the 20th year of Artaxerxes for the terminus a quo. Zöckler reports that Polychronius (d. ca. A.D. 430) held a modified view of this. "Polychronius... reckons the first 7 weeks from Darius Medus to the 9th year of Darius Hystaspia, when Zerubbabel's temple is said to have been completed, the 62 weeks from the 20th year of Artaxerxes to the birth of Christ, and the final week from that date to Titus, while the death of Christ falls in its central point" (*Daniel* p. 207). Also Theodoret of Cyrus (ca. A.D. 433) took a similar view (see *Theodoret of Cyrus: Commentary on Daniel* trans. by Robert C. Hill, (Atlanta: Society of Biblical Literature, 2006, pp. 239–61). However, he counted the 62 weeks first and then the 7 weeks, with the latter (49 years) leading up to the beginning of Christ's public ministry.

A.D. 70 or suggest how the 70th Week in Daniel 9:27 relates to his view.

It wasn't until the 3rd-century, during the reign of Emperor Septimius Severus (A.D. 193–211A.D.), that an actual Christian commentary on the Book of Daniel appeared. *Eusebius' Ecclesiastical History* reports that "during the reign of the Emperor Septimius Severus, a certain Judas, otherwise unknown, composed a chronicle in the form of a commentary on Daniel 9:24-27… Judas' chronicle marks the first attested case in which Daniel's Apocalypse of 70 Weeks underpinned a Christian chronicle."[338]

Even though Eusebius says very little about Judas' commentary, He does remark about the historical conditions that influenced it. His comment is probably the very first recorded psychosocial explanation of apocalyptic thought. As Eusebius recorded, "the persecution which was then stirred up against us disturbed the minds of the many," he concluded that Judas was caught up in the hysteria of his time.[339]

It is clear from the history of Jewish and Christian interpretation of Daniel 9 that part of its psychological impact was in promising some immediate resolution of and hence emotional relief from a current crisis. But once it was established that the outcome of the prophecy was known and realized in the epochal events of the first centuries, its value as consolation in a current crisis was blunted.[340]

---

[338] *The Apocalyptic Survey of History Adapted by Christians: Daniel's Prophecy of 70 Weeks* by William Adler, *The Jewish Apocalyptic Heritage In Early History* by James C. VanderKam and William Adler, ed., Assen: Van Gorcum & Comp. B.V., 1996, p. 201

[339] *The Apocalyptic Survey of History Adapted by Christians: Daniel's Prophecy of 70 Weeks* by William Adler, *The Jewish Apocalyptic Heritage In Early History* by James C. VanderKam and William Adler, ed., Assen: Van Gorcum & Comp. B.V., 1996, p. 201

[340] *The Apocalyptic Survey of History Adapted by Christians: Daniel's Prophecy of 70 Weeks* by William Adler, *The Jewish Apocalyptic Heritage In Early*

Soon after Judas' commentary, the universal chronicler, Julius Africanus (ca. A.D.160–A.D. 240), claimed to have observed a foreshadowing of Messiah in Daniel's apocalyptic vision. This is the first time that Daniel 9 is associated with Messiah Yahshua.[341] "I am shocked," he writes after an extensive chronological analysis of Daniel 9, "at the Jews who say that the Messiah has not arrived, and the Marcionites who say that there was no prediction of him in the prophecies."[342]

It isn't until the 3rd and 4th centuries that we see an increase in the number of commentaries, which handled the 70 Week Prophecy of Daniel 9. These tended to forgo the future promises and instead were more retrospective and messianic in nature. It is also during this time that, "the interpretation of Daniel 9 moved from eschatological to historical, from matters of the future to events of the past. Instead of the prophecy providing comfort and support through its descriptions of events that lay ahead, it became interpreted as describing historical events that had been completed."[343]

This change occurred as, "it was established that the outcome of the prophecy was known and realized in the epochal events of the first centuries, its value as consolation in a current crisis was blunted. This change in attitude lay behind

---

*History* by James C. VanderKam and William Adler, ed., Assen: Van Gorcum & Comp. B.V., 1996, p. 221

[341] *IS DANIEL'S SEVENTY-WEEKS PROPHECY MESSIANIC? PART 1* by J. Paul Tanner, 2009, p. 15. http://paultanner.org/English%20HTML/Publ%20Articles/Daniel%27s%2070th%20Wk%20-%20BibSac%20Article%201%20-%20Dr%20Tanner.pdf (You will have to enter *"Daniel's Seventy-Weeks Prophecy Messianic"* in the search engine when you arrive at this link)

[342] *The Apocalyptic Survey of History Adapted by Christians: Daniel's Prophecy of 70 Weeks* by William Adler, *The Jewish Apocalyptic Heritage In Early History* by James C. VanderKam and William Adler, ed., Assen: Van Gorcum & Comp. B.V., 1996, p. 202

[343] *The Bible—God's Word or Man's? Does This Book Answer the Question? Critique of Chapter 9: Prophecies That Came True* by Doug Mason, 2010, pp. 15-16. http://www.jwstudies.com/Critique_of_GM_on_Daniel_9.pdf

a gradual change in Christian Exegesis from the beginning of the 3rd-century."[344]

Interestingly, another factor influenced the change to the more retrospective messianic historical view and that was the wide distribution of Theodotion's A.D. 150 translation of the Scriptures. By A.D. 40, Jerome recorded in his Preface to Daniel that Christians had already rejected the *Septuagint's* version of that book in favor of the one found in Theodotion's. "The Theodotionic version of Daniel that came to be favored in the early church partly contributed to the increasing popularity of the retrospective messianic/historical treatment of Daniel 9."[345]

Theodotion's translation was used almost universally in the Greek speaking church and it encouraged a different understanding of Daniel's 70 Weeks. It blurred the demarcation between the first 7 weeks and the following 62 weeks—making them into a continuous 69-week period. This had a profound impact on Christian Exegesis and resulted in Christian translators rarely seeing the implications of distinguishing between the two periods.

The early church fathers, Clement, Tertullian, Hippolytus, Julianus Africanus, Origen, and Eusebius all chased after chronologies based upon Yahshua's advent. However, they all disagreed on the starting point from which to count. For example, Clement began with the 2nd year of Cyrus; Hippolytus, the 1st year of Darius the Mede; Julius Africanus preferred the 20th year of Artexerxes as his starting point. As stated by James Montgomery, most of these interpretations

---

[344] *The Apocalyptic Survey of History Adapted by Christians: Daniel's Prophecy of 70 Weeks* by William Adler, *The Jewish Apocalyptic Heritage In Early History* by James C. VanderKam and William Adler. ed., Assen: Van Gorcum & Comp. B.V., 1996, p. 221

[345] *The Apocalyptic Survey of History Adapted by Christians: Daniel's Prophecy of 70 Weeks* by William Adler, *The Jewish Apocalyptic Heritage In Early History* by James C. VanderKam and William Adler, ed., Assen: Van Gorcum & Comp. B.V., 1996, p. 218

followed a pattern where, "the climax of the Weeks is generally found in Christ's death, in which there was the cancellation of the Jewish ritual, but with a balance of 3½ years left over which is treated most vaguely; it is often regarded as representing the period down to the destruction of Jerusalem, or, after ancient precedent, it is understood as of the era of Antichrist."[346]

Let's wrap this up. As James Montgomery said, this is nothing but a *swamp* of wrong views and compounded misconceptions. The tragic part being, it has been passed down to our spiritual leaders *to this day*. When you build on a faulty foundation, you too, will have problems. Let me say this before we go forward. I have learned many things from many different teachers. It is not my intention to shame any of them for studying and trying to understand the Scriptures. On the contrary, it is my hope they will read this and learn the truth of this prophecy and begin to share it with those that they teach. Sincerely, it is not my aim to humiliate any of them for doing their best to understand what Yehovah has given us. But to understand the full impact of this prophecy will humble, sober, and terrify all of us. And to understand the time we are in, will terrify us all the more still.

But as the Angel told Daniel, these things have been sealed for the Last Days. We are in the Last Days and it is now time to have this prophecy revealed.

In general, most modern day teachers begin this prophecy from the decree to restore and rebuild Jerusalem and they date this to 447 B.C., 445 B.C., or 444 B.C. They then tie this into the Baptism of Yehshua, His entry into Jerusalem on a colt, or the death of Yehshua. As you continue reading, you will see they all have different dates for that. It is not the purpose of this book to debate the date of His birth[347] or death.[348] The

---

[346] *A Critical and Exegetical Commentary on THE BOOK OF DANIEL* by James Montgomery, New York: C. Scribner, 1927, p. 398

[347] Conjunction or Sighted, Which? http://www.sightedmoon.com/?page_id=22 & http://sightedmoon.com/conjunction-or-sighted-which/ & The Return of Yehshua http://www.sightedmoon.com/?page_id=20 & http://sightedmoon.com/the-return-of-yahshua/

[348] The Sign of Jonah http://sightedmoon.com/the-sign-of-jonah/ & http://www.

reader can go to my website to read my views on this point; but I firmly believe the birth of Yehshua to have taken place on September the 11th, 3 B.C. and His death to have taken place on Nisan 14th as Passover was about to begin on the 15th, 31 C.E. Please see the articles in the footnotes, for more information.

If you were to do the actual math on many of these timelines for Daniel, you will see they do not add up. All of them leave us hanging with 3½ years that can touch down at any time in the future. It is what you have already read about and is called the Gap Theory.

In 539 B.C., as I have already told you, Cyrus defeated the Babylonians. And this ended the 70 years in which Judah was under the Babylonian authority. So when you read Ezra 1 it sure sounds like this is what Daniel was talking about in Daniel 9:24-27, but with one problem—Daniel, was not speaking about the coming of Yehshua the Messiah. Neither Yehshua, nor the apostles spoke of this prophecy in reference to His coming.

> *1 And in the first year of Koresh sovereign of Persia, that the word of יהוה by the mouth of Yirmeyah might be accomplished, יהוה stirred up the spirit of Koresh sovereign of Persia, to proclaim throughout all his reign, and also in writing, saying, 2 Thus said Koresh sovereign of Persia, "יהוה Elohim of the heavens has given me all the reigns of the earth. And He has commanded me to build Him a house in Yerushalayim which is in Yehudah. 3 Who is among you of all His people? His Elohim be with him! And let him go up to Yerushalayim, which is in Yehudah, and build the House of יהוה Elohim of Yisra'ěl—He is Elohim—which is in Yerushalayim. 4 And whoever is left from all the places where he sojourns, let the men of his place help him with silver and gold, with goods and livestock, besides the voluntary offerings for the House of Elohim which is in Yerushalayim." (Ezra 1:1-4)*

All you have to do now then is take 539 B.C. and subtract 483 years from this and you get 56 B.C. The reason they use the 483 number is

---

sightedmoon.com/?page_id=19

because Yehshua's ministry was 3½ years and then when the Tribulation comes it is going to be another 3½ years. This is the current logic that pervades all of those who use this theory, but not us, once all has been revealed.

As you can see 56 B.C. does not come close to even the birth of Yehshua, *let alone* the crucifixion, so this decree cannot be right.

The next date we have to work with is when the building was stopped (as told to us in Ezra 4:6-13) and, when all was said and done, King Darius decreed in his second year to rebuild the house.

> *24 Then the work of the House of Elah which is at Yerushalayim ceased, and it ceased until the second year of the reign of Dareyawesh sovereign of Persia.* (Ezra 4:24)

You now know Darius became King in 522 B.C., which would make 520 the second year in which the work ceased and the exchange of letters in the Book of Ezra took place. This decree is told to us in Ezra 6.

> *8 And I make a decree as to what you should do for the elders of these Yehudim, for the building of this House of Elah: Let the exact expense be paid to these men from the sovereign's resources, out of the taxes beyond the River, so that they are not stopped. 9 And whatever they need—both young bulls and rams, and lambs for the burnt offerings of the Elah of heaven, wheat, salt, wine, and oil, according to the request of the priests who are in Yerushalayim—let it be given them day by day without fail, 10 so that they bring pleasing offerings to the Elah of heaven, and pray for the life of the sovereign and his sons. 11 And I make a decree that whoever changes this word, let a timber be pulled from his house, and let him be impaled, hanged on it. And let his house be made a dunghill because of this. 12 And Elah, who has caused His Name to dwell there does overthrow any sovereign or people who put their hand to change, to destroy this House of Elah which is in Yerushalayim! I Dareyawesh make the decree—let it be done promptly.* (Ezra 6:8-12)

Doing the math once again we have 520 B.C. and must subtract 483 years from this, which brings us to the year 37 B.C. Again, this is not even at Yehshua's birth and therefore this one as well cannot be used for this theory.

Now some will try to tell you that these decrees were put into effect to build the House of Yehovah. And as you can see below in Ezra the House was completed in the sixth year of Darius or 516 B.C.

> *15 And this House was completed on the third day of the month of Adar, which was in the sixth year of the reign of Sovereign Dareyawesh.* (Ezra 6:15)

The third decree theorists of today use, in order to understand Daniel 9, is the decree found in Ezra 7 in the seventh year of Artaxerxes.[349] He became King in 465 B.C., making his seventh year, 458 B.C.

> *8 And he came to Yerushalayim in the fifth month, which was in the seventh year of the sovereign. 9 For on the first day of the first month he began to go up from Babel, and on the first day of the fifth month he came to Yerushalayim, according to the good hand of his Elohim upon him. 10 For Ezra had prepared his heart to seek the Torah of יהוה, and to do it, and to teach laws and right-rulings in Yisra'ĕl. 11 And this is the copy of the letter that Sovereign Artaḥshashta gave Ezra the priest, the scribe, a scribe in the words of the commands of יהוה, and of His laws to Yisra'ĕl: 12 Artaḥshashta, sovereign of sovereigns, to Ezra the priest, a perfect scribe of the law of the Elah of heaven. And now, 13 I make a decree that all those of the people of Yisra'ĕl and the priests and Lĕwites in my reign, who volunteer to go up to Yerushalayim, go with you.* (Ezra 7:8-13)

> *14 Since you are being sent by the sovereign and his seven counselors to inquire about Yehudah and Yerushalayim, with regard to the law of your Elah which is in your hand;*

---

[349] http://en.wikipedia.org/wiki/Artaxerxes_I_of_Persia & http://www.britannica.com/EBchecked/topic/36741/Artaxerxes-I

*15 and to bring the silver and gold which the sovereign and his counselors have voluntarily given to the Elah of Yisra'ĕl, whose dwelling is in Yerushalayim, 16 and all the silver and gold that you find in all the province of Babel, along with the gift of the people and the priests, voluntarily given for the House of their Elah in Yerushalayim, 17 therefore, with this silver promptly buy bulls, rams, lambs, with their grain offerings and their drink offerings, and offer them on the altar of the House of your Elah in Yerushalayim. 18 And whatever seems good to you and your brothers to do with the rest of the silver and the gold do it according to the desire of your Elah. 19 And the utensils that are given to you for the service of the House of your Elah, put back before the Elah of Yerushalayim. 20 And the rest of the needs for the House of your Elah, which falls to you to give, give from the sovereign's treasure-house.* (Ezra 7:14-20)

*21 And I, I Artaḥshashta the sovereign, do make a decree to all the treasurers who are beyond the River, that whatever Ezra the priest, the scribe of the law of the Elah of heaven, does ask of you, let it be done promptly, 22 up to one hundred talents of silver, and up to one hundred kors of wheat, and up to one hundred baths of wine, and up to one hundred baths of oil, and salt without reckoning. 23 Whatever is commanded by the Elah of heaven, let it be diligently done for the House of the Elah of heaven. For why should there be wrath against the reign of the sovereign and his sons? 24 We further inform you that there is no authority to impose tax, excise, or toll on any of the priests and Lĕwites, singers, gatekeepers, Nethinim, and servants of this House of Elah. 25 And you, Ezra, according to the wisdom of your Elah that is in your hand, appoint magistrates and judges to judge all the people who are beyond the River, all such as know the laws of your Elah. And teach those who do not know them. 26 And whoever does not do the law of your Elah and the law of the sovereign, let judgment be promptly executed on him, whether it be death, or banishment, or confiscation of goods, or imprisonment.* (Ezra 7:21-26)

Doing the math we start at 458 B.C., subtract 483 years and arrive at 26 C.E. Keep in mind that you must add one year for the year zero. This is fine if you can prove that the Messiah died in the year 30 C.E. Many are coming to the understanding that HE *had to have died* in 31 C.E., which is the position I hold also.

And yet, this is the date (458 B.C.) that many of theologians of our time begin to fudge with, in order to get the year that best suits their interpretation of when Yehshua's ministry began. They will maintain that Artaxerxes seventh year was 457 B.C. allowing for the accessional year. Others will maintain it was 456 B.C. If we use the year 457 B.C., then we arrive at the year 27 C.E.—which would be when the Messiah was anointed in the fall. The next thing we read is that he read the Isaiah scroll in which HE says *this* is the acceptable year. The year Yehshua did this was 28 C.E. and that year was a Sabbatical Year—or an acceptable year.

So 3½ years from the fall of 27 C.E. is Passover 31 C.E. when Yehshua was killed. So if one misses the seventh year of Artaxerxes by one year then this works out reasonably well. Together, we have now covered the 483 years and then the next 3½ years leading to His death giving us a total of 486 ½ years. But now we have the last 3½ years to account for. The Gap Theory has now expanded out to be a total of 1,982 years, going from 31 C.E. to the year of the writing of this book in 2013.

And below we find the last decree to be the one presented to Nehemiah in Chapter 2 of the same book.

> *1 And it came to be in the month of Nisan, in the twentieth year of Artaḥshashta the sovereign, when wine was before him, that I took the wine and gave it to the sovereign. And I had never been sad in his presence. 2 And the sovereign said to me, "Why is your face sad, since you are not sick? This is none else but sorrow of heart." Then I was very much afraid, 3 and said to the sovereign, "Let the sovereign live forever! Why should my face not be sad, when the city, the place of my fathers' tombs, lies waste, and its gates are burned with fire?" 4 And the sovereign said to me, "What are you asking*

*for?" Then I prayed to the Elohim of the heavens, 5 and said to the sovereign, "If it seems good to the sovereign, and if your servant is pleasing before you, I ask that you send me to Yehudah, to the city of my fathers' tombs, so that I build it." 6 And the sovereign, with the sovereigness sitting beside him, said to me, "How long would your journey take? And when do you return?" So it seemed good before the sovereign to send me. And I set him a time. 7 And I said to the sovereign, "If it seems good to the sovereign, let letters be given to me for the governors beyond the River, that they should let me to pass through 'til I come to Yehudah, 8 and a letter to Asaph the keeper of the sovereign's forest, that he should give me timber to make beams for the gates of the palace that belongs to the House, and for the city wall, and for the house I would enter." And the sovereign gave them to me according to the good hand of my Elohim upon me.* (Nehemiah 2:1-8)

Artaxerxes came to power as in 465 B.C., as I've already pointed out, making his twentieth year, 445 B.C. From 445 you then subtract 483 to arrive at the year 39 C.E. This, however, is way beyond all dates used for the crucifixion and so it must be discarded.

There you have it. Everyone looks at all four of these and then decides that the third one is the right one. "It just has to be this one," so they pick it. And now we all just wait for the last 3½ years to come and some think it will be 2013 or 2014.

Having now looked at this, I have an important question to leave you with. How was it that the Magi knew, without referring to this section of Daniel, when the Messiah was to be born? The Messiah was born September 11th, 3 B.C.[350] and the Magi showed up two years later in 1 B.C. They did not have to rely on this misapplied prophecy. But this is another discussion for another time. But you can think upon this until then.

---

[350] Conjunction or Sighted, Which? http://www.sightedmoon.com/?page_id=22
http://sightedmoon.com/conjunction-or-sighted-which/

I tried to pull us out of this primordial soup of prophetic ideas a few pages back, only to get caught up myself in the present outgrowth of such faulty theories that have evolved resulting in false prophecies. It is time to see the truth and once you have seen the real thing then all of these ever evolving and transitory ideas that change with each new generation and each new world crisis will vaporize into the methane gas that they really are and always have been.

# Chapter 5 | What Does "Weeks" Mean?

*24 "Seventy weeks are decreed for your people and for your set-apart city, to put an end to the transgression, and to seal up sins, and to cover crookedness, and to bring in everlasting righteousness, and to seal up vision and prophet, and to anoint the Most Set-apart. 25 Know, then, and understand: from the going forth of the command to restore and build Yerushalayim until Messiah the Prince is seven weeks and sixty-two weeks. It shall be built again, with streets and a trench, but in times of affliction. 26 And after the sixty-two weeks Messiah shall be cut off and have naught. And the people of a coming prince shall destroy the city and the set-apart place. And the end of it is with a flood. And wastes are decreed, and fighting until the end. 27 And he shall confirm a covenant with many for one week. And in the middle of the week he shall put an end to slaughtering and meal offering. And on the wing of abominations he shall lay waste, even until the complete end and that which is decreed is poured out on the one who lays waste.[1]"* [Footnote: [1]Matthew 24:15 (Daniel 9:24-27)]

We are now over 300 pages into this subject of Daniel's 70 Weeks Prophecy and yet, we have only covered the first seven words of this prophesy.

*"Seventy weeks are decreed for your people."*

I have explained who Daniel's people are. They are all of Israel and I have explained who they are today. They are the descendants of the Celtic people and they are the Nation of Britain and the British Commonwealth—as well as the United States of America and the State of Israel. It is extremely important to understand who this prophecy is speaking about.

I have already shown you why the 70 Weeks is not 70 x 7—which would give you an invalid total of 490 years. People have been using this information for every time of trial for over the past 2,000 years and it has *never* proven true. Nor will it. It cannot be plugged into any current theories and it also falls short in the context of using it to rectify and bridge any remaining gaps in the so-called "Gap Theory."

So what then is the answer to this riddle of riddles?

It is actually quite simple and it comes from a proper understanding of the words spoken. When you understand this word "week," the meaning is extremely deep. Prepare to have the tent pegs of your mind stretched as we begin by examining the word "weeks" for insight and clarity.

Here is this first sentence again with the Strong's Hebrew notes:

> 24 Seventy$^{H7657}$ weeks$^{H7620}$ are determined$^{H2852}$ upon$^{H5921}$ thy people. $^{H5971}$ (Daniel 9:24)

The word "seventy" is very easy to understand and it is:

**H7657**[351]—shib'ı ym *shib-eem'*

Multiple of **H7651**: *Seventy:* Seventy, threescore and ten (+ -teen).

But remember, it is the word *"weeks"* that is the primary focus of this chapter. When you look it up in *Strong's Concordance*, you immediately find there are a number of words to investigate.

---

[351] *Strong's Concordance*, Esword.

**H7620**—*shaw-boo'-ah, shaw-boo'-ah, sheb-oo-aw'*

Properly passive participle of **H7650** as a denominative of **H7651**: Literally *sevened*, that is, a *week* (specifically of years): Seven, week.

**H7650**—*shaw-bah'*

A primitive root; properly to *be complete*, but used only as a denominative from **H7651**: To *seven* oneself, that is, *swear* (as if by repeating a declaration seven times): Adjure, charge (by an oath, with an oath), feed to the full [by mistake for **H7646**], take an oath, X straitly, (cause to, make to) swear.

**H7646**—*saw-bah', saw-bay'-ah*

A primitive root; to *sate*, that is, *fill* to satisfaction (literally or figuratively): Have enough, fill (full, self, with), be (to the) full (of), have plenty of, be satiated, satisfy (with), suffice, be weary of.

**H7651**—*sheh'-bah, shib-aw'*

From **H7650**: A primitive cardinal number; *seven* (as the sacred *full* one); also (adverbially) *seven times*; by implication a *week*; by extension an *indefinite* number: (+ by) seven ([-fold], -s, [-teen, -teenth], -th, times). Compare **H7658**.

**H7658**—*shib-aw-naw'*

Prolonged for the masculine of **H7651**: *Seven:* Seven.

Above then you have the definition of this word commonly known as "weeks." Before I say anything further to influence your thoughts one way or another, I will first have you look where else this same word is used in the Bible. *Strong's Concordance* maintains it is used a total of nineteen times. In eleven of these nineteen instances, we are provided with a clear example of the word and its proper meaning.

**H7620** *shaw-boo'-ah, shaw-boo'-ah, sheb-oo-aw'*

**Total KJV Occurrences:** 19

**Weeks (15)**

Exodus 34:22 (1), Leviticus 12:5 (1), Numbers 28:26 (1), Deuteronomy 16:9-10 (3), Deuteronomy 16:16 (1), 2 Chronicles 8:13 (1), Daniel 9:24-26 (5), Daniel 10:2-3 (2)

**Week (4)**

Genesis 29:27-28 (2), Daniel 9:27 (2)

Our first example in Exodus plainly reveals to us it is speaking of the "Feast of Weeks."

> 22 *"And perform the **Festival of Weeks** for yourself, of the first-fruits of wheat harvest, and the Festival of Ingathering at the turn of the year."* (Exodus 34:22)

The second verse the word "weeks" is found in is Leviticus 12:5, but it does not meet the criteria of what I am talking about here. However, the next verse in Numbers does and clearly, it too is talking about the Feast of Weeks.

> 26 *"And on the day of the first-fruits, when you bring a new grain offering to* יהוה *at your **Festival of Weeks**, you have a set-apart gathering, you do no servile work."* (Numbers 28:26)

The fourth, fifth, sixth and seventh verses resulting from our word search for the word "weeks" originate in the Book of Deuteronomy and they too, without a doubt, are speaking about this Feast of "Weeks."

> 9 *"Count seven weeks for yourself. Begin to count seven weeks from the time you begin to put the sickle to the*

> *grain. 10 And you shall perform the **Festival of Weeks** to יהוה your Elohim, according to the voluntary offering from your hand, which you give as יהוה your Elohim blesses you."* (Deuteronomy 16:9-10)

> *16 "Three times a year all your males appear before יהוה your Elohim in the place which He chooses: at the Festival of Unleavened Bread, and at the **Festival of Weeks**, and at the Festival of Booths. And none should appear before יהוה empty-handed."* (Deuteronomy 16:16)

Our eighth usage of the word "weeks" is found again in 2 Chronicles. Are you seeing a pattern here?

> *13 "... even as the duty of every day required, offering according to the command of Mosheh, for the Sabbaths, and for the New Moons, and for the appointed times three times a year: the Festival of Unleavened Bread, and the **Festival of Weeks**, and the Festival of Booths."* (2 Chronicles 8:13)

Up to this point, all of the examples given to us are decidedly talking about the Feast of Weeks with one exception. The Scriptures that follow are the ones we are determining their proper meaning concerning the 70 Weeks of Daniel 9. Out of the nineteen verses with the word 'weeks,' there are twelve which describe to us the **Feast of Weeks,** with seven of those occurrences taking place in the very set of scriptures we are examining—that is, Daniel 9:24-26.

> *24 "Seventy **weeks** are decreed for your people and for your set-apart city, to put an end to the transgression, and to seal up sins, and to cover crookedness, and to bring in everlasting righteousness, and to seal up vision and prophet, and to anoint the Most Set-apart. 25 Know, then, and understand: from the going forth of the command to restore and build Yerushalayim until Messiah the Prince is seven **weeks** and sixty-two **weeks**. It shall be built again, with streets and a trench, but in times of affliction. 26 And after the sixty-two **weeks** Messiah shall be cut off and have naught. And the*

*people of a coming prince shall destroy the city and the set-apart place. And the end of it is with a flood. And wastes are decreed, and fighting until the end. 27 And he shall confirm a covenant with many for one week. And in the middle of the week he shall put an end to slaughtering and meal offering. And on the wing of abominations he shall lay waste, even until the complete end and that which is decreed is poured out on the one who lays waste."* (Daniel 9:24-27)

There are also four more verses where the word "week" is found. Daniel 10:2-3 (2), Genesis 29:27-28 (2), which in both instances is speaking of an actual 7 day period of time. In Chapter 11, I will present to you the two instances of the word 'week' that are found in Daniel 9:27—again, in the context of part of the verses we are examining. This is very remarkable.

Given the fact many of you may not know what the "Feast of Weeks" is exactly, I will now direct you to Leviticus 23 where we are told of each of the Festivals we are to keep according to Yehovah's Biblical Calendar with His holy, appointed times.

*5 "In the first month, on the fourteenth day of the month, between the evenings, is the Passover to יהוה. 6 And on the fifteenth day of this month is the Festival of Unleavened Bread to יהוה—seven days you eat unleavened bread. 7 On the first day you have a set-apart gathering, you do no servile work. 8 And you shall bring an offering made by fire to יהוה for seven days. On the seventh day is a set-apart gathering, you do no servile work."* (Leviticus 23:5-8)

*9 And יהוה spoke to Mosheh, saying, 10 "Speak to the children of Yisra'ĕl, and you shall say to them, 'When you come into the land which I give you, and shall reap its harvest, then you shall bring a sheaf of the first-fruits of your harvest to the priest. 11 And he shall wave the sheaf before יהוה, for your acceptance. On the morrow after the Sabbath the priest waves it. 12 And on that day when you wave the sheaf, you shall prepare a male lamb a year old, a perfect one, as a*

> burnt offering to יהוה, 13 and its grain offering: two-tenths of an ĕphah of fine flour mixed with oil, an offering made by fire to יהוה, a sweet fragrance, and its drink offering: one-fourth of a hin of wine. 14 And you do not eat bread or roasted grain or fresh grain until the same day that you have brought an offering to your Elohim—a law forever throughout your generations in all your dwellings.'" (Leviticus 23:9-14)

> 15 "'And from the morrow after the Sabbath, from the day that you brought the sheaf of the wave offering, you shall count for yourselves: seven completed Sabbaths. 16 Until the morrow after the seventh Sabbath you count fifty days, then you shall bring a new grain offering to יהוה. 17 Bring from your dwellings for a wave offering two loaves of bread, of two-tenths of an ĕphah of fine flour they are, baked with leaven, first-fruits to יהוה. 18 And besides the bread, you shall bring seven lambs a year old, perfect ones, and one young bull and two rams. They are a burnt offering to יהוה, with their grain offering and their drink offerings, an offering made by fire for a sweet fragrance to יהוה. 19 And you shall offer one male goat as a sin offering, and two male lambs a year old, as a peace offering. 20 And the priest shall wave them, besides the bread of the first-fruits, as a wave offering before יהוה, besides the two lambs. They are set-apart to יהוה for the priest. 21 And on this same day you shall proclaim a set-apart gathering for yourselves, you do no servile work on it—a law forever in all your dwellings throughout your generations.'" (Leviticus 23:5-21)

You are commanded to keep the Passover. Then, from the Sunday during the Days of Unleavened Bread, you are to count seven Sabbaths and after the seventh Sabbath you are to count to the fiftieth day.

> 15 "And from the morrow after the Sabbath, from the day that you brought the sheaf of the wave offering, you shall count for yourselves: seven completed Sabbaths. 16 Until the morrow after the seventh Sabbath you count fifty days,

*then you shall bring a new grain offering to יהוה."* (Leviticus 23:15-16)

In Christendom this is referred to as Pentecost—Pentecost Sunday to be exact. It is also known in Hebrew as Shavuot.

In Luke we can read of this time when the counting of the weeks was taking place.

> *And it happened on the second chief sabbath, He went through the grainfields. And His disciples plucked the heads of grain and ate, rubbing them in their hands.* (**Luke 6:1**)

When you look up the word for the chief Sabbath in the Strong's Concordance it tells you the following.

> **G1207** deuteroprōtos *dyoo-ter-op'-ro-tos*
>
> From G1208 and G4413; *second first*, that is, (specifically) a designation of the Sabbath immediately after the Paschal week (being the *second* after Passover day, and the *first* of the seven Sabbaths intervening before Pentecost): - second... after the first.
>
> *Shavuot* is the plural of *shabua*. The Jewish Feast of Pentecost, or Festival of Weeks, is called in Hebrew, *Shavuot*.[352]
>
> The Festival of Weeks, commonly shortened to *Shavuot* (Weeks). *Shavuot* is the plural of *shabua*. A *shabua* in Hebrew is a collection of seven (just as a decade is a collection of ten in English). *Shavuot* in this instance is a collection of seven seven-day weeks.[353]

The word "weeks" is the plural of the word "week." Our word in Daniel 9:24 is the plural word and in Hebrew this word "week" is

---

[352] http://www.prophecyfulfillment.com/en014a.html
[353] http://www.prophecyfulfillment.com/en014a.html

"Shabua" and the plural for "Shabua" is "Shabuot" or "Shavuot"—the "v" and "b" sounding the same.

> **Shavuot** *or* **Shabuoth** (ʃəˈvuːəs, -əʊs, *Hebrew* ʃavuːˈɔt, ʃəˈvuːəs, -əʊs, *Hebrew* ʃavuːˈɔt)
>
> *n.* the Hebrew name for Pentecost
>
> [from Hebrew *shābhū'ōth,* plural of *shābhūā`* week][354]

It stands to reason then, to say that this verse is saying Seventy Shavuot. The following passage in Jeremiah is also a point of interest not noted earlier that is deserving of merit.

> 24 *And they do not say in their heart, "Let us now fear* יהוה *our Elohim, who gives rain, both the former and the latter, in its season. He guards for us the appointed weeks of the harvest."* (Jeremiah 5:24)

Here in Jeremiah this word "weeks" is called SHAVUOT.[355]

So, instead of saying *"Seventy weeks are decreed for your people,"* you could say *"Seventy Shavuot are decreed for your people."*

I will now take you on a bit of a detour to help you gain an even deeper understanding of what Shavuot is really all about. To some people it is simply the day when Yehovah gave the Ten Commandments to Moses and the Nation of Israel and although this is true, it is not the whole truth (Exodus 19-20). To most Christians this is the day the Holy Spirit was imparted to the Apostles in Acts 2 and this is *also* true, but what most people do not realize is what this day means to Yehovah Himself. We have three names for the Feast of Shavuot—also known as the Feast of Pentecost.

1. Chag haKatzir—Festival of the Harvest (Exodus 23:16)

---

[354] *Collins-World English Dictionary,* http://dictionary.reference.com/browse/Shavuot
[355] http://biblesuite.com/hebrew/shevuot_7620.htm

2. Yom Habikkurim—Day of First-fruits (Numbers 28:26)
3. Chag haShavuot—Festival of Weeks (Deuteronomy 16:10)

The least common name connection to Shavuot,[356] however, is "The Feast of Oaths."[357]

But getting back to where we were, let us now look at the definition of the word "weeks."

> **H7620**—Taken from *Brown-Driver-Briggs*, שׁבעה / שׁבע / שׁבוּע, shâbûa' / shâbûa' / shebû'âh, BDB Definition:
>
> 1. Seven, period of seven (days or years), heptad, week
>    1a. Period of seven days, a week
>    1a1. Feast of Weeks
>    1b. Heptad, seven (of years)
>
> Part of Speech: Noun masculine, a related word by BDB/Strong's Number: Properly, passive participle of.
>
> **H7650**—As a denominative of **H7651**. Same word by TWOT Number: 2318d

Just like in the beginning, we are led to another root word that ties into the word "week" or "Shabua" and this is the word "Shaba."

> **H7650**—*Brown-Driver-Briggs* שׁבע, shâba, BDB Definition:
>
> 1. To swear, adjure.
>    1a. (Qal) sworn (Participle)
>    1b. (Niphal)
>    1b1. To swear, take an oath.
>    1b2. To swear (of Elohim by Himself).
>    1b3. To curse.
>    1c. (Hiphil)

---

[356] This is adapted from a PowerPoint teaching by my friend Rico Cortez of: http://wisdomintorah.com
[357] http://thekeyofknowledge.net/downloads/Feasts/daniel-shavuot-feastofoaths.pdf

1c1. To cause to take an oath.
1c2. To adjure, Part of Speech: Verb

**H7650**—*Strong's* שׁבע, shâba, shaw-bah'

A primitive root; properly to be complete, but used only as a denominative from **H7651**; to seven oneself, that is, swear (as if by repeating a declaration seven times): adjure, charge (by an oath, with an oath), feed to the full [by mistake for **H7646**], take an oath, X straitly, (cause to, make to) swear.

By investigating just these three Hebrew words (**H-7620**, **H-7650** and **H-7651**) alone, which stem from the word "Shavuot," we now have a sound basis and very strong case for seeing the correlation between the three Hebrew words and their connection to the "Feast of Oaths." When you seven yourself, you are making an oath.

We read in *The Book of Customs*:

> *The Book of Jubilees*, an ancient text that survived in part in the *Dead Sea Scrolls* and in its entirety in the ancient Ethiopian language Ge'ez, gives an entirely different spin on Shavuot. The word 'shavua,' (or) 'week' is a near-homonym to the word for 'oath' ('shevuah'), and the anonymous author of Jubilees says that Shavuot was, in fact, the "Feast of Oaths."[358]

Nissan Mindel confirms this meaning of Shavuot in his book:

> Shavuot means not only 'weeks' but also 'oaths.' The name indicates the two oaths, which G-d and the Jewish people exchanged, upon the day of the Giving of the Torah, to remain faithful to each other forever.[359]

---

[358] *The Book of Customs, A Complete Handbook for the Jewish Year* by Scott-Martin Kosofsky, p. 164

[359] *The Complete Story of Shavuot* by Nissan Mindel, p. 72, Kehot Publication's Society (November 1998)
ISBN-10: 0826603211 ISBN-13: 978-0826603210

What does "swearing an oath" mean in the light of Ancient Near Eastern Covenant structure and context? The answer to this is revealed to us in Exodus, Chapters 19-24—the tenets of which are drawn up in a Suzerain-Vassal Covenant Treaty format.

A Suzerain-Vassal Treaty is a conditional covenant where a great King or Nation (Suzerain) rules over a Lesser Servant King/Nation (Vassal)—whereas the Vassal himself pledges or vows an *oath* of love and loyal allegiance alongside of upholding all the commitments laid forth by the Great King-Suzerain. While this was common knowledge in the Ancient Near East within covenant making between nations, we can now begin to see just how much more depth a Covenant Kingdom has in the Eyes of our Creator.

A Suzerain Treaty requires that the following seven conditions be fulfilled:

1. Identification or Preamble of those involved in the treaty.
2. Prologue listing deeds performed by the Suzerain King already done for the Vassal nation.
3. Commitments to be honored by the Vassal for the duration of the treaty.
4. Terms for the annual reading to the nation of the treaty as wells as terms to renew allegiance to the treaty and the Suzerain.
5. Divine witness to the treaty. In our case, YHWH would be our Witness.
6. Blessings for obedience and Curses for disobedience to the Covenant Treaty.
7. *A Ratification Ceremony* with *oaths* and a sacrificial meal to show participation of those involved in the Covenant Treaty.

# "Oath of Compliance"

From George E. Mendenhall's, *Ancient Israel's Faith and History*[360] description of the sixth typical section in common ANE Treaty structure.

---

[360] Ancient Israel's Faith and History by George E. Mendenhall, p. 69, Section 6

A treaty is a text but an oath is the actual mechanism whereby the text is ratified and brought to life, no longer just words in a document but a functioning reality in the lives of actual people. We have ample evidence of treaties concluding with rituals of compliance, usually spoken oaths but sometimes physical gestures. In much the same way, treaties today are ratified by signatures and handshakes activating the new relationships and its terms. It should not be surprising that the biblical story of the Covenant at Mount Sinai reaches its climax with the escaped slaves pledging to abide by the covenant obligations thereby defining and activating themselves as the people of YHWH (See Exodus 24: 3-8).

> 3 And Mosheh came and related to the people all the Words of יהוה and all the right-rulings. And all the people answered with one voice and said, "All the Words which יהוה has spoken we shall do." 4 And Mosheh wrote down all the Words of יהוה, and rose up early in the morning, and built an altar at the foot of the mountain, and twelve standing columns for the twelve tribes of Yisra'ĕl. 5 And he sent young men of the children of Yisra'ĕl, and they offered burnt offerings and slaughtered peace slaughterings of bulls to יהוה. 6 And Mosheh took half the blood and put it in basins, and half the blood he sprinkled on the altar. 7 And he took the Book of the Covenant and read in the hearing of the people. And they said, "All that יהוה has spoken we shall do, and obey." 8 And Mosheh took the blood and sprinkled it on the people, and said, "See, the blood of the covenant which יהוה has made with you concerning all these Words." (Exodus 24:3-8)

Speaking on the Covenant at Sinai and Near Eastern covenants Rene Lopez[361] says:

> Foundationally, Beri't ("covenant") signifies a binding agreement between two parties... The function of Beri't is

---

[361] *Israelite Covenants In the Light of Ancient Near Eastern Covenants* (Part 2 of 2) by René Lopez, p. 1 http://chafer.nextmeta.com/files/v10n1_5lopez_covenants2israelite_covenants.pdf

basically that of an oath, commitment, or bond between two parties.

The oath. At the conclusion of a covenant, the vassal usually uttered an oath. This gave assurance to the suzerain that the stipulations of the treaty would be kept. Furthermore, an oath ceremony also served to secure bilateral faithfulness of the parties.[362]

Oaths were usually uttered at the conclusion of a treaty, which implied acceptance of its terms. However, Israel invoked an oath in Exodus 19:8, "All that the YHWH has spoken we will do," before hearing the covenant. Then, after hearing the covenant in 24:3, 7, they consented again.

So oaths and stipulations are correlated expressions of the concluded covenant itself, or the oath is the divine sanction of the agreement as affirmed in the covenant declaration and as laid down in the stipulations.[363]

We can read of this "Oath" made by our King, our Suzerain, Yehovah at Shavuot, during the Feast of Weeks at Mount Sinai.

*3 And Mosheh went up to Elohim, and יהוה called to him from the mountain, saying, "This is what you are to say to the house of Ya'aqob, and declare to the children of Yisra'ěl: 4 'You have seen what I did to the Mitsrites, and how I bore you on eagles' wings and brought you to Myself. 5 And now, if you diligently obey My voice, and shall guard My covenant, then you shall be My treasured possession above all the peoples—for all the earth is Mine—6 and you shall be to Me a reign of priests and a set-apart nation.' Those are the words which you are to speak to the children of Yisra'ěl." 7 And Mosheh came and called for the elders of the people,*

---

[362] *Israelite Covenants In the Light of Ancient Near Eastern Covenants* (Part 2 of 2) by René Lopez, p. 87

[363] *Israelite Covenants In the Light of Ancient Near Eastern Covenants* (Part 2 of 2) by René Lopez, p. 88

*and set before them all these words which יהוה commanded him.* (Exodus 19:3-7)

The Covenant Yehovah forged with His chosen ones at Mount Sinai is intricately intertwined with a direct Oath and Covenant made by Yehovah with Abraham, Isaac, and Jacob.

*15 And the Messenger of יהוה called to Abraham a second time from the heavens, 16 and said, "By Myself I have sworn, declares יהוה, because you have done this, and have not withheld your son, your only son, 17 that I shall certainly bless you, and I shall certainly increase your seed as the stars of the heavens and as the sand which is on the seashore, and let your seed possess the gate of their enemies. 18 And in your seed all the nations of the earth shall be blessed, because you have obeyed My voice."* (Genesis 22:15-18)

Is this not exactly what Paul is talking about also in Hebrews 6?

*13 For Elohim, having promised Abraham, since He could swear by no one greater, swore by Himself, 14 saying, "Truly, blessing I shall bless you, and increasing I shall increase you." 15 And so, after being patient, he obtained the promise. 16 For men do indeed swear by the one greater, and an oath for confirmation is for them an end of all dispute. 17 In this way Elohim, resolving to show even more clearly to the heirs of promise the unchangeableness of His purpose, confirmed it by an oath, 18 so that by two unchangeable matters in which it is impossible for Elohim to lie, we might have strong encouragement, we who have fled for refuge to lay hold of the expectation set before us, 19 which we have as an anchor of the life, both safe and firm, and entering into that within the veil, 20 where יהושע has entered as a forerunner for us, having become High Priest forever according to the order of Malkitsed.* (Hebrew 6:13-20)

The Covenant that Yehovah made with Abraham as described in Genesis 15 is a Blood Covenant, of which you would do well to understand. Abraham wanted to know what his great reward was because he had no children.

> 7 And He said to him, "I am יהוה, who brought you out of Ur of the Chaldeans, to give you this land to inherit it." 8 And he said, "Master יהוה, whereby do I know that I possess it?" 9 And He said to him, "Bring Me a three-year-old heifer, and a three-year-old female goat, and a three-year-old ram, and a turtledove, and a young pigeon." 10 And he took all these to Him and cut them in the middle, and placed each half opposite the other, but he did not cut the birds. 11 And the birds of prey came down on the carcasses, and Aḇram drove them away. (Genesis 15:7-11)

> 17 And it came to be, when the sun went down and it was dark, that see, a smoking oven and a burning torch passing between those pieces. 18 On the same day יהוה made a covenant with Aḇram, saying, "I have given this land to your seed, from the river of Mitsrayim to the great river, the River Euphrates." (Genesis 15:17-18)

Here you have an oath that began with Yehovah making a promise to Abraham, and this oath was in turn, spoken to Isaac and Jacob and was finally ratified in blood at Mount Sinai 50 days after the Passover and the Exodus by the people themselves agreeing to it. Many people already know the passage in Romans below by heart, but few, if any, understand what it really means. We read in Romans, Chapter 10:

> 9 That if you confess with your mouth the Master יהושע and believe in your heart that Elohim has raised Him from the dead, you shall be saved. (Romans 10:9)

This word "confess," means something entirely different than just saying the name of Jesus out loud. It is the Greek word **G3670** ὁμολογέω homologeo⁻ hom-ol-og-eh›-o

From a compound of the base of **G3674** and **G3056**; to assent, that is, covenant, acknowledge: con-(pro)-fess, confession is made, give thanks, promise.

Taken in context this means one who is "confessing"/"professing" a genuine faith in Yehshua. Also, one who is coming into Covenant and binding themselves by oath with Him and agrees to the Covenant Yehshua presented at Mount Sinai. As the "Lesser King" or "Master" to the Suzerain Yehovah, Yehshua's Covenant is the *same as* the Father's, which means you are entering into an agreement to keep and be loyal to the Torah and you are then reconciled to Him and restored back into the Kingdom! Remember we showed you earlier that Yehovah is Yehshua.

When you confess in the Messiah as Romans 10:9 says, you are in fact admitting that you have broken the commandments made at Mount Sinai and want to come back into that covenant arrangement. You want to be forgiven your sin of not keeping this covenant agreement.

Keep in mind that in Ancient world culture and context, when a covenant was cut between a Suzerain and vassal, that meant that as long as the vassal was keeping the commitments of the covenant with the King, no one else could come against that nation or vassal without having to face the full Sovereignty of the Suzerain King and all of his resources.

On the other hand, it also meant that if the vassal broke the commitments of the Covenant, the Vassal would suffer the consequences invoked by the Suzerain King.

The entire Book of Deuteronomy is structured as a typical Suzerain-Vassal Covenant Document, which is a more detailed reiteration of the Covenant at Mount Sinai to the second generation in the wilderness prior to entering Eretz Yisrael (the Promised Land).

When you confess your sins you are, in fact, admitting to having broken the Covenant made at Mount Sinai and are wishing to return to the terms of that Covenant as originally agreed. By doing this, you escape the curses that you are now under.

Avinu, Malkeinu (Our Father, Our KING) states HIS oath to Israel again in Chapter 29:

> *9 "Therefore you shall guard the words of this covenant, and do them, so that you prosper in all that you do. 10 All of you are standing today before יהוה your Elohim: your leaders, your tribes, your elders and your officers, all the men of Yisra'ěl, 11 your little ones, your wives, and your sojourner who is in the midst of your camp, from the one who cuts your wood to the one who draws your water, 12 so that you should enter into covenant with יהוה your Elohim, and into His oath, which יהוה your Elohim makes with you today, 13 in order to establish you today as a people for Himself, and He Himself be your Elohim, as He has spoken to you, and as He has sworn to your fathers, to Aḇraham, to Yitsḥaq, and to Ya'aqoḇ. 14 And not with you alone I am making this covenant and this oath, 15 but with him who stands here with us today before יהוה our Elohim, as well as with him who is not here with us today."* (Deuteronomy 29:9-15)

Those who confess the name of Yehshua, as we are told in Romans 10:9 which we just read, confess to breaking this Covenant and want to come back and begin to obey it.

The nation of Israel, our ancestors, gave an Oath to obey three different times. Three times we swore to keep all that Yehovah had said concerning the Covenant. The first time again, was prior to hearing the Commandment by Yehovah.

> *8 And all the people answered together and said, "All that יהוה has spoken we shall do." So Mosheh brought back the words of the people to יהוה.* (Exodus 19:8)

The second time is at the ratification ceremony prior to the Offerings.

> *3 And Mosheh came and related to the people all the Words of יהוה and all the right-rulings. And all the people answered*

> *with one voice and said, "All the Words which יהוה has spoken we shall do." (Exodus 24:3)*

The third time is at the ratification prior to the sprinkling of the blood again making this a Blood Covenant.

> *7 And he took the Book of the Covenant and read in the hearing of the people. And they said, "All that יהוה has spoken we shall do, and obey." (Exodus 24:7)*

I want to point out to you what was said in the last part of Deuteronomy. This covenant was made with those standing there at that time and also with those who were not yet born. That is with us today.

> *14 And not with you alone I am making this covenant and this oath, 15 but with him who stands here with us today before יהוה our Elohim, as well as with him who is not here with us today." (Deuteronomy 29:9-15)*

Acts 2 is also an affirmation of the Covenant on Shavuot! And let me go even further and say that by keeping Pentecost or Shavuot, you are in fact, *sevening* yourself each year. You are reaffirming your commitment to the Covenant our ancestors made on our behalf back at Mount Sinai over 3,391 years ago in 1337 B.C.

> *1 And when the Day of the Festival of Weeks had come, they were all with one mind in one place. 2 And suddenly there came a sound from the heaven, as of a rushing mighty wind, and it filled all the house where they were sitting. 3 And there appeared to them divided tongues, as of fire, and settled on each one of them. 4 And they were all filled with the Set-apart Spirit and began to speak with other tongues, as the Spirit gave them to speak. 5 Now in Yerushalayim there were dwelling Yehudim, dedicated men from every nation under the heaven. (Acts 2:1-5)*

> *1 And when the Day of the Festival of Weeks had come, they were all with one mind in one place. (Acts 2:1)*

Many of you may know that there was a specific service and set of prayers done at the Beit HaMikdash (The Holy Temple) on Shavuot, including a recitation of the Ten Commandments.[364]

Everyone who was there at the Temple during the time of Shavuot was recommitting themselves to Yehovah and the Covenant that was made at Mount Sinai. All with one mind, in one accord and in one place!

Ancient Covenants were often ratified or enacted by the incorporation of multiple elements—some of which included the oaths spoken by both parties, usually followed by a sacrifice and a shared meal. Additionally, there were normally stipulations included in the Covenant that underscored the importance of reciting and reviewing the Covenant annually, and/or at the time of a new Vassal King in order for renewal and remembrance of the Covenant made with the Suzerain KING!

Each year at Shavuot, the Feast of Pentecost, we review the Ten Commandments found in Exodus 20 and expanded in Exodus 34.

The Covenant made at Mount Sinai was a Blood Covenant. Read what Henry Trumbull has to say on this.

> A "covenant union in sacrifice" is an indefinite and ambiguous term. It may mean a covenant union wrought by sacrifice, or a covenant union accompanied by sacrifice, or a covenant union exhibited in sacrifice. But, in whatever sense it is employed, the fact remains true, that, wherever a bloody offering is made in connection with sacrifice and with covenanting, it is the blood-drinking, the blood-pouring, or the blood-touching, that represents the covenant-making; while eating the flesh of the victim, or of the feast otherwise provided, represents the covenant-ratifying, or the covenant-showing…[365]

---

[364] Listen to Rico Cortes's teaching on the Book of Acts, Part 3, Chapter 2 http://wisdomintorah.com/?s=study+on+the+book+of+acts+chapter+1&search_404=1

[365] *The Blood Covenant* by Henry Trumbull, pp. 350-351, Kessinger Publishing

Thus, at Sinai the formal covenanting of the Lord with His people was accompanied by sacrificing. Representatives of the people of Israel offered burnt-offerings, and sacrificed peace-offerings of oxen unto the Lord. Nothing is here said of the technical sin-offering, but the whole burnt-offering and the peace-offering are included. The blood-outpouring and the blood-sprinkling preceded any feasting. And as if to make it clear that "by sprinkling the blood" and not "by eating the flesh of the victim," the "covenant union in [this] sacrifice was represented," Moses took a portion of the blood and "sprinkled [it] on the altar," and another portion "and sprinkled it on the people," saying as he did so, "Behold the blood of the covenant, which the Lord hath made with you." It was not until after this covenanting by blood, that the people of Israel, by their representatives, did eat and drink "in ratification, or in proof, or in exhibit, of the covenant thus wrought by blood."

We have these exact same things spelled out to us in Exodus. It is Yehovah and the Nation of Israel making a Blood Covenant on the Day of Shavuot. Yehovah spoke these Commandments in person on Shavuot, so that all of Israel heard them in Exodus 20. He then wrote them on stone in Exodus 24.

> *1 And to Mosheh He said, "Come up to* יהוה, *you and Aharon, Naḏaḇ and Aḇihu, and seventy of the elders of Yisra'ěl, and you shall bow yourselves from a distance. 2 "But Mosheh shall draw near to* יהוה *by himself, and let them not draw near, nor let the people go up with him." 3 And Mosheh came and related to the people all the Words of* יהוה *and all the right-rulings. And all the people answered with one voice and said, "All the Words which* יהוה *has spoken we shall do." 4 And Mosheh wrote down all the Words of* יהוה, *and rose up early in the morning, and built an altar at the foot of the mountain, and twelve standing columns for the twelve tribes of Yisra'ěl. 5 And he sent young men of the children*

---

(March 10th, 2003)
ISBN-10: 0766139832 ISBN-13: 978-0766139831

> *of Yisra'ěl, and they offered burnt offerings and slaughtered peace slaughterings of bulls to* יהוה. *6 And Mosheh took half the blood and put it in basins, and half the blood he sprinkled on the altar.* (Exodus 24:1-6)

> *7 And he took the Book of the Covenant and read in the hearing of the people. And they said, "All that* יהוה *has spoken we shall do, and obey." 8 And Mosheh took the blood and sprinkled it on the people, and said, "See, the blood of the covenant which* יהוה *has made with you concerning all these Words." 9 And Mosheh went up, also Aharon, Nadab, and Abihu, and seventy of the elders of Yisra'ěl, 10 and they saw the Elohim of Yisra'ěl, and under His feet like a paved work of sapphire stone, and like the heavens for brightness. 11 Yet He did not stretch out His hand against the chiefs of the children of Yisra'ěl! And they saw Elohim, and they ate and drank. 12 And* יהוה *said to Mosheh, "Come up to Me on the mountain and be there, while I give you tablets of stone, and the Torah and the command which I have written, to teach them."* (Exodus 24:7-11)

And after Moses broke those stones, Yehovah wrote them again on both sides of the stone in Exodus 34.

This is exactly what the Apostle Paul is discussing in Chapter 9 of the Book of Hebrews, connecting the Ratification Ceremony at Mount Sinai with Yehshua, the Mashiach, our Redeemer and Mediator of the *Renewed Covenant!*

> *1 Now the first covenant indeed had regulations of worship and the earthly set-apart place. 2 For a Tent was prepared: the first part, in which was the lampstand, and the table, and the showbread, which is called the Set-apart Place. 3 And after the second veil, the part of the Tent which is called Most Set-apart, 4 to which belonged the golden censer, and the ark of the covenant overlaid on all sides with gold, in which were the golden pot that held the manna, and the rod of Aharon that budded, and the tablets of the covenant, 5*

*and above it the kerubim of esteem were overshadowing the place of atonement—about which we do not now speak in detail. 6 And these having been prepared like this, the priests always went into the first part of the Tent, accomplishing the services.* (Hebrews 9:1-6)

*7 But into the second part, the high priest went alone once a year, not without blood, which he offered for himself and for sins of ignorance of the people, 8 the Set-apart Spirit signifying this, that the way into the Most Set-apart Place was not yet made manifest while the first Tent has a standing, 9 which was a parable for the present time in which both gifts and slaughters are offered which are unable to perfect the one serving, as to his conscience, 10 only as to foods and drinks, and different washings, and fleshly regulations imposed until a time of setting matters straight.*(Hebrews 9:7-9)

*11 But Messiah, having become a High Priest of the coming good matters, through the greater and more perfect Tent not made with hands, that is, not of this creation, 12 entered into the Most Set-apart Place once for all, not with the blood of goats and calves, but with His own blood, having obtained everlasting redemption. 13 For if the blood of bulls and goats and the ashes of a heifer, sprinkling the defiled, sets apart for the cleansing of the flesh, 14 how much more shall the blood of the Messiah, who through the everlasting Spirit offered Himself unblemished to Elohim, cleanse your conscience from dead works to serve the living Elohim?* (Hebrews 9:11-14)

*15 And because of this, He is the Mediator of a renewed covenant, so that, death having taken place for redemption of the transgressions under the first covenant, those who are called might receive the promise of the everlasting inheritance. 16 For where a covenant is, it is necessary for the death of the covenanted one to be established. 17 For a covenant over those dead is firm, since it is never valid while* *the covenanted one is living. (Deuteronomy 24, Numbers 5, Romans 7)\*18 Therefore, not even the first covenant was instituted without blood. 19 For when, according to Torah, every command had been spoken by Mosheh to all the people, he took the blood of calves and goats, with water, and scarlet wool, and hyssop, and sprinkled both the book itself and all the people, 20 saying, "This is the blood of the covenant which Elohim commanded you."* (Hebrews 9:15-20)

*21 And in the same way he sprinkled with blood both the Tent and all the vessels of the service. 22 And, according to the Torah, almost all is cleansed with blood, and without shedding of blood there is no forgiveness. 23 It was necessary, then, that the copies of the heavenly ones should be cleansed with these, but the heavenly ones themselves with better slaughter offerings than these. 24 For Messiah has not entered into a Set-apart Place made by hand—figures of the true—but into the heaven itself, now to appear in the presence of Elohim on our behalf, 25 not that He should offer Himself often, as the high priest enters into the Set-apart Place year by year with blood not his own. 26 For if so, He would have had to suffer often, since the foundation of the world. But now He has appeared once for all at the end of the ages to put away sin by the offering of Himself. 27 And as it awaits men to die once, and after this the judgment, 28 so also the Messiah, having been offered once to bear the sins of many, shall appear a second time, apart from sin, to those waiting for Him, unto deliverance.* (Hebrews 9:21-28)

As I have shown, Shavuot is also the portrait of an intimate, loving relationship between Yehovah and Israel. This is Israel marrying her KING, coming under the Chuppah of Mount Sinai, accepting the Ketubah (Wedding Contract) of the Creator of the Universe. Even though Yehovah would know that we would violate this marriage, that we would commit idolatry and spiritual adultery by going after other mighty ones, HE nevertheless instilled provisions for the complete Restoration of His Bride through Yehshua the Messiah!

It was also on Shavuot in Acts, Chapter 2 when a new facet of our Marriage Covenant was brought to life and became a reality when the Spirit of the Torah—the Ruach HaQodesh (Holy Spirit) was given and recognized as the counterpart to the Letter of the Torah that was given at Mount Sinai. The Ruach is our Seal from the KING that we have been marked for redemption to enter the Kingdom of Yehovah by the work of Yehshua the Messiah!

Did Yehovah our Groom, our King, give His Vassal-Israel a Signet/Wedding Ring, or a sign to the Nations that we, as His Bride, are married to the Great King in which accompanies the Seal of the Ruach HaQodesh?

> *13 And you, speak to the children of Yisra'ěl, saying, "My Sabbaths you are to guard, by all means, for it is a sign between Me and you throughout your generations, to know that I, יהוה, am setting you apart. 14 And you shall guard the Sabbath, for it is set-apart to you. Everyone who profanes it shall certainly be put to death, for anyone who does work on it, that being shall be cut off from among his people. 15 Six days work is done, and on the seventh is a Sabbath of rest, set-apart to יהוה. Everyone doing work on the Sabbath day shall certainly be put to death. 16 And the children of Yisra'ěl shall guard the Sabbath, to observe the Sabbath throughout their generations as an everlasting covenant. 17 Between Me and the children of Yisra'ěl it is a sign forever. For in six days יהוה made the heavens and the earth, and on the seventh day He rested and was refreshed." 18 And when He had ended speaking with him on Mount Sinai, He gave Mosheh two tablets of the Witness, tablets of stone, written with the finger of Elohim.* (Exodus 31:13-18)

> *13 And you, speak to the children of Yisra' ěl, saying, "My Sabbaths you are to guard, by all means, for it is a sign between Me and you throughout your generations, to know that I, יהוה, am setting you apart."* (Exodus 31:13)

> *19 "I am יהוה your Elohim. Walk in My laws, and guard My right-rulings, and do them. 20 And set apart My Sabbaths, and they shall be a sign between Me and you, to know that I am יהוה your Elohim."* (Ezekiel 20:19-20)

The Fourth Commandment is the one part of The Law most will not keep. It includes the weekly Sabbath and the Annual Holy Days as listed in Leviticus 23 and it also includes the Sabbatical and Jubilee Years as told to us in Leviticus 25.

Before I move on, I must point out that the night before Passover in the year Yehshua was to be killed, He had a meal (His last Supper) with His disciples and told them that the wine represented His blood and that the bread represented His flesh. All the ingredients used to make a covenant; or, a Suzerain-Vassal Treaty.

> *27 And He took the cup and gave thanks, and gave it to them, saying, "Drink all of it. 28 For this is My blood of the new covenant, which is shed for many for the remission of sins."* (Matthew 26:27-28)

> *19 And He took bread and gave thanks, and He broke it and gave it to them, saying, "This is My body which is given for you, this do in remembrance of Me." 20 In the same way He took the cup, after having dined, saying, "This cup is the new covenant in My blood, which is being poured out for you."* (Luke 22:19-20)

His body was not broken until that next day and His blood was spilled out on the ground in the exact same way an animal's blood runs on the ground in a covenant treaty. This happened at the exact same time when the Passover Lambs were killed at 3pm on the 14th of Aviv and their blood spilled on the ground each year renewing the Covenant.

The Covenant that He was renewing was, again, the very same one from Mount Sinai, which He spoke to the Israelites. The same one which on the day of His Ascension on that Sunday Morning began the process of counting to the seven weeks of Sabbaths; the fifty days until

Pentecost, or the time of swearing our oaths renewed again that we will keep the Torah, only now in a way that's been written on our hearts. In other words, the Feast of Oaths is a time during which we seven ourselves to Yehovah again, as we are renewing our vows each year at Shavuot, again, also known as Pentecost.

And like a bride who has taken on the name of her husband, we are told not to take the name of Yehovah in vain. That is, we do not become His Bride only to keep dragging His name back down into the bog of idolatry we have been delivered out of. Instead, we are to renew our vows to keep those same laws spoken to us and given to us at Mount Sinai that Yehshua said were the two greatest Commandments. To love Yehovah which are the first four and to love your fellow man which are the last six.

Yehshua Himself told us:

> *15 If you love Me, keep My commandments... 21 He who has My commandments and keeps them, he it is who loves Me. And he who loves Me shall be loved by My Father, and I will love him and will reveal Myself to him.* (John 14:15, 21)

I have now provided you with a sound basis and solid foundation by which to more closely and critically examine this word "weeks," and with a much greater chance of you arriving at an accurate conclusion. In addition, I have shown you that "weeks" means the "Feast of Weeks"—also called "Shavuot." I have also helped you come to understand how this is a very special time when we make a solemn oath to guard His Commandments in order to remain in His blessings. That being said let us now begin to understand what is being foretold in this prophecy. Keep in mind as we go forward that this Daniel 9 prophecy has a great deal to do with having broken the oath we agreed to at Mount Sinai and very little to do with the coming of the Messiah. I can't stress this enough, for most of us have had it so deeply engrained within us to think it is the latter and not the former.

*"Seventy weeks are decreed for your people."*

Seventy Shavuots are decreed for your people. A Shavuot is forty-nine days. Therefore, seventy forty-nines are decreed for your people.

$$70 \times 49 = 3{,}430$$

Now when the Bible says a "year is as a day" as it does in Ezekiel,[366] we then have 3,430 years to reckon with and not the 490 years that most try to rationalize. A Jubilee Cycle is also forty-nine years in length of time in the *same way* the Feast of Weeks is.

Now how do we prove that these 3,430 years, which are the same as seventy Jubilee cycles are in fact the correct way to understand what Daniel is saying; Seventy Shavuot or 70 weeks? We do so by those things we are now going to explain in the following chapters. By reading what these four verses actually do say and not dropping those sections that do not fit our theory. It all must fit without being forced and we will show you this in the coming chapters.

---

[366] "I have assigned you the same number of days as the years of their sin. So for 390 days you will bear the sin of the house of Israel…and bear the sin of the house of Judah. I have assigned you 40 days, a day for each year." (Ezekiel 4:5-6b).

# Chapter 6 | Why Daniel's Book Has Been Sealed Until the Last Days & the Jubilee Cycle Explained

*24 "Seventy weeks are decreed for your people and for your set-apart city, to put an end to the transgression, and to seal up sins, and to cover crookedness, and to bring in everlasting righteousness, and to seal up vision and prophet, and to anoint the Most Set-apart. 25 Know, then, and understand: from the going forth of the command to restore and build Yerushalayim until Messiah the Prince is seven weeks and sixty-two weeks. It shall be built again, with streets and a trench, but in times of affliction. 26 And after the sixty-two weeks Messiah shall be cut off and have naught. And the people of a coming prince shall destroy the city and the set-apart place. And the end of it is with a flood. And wastes are decreed, and fighting until the end. 27 And he shall confirm a covenant with many for one week. And in the middle of the week he shall put an end to slaughtering and meal offering. And on the wing of abominations he shall lay waste, even until the complete end and that which is decreed is poured out on the one who lays waste.[1]"* [Footnote: [1]Mt. 24:15 (Daniel 9:24-27)]

In Chapter 5, I just shared with you three of the key things you need to know to come into a fundamental and revolutionary understanding of things that will enable you to finally unlock this Daniel 9 Prophecy.

The first is that this "weeks" (Shavuot plural for week or Shabua) being spoken of is *The Feast of Weeks*. Second of extreme importance is that this "weeks" is also known as *The Feast of Oaths* and by this it is constantly referring us back to the covenant we made at Mount Sinai. The third key to understanding this prophecy is that *"seventy weeks"* means 70 X 49, which totals 3430 Years.

I want to ensure, however, that I leave no stone unturned and make sure you get it and understand it, so let me proceed to explain some additional points to back up my claims.

We read in Daniel 12 of some more prophetic events and twice Daniel is being told that these things are for the time of the end.

> *1 And at that time Michael shall stand up, the great ruler who stands for the sons of your people. And there shall be a time of trouble, such as never was since there was a nation; until that time. And at that time your people shall be delivered, every one that shall be found written in the book. 2 And many of those who sleep in the dust of the earth shall awake, some to everlasting life, and some to shame and everlasting contempt. 3 And those who are wise shall shine as the brightness of the sky; and those who turn many to righteousness shall shine as the stars forever and ever. 4* **But you, O Daniel, shut up the words and seal the book, even to the time of the end.** *Many shall run to and fro, and knowledge shall be increased.* (Daniel 12:1-4)

> *5 Then I Daniel looked, and behold, there stood another two, the one on this side, and the one on that side of the bank of the river. 6 And one said to the man clothed in linen on the waters of the river: "Until when shall be the end of these wonders?" 7 And I heard the man clothed in linen, who was on the waters of the river, when he held up his right and his*

> *left hand to Heaven, and swore by Him who lives forever that it shall be for a time, times, and a half. And when they have made an end of scattering the power of the holy people, all these things shall be finished. 8 And I heard, but I did not understand.* **Then I said, "O my lord, what shall be the end of these things?" 9 And He said, "Go, Daniel! For the words are closed up and sealed until the end-time."** *10 Many shall be purified, and made white, and tried. But the wicked shall do wickedly. And none of the wicked shall understand, but the wise shall understand.* (Daniel 12:5-10)

I am here writing this book to you, the reader in this year of 2013 C.E., which is the 5849th[367] year since the creation of Adam. My claim here is basically that now is the time when Yehovah has chosen to reveal to us the secrets of this understanding.

That is a very bold and defining statement, is it not? So how can I stand here and make such a statement?

The first time Daniel is told "this is for the time of the end" in this chapter we are told something in the preceding verse:

> *3 And those who are wise shall shine as the brightness of the sky; and those who turn many to righteousness shall shine as the stars forever and ever.* (Daniel 12:3)

The question at this point is: "Who are the 'wise' and how do they turn many to righteousness?" *The* wise must also be righteous if they can "turn others TO righteousness." What does Scripture tell us? What is wisdom and what is righteousness as defined by Scripture?

> *7 The Torah of* יהוה *is perfect, bringing back the being; the witness of* יהוה *is trustworthy, making wise the simple.* (Psalm 19:7)

---

[367] See Prophecies of Abraham and Remembering the Sabbatical Year of 2016 for proof according to the Sabbatical and Jubilee year cycles as to which year in Yehovah's 7000 year plan of salvation we are in.

> *97 O how I love Your Torah! It is my study all day long. 98 Your commands make me wiser than my enemies; for it is ever before me. 99 I have more understanding than all my teachers, for Your witnesses are my study. 100 I understand more than the aged, for I have observed Your orders.* (Psalm 119:97-100)

According to these two Psalms, Yehovah's Law, or the keeping of His Laws, makes us wise and gives us understanding above all others. The keeping of the Commandments is what makes us wise; but what about being righteous?

> *172 My tongue sings of Your word, for all Your commands are righteousness* (Psalms 119:172)

Here again, in order to be righteous we are being told that we have to keep the Commandments. It is the keeping of the Commandments that makes us righteous and wise. I want to make sure you get this. This is *Yehovah's definition* of righteousness and His definition of wisdom straight from Bible.

It is no wonder then that these things of Daniel have been sealed and closed until the time of the end. If only the wise and the righteous could understand, it has only been in the last century that people have been turning back to keeping all ten of the Commandments. Yes, they kept them for the most part all along, but they never would keep the fourth one. That is the one that says we must keep the seventh day Sabbath—Saturday. But, just as Yehshua expanded on adultery and murder in the context of not only acting it out but even with regard to the tendency to look upon a person with such intent, so has the Fourth Commandment been expanded to not only include the Holy Days of Leviticus 23 and not adding any other holidays to them, but also, just as importantly, the Sabbatical and Jubilee Years of Leviticus 25.

Starting in the late 1800's the Sabbath was being kept by many of what are now called the Seventh Day Adventists. It was after the 1930's that many others began to keep both the Seventh Day Sabbath and the Holy Days of Leviticus 23. It was not until sometime after the 1990's that some began to keep the Holy Days according to the barley being ripe in Israel and the sighting of the Moon, to begin the month and the count to each of the Holy Days. This had not been done since before the Temple was destroyed in 70 C.E. And it was not until I began to tell people in 2005 about the importance of keeping the Sabbatical Years and actually keeping them in 2009-2010, that the final part of this Commandment was fully kept as far as I know.

The keeping of the Fourth Commandment entails the weekly Saturday Sabbath, the Holy Days and the Sabbatical and Jubilee Years.

> *24 And יהוה commanded us to do all these laws, to fear יהוה our Elohim, for our good always, to keep us alive, as it is today. 25 And it is righteousness for us when we guard to do all this command before יהוה our Elohim, as He has commanded us.* (Deuteronomy 6:24-25)

> *9 He sent redemption to His people, He has commanded His covenant forever. Set-apart and awesome is His Name. 10 The fear of יהוה is the beginning of wisdom. All those doing them have a good understanding. His praise is standing forever.* (Psalm 111:9-10)

It is when we are keeping and doing all of His Commandments that we have a respectful fear of Yehovah. It is by doing these Commandments that we gain righteousness and understanding and wisdom above all those who do not keep them.

We are told in Revelation that Satan is going to attack those who keep the Commandments. And we are also told in Revelation that those who are, at that time, keeping those Commandments will be the ones who have true faith in Yehovah.

> *12 Here is the endurance of the set-apart ones, here are those guarding the commands of Elohim and the belief of עשוהי.* (Revelation 14:12)

> *17 And the dragon was enraged with the woman, and he went to fight with the remnant of her seed, those guarding the commands of Elohim and possessing the witness of* יהושע *Messiah.* (Revelation 12:17)

There are many who say the Commandments were nailed to the cross and done away with. Revelation clearly tells us that they are not. Paul was not one of those who said the Law was nailed to the cross either, for he says that the Law and the Commandments are Holy and are what make us righteous.

> *12 So that the Torah truly is set-apart, and the command set-apart, and righteous, and good.* (Romans 7:12)

In the first three chapters I have already shown you who Israel is today. Today, you Israel, need to hear the words of Yehovah in order to return to being righteous, in order to return to being Holy, in order to return to being wise and in order to return to a sound understanding of biblical prophecy.

> *1 "And now, O Yisra'ĕl, listen to the laws and the right-rulings which I am teaching you to do, so that you live, and shall go in and possess the land which* יהוה *Elohim of your fathers is giving you. 2 Do not add to the Word which I command you, and do not take away from it,[1] so as to guard the commands of* יהוה *your Elohim which I am commanding you."* [Footnote: [1]See also: Deuteronomy 12:32, Proverbs 30:6, Revelation 22:18-19 (Deuteronomy 4:1-2)].

> *3 Your eyes have seen what* יהוה *did at Ba'al Pe'or, for* יהוה *your Elohim has destroyed from your midst all the men who followed Ba'al Pe'or. 4 But you who are clinging to* יהוה *your Elohim are alive today, every one of you. 5 See, I have taught you laws and right-rulings, as* יהוה *my Elohim commanded me, to do thus in the land which you go to possess. 6 And you shall guard and do them, for this is your wisdom and your understanding before the eyes of the peoples who hear all these laws, and they shall say, "Only a wise and*

*understanding people is this great nation! 7 For what great nation is there which has Elohim so near to it, as יהוה our Elohim is to us, whenever we call on Him? 8 And what great nation is there that has such laws and righteous right-rulings like all this Torah which I set before you this day? 9 Only, guard yourself, and guard your life diligently, lest you forget the Words your eyes have seen, and lest they turn aside from your heart all the days of your life. And you shall make them known to your children and your grandchildren."* (Deuteronomy 4:3-9)

It is by keeping Yehovah's Commandments that we acquire the wisdom that is so desperately needed in these Last Days to be able to adequately understand what has been sealed up in Daniel's prophecies. As you have just read, *"4 But you who are clinging to יהוה your Elohim are alive today, every one of you."* This is what will keep us alive in the coming cycle of war.

Having said this, it was not until I myself came into an understanding of the Sabbatical and Jubilee Cycles—and when they had occurred in the past—that I was able to fully understand the Daniel 9 Prophecy. It is because of this understanding that I am now sharing this information with you.

Moving on, in the previous chapter I explained to you what the Seventy Weeks actually were.

*"Seventy weeks are decreed for your people."*

In other words, Seventy Shavuots are decreed for your people. A Shavuot is forty-nine days. Seventy "forty-nines" are decreed for you people.

$$70 \times 49 = 3{,}430$$

Now when you apply the Day-Year Principle[368] as put forth in Ezekiel, Chapter 4, you then have 3,430 years to deal with and *not* the

---

[368] http://en.wikipedia.org/wiki/Day-year_principle Also known as year-day

490 years that most try to rationalize. A Jubilee Cycle is also a forty-nine year block of time in the very same way the Feast of Weeks is. 3,430 years can also be understood to be 70 Jubilee Cycles.

I have to bring this up so that you understand it, because this is a vital clue you need to be aware of in order to understand when this Seventy Weeks, or seventy forty-nines, or Seventy Jubilee Cycles begins. But before I take you there, I must explain the Jubilee Cycles.

The Jubilee Cycles are the foundational subject of my DVD entitled, *The Chronological Order of Prophecy In the Jubilees,* which came out in 2008 and also, my book, *The Prophecies of Abraham,* which came out in 2010, and my second book, *Remembering the Sabbatical Year of 2016,* which became available in 2013. Those same Jubilee Cycles are the basis for this book *The 2300 Days of Hell* and the video series we recorded at Sukkot in the fall of 2013, which you can view for free at my web site www.sightedmoon.com I strongly recommend you watch or read each of them as I am taking special care to not repeat all the information in them here again in this book. I am not going to explain them again here in detail and prove them as I have in the other books. You can study these things in greater detail in my previous two books and in watching my videos.

The first mention of the Sabbatical Years can be found in Genesis:

> *3 And יהוה said, "My Spirit shall not strive with man forever in his going astray. He is flesh, and his days shall be one hundred and twenty years."* (Genesis 6:3)

The word for "years" here is "shaneh."

**H8141** שנה שנה shâneh, shânâh, shaw-neh', shaw-naw'

---

principle or year-for-a-day principle, this is a method of interpretation of Bible prophecy in which the word *day* in prophecy is symbolic for a *year* of actual time. It is used principally by the Historicist School of Prophetic Interpretation.

(The first form being in plural only, the second form being feminine); from

**H8138**—A year (as a revolution of time): Whole age, X long, old, year (X -ly).

Genesis 6:3 is telling us that man will have 120 periods of time. It is the *only* place this is said. Many people use this to then jump to the following conclusion:

$$120 \times 50 = 6{,}000 \text{ Years}$$

I have demonstrated beyond all reasonable doubt why the Jubilee Cycles are forty-nine years and then followed by the fiftieth year, which is also the first year in the next count of forty-nine years. But I urge you again to read these things in *Remembering the Sabbatical Year of 2016*.

These 120 periods of time are, in fact, $120 \times 49 = 5{,}880$ years and not the 6,000 years many have presumed them to be.

Moses knew that when the Israelites entered into the Promised Land it would be a Jubilee Year. Because of this, he had to explain the Jubilee Year Laws to them.

How did he know this?

All you have to do is to add up all the years from the creation of Adam to the time of the forty year curse of wandering in the wilderness comes to a close and you too will then be able to see it would most definitely be a Jubilee Year when the Israelites are able to cross the Jordan and enter the Land.

In my book, *Remembering the Sabbatical Year of 2016*, I have gone through an extensive explanation showing the proper chronology from Adam up until the Israelites entered the Promised Land. That year was 2,500 years from the creation of Adam until they crossed the Jordan. I then show you how to connect this chronology to the modern Common Era.

Let me now quote to you Chapter 18 from *Remembering the Sabbatical Year of 2016*.

You are most likely wondering, at this point, *when* the Jubilee Years were in the past, when the *next one* is going to occur and *how* to know or how to *prove* it, as this is what we *all* must do.

There is a great deal of confusion out there about the Sabbatical Years and it is because of this confusion most of us today are unable to figure it out. In order to find the truth before it was adulterated, one must go back in time to a source that is true. One must go back to Scripture itself and to Yehovah's very own words spoken by Himself. From this point on, we can *then* go forward (and backward) to know *when* the Sabbatical and Jubilee Years were and which ones are still to come.

Respected Chronologist, Edwin R. Thiele wrote the book, *The Mysterious Numbers of the Hebrew Kings*.[369] In it he states how there are *only* two dates in all of Hebrew chronology that can be confirmed by outside sources.

In the Old Testament, no absolute dates are given for the Hebrew kings and it becomes a true Berean's task to establish, if he or she can, an absolute date in the history of Israel that can be used as a starting place to establish other dates in the desired chronological scheme. One's only hope of doing this in the instances where there exists historical gaps which cannot be accounted for, is to isolate an intersecting principal point of contact where Hebrew history correlates with certainty to the history of another nation whose chronology, for a given space and time, is more well-known.

In the early history of the Hebrew monarchies, the two most well documented examples of this were the Assyrians first and the Babylonians second. Fortunately for us, the chronologies of these two nations as they pertain to the time periods we will be concerning ourselves with the most have been very thoroughly established.[370]

---

[369] http://www.amazon.com/Mysterious-Numbers-Hebrew-Kings/dp/082543825X
[370] *The Mysterious Numbers of the Hebrew Kings* by Edwin R. Thiele; p.67

One is the Battle of Qarqar in 853 B.C. in which King Ahab died. This story is found in I Kings 22. The reason this date is important is because of *who* Ahab was fighting against. He and his regiment were fighting against Assyria.

Assyrian chronology dating back to the beginning of the 9th-century B.C. rests on a highly dependable and exceptionally solid foundation. All the essentials for a sound chronology are present. Therefore, scholars have been able to come up with a sound chronological system for the nation of Assyria.[371]

The only other date that ties into other chronologies is 701 B.C. when King Sennacherib attacks Judah in the fourteenth year of King Hezekiah's reign.

A solid synchronism between Judah and Assyria in which our pattern of Hebrew dates could begin is 701 B.C. This is a definitely fixed date in Assyrian history and is the year in which King Sennacherib, in his third campaign, "went against the Hittite-land" (Aram), and shut up King Hezekiah the Jew... like a caged bird in Jerusalem, his royal city. This took place in the fourteenth year of King Hezekiah's reign (II Kings 18:13), that is, in the year 701 B.C.[372]

The Assyrians adhered to a practice of appointing to the office of Eponym, or Limmu, some high official of the court such as the governor of a province or the king himself. The Limmu held office for a calendar year and to that year was given the name of the individual then occupying the position of Limmu.[373]

From the ruins of Nineveh we have four Assyrian chronologies called *Eponym* with which we can date from 911 B.C.–701 B.C.—each of which overlap the others.

We also have seven Assyrian chronologies called *Limmu Lists* which cover the years from 891 B.C.–648 B.C. and they too have astronomical

---

[371] *The Mysterious Numbers of the Hebrew Kings* by Edwin R. Thiele; p.67
[372] *The Mysterious Numbers of the Hebrew Kings* by Edwin R. Thiele; p.78
[373] *The Mysterious Numbers of the Hebrew Kings* by Edwin R. Thiele; p.68

events that can be used to pinpoint the exact time in history that an event itself took place and the king that existed at that time.

There are also two other documents known as the *Khorsabad King List* from Sargon and the *SDAS King List* which not only are in agreement with each other, but are also in agreement with the *Eponym* and *Limmu Lists* previously mentioned.

And if all of the above isn't enough, to all of this we can then add *Ptolemy's Canon* which is a chronology of Babylonian, Persian and Grecian kings dating from 747 B.C.–161 C.E. But even this is not the end of it. Ptolemy also authored over eighty astronomical recordings including their dates and their relationship to the rulers at that time. These astronomical recordings can then be used to double-check the accuracy of the list of kings and confirm when they ruled in human history.

It is *only* with these lists of chronologies, recovered from the ruins of Nineveh, that we are able to have a reliable chronological record of *any* of the Hebrew kings.

Having the lists of Assyrian rulers at our disposal only matters, however, when we can connect one or more Israelite kings to it and, remarkably, this has been done with the Battle of Qarqar *and* the Assyrian attack on King Hezekiah. Except for these two events tying directly into the known Assyrian chronology, we would have *no* date by which to reckon the kings of Israel to, for they left no records to us.

Why, you may ask, is any of this important?

For one, the reference above with regard to King Sennacherib's attack on King Hezekiah is recorded in the Assyrian chronologies. This recording is an absolute benchmark year and from that year we can determine when all the other kings of Israel reigned. We could also use the Battle of Qarqar, but the one involving King Hezekiah is much more important to us in the context of the Sabbatical and Jubilee Years.

In this well-documented account, King Sennacherib, in his third campaign, "went against the Hittite-land Aram, and shut up King Hezekiah the Jew... like a caged bird in Jerusalem, his royal city." This took place in the fourteenth year of King Hezekiah's reign (II Kings 18:13). This was the year 701 B.C.

As I also stated earlier, but in more general terms, 701 B.C. is an absolute chronological benchmark date in history. It is irrefutable. It is provable beyond scrutiny. Knowing this, let us now read about the events leading up to this dramatic event.

> *1 And it came to be in the third year of Hoshĕa son of Ělah, sovereign of Yisra'ĕl, that Ḥizqiyahu son of Aḥaz, sovereign of Yehuḏah, began to reign. 2 He was twenty-five years old when he began to reign, and he reigned twenty-nine years in Yerushalayim. And his mother's name was Aḇi, daughter of Zeḵaryah. 3 And he did what was right in the eyes of* יהוה*, according to all that his father Dawiḏ did. 4 He took away the high places and broke the pillars, and cut down the Ashĕrah, and broke in pieces the bronze serpent which Mosheh had made, for until those days, the children of Yisra'ĕl burned incense to it, and called it Neḥushtan (a bronze trifle). 5 He put his trust in* יהוה *Elohim of Yisra'ĕl, and after him was none like him among all the sovereigns of Yehuḏah, nor who were before him, 6 and he clung to* יהוה*. He did not turn away from following Him, but guarded His commands, which* יהוה *had commanded Mosheh. 7 And* יהוה *was with him—wherever he went, he acted wisely. And he rebelled against the sovereign of Ashshur and did not serve him. 8 He smote the Philistines, as far as Azzah and its borders—from watchtower unto the walled city.* (II Kings 18:1-8)

> *13 And in the fourteenth year of Sovereign Ḥizqiyahu, Sanḥĕriḇ sovereign of Ashshur came up against all the walled cities of Yehuḏah and captured them. 14 And Ḥizqiyahu sovereign of Yehuḏah sent to the sovereign of Ashshur at Laḵish, saying, "I have done wrong, turn away from me. I*

shall bear whatever you impose on me." And the sovereign of Ashshur imposed upon Ḥizqiyahu, the sovereign of Yehuḏah, three hundred talents of silver and thirty talents of gold. 15 And Ḥizqiyahu gave him all the silver that was found in the House of יהוה and in the treasuries of the sovereign's house. (II Kings 18:13-15)

16 At that time Ḥizqiyahu cut off the doors of the Hĕḵal of יהוה, and the doorposts which Ḥizqiyahu sovereign of Yehuḏah had overlaid (with gold), and gave it to the sovereign of Ashshur. 17 And the sovereign of Ashshur sent the Tartan, and the Raḇsaris, and the Raḇshaqĕh from Laḵish, with a great army against Yerushalayim, to Sovereign Ḥizqiyahu. And they went up and came to Yerushalayim. And when they had come up, they came and stood by the channel of the upper pool, which was on the highway to the Launderer's Field. (II Kings 18:16-17)

18 And they called to the sovereign. And Elyaqim son of Ḥilqiyahu, who was over the household, and Sheḇnah the scribe, and Yo'aḥ son of Asaph, the recorder, came out to them. 19 And the Raḇshaqĕhm said to them, "Please say to Ḥizqiyahu, 'Thus said the great sovereign, the sovereign of Ashshur, what is this trust in which you have trusted?' 20 You have spoken of having counsel and strength for battle, but they are only words of the lips! And in whom do you trust, that you rebel against me? 21 Now look! You have put your trust in the staff of this crushed reed, Mitsrayim, on which if a man leans, it shall go into his hand and pierce it. So is Pharaoh, sovereign of Mitsrayim to all who trust in him. 22 But when you say to me, 'We trust in יהוה our Elohim,' is it not He whose high places and whose altars Ḥizqiyahu has taken away, and said to Yehuḏah and Yerushalayim, 'Bow yourselves before this altar in Yerushalayim?' 23 And now, I urge you, give a pledge to my master the sovereign of Ashshur, then I give you two thousand horses, if you are able to put riders on them!" (II Kings 18:18-23)

*24 "And how do you turn back the face of one commander of the least of my master's servants, and trust in Mitsrayim for chariots and horsemen? 25 Have I now come up without* יהוה *against this place to destroy it?* יהוה *said to me, 'Go up against this land, and you shall destroy it.'" 26 Then said Elyaqim son of Ḥilqiyahu, and Sheḇnah, and Yo'aḥ to the Raḇshaqēh, "Please speak to your servants in Aramaic, for we understand it. And do not speak to us in the language of Yehuḏah, in the ears of the people on the wall." 27 And the Raḇshaqēh said to them, "Has my master sent me to your master and to you to speak these words, and not to the men sitting on the wall to eat their own dung and drink their own urine, with you?"* (II Kings 18:24-27)

*28 And the Raḇshaqēh stood and called out with a loud voice in the language of Yehuḏah, and spoke and said, "Hear the word of the great sovereign, the sovereign of Ashshur!" 29 Thus said the sovereign, "Do not let Ḥizqiyahu deceive you, for he is unable to deliver you out of his hand, 30 and do not let Ḥizqiyahu make you trust in* יהוה*, saying, '*יהוה* shall certainly deliver us, and this city is not given into the hand of the sovereign of Ashshur.' 31 Do not listen to Ḥizqiyahu," for thus said the sovereign of Ashshur, "Make peace with me by a present and come out to me, and let each of you eat from his own vine and each from his own fig tree, and each of you drink the waters of his own cistern, 32 until I come. Then I shall take you away to a land like your own land, a land of grain and new wine, a land of bread and vineyards, a land of olive trees and honey, and live, and not die. But do not listen to Ḥizqiyahu, when he misleads you, saying, '*יהוה* shall deliver us.' 33 Have any of the mighty ones of the nations at all delivered its land from the hand of the sovereign of Ashshur?"* (II Kings 18:29-33)

*34 "Where are the mighty ones of Ḥamath and Arpaḏ? Where are the mighty ones of Sepharwayim and Hēna and Iwwah? Did they deliver Shomeron from my hand? 35 Who among all the mighty ones of the lands have delivered their* land out of my hand, that יהוה should deliver Yerushalayim from my hand?" 36 But the people were silent and did not answer him a word, for the command of the sovereign was, "Do not answer him." 37 And Elyaqim son of Ḥilqiyah, who was over the household, and Sheḇnah the scribe, and Yo'aḥ son of Asaph, the recorder, came to Ḥizqiyahu with their garments torn, and they reported to him the words of the Raḇshaqĕh. (II Kings 18:34-37)

1 And it came to be, when Sovereign Ḥizqiyahu heard it, that he tore his garments, and covered himself with sackcloth, and went into the House of יהוה, 2 and sent Elyaqim, who was over the household, and Sheḇnah the scribe, and the elders of the priests, covering themselves with sackcloth, to Yeshayahu the prophet, son of Amots. 3 And they said to him, "Thus said Ḥizqiyahu, 'This day is a day of distress and rebuke and scorn, for the children have come to birth but there is no power to bring forth. 4 It could be that יהוה your Elohim does hear all the words of the Raḇshaqĕh, whom his master the sovereign of Ashshur has sent to reproach the living Elohim, and shall rebuke the words which יהוה your Elohim has heard. Therefore lift up your prayer for the remnant that is left.'" (II Kings 19:1-4)

5 And the servants of Sovereign Ḥizqiyahu came to Yeshayahu, 6 and Yeshayahu said to them, say this to your master, "Thus said יהוה, 'Do not be afraid of the words which you have heard, with which the servants of the sovereign of Ashshur have reviled Me. 7 See, I am putting a spirit upon him, and he shall hear a report and return to his own land. And I shall cause him to fall by the sword in his land.'" 8 And the Raḇshaqĕh returned and found the sovereign of Ashshur fighting against Liḇnah, for he had heard that he had left Lakish. 9 And when the sovereign heard concerning Tirhaqah sovereign of Kush, "See, he has come out to fight against you," he again sent messengers to Ḥizqiyahu, saying, 10 "Speak to Ḥizqiyahu sovereign of Yehuḏah, saying, 'Do not let your Elohim in whom you trust deceive you, saying

*Yerushalayim is not given into the hand of the sovereign of Ashshur.'"* (II Kings 19:5-10)

*11 "See, you have heard what the sovereigns of Ashshur have done to all lands by putting them under the ban. And are you going to be delivered? 12 Have the mighty ones of the nations delivered those whom my fathers have destroyed: Gozan and Ḥaran (of Mesopotamia) and Retseph, and the sons of Ĕḏen who were in Telassar? 13 Where is the sovereign of Ḥamath, and the sovereign of Arpaḏ, and the sovereign of the city of Sepharwayim, Hĕna, and Iwwah?" 14 And Ḥizqiyahu received the letters from the hand of the messengers, and read them, and went up to the House of יהוה. And Ḥizqiyahu spread it before יהוה. 15 And Ḥizqiyahu prayed before יהוה, and said, "O יהוה Elohim of Yisra'ĕl, the One who dwells between the keruḇim, You are Elohim, You alone, of all the reigns of the earth. You have made the heavens and earth. 16 Incline Your ear, O יהוה, and hear. Open Your eyes, O יהוה, and see. And hear the words of Sanḥĕriḇ, which he has sent to reproach the living Elohim. 17 Truly, יהוה, the sovereigns of Ashshur have laid waste the nations and their lands, 18 and have put their mighty ones into the fire, for they were not mighty ones, but the work of men's hands, wood and stone, and destroyed them. 19 And now, O יהוה our Elohim, I pray, save us from his hand, so that all the reigns of the earth know that You are יהוה Elohim, You alone."* (II Kings 19:11-19)

*21 Then Yeshayahu, son of Amots, sent to Ḥizqiyahu, saying, Thus said יהוה Elohim of Yisra'ĕl, "Because you have prayed to Me against Sanḥĕriḇ sovereign of Ashshur, 22 this is the word which יהוה has spoken concerning him, 'The maiden, the daughter of Tsiyon, has despised you, mocked you; the daughter of Yerushalayim has shaken her head behind you! 23 Whom have you reproached and reviled? And against whom have you raised your voice, and lifted up your eyes in pride? Against the Set-Apart One of Yisra'ĕl!' 24 By the hand of your servants you have reproached יהוה, and said, 'With my many chariots I have come up to the height of the* mountains, to the limits of Leḇanon. And I cut down its tall cedars and its choice cypress trees. And I enter its farthest height, its thickest forest. 25 I have dug and drunk water, and with the soles of my feet I have dried up all the streams of defense.' 26 Have you not heard long ago how I made it, from days of old, that I formed it? Now I have brought it about, that you should be for crushing walled cities into heaps of ruins." (Isaiah 37:21-26)

27 "And their inhabitants were powerless, they were overthrown and put to shame. They were as the grass of the field and as the green plant, as the grass on the house-tops and as grain blighted before it is grown. 28 But I know your sitting down, and your going out and your coming in, and your rage against Me. 29 Because your rage against Me and your pride have come up to My ears, I shall put My hook in your nose and My bridle in your lips, and I shall turn you back by the way which you came. **30 And this shall be the sign for you: This year you eat such as grows of itself, and the second year what springs from that, and in the third year sow and reap, plant vineyards, and eat the fruit of them.** 31 And the remnant who have escaped of the house of Yehuḏah shall again take root downward, and bear fruit upward." (Isaiah 37:27-31)

32 "For out of Yerushalayim comes forth a remnant, and those who escape from Mount Tsiyon—the ardor of יהוה of hosts does this. 33 Therefore thus said יהוה concerning the sovereign of Ashshur, 'He does not come into this city, nor does he shoot an arrow there, nor does he come before it with shield, nor does he build a siege mound against it. 34 By the way that he came, by the same he turns back. And into this city he does not come,' declares יהוה. 35 'And I shall defend this city, to save it for My own sake and for the sake of My servant Dawiḏ.'" 36 And a messenger of יהוה went out, and killed in the camp of Ashshur one hundred and eighty-five thousand. And they arose early in the morning, and saw all of them, dead bodies. 37 And Sanḥĕriḇ the sovereign of

*Ashshur broke camp and went away, and turned back, and remained at Nineweh.* (Isaiah 37:27-37)

What Isaiah has just said is also repeated and confirmed in II Kings 19:29.

**29 And this is the sign for you: This year you eat what grows of itself, and in the second year what springs from that, and in the third year sow and reap and plant vineyards and eat their fruit. (II Kings 19:29)**

*1 In those days Ḥizqiyahu was sick unto death. And Yeshayahu the prophet, son of Amots went to him and said to him, "Thus said יהוה, 'Set your house in order, for you are going to die, and not live.'" 2 And he turned his face toward the wall, and prayed to יהוה, saying, 3 "I pray to You, O יהוה, remember how I have walked before You in truth and with a perfect heart, and have done what was good in Your eyes." And Ḥizqiyahu wept bitterly. 4 And it came to be, before Yeshayahu had gone out into the middle court, that the word of יהוה came to him, saying, 5 "Return and say to Ḥizqiyah the leader of My people, 'Thus said יהוה, the Elohim of Dawiḏ your father, I have heard your prayer, I have seen your tears. See, I am going to heal you. On the third day go up to the House of יהוה. 6 And I shall add to your days fifteen years, and deliver you and this city from the hand of the sovereign of Ashshur, and shall defend this city for My own sake, and for the sake of Dawiḏ My servant.'"* (II Kings 20:1-6)

*7 And Yeshayahu said, "Take a cake of figs." And they took and laid it on the boil, and he recovered. 8 And Ḥizqiyahu said to Yeshayahu, "What is the sign that יהוה does heal me, and that I shall go up to the House of יהוה the third day?" 9 And Yeshayahu said, "This is the sign for you from יהוה, that יהוה does the word which He has spoken: shall the shadow go forward ten degrees or go backward ten degrees?" 10 And Ḥizqiyahu said, "It would be easy for the shadow to go down ten degrees; no, but let the shadow go backward ten degrees." 11 And Yeshayahu the prophet cried out to יהוה, and He brought the shadow ten degrees backward, by which it had gone down on the sundial of Aḥaz.* (II Kings 20:7-11)

This is the full account of the events surrounding King Hezekiah and the attack on Judah by the Assyrians.

The most important passage of Scripture in this section is found in II Kings 19:29. I encourage you to look at this verse point by point with me to get a much closer look at its meaning.

And this is the sign for you:

- *This* year you eat what grows of itself…
- And in the *second year* what springs from that…
- And in the *third year* sow and reap and plant vineyards and eat their fruit.

We are given a very large clue in the first line. "This is the sign for you."

For now, just know that Yehovah's sign is His Sabbaths and He is intimating here to King Hezekiah that His sign to him has something to do with the Sabbaths. Keep in mind that I have already discussed the sign or mark of Yehovah, which are His weekly and annual Sabbaths and Holy Days. The Sabbatical Years are *also* part of those signs that identify those who keep them as His. I also shared with you what Satan's sign or mark is. It is *any other* days or holi-days that are *not* listed in the Bible in Leviticus 23.

Yehovah is telling King Hezekiah that this sign has something to do with these Holy Appointments that we have learned about in Leviticus 23 and 25.

"This year you eat what grows of itself" is telling us that *no one* has planted or harvested in this first year.

"... and in the second year, what springs from that" is showing us that for two years in a row we do *not* plant or harvest crops. To most people this is very peculiar unless—well, unless you are familiar with the Sabbatical Cycles of Yehovah.

"... and in the third year, sow and reap and plant vineyards and eat their fruit." With this closing line in Yehovah's promise to King Hezekiah we see they can now plant, sow and harvest crops.

What you have just read is Yehovah's injunction that for two years His people were commanded not to plant or harvest. There are *only two years* in a Sabbatical Cycle when you *cannot* plant or harvest and that is the forty-ninth and fiftieth years of the Jubilee Cycle.

But as to the II Kings 19:29 opener, "And this is the sign for you," this is speaking about the Sabbatical and Jubilee Years, which are part of the Sabbaths and Holy Days that go into keeping the Fourth Commandment—a sign that we are His.

But as to how this scripture pertains to any kind of timeline or chronology, I will now explain:

"This year you eat what grows of itself."

The year Sennacherib attacked Jerusalem and Hezekiah, was, as I have shown you, one of the most documented and undisputable years in history. It was 701 B.C.

"... and in the second year what springs from that."

Knowing what year Sennacherib attacks then makes this second line the year 700 B.C.

"... and in the third year sow and reap and plant vineyards and eat their fruit."

So the logical conclusion is that this third year is 699 B.C.

As I have reiterated already, these are proven historical years which match up with other known chronological histories.

701 B.C. is a proven historical date that can be successfully corroborated with a proven Assyrian date. We can now tie the succession of Hebrew kings in with a *known* chronology. Even more importantly, we can also use this exact same date to know when a Sabbatical Year was, which was followed by another Sabbatical Year, which was, in fact, a Jubilee Year.

This information is truly *groundbreaking* and so pivotal, yet no one wants to look at it or acknowledge it. Very few seem to be operating under the conviction of just *how paramount* the Sabbatical and Jubilee Years are with regard to biblical history and prophecy, yet their importance is not to be denied and they can be found throughout the Bible if you know how to look for them and where.

Just *how* important are the Sabbatical and Jubilee Years to Yehovah? Do they even matter? Did anyone even keep them? We do not read of them in the Bible, do we? But *if* we do, *why* do they matter?

The passages below (and the answers contained therein) are central to gaining an understanding of and insight into the pointed questions I have just asked.

> *19 And they burned the House of Elohim, and broke down the wall of Yerushalayim, and burned all its palaces with fire, and destroyed all its valuable utensils. 20 And those who escaped from the sword he exiled to Babel, where they became servants to him and his sons until the reign of the reign of Persia, 21 in order to fill the word of יהוה by the mouth of Yirmeyahu, until the land had enjoyed her Sabbaths. As long as she lay waste she kept Sabbath, until seventy years were completed.* (II Chronicles 36:19-21)

> *11 "And all this land shall be a ruin and a waste, and these nations shall serve the sovereign of Babel seventy years. 12 And it shall be, when seventy years are completed, that I*

> *shall punish the sovereign of Babel and that nation, the land of the Chaldeans, for their crookedness," declares* יהוה, *"and shall make it everlasting ruins. 13 And I shall bring on that land all My words which I have pronounced against it, all that is written in this book, which Yirmeyahu has prophesied concerning all the nations."* (Jeremiah 25:11-13)

> *10 For thus said* יהוה, *"When seventy years are completed, at Babel I shall visit you and establish My good word toward you, to bring you back to this place. 11 For I know the plans I am planning for you," declares* יהוה, *"plans of peace and not of evil, to give you a future and an expectancy. 12 Then you shall call on Me, and shall come and pray to Me, and I shall listen to you. 13 And you shall seek Me, and shall find Me, when you search for Me with all your heart."*[1] [Footnote: [1]Deuteronomy 4:29, Joel 2:12 (Jeremiah 29:10-13)]

So again I ask you, *DO* the Sabbatical and Jubilee Years even matter? Jeremiah warned them they would be captives seventy years and 2 Chronicles explains why—for *not* keeping seventy Sabbatical Years *prior to* this outcome.

This captivity took place in 586 B.C. You must be mindful to factor in the Jubilee Years when you count the Sabbatical Years—the Seventy Sabbatical Years being no different. So Seventy Sabbatical Years from 586 B.C. takes you back far enough, at the very least, to the time when David became king in 1010 B.C.[374] If the Israelites kept some of the Sabbatical Years and not others, then we can speculate they never kept them from the time of Joshua, which was fifty-three Sabbatical Years *before* King David.

What we are seeing here is the fact that, if no one else kept track of the Sabbatical and Jubilee Years, Yehovah did. He kept track of precisely how many Sabbatical Years the Earth was owed. One might think it strange that the Earth would be "owed" anything. Yet, this is what Yehovah is impressing upon us in His Word, even though it keeps falling on deaf ears. Yet, the simple truth of the matter is this: each year

---

[374] http://www.aboutbibleprophecy.com/e8.htm

the Earth has to work while it grows your food on the Sabbath while you are resting. It misses fifty-two Shabbats a year as a result. Unlike us, it is not possible for the Earth to cease and desist from growing your food once a week to observe the weekly Sabbath rest.

When you multiply 52 weeks x 7 years you get 364 Sabbath Days that the Earth misses, or:

$$52 \times 7 = 364$$

The Sabbatical Year is when the Earth *finally* is allowed to rest from and make up for all the Sabbaths it had to work growing your food on the weekly Sabbath.

Do these years which are so vital to the Earth's ongoing, overall well-being matter to Yehovah? You bet your life they do. And if you wish to keep benefiting from the Earth being in a position to continue to yield its sustenance, then these years should matter to you too—every bit as much.

It is after Judah returned to the land of Israel that we begin to see the Jews getting on board with observing and keeping the Sabbatical Years—along with the other Holy Days and the weekly Sabbath—something they did *not* do *before* their captivity. They are now becoming zealous about obeying them. And it is only *after* this time that we are actually able to find references to the Sabbatical Years in biblical history.

The following are historically recorded Sabbatical Years, with the *last four* being artifacts that mention a Sabbatical Year.

After Judah went into captivity for seventy years, the Jews returned to the Land and were more zealous than ever to keep the Sabbatical Years, the weekly Sabbath and the Holy Days than before their captivity when they made little or no effort to keep them. So again, it is only *after* their captivity we find artifacts and records of Judah keeping the

Sabbatical Years. But you will notice also that after the Bar Koch-Bah Revolt we do not have any records.

| **Historically Recorded Sabbatical Years** ||
|---|---|
| 701 B.C. | Sennacherib Attacks Judah (II Kings 19:29) |
| 700 B.C. | A Jubilee Year (II Kings 19:29) |
| 456 B.C. | Nehemiah 8:18 |
| 162 B.C. | I Maccabees 16:14 & Josephus Antiquities |
| 134 B.C. | I Maccabees & Josephus Antiquities |
| 43 B.C. | Julius Caesar & Josephus Antiquities |
| 36 B.C. | Josephus Antiquities 14:16:2 |
| 22 B.C. | Josephus Antiquities 15:9:1 |
| 42 C.E. | Josephus Antiquities 18 |
| 56 C.E. | A Note of Indebtedness In Nero's Time. |
| 70 C.E. | The Sabbath Year of 70 C.E.-71 C.E. |
| 133 C.E. | Rental Contracts Before Bar Koch-Bah Revolt |
| 140 C.E. | Rental Contracts Before Bar Koch-Bah Revolt |

It was brought to our attention of two more recorded Sabbatical years in the fall of 2013. These two records are found on two tombstones located at the south end of the Dead Sea. They are currently located in the Jerusalem Museum.

The first is titled;

> Tombstone of Hannah
> Zoar, southern Dead Sea, 438 C.E.[375] sandstone and red pigment
> Gift of Max Ratner, Cleveland, to America Friends of the Israel Museum

---

[375] The reason they have 438 C.E. is because they are basing the year from Rosh Hashanah and not Aviv, which is the month Yehovah tells us to begin our year with in Exodus 12:2. Rosh Hashanah begins on the 1st day of the seventh month and Aviv begins in the month of Passover, a difference of six months. *This month shall be to you the beginning of months. It shall be the first month of the year to you.* (Exodus 12:2)

> "This is the tombstone of Hannah, daughter of Ha{niel} the preist, who died on the Sabbath, the first festival of Passover, the fifteenth day of the month of Nisan, in the year of the Sabbatical cycle, which is the year three hundred and sixty-nine years after the destruction of the Temple. May her soul rest. Peace."

When you add 369 years to the year the temple was destroyed you arrive at 439. And when you check with the Sabbatical and Jubilee chronology in the Prophecies of Abraham you will see that 439 C.E. was indeed the 5th year of that Sabbatical cycle.

The second tombstone read as follows;

> Tombstone of Hasadiah the Priest
> Zoar, southern Dead Sea, 514 C.E.[376] sandstone and red pigment
> Gift of Max Ratner, Cleveland, to America Friends of the Israel Museum
>
> "May the soul of Hasadiah the priest son of Dematin rest, who died on Thursday the fifth of Av, in the fourth year of the sabbatical cycle, which is the year four hundred and forty-five after the destruction of the temple. Peace on Israel. Peace.

Again when we add 445 to 70 we arrive at 515 C.E., which is indeed the 4th year of the Sabbatical cycle.

> *17 And the entire assembly of those who had come back from the captivity made booths and sat under the booths, for since the days of Yehoshua, son of Nun until that day, the children of Yisra'ĕl had not done so. And there was very great rejoicing. 18 And day by day, from the first day until the last day, he read from the Book of the Torah of Elohim. And they performed*

---

[376] The reason they have 514 C.E. is because they are basing the year from Rosh Hashanah and not Aviv, which is the month Yehovah tells us to begin our year with in Exodus 12:2. Rosh Hashanah begins on the 1st day of the seventh month and Aviv begins in the month of Passover, a difference of six months. *This month shall be to you the beginning of months. It shall be the first month of the year to you.* (Exodus 12:2)

> *the festival seven days. And on the eighth day there was an assembly, according to the right-ruling.* (Nehemiah 8:17-18)

From the days of Joshua until Nehemiah they had *not* kept the Feast of Booths. If they never kept Sukkot, then how would they know or remember to keep the Sabbatical and Jubilee Years?

> *10 And Mosheh commanded them, saying, "At the end of seven years, at the appointed time, the year of release, at the Festival of Booths, 11 when all Yisra'ĕl comes to appear before יהוה your Elohim in the place which He chooses, read this Torah before all Yisra'ĕl in their hearing. 12 Assemble the people, the men and the women and the little ones, and your sojourner who is within your gates, so that they hear, and so that they learn to fear יהוה your Elohim and guard to do all the Words of this Torah. 13 And their children, who have not known it, should hear and learn to fear יהוה your Elohim as long as you live in the land you are passing over the Yardĕn to possess."* (Deuteronomy 31:10-13)

Moses commanded the Israelites to read the Torah every seventh year during Sukkot. And this is also what Nehemiah was doing. This was the "Year of Release."

Qadesh La Yahweh Press in their book, *The Sabbath and Jubilee Cycle*[377] examines the theories stemming from the Zuckermann-Schurer school of thought and also, the Marcus-Wacholder interpretation method, as well as others in extreme detail. This book is 445 pages in length and is free to download and read from their website. I highly recommend this book. We will begin to look at some of the theories these men have put forward and show where they have erred in their understanding of the Sabbatical and Jubilee Years. (In *Remembering the Sabbatical Years of 2016*).

I have repeated one chapter from my previous book here for your benefit. It is well worth reading a number of times.

---

[377] http://www.yahweh.org/yahweh2.html

For the sake of brevity and to avoid repeating a number of other chapters from my previous publications where I have explained these things, I am going to be as succinct as possible and hope you will take the initiative and learn more about this amazing subject in those books.

Once you have established that 701 B.C. is the 49th Sabbatical Year and 700 B.C. is the 50th Year Jubilee, you can then go forward and backward and list *all* the Sabbatical and Jubilee Years throughout history. Keep in mind there are only going to be 5,880 years from the creation of Adam until the end of the sixth day. As I shared before, this is 120 x 49 = 5,880 years with 5881 being the 120th Jubilee Year. The year 5881 from the creation of Adam is the year 2045 C.E. on the Gregorian calendar.

In the chart three pages back I have listed all the known historically recorded Sabbatical Years. When you count from 701 B.C. by seven you will land on each of these known years—whereas, if you start from 700 B.C. and count by fifty onward, you will *not* match any of these recorded years, because 700 B.C. is *also* the first year of the *next* Jubilee Cycle. The fiftieth year and the first year are the same year.

Utilizing this information and that of Joshua entering the Promised Land in the 2,500th year from the creation of Adam, *which consequently, was a Jubilee Year*, one can then connect our modern chronology with the chronology put forth in Genesis. Again, this is explained in much greater detail in my previous books.

The year Joshua entered the Promised Land was the year 1337 B.C., a *Jubilee Year*.

The year of the Exodus was the year 1379 B.C. therefore, the beginning of this Jubilee Cycle in which the Exodus took place was the year 1386 B.C. The year 1386 B.C. just so happens to be the 50th Jubilee Cycle since the creation of Adam.

This will all come together and begin to make sense shortly, so please be patient and just dwell on the things I have shown you thus far. If you're questioning the math in general, or any of my calculations specifically, then know I have again, for brevity's sake, assumed you would look these things up in my previous books where they are proven in detail.

# Chapter 7 | The Apple of His Eye (Daniel 9:24)

> 24 *"Seventy weeks are decreed for your people and for your set-apart city, to put an end to the transgression, and to seal up sins, and to cover crookedness, and to bring in everlasting righteousness, and to seal up vision and prophet, and to anoint the Most Set-apart. 25 Know, then, and understand: from the going forth of the command to restore and build Yerushalayim until Messiah the Prince is seven weeks and sixty-two weeks. It shall be built again, with streets and a trench, but in times of affliction. 26 And after the sixty-two weeks Messiah shall be cut off and have naught. And the people of a coming prince shall destroy the city and the set-apart place. And the end of it is with a flood. And wastes are decreed, and fighting until the end. 27 And he shall confirm a covenant with many for one week. And in the middle of the week he shall put an end to slaughtering and meal offering. And on the wing of abominations he shall lay waste, even until the complete end and that which is decreed is poured out on the one who lays waste[1]."* [Footnote: [1]Matthew 24:15 (Daniel 9:24-27)]

We have learned in the first three chapters that Israel today consists of the USA, Britain, Scotland, Ireland, Wales, Canada, Australia, New Zealand, South Africa, Holland, Denmark, Switzerland, Sweden, parts of France, Norway and Finland. In chapter 4 we learned where the misinterpretation of this passage of Daniel first took place and how it was compounded with each new drama. In chapter 5 we learned that this "weeks" (Shavuot plural for week or Shabua) being spoken of is *The Feast of Weeks*. Secondly that this "weeks" is also known as *The Feast of Oaths* and by this, is constantly referring us back to the covenant we made at Mount Sinai. The third key to understanding this prophecy is that *"seventy weeks"* is seventy Shavuot and means 70 X 49, which totals 3430 Years. In chapter 6 we covered briefly how many Jubilee cycles there are by understanding Genesis 6:3, which tells us there are only 120 for the 6 days of man. And finally we learned by doing the chronology of Genesis that the Exodus took place during the 50th Jubilee Cycle.

In keeping with all I have covered so far let us once again go back and reread what is written in the beginning of the above passage in Daniel.

> 24 *"Seventy weeks are decreed for your people and for your set-apart city, to put an end to the transgression, and to seal up sins, and to cover crookedness, and to bring in everlasting righteousness, and to seal up vision and prophet, and to anoint the Most Set-apart."* (Daniel 9:24)

*"Seventy Weeks,"* as we have seen, is Seventy Shabua and is 70 x 49 which is 3,430 years. Those 3,430 years are also 70 Jubilee Cycles.

*"Are Decreed."*

H2852: châthak *khaw-thak'*

A primitive root; properly to *cut* off, that is, (figuratively) to *decree:* determine.

Now this is extremely interesting. Seventy Jubilee Cycles are decreed—seventy Jubilee Cycles until Israel is cut off. Seventy Jubilee Cycles until the USA, until the UK, until Canada, and until Australia are all cut off. I will elaborate on this more as we delve into the next round of Bible verses.

*"For Your People"*

I went through three long chapters for you in order to prove *exactly* who Daniel's people are. They are not only the Jewish people, who today comprise the State of Israel, but they are also the Northern Ten Tribes that went into exile or captivity. They are the USA, UK, Canada, Australia, New Zealand, Scotland, Ireland, Wales, South Africa, Holland, Denmark, Belgium, Sweden, Switzerland, Norway, Finland, and parts of France.

*"And For Your Set-Apart City."*

You all know what city this is but, in the context of this book, it is important that we prove it. Clearly, there is only one city on Earth that fits the following description:

> 5 *"From the day that I brought My people out of the land of Mitsrayim, I have chosen no city from any tribe of Yisra'ĕl in which to build a house for My Name to be there, nor did I choose any man to be a leader over My people Yisra'ĕl. 6 But I have chosen Yerushalayim, for My Name to be there. And I have chosen Dawid to be over My people Yisra'ĕl."* (2 Chronicles 6:5-6)

> 7 *"And he placed a carved image of the idol which he had made, in the House of Elohim, of which Elohim had said to Dawid and to Shelomoh his son, "In this house and in Yerushalayim, which I have chosen out of all the tribes of Yisra'ĕl, I put My Name forever, 8 and no more shall I remove the foot of Yisra'ĕl from the soil which I have appointed for your fathers—only if they guard to do all that I have commanded them, according to all the Torah and the laws and the right-rulings by the hand of Mosheh."* (2 Chronicles 33:7-8)

Yehovah has set apart Jerusalem from every other city in the world. He has placed His name there. When Yehshua came to Jerusalem He had something to say to her as well.

> *37 "Yerushalayim, Yerushalayim, killing the prophets and stoning those who are sent to her! How often I wished to gather your children together, the way a hen gathers her chickens under her wings, but you would not!"* (Matthew 23:37; Luke 13:34)

All of us have been asked to pray for Jerusalem. No other city has had the distinction of having Yehovah claim it as His own, in which His name shall be forever.

> *6 Pray for the peace of Yerushalayim, let those who love You be at rest.* (Psalm 122:6)

Returning to the Daniel 9 Prophecy, we can now read the remainder of this verse.

> *24 "...to put an end to the transgression, and to seal up sins, and to cover crookedness, and to bring in everlasting righteousness, and to seal up vision and prophet, and to anoint the Most Set-apart."* (Daniel 9:24)

It is *this* section of *this* prophecy, I have to ask those who are supporting the 490-Year Theory, a number of questions. That is, those who believe that at the 483 year mark of this 490-Year Theory proves that this is speaking of the Messiah when He arrived in Jerusalem for His 3½ year ministry beginning in 27 C.E.

My question is if this prophecy truly represents the arrival of Yehshua in 27 C.E., did Yehshua put an end to transgression, for once & for all?

The answer is obviously no. People are continuing to transgress (sin), as well as be transgressed (sinned against), and people everywhere are still transgressing the 10 Commandments, so this 490-Year Theory did not, by any stretch of the term, put an end to ALL transgression. But then there are those who currently maintain that from 2013-2017 are the last 3½ years and use this Gap Theory to justify themselves.

Which brings me to my next question: Are sins sealed up?

Again, all one need do is tune into the Nightly News and it practically goes without saying that sin is running rampant throughout the entire world.

> *4 Everyone doing sin also does lawlessness, and sin is lawlessness.* (1 John 3:4)

At this late date sin still rules and the world does not keep The Commandments nor has the world any intentions of keeping them. Therefore, this part of Daniel 9:24 could not possibly have been fulfilled by the ministry of Yehshua. It has to be something *else* that this prophecy is telling us.

> *"And To Cover Crookedness."*

To truly grasp what is being conveyed here and the true meaning behind it all, you must know about the Holy Days as told to us in Leviticus 23—the Day of Atonement in particular.

The word "cover" here is H3722: kâphar *kaw-far'*

> A primitive root; to *cover* (specifically with bitumen); figuratively to *expiate* or *condone*, to *placate* or *cancel:* Appease, make (an) atonement, cleanse, disannul, forgive, be merciful, pacify, pardon, to pitch, purge (away), put off, (make) reconcile (-liation).

You can see how "kaphar" sounds just like our English word "cover." The Day of Atonement is known as Yom Kippur—again having to do with the *covering of sins*. Most of those using this Daniel 9:24 Prophecy say it was to announce the arrival of Yehshua and His ministry and that He died on Passover to pay the price for mankind's sins.

Yes this is what Yehshua did; He did pay the debts we owed for breaking the "Blood Covenant." Instead of us paying for our trespasses He did in our place as the Redeemer. But this did not *cover* the sins. Our sins are not covered over until the ceremony of the Day of Atonement is acted out in real time and in real life. And this has to do with the laying on of hands on the Azazel Goat, which represents Satan and placing the guilt upon the one that is guilty. That being is Satan. This takes place on the Day of Atonement and is a future event still yet to come that is described in the Book of Revelation.

*"To Make Atonement For Iniquity."*

The above headline is what is said in the modern King James about this section of Daniel 9:24. The Day of Atonement is told to us even more in depth, however, in Leviticus 23.

> *26 And יהוה spoke to Mosheh, saying, 27 "On the tenth day of this seventh month is the Day of Atonement. It shall be a set-apart gathering for you. And you shall afflict your beings, and shall bring an offering made by fire to יהוה. 28 And you do no work on that same day, for it is the Day of Atonement, to make atonement for you before יהוה your Elohim. 29 For any being who is not afflicted on that same day, he shall be cut off from his people. 30 And any being who does any work on that same day, that being I shall destroy from the midst of his people. 31 You do no work—a law forever throughout your generations in all your dwellings. 32 It is a Sabbath of rest to you, and you shall afflict your beings. On the ninth day of the month at evening, from evening to evening, you observe your Sabbath."* (Leviticus 23:26-32)

We read in Leviticus 16 of the ceremony of the two goats and how the Azazel Goat was led off into the wilderness. Now compare that word picture to the passage in Revelation below.

> *1 And I saw a messenger coming down from the heaven, having the key to the pit of the deep and a great chain in his hand. 2 And he seized the dragon, the serpent of old, who is the Devil and Satan, and bound him for a thousand years, 3 and he threw him into the pit of the deep, and shut him up, and set a seal on him, so that he should lead the nations*

> *no more astray until the thousand years were ended. And after that he has to be released for a little while.* (Revelation 20:1-3)

The question I am raising here is this: Has Satan been taken away and locked up yet? The answer is "No!" and therefore, we have to conclude that the making of atonement for sin has not taken place yet either. This is yet a future event still yet to happen.[378]

*"And To Bring In Everlasting Righteousness."*

This everlasting righteousness is what many have claimed and continue to claim took place when Messiah arrived. Is that right?

> *142 Your righteousness is righteousness forever, and Your Torah is truth.* (Psalm 119:142)

Today many believe this part of this verse justifies the arrival of the Messiah. If that is indeed the case and they are right, then for the past 2,000 years where is the evidence of that righteousness? Where are a given nation's or a given people's righteous laws? It is not anywhere to be found. They are only in the Bible and are not part of the law of the land in every country on this Earth. This is speaking of the coming Kingdom during the 7$^{th}$ Millennium when He will rule on this Earth and there will be righteous Laws and ruler-ship then. But there is none of that in place now and it has not been for the past 2,000 years, as many would have us believe.

This part of the prophecy also points us to the time just in front of us when the 7$^{th}$ Millennium is to begin. The 7$^{th}$ Millennium clearly, has not yet started.

*"And To Seal Up Vision and Prophet."*

---

[378] To learn when this is take place according to the Sabbatical Cycles read *The Prophecies of Abraham*. http://bookstore.authorhouse.com/Products/SKU-000366309/The-Prophecies-of-Abraham.aspx

Have visions and prophets been sealed up? All a person need do is look to the Apostle Peter to find the answer.

> *16 But this is what was spoken by the prophet Yo'ĕl: 17 "And it shall be in the last days, says Elohim, that I shall pour out of My Spirit on all flesh. And your sons and your daughters shall prophesy, and your young men shall see visions, and your old men shall dream dreams, 18 and also on My male servants and on My female servants I shall pour out My Spirit in those days, and they shall prophesy."* (Acts 2:16-18)

This event was to take place in the Last Days. If this was to happen at a future time how could the arrival of the Messiah in 27 C.E. seal up all prophecy? It did not and therefore, we must conclude once again that this Daniel 9:24 prophecy did not pertain to the arrival of the Messiah in 27 C.E.

*"And To Anoint the Most Set-Apart."*

We know who the Most Set-apart is, or do we? Let's take a look at what your Bible says and not just assume. Many of you believe this is the anointing of Jesus but is this correct?

The word for anoint here is Mashiak and in this case those who have interpreted the Bible have done so correctly for this is speaking of the anointing of the holy.

H4886: Mâshach *Maw-shakh'*

A primitive root; to *rub* with oil, that is, to *anoint*; by implication to *consecrate*; also to *paint:* anoint, paint.

In the Hebrew, the words used are: Qodesh, Qodesh or Holy, Holy.

H6944: Qôdesh *Ko'-desh*

From H694: A *sacred* place or thing; rarely abstractly *sanctity:* consecrated (thing), dedicated (thing), hallowed (thing), holiness, (X most) holy (X day, portion, thing), saint, sanctuary.

When Daniel was shown this, the Ark from the Holy of Holies had been hidden away by Jeremiah in 586 B.C. before the Babylonian invasion. It was not there when Yehshua came to the Temple. Once again, I do not believe this part of this prophecy applies to Yehshua. I do believe it applies to the 144,000 in the Book of Revelation at the end of this 3,430 year time period. The reason I say this is because one of the translations of the word "Qodesh" is "saint."

We are to be a Holy Nation and we are to be Holy.

> *9 But you are a chosen race, a royal priesthood, a set-apart nation, a people for a possession, that you should proclaim the praises of Him who called you out of darkness into His marvellous light.* (1 Peter 2:9)

> *15 "...instead, as the One who called you is set-apart, so you also should become set-apart in all behaviour, 16 because it has been written, "Be set-apart, for I am set-apart."* (1 Peter 1:15-16)

We have been called and set apart to do a job for Yehovah.

> *5 "Before I formed you in the belly I knew you, and before you came out of the womb I did set you apart—I appointed you a prophet to nations."* (Jeremiah 1:5)

> *24 But I say to you, "You are going to possess their land, and I Myself give it to you to possess it, 'a land flowing with milk and honey.' I am יהוה your Elohim, who has separated you from the peoples."* (Leviticus 20:24)

> *1 I call upon you, therefore, brothers, through the compassion of Elohim, to present your bodies a living offering—set-apart, well-pleasing to Elohim—your reasonable worship. 2 And do not be conformed to this world, but be transformed*

*by the renewing of your mind, so that you prove what is that good and well-pleasing and perfect desire of Elohim.* (Romans 12:1-2)

*2 And as they were doing service to the Master and fasted, the Set-apart Spirit said, "Separate unto Me Barnabah and Sha'ul for the work to which I have called them."* (Acts 13:2)

*26 "And you shall be set-apart to Me, for I יהוה am set-apart, and have separated you from the peoples to be Mine."* (Leviticus 20:26)

*8 יהוה does perfect for me. O יהוה, Your kindness is everlasting. Do not forsake the works of Your hands.* (Psalm 138:8)

*13 The sons of Amram: Aharon and Mosheh. And Aharon was set apart, he and his sons forever, that he should set apart the most set-apart, to burn incense before יהוה, to serve Him, and to give the blessing in His Name forever.* (1 Chronicles 23:13)

It is the Holy Saints that are to be anointed, not the Messiah, but the saints. And if you are worthy to be counted as one of the 144,000, then it will be you and them at the end of this age, at the end of the 3,430 years, and at the end of the 70 x 49 who will be anointed with oil.

In conclusion, what I am arguing is that the verse in Daniel 9:24 clearly does not apply to the arrival of Yehshua in 27 C.E. In other words, what I am getting at is that this verse is a *general statement* by which to cover the entire timeframe in which these things will be accomplished; that time being, 3,430 years or 70 x 49 or 70 Shavuot. When this time actually began and when this time period is prophesied to end will be explained in more depth in the next chapter where I will have you take a closer look at verse 25.

# Chapter 8 | The Burning Bush, the Moat & the Akra (Daniel 9:25)

*24 "Seventy weeks are decreed for your people and for your set-apart city, to put an end to the transgression, and to seal up sins, and to cover crookedness, and to bring in everlasting righteousness, and to seal up vision and prophet, and to anoint the Most Set-apart. 25 Know, then, and understand: from the going forth of the command to restore and build Yerushalayim until Messiah the Prince is seven weeks and sixty-two weeks. It shall be built again, with streets and a trench, but in times of affliction. 26 And after the sixty-two weeks Messiah shall be cut off and have naught. And the people of a coming prince shall destroy the city and the set-apart place. And the end of it is with a flood. And wastes are decreed, and fighting until the end. 27 And he shall confirm a covenant with many for one week. And in the middle of the week he shall put an end to slaughtering and meal offering. And on the wing of abominations he shall lay waste, even until the complete end and that which is decreed is poured out on the one who lays waste[1]."* [Footnote: [1]Matthew 24:15 (Daniel 9:24-27)]

*25 "Know, then, and understand: from the going forth of the command to restore and build Yerushalayim until Messiah the Prince is seven weeks and sixty-two weeks. It shall be built again, with streets and a trench, but in times of affliction."* (Daniel 9:25)

Now that I've explained what verse 24 means in the seven chapters prior to this one, verse 25 contains some amazing truths waiting to be discovered once we come to know what the words actually mean. Keep in mind that many have tried to conform this translation into a construct that best fits their incomplete understanding of it—thus, predicting the Messiah 490 years later. And even after all this time, some are *still* changing the order of verse 25 to suit their own teachings today.

*"Know, then, and understand."*

This first expression is fairly basic.

H3045: *yaw-dah'*

A primitive root; to *know* (properly to ascertain by *seeing*); used in a great variety of senses, figuratively, literally, euphemistically and inferentially (including *observation, care, recognition*; and causatively *instruction, designation, punishment*, etc.): acknowledge, acquaintance (-ted with), advise, answer, appoint, assuredly, be aware, [un-] awares, can [-not], certainly, for a certainty, comprehend, consider, X could they, cunning, declare, be diligent, (can, cause to) discern, discover, endued with, familiar friend, famous, feel, can have, be [ig-] norant, instruct, kinsfolk, kinsman, (cause to, let, make) know, (come to give, have, take) knowledge, have [knowledge], (be, make, make to be, make self) known, + be learned, + lie by man, mark, perceive, privy to, X prognosticator, regard, have respect, skilful, shew, can (man of) skill, be sure, of a surety, teach, (can) tell, understand, have [understanding], X will be, wist, wit, wot.

The key part of this is "to *know* (properly to ascertain by *seeing*)." How do you do this? You do this the exact same way I have. By taking the time to actually do the work and lay out the Sabbatical and Jubilee

Year chronology from Adam up to our time.[379] These charts can be found in the back of my book, *The Prophecies of Abraham*. The calculations have been explained on my DVD, *The Chronological Order of the Prophecies In the Jubilees* and in my recent book, *Remembering the Sabbatical Years of 2016*[380].

Each and every one who has read these books, seen my DVD, and then followed it up by doing the actual work of figuring out the chronology, have all proven it true and in so doing, now KNOW, and they all KNOW because they have seen it with their own eyes. They no longer say this is Joe Dumond's calculations or Joe Dumond's "opinion"; but instead they say these are facts based on the Torah because they all have done the actual legwork themselves to prove it.

The part about "understand" is also interesting, yet basic.

H7919: *saw-kal'*

A primitive root; to *be* (causatively *make* or *act*) *circumspect* and hence *intelligent:* - consider, expert, instruct, prosper, (deal) prudent (-ly), (give) skill (-ful), have good success, teach, (have, make to) understand (-ing), wisdom, (be, behave self, consider, make) wise (-ly), guide wittingly.

Once you know this and can grasp it and understand it, then you are to act accordingly—carefully considering what all this means; being circumspect about the times we are now in.

*"From the going forth of the command."*

H4161: מצא מוצא môtsâ' môtsâ' mo-tsaw,' mo-tsaw'

From H3318; a going forth, that is, (the act) an egress, or (the place) an exit; hence a source or product; specifically dawn, the rising of the sun (the East), exportation, utterance, a gate,

---

[379] http://www.authorhouse.co.uk/Bookstore/BookDetail.aspx?Book=286642
[380] http://bookstore.xlibris.com/Products/SKU-0125561003/Remembering-The-Sabbatical-Years-of-2016.aspx

a fountain, a mine, a meadow (as producing grass): brought out, bud, that which came out, east, going forth, goings out, that which (thing that) is gone out, outgoing, proceeded out, spring, vein, [water-] course [springs].

Notice the words used here to describe this Hebrew word "Motsa."

"Exit at dawn," "exit at the rising of the sun," "East," "brought out," "that which came out, east," and "going forth."

None of the commentators on this verse mention this glaring fact. They say "from the going forth of the decree" is referring to the decree by King Artaxerxes. The commentators all ignore the fact that Ezra and Nehemiah never exited at dawn and never headed east. They instead headed west toward Jerusalem!

I am telling you this decree, this command, was never about Nehemiah or Ezra rebuilding Jerusalem or the Temple. As you are about to see it applies to one specific group at one very specific time.

We have a root word of the word *"Motsa"* to look at as well.

H3318: *yaw-tsaw'*

A primitive root; to *go* (causatively *bring*) *out*, in a great variety of applications, literally and figuratively, direct and proximate: X after, appear, X assuredly, bear out, X begotten, break out, bring forth (out, up), carry out, come (abroad, out, thereat, without), + be condemned, depart (-ing, -ure), draw forth, in the end, escape, exact, fail, fall (out), fetch forth (out), get away (forth, hence, out), (able to, cause to, let) go abroad (forth, on, out), going out, grow, have forth (out), issue out, lay (lie) out, lead out, pluck out, proceed, pull out, put away, be risen, X scarce, send with commandment, shoot forth, spread, spring out, stand out, X still, X surely, take forth (out), at any time, X to [and fro], utter.

Again, notice the meaning of this word in relation to "Motsa."

*"To go out," "break out," "come out," "escape," "get away," "pluck out."*

Before we put this piece in place, let's look at the next part of this same verse.

*"Of the Commandment."*

H1697: דבר **dâbâr daw-bawr'**

From H1696: a word; by implication a matter (as spoken of) of thing; adverbially a cause: act, advice, affair, answer, X any such (thing), + because of, book, business, care, case, cause, certain rate, + chronicles, commandment, X commune (-ication), + concern [-ing], + confer, counsel, + dearth, decree, deed, X disease, due, duty, effect, + eloquent, errand, [evil favoured-] ness, + glory, + harm, hurt, + iniquity, + judgment, language, + lying, manner, matter, message, [no] thing, oracle, X ought, X parts, + pertaining, + please, portion, + power, promise, provision, purpose, question, rate, reason, report, request, X (as hast) said, sake, saying, sentence, sign

We have a Commandment, a word "to escape," "to pluck out," "to come out and get away," "to leave at dawn," "to get out at sunrise," and "to go east."

This does not sound *anything* like a decree from King Artaxerxes. No, this is *much bigger* than that! Let's continue to learn the meaning of each word and see what we are being told here.

*"To restore."*

H7725: שוב **shûb shoob**

A primitive root; to turn back (hence, away) transitively or intransitively, literally or figuratively (not necessarily with the idea of return to the starting point); generally to retreat; often adverbially again: (break, build, circumcise, dig, do anything, do evil, feed, lay down, lie down, lodge, make, rejoice, send, take, weep) X again, (cause to) answer (+ again), X in any case (wise), X at all, averse, bring (again, back, home again), call [to mind], carry again (back), cease, X certainly, come again (back) X consider, + continually, convert, deliver (again), + deny, draw back, fetch home again, X fro, get [oneself] (back) again, X give (again), go again (back, home), [go] out, hinder, let, [see] more, X needs, be past, X pay, pervert, pull in again, put (again, up again), recall, recompense, recover, refresh, relieve, render (again), X repent, requite, rescue, restore, retrieve, (cause to, make to) return, reverse, reward, + say nay, send back, set again, slide back, still, X surely, take back (off), (cause to, make to) turn (again, self again, away, back, back again, backward, from, off), withdraw.

Do you see what is taking place here?

Know, then, and understand; "that which came out," "east," "going forth by the Word," "bring again," "back," "home again," "draw back," "fetch home again," "go again" (back, home).

*Who* is this talking about? *Who* is speaking and to *whom* are they speaking?

This Commandment is issuing forth from Yehovah to Moses, to go and get the Israelite captives and escape from Egypt heading *east* through the Red Sea.

> 9 *"And now, see, the cry of the children of Yisra'el has come to Me, and I have also seen the oppression with which the Mitsrites oppress them. 10 And now, come, I am sending you to Pharaoh, to bring My people, the children of Yisra'el, out of Mitsrayim."* (Exodus 3:10)
>
> 15 *And Elohim said further to Mosheh, "Thus you are to say to the children of Yisra'el,* 'יהוה' *Elohim of your fathers, the*

*Elohim of Abraham, the Elohim of Yitshaq, and the Elohim of Ya'aqob, has sent me to you. This is My Name forever, and this is My remembrance to all generations.' 16 Go, and you shall gather the elders of Yisra'el together, and say to them, 'יהוה Elohim of your fathers, the Elohim of Abraham, of Yitshaq, and of Ya'aqob, appeared to me, saying, I have indeed visited you and seen what is done to you in Mitsrayim; 17 and I say: I am bringing you up out of the affliction of Mitsrayim to the land of the Kena'anite and the Hittite and the Amorite and the Perizzite and the Hiwwite and the Yebusite, to a land flowing with milk and honey. 18 And they shall listen to your voice. And you shall come, you and the elders of Yisra'el, to the sovereign of Mitsrayim, and you shall say to him, ' יהוה Elohim of the Hebrews has met with us. And now, please, let us go three days' journey into the wilderness to slaughter to יהוה our Elohim.'"* (Exodus 3:15-18)

When you read the Exodus account carefully you will also understand that they fled Egypt in the morning after the first-born had been killed again fulfilling the meaning of the word *"motsa."*[381]

---

[381] http://truthsearch.org/ContentsLeaveEgyptatNight.html The word <brought #03318> in Deuteronomy 16:1 can have a figurative application – as explained earlier. The fact that the word supports a figurative usage does away with any absolute requirement to understand it literally. If one does a study of each time the bible uses the phrase "God brought you out of Egypt" – you will see the strength and power of <God> behind that thought. What did God do that night that made it possible for the Israelites to come out of Egypt? Of course, we all know the answer; He slew the firstborn of Egypt.

Consider, the verse does not say that *Israel went out of Egypt that night,* but that *God brought them out of Egypt by night.* Some have assumed that God literally brought the Israelites out of Egypt that night. There is a world of difference in these two statements.

One is literal; the other could be literal or it could be a figure of speech. The Hebrew Hiphil Perfect indicates a figure of speech, for the verb brought. The full thrust of the Hebrew is that God "caused them to be brought out" of Egypt by night. In other words, God's actions to bring Israel out of Egypt took place by night.

The language the bible uses for the departure of Israel suggests a morning departure.

There is a Hebrew word for <night>, and there is a Hebrew word for <morning>. There has to be a point when it is no longer night, and morning has begun. The morrow, as in Numbers 33:3 begins with daybreak. There was no reason for the Israelites to linger.

Pharaoh either came to Moses or sent an official with the message to "rise up and depart from among his people". Moses could not leave his house until daybreak, and Pharaoh had told him that he would kill him if he ever saw him again. Therefore, the implication is that Pharaoh came to Moses officially, if not literally, and was urgent for him to leave Egypt with all the Israelites. Moreover, the Egyptians followed Pharaoh' lead and urged the Israelites to leave the land in haste. They were not to leave Egypt until morning, but once daybreak arrived, they were free to go and there was no reason for them to hesitate. The whole tenor of the occasion implies a quick get-away at daybreak. The phrase "And he (Pharaoh) called for Moses" is more correctly translated, "And he called to Moses". The Septuagint has, "And Pharaoh called Moses and Aaron by night" leaving out the preposition altogether. The Hebrew does use an inseparable preposition hv,mol. (to Moses) and !roh]a;l.W (and to Aaron). The same Hebrew preposition l. stands for many different English prepositions – <for> is among them. However, <to> seems to be the best preposition for this context.

*Exodus 12:29 And it came to pass, that at midnight the LORD smote all the firstborn in the land of Egypt, from the firstborn of Pharaoh that sat on his throne unto the firstborn of the captive that [was] in the dungeon; and all the firstborn of cattle.*

*30 And Pharaoh rose up in the night, he, and all his servants, and all the Egyptians; and there was a great cry in Egypt; for [there was] not a house where [there was] not one dead.*

*31 And he called for (to) Moses and Aaron by night, and said, Rise up, [and] get you forth from among my people, both ye and the children of Israel; and go, serve the LORD, as ye have said.*

LXX:

*Exodus 12:31 And Pharao called Moses and Aaron by night, and said to them, Rise and depart from my people, both ye and the children of Israel. Go and serve the Lord your God, even as ye say.*

*Exodus 12:33 And the Egyptians were urgent upon the people, that they might send them out of the land in haste; for they said, We [be] all dead [men].*

*Deuteronomy 16:1 Observe the month of Abib, and keep the Passover unto the LORD thy God: for in the month of Abib the LORD thy God brought thee forth out of Egypt by night (03915).*

\*\*\*\*\*\*\*\*\*\*\*\*\*\*\*\*\*\*\*\*\*\*\*\*\*\*\*\*\*\*\*\*\*\*\*\*\*\*\*\*\*\*\*\*\*\*\*\*\*\*\*\*\*\*\*\*\*\*\*\*

*03915 layil {lah'-yil} or (Isa. 21:11) leyl {lale} also lay@lah {lah'- yel-aw} from the same as 03883; TWOT - 1111; n m*

*AV - night 205, nights 15, midnight + 02677 4, season 3,midnight + 02676 2, night + 01121 2, midnight 1, midnight + 08432 1; 233*

*1) night*

*1a) night (as opposed to day)*

The mountain Moses was to bring the Israelites to, was east of Egypt in Midian in Saudi Arabia. It is called Jabel al Lawz.[382]

> *12 And He said, "Because I am with you. And this is to you the sign that I have sent you: When you have brought the people out of Mitsrayim, you are to serve Elohim on this mountain."* (Exodus 3:12)

This is the Commandment from Yehovah to Moses to go and get the Israelites. This is the commencement of the prophecy of Daniel 9:24-27. It starts at *this time* in history.

When Israel left Egypt, they traveled east through the Red Sea by the Word of Yehovah on their way back home to the Land of Israel. The Land Yehovah had promised to give to Abraham, Isaac and Jacob, and this Land was *east* of Egypt.

Chances are, I am now going to upset many people and their dearly held perspectives. No doubt, I will be presenting crucial information that might be an affront to many people's "sacred cows." But this is the

---

*1b) of gloom, protective shadow (fig.)*
*************************************************************
Morning is the break of day, the <end> of night.
*Ex 12:22 And ye shall take a bunch of hyssop, and dip it in the blood that is in the bason, and strike the lintel and the two side posts with the blood that is in the bason; and none of you shall go out at the door of his house until the morning (1242).*
*************************************************************
*01242 boqer {bo'-ker} from 01239; TWOT - 274c; n m*
*AV - morning 191, morrow 7, day 3, days + 06153 1, early 3; 205*
*1) morning, break of day*
*1a) morning*
*1a1) of end of night*
*1a2) of coming of daylight*
*1a3) of coming of sunrise*
*1a4) of beginning of day*
*1a5) of bright joy after night of distress (fig.)*
*1b) morrow, next day, next morning*

[382] http://www.youtube.com/watch?v=18gvJwx8VyI & http://www.youtube.com/watch?v=-mB5Awl4e4M

stuff uncovering the truth and getting to the bottom of things is made of! That being said, let us look at the meaning of the words and search for the truth, the whole truth and nothing but the truth—no matter where it might take us.

*"Until Messiah."*

H4899: משיח mâshîyach maw-shee'-akh

From H4886: anointed; usually a consecrated person (as a king, priest, or saint); specifically the Messiah: anointed, Messiah.

H4886: משח mâshach maw-shakh'

A primitive root; to rub with oil, that is, to anoint; by implication to consecrate; also to paint: anoint, paint.

We are told that this word "Mashiyach" can be a king, a priest or a saint. But today's most prevalent and common understanding of this word is "Messiah." But *is this*, given the context of this passage in Daniel, the *right* understanding of this word? I am here to tell you it is *not* the Messiah! Let us now look at the next word much more closely to gain a deeper and far more complete understanding of the word "Mashiyach."

*"The Prince"*

H5057: נגיד נגד nâgîyd nâgid naw-gheed,' naw-gheed'

From H5046: A commander (as occupying the front), civil, military or religious; generally (abstract plural), honorable themes: captain, chief, excellent thing, (chief) governor, leader, noble, prince, (chief) ruler.

*None* of these words for the Prince refer to the Messiah. We just *assume* they do, and we all know what "ass-u-me" means. I am about to show you that this anointed saint and anointed king is none other than

King David. King David was anointed not once, not twice but *three times* for the position that he was chosen for and that was the office of king.

"Is seven weeks and sixty-two weeks."

The word "weeks" I have already discussed and gone over with you but will review it here once again.

> H7620: שבעה שבע שבוע **shâbûa'** shâbûa' shebû'âh shaw-boo'-ah, shaw-boo'-ah, sheb-oo-aw'
>
> Properly passive participle of H7650 as a denominative of H7651; literally sevened, that is, a week (specifically of years): seven, week.

The word *"week"* is *Shabua* but the expression is *"Seven weeks,"* seven Feast of Weeks, or Seven Shavuot. One Shavuot is 49 days. This can then be denoted as: 7 x 49 = 343 years.

This prophecy of Daniel begins with the word or the Commandment "to go" and "bring back" the Israelites, "drawing them back" by "leaving at dawn," or at "sunrise" and "heading east." Scripture is telling us that the time this Commandment was given to go get them, until the anointing of King David, would encompass a period of 343 years or seven weeks. That is, seven Feasts of Weeks or: 7 x 49.

In other words, you are being told that from the time when Yehovah told Moses to go and get the Israelites until the time when King David would be King over them, would be seven Jubilee Cycles.

I have demonstrated to you in great detail the chronology from the creation of Adam up to the Exodus—followed by the Israelites entering into the Promised Land led by Joshua. Moreover, I have reckoned that chronology based on the passage below in Genesis, which states that:

*3 And said, "My Spirit shall not strive with man forever in his going astray. He is flesh, and his days shall be one hundred and twenty years."* (Genesis 6:3)

These *120 years* is actually the term 120 *"shaneh."*

H8141: *shaw-ne,' shaw-naw'*

(The first form being in plural only, the second form being feminine); from H8138; a *year* (as a *revolution* of time): + whole age, X long, + old, year (X -ly).

120 periods of time is also 120 Jubilee Cycles. Having adequately explained this in my two previous books and my DVD, I am not going to do so here.

I will post portions of the charts below, however, so you can more easily see what I am getting at and understand what I am saying. The year of the Exodus was 1379 B.C. In order to bring all ten of the plagues to pass, Moses and Aaron had to work in Egypt for a *minimum* of three years prior to the Exodus, which brings us to the year 1382 B.C. The Jubilee Cycle in which the Exodus and the plagues took place began in 1386 B.C.

| | | | | | | | -1337 | 51 |
|---|---|---|---|---|---|---|---|---|
| Sabbath | 6th Cycle | 5th Cycle | 4th Cycle | 3rd Cycle | 2nd Cycle | 1st Cycle | | |
| -1338 | -1345 | -1352 | -1359 | -1366 | -1373 | -1380 | | |
| -1339 | -1346 | -1353 | -1360 | -1367 | -1374 | -1381 | | |
| -1340 | -1347 | -1354 | -1361 | -1368 | -1375 | -1382 | | |
| -1341 | -1348 | -1355 | -1362 | -1369 | -1376 | -1383 | | |
| -1342 | -1349 | -1356 | -1363 | -1370 | -1377 | -1384 | | |
| -1343 | -1350 | -1357 | -1364 | -1371 | -1378 | -1385 | | |
| -1344 | -1351 | -1358 | -1365 | -1372 | -1379 | -1386 | | |
| | | | | | | | -1386 | 50 |

The counting of Jubilee Cycles in the chart above is on right hand side. 1386 B.C. was the Jubilee Year. The total number of Jubilees since the creation of Adam is fifty Jubilee Cycles in all.

The chart below is the *exact same* chart as the one above, except that it is numbered from the creation of Adam. I am placing it here for you, so that you can compare the two and see the year Joshua entered the

Promised Land—which was also the 2,500th year *after* creation (A.C.) and this year is *also* 1337 B.C. Both 1337 B.C. and 2500 A.C. are the *same* year and *both* are the 51st Jubilee Year. This is part of the Third Millennial Day. The shaded area from 1377 B.C. up to 1338 B.C. are the forty years of wandering in the wilderness. 1379 B.C. is the year of the Exodus.

Again, you can see the full chart in my book, *The Prophecies of Abraham* and I highly recommend you obtain a copy of this book right away.

| 51 | | | | | | | 2500 |
|---|---|---|---|---|---|---|---|
| | Sabbath | 6th Cycle | 5th Cycle | 4th Cycle | 3rd Cycle | 2nd Cycle | 1st Cycle |
| | 2499 | 2492 | 2485 | 2478 | 2471 | 2464 | 2457 |
| | 2498 | 2491 | 2484 | 2477 | 2470 | 2463 | 2456 |
| | 2497 | 2490 | 2483 | 2476 | 2469 | 2462 | 2455 |
| | 2496 | 2489 | 2482 | 2475 | 2468 | 2461 | 2454 |
| | 2495 | 2488 | 2481 | 2474 | 2467 | 2460 | 2453 |
| | 2494 | 2487 | 2480 | 2473 | 2466 | 2459 | 2452 |
| | 2493 | 2486 | 2479 | 2472 | 2465 | 2458 | 2451 |
| 50 | | | | | | | 2451 |

Moses began his real work *at least* three years *prior to* the Exodus. This is based on the fact the cattle were all killed off three times during the curses that ensued before the Exodus[383] and also based on the fact that, like the Two Witnesses spoken of in Revelation, Moses and Aaron worked for 3-½ **years** *before* the actual Exodus. This will bring us to 1382 B.C. or 1383 B.C.

> *7 Now Mosheh was eighty years old and Aharon eighty-three years old when they spoke to Pharaoh.* (Exodus 7:7)

> *3 "...see, the hand of* יהוה *is on your livestock in the field, on the horses, on the donkeys, on the camels, on the cattle, and on the sheep—a very grievous pestilence. 4 And* יהוה *shall separate between the livestock of Yisra'el and the livestock of Mitsrayim, and let no matter die of all that belongs to the children of Yisra'el. 5 And* יהוה *set an appointed time, saying, 'Tomorrow* יהוה *is going to do this word in the land.' 6 And* יהוה *did this word on the next day, and all the livestock of*

---

[383] http://www.sightedmoonnl.com/?page_id=773 & http://sightedmoon.com/moses-120-years-and-deleavening-our-homes-and-our-minds/

> *Mitsrayim died, but of the livestock of the children of Yisra'el, not one died. 7 Then Pharaoh sent, and see, not even one of the livestock of the Yisra'elites was dead. But the heart of Pharaoh was hardened, and he did not let the people go."* (Exodus 9:3-7)

Notice that *all* the cattle died. But in the following curse, once again, the cattle are to be afflicted. You need time to bring in more cattle and to have them reproduce in the fields. So it is my opinion that *at least* one year had to have passed in order to obtain new cattle and have them grow in number again.

> *18 "See, tomorrow about this time I am causing very heavy hail to rain down, such as has not been in Mitsrayim, from the day of its founding until now. 19 And now send, bring your livestock to safety, and all that you have in the field, for the hail shall come down on every man and every beast which is found in the field and is not brought home, and they shall die." 20 Those among the servants of Pharaoh who feared the word of יהוה made their servants and livestock flee to the houses. 21 But those who did not set their heart on the word of יהוה left their servants and livestock in the field. 22 Then יהוה said to Mosheh, "Stretch out your hand toward the heavens, and let there be hail in all the land of Mitsrayim—on man, and on beast, and on every plant of the field, throughout the land of Mitsrayim." 23 Then Mosheh stretched out his rod toward the heavens. And יהוה sent thunder and hail, and fire came down to the earth. And יהוה rained hail on the land of Mitsrayim. 24 Thus there came to be hail, and fire flashing continually in the midst of the hail, very heavy, such as had not been in all the land of Mitsrayim since it became a nation. 25 And the hail smote in all the land of Mitsrayim all that was in the field, both man and beast. And the hail smote every plant of the field and broke every tree of the field.* (Exodus 9:18-25)

We then read once again of the cattle being killed and this time it was the firstborn of the cattle. So they had to replace a significant number of cattle and the cows had to have time to give birth to the firstborn in order for them to be killed on the night of Passover.

> *29 And it came to be at midnight that יהוה smote all the firstborn in the land of Mitsrayim, from the firstborn of Pharaoh who sat on his throne to the firstborn of the captive who was in the dungeon, and all the firstborn of livestock. 30 And Pharaoh rose up in the night, he and all his servants, and all the Mitsrites. And there was a great cry in Mitsrayim, for there was not a house where there was not a dead one.* (Exodus 12:29-30)

It is based on these Scriptures then that I am forced to conclude Moses and Aaron must have been working amongst the Egyptians for more than one year, at the very least, and maybe for as long as three years!

Returning to the prophecy in Daniel:

> *25 "Know, then, and understand: from the going forth of the command to restore and build Yerushalayim until Messiah the Prince is seven weeks and sixty-two weeks. It shall be built again, with streets and a trench, but in times of affliction."* (Daniel 9:25)

From the Commandment of Yehovah given to Moses out of the burning bush until the coming of the Anointed Prince is: 7 x 49 = 343 years. And yes, I am stating that Moses was given this Commandment to go and deliver the Israelites *at* the burning bush.

> *9 "And now, see, the cry of the children of Yisra'el has come to Me, and I have also seen the oppression with which the Mitsrites oppress them. 10 And now, come, I am sending you to Pharaoh, to bring My people, the children of Yisra'el, out of Mitsrayim."* (Exodus 3:9-10)

The year Moses heard Yehovah speak to him from the burning bush was roughly around or during the year 1383 B.C. Then, if we add 343 years to the equation, we arrive at the year 1040 B.C. This is the first part of the prophecy of Daniel that most skip over not knowing exactly what to do with it. And some today have even turned it around and tack it on at the end. But it reads the seven weeks, or the seven Shavuot—the 7 x 49 being the first part of the prophecy, spanning a 343 year period of time from when Yehovah spoke to Moses from the burning bush.

What took place then in 1040 B.C. exactly?

We know King David was king over Judah seven years and then over *all of* Israel an additional thirty-three years, bringing his reign to a total of forty years. We also know King Solomon reigned forty years and died in 931 B.C.[384] Forty years before this is 970 B.C. when King Solomon began his reign. King David also reigned forty years and if we count back from 971 B.C., we arrive at 1010 B.C.

> *4 Dawid was thirty years old when he began to reign, and he reigned forty years. 5 In Hebron he reigned over Yehudah seven years and six months, and in Yerushalayim he reigned thirty-three years over all Yisra'el and Yehudah.* (2 Samuel 5:4-5)

> *10 And Dawid slept with his fathers, and was buried in the City of Dawid. 11 And the days that Dawid reigned over Yisra'el (were) forty years. He reigned seven years in Hebron, and in Yerushalayim he reigned thirty-three years. 12 And Shelomoh sat on the throne of his father Dawid. And his reign was firmly established.* (1 Kings 2:10-12)

|  |  |  |  |  |  | -994 | 58 |
|---|---|---|---|---|---|---|---|
| Sabbath | 6th Cycle | 5th Cycle | 4th Cycle | 3rd Cycle | 2nd Cycle | 1st Cycle |  |
| -995 | -1002 | -1009 | -1016 | -1023 | -1030 | -1037 |  |
| -996 | -1003 | -1010 | -1017 | -1024 | -1031 | -1038 |  |
| -997 | -1004 | -1011 | -1018 | -1025 | -1032 | -1039 |  |
| -998 | -1005 | -1012 | -1019 | -1026 | -1033 | -1040 |  |
| -999 | -1006 | -1013 | -1020 | -1027 | -1034 | -1041 |  |
| -1000 | -1007 | -1014 | -1021 | -1028 | -1035 | -1042 |  |
| -1001 | -1008 | -1015 | -1022 | -1029 | -1036 | -1043 |  |
|  |  |  |  |  |  | -1043 | 57 |

---

[384] *The Mysterious Number of the Hebrew Kings* by Edwin R. Thiele, p. 217

If King David began to reign in the year 1010 B.C. and he was thirty years of age, then he was born in 1040 B.C.

> *20 I have found My servant Dawid; with My set-apart oil I anointed him.* (Psalm 89:20)

King David is the anointed Prince spoken of in Daniel 9:25 *"...until Messiah the Prince is seven weeks."* Again as we explained in chapter 4 it was not until the early church fathers, around 200 C.E., began to interpret this verse to mean *"the Messiah,"* that this word "anointed" took on a different meaning than what it actually said. It is not about the Messiah, but it is all about the coming King over Israel, and that king was King David.

As I have already shared with you, this saying is not Messiah the Prince, but the Anointed Prince or King and that person, who comes into the forefront 343 years *after* Yehovah spoke to Moses out of the burning bush, is King David who, as a shepherd boy, was anointed by Samuel.

> *1 And יהוה said to Shemu'el, "How long are you going to mourn for Sha'ul, seeing I have rejected him from reigning over Yisra'el? Fill your horn with oil, and go, I am sending you to Yishai the Beyth Lehemite. For I have seen among his sons a sovereign for Myself." 2 And Shemu'el said, "How would I go? When Sha'ul hears it, he shall kill me." And יהוה said, "Take a heifer with you, and say, 'I have come to slaughter to יהוה.' 3 And you shall invite Yishai to the slaughtering, then let Me show you what to do. And you shall anoint for Me the one I say to you." 4 And Shemu'el did what יהוה said, and went to Beyth Lehem. And the elders of the town trembled at his coming, and said, "Do you come in peace?" 5 And he said, "In peace. I have come to slaughter to יהוה. Set yourselves apart, and you shall come with me to the slaughtering." And he set Yishai and his sons apart, and invited them to the slaughtering.* (1 Samuel 16:1-5)

> *6 And it came to be, when they came, that he saw Eliyab and thought, "The anointed of* יהוה *is indeed before Him." 7 But* יהוה *said to Shemu'el, "Do not look at his appearance or at the height of his stature, because I have refused him, for not as man sees, for man looks at the eyes, but* יהוה *looks at the heart." 8 Then Yishai called Abinadab, and made him pass before Shemu'el. And he said, "Neither has* יהוה *chosen this one." 9 Next Yishai made Shammah pass by. And he said, "Neither has* יהוה *chosen this one." 10 And Yishai made seven of his sons pass before Shemu'el. And Shemu'el said to Yishai, "*יהוה *has not chosen these." 11 And Shemu'el said to Yishai, "Are these all the young men?" And he said, "There remains yet the youngest, and see, he is tending the sheep." And Shemu'el said to Yishai, "Send and bring him, for we do not turn round (until) he comes here." 12 And he sent and brought him in. And he was ruddy, with bright eyes, and good-looking. And* יהוה *said, "Arise, anoint him, for this is the one!" 13 And Shemu'el took the horn of oil and anointed him in the midst of his brothers. And the Spirit of* יהוה *came upon Dawid from that day and onwards. And Shemu'el arose and went to Ramah.* (1 Samuel 16:6-13)

Most of the shepherds in the Middle East are the *youngest* of the children *even today*. While I was in Eastern Turkey visiting Noah's Ark, the children shepherding the sheep in the mountains of Ararat were mostly under seven years of age. While I was there, we had a huge downpour and about thirty shepherds were swept away in the resulting floods. They were all about five years of age out in the field watching the sheep for the family.

Although there is no hard proof or concrete biblical text to support it, there exists every reason to believe David was a young boy when Samuel anointed him.

We next read of David being anointed once again when he became king over Judah in 1010 B.C.

> *1 And it came to be afterwards that Dawid inquired of יהוה, saying, "Do I go up to any of the cities of Yehudah?" And יהוה said to him, "Go up." And Dawid said, "Where should I go up?" And He said, "To Hebron." 2 And Dawid went up there, as well as his two wives, Ahino'am the Yizre'elitess, and Abigayil the widow of Nabal, the Karmelite. 3 And Dawid brought up the men who were with him, each man with his household, and they dwelt in the cities of Hebron. 4 And the men of Yehudah came, and anointed Dawid sovereign over the house of Yehudah there. They also reported to Dawid, saying, "The men of Yabesh Gil'ad are they who buried Sha'ul."* (2 Samuel 2:1-4)

This resulted in a war with the other 10 Tribes of Israel who *only* came to make David the king over both houses once Ishbosheth the son of Saul was dead, which was seven years *after* David was first anointed king over Judah.

> *3 And all the elders of Yisra'el came to the sovereign at Hebron, and Sovereign Dawid made a covenant with them at Hebron before יהוה. And they anointed Dawid sovereign over Yisra'el.* (2 Samuel 5:3)

We have now read of all three anointings that happened to King David. The first time when he was a child tending the sheep by Samuel. Next, when he began to reign over Judah and the third time when he began to reign over Judah *and* Israel in 1017 B.C.

> *25 "Know, then, and understand: from the going forth of the command to restore and build Yerushalayim until Messiah the Prince is seven weeks and sixty-two weeks. It shall be built again, with streets and a trench, but in times of affliction."* (Daniel 9:25)

This Command originated from Yehovah and was given to Moses. This time period begins in the 50th Jubilee Cycle, which began in 1386 B.C. David is then born, 343 years later, and anointed three times to be king—all of which took place during the 57th Jubilee Cycle. That is seven Shavuot or *seven weeks* later.

From the time of the Exodus, they were to go and capture the Land of Israel. But they never did actually capture it all. Moreover, the restoring and rebuilding of Jerusalem had not yet taken place.

The word "restore" is:

H7725: *shoob*

> A primitive root; to *turn* back (hence, away) transitively or intransitively, literally or figuratively (not necessarily with the idea of *return* to the starting point); generally to *retreat*; often adverbially *again:* (break, build, circumcise, dig, do anything, do evil, feed, lay down, lie down, lodge, make, rejoice, send, take, weep) X again, (cause to) answer (+ again), X in any case (wise), X at all, averse, bring (again, back, home again), call [to mind], carry again (back), cease, X certainly, come again (back) X consider, + continually, convert, deliver (again), + deny, draw back, fetch home again, X fro, get [oneself] (back) again, X give (again), go again (back, home), [go] out, hinder, let, [see] more, X needs, be past, X pay, pervert, pull in again, put (again, up again), recall, recompense, recover, refresh, relieve, render (again), X repent, requite, rescue, restore, retrieve, (cause to, make to) return, reverse, reward, + say nay, send back, set again, slide back, still, X surely, take back (off), (cause to, make to) turn (again, self again, away, back, back again, backward, from, off), withdraw.

> Once again here are the key words to be taken from this word *"shoob"* draw back, fetch home again, get [oneself] (back) again, go again (back, home), recover, refresh, relieve, rescue, restore, retrieve, (cause to, make to) return, take back.

In order for Jerusalem to be *returned* to Israel or *go back home again* to it or *recover* it and *restore* it implies that it *at one time* belonged to them. When was that?

> The word build is:
>
> H1129: *baw-naw'*
>
> A primitive root; to *build* (literally and figuratively): (begin to) build (-er), obtain children, make, repair, set (up), X surely.

They were to go back home to Jerusalem to restore it, retrieve it, build it back up again and repair it. But since the Exodus, they had not captured Jerusalem, which was being held by the Jebusites. And Abraham, Isaac and Jacob never even lived in Jerusalem!

When did it belong to Israel then?

We read about "Jeru Salem" the city of Salem, for the first time, *after* Abraham had defeated the Kings of the North, when Melchizedek, the King of Salem, came out to greet Abraham.

Melchizedek was the son of Noah and called Shem. We read in Genesis 11 about Shem:

> *10 This is the genealogy of Shem: Shem was a hundred years old and brought forth Arpakshad, two years after the flood. 11 And after he brought forth Arpakshad, Shem lived five-hundred years, and brought forth sons and daughters.* (Genesis 11:10-11)

The Flood of Noah took place in 2181 B.C. and by the time Shem died in 1679 B.C., all of his descendants had already died from Arphaxad down to Abraham. Shem had outlived them all. That comes to nine generations in all that he outlived. It is *no wonder then* no one knew who his parents were! How many of you can honestly say you know the names of your grandparents dating back nine generations ago or those who lived 500 years ago?

> *1 For this Malkitsedeq, sovereign of Shalem, priest of the Most High Elohim, who met Abraham returning from the slaughter of the sovereigns and blessed him, 2 to whom also Abraham gave a tenth part of all, his name being translated, indeed, first, 'sovereign of righteousness,' and then also sovereign of Shalem, that is,'sovereign of peace,' 3 without father, without mother, without genealogy, having neither beginning of days nor end of life, but having been made like the Son of Elohim, remains a priest for all time.* (Hebrews 7:1-3)

Even Isaac and Jacob would have known of Shem as they were born when Shem was still King of Jeru Salem.

It was eighty years after the death of Shem in 1679 B.C. that the children of Jacob went down to Egypt and then sojourned there from 1599 B.C., the second year of the famine, until the Exodus in 1379 B.C.—making for a total of 220 years. Isaac, having died in 1609 B.C., or two years *before* the seven years of plenty began.

This is how long Jerusalem was without a righteous king—from the time of Shem's death until the time King David recaptured the city and made it his fortress.

Shem in Hebrew means "The Name."

> H8035: shem *shame*

> The same as H8034; *name*; *Shem*, a son of Noah (often including his posterity): Sem, Shem.

> H8034: shem *shame*

> A primitive word (perhaps rather from H7760 through the idea of definite and conspicuous *position*; compare H8064); an *appellation*, as a mark or memorial of individuality; by implication *honor*, *authority*, *character:* + base, [in-] fame [-ous], name (-d), renown, report.

We are told that Jerusalem is the one city on the whole of planet Earth where Yehovah is going to place His name. Have you ever seriously considered what this means?

> *11 And it shall be, that unto the place which יהוה your Elohim chooses to make His Name dwell there, there you are to bring all that I command you: your burnt offerings, and your offerings, and your tithes, and the contributions of your hand, and all your choice offerings which you vow to יהוה. 12 "And you shall rejoice before יהוה your Elohim, you and your sons and your daughters, and your male servants and your female servants, and the Lewite who is within your gates, since he has no portion nor inheritance with you.* (Deuteronomy 12:11-12)

> *36 "And to his son I give one tribe, so that My servant Dawid shall always have a lamp before Me in Yerushalayim, the city which I have chosen for Myself, to put My Name there."* (1 Kings 11:36)

> *29 "For Your eyes to be open toward this House night and day, toward the place of which You said, 'My Name is there,' to listen to the prayer which Your servant makes toward this place."* (1 Kings 8:29)

> *4 And he built altars in the House of יהוה, of which יהוה had said, "In Yerushalayim I put My Name."* (2 Kings 21:4)

Today, Jews the world over will not pronounce the true or actual name of God, in accordance with the Tetragrammaton. It is my understanding, however, His name is spelled and pronounced Yehovah. The Jews instead will say Ha Shem, which again means, "The Name."

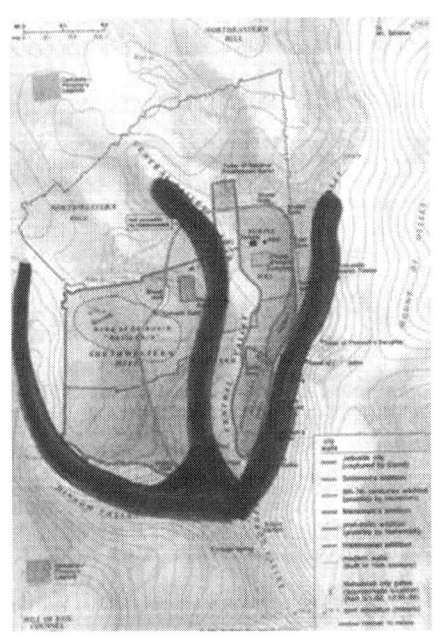

There is something else you should be aware of.

The letter "shin" is written as ש. It is the twenty-first letter of the Hebrew alphabet.

"Shin" also stands for the word "Shaddai," a name for God. Because of this, a kohen (priest) forms the letter shin with his hands as he recites the Priestly Blessing. The letter "shin" is often inscribed on the case containing a Mezuzah, a scroll of parchment with Biblical text written on it. The text contained in the Mezuzah is the *Shema Yisrael Prayer*, which calls the Israelites to love their God with all their heart, soul and strength.[385] The Mezuzah is situated upon all the doorframes in a home or establishment. Sometimes the word *Shaddai*, in all its entirety, will be written out.

The *Shema Yisrael Prayer* also commands the Israelites to write God's Commandments on their hearts (Deuteronomy 6:6). The shape of the letter "shin" mimics the structure of the human heart: the lower, larger left ventricle (which supplies the full body) and the smaller right ventricle (which supplies the lungs) are positioned like the lines of the letter "shin."

> A religious significance has been applied to the fact that there are three valleys (as pictured above)[386] which comprise the city of Jerusalem's geography: (1) the Valley of Ben Hinnom, (2) the Tyropoeon Valley, and (3) the Kidron Valley, and

---

[385] 4 Hear, O, Israel. Jehovah our God *is* one Jehovah. 5 And you shall love Jehovah your God with all your heart and with all your soul and with all your might. (Deuteronomy 6:4-5)

[386] http://promisedlandministries.files.wordpress.com/2010/03/anc-jerusalem-2-2.jpg

that these valleys converge to also form the shape of the letter shin. This is seen as a fulfillment of passages such as Deuteronomy 16:2 that instructs Jews to celebrate the Pasach at: *"the place the LORD will choose as a dwelling for his Name."* (NIV)[387]

Jerusalem sits upon the name of Yehovah. One of the hills in the City of David, which is Jerusalem, is called the Ophel. Ophel in Hebrew means: My Fortress, Tower and Stronghold—all of which are names of Yehovah.

> *2 יהוה is my rock and my stronghold and my deliverer; my El is my rock, I take refuge in Him; my shield and the horn of my deliverance, my high tower.* (Psalm 18:2)

> Zion means: the Mark, the Sign, the Waymark, the Pillar

> Moriah means: To see Yehovah, or to be seen of Yehovah. Today, Mount Moriah is called the Mount of Olives and the Mount of Offense.

We know this because when Abraham went to sacrifice Isaac, the city of Jerusalem was *already there* because that is where King Melchizedek lived; which means Abraham set out to sacrifice Isaac at the very same place Yehshua was sacrificed on the Mount of Olives across from the Temple in Jerusalem, the City of David—namely, the Mount of Offense.

The fact Yehovah actually has His name placed there in the form of the three valleys that form up around Jerusalem is highly significant and no coincidence—a detail that was clearly authored by Yehovah and did not escape Yehshua's notice in the least.

> *37 And as He was coming near, already at the descent of the Mount of Olives, the entire crowd of the taught ones began, to praise Elohim, rejoicing with a loud voice for all the miracles they had seen, 38 saying, "Blessed is the Sovereign who is*

---

[387] http://en.wikipedia.org/wiki/Shin_(letter)

*coming in the Name of יהוה! Peace in heaven and esteem in the highest!" 39 And some of the Pharisees from the crowd, said to Him, "Teacher, rebuke Your taught ones." 40 But He answering, said to them, "I say to you that if these shall be silent, the stones would cry out."* (Luke 19:37-40)

Yehshua knew the true meaning of this place.

From the time of Shem's death in 1679 B.C. until the time when David captured the city in 1017 B.C., 662 years had already passed and the city was overtaken by the Jebusites at some point during that time and Jerusalem was trampled down. The name Jebus comes from the Hebrew verb (bus) meaning "to trample down" and "polluted."

We now have another point to consider. Yehovah has placed His name upon the children of Israel in a similar fashion to how Shem meant "the name."

> *23 Speak to Aaron and to his sons saying, In this way you shall bless the sons of Israel, saying to them, 24 יהוה bless you and keep you. 25 יהוה make His face shine upon you and be gracious to you. 26 יהוה lift up His face to you and give you peace. 27 And they shall put My name upon the sons of Israel. And I, I will bless them.* (Numbers 6:23-27)

> *14 if My people, who are called by My name, shall humble themselves and pray, and seek My face, and turn from their wicked ways, then I will hear from Heaven and will forgive their sin and will heal their land.* (2Chronicles 7:14)

> *6 I will say to the north, Give up; and to the south, Do not keep back; bring My sons from far and My daughters from the ends of the earth; 7 everyone who is called by My name; for I have created him for My glory, I have formed him; yea, I have made him.* (Isaiah 43:6-7)

> *9 יהוה shall establish you a holy people to Himself, as He has sworn to you, if you shall keep the commandments of יהוה*

*your God and walk in His ways. 10 And all the peoples of the earth shall see that you are called by the name of יהוה, and they shall be afraid of you.* (Deuteronomy 28:9-10)

This now brings us to the time when King David, who has already set up his capital in Hebron, now comes up to take Jerusalem and the name of Yehovah, which is both stamped on the city of Jerusalem and the children of Israel will be brought together removing the Jebusites who are trampling down Yehovah's city and polluting it.

*6 And the sovereign and his men went to Yerushalayim against the Yebusites, the inhabitants of the land. And they spoke to Dawid, saying, "Except you take away the blind and the lame, you are not going to come in here," thinking, "Dawid is not going to come in here." 7 But Dawid captured the stronghold of Tsiyon, the City of Dawid. 8 And Dawid said on that day, "Anyone who smites the Yebusites, let him go by the water-shaft and take the lame and the blind, who are hated by Dawid's being." That is why they say, "The blind and the lame do not come into the house." 9 And Dawid dwelt in the stronghold, and called it the City of Dawid. And Dawid built all around from the Millo and inward.* (2 Samuel 5:6-9)

It says David lived in the fort and I just cited earlier in this chapter how the Ophel in Hebrew means: my Fortress, my Tower, my Stronghold—all of which are names of Yehovah. Let us pause to take a closer look at this important rabbit trail for a moment.

*7 And Dawid dwelt in the stronghold, so they called it the City of Dawid. 8 And he built the city around it, from Millo round about, and Yo'ab revived the rest of the city. 9 And Dawid went on and became great, and יהוה of hosts was with him.* (1 Chronicles 11:7-9)

I am now going to have you take a look at the three things mentioned about the City of David—also called Jerusalem. The first is the Ophel, the second is the Millo and the third is the Akra. Concerning this prophecy of Daniel 9:25, you need to understand the *proper meaning* of these three places and what they represent. Then and *only then*, will you be able to rightly unravel another layer of the Daniel 9:25 Prophecy.

*International Standard Bible Encyclopedia*

# OPHEL

O'-fel (ha-'ophel (2 Chronicles 27:3; 2 Chronicles 33:14; Nehemiah 3:26; Nehemiah 11:21; and without article, Isaiah 32:14 and Micah 4:8; also 2 Kings 5:24):

1. Meaning of Name: There has been considerable divergence of opinion with regard to the meaning of this name. Thus, in all the references given above with the article, the Revised Version (British and American) has simply "Ophel," but the King James version adds in margin "the tower," in Isaiah 32:14, "the hill" with margin "Ophel," but the King James version "the forts," margin "clifts"; Micah 4:8, "the hill," margin "Hebrew: Ophel," but the King James Version "the stronghold"; 2 Kings 5:24, "the hill," margin "Hebrew: Ophel," but the King James Version "the tower," margin "secret place." It is true that the other occurrences of the word in 1 Samuel 5:9, 12; 1 Samuel 6:5, where it is translated "tumors," and Habakkuk 2:4, where a verbal form is translated "puffed up," seem to imply that one meaning assigned to the root may be that of "swelling." Recently, Dr. Burney (PEF, January, 1911) has produced strong arguments in favor of Ophel, when used as the name of a locality, meaning "fortress."

2. Three Ophels: Three places are known to have received this name:

    (a) A certain place on the east hill of Jerusalem, south of the Temple; to this all the passages quoted above—except for one—refer to.

(b) The "Ophel," translated "hill," situated apparently in Samaria (compare to 2 Kings 5:3), where Gehazi took his ill-gotten presents from the hands of the servants of Naaman the Syrian. The translation "tower" would suit the sense at least as well. It was some point probably in the wall of Samaria, perhaps the citadel itself.

(c) The third reference is not biblical, but on the Moabite Stone, an inscription of Mesha, King of Moab, contemporary (of) Omri. He says: "I built Q-R-CH-H (Karhah), the wall of yea'rim, and the wall of Ophel and I built its gates and I built its towers." In comparing the references to (a) and (c), it is evident that if Ophel means a "hill," it certainly was a fortified hill, and it seems highly probable that it meant some "artificial swelling in a fortification," (e.g., a bulging or rounded keep or enceinte).[388]

In Isaiah we read:

*14 "... for the palace is abandoned, the crowded city deserted. Hill and watchtower serve as caves forever."* (Isaiah 32:14)

Here we have the terms: palace, city and watchtower—all the handiwork of the builder. Does it not seem probable then that the Ophel belongs to the same category?

3. The Ophel of Jerusalem: The situation of the Ophel of Jerusalem is very definitely described. It was clearly, from the references (Nehemiah 3:26-27; 2 Chronicles 27:3; 2 Chronicles 33:14) on the east hill south of the Temple. Josephus states[389] that the eastern wall of the city ran from Siloam "and reaches as far as a certain place which they called Ophlas when it was joined to the eastern cloister of the Temple." In BJ, V, vi, 1, it states that, "John held the Temple and the parts thereto adjoining, for a great way, as also 'Ophla,' and the valley called the 'Valley of the Cedron.'"

---

[388] Dr. Burney, loc. cit.
[389] *Jewish Wars*, Vol. 5, pp. iv & 2

It is noticeable that this is not identical with the "Acra" and "Lower City" which was held by Simon. There is not the slightest ground for applying the name Ophel, as has been so commonly done, to the whole southeastern hill.

In the days of Josephus, it was a part of the hill immediately south of the Temple walls, but the Old Testament references suit a locality nearer (to) the middle of the southeastern hill. In the article ZION (which see) it is pointed out that (this) name does not occur (except in reference to the Jebusite city) in the works of the chronicler, but that "the Ophel," which occurs almost alone in these works, is apparently used for it. Micah 4:8 margin seems to confirm this view: "O tower of the flock, the Ophel of the daughter of Zion." Here the "tower of the flock" may well refer to the shepherd David's stronghold, and the second name appears to be a synonym for the same place. Ophel then was probably the fortified site, which in earlier days, had been known as "Zion" or "the City of David." King Jotham "built much" "on the wall of Ophel" (2 Chronicles 27:3). King Manasseh "built an outer wall to the city of David, on the west side of Gihon, in the valley, even to the entrance at the Fish Gate; and he compassed Ophel about with it, and raised it up to a very great height." (2 Chronicles 33:14). It was clearly a fortified place of great importance, and its situation must have been so near that of the ancient "Zion" that scarcely any other theory is possible except that it occupied the site of that ancient fortress.[390]

The Millo was a structure in Jerusalem first mentioned in the Book of 2 Samuel 5:9 and corresponding passages in the Book of Chronicles and the Book of Kings. However, it is mentioned as being part of the City of David[391] and seems to have been a *rampart* built by the Jebusites *prior to* Jerusalem's being conquered by the Israelites.[392] The texts

---

[390] E. W. G. Masterman
[391] 2 Samuel 5:9
[392] http://www.keyway.ca/htm2003/20030728.htm

also describe a Millo built by (King) Solomon[393] and repaired by (King) Hezekiah,[394] without giving an explanation of what exactly the Millo was. There is some debate among scholars as to the Millo's specific nature. The most common assumption among archaeologists and historians of ancient Israel is that the Millo is the Stepped Stone Structure uncovered by Kathleen Kenyon and demonstrated by Eilat Mazar to be connected to the recently uncovered Large Stone Structure.[395]

A recent excavation by Eilat Mazar directly above the Stepped Stone Structure shows that the structure connects with and supports the Large Stone Structure.[396] Mazar presents evidence that the Large Stone Structure was an Israelite royal palace in continuous use from the 10th-century until 586 B.C.E. Her conclusion that the Stepped Stone Structure and the Large Stone Structure are parts of a single, massive royal palace makes sense of the biblical reference to the Millo as the House of Millo in 2 Kings 12:21 and 2 Chronicles 24:25 as the place where King Joash was assassinated in 799 B.C.E. while he slept in his bed. Millo is derived from "fill," (Hebrew *milui*). The Stepped Stone (support) Structure is built of fills.[397]

In the Book of Samuel, Millo is mentioned as boundary of King David's construction while building up the City of David after the capture of Jerusalem from the Jebusites.[398] The King James Version (English translation) footnotes Millo

---

[393] 1 Kings 9:24
[394] 2 Chronicles 32:4-5
[395] http://en.wikipedia.org/wiki/Large_Stone_Structure
[396] *Excavations At the Summit of the City of David, Preliminary Report of Seasons 2005-2007* by Eilat Mazar, Shoham, Jerusalem and New York, 2009.
[397] *Excavations at the Summit of the City of David, Preliminary Report of Seasons 2005-2007* by Eilat Mazar, Shoham, Jerusalem and New York, 2009. p. 67
[398] 2 Samuel 5:9

as literally, "the landfill,"[399] while the New International Version translates it to "supporting terraces."[400]

(King) Hezekiah's repair of the Millo is mentioned within a list of repairs to military fortifications, and several scholars generally believe that it was something connected to military activity, such as a tower, citadel, or simply a significant part of a wall.[401] However, taking into account that the potentially cognate term *mulu*, from Assyrian, refers to "earthworks,"[402] it is considered more likely that it was an embankment, which flattened the slope between Ophel and the Temple Mount.[403]

From the above descriptions, we can now see that the Millo was an earthworks structure and the Ophel was a fortress. In other words, it was a stepped wall and was filled with earth to give it strength from battering rams and the like. To better help you understand this, consider the castles of England and how some of them are built upon mountain cliffs and the defensive structures these steep cliffs afford. This should help you as we continue.

Below is another description I'd like to share with you with regard to the Millo and the Akra.

---

[399] 2 Samuel 5:9 (NKJV)
[400] 2 Samuel 5:9 (NIV)
[401] *Peake's Commentary On the Bible*; *Jewish Encyclopedia*
[402] *Jewish Encyclopedia*
[403] http://en.wikipedia.org/wiki/Millo

## THE MILLO & THE AKRA

> *9 So David lived in the fortress, and called it the city of David. And David built around from the Millo inward.* (2 Samuel 5:9 | NKJV)

> *9 And Dawid dwelt in the stronghold, and called it the City of Dawid. And Dawid built all around from the Millo and inward.* (2 Samuel 5:9)

> *33 Then they fortified the city of David with a great strong wall and towers, and it became their citadel.* (1 Maccabees 1:33)

There have been two fortresses, the locations of which have puzzled biblical scholars for years. Where exactly was (King) David's Millo and later, the Akra, which were closely associated with the "City of David?" They were naturally considered different structures and everyone has looked in different places for each of them.

What is even more puzzling is the fact that they ignored the Greek version of the above text in the Septuagint. For plain to see is that version's translation of "Millo" = AKRA! It is a truism of history. Fortresses, Temples and Palaces were built on strategic sites and they remained strategic throughout history. If David had found a stronghold in his time, it is natural that its location would remain strategic throughout history. And so it was. What was earlier known as Millo later became the Akra.[404]

Here is what we have learned so far. The City of David had a pre-existing structure built by the Jebusites and it seems to have been a rampart. It is also called the Millo and this is due to the earthen fill put in the walls of this stepped wall. But it also appears to be called the Ophel. But I must include one more report before I conclude with regard to this section.

---

[404] http://www.biblemysteries.com/lectures/akra.htm

By the Late Bronze Age, Jerusalem (later, the City of David) was heavily fortified and covered an area of about ten acres. Another city, called Shechem, also was heavily fortified in the Late Bronze Age and it covered an area of only about seven acres. Judges 9:6 says, "And all the men of Shechem gathered together, and all the house of Millo, and went, and made Abimelech king..." Notice the repetition—"And all the men of Shechem..."—"and all the house of Millo..." This repetition occurs again, twice, in verse 20—"...let fire come out from Abimelech, and devour the men of Shechem, and the house of Millo; and let fire come out from the men of Shechem, and from the house of Millo, and devour Abimelech." The word "house," in these verses, is translated "family," "household," "inside," "place"... according to Strong's Concordance (#1004). The word "Millo" is translated as "rampart" (as filled in) (#4407) and is from (#4390) "to fill" or "to be full of," "be fenced," "fill," "full," "overflow," "fullness," "gather selves together," "have wholly." "House of Millo" therefore, could be rendered "household of full rampart" and is simply a way of repeating "men of Shechem." Millo, in this instance, is a reference to *the entire fortified city* of Shechem and, being only seven acres in size, was probably rather crowded at times (full).

Now we come to another city, which is called Millo in the Bible: the City of David. II Chronicles 32: 5 says, "Also he strengthened himself, and built up the wall that was broken, and raised it up to the towers, and another wall without, and repaired Millo *in* the city of David." Notice the word "in" is written in *italics*. In the back of my old King James Bible it states, "The words in italics are words that do not have any equivalents in the Hebrew or Greek text. They are words which have been supplied by the translators in order to make the meaning of the sentence clearer, or in order to make the passage read more smoothly in English." Knowing this, it is acceptable to read this verse again, omitting the word "*in*." Now the verse can be read, "...and repaired Millo the city of David." II Samuel 5: 9 says, "So David dwelt in the fort (rampart), and called it the city of David. And David built roundabout from Millo and inward." Interestingly, the word "inward" in this verse is the same Hebrew word used as "house" (three times) in Judges 9 (Strong's #1004)! Knowing this, it is acceptable to read this verse again, changing the word "inward" to "house." Now the verse can be read, "... And David built roundabout from Millo and house." 2 Kings 12:20 also refers to the "House of Millo," "And his servants arose, and made a conspiracy, and slew Joash in the house of Millo, which goeth down to Silla." "Silla" is a reference to Silwan which today lies east and south of the City of David. 1 Chronicles 11:8 is another example of repetition in a verse, "And he built the city roundabout, even from Millo round about..." "Millo," in this instance, is equal to "city."

Other references to "Millo" in the Bible are found in 1 Kings 9:15, 24 and 1 Kings 11: 27. In every instance we can associate it with the "full rampart" (the entire city).

In Scripture, David accurately described Jerusalem (the city of David) before the expansion to the north by his son, Solomon:

*3 Jerusalem is builded as a city that is compact together.* (Psalm 122:3)[405]

*3 Yerushalayim is built as a city that is bound together.* (Psalm 122:3)

This is a picture of Shechem. I have provided you with an image below so you can see the actual rampart. It is the section of outer wall with earthen fill to strengthen it. Notice the rooms attached to the wall. In times of peace people lived in them. But as war was approaching, they would remove the house and fill the rooms with earth to strengthen

---

[405] http://www.biblicalarchaeologytruth.com/millo.html

the walls. This was shown to those of us in my group in the City of Two Gates when I went to visit it in Israel in 2011 and 2012.[406]

Shechem, seen below has a moat. Moats could be filled with water or used as what is called a dry moat. You see this same defensive structure throughout the castles of Europe and England.

Here is the Bible Dictionary-based definition of the meaning of the Millo and another set of quotes that define what it is.

*Bible Dictionary*
Millo (Definition)

> (Hebrew—always with the article, "the" Millo). (1) Probably the Canaanite name of some fortification, consisting of walls filled in with earth and stones, which protected Jerusalem on the north as its outermost defense. It is always rendered Akra (i.e., "the citadel,") in the LXX. It was already existing when David conquered Jerusalem (2 Samuel 5:9). He extended it to the right and left, thus completing the defense of the city. It was rebuilt by (King) Solomon (1 Kings 9:15, 24; 11:27) and repaired by (King) Hezekiah (2 Chronicles 32:5). (2) In Judges 9:6, 20 it is the name of a rampart in Shechem, probably the "Tower of Shechem." (Judges 9:46, 49)[407]

> "David's building of the Millo was considered by the biblical writers to be one of this king's major accomplishments."[408]

---

[406] The Elah Fortress (Khirbet Qeiyafa in Arabic), possibly providing hints to the existence of the city of Sha'arayim, (Hebrew for "Two Gates").
[407] http://dictionary.reference.com/browse/Millo
[408] http://tinyurl.com/cj23f2a

"David rebuilt the upper town of Sion, the citadel or Millo, and all the neighboring quarters."[409]

"David built round about Millo inward: Millo was the central fortification of the city. David extended it by enlarging the city wall, also by enlarging the fortress itself."[410]

Why have we gone through this long section on the Milo, Ophel and Akra? Because this is the section of Daniel 9:25, which proves this is speaking of King David and not the Messiah that everyone is trying to convince you that it is.

> *"It shall be built again, with streets and a trench, but in times of affliction."* (Daniel 9:25)

"Street" is Strong's –H7339—*rĕchob* and actually means "broad or open place or plaza."

"Wall" is Strong's –H2742—*charuwts* and means, "trench, moat, ditch."

I have now covered the section that shows us that in the 7th Jubilee Cycle, after Moses was commanded to take the people out, to head east, and return to and rebuild Jerusalem that King David, once he became king, did *in fact* capture Jerusalem *during* this 7th Jubilee Cycle. And even more intriguing is the fact that King David *did* built a rampart, which has a "moat" (another name for a ditch) around the fortification. In the Bible this was originally called the Millo, later it became known as the Akra, and may have been the Ophel. It is my personal opinion that the Akra was to the southeast, with the Millo as the protective moat, was a fortification of the City of David, which enclosed the Akra. The Ophel was to the north and it was this Millo that King Solomon filled in, leveled and compacted it in order to build upon the Milo and the Ophel (the Temple), the *Tower of Strength*.

---

[409] http://tinyurl.com/d82pwey
[410] http://tinyurl.com/czxywze

As a side note, many will be asking, "Where are the Akra and this Millo—also called Zion and King David's citadel? What happened to them?"

The answer is one of the greatest things I have discovered in my journeys to Israel and in my studies.

> The first Book of Maccabees tells us that at the beginning of Simon's reign (after he dislodged the Macedonians from the Akra on the southern tip of the Crescent Ridge), he first began to reinforce the Akra and the original Temple Mount.[411] This initial action of Simon returned the geographical situation to the status quo that had existed before the time when Antiochus Epiphanes desolated the Temple in 167 B.C.E. But to Simon, this former status quo presented a problem of the first magnitude concerning the security of the Jewish people at their capital of Jerusalem. This former geographical situation left the Akra in a location of invulnerability and potentially it was still a fortress that could be used to threaten Israel at a future time if the Gentiles would recapture it. It was because of this future possibility, among other things that I will soon relate, that Simon devised a momentous plan.
>
> Simon decided to change his mind about the Akra. After securing all of Jerusalem, he stopped the rebuilding of the Akra (which the Jews were again fortifying). Josephus states that Simon consulted with the authorities in Jerusalem and they all confirmed it was better for the protection of the nation and the Temple that the Akra should have its summit reduced in size.[412] They then assigned men to begin the destruction of that southern summit. As Josephus stated: "So they all set to and began to level the hill."[413] After accomplishing this leveling, the result made the adjacent hill called the Ophel (on which the Temple stood) higher than the former Akra.[414]

---

[411] 1 Maccabees 14:37
[412] *War*, Vol.4, p. 1
[413] *Antiquities* XIII. pp. 6-7
[414] *War*, Vol.4, p. 1

But Simon went even further than this. He thought it was prudent if he thoroughly leveled the Akra to the ground, to the very bedrock. And this he did. Josephus said they continued their work and finally "raised the Akra to the ground."[415] Josephus said; "So they all set to and began to level the hill [the Akra], and without stopping work night and day, after three whole years, brought it down to the ground and the surface of the plain."[416]

They cut to the bedrock the Akra. This meant that the Ophel knoll just to the north (on which the Temple stood) was then higher in elevation than the Akra as Josephus stated.[417]

They cut to the bedrock the Akra.[418]

When you go to Israel today, you can still see the very bedrock that they dug down to. It is upon this bedrock that the Akra stood. It is upon this bedrock that the Citadel of David once stood. It is upon this bedrock that was once called Mount Zion. And when we go to 2 Chronicles, it confirms this by telling us the very place in which the Pool of Siloam is—directly west of the City of David.

> *30 And Hizqiyahu himself had stopped the upper outlet of the waters of Gihon, and directed them to the west side of the City of Dawid. And Hizqiyahu prospered in all his work.* (2 Chronicles 32:30)

There now remains just one more part to verse 25 to look at. I have explained that the going forth was when the command was given to Moses at the burning bush in the 50th Jubilee Cycle. I have also explained to you that Messiah the Prince is *not* The Messiah but it is the Anointed King David. It was King David, who after seven weeks or seven Shavuot or seven Jubilee Cycles, was anointed and captured Jerusalem and rebuilt both the rampart and the moat. *Nowhere else*

---

[415] *War*, I.2, 2.
[416] *Antiquites* XIII. pp. 6-7 (words in brackets mine).
[417] *War,* Vol. 4, p. 1, see Whiston and Cornfield translations.
[418] *The Temples That Jerusalem Forgot* by Ernest L. Martin, pp. 340-341

do we have this recorded as being done! Yehshua, in the 490-Years-Prophecy, never digs a moat or builds a rampart! Nor is this mentioned or suggested by anyone holding to this Theory of the 483rd Year followed by a seven year gap that is to begin at some mysterious point in the future that no one knows. But I have just shown you that King David did, *in fact*, build this rampart and also extended it and the moat as well.

What I have not gone over with you yet is the sixty-two weeks. I will do that now by prefacing it first with the following passage in Scripture:

> *25 Know, then, and understand: from the going forth of the command to restore and build Yerushalayim until Messiah the Prince is seven weeks and sixty-two weeks. It shall be built again, with streets and a trench, but in times of affliction.* (Daniel 9:25)

I have shown you that Moses was given the Command in the 50th Jubilee Cycle at some point right before or during the year 1383 B.C.

| | | | | | | -1337 | 51 |
|---|---|---|---|---|---|---|---|
| Sabbath | 6th Cycle | 5th Cycle | 4th Cycle | 3rd Cycle | 2nd Cycle | 1st Cycle | |
| -1338 | -1345 | -1352 | -1359 | -1366 | -1373 | -1380 | |
| -1339 | -1346 | -1353 | -1360 | -1367 | -1374 | -1381 | |
| -1340 | -1347 | -1354 | -1361 | -1368 | -1375 | -1382 | |
| -1341 | -1348 | -1355 | -1362 | -1369 | -1376 | -1383 | |
| -1342 | -1349 | -1356 | -1363 | -1370 | -1377 | -1384 | |
| -1343 | -1350 | -1357 | -1364 | -1371 | -1378 | -1385 | |
| -1344 | -1351 | -1358 | -1365 | -1372 | -1379 | -1386 | |
| | | | | | | -1386 | 50 |

Then we see where Daniel 9:25 reads seven weeks, which is seven Shavuot, as I have shown you. This is: 7 x 49 = 343 years and this takes you from the time of Moses being told to go and deliver the Israelites to the time when David is born. In this 57th Jubilee Cycle, David is born anointed three times and then as that *Anointed King* captures Jerusalem from the Jebusites and rebuilds and extends the rampart and the moat *just as* the Daniel 9:25 Prophecy said he would.

| Sabbath | 6th Cycle | 5th Cycle | 4th Cycle | 3rd Cycle | 2nd Cycle | 1st Cycle | |
|---|---|---|---|---|---|---|---|
| | | | | | | -994 | 58 |
| -995 | -1002 | -1009 | -1016 | -1023 | -1030 | -1037 | |
| -996 | -1003 | -1010 | -1017 | -1024 | -1031 | -1038 | |
| -997 | -1004 | -1011 | -1018 | -1025 | -1032 | -1039 | |
| -998 | -1005 | -1012 | -1019 | -1026 | -1033 | -1040 | |
| -999 | -1006 | -1013 | -1020 | -1027 | -1034 | -1041 | |
| -1000 | -1007 | -1014 | -1021 | -1028 | -1035 | -1042 | |
| -1001 | -1008 | -1015 | -1022 | -1029 | -1036 | -1043 | |
| | | | | | | -1043 | 57 |

We are also told in this same verse about the *"sixty-two weeks."*

This is extremely exciting and critical to understand. I will address the sixty-two weeks part first. Sixty-two weeks is the similar to the 7 x 49, only now it is 62 x 49—which is a total of 3,038 years. These 3,038 years are to be added to the Jubilee Cycle in which David is born and rules; that is Jubilee Cycle #57, which is *also* the year 1043 B.C. This now brings us to the year 1996 C.E. and I will explain what this means in the next chapter.

The exciting part being: understanding and comprehending that King David was to come in the seventh Jubilee cycle after Moses was commanded to go and bring the Israelites out eastwards. Because you now understand that the subject of this verse is speaking of King David and have now proven that it was in fact King David who came after the first seven weeks, then the same subject of this verse, King David, is going to come again after another sixty-two weeks have past. Stop and consider this. Most, if not all Christians, assume Yehshua is going to come and rule during the 7th Millennium, but is this right? And if it is as Revelation indicates, then we *also* must understand that King David is going to rule *with* Him.

Let me share with you some scriptures to challenge you and broaden your understanding once again. King David made a statement in Psalm 17 that we should consider. He knew he would one day be woken up:

| Sabbath | 6th Cycle | 5th Cycle | 4th Cycle | 3rd Cycle | 2nd Cycle | 1st Cycle | 6th |
|---|---|---|---|---|---|---|---|
| | | | | | | 2045 | 120 |
| 2044 | 2037 | 2030 | 2023 | 2016 | 2009 | 2002 | Millennial |
| 2043 | 2036 | 2029 | 2022 | 2015 | 2008 | 2001 | Day |
| 2042 | 2035 | 2028 | 2021 | 2014 | 2007 | 2000 | Ended |
| 2041 | 2034 | 2027 | 2020 | 2013 | 2006 | 1999 | |
| 2040 | 2033 | 2026 | 2019 | 2012 | 2005 | 1998 | |
| 2039 | 2032 | 2025 | 2018 | 2011 | 2004 | 1997 | |
| 2038 | 2031 | 2024 | 2017 | 2010 | 2003 | 1996 | |
| | | | | | | 1996 | 119 |

> *15 As for me, let Me see Your face in righteousness; I am satisfied to see Your appearance when I awake.* (Psalm 17:15)

In Hosea, however, we have a very interesting verse. We have had no Temple since 70 C.E. when it was destroyed for the second time. Also, there has not yet been a king to unite both the House of Israel and the House of Judah. Yet, we are told that we will in the last days (note it is the last days) have a King and that King will be David. When Israel returns and seeks Yehovah, then at that time they will also seek David their King. That time is almost upon us.

> *4 For many days the children of Yisra'el are to remain without sovereign and without prince, and without slaughtering, and without pillar, and without shoulder garment or house idols. 5 Afterward the children of Yisra'el shall return, and seek יהוה their Elohim, and Dawid their sovereign, and fear יהוה and His goodness, in the latter days.* (Hosea 3:4-5)

Shifting our focus to Ezekiel, we read about all the dead of Israel who will be raised up and then we read that the one leading them is King David. We have to ask ourselves, *when* does this happen? Even as we read it, we are given a clue. It will happen the same time of year as when the Holy Spirit was given once before at Pentecost. In fact, when you understand the deep meaning of Pentecost and the Wave Offering it represents, then you will know that it is on Pentecost they will be raised up.[419] The year this takes place is explained in *The Prophecies of Abraham*[420] and is too big a subject to revisit for this book.

---

[419] *Pentecost's Hidden Meaning*, http://www.sightedmoon.com/?page_id=21
[420] *The Prophecies of Abraham*, http://www.authorhouse.co.uk/Bookstore/

*3 And He said to me, "Son of man, would these bones live?" And I said, "O Master יהוה, You know." 4 Again He said to me, "Prophesy to these bones and you shall say to them, 'O dry bones, hear the word of יהוה!'" 5 Thus said the Master יהוה to these bones, "See, I am bringing into you a spirit, and you shall live. 6 And I shall put sinews on you and bring flesh upon you, and cover you with skin and put a spirit in you, and you shall live. And you shall know that I am יהוה." 7 And I prophesied as I was commanded. And as I prophesied, there was a noise, and there was a rattling. And the bones came together, bone to bone. 8 And I looked and saw sinews and flesh came upon them, and skin covered them, but there was no spirit in them. 9 He then said to me, "Prophesy to the spirit, prophesy, son of man, and you shall say to the spirit, 'Thus said the Master יהוה, Come from the four winds, O spirit, and breathe on these slain, so that they live.'"* (Ezekiel 37:3-9)

*10 And I prophesied as He commanded me, and the spirit came into them, and they lived, and stood upon their feet, a very great army. 11 And He said to me, "Son of man, these bones are all the house of Yisra'el. See, they say, 'Our bones are dry, our expectancy has perished, and we ourselves have been cut off!' 12 Therefore prophesy, and you shall say to them, 'Thus said the Master יהוה, See, O My people, I am opening your graves, and shall bring you up from your graves, and shall bring you into the land of Yisra'el. 13 And you shall know that I am יהוה, when I open your graves, O My people, and bring you up from your graves. 14 And I shall put My Spirit in you, and you shall live, and I shall settle you in your own land. And you shall know that I יהוה have spoken, and I have done it,'" declares יהוה.* (Ezekiel 37:10-14)

*23 "And I shall raise up over them one shepherd, My servant Dawid, and he shall feed them. He shall feed them and be their shepherd. 24 And I, יהוה, shall be their Elohim, and My servant Dawid a prince in their midst. I, יהוה, have spoken. 25 And I shall make a covenant of peace with them, and make*

---

BookDetail.aspx?Book=286642

> *evil beasts cease from the land. And they shall dwell safely in the wilderness and sleep in the forest. 26 And I shall make them and the places all around My hill a blessing, and shall cause showers to come down in their season—showers of blessing they are. 27 And the trees of the field shall yield their fruit and the earth yield her increase and they shall be safe in their land. And they shall know that I am יהוה, when I have broken the bars of their yoke. And I shall deliver them from the hand of those who enslaved them."* (Ezekiel 34:23-27)

We also read in Amos how Yehovah is going to restore the ruins of King David. Does this mean that the Akra is going to be rebuilt? I do not know.

> *11 In that day I shall raise up the booth of Dawid which has fallen down. And I shall repair its breaches and raise up its ruins. And I shall build it as in the days of old, 12 so that they possess the remnant of Edom, and all the gentiles on whom My Name is called," declares יהוה who does this.* (Amos 9:11-12)

In the next chapter I am going to warn you once again of the coming captivity of Israel—that is, *all* 12 Houses (or Tribes) as I have explained them. It is from this captivity that those of us who survive will witness the king who is going to rule over us—the very king who it was once prophesied was going to come seven Jubilee cycles after Moses led the Israelites out of Egypt and this same King who would once again come after another sixty two Jubilee cycles to be King. This is none other than King David.

> *3 "For look, the days are coming," declares יהוה, "when I shall turn back the captivity of My people Yisra'el and Yehudah," declares יהוה, "and I shall bring them back to the land that I gave to their fathers, and let them possess it... 8 "And it shall be in that day," declares יהוה of hosts, "that I break his yoke from your neck, and tear off your bonds, and foreigners no more enslave them. 9 And they shall serve יהוה their Elohim and Dawid their sovereign, whom I **raise up** (akim lahem) for them."* (Jeremiah 30:3, 8-9)

# Chapter 9 | The Saints Destroyed (Daniel 9:26)

*24 Seventy weeks are decreed for your people and for your set-apart city, to put an end to the transgression, and to seal up sins, and to cover crookedness, and to bring in everlasting righteousness, and to seal up vision and prophet, and to anoint the Most Set-apart. 25 Know, then, and understand: from the going forth of the command to restore and build Yerushalayim until Messiah the Prince is seven weeks and sixty-two weeks. It shall be built again, with streets and a trench, but in times of affliction. 26 And after the sixty-two weeks Messiah shall be cut off and have naught. And the people of a coming prince shall destroy the city and the set-apart place. And the end of it is with a flood. And wastes are decreed, and fighting until the end. 27 And he shall confirm a covenant with many for one week. And in the middle of the week he shall put an end to slaughtering and meal offering. And on the wing of abominations he shall lay waste, even until the complete end and that which is decreed is poured out on the one who lays waste.[1]* [Footnote: [1]Matthew 24:15 (Daniel 9:24-27)]

*26 And after the sixty-two weeks Messiah shall be cut off and have naught. And the people of a coming prince shall destroy the city and the set-apart place. And the end of it is with a flood. And wastes are decreed, and fighting until the end.* (Daniel 9:26)

For me, this is, hands down, the most terrifying verse in the entire Bible. Each time I share the meaning of this verse, it fills me with dread. I pray that with all the information I have shared with you thus far that, *you too*, once you have finished reading this chapter, will see the real danger directly ahead.

I have already shown you that the 62 weeks is 62 Shavuot or 3,038 years. That is 62 x 49 = 3,038 years and these are to be added to the 7 x 49 which equals the 343 years that we discussed previously. This entire 69 weeks, or 69 Shavuot, or 3381 years, began from the time Moses was given the command to "go" and deliver the Israelites from Egypt and bring them back to the Promised Land—an event which consequently transpired after the 50$^{th}$ Jubilee Cycle ended, counting from the creation of Adam, and the 51$^{st}$ Jubilee Cycle began in 1386 B.C.

When you add up these years, 1386 B.C. + 3381 you should arrive at 1996 C.E. (Keep in mind there is no year zero.) Thus 1996 is the beginning of this current and last Jubilee Cycle. So what this verse is saying is that after the 62 weeks, or after the 3,038 years from the Jubilee Cycle which showed us the birth and anointing of King David, *then* the Messiah will be cut off.

This verse is also saying that after the total of 69 weeks or 69 Shavuot, or after the 69 Jubilee Cycles which was the year 1996, *then* the Messiah will be cut off.

Am I really saying that the Messiah is going to be cut off again after 1996? If I am then many of you will stop reading right here. We know for sure the 69 Shavuot is correct and begins with Yehovah's command to Moses at the burning bush. What I am about to show you is what "*then* the Messiah will be cut off" actually does mean.

Many have believed the current understanding that this is referring to Yehshua being killed on the tree on the Mount of Offense (Olives) in 31 C.E., but *is this correct*?

I have shown you that the entire prophecy of Daniel 9:24-25 has been about something *other* than what those who hold to the commonly held view have been maintaining for the past 2000 years and how it lines up much better with those things I have explained to you thus far.

Again, in Genesis 6:3 we read of the 120 periods of time. The word for "years" is the Hebrew word, "Shanah."

> H8141: *shaw-neh,' shaw-naw'*
>
> (The first form being in plural only, the second form being feminine); from H8138; a *year* (as a *revolution* of time): −+ whole age, X long, + old, year (X -ly).

"Shanah" can also mean a revolution of time or 120 Jubilee Cycles.

> *3 And יהוה said, "My Spirit shall not strive with man forever in his going astray. He is flesh, and his days shall be one hundred and twenty years."* (Genesis 6:3)

From the creation of Adam to the year 1386 B.C. was a total of 50 Jubilee Cycles. In the first few years of that 51st Jubilee Cycle beginning with the burning bush, and the call upon Moses to deliver the Israelites from Egypt and travel east through the Red Sea was the start of Daniel's 70 Shavuot. Daniel's 70 Shavuot is 70 Jubilee Cycles and will take us right up to the year 2045. 2045 is the end of the 70th week of Daniel's prophecy.

Daniels 70 weeks or 70 Jubilee cycles is added to the 50 Jubilee cycles counting from Adam up to just before the Exodus. 50 + 70 = 120 Jubilee Cycles, which will bring us to the year 2045. *This* is what Genesis 6:3 is referring to:

> *Yet his days shall be a hundred and twenty years.*
> *Yet his days shall be a hundred and twenty periods of time.*
> *Yet his days shall be a hundred and twenty Jubilee Cycles.*

Yehovah will put up with man's rebellious attitude for 120 Jubilee Cycles, or six Millennial Days. 1996 was the beginning of the 119th Jubilee Cycle.

In the very same way a child does not actually turn one until after having lived one full year and then is subsequently considered to be in the second year of life from that first birthday onward, so it is with the Jubilee Cycle. The 119th Jubilee Cycle, which was 1996, is in fact, the *end of* the 119th Jubilee Cycle. We are currently in the 120th one but do not celebrate the 120th Jubilee Year until we have completed this cycle which is in 2045. 2045 is *also* the *next* Jubilee Year and the first year of the 7th Millennium. So this Jubilee Cycle is the *last one* before the 7th Millennium begins and the Messiah and King David rule over Israel and this Earth.

Just by correctly adding up all of the known history, one can, with certainty, arrive at this conclusion also, especially given what I have already shown you in *The Prophecies of Abraham*[421] and *Remembering the Sabbatical Years of 2016.*[422]

If what I am saying thus far is true, and I *do* believe it is, then what does the word "Messiah" actually mean in verse 26 of Daniel 9? For surely the Messiah can't be cut off *again* having already died once already in 31 C.E.!

Let us once again go back to the Hebrew and look at each of the words in this phrase to examine them and learn the truth.

*"Messiah"*

H4899: *maw-shee'-akh*

H4886: *anointed*; usually a *consecrated* person (as a king, priest, or saint); specifically the *Messiah:* anointed, Messiah.

H4886: *maw-shakh'*

---

[421] *The Prophecies of Abraham* by Joseph Dumond http://www.authorhouse.co.uk/Bookstore/BookDetail.aspx?Book=286642

[422] *Remembering the Sabbatical Years of 2016* by Joseph Dumond http://www.amazon.com/gp/product/147977037X/ref=s9_simh_gw_p14_d13_i1?pf_rd_m=ATVPDKIKX0DER&pf_rd_s=center-2&pf_rd_r=10FEQZAVE0WWRWHZ2WJ0&pf_rd_t=101&pf_rd_p=1630083502&pf_rd_i=507846

> A primitive root: to *rub* with oil, that is, to *anoint*; by implication to *consecrate*; also to *paint:* anoint, paint.

I have already given you a close look at this word, "Mashiyach" in a previous chapter and "Messiah" is what the translators have told us it means. Yet, what many do not realize is it *also* means king, priest and/or saint, as well as someone who is anointed or rubbed with oil, as I explained to you and went over with you in the last chapter.

I showed you in the previous study in verse 25 that in that case, "Mashiyach" was referring to King David and *not* the Messiah. So who exactly is the *anointed one* who is being referred to in verse 26? Also, who is the *anointed one* who is going to be cut off? It can't be the Messiah who is cut off again.

We must go to the Bible to find the answers.

We read in many places about *"the Lord's anointed."* This is a reference to the kings of the nation of Israel (1 Samuel 12:3 & 5, 24:6 & 10, 26:9, 11, 16, & 23; 2 Samuel 1:14 & 16, 19:21) David respected King Saul's anointed status despite King Saul's treacherous dealings with him and did not think to take matters into his own hands. Why? Because King Saul was Yehovah's anointed. Even Abishai knew that he had cursed the king and was in danger of losing his life for having done so.

Yehovah saves His anointed. He hears them when they pray. Those who do not keep His Laws, He does not hear, which means they are not anointed.

> *6 Now I know that* יהוה *shall save His Anointed; He answers him from His set-apart heavens with the saving might of His right hand.* (Psalm 20:6)

> *31 And we know that Elohim does not hear sinners. But if anyone fears Elohim and does His desire, He hears him.* (John 9:31)

*9 He who turns away his ear from hearing the Torah, even his prayer is an abomination.[1]* [Footnote: [1]See also Proverbs 15:29, Isaiah 59:1-2, John 9:31, 1 John 3:22 (Proverbs 28:9)]

We know Yehovah hears the anointed, those who keep and do His Torah—those who are no longer counted as sinners. But we have a troubling report in Lamentations after Jeremiah had witnessed the destruction of Jerusalem.

*1 How dim the gold has become, the fine gold changed! The stones of the set-apart place are scattered at the head of every street. 2 The precious sons of Tsiyon who were weighed against fine gold, how they have been reckoned as clay pots, the work of the hands of the potter! 3 Even jackals have presented their breasts, they have nursed their young. The daughter of my people has become as cruel, as ostriches in the wilderness. 4 The tongue of the infant has clung to the roof of its mouth for thirst; children asked for bread, no one breaks it for them. 5 Those who ate delicacies have been laid waste in the streets; those who were brought up in scarlet have embraced dunghills. 6 And the crookedness of the daughter of my people is greater than the punishment of the sin of Sedom, which was overthrown in a moment, and no hands were wrung over her! 7 Her Nazirites were brighter than snow and whiter than milk; more ruddy in body than rubies, their cut like sapphire. 8 Their appearance has become blacker than soot; they have become unrecognized in the streets; their skin has shriveled on their bones, it has become dry, it has become as wood.* (Lamentations 4:1-8)

*9 Better off were those pierced by the sword than those pierced by hunger; for these pine away, pierced through for lack of the fruits of the field. 10 The hands of the compassionate women have boiled their own children; they became food for them in the destruction of the daughter of my people. 11 יהוה has completed His wrath, He has poured out His burning displeasure. And He kindled a fire in Tsiyon, and it consumed her foundations. 12 The sovereigns of the earth did not believe, nor any of the inhabitants of the world, that an adversary and enemy would enter the gates of Yerushalayim.13 It was because of the sins of her prophets, the crookednesses of her priests, who shed in her midst the blood of the righteous. 14 They staggered, blind, in the streets; they have defiled themselves with blood, so that no one was able to touch their garments. 15 They shouted at them, "Away! Unclean! Away! Away! Touch not!" When they fled and staggered, they said, among the gentiles, "They shall stay no longer."* (Lamentations 4:9-15)

*16 The face of יהוה scattered them. He no longer regards them. They showed no respect for the priests nor favor to the elders. 17 While we exist, our eyes are consumed, watching vainly for our help. In our watchtower we watched for a nation that could not save. 18 They have hunted our steps from going in our streets. Our end was near; our days were completed, for our end had come. 19 Our pursuers were swifter than the eagles of the heavens. They came hotly after us on the mountains and lay in wait for us in the wilderness. 20 The breath of our nostrils, the anointed of יהוה, was caught in their pits, in whose shadow we had thought to live among the gentiles. 21 Rejoice and be glad, O daughter of Edom, you who dwell in the land of Uz! The cup is to pass over to you too, so that you become drunk and make yourself naked. 22 Your crookedness has been completed, O daughter of Tsiyon. He no longer prolongs your exile. He shall punish your crookedness, O daughter of Edom, He shall uncover your sins!* (Lamentations 4:16-22)

We read in verse 20 that those Jews who were slaughtered and those who had escaped and were reduced to eating their own children were, in fact, the anointed of Yehovah.

*20 The breath of our nostrils, the anointed of יהוה, was caught in their pits, in whose shadow we had thought to live among the gentiles.* (Lamentations 4:20)

It is glaringly obvious they had fallen out of Yehovah's grace however, and even still, Jeremiah refers to them as His anointed. So even though they were clearly *not* keeping Torah, they were *still* considered His anointed. When did this take place? We can see that Abraham, Isaac and Jacob were anointed by the protection they received and the comments that are made in Psalms 105.

> *7 He is* יהוה *our Elohim; His right-rulings are in all the earth. 8 He has remembered His covenant forever, the Word He commanded, for a thousand generations, 9 The covenant He made with A*ḇ*raham, a*nd *His oath to Yitsḥaq, 10 and established it to Ya'aqo*ḇ *for a law, to Yisra'ěl—an everlasting covenant, 11 saying, "To you I give the land of Kena'an, the portion of your inheritance." 12 When they were few in number, few indeed, and sojourners in it, 13 and they went about from one nation to another, from one reign to another people, 14 He allowed no one to oppress them, and He reproved sovereigns for their sakes.15 saying, Touch not my* **anointed**, *and do My prophets no harm.* (Psalms 105:7-15)

And from this statement we can see that the ancestry of Abraham, Isaac, and Jacob was also anointed because of the inclusion of the prophets in this statement. They too were anointed and the prophets where chosen from amongst the people.

Also notice in this Scripture that Yehovah protected His anointed (they were the Israelites and His prophets) from the enemies of Israel who wanted to cause them harm.

We can safely conclude then that all of Israel is also known as the anointed, but there is more to this because we read in 2 Corinthians that those who believe in Yehshua are *also* anointed. But this means they not only believe, but *also* obey and keep the Torah as well.

> *20 For as many promises as are of Elohim, in Him they are Yea, and in Him Aměn, to the esteem of Elohim through us. 21 But He who establishes us with you in Messiah and has*

> *anointed us is Elohim, 22 who also sealed us, and gave the Spirit in our hearts as a pledge.* (2 Corinthians 1:20-22)

When you are keeping the Torah, obeying it in everyday life, and are not just talking the talk but actually walking the walk, then His Spirit is upon you, and *this too*, is an anointing. The Holy Spirit is like the anointing oil used on the kings of Israel.

> *12 For as the body is one and has many members, but all the members of that one body, being many, are one body, so also is the Messiah. 13 For indeed by one Spirit* **we were all immersed** *into one body, whether Yehudim or Greeks, whether slaves or free, and we were all made to drink into one Spirit. 14 For indeed the body is not one member but many.* (1 Corinthians 12:12-14)

> *19 They went out from us, but they were not of us, for if they had been of us, they would have stayed with us—but in order that it might be made manifest that none of them were of us. 20 And* **you have an anointing from the Set-apart One**, *and you know all. 21 I did not write to you because you do not know the truth, but because you know it, and because no falsehood is of the truth. 22 Who is the liar, except the one denying that* יהושע *is the Messiah? This is the anti-messiah, the one denying the Father and the Son. 23 No one denying the Son has the Father. The one confessing the Son has the Father as well. 24 As for you, let that stay in you which you heard from the beginning. If what you heard from the beginning stays in you, you also shall stay in the Son and in the Father. 25 And this is the promise that He has promised us: everlasting life. 26 I have written this to you concerning those who lead you astray. 27* **But the anointing which you have received from Him stays in you,** *and you have no need that anyone should teach you. But as* **the same anointing does teach you** *concerning all, and is true, and is no falsehood, and even as it has taught you, you stay in Him.* (1 John 2:19-27)

> *8 יהוה is the strength of His people, and He is the stronghold of deliverance of **His anointed.*** (Psalm 28:8)

These are the ones Peter referred to when he wrote:

> *9 But you are a chosen race, a royal priesthood, a set-apart nation, a people for a possession, that you should proclaim the praises of Him who called you out of darkness into His marvelous light.* (1 Peter 2:9)

David saw the entire nation of Israel to be Yehovah's anointed and this is why He said, *"do not touch my anointed."* We, the physical descendants of Jacob, all twelve tribes are the anointed; but only those who keep the Torah will be saved. Those not keeping the Torah are to be cut off, as we are about to learn as we read the rest of the verse.

> *26 And after the sixty-two weeks Messiah shall be cut off and have naught.* (Daniel 9:26)

*"Be cut off"* is from the word "Kawrath."

H3772: כרת kârath kaw-rath'

> A primitive root: to cut (off, down or asunder); by implication to destroy or consume; specifically to covenant (that is, make an alliance or bargain, originally by cutting flesh and passing between the pieces): be chewed, be con- [feder-] ate, covenant, cut (down, off), destroy, fail, feller, be freed, hew (down), make a league ([covenant]), X lose, perish, X utterly, X want.

Do you see what this meaning of this word entails? One expression is to "Destroy." But here is the very real and altogether sobering expression; "make an alliance or bargain, originally by cutting flesh and passing between the pieces."

This is referring us right back to the very beginning when Yehovah made the Covenant with Abraham. And Yehovah walked between the two halves of the animals that were cut.

*8 And he said, "Master יהוה, whereby do I know that I possess it?" 9 And He said to him, "Bring Me a three-year-old heifer, and a three-year-old female goat, and a three-year-old ram, and a turtledove, and a young pigeon." 10 And he took all these to Him and cut them in the middle, and placed each half. 11 And the birds of prey came down on the carcasses, and Aḇram drove them away. 12 And it came to be, when the sun was going down, and a deep sleep fell upon Aḇram, that see, a frightening great darkness fell upon him. 13 And He said to Aḇram, "Know for certain that your seed are to be sojourners in a land that is not theirs, and shall serve them, and they shall afflict them four hundred years. 14 But the nation whom they serve I am going to judge, and afterward let them come out with great possessions. 15 Now as for you, you are to go to your fathers in peace, you are to be buried at a good old age. 16 Then, in the fourth generation they shall return here, for the crookedness of the Amorites is not yet complete." 17 And it came to be, when the sun went down and it was dark that see, a smoking oven and a burning torch passing between those pieces. 18 On the same day יהוה made a covenant with Aḇram, saying, "I have given this land to your seed, from the river of Mitsrayim to the great river, the River Euphrates, 19 with the Qěynite, and the Qenizzite, and the Qaḏmonite, 20 and the Ḥittite, and the Perizzite, and the Repha'im, 21 and the Amorite, and the Kena'anite, and the Girgashite, and the Yeḇusite."* (Genesis 15:8-21)

This is when Yehovah went between them and made the Covenant with Abraham. This is a Blood Covenant between Yehovah and Abraham and his descendants. But this is *not* the Blood Covenant that Daniel 9:26 is referring to.

Just so that you understand, in a blood covenant, should either party break that covenant, then the other has the inalienable right to kill them. The party that breaks this covenant will pay for doing so with their very lives.

Covenant in Hebrew means a "cut-where-blood-flows." The purpose of covenant was to create a binding agreement, more powerful than a contract or agreement. This was to be forever—the lifespan of the participants, it was to be holy (and) sacred. To violate the covenant would mean death. The blood covenant was the ultimate insurance of loyalty and fidelity. There were variances of rituals but the common base was a "cut-where-blood-flows" and the mingling of these two bloods by the cuts being rubbed against each other. A cup of wine would be held under the cuts to catch the dripping blood, which was stirred into the wine by an officiating priest, then each participant would drink from the cup. In many cases the witnesses to the covenant would also drink from the cup of the blood and wine. In the minds of the covenant participants they had become one blood and one identity with each other. They would give each other their children to raise in utter confidence that the covenant partner would raise the child as their own.

The blood covenant has been used for centuries as a means by which any two people, families, tribes, villages or towns could enter into a binding, unending agreement. Covenant between two persons could end with the death of a participant on either side.

The participants would sacrifice several animals and cut the carcasses lengthwise down the spine and lay the animal halves opposite of each other about three feet apart. There being several animals involved, a path (was) formed with half a carcass on the left side and half a carcass on the right side with a three foot space between. After three hours, the three foot space between the animal halves would fill with blood that drained from the carcasses. The participants stand facing each other at each end of the path. Each removes their sandals and stand in their bare feet. Each will walk through the path of blood twice. The first participant walks the path through the animal halves to the other. Upon reaching the end of the path, makes a declaration to the other participant that he has just symbolically died and all his (list agreed upon prior) goods listed in will now belong to the other. He then walks back to his starting place through the path of blood, which is now a symbolic birth canal and is now born, is the new, (mutually) agreed upon identity.

The blood covenant, while somewhat gory, has at its base a death–rebirth process. Each participant will symbolically die, thus ending their former identity. They will then, in the ceremony, go through a symbolic rebirth. They are "born" or "reborn" into a new identity the two participants have chosen. Each of the participants will each write out their contribution to the covenant and this written document will be the same as the last will and testament that is enacted after the death of the writer of the will.

DEATH: The two being joined together into one, each make out a will as what will belong to the other upon death, the death that will take place during the ceremony is symbolic because animals will be sacrificed and the animals' deaths take the place of the persons being joined together. After each makes out their will, they then discuss at length with the other exactly what each side is gain from the covenant. The normal time from the decision to enter into covenant to the ceremony is about one year.

When two individuals are joined in covenant, they may choose to take one last name to show their common identity. In almost every instance when two families are joined together by covenant, they choose one common last name or they put their last names together and place a hyphen between the names.

Covenant in the Hebrew language means a "cut-where-blood-flows." The blood was the seal of the covenant. The purpose of covenant was to join two persons/families in a permanent relationship that had no way out. Contracts and agreements have been recorded back to the most ancient of times. The ruins of Summer, the pre-Babylonian Empire that ruled the Tigris and Euphrates Valley, have yielded stone contracts for harvests of wheat, rye and barley. No argument can be made that the people were too unsophisticated to have contracts and that is why they entered into so many covenants.

Marriage is the closest agreement to the blood covenant in modern society, and marriage is today, closer to a contract than a covenant.[423]

The blood means *death* if you break the covenant:

*18 "So even the... first covenant... was not inaugurated and ratified and put in force without the shedding of blood. 19 For when every command of the (Torah) had been read out by (Moshe) to all the people, he took the blood of slain calves and goats, together with water and scarlet wool and with a bunch of hyssop, and sprinkled both the Book [the roll of the (Torah) and covenant] itself and all the people, 20 Saying these words: This is the blood that seals and ratifies the... covenant which (Yah) commanded [me to deliver to] you.[424] 21 And in the same way he sprinkled with the blood both the tabernacle and all the [sacred] vessels and appliances used in [divine] worship. 22 [In fact] under the (Torah) almost everything is purified by means of blood, and without the shedding of blood there is neither release from sin and its guilt nor the remission of the due and merited punishment for sins."* [(Hebrews 9:18-22 | Amplified Bible) Hebraically Revised]

Another name of a blood covenant is a "blood oath." The symbolism of the blood is simple—"if you break this covenant you will die." In covenants between human beings,

---

[423] http://home.comcast.net/~kendelany/Phila/CovenantWeb.html
[424] 6 And Mosheh took half the blood and put it in basins, and half the blood he sprinkled on the altar. 7 And he took the Book of the Covenant and read in the hearing of the people. And they said, "All that יהוה has spoken we shall do, and obey." 8 And Mosheh took the blood and sprinkled it on the people, and said, "See, the blood of the covenant which יהוה has made with you concerning all these Words." (Exodus 24:6-8)

this simply meant that if the one party broke the covenant, it was the right and obligation of the other party to kill the offending party—that simple.

That remains the meaning of covenant today—this was why Yahooshua had to die such a brutal death to take our place because of our sins.

In Genesis 15, we read of Yah entering into covenant with Abram whom He renamed Abraham. Abram slaughtered some animals and the Spirit of Yah walked between the halves of the animals in the blood in order to consummate the covenant.

Cutting an animal in two and walking between the halves was a common way of cutting covenant in those days. Part of the symbolism was "If you break this covenant, I will slaughter you like this animal."[425]

Yehovah tells Jeremiah when this Covenant was made; the very same one Daniel 9:26 is referring to. Those who did not and would not keep it were going to pay for not doing so with their very own lives.

> *13 Thus said יהוה the Elohim of Yisra'el, "I Myself made a covenant with your fathers in the day that I brought them out of the land of Mitsrayim, out of the house of bondage, saying, 14 'At the end of seven years each one should set free his Hebrew brother, who has been sold to him. And when he has served you six years, you shall let him go free from you.' But your fathers did not obey Me nor incline their ear. 15 And you recently turned and did what was right in My eyes, each man proclaiming release to his neighbor. And you made a covenant before Me in the house which is called by My Name. 16 But you turned back and profaned My Name, and each one of you took back his male and female slaves, whom he had set free, at their pleasure, and brought them into subjection, to be your male and female slaves." 17 Therefore,*

---

[425] http://tinyurl.com/af7efg2

> *thus said יהוה, "You have not obeyed Me in proclaiming release, each one to his brother and each one to his neighbor. See, I am proclaiming release to you," declares יהוה, "to the sword, to the pestilence, and to the scarcity of food! And I shall make you a horror to all reigns of the earth. 18 And I shall give the men who are transgressing My covenant, who have not established the words of the covenant which they made before Me, when they cut the calf in two and passed between the parts of it: 19 the heads of Yehudah, and the heads of Yerushalayim, the eunuchs, and the priests, and all the people of the land who passed between the parts of the calf. 20 And I shall give them into the hand of their enemies and into the hand of those who seek their life. And their corpses shall be for food to the birds of the heavens and the beasts of the earth."* (Jeremiah 34:13-20)

What Daniel 9:26 is telling us is that Israel, the anointed—all 12 Tribes—which include the State of Israel, the U.S.A., the U.K. and her Commonwealth, will be cut off, cut down, destroyed and utterly consumed.

When you break any kind of blood covenant, you pay for breaking it with your very life. What you are, in fact, saying is this: "May I pay with my life if this covenant is broken."

This Covenant that Daniel 9 is speaking of is the one from Mount Sinai. We read how Moses sprinkled the blood of this Covenant upon the people *after* they had unanimously agreed to keep it. After this, the leaders of Israel then ate a meal with Yehovah all in accordance with the making of a Blood Covenant.

> *1 And to Mosheh He said, "Come up to יהוה, you and Aharon, Nadab and Abihu, and seventy of the elders of Yisra'el, and you shall bow yourselves from a distance. 2 But Mosheh shall draw near to יהוה by himself, and let them not draw near, nor let the people go up with him." 3 And Mosheh came and related to the people all the Words of יהוה and all the right-rulings. And all the people answered with one voice*

> and said, "All the Words which יהוה has spoken we shall do."
> 4 And Mosheh wrote down all the Words of יהוה, and rose up early in the morning, and built an altar at the foot of the mountain, and twelve standing columns for the twelve tribes of Yisra'el. 5 And he sent young men of the children of Yisra'el, and they offered burnt offerings and slaughtered peace slaughterings of bulls to יהוה. 6 And Mosheh took half the blood and put it in basins, and half the blood he sprinkled on the altar. 7 And he took the Book of the Covenant and read in the hearing of the people. And they said, "All that יהוה has spoken we shall do, and obey." 8 And Mosheh took the blood and sprinkled it on the people, and said, "See, the blood of the covenant which יהוה has made with you concerning all these Words." 9 And Mosheh went up, also Aharon, Nadab, and Abihu, and seventy of the elders of Yisra'el, 10 and they saw the Elohim of Yisra'el, and under His feet like a paved work of sapphire stone, and like the heavens for brightness. 11 Yet He did not stretch out His hand against the chiefs of the children of Yisra'el! And they saw Elohim, and they ate and drank. (Exodus 24:1-11)

But there is more. Many of you who claim to be followers of Yehshua are *also* under a binding Blood Covenant with Him. At the Last Supper, the day before the Passover Lamb was to be killed, Yehshua sat and ate with His disciples and they also drank the wine. And what did Yehshua say of this night?

> 26 And as they were eating, יהושע took bread, and having blessed, broke and gave it to the taught ones and said, "Take, eat, this is My body." 27 And taking the cup, and giving thanks, He gave it to them, saying, "Drink from it, all of you. 28 For this is My blood, that of the renewed covenant, which is shed for many for the forgiveness of sins." (Matthew 26:26-28)

This entailed everything the ceremony of the ancient Blood Covenant entailed. And it was not completed until the next day when Yehshua was killed. Read about the symbolism of this event by John D. Keyser:

### The Blood On the Ground!

How, then, did the Messiah die? HOW did He shed His precious blood for humankind?

During the Passover Seder the shed blood of the Messiah is emphasized time and time again. Did the blood our Savior lost while being SCOURGED by the Romans qualify for our atonement? True, He probably lost quite a bit of blood during this ordeal; but the Old Testament shows that His blood had to be shed at the PLACE OF HIS DEATH!

The sacrifice of the RED HEIFER clearly points to this. During this ceremony, the Red Heifer, which PREFIGURED THE MESSIAH, was taken EAST from the Temple in Jerusalem, across the arched bridge over the Kidron Valley, to the MIPHKAD ALTAR located on the slopes of the Mount of Olives. (For further details, read our article, *Just Where In Jerusalem Did Our Savior Die?*) Here it was killed and the BLOOD SPRINKLED SEVEN TIMES ON THE GROUND before the east entrance of the Temple. Obviously, the scourging the Messiah received did NOT fulfill this, because it occurred within the city—WITHIN THE CAMP.

What about the blood released from the Messiah's hands and feet when He was nailed to the tree? Would this qualify? A recent article published by the *Journal of the American Medical Association* (March 21st, 1986) shows that VERY LITTLE BLOOD was released by the crucifixion itself: "Although scourging may have resulted in considerable blood loss, crucifixion per se was a RELATIVELY BLOODLESS PROCEDURE, since no major arteries, other than PERHAPS the deep plantar arch, pass through the favored anatomic sites of transfixion."

Ernest L. Martin verifies this:

It has always been a mystery why so much EMPHASIS is given in the New Testament to the SPILLING OF CHRIST'S BLOOD, while in normal crucifixions, LITTLE BLOOD EVER REACHED THE GROUND. Only a SMALL AMOUNT of blood would ordinarily have issued from Christ's wounds in His hands or feet while He was hanging on the tree (the blood that came forth by use of the spear WOULD NOT COUNT in a theological sense because that occurred AFTER HIS DEATH).[426]

What, *then*, occurred to the Messiah, while He was hanging on the tree, that would FULFILL the sacrifice of the Red Heifer—which PREFIGURED His own death?

**The Marring of the Front of the Messiah's Body**

Remember that Pontius Pilate was ASTONISHED the Messiah had died so early—BEFORE the two robbers crucified with Him. SOMETHING ELSE caused the Messiah to die more quickly, and it was this "something" which fulfilled the sacrifice of the Red Heifer.

Notice Isaiah 53:5-6:

But He was WOUNDED for our transgressions, He was BRUISED for our INIQUITIES; the chastisement for our peace was upon Him, and by His STRIPES we are healed. We all, like sheep, have gone astray; we have turned, every one, to his own way; and the Lord has LAID ON HIM the INIQUITY of us all.

In the margin of the *New King James Bible*, published by Thomas Nelson (1983), the following words are given an ALTERNATE translation, as follows: "Wounded," PIERCED THROUGH; "bruised," CRUSHED; "stripes," BLOWS THAT CUT IN; and "laid on Him," CAUSED TO LAND ON HIM. Using these ALTERNATE words

---

[426] *Secrets of Golgotha*, p. 202.

in the above verses we get this: "But He was PIERCED THROUGH for our transgressions, He was CRUSHED for our iniquities; the chastisement for our peace was upon Him, and by His BLOWS THAT CUT IN we are healed. We all, like sheep, have gone astray; we have turned, everyone, to his own way; and the Lord has CAUSED TO LAND ON HIM the iniquity of us all." The phrase "pierced through for our transgressions" obviously refers to the CRUCIFIXION process itself, while "blows that cut in" must refer to the SCOURGING Yeshua received.

But what about the phrase "CRUSHED for our iniquities?" If we couple this with the last phrase (both verses are talking about "our iniquities"), we can readily see that whatever CRUSHED OR BRUISED our Savior was (also) CAUSED TO LAND ON HIM! Now, WHAT could that be? Let's look at Isaiah 52:14: "Just as many were astonished at you, so His VISAGE WAS MARRED more than any man, and His FORM more than the sons of men; so shall HE SPRINKLE many nations." Here we see His face and His body were MARRED and He SPRINKLED His blood for "many nations."

According to **Strong's Exhaustive Concordance**, the Hebrew word for "marred" is *"moshchath,"* meaning "disfigurement: corruption, marred" (#4893). This word comes from *"shachath,"* a word that can mean "BATTER." It is easy to deduce that the Messiah's FACE AND BODY were disfigured BY BATTERING. WHAT caused this battering?

Another clue can be gleaned from Psalm 22, which also highlights the suffering of the Messiah: "They pierced My hands and My feet; I CAN COUNT ALL MY BONES. They look and stare at Me." Think about this a minute. This "battering" that so marred the face and body of the Messiah by "crushing" or "bruising" had to have occurred ON THE FRONT OF HIS BODY! How *else* could He "count all [his] bones" that were exposed by whatever was "CAUSED TO LAND ON HIM?!"

Consider this: the Messiah's FACE and the FRONT PART OF HIS BODY could NOT have been so marred by the scourging He received! To undergo the scourging, He was tied to a large flogging post THAT COVERED, AND THEREBY PROTECTED, THE FRONT PART OF HIS BODY from the Roman whip! Also, the face was NOT flogged. The report in the *Journal of the American Medical Association* explains this: "For scourging, the man was stripped of his clothing, and his hands were tied to an upright post. The BACK, BUTTOCKS, AND LEGS were flogged either by two soldiers (lictors) or by one who alternated positions." Even Isaiah 50:6 shows it was the BACK PART of the Messiah that received the whipping: "I gave MY BACK to those who struck Me."

Another point to consider is the SPRINKLING of the Messiah's blood. To fulfill the SACRIFICE OF THE RED HEIFER, our Savior was crucified FACING WEST toward the Temple and the Holy of Holies; and His blood was sprinkled on the ground BEFORE the Temple—BETWEEN Himself and the Temple. This, in (and of) itself, ELIMINATES SCOURGING as the agent responsible for the shedding of His atoning blood. The blood obviously had to come from the FRONT OF HIS BODY—AND AT THE SCENE OF THE CRUCIFIXION! So WHAT was it that so BATTERED AND BRUISED the front of the Messiah's body?

### The Key To the Enigma!

The Book of John contains the key:

As soon as the chief priests and their officials saw Him [the Messiah], they shouted, "Crucify! Crucify!" But Pilate answered, "You take Him and crucify Him. As for me, I find no basis for a charge against Him." The Jews insisted, [saying] "WE HAVE A LAW, AND ACCORDING TO THAT LAW HE MUST DIE because He claimed to be the Son of God." (John 19:7)

What was this LAW the Jews were talking about? Leviticus 24:16 reveals the answer: "And he that BLASPHEMES the name of the Lord, he shall surely be put to death, and all the congregation shall certainly STONE HIM: as well as the stranger, as he that is born in the land, when he blasphemes the name of the Lord, shall be put to death." The ***Acts of Pilate***[427] (a 4th-century apocryphal work) contains verses PARALLELING John 19:7 that irrefutably prove the Jews were indeed referring to the Law in Leviticus 24:16.

In these verses, Pilate could not see any blasphemy in the utterance of Yeshua:

If this word is blasphemy, take Him, bring Him into *your* synagogue, and JUDGE HIM ACCORDING TO *YOUR* LAW. The Jews answered Pilate: "It is contained in our Law, that if a man sins against a man, he must receive forty strokes save one, BUT HE WHO BLASPHEMES AGAINST GOD MUST BE STONED." Pilate said to them: "Take Him yourselves and punish Him as you wish."

THE REASON THE FRONT PART OF THE MESSIAH'S FACE AND BODY WAS SO "CRUSHED" AND "BRUISED" BY OBJECTS THAT WERE "CAUSED TO LAND ON HIM" WAS BECAUSE HE WAS STONED IN ACCORDANCE WITH THE LAW OF MOSES!

Was the Messiah accused of blasphemy? Indeed He *was*! Notice Matthew 26:63-66 (below):

*The high priest said to him, "I charge you under oath by the living God: Tell us if you are the Christ, the Son of God." "Yes, it is as you say," Jesus replied. "But I say to all of you: In the*

---

[427] *The Acts of Pilate*, **Vol.** or **Ch.** IV, pp.3-4

*future you will see the Son of Man sitting at the right hand of the Mighty One and coming on the clouds of heaven."* Then the high priest tore his clothes and said, *"HE HAS SPOKEN BLASPHEMY! Why do we need any more witnesses?: Look, now you HAVE HEARD THE BLASPHEMY. What do you think?" "HE IS WORTHY OF DEATH,"* they answered.

And what was the PENALTY for blasphemy? STONING!

Ernest Martin notes, in his book, ***Secrets of Golgotha***, that this was NOT the first time the Jews tried to stone Him:

During the time of Christ's ministry, many of the people who did not like His teachings had tried to carry out this Mosaic Law against Him SEVERAL TIMES. "Then they took up STONES to cast at Him: but Jesus hid Himself, and went out of the Temple, going throughout the midst of them, and so passed by." (John 8:59) "Then the Jews TOOK UP STONES AGAIN TO STONE HIM. Jesus answered them, "Many good works have I showed you from my Father; for which of those works do you STONE ME?" The Jews answered Him, saying, "For a good work we STONE you not; but FOR BLASPHEMY; and because you, being a man, make yourself God." (John 10:31-33) The fact is, TIME AND TIME AGAIN, the authorities were trying to KILL HIM BY STONING. "His disciples (said) unto Him, 'Master, the Jews of late sought TO STONE YOU; and go you [to Judea] again?'" (John 11:8). It is made clear in the Gospel record that the people who were hostile to Christ were looking for EVERY OPPORTUNITY TO STONE HIM FOR HIS BLASPHEMY (as they considered it). And, THEY FINALLY GOT THEIR WISH when they went to Pilate and said: "We have a law, AND BY THAT LAW HE OUGHT TO DIE." (John 19:7)[428]

Reading through the Gospel of John, it becomes readily apparent the Jews were *indeed* out to kill Yeshua by

---

[428] *Secrets of Golgotha*, p. 188

STONING from an early date. The first mention of the Jews plotting to kill Him is found in (John) 5:18 (below):

"For this reason the Jews tried all the harder TO KILL HIM; not only was He breaking the Sabbath, but He was even calling God His own Father, MAKING HIMSELF EQUAL WITH GOD."

In the eyes of the religious authorities, this amounted to BLASPHEMY—the worst crime imaginable! And, as we have seen, the Law of Moses required the penalty of STONING for blasphemy!

Later on, in (John) 7:1, we find this statement:

"After this, Jesus went around Galilee, PURPOSELY staying away from Judea BECAUSE THE JEWS THERE WERE WAITING TO TAKE HIS LIFE."

And how were they planning to take His life? BY STONING!

Now notice (John) 7:30 (below):

"At this they tried to seize Him, but no one laid a hand on Him, BECAUSE HIS TIME [HOUR] HAD NOT YET COME."

What "time" is John talking about? The "time" for the Messiah TO BE KILLED—to be sacrificed according to the preordained schedule of His Father!

We see this again in John 8:20 (below):

"Yet no one seized Him, BECAUSE HIS TIME HAD NOT YET COME." The "time" for the Messiah to die and fulfill ALL the Old Testament prophecies pertaining to Himself had not yet arrived!

In (John) 8:58, we see the Jews becoming so upset they tried to stone Him on the spot!

"I tell you the truth," Yeshua answered, "before Abraham was born, I Am!" At this, THEY PICKED UP STONES TO STONE HIM, but Yeshua hid Himself, slipping away from the Temple guards.

In (John) 10:30-33, 39, it is PLAINLY revealed the Jews were trying to STONE HIM FOR BLASPHEMY:

"I and the Father are one." Again the Jews PICKED UP STONES TO STONE HIM, but Jesus said to them, "I have shown you many great miracles from the Father. For which of these do you STONE me?" "We are not STONING you for any of these," replied the Jews, "but for BLASPHEMY, because you, a mere man, CLAIM TO BE GOD." Again they tried to seize Him, but He escaped their grasp.

The disciples became very concerned and were aghast when Yeshua determined to return to Judea: "Then He said to His disciples, 'Let us go back to Judea.' 'But Rabbi,' they said, 'a short while ago the Jews tried to STONE you, and yet you are going back there?'" (John 11:7).

(Yet) the Messiah knew exactly what He was doing—His "time" had arrived and the events were to move inexorably toward the conclusion of His ministry and His life.

Putting all this together, we can CLEARLY see the authorities were out to STONE the Messiah FOR BLASPHEMY, and from an early date. But they were not permitted to carry out their plan UNTIL THE MESSIAH'S TIME HAD ARRIVED—the time set aside at the end of a long series of events that had to be fulfilled before the Son of God could be offered up on our behalf. And when that time arrived, the Jews WERE NO LONGER HELD BACK FROM STONING

THE MESSIAH FOR WHAT THEY CONSIDERED TO BE BLASPHEMY!

Haim Cohn came to the same conclusion! Notice what he says:

Two incidents, reported only in John, are often cited to prove JEWISH ENMITY against Jesus: they are INCIDENTS OF STONING, when that animus took violent form. When they heard Him say in the Temple—of all places—that He had been before Abraham, the Jews "took up stones to cast at Him" (John 8:59); and again, when He proclaimed that He and God, His father, were one, "the Jews took up stones again to stone Him" (John 10:31)... (yet) when Jesus had spoken and taught in the Temple, "no man laid hands on Him, for His hour WAS NOT YET COME" (John 7:30; John 8:20). How then can it be that, though HIS HOUR WAS NOT YET COME and no man could lay hands on Him, THE JEWS STONED HIM? If His hour was not yet come, why did they seek to take Him, and He had to escape out of their hands? (John 10:39)

The words "for His hour was not yet come" carry a DOUBLE MEANING. On the one hand, they PREPARE THE GROUND FOR WHAT WILL HAPPEN WHEN THE HOUR COMES: then, it appears, THE JEWS WILL BE FREE FROM ALL INHIBITIONS AND GIVE FULL PLAY TO THEIR MURDEROUS AGGRESSIONS. On the other, there is a hint of the predestination of JESUS' FATE, as if it were not the hostility and contumaciousness [rebelliousness, stubborn disobedience] of the Jews which DETERMINED THE EVENT [STONING], but *solely* the will of God, Who appointed His *own* time and CHOSE HIS *OWN* INSTRUMENTS.[429]

There is absolutely no doubt that this is what the Jewish authorities were petitioning Pilate for permission to do.

---

[429] *The Trial and Death of Jesus*, p. 64.

And what did Pilate do? "Pilate said, 'Take Him yourselves and JUDGE HIM BY YOUR OWN LAW.'" (John 18:31) In saying this, Pilate permitted the Jews to execute Yeshua ACCORDING TO THE BIBLICAL LAW. This was an UNCOMMON allowance because it subjected the Messiah to suffer BOTH the Roman method of execution (crucifixion) for sedition and treason, and the scriptural (Mosaic) execution (STONING) for blasphemy, thus fulfilling all the Old Testament prophecies. To die for ALL of us—BOTH Jew *and* Gentile—He had to DIE ACCORDING TO *BOTH* JEWISH *AND* GENTILE LAW!

The Apostle Paul, in the sixth chapter of Galatians, affirms that our Savior died as a result of STONING. This is what he claims: "Finally, let no one cause me trouble, FOR I BEAR ON MY BODY THE MARKS [SCARS] OF JESUS." (Galatians 6:17) Obviously, these "marks" could NOT be the result of crucifixion—Paul was never crucified; and, if he had been, he would NEVER have lived to tell the tale! Paul's scars, therefore, were the result of something else.

The Book of Acts reveals that Paul was STONED about four years prior to his statement in the New Testament. The very first act of persecution against Paul that's recorded in the New Testament was STONING—see Acts 14:19-20. During this incidence, which occurred in Galatia, Paul was STONED and left for dead. By a miracle from YEHOVAH God, he got up and walked away from it, but suffered for many years as a result of the terrible punishment his body received.

### Our Savior Was Blinded!

Just like the Messiah, Paul's face and EYES were the PRIME TARGETS of those hurling the stones. Paul mentions this in Galatians 4:13-15:

And you know that on account of a PHYSICAL INFIRMITY [Gr. WEAKNESS OF THE FLESH], I preached the Gospel to you formerly; and though I was a trial to you IN MY FLESH, you did not reject or despise me; but you received me as an angel of God, EVEN AS CHRIST JESUS. Where then is your self congratulation? For I bear you witness that, if possible, you would have PLUCKED OUT YOUR VERY EYES AND GIVEN THEM TO ME.

It was to the HEAD AND EYES that the stones were mainly thrown, especially during the initial phases of the execution (see Mark 12:4); and remarkably, Paul indicates, in these verses, that his principal affliction had SOMETHING TO DO WITH HIS EYES!

Ernest Martin elaborates on this:

Since it was common for hostile people to hurl stones at the FACE of a person, it can readily be understood why such a stoning could have ALMOST BLINDED Paul. He wrote with LARGE ALPHABETIC LETTERS (Galatians 6:11), and this may well indicate that he had difficulty seeing clearly. The lacerations had apparently so injured Paul that there was permanent damage TO HIS EYES AND FACE. When he told the Galatians that "my trial in my flesh ye despised not, nor rejected," it STRONGLY implies that his wounds (even four years after his stoning) were ostensibly so bad and unattractive that the common thing for people to do would be to reject him from being in their company. The Galatians, however, did *not* reject him, but treated him like an angel of God, "EVEN AS CHRIST JESUS" (BECAUSE THEY KNEW THAT CHRIST WAS *ALSO* STONED AND BLINDED). Since there were no plastic surgeons to improve Paul's outward appearance, this is, no doubt, why Paul made a special point in telling the Galatians that he BORE THE SCARS OF JESUS IN HIS BODY (Galatians 6:17). Those SCARS, no doubt, CAME FROM THE WOUNDS HE SUFFERED DURING HIS STONING.[430]

---

[430] *Secrets of Golgotha*, p. 198.

YES, THE MESSIAH WAS STONED IN THE FACE AND BLINDED!

Notice Psalm 38, which is a prophecy of HOW the Messiah would have to suffer:

"For thine arrows [piercers—to chop into, pierce or sever] stick fast in Me, and thy hand presseth Me sore… My heart panteth, My strength faileth me: AS FOR THE LIGHT OF MINE EYES, IT ALSO IS GONE FROM ME." (Psalm 38:2, 10)

Psalm 69:3, which is FULL of references to the sufferings of the Messiah, also indicates this! "I am weary with my crying; my throat is dry; MY EYES FAIL while I wait for my God."

These verses show that the Messiah WAS TO BE BLINDED; and there can hardly be a doubt that sometime during the six hours the Messiah hung on the tree, constantly being struck by stones, (that) some of them hit His eyes and blinded Him!

**Mangled Beyond Recognition!**

His "visage" and His "form"—the front parts of his body—were MARRED BEYOND RECOGNITION. How do you account for the fact that Mary couldn't recognize her Master at the tomb?

They [the angels] asked her, "Woman, why are you crying?" "They have taken my Lord away," she said, "and I don't know where they have put Him." At this, she turned around and saw Jesus standing there, BUT SHE DID NOT REALIZE THAT IT WAS JESUS. "Woman," He said, "why are you crying? Who is it you are looking for?" THINKING HE WAS THE GARDENER, she said, "Sir, if you have carried Him away, tell me where you have put Him, and I will get Him." Jesus said to her, "Mary." She turned toward Him and cried out in Aramaic, "Rabboni!" (which means teacher). (John 20:13-16)

The Messiah's flesh was so mangled and His body so disfigured that even a close friend could not recognize Him! "His visage was so marred more than any man" (Isaiah 52:14). For six long hours our Savior was tormented by volleys of small, sharp, flint stones (such as are found on the Mount of Olives to this day) hurled at the front parts of His naked body while He was nailed to the tree—facing the East Gate of the Temple and the great curtain that hung from the eastern portal. These stones struck His face, His midsection and His legs, breaking the skin and dislodging the flesh—crushing and bruising and tearing, but without the force to break His bones. No wonder the Messiah was marred more than any man!

**The Seder Symbolism**

The Passover Seder or service has long puzzled scholars. They have been unable to see how breaking off pieces of matzos (unleavened bread) could in any way represent the body of the Messiah at His crucifixion.

Ernest Martin explains:

When Christ instituted the Lord's Supper on the eve of His crucifixion, He took bread and BROKE it and He said this BREAKING was like His body WOULD BE BROKEN for them (Matthew 26:26). He spoke of the BREAKING of His body in the same context as the wine which represented His BLOOD which was shed at His crucifixion for the remission of sins... Since the New Testament specifically states that NO BONES in His body would be broken (John 19:36), many scholars can see no reference whatsoever to the death of Christ in the BREAKING of the unleavened bread... There are a number of Greek manuscripts and writings of several Church Fathers which provide a comment of explanation to the text of 1 Corinthians 11:24 concerning the BREAKING of the bread at the Lord's Supper and they associated it with the BREAKING of Christ's body at His crucifixion. They added their comments that the bread represented Christ's body: "WHICH IS BROKEN FOR YOU"[431] THIS MEANS THAT THERE WERE EARLY BELIEFS THAT THE "BROKEN BREAD" IN THE CEREMONY OF THE LORD'S SUPPER DID INDEED REPRESENT THE "BROKEN BODY" OF CHRIST AT THE TIME OF HIS CRUCIFIXION…

Thus, we have the beliefs of early Christians and the prophecy of Isaiah itself that Christ's body would *indeed* be BROKEN like BREAKING OFF pieces of unleavened bread. But the scourging of the soldiers before His crucifixion or the simple act of (the) crucifixion itself COULD NOT ACCOUNT FOR SUCH BREAKING OFF OF PIECES OF HIS BODY. But the act of STONING would fit the description precisely. The hurling of small and sharp stones at Christ's body would tear away pieces of His flesh ever so slowly until, after about six hours of such treatment, He would have been hanging on the tree of crucifixion as a person whose VISAGE AND FORM would have been so marred that He would not have resembled a normal human any longer. This is how Isaiah 52:14 describes the Suffering Servant, whom all the New Testament writers identified with Christ Jesus, and I see no reason for not believing it. THIS IS JUST ANOTHER EVIDENCE THAT CHRIST MET HIS DEATH BY STONING (His body torn to shreds in its frontal areas) and that He DID NOT DIE BY CRUCIFIXION ALONE.[432]

The next time you observe the Passover Seder remember how, when you BREAK the unleavened bread, our Passover Lamb was TORMENTED for hours by the constant barrage of sharp, flint-like stones that bruised… crushed… gouged and BROKE OFF pieces of His flesh, SPRINKLING His

---

[431] *Greek New Testament*, UBS, p. 604
[432] *Secrets of Golgotha*, pp. 189-190

atoning blood on the ground before the presence of his Father's Shekinah Glory in the Temple.

Remember, the sacrifice of the Red Heifer, which PREFIGURED the Messiah's death so accurately, (it) did so right down to the very LOCATION of His death!

Remember that the Messiah died for the ENTIRE human race—you *and* me, Gentile *and* Jew (Israelite)—and in so doing, had to die ACCORDING TO GENTILE *AND* JEWISH LAW. Crucifixion satisfied the Gentile (Roman) Law and the STONING satisfied Jewish (Mosaic) Law. Without the stoning, the Messiah would have died for Gentiles ONLY! Remember that!

**Jewish & Other Evidence**

Are there other sources of information that show the Messiah died as a result of STONING? Indeed there are. The early Jewish people have long known that this was *the way* the Messiah was put to death. The ***Talmud*** (body of Jewish civil and religious law) has an account of His very death:

On the eve of Passover, Yeshua the Nazarean WAS HANGED. For forty days before the execution took place, a herald went forth and cried, "He is going forth TO BE STONED because He has practiced sorcery and enticed Israel to apostasy. Anyone who can say anything in His favor let him come forward and plead on His behalf." But since nothing was brought forward in His favor, HE WAS HANGED on the eve of Passover.[433]

The word "hanged" in this instance does NOT refer to hanging by the neck, but to being "attached" or "transfixed" to a tree. This historical reference in the Talmud shows that the Jews were aware that Yeshua the Messiah was actually STONED WHILE HANGING on the tree of crucifixion.

---

[433] *Sanhedrin*, 43b

It is interesting to note that the Jewish authorities in Jerusalem had been PUBLICLY PROCLAIMING (during the forty days *before* the Passover in A.D. 31) that Yeshua deserved to be STONED for His teachings and statements. The Book of John shows that the apostles were well aware of this pronouncement and constantly reminded the Messiah of it. Notice John 11:8 once again: "But Rabbi," they said, "a short while ago the Jews tried to STONE you, and yet you are going back there [to Judea]?"

(John) 11:55-57 shows that the chief priests and Pharisees had issued orders for His arrest: "When it was almost time for the Jewish Passover, many went up from the country to Jerusalem for their ceremonial cleansing before the Passover. They kept looking for Jesus, and as they stood in the Temple area, they asked one another, 'What do you think? Isn't He coming to the Feast at all?' But the chief priests and Pharisees HAD GIVEN ORDERS that if anyone found out where Jesus was, he should report it so that they might arrest Him." And true to the words of the *Talmud*, they had Yeshua STONED while hanging on the tree of crucifixion in order to fulfill the Law of Moses regarding a person who BLASPHEMED against YEHOVAH God.

In the book **Rabbinic Essays**,[434] we find FURTHER EVIDENCE our Savior died as a result of stoning. Recalling a Jewish *Baraita* (Jewish teaching that was not codified when the first part of the *Talmud* was put together), the author states that the Messiah met His death BY STONING and NOT by crucifixion *alone*. After a long discussion on this subject, the *Baraita* says: "He [the Messiah] is going out TO BE STONED," followed by, "they hanged Him." () This early Jewish tradition PLAINLY SHOWS that our Passover Lamb was indeed STONED TO DEATH while hanging on the "accursed tree."

In Luke 23:27-28 we read:

---

[434] Rabbinic Essays by Jason Z. Lauterback, pp. 494-497

And a great multitude of the people followed Him [to Golgotha], and WOMEN WHO ALSO MOURNED AND LAMENTED HIM. But Jesus, turning to them, said, "Daughters of Jerusalem, do not weep for Me, but weep for yourselves and for your children."

Mark notes what happened when the Messiah and the women arrived at the execution site: "Then they gave Him WINE MINGLED WITH MYRRH to drink, but He did not take it." (Mark 15:23) The "wine mingled with myrrh" was given to the condemned to deaden the pain, and was part of an old Jewish custom.

Haim Cohn explains this:

From Luke we know that "there followed Him a great company of people, AND OF WOMEN, which also bewailed and lamented Him" (Luke 23:27), and they would of a surety have followed Him all the way to Golgotha. Combining both traditions [Luke 23:2, Mark 15:23], it may, I think, be permissible to infer that it was the WOMEN ACCOMPANYING JESUS on His way to execution, and attending Him in His last hours on the cross, who BROUGHT THE WINE AND BEGGED HIM TO DRINK: it was an ancient Jewish custom that a condemned man, when led to the place of execution, had to be given a DRAFT OF WINE WITH INCENSE IN IT, "in order that He may lose His mind," that is, become unconscious; and it was "the dear women of Jerusalem who volunteered and brought the wine" and offered it to Him.[435] This custom is told in the Talmud IN CONNECTION WITH CONVICTS ABOUT TO BE STONED... "the dear women of Jerusalem" saw to it that... a man ABOUT TO DIE BY STONING should be anesthetized against excess of pain.[436]

---

[435] B Sanhedrin, 43a
[436] *The Trial and Death of Jesus*, KTAV Publishing House, N.Y., 1977, pp. 217-218.

This custom passed into law, Maimonides (Jewish philosopher of the 12th-century) ruling that, when being led to his execution BY STONING, the convict had to be given a DRINK OF WINE WITH INCENSE, so that he may get intoxicated and insensible—and ONLY THEN was he to be STONED. (***Mishneh Torah***, *Hilkhot Sanhedrin 13, 2*). This is FURTHER PROOF the Messiah suffered according to the Mosaic Law AND Roman law!

Ernest Renan, one of the leading biographers of Yeshua during the nineteenth century, understood clearly that the Messiah had been STONED as He hung on the gallows or tree:

> And if ever a crime was that of a nation, it was the murder of Jesus. It was a "legal" murder, in the sense that its primary cause was THE LAW WHICH WAS THE VERY *SOUL* OF THE NATION. The MOSAIC LAW pronounced the death penalty for any attempt to CHANGE the established cult. Jesus, no doubt, attacked that cult and aspired to destroy it... Christianity has been intolerant; but intolerance is not essentially Christian. It is Jewish, in this sense that Judaism was the first to vest religion with a theory of the absolute, postulating that every reformer—EVEN THOUGH SUPPORTING HIS DOCTRINE WITH MIRACLES—MUST BE DRAGGED TO THE GALLOWS [TREE, CROSS] AND STONED BY ALL AND SUNDRY.[437]

### The Final Fulfillment

Once we realize that people were throwing sharp, flint-like stones (such as those found on the Mount of Olives) at Yeshua's naked body for almost SIX HOURS, we can easily understand WHY He died so quickly. Isaiah 52 and 53 were PERFECTLY fulfilled. His flesh was so TORN AWAY from the bones on the front part of His body that bystanders could hardly tell He was a human being. His flesh was so mangled

---

[437] ***La Vie de Jesus***, 8th ed., Paris, 1863, pp. 411-412.

and His body so DISFIGURED that it was almost impossible to recognize Him. "His VISAGE was so marred MORE than any man, and His FORM more than the sons of man." (Isaiah 52:14)

In the initial stages of the stoning the head received the brunt of the punishment; and there can be no doubt several of the stones at least struck His eyes and BLINDED Him, thus fulfilling Psalm 38.

His body was truly BROKEN FOR US; and it is this terrible stoning that we commemorate when we break the matzos during the Passover Seder. How much *MORE* MEANING the Passover service will have for us now that we understand this crucial truth about the death of our Passover Lamb!

The tremendous symbolism pictured by the sacrifice of the Red Heifer really comes to life when we see how the Messiah SPRINKLED His blood on the ground before the Sanctuary. And the only action that could sprinkle the blood on the ground in such a manner, was the STONING He received. THE MESSIAH DIED FOR US PRIMARILY AS A RESULT OF THE TERRIBLE STONING HE ENDURED AS HE HUNG ON THE TREE—THUS BECOMING AN ATONEMENT FOR BOTH JEW (ISRAELITE) AND GENTILE!

We should thank our Heavenly Father for giving up His only begotten Son; and thank our Lord and Savior for the SACRIFICE He made on our behalf so we can qualify to become members of the God family and inherit the entire universe. May YEHOVAH God help us to continually keep this in mind![438]

Daniel 9:26 is going to happen to those of us who have *not* kept the Ten Commandments as we agreed to keeping at Mount Sinai. Yet, many

---

[438] http://hope-of-israel.org/stonejes.htm, Hope of Israel Ministries (Ecclesia of YEHOVAH)

of you will say you are under the New Covenant and will not have to pay the price for failing or opting not to keep Yehovah's Commandments.

Yet Yehshua says:

> 17"Do not think that I came to destroy the Torah or the Prophets. I did not come to destroy but to complete. 18 For truly, I say to you, until the heaven and the earth pass away, one jot or one tittle shall by no means pass from the Torah until all be done. 19 Whoever, then, breaks one of the least of these commands, and teaches men so, shall be called least in the reign of the heavens; but whoever does and teaches them, he shall be called great in the reign of the heavens." (Matthew 5:17-19)

Yehshua Himself *also* said, "If you love Me, keep My Commandments." (John 14:15) We also read earlier that if you claim to love Yehshua and be one of His followers, then you are also going to be keeping the Father's Commandments—the very same ones the finger of Yehovah inscribed on tablets of stone and bestowed upon Moses from atop Mount Sinai.

> 21 "He who has My commandments and keeps them, he it is who loves Me. And he who loves Me shall be loved by My Father, and I will love him and will reveal Myself to him." (John 14:21)

> 24 "He who does not love Me does not keep My Words, and the Word which you hear is not Mine, but the Father's who sent Me." (John 14:24)

> 3 And by this we know that we have known Him, if we keep His commandments. 4 He who says, "I have known Him," and does not keep His commandments, is a liar, and the truth is not in him. 5 But whoever keeps His Word, truly in this one the love of God is perfected. By this we know that we are in Him. 6 He who says he abides in Him ought himself also to walk even as He walked. (1 John 2:3-6)

The Covenant inscribed in stone atop Mount Sinai was also going to be written on the hearts of men at a future time. This is the Covenant of which Yehshua made. The Law has *not* been done away with, but now is to be inscribed indelibly on the hearts and innermost being of all who call upon and believe upon Yehshua!

> *30 But each one shall die for his own crookedness—whoever eats sour grapes, his teeth shall be blunted. 31 "See, the days are coming," declares יהוה, "when I shall make a new covenant with the house of Yisra'el and with the house of Yehudah, 32 not like the covenant I made with their fathers in the day when I took them by the hand to bring them out of the land of Mitsrayim, My covenant which they broke, though I was a husband to them," declares יהוה. 33 "For this is the covenant I shall make with the house of Yisra'el after those days, declares יהוה: I shall put My Torah in their inward parts, and write it on their hearts. And I shall be their Elohim, and they shall be My people. 34 And no longer shall they teach, each one his neighbor, and each one his brother, saying, 'Know יהוה,' for they shall all know Me, from the least of them to the greatest of them," declares יהוה. "For I shall forgive their crookedness, and remember their sin no more." 35 Thus said יהוה, who gives the sun for a light by day, and the laws of the moon and the stars for a light by night, who stirs up the sea, and its waves roar— יהוה of hosts is His Name: 36 "If these laws vanish from before Me," declares יהוה, "then the seed of Yisra'el shall also cease from being a nation before Me forever." (Jeremiah 31:30-36)*

Again, when we look at what the Book of Hebrews has to say on the matter, we are reminded of the judgment that we stand to bring upon ourselves.

> *26 For if we sin purposely after we have received the knowledge of the truth, there no longer remains a slaughter offering for sins, 27 but some fearsome anticipation of judgment, and a fierce fire which is about to consume the opponents. 28 Anyone who has disregarded the Torah of*

> *Mosheh dies without compassion on the witness of two or three witnesses. 29 How much worse punishment do you think shall he deserve who has trampled the Son of Elohim underfoot, counted the blood of the covenant by which he was set apart as common, and insulted the Spirit of favor?* (Hebrews 10:26-29)

Even though you claim to be under the "New Covenant," you fail entirely to take into account the fact that the New Covenant is a RENEWED Covenant of Mount Sinai taking the same laws written on stone and transferring them, through the Holy Spirit, to being written and inscribed on your hearts. Therefore, if you do not and will not keep all Ten Commandments, then you too, can look forward to the very same judgment that will come upon those Daniel 9:26 is referring to if you are counted amongst those found breaking the Covenant agreement.

Let us again read the following verse in Daniel 9:

> *26 And after the sixty-two weeks Messiah shall be cut off and have naught.* (Daniel 9:26)

Here is what this is telling you and me one more time:

After sixty-two Shabua, or after the year 1996 (in the last Jubilee Cycle), Israel, the anointed of Yehovah, who agreed at Mount Sinai to the Covenant and then broke faith with Yehovah and, in like manner, those of us who came after who continue to break faith with Yehovah, will be cut off; that is, cut down and destroyed, so that they, utterly *perish* for having not kept the very same Torah that we agreed to at Mount Sinai; our marriage contract that we have broken.

Yes, we were redeemed and the Messiah paid the ultimate price at the tree when He was crucified in our stead. But this was for those of us who *repented* and *returned* to keeping that very same Torah that we had broken. It does not allow us to continue to not keep the Law now! Those of us who continue to break the Torah will have to pay the price of breaking the Blood Covenant of Mount Sinai with our very own lives! But those of us who repent have already had our sin debt paid for in full by Yehshua.

But we are not done with this verse yet. It also says:

- "Messiah shall be cut off and have naught."
- "Shall be cut off, but not for Himself" is from the *N.K.J.V.*
- "Will be cut off and have nothing" is from *C.J.B.*

But here is the *actual* meaning. Read it:

H369: אַיִן 'ayin ay'-yin

> As if from a primitive root meaning to be nothing or not exist; a non-entity; generally used as a negative particle: else, except, fail [father-] less, be gone, in [-curable], neither, never, no (where), none, nor (any, thing), not, nothing, to nought, past, un [-searchable], well-nigh, without, compare H370.

Israel is going to be cut off, cut down, destroyed and consumed. They will be as though they never existed. They will be no more; they will be fatherless. That is without our Father Yehovah.

What you're reading is that the State of Israel, *along with* the U.S.A. and the U.K., will be so utterly destroyed that they will be as if they had not existed. They will be wiped off the face of the Earth!!! They will be completely gone!

I have explained in detail in *The Prophecies of Abraham* how, 90% of the U.S.A., 90% of the U.K., 90% of Canada, 90% of Australia and 90% of the State of Israel will be, for all practical intents and purposes, gone entirely—or, in other words, 270 million Americans, 54,000,000 Britons, 27,000,000 Canadians, 22,000,000 Australians and over 1,000,000 Jews destroyed and killed

Assyria in the Bible is today known as the nation of Germany and it is by Germany, the rod of Yehovah that we must *all* pass under.

> *5 "Woe to Ashshur, the rod of My displeasure and the staff in whose hand is My displeasure. 6 Against a defiled nation I send him, and against the people of My wrath I command him to seize the spoil, to take the prey, and to tread them down like the mud of the streets."* (Isaiah 10:5-6)

But this rod has another job as well as we are told in Ezekiel. Only every tenth one will be saved. The rest will be destroyed.

> *33 "As I live," declares the Master יהוה, "do not I, with a mighty hand, with an outstretched arm, and with wrath poured out, reign over you? 34 And I shall bring you out from the peoples and gather you out of the lands where you are scattered, with a mighty hand, and with an outstretched arm, and with wrath poured out. 35 And I shall bring you into the wilderness of the peoples, and shall enter into judgment with you face to face there. 36 As I entered into judgment with your fathers in the wilderness of the land of Mitsrayim, so I shall enter into judgment with you," declares the Master יהוה. 37 "And I shall make you pass under the rod, and shall bring you into the bond of the covenant, 38 and purge the rebels from among you, and those who transgress against Me. From the land where they sojourn I bring them out, but they shall not come into the land of Yisra'ĕl. And you shall know that I am יהוה."* (Ezekiel 20:33-38)

We can go back to the times of Jacob to find out *why* this is the way it is—why today when we are in the time known as "Jacob's Trouble," of which only 10% will be saved out of it.

> *22 (T)hen this stone which I have set as a standing column shall be Elohim's house, and of all that You give me, I shall certainly give a tenth to You.* (Genesis 28:22)

Many think this is speaking of tithing and they use it to justify tithing to the church. But is this *really* what is being spoken of here? In the first half of the verse is the pillar stone upon which every King of Israel would come and be anointed as they vowed to keep the Torah in front of Yehovah. These kings came forth from the loins of Jacob. The tenth that Jacob was vowing here were of his descendants—a tenth part or 10%. Consequently, it is *this* 10% that we see being spared in the prophecy of Daniel.

I still have more information in this verse 26 for you to come to grips with on top of this terrible news I have just shared with you.

> *26 And the people of a coming prince shall destroy the city and the set-apart place. And the end of it is with a flood. And wastes are decreed, and fighting until the end.* (Daniel 9:26)

The people are the army of the prince and it is my strong opinion that this "prince" is the King of the North who is coming, who will destroy the city of Jerusalem. It is the one city these verses have been talking about.

But now we have a problem with the word being used to denote the sanctuary.

> The word is H6944: *ko'-desh*

> H6942: a *sacred* place or thing; rarely abstractly *sanctity*: —consecrated (thing), dedicated (thing), hallowed (thing), holiness, (X most) holy (X day, portion, thing), saint, sanctuary.

> H6942: *kaw-dash'*

> A primitive root: to *be* (causatively *make, pronounce* or *observe* as) *clean* (ceremonially or morally): appoint, bid, consecrate, dedicate, defile, hallow, (be, keep) holy (-er, place), keep, prepare, proclaim, purify, sanctify (-ied one, self), X wholly.

People presume this to be the Holy of Holies or the Temple in Jerusalem. And many assume that this means a new Temple is going to soon be rebuilt. But is this *really* what Daniel was being told?

It says this prince is going to destroy the city and "the holy." If it meant the Holy of Holies it would have said "Kadosh Kadosh." But it only says "the holy," which could mean "the saints" and this is *exactly* what one of the acceptable translations of this word *does* mean. Both the words, "saints" and "sanctified" are speaking of the anointed of Israel- all 12 tribes in these last days.

Young's Literal Translation has it as:

> *26 And after the sixty and two weeks, cut off is Messiah, and the city and the holy place are not his, the Leader who hath come doth destroy the people; and its end is with a flood, and until the end is war, determined are desolations.* (Daniel 9:26 YLT)

We read in Daniel of something that is troublesome and yet it supports what I am saying here. We read in Daniel 7 how this king wears out the saints and then in Daniel 8 how this king destroys the Holy people. We then read again in Revelation how this great power destroys the saints and also, in Revelation 17, how "she was drunk with the blood of the saints." So, to me, this verse in Daniel 9:26 is *not* speaking of the Holy of Holies being destroyed, it is speaking of *the saints* being destroyed. These are the "anointed" of Yehovah. Again, it does *not* say "Kadosh Kadosh" for Holy Place.

> *25 "... and it speaks words against the Most High, and it wears out the set-apart ones of the Most High, and it intends to change appointed times[1] and law[2], and they are given into its hand for a time and times and half a time.* [Footnotes: [1]This is another word for festivals. [2]Changing the law amounts to lawlessness. Read in 2 Thessalonians 2:3-12 about "the lawless one" and the "lawlessness" which would take over (indeed, it has already taken over!) in the set-apart place, and also about Messiah's judgment upon the lawless "prophets" in Matthew 7:23, and the lawless "believers" in Matthew 13:41! (Daniel 7:25)]

The saints are given into the hand of the Beast power until the Tribulation period; until the time when the woman who is Israel flees into the Wilderness.

> *23 And in the latter time of their rule, when the transgressors have filled up their measure, a sovereign, fierce of face and skilled at intrigues, shall stand up. 24 And his power shall be mighty, but not by his own power, and he shall destroy incredibly, and shall prosper and thrive, and destroy mighty men, and the set-apart people. 25 And through his skill, he shall make deceit prosper in his hand, and hold himself to be great in his heart, and destroy many who are at ease, and even stand against the Prince of princes—yet without hand he shall be broken.* (Daniel 8:23-25)

> *7 And it was given to him to fight with the set-apart ones and to overcome them. And authority was given to him over every tribe and tongue and nation. 8 And all those dwelling on the earth, whose names have not been written in the Book of Life of the slain Lamb, from the foundation of the world shall worship him. 9 If anyone has an ear, let him hear. 10 He who brings into captivity shall go into captivity, he who kills with the sword has to be killed with the sword. Here is the endurance and the belief of the set-apart ones.* (Revelation 13:7-10)

> *6 And I saw the woman, drunk with the blood of the set-apart ones, and with the blood of the witnesses of יהושע. And having seen her, I marveled—greatly marveled!* (Revelation 17:6)

If this word used here in Daniel 9:26 was speaking of the Holy of Holies, then it would seem that the word used for "sanctuary" would have been "Miq qedosh" and not "qedosh," which is what is used. The "Qedosh" in this verse is clearly speaking of the saints. The saints will be attacked and killed.

> Strong's 4720: מקדש **miqdash {mik-dawsh'}** or, מקדש **miqqedash (Exodus** 15:17) {mik-ked-awsh'} from 06942;

TWOT–1990f; n m A–sanctuary 69, holy place 3, chapel 1, hallowed part 1; 74 1) Sacred place, sanctuary, holy place 1a) Sanctuary 1a1) of the Temple 1a2) of the Tabernacle 1a3) of Ezekiel's Temple 1a4) of Jehovah.

There are a number of other verses we can look at in the Hebrew to be even surer of the true meaning of the word "qodesh."

In all of the following verses, saints is "qodesh":

> *2 And he said, "יהוה came from Sinai, and rose from Sĕʻîr for them. He shone forth from Mount Paran, and came with ten thousands of set-apart ones (H6944 ko desh Saints)—at His right hand a law of fire for them." 3 Indeed, He loves the peoples, all His set-apart ones (H6944 ko desh Saints) are in Your hand. And they, they sat down at Your feet, receiving Your Words.* (Deuteronomy 33:2-3)

> *41 And now, arise, O יהוה Elohim, to Your resting place, You and the ark of Your strength. Let Your priests, O יהוה Elohim, be robed with deliverance, and let Your kind ones rejoice in goodness.* (2 Chronicles 6:41)

> *1 Call out, please, is there anyone to answer you? And to which of the set-apart ones* (H6918 qâdôsh qâdôsh holy (One), saint) *would you turn?* (Job 5:1)

> *15 Look, He puts no trust in His set-apart ones,* (H6918 qâdôsh qâdôsh holy (One), saint) *and the heavens are not clean in His eyes.* (Job 15:15)

> *3 "As for the set-apart ones* (H6918 qâdôsh qâdôsh holy (One), saint.) *who are on the earth, they are the excellent ones, in whom is all my delight."* (Psalm 16:3)

> *12 "Ephrayim has surrounded Me with lying, and the house of Yisra'ĕl with deceit. But Yehuḏah is still wandering with*

*Ěl, and is true to the Set-apart One."* (Hosea 11:12) (H6918 qâdôsh qâdôsh holy (One), saint)

*5 "And you shall flee to the valley of My mountain—for the valley of the mountains reaches to Atsal. And you shall flee as you fled from the earthquake in the days of Uzziyah sovereign of Yehud̲ah." And* יהוה *my Elohim shall come—all the set-apart ones* (H6918 qâdôsh qâdôsh holy (One), saint) *with You.* (Zechariah 14:5)

There are more, but this is the short version of this list.

Now, to prove my point that Daniel is writing about the saints and *not* the sanctuary or Holy of Holies, let's look to Daniel himself who wrote of a sanctuary in other verses and did *not* use the word "qodesh." He used the word "miqdash," which tells us Daniel, in all certainty, knew which was which. If Daniel was speaking of the *Holy of Holies*, he used the word "miqdash." However, when he spoke of *the saints*, he used the word "qadosh."

The word for "sanctuary" is "miqdash," or Strong's #4720, as I have shown you above. The "miqdash" is the word "qodesh," but with a mem prefix.

Daniel uses this word "miqdash" for "sanctuary" in the following verses:

*11 It even exalted itself as high as the Prince of the host. And it took that which is continual away from Him, and threw down the foundation of His set-apart place.* (Daniel 8:11)

*17 And now, our Elohim, hear the prayer of Your servant, and his supplications, and for the sake of* יהוה *cause Your face to shine on Your set-apart place, which is laid waste.* (Daniel 9:17)

*31 And strong ones shall arise from him and profane the set-apart place, the stronghold, and shall take away that which is continual, and set up the abomination that lays waste.* (Daniel 11:31)

In Daniel 9:26, he most obviously did not use the word "miqdash," but "qodesh" and Daniel, as I have now sufficiently proven to you, knew the difference. He meant "qodesh" and *not* "miqdash." He meant "set-apart" and *not* "set-apart place." Daniel was talking about the saints, the people of Israel and *not* the Holy of Holies.

Daniel 8:13 is interesting because the first "qodesh" is translated as "saint" but the second "qodesh" is translated as "sanctuary" and yet, the word the translators have used is not the word for "sanctuary," at all, which is the word #4720:

> *13 Then I heard a certain holy one speaking, and another holy one said to that one who spoke, "Until when shall the vision last, concerning the daily sacrifice and the transgression that astounds, to give both the sanctuary and the host to be trampled?"* (Daniel 8:13)

Even in this verse then, when you understand the proper use of the word "qodesh," it is still referring to *"the saints; the entire host of the saints who are going to be trampled,"* so these translations are not good (this is K.J.V.) and they primarily seek to promote the ideology of *those* doing the translation.

Surprisingly (I am shocked), Daniel 8:14 has *always* been translated "sanctuary" but… in the Hebrew (or Aramaic)… Daniel did not write "miqdash!!!" He wrote "qodesh." This, to me, *completely changes* the way so many have misread this.

> *13 Then I heard a certain set-apart one speaking. And another set-apart one said to that certain one who was speaking, "Until when is the vision, concerning that which is continual, and the transgression that lays waste, to make both the set-apart place and the host to be trampled underfoot?¹"* [Footnote: ¹See Daniel 11:31, Matthew 24:15 (Daniel 8:13)]

*14 And he said to me, "For two thousand three hundred days, then that which is set-apart shall be made right."* (Daniel 8:14)

Now compare the word "Qadosh" to the word "Qedosh":

H6918: *kaw-doshe,' kaw-doshe'*

H6942: *sacred* (ceremonially or morally); (as noun) *God* (by eminence), an *angel*, a *saint*, a *sanctuary:* holy (One), saint.

H6944: *ko'-desh*

H6942: a *sacred* place or thing; rarely abstractly *sanctity:* consecrated (thing), dedicated (thing), hallowed (thing), holiness, (X most) holy (X day, portion, thing), saint, sanctuary.

I am 100% convinced at this point… that Daniel in Daniel 9:26 was most certainly *not* writing about a sanctuary… but instead was writing about the saints or set-apart (ones).

Because we made this "Blood Covenant" with Yehovah via with Moses, at Mount Sinai and our ancestry agreed with the conditions of this Covenant and now, even to this day, we have not kept it nor have we and our nations repented and returned to this agreement, we now must pay the price and that is death. If we repent, then Yehshua, who died in our stead, has already paid for our death penalty; but we *must* repent if we want to have *any hope whatsoever* of escaping these things.

Daniel has made it clear to us that after the 69 Shavuot or 69 Jubilee Cycles, from the time that Moses was told to go and deliver Israel from Egypt and bring them back to rebuild Jerusalem, that after this 69th Jubilee Cycle, which ended in 1996 and during this 70th Jubilee Cycle, that we would then have to pay dearly and in full for violating Yehovah's Covenant.

This time period that we are going to be trampled for is 2,300 days in all.

> *14 And he said to me, "For two thousand three hundred days, then that which is set-apart shall be made right."* (Daniel 8:14)

The word for "cleansed" is:

H6663: *tsaw-dak'*

A primitive root: to *be* (causatively *make*) *right* (in a moral or forensic sense): cleanse, clear self, (be, do) just (-ice, -ify, -ify self), (be, turn to) righteous (-ness).

At the end of those 2,300 days, which is 6¼ years, the saints will have been perfected or made righteous.

> *13 Then I heard a certain set-apart one speaking. And another set-apart one said to that certain one who was speaking, "Until when is the vision, concerning that which is continual, and the transgression that lays waste, to make both the set-apart place and the host to be trampled underfoot?"* (Daniel 8:13)

The word for "sanctuary" is "saints" and the word for "host" is:

H6635: *tsaw-baw,' tseb-aw-aw'*

H6633: a *mass* of persons (or figurative things), especially regularly organized for war (an *army*); by implication a *campaign*, literally or figuratively (specifically *hardship*, *worship*): appointed time, (+) army, (+) battle, company, host, service, soldiers, waiting upon, war (-fare).

H6633: *tsaw-baw'*

A primitive root: to *mass* (an army or servants): assemble, fight, perform, muster, wait upon, war.

The whole host or army of the saints will be trampled underfoot 2,300 days.

Now let us read verse 26 with this new understanding in mind:

> *26 And after the sixty-two weeks, Messiah shall be cut off and have naught. And the people of a coming prince shall destroy the city and the set-apart place. And the end of it is with a flood. And wastes are decreed, and fighting until the end.* (Daniel 9:26)

After 62 Jubilee Cycles from David which is seven Jubilee Cycles *after* Moses was told to go and get the Israelites, then the saints, Israel, all 12 Tribes, will be cut off and be as if they never were. And the army of the King of the North shall destroy Jerusalem and the saints for 2,300 days or 6¼ years.

> "…and the end[H7093] thereof shall be with a flood,[H7858] and unto[H5704] the end[H7093] of the war[H4421] desolations[H8074] are determined." [H2782] (Daniel 9:26)

The word "flood" is:

H7858: *sheh'-tef, shay'-tef*

H7857: a *deluge* (literally or figuratively): flood, outrageous, overflowing.

H7857: *shaw-taf*

A primitive root: to *gush*; by implication to *inundate, cleanse*; by analogy to *gallop, conquer:* drown, (over-) flow (-whelm), rinse, run, rush, (thoroughly) wash (away).

This King of the North will overwhelm, inundate and conquer the saints until the end of the war.

This word "war" is:

>H4421: *mil-khaw-maw'*

>H3898: (in the sense of *fighting*); a *battle* (that is, the *engagement*); generally *war* (that is, *warfare*): battle, fight, (-ing), war ([-rior]).

>H3898: *law-kham'*

>A primitive root: to *feed* on; figuratively to *consume*; by implication to *battle* (as *destruction*): devour, eat, X ever, fight (-ing), overcome, prevail, (make) war (-ring).

This King of the North will overwhelm, inundate and conquer the saints. Right up until the very end he will war against, consume and devour the saints.

The last expression, "desolations[H8074] are determined.[H2782]"

>H8074: *shaw-mame'*

>A primitive root; to *stun* (or intransitively *grow numb*), that is, *devastate* or (figuratively) *stupefy* (both usually in a passive sense): make amazed, be astonished, (be an) astonish (-ment), (be, bring into, unto, lay, lie, make) desolate (-ion, places), be destitute, destroy (self), (lay, lie, make) waste, wonder.

>H2782: *khw-rats'*

>A primitive root: properly to *point* sharply, that is, (literally) to *wound*; figuratively to *be alert*, to *decide:* bestir self, decide, decree, determine, maim, move.

This King of the North will overwhelm, infiltrate, inundate and conquer the saints. Right up until the very end he will war, consume and utterly devour the saints.

The saints will be stunned, stupefied, astonished and utterly dismayed at the devastation all around them. They will be astonished and dumbfounded at the utter destruction and complete destitution of their once mighty nations.

Before we proceed to move on to verse 27 we must first learn when the 2,300 days begins and when we are going to have to start paying for having broken the Blood Covenant of Mount Sinai, that we agreed to with Yehovah, as well as a number of other important things I haven't brought to your attention just yet.

# Chapter 10 | The 2,300 Days of Hell, Joseph's 7 Years of Plenty & 7 Years of Famine, & the Meal Offering (Daniel 9:27)

*24 Seventy weeks are decreed for your people and for your set-apart city, to put an end to the transgression, and to seal up sins, and to cover crookedness, and to bring in everlasting righteousness, and to seal up vision and prophet, and to anoint the Most Set-apart. 25 Know, then, and understand: from the going forth of the command to restore and build Yerushalayim until Messiah the Prince is seven weeks and sixty-two weeks. It shall be built again, with streets and a trench, but in times of affliction. 26 And after the sixty-two weeks, Messiah shall be cut off and have naught. And the people of a coming prince shall destroy the city and the set-apart place. And the end of it is with a flood. And wastes are decreed, and fighting until the end. 27 And he shall confirm a covenant with many for one week. And in the middle of the week he shall put an end to slaughtering and meal offering. And on the wing of abominations he shall lay waste, even until the complete end and that which is decreed is poured out on the one who lays waste.[1]* [Footnote: [1]Matthew 24:15 (Daniel 9:24-27)]

*27 And he shall confirm a covenant with many for one week. And in the middle of the week he shall put an end to slaughtering and meal offering. And on the wing of abominations he shall lay waste, even until the complete end and that which is decreed is poured out on the one who lays waste.* (Daniel 9:27)

First, I would like to take a look at the middle sentence in this verse because there is a whole lot more than meets the eye to this verse.

*27 And in the middle of the week he shall put an end to slaughtering and meal offering.* (Daniel 9:27)

Many believe and assume the Slaughtering and Meal Offering are just that, animal sacrifices and grain offerings. On that count alone, at some point during this last Jubilee Cycle, one would expect the temple sacrifices to be reinstated for a period of time. The question is "when?" I am not going to take the time to address when the temple sacrifices may be set up mainly because I am uncertain that is what this verse is referring to. It is possible, yes. However, after having given the matter much study and thought, I consider it highly unlikely. It is my belief this verse is telling us something entirely different which will line up with other verses I am about to show you which say the very same thing.

There are groups out there who have used this Daniel 9 Prophecy and the *2,000 Years Gap Theory* to speculate that these sacrifices would begin with the Festival of Purim in 2013 or Passover in 2014. At the time of this writing, they have yet to happen. They also speculate on how this will purportedly usher in the last 3½ year time period commonly known as the Great Tribulation that they are to wait and keep watch for.

Still other groups use the founding of Israel in 1947 and then add the seventy weeks of Daniel 9 to the year 1947 and arrive at 2017 as the end of this age. They claim the seventy weeks is seventy Shavuot and as such, they claim there is one Shavuot or one Feast of Pentecost each year, and it is by this reasoning they justify the seventy years being added to the year of Israel's founding by the United Nations in 1947. From 2017 they then count back 3½ years and arrive at Passover 2014 as the start date for the Great Tribulation. They say the last seven years, from 2010 to 2017, is this *last week* (Daniel 9:27), and that in the *midst* of this week the Tribulation begins—again, in 2014.

As I have indicated in previous chapters of this book, I do not hold to these theories. The 7 Shavuot (weeks) comes first, followed by the 62 Shavuot as I have shown you in earlier chapters, and finally, the 70th Shabua or "week."

Although I do not deny that the sacrifices could rightfully be set up again and put in place at some point, there is also another view I subscribe to that I'd like to now share with you.

*27 And in the middle of the week.* (Daniel 9:27)

The word "middle" here is:

H2677: *khay-tsee'*

From H2673: the *half* or *middle:* –half, middle, mid [-night], midst, part, two parts.

Knowing that the word "week" is a Shabua (the word *week* is Shabua and the word *weeks* is Shavuot in Hebrew), or one Jubilee Cycle consisting of a forty-nine year period of time, then the middle of this Shabua is 24½ years. Also, knowing that the 69th Shabua was in 1996, then all we have to do is add 24½ years to 1996 to arrive at the year these sacrifices will be cut off—which brings us to the year 2020 C.E. And the ½ year time frame would take us to the fall of the year; generally the seventh month of the Hebrew calendar. But I still believe the 9th of the 5th month, Tisha B'Av, (around August) is a date worthy of serious consideration. It was on this date that Yehovah instituted the forty-year curse upon Israel to wander in the Wilderness. Also, on this very same date, the first Temple was destroyed in 586 B.C. and the second Temple in 70 C.E.

With the saints *themselves* being the Temple of the living Yehovah, I am about to show you that it is not the Temple *building* that is going to be destroyed, but the *saints* (as I have been describing to you in the previous chapters). In other words, in the midst of this final Shabua, the saints will be cut off!

But this word "chetsiy or khay-tsee" does not *always* mean, "middle." It sometimes simply means "in the midst" as "within a particular timeframe." In Exodus, the word "midnight" is derived from this same word used for "middle" or "midst" as referenced in Daniel 9:

> *29 And it came to be at midnight that* יהוה *smote all the first-born in the land of Mitsrayim, from the first-born of Pharaoh who sat on his throne to the first-born of the captive who was in the dungeon, and all the first-born of livestock.* (Exodus 12:29)

This word middle is:

H2677: *khay-tsee'*

From H2673: the *half* or *middle:* –half, middle, mid [-night], midst, part, two parts.

H2673: *khaw-tsaw'*

A primitive root (compare H2686): to *cut* or *split* in two; to *halve:* –divide, X live out half, reach to the midst, part.

H2686: *khaw-tsats'*

A primitive root (compare H2673): properly to *chop* into, pierce or sever; hence to *curtail*, to *distribute* (into ranks); as denominative from H2671; to *shoot* an arrow: –archer, X bands, cut off in the midst.

H2671: *khayts*

From H2686: properly a *piercer*, that is, an *arrow*; by implication a *wound*; figuratively (of God) thunder *bolt*; (by interchange for H6086) the *shaft* of a spear: –+ archer, arrow, dart, shaft, staff, wound.

This last meaning of this word H2686 is very interesting. One of the teachings I expound upon pertains to the god Thor, who he represents and where he comes from. One of the symbols of Thor is the hammer (also known as the swastika) and the thunderbolt. This god and these symbols represent the nation of Germany, who is known in the Bible as the Assyrians. Having said that, what this is indicating to us is that in the midst of this 70th week, Germany will afflict the 12 Tribes of Israel with arrows or missiles and pierce her.

The other meanings for this same word show us how these same 12 Tribes are going to be chopped into pieces, split up divided and severely wounded.

It is with these meanings that I am drawn once again to the prophecy about the House of Joseph. I explained who Joseph was in the first three chapters of this book. Today, the Tribe of Joseph is regarded as the leading tribe of the Ten Lost Tribes of Israel, made up of the USA and UK nations. Look at the prophecy Joseph is given by his father.

> *22 Yosĕph is an offshoot of a fruit-bearing tree, an offshoot of a fruit-bearing tree by a fountain, his branches run over a wall. 23 And the archers have bitterly grieved him, shot at him and hated him. 24 But his bow remained in strength, and the arms of his hands were made strong by the hands of the Mighty One of Ya'aqob—from there is the Shepherd, the Stone of Yisra'ĕl—25 from the Ĕl of your father who helps you, and by the Almighty who blesses you with blessings of the heavens above, blessings of the deep that lies beneath, blessings of the breasts and of the womb. 26 The blessings of your father have excelled the blessings of my ancestors, up to the limit of the everlasting hills. They are on the head of Yosĕph, and on the crown of the head of him who was separated from his brothers.* (Genesis 49:22-26)

So, in the midst of this last Shabua, Joseph will be cut off by arrows. Arrows in the Bible today are known as *missiles*. Also we are told that Joseph is going to be *"hated."* Isn't this amazing to see that today, both Joseph and Judah are hated around the world? Joseph today is the U.S.A., the U.K. and her commonwealth countries. The Muslim world calls the U.S.A. the "Great Satan" and they call the state of Israel the "little Satan." They do this because both are sons of Jacob and brothers. With that in mind, let us continue to understand what is written here.

> *27 And in the middle of the week he shall put an end to slaughtering and meal offering.* (Daniel 9:27)

*"He"* in this verse is referring to the coming world leader or Satan.

The word for "slaughtering" in other versions is the word "sacrifice" and this word is:

H2077: zebach *zeh'-bakh*

From H2076: properly a *slaughter*, that is, the *flesh* of an animal; by implication a *sacrifice* (the victim or the act): – offer (-ing), sacrifice.

H2076: *zaw-bakh'*

A primitive root: to *slaughter* an animal (usually in sacrifice): –kill, offer, (do) sacrifice, slay.

The word "zabach" means "sacrifice," but is generic. It is generic and associated with offerings of ***all*** types.

The word we use for *"Meal Offering"* is also very interesting and will help you to better understand on a deeper level what I'm trying to convey. "Meal Offering" is known in Hebrew as *Min Kah* and it is where we get the word *Minchah*.

H4503: *min-khaw'*

From an unused root meaning to *apportion*, that is, *bestow*; a *donation*; euphemistically *tribute*; specifically a sacrificial *offering* (usually bloodless and voluntary): –gift, oblation, (meat) offering, present, sacrifice.

Daniel is talking about a "Minchah Offering," or a "Minchah Sacrifice Offering," in other words.

In the midst of this 70th Shabua (or this last forty-nine year period), he (the prince) will put an end to all sacrifices and offerings. What are these sacrifices and offerings otherwise called Minchah offerings?

> The burnt offerings are described in Leviticus 1 and 2 and they are listed according to the wealth of the one making the gift. The most wealthy offering a bullock, the less well off (offering) birds, and the poorest, an offering of flour. This last of the offerings made by fire is the sacrifice we usually refer to as the *Korban Minchah*, the "Meal Offering." Though the term "*Minchah*" was originally used to describe any ritual offering, it is used in *Parshah Vayikra* to denote an offering of unleavened bread made using flour and oil. The word has since come to denote the afternoon prayer service, which replaced the afternoon Sanctuary/Temple sacrifice.[439]

Since 70 C.E. when the Temple was destroyed, there have not been any animal sacrifices made to Yehovah. They have not had a fitting place by which to do so. Because of this fact, that there have been no sacrifices since 70 C.E., then we must question whether or not this is even speaking of the animal sacrifices. Many assume they must be restored in order for this prophecy to be fulfilled, but is this line of thinking logical. The daily sacrifices have already been taken away, but not in the midst of the 70th Shabua or week. The daily sacrifices were made in the morning and in the late afternoon, at 9 a.m. and 3 p.m.

Keep in mind that Yehshua was hung on the tree at 9 a.m. in the middle of the week. This was a Wednesday and He died at 3 p.m. that

---

[439] http://jewishcontemplatives.blogspot.com/2011/03/korban-minchah-finest-flour-march-2011.html?m=1

afternoon. He was an example to us of the ultimate sacrifice and was offered at these two precise times in the *midst,* the *middle* of the week on the Wednesday. This is also symbolic of when Israel too, like Yehshua, will be cut off. The nation of Israel as well was cut down in 723 B.C. when it fell to the Assyrians. This date was the middle of that Jubilee Cycle.

> Besides the intrinsic ingredients of the bread itself, the meal offering included the pouring of oil and the laying of frankincense. This would increase the visual intensity of the flames and would produce a strong-smelling cloud of smoke when the offering was set on fire. Oil is one of the symbols for joy and also of consecration. Frankincense is one of the symbols of purification and of devoted prayer. All sacrifices were offered with salt as well, another symbol of cleansing but also of self-sacrifice and of wealth. If we remember that a sacrifice is an act of *Korban*, of the drawing close of God and Israel, we could say that:
>
> **Flour and Oil**: The sacrifice of our prayer is most acceptable when we offer it in joy and as a part of a dedicated life, not as a separate act. (Our *entire lives* should be an act of worship).
>
> **Oil and Frankincense**: Our own effort, our "labor," is blended with the fire of God's overwhelming love and the inspiration of His breath so that we might "burn" more brightly in His service.
>
> **Salt**: If we perform this kind of sacrifice to the best of our ability, it will serve to purify our hearts to make the drawing close of our souls with God a possibility. The giving of charity and the nullification of our own self-importance will complete the sacrificial act and make our prayers a potential atonement for ourselves and for those for whom we pray.
>
> In Leviticus 2:3 and Leviticus 2:10 we are told that the Minchah Offering is the "*most* holy of all the offerings made by fire." Here is the reason for you to consider why this might be:

We are told that the offering should be of "fine flour" (*Solet*). As the *Minchah* offering was the sacrifice brought by the very poorest people, it is significant that despite their poverty, the best grain available was to be selected. It reminds us that even in (physical or spiritual) poverty we can always afford to select the very best we have to give as our offering to God. This applies especially to the way we observe *Mitzvot*. Our intention is to "beautify" the *Mitzvos* to the best of our ability and we do this by making full use of whatever expertise, intellect, or artistic skill we might be blessed with in performing the act of service we are engaged in. For contemplative Jews, this is especially so when we pray or when we study in Hegyon Ha-Lev (*meditative scriptural reflection*). The hurried performance of liturgy or a skimped, half-attentive period of Torah study are like inappropriate fast-food or a cake made from a packet. We are to bring only the *finest* ingredients... even though we are poor in the sense that our personal resources are often limited (and always imperfect), we are asked to select only the best we can offer.

An animal sacrifice involves a lot of violent drama and splashed blood and is unavoidably spectacular. To a modern sensibility it is also an emotional event. It is not just a symbol of surrendered wealth, it is also the taking of a life and the destruction of an animals "soul." Some may feel that the drama and enormity of the action is a sign that animal sacrifice is in some way more momentous or even superior, but the text obviously sees things in a different light. The sacrifice of Minchah is not the taking of life, nor the expending of an item of great financial value, nor is it performed on a grand scale. These are highly significant factors which indicate that a much more spiritual theology of sacrifice is at work. That which distinguishes the meal offering, and therefore indicates why it is singled out as being of special value, is that a cake of wheat-meal is **the product of human labor**. It is a sacrifice of the humblest human effort (unleavened bread) offered with holy joy (consecrating oil) and the devotion of those cleansed of self-interest (the purifying Frankincense of prayer).

The Korban Minchah is the gift of a poor, but devoted soul, to a God who has and gives *everything*. It is a personal offering which is an act of allegiance and a statement of trust in God. It is an act of allegiance because it involves a person "presenting" himself before the altar (performing a religious commandment). It is an act of trust because the "poor one" making the offering has chosen the finest ingredients despite the cost.

When we say the blessing over bread which we are about to eat, we always use a formula which declares that God is the one who "brings forth bread from the earth." It is clear that this "bringing forth" involves a great deal of *human* work and that we are not referring to a miraculous *manna*. This is to teach us (at least) two things.

*Firstly*: all our offerings are made from things which are already God's to start with. We provide nothing but our labor. All creation is His gift and the life which beats even in the molecules of a grain of wheat is not simply a matter of physical activity, it is simultaneously a life which is one of God's "garments." We ourselves only exist by His life-giving breath, and the impulse to serve is often as much a matter of inspiration as of any independent effort on our behalf.

*Secondly*: it is to encourage us by reminding us that, paradoxically, our partnership in the "life" and "work" of God is by no means insignificant. It is precisely *because* we have collaborated intensively in the production of the bread that the *Minchah* sacrifice is declared the most acceptable and most valuable of all the sacrifices of the Temple. It represents an ideal balance between *Bitachon* and *Hishtadlus*—between relying on Providence and taking the initiative ourselves.

The flour, which makes our meal offering, is the ***finest*** flour when it has been purified and processed in humility and yet still represents the very best we each have to offer. In return for our acceptance that we are literally paupers who rely on Providence at every moment, another bread falls… the *manna, which* is our spiritual sustenance.

The ***finest*** flour is also a symbol of which kind of prayer is the most valued. We may use a formulaic liturgy—but without the work of our own *Kavannah*, our own attention to the task of prayers and to the discipline of "creating" a liturgy afresh each day … our offering would be lacking. If we make the *Avodat HaKodesh* … our *best* labor then we will have understood the core meaning of the meal offering, and why it is declared the "most holy."

And yet, however "holy" a sacrifice is we know that our intentions, our words, our acts of love, our efforts are only actually of value in the processes of atonement or worship as *signs* of our willing service. This is what I meant earlier when I pointed out that our prayer is most valuable when it is offered as a part of an entire way of life that is "holy."

Our acts of restorative justice and the creation of a channel for grace in our everyday relationships and business dealings are what make our "atonement" a reality, not just our holy words and rituals. The drawing close of man and God is a ***part*** of God not some "thing" we burn or wave at Him to get our own way. He initiates both forgiveness and pardon on the evidence of our *heart* and our *will*, and *not* on the offering of promises, presents, or bribes. In the end, atonement is an activity of God's mercy, freely given. In *Haftarah Vayikra* we read:

*25 "I, I am He who blots out your transgressions for My own sake, and remembers your sins no more."* (Isaiah 43:25)

Our prayers are both an *Olah* (an ascent) of praise and petition and a vehicle for the descent of God's mercy in the form of a heavenly manna. In other words, we present the finest flour of devotion and trust in His Providence. He blesses us with the daily sustenance, which we need in order to serve Him. We are given just enough faith and trust to enable us to follow one step at a time.

But perhaps the *most* important aspect of the meal offering is that it is the offering of one who is "poor." By poor I mean: clear sighted in humility before God who creates and owns all (*Koneh Hakol*). Whatever its theological dynamics or liturgical significance... the thing which makes the *Korban Minchah* most special for me is that it is not an offering demonstrating the sacrifice of one's own "wealth:" but it is **a demonstration of one's intent to give the best one can**. That is an act by which we remember God's overwhelming kindness and through which we hope He will regard us as being His faithful servants. And it is a prayerful act of sacrifice, a *Korban Minchah* of the finest flour, which anyone can offer.

The small contribution we make in any offering to God is our ***effort***. And though it is a small offering, in God's eyes it is far from insignificant. *Parshas Vayikra* describes the person who offers the *Korban Minchah* as "*Nefesh*" (a soul) not as "*ish*" or "*Adam*" (a man). In the Talmud we read:

> ***For what reason is the introduction to the Mincha changed, to say 'Nefesh?' The Holy One said, "Who is it who usually brings a Mincha? A poor person. I will therefore consider it as though he sacrifices his soul (Nefesh) before Me."*** (Menachot 104b)[440]

It is our prayers that we offer up at 9 a.m. and 3 p.m. daily that are the "Zabach" and "Minchah" offering, the "Slaughtering and Meal Offering." Keep in mind as you read this that you are also likened to the wheat amongst the tares. The wheat is to be gathered and stored in

---

[440] http://jewishcontemplatives.blogspot.com/2011/03/korban-minchah-finest-flour-march-2011.html?m=1 by N. R. Davies, March 8th, 2011.

the barn while the tares are burned. It is from the finest of the wheat that the best of the flour comes which is used in the Minchah or Grain Offering. It is the best of your prayers.

And if you will recall the service of Pentecost, it too is at the beginning of the wheat harvest, when the Holy Spirit was poured out and when the Torah was given at Mount Sinai.

The Minchah is a gift or tribute, and nearly *always* associated with grain—that is, the *very best* of the flour.

Our prayers and our praises are *important* to Yehovah.

> *3 Yet You are set-apart, enthroned on the praises of Yisra'ĕl.* (Psalm 22:3)

Minchah has come to mean literally "morning and afternoon prayers." This should teach us something in and of itself. We should be doing our prayers at this time—at the time of the morning and evening prayer, which would be around 9 a.m. and 3 p.m. and *not* at those times when we are about to go to sleep—a time that is not our very best time to pray.

> *2 Let my prayer be prepared before You as incense, the lifting up of my hands as the evening offering.* (Psalm 141:2)

**As Incense**—Incense was offered every morning and evening before the Lord, on the golden altar, before the veil of the sanctuary. Exodus 29:39, and Numbers 28:4.

**As the Evening Sacrifice**—This was a burnt-offering, accompanied with flour and salt. But it does not appear that David refers to any sacrifice, for he uses not זבח Zebach, which is almost universally used for a slaughtered animal; but מנחה Minchah, which is generally taken for a gratitude offering or unbloody sacrifice. The literal translation of the passage is, "Let my prayer be established for incense before thy faces; and the lifting up of my hands for the evening oblation." The psalmist appears to have been, at this time, at a distance from the sanctuary, and therefore could not perform the Divine worship in the way prescribed by the Law. What could he do? Why, as he could not worship according to the Letter of the Law, he will worship God according to the Spirit (of the Law); then prayer is accepted in the place of incense; and the lifting up of his hands, in gratitude and self-dedication to God, is accepted in the place of the evening Minchah or Oblation. Who can deplore the necessity that obliged the psalmist to worship God in this way?[441]

Numbers 28 talks about offerings that are daily and continual as well. The grain (meat, Minchah) offering is one of those. We also read of this in Exodus.

*38 And this is what you prepare on the altar: two lambs, a year old, daily, continually. 39 Prepare the one lamb in the morning, and the other lamb you prepare between the evenings, 40 and one-tenth of an ĕphah of flour mixed with one-fourth of a hin of pressed oil, and one-fourth of a hin of wine as a drink offering, with the one lamb. 41 And prepare the other lamb between the evenings. And with it prepare the grain offering and the drink offering, as in the morning, for a sweet fragrance, an offering made by fire to יהוה—42 a continual burnt offering for your generations at the door of the Tent of Meeting before יהוה, where I shall meet with you to speak with you. 43 And there I shall meet with the children of Yisra'ĕl, and it shall be set apart by My esteem. (Exodus 29:38-43)*

*1 Give ear to my prayer, O Elohim, and do not hide Yourself from my plea. 2 Give heed to me, and answer me; I wander and moan in my complaint, 3 because of the noise of the enemy, because of the outcry of the wrong; for they bring down wickedness upon me, and in wrath they hate me. 4 My heart is pained within me, and the frights of death have fallen upon me. 5 Fear and trembling have come upon me,*

---

[441] http://clarke.biblecommenter.com/psalms/141.htm

*and shuddering covers me. 6 And I said, "Who would give me wings like a dove! I would fly away and be at rest. 7 See, I would wander far off, I would lodge in the wilderness. Selah." 8 "I would hasten my escape from the raging wind and storm. 9 Confuse, O* יהוה*, divide their tongues, for I saw violence and strife in the city. 10 Day and night they go around it on its walls; wickedness and trouble are also in the midst of it. 11 Covetings are in its midst; oppression and deceit do not vanish from its streets. 12 It is not an enemy who reproaches me—that I could bear; nor one who hates me who is making himself great against me—then I could hide from him. 13 But it was you, a man my equal, my companion and my friend. 14 We took sweet counsel together, we walked to the House of Elohim in the throng. 15 Let death come upon them; let them go down into the grave alive, for evil is in their dwellings, in their midst. 16 I, I call upon Elohim, and* יהוה *saves me. 17* **Evening and morning and at noon I complain and moan, and He hears my voice.** (Psalm 55:1-17)

*36 And it came to be,* **at the time of bringing the evening offering,** *that Ěliyahu the prophet came near and said, "*יהוה *Elohim of Aḇraham, Yitsḥaq, and Yisra'ěl, let it be known today: You are Elohim in Yisra'ěl, and I Your servant, have done all these matters by Your word." (1 Kings 18:36)*

*8 And it came to be, that while he was serving as priest before Elohim in the order of his division, 9 according to the institute of the priesthood, he was chosen by lot to burn incense when he went into the Dwelling Place of* יהוה*. 10 And the entire crowd of people* **was praying outside at the hour of incense**. *11 And a messenger of* יהוה *appeared to him, standing on the right side of the altar of incense.* (Luke 1:8-11)

*8 And when He took the scroll, the four living creatures and the twenty-four elders fell down before the Lamb, each*

> *holding a harp, and **golden bowls filled with incense, which are the prayers of the set-apart ones***. (Revelation 5:8)

> *1 And when He opened the seventh seal, there came to be silence in the heaven for about half an hour. 2 And I saw the seven messengers who stand before Elohim, and to them were given seven trumpets. 3 And another messenger came and stood at the altar, holding a golden censer, and much incense was given to him, that he should offer it with the prayers of all the set-apart ones upon the golden altar which was before the throne. 4 **And the smoke of the incense, with the prayers of the set-apart ones, went up before Elohim from the hand of the messenger***. (Revelation 8:1-4)

It seems that in the midst of that 70th Shavuot, the Minchah sacrifice will cease. That is, the prayers will cease. Is such a thing possible; and if so, how? I think I have found a possible answer, which I will explain below.

We are also told that *instead of* sacrifices, Yehovah would have *preferred* our prayers instead.

> *1 O Yisra'ĕl, return to יהוה your Elohim, for you have stumbled by your crookedness. 2 Take words with you, and return to יהוה. Say to Him, "Take away all crookedness, and accept what is good, and we render the bulls of our lips."*[1] [Footnote: [1]Hebrews 13:15—bulls, referring to offerings (Hosea 14:1-2)]

> *15 Through Him then, let us continually offer up a slaughter offering of praise to Elohim, that is, the fruit of our lips, giving thanks to His Name.* (Hebrews 13:15)

Sacrifice and prayer are an *essential* part of worshiping and getting to know Yehovah and letting us be known by Him. Being known by Him is *every bit as* important as knowing Him, so that He does not say unto us on that day, "Depart from me, I never *knew* you."

*6 "For I delight in kindness and not slaughtering, and in the knowledge of Elohim more than burnt offerings."* (Hosea 6:6)

*2 All a man's ways are right in his own eyes, but יהוה weighs the hearts. 3 To do righteousness and right-ruling is more acceptable to יהוה than a slaughtering.* (Proverbs 21:2-3)

It is with all of these Scriptures in mind that I believe the morning and evening sacrifices will be (and already are) the prayers of the saints at 9 a.m. and 3 p.m. each day; at the time of the incense offering and at the same time as when the lambs were sacrificed on a daily basis.

The ceasing of this offering can only support and enforce what I have been saying in previous chapters; that the saints, those of the House of Israel, will be destroyed and it is at such a time as this that the continual or daily prayers will cease.

We are also commanded to go up to Jerusalem three times a year to keep the Feasts. Passover would represent the morning offering, Pentecost would represent the prayers made at noon, and the Feast of Tabernacles would represent the evening offering, which take place in the fall. When the saints are being destroyed and hunted down, no one will be able to gather in order to worship during these three special times of the year, when we would be gathering to keep each Feast. It would be just too dangerous or impossible to do.

This is reminiscent of what Moses had said to Pharaoh, to let the people go, so they could go and worship Yehovah.

> *And you shall say to him, Jehovah, the God of the Hebrews has sent me to you, saying, Let My people go so that they may serve Me in the wilderness. And, behold, until now you would not hear.* (Exodus 7:16)

> *And Jehovah spoke to Moses, Go to Pharaoh, and say to him: Thus says Jehovah, Let my people go so that they may serve Me.* (Exodus 8:1)

*And Pharaoh called for Moses and Aaron, and said, Pray to Jehovah that He may take away the frogs from me and from my people. And I will let the people go, so that they may sacrifice to Jehovah.* (Exodus 8:8)

*And Jehovah said to Moses, Rise up early in the morning and stand before Pharaoh. Lo, he comes forth to the water. And say to him, Thus says Jehovah: Let My people go, so that they may serve Me.* (Exodus 8:20)

*And Pharaoh called for Moses and for Aaron, and said, Go sacrifice to your God in the land. 26 And Moses said, It is not right to do so, for we shall sacrifice the abomination of the Egyptians to Jehovah our God. Lo, shall we sacrifice the abomination of the Egyptians before their eyes, and will they not stone us? 27 We will go three days' journey into the wilderness, and sacrifice to Jehovah our God, as He shall command us. 28 And Pharaoh said, I will let you go so that you may sacrifice to Jehovah your God in the wilderness. Only you shall not go very far away. Pray for me.* (Exodus 8:25-28)

*And Jehovah said to Moses, Go in to Pharaoh and tell him, Thus says Jehovah, the God of the Hebrews: Let My people go so that they may serve Me.* (Exodus 9:1)

*And Jehovah said to Moses, Rise up early in the morning, and stand before Pharaoh, and say to him, So says Jehovah, the God of the Hebrews, Let My people go, so that they may serve Me.* (Exodus 9:13)

*And Moses and Aaron came in to Pharaoh and said to him, So says Jehovah, the God of the Hebrews, How long will you refuse to humble yourself before Me? Let My people go, so that they may serve Me.* (Exodus 10:3)

*And Moses and Aaron were brought again to Pharaoh, and he said to them, Go! Serve Jehovah your God. Who are the ones that shall go? 9 And Moses said, We will go with our young and with our old, with our sons and with our daughters. We will go with our flocks and with our herds. For we must hold a feast to Jehovah. 10 And he said to them, May Jehovah be so with you, as I send you and your little ones away. Watch out, for evil is before you. 11 Not so! You men go now and serve Jehovah, for it is you who desired it. And they were driven out from Pharaoh's presence.* (Exodus 10:8)

*And Pharaoh called to Moses, and said, You go serve Jehovah. Only let your flocks and your herds be left. Let your little ones also go with you. 25 And Moses said, You must give us also sacrifices and burnt offerings, so that we may sacrifice to Jehovah our God. 26 Our cattle also shall go with us. There shall not be a hoof left behind. For we must take from them to serve Jehovah our God. And we do not know with what we must serve Jehovah until we come there.* (Exodus 10:24-26)

In the same way that Egypt prevented Israel from keeping the feasts while they were slaves, so will the future world ruling empire led by Satan prevent the saints from keeping any feasts to Yehovah while they are being hunted and destroyed. Before the time of the Exodus, Israel was not able to keep any feasts until they kept the Feast of Passover in the land of Egypt and then fifty days later, when they arrived at Mount Sinai they kept the Feast of Pentecost.

From the middle of this 70th Shabua, from the year of 2020 onward, no one will be able to keep any Feasts as a group of people because they will be hunted and killed. The next question you should be asking is "for how long?"

In explaining this part of Daniel's Prophecy, *"And in the middle of the week he shall put an end to slaughtering and meal offering,"* I am compelled to have you take a closer look at another prophecy of Daniel, which is found in Chapter 8.

Let us first read the Scripture below to get the context of what I am talking about. Again, it is the daily offerings, also known as 'the daily':

> *3 And I lifted my eyes and looked and saw a ram standing beside the river, and it had two horns, and the two horns were high. And the one was higher than the other, and the higher one came up last. 4 I saw the ram pushing westward, and northward, and southward, so that no beast could stand before him, and there was no one to deliver from his hand, while he did as he pleased and became great. 5 And I was observing and saw a male goat came from the west, over the surface of all the earth, without touching the ground. And the goat had a conspicuous horn between his eyes. 6 And he came to the ram that had two horns, which I had seen standing beside the river, and ran at him in the rage of his power. 7 And I saw him come close to the ram, and he became embittered against him, and smote the ram, and broke his two horns. And there was no power in the ram to withstand him, but he threw him down to the ground and trampled on him. And there was no one to deliver the ram from his hand. 8 And the male goat became very great. But when he was strong, the large horn was broken, and in place of it four conspicuous ones came up toward the four winds of the heavens.* (Daniel 8:3-8)

> *9 And from one of them came a little horn which became exceedingly great toward the south, and toward the east, and toward the Splendid Land. 10 And it became great, up to the host of the heavens. And it caused some of the host and some of the stars to fall to the earth, and trampled them down. 11 It even exalted itself as high as the Prince of the host. And it took that which is continual away from Him, and threw down the foundation of His set-apart place.* (Daniel 8:9-11)

The Two Witnesses and the Angel Gabriel are about to explain some things to us, but I must point out that in v. 10 of the above passage, we read of those who are trampled and then we read how the daily sacrifices, or the prayers, (*that which is continual*), the Feasts are taken away.

*12 And because of transgression, an army was given over to the horn to oppose that which is continual. And it threw the truth down to the ground,[1] and it acted and prospered.* [Footnote: [1]Isaiah 59:14 (Daniel 8:12)]

*13 Then I heard a certain set-apart one speaking. And another set-apart one said to that certain one who was speaking, "Until when is the vision, concerning that which is continual, and the transgression that lays waste, to make both the set-apart place and the host to be trampled underfoot?"[1]* [Footnote: [1]See Daniel 11:31, Matthew 24:15 (Daniel 8:13)]

The *Host to be trampled* are the descendants of Abraham and are in fact, the Tribes of Israel. It is *these saints* who are to be trampled into the ground. We read of this when Yehovah showed Abraham how innumerable his heirs would be.

*3 And Aḇram said, "See, You have given me no seed, and see, one born in my house is my heir!" 4 And see, the word of יהוה came to him, saying, "This one is not your heir, but he who comes from your own body is your heir." 5 And He brought him outside and said, "Look now toward the heavens, and count the stars if you are able to count them." And He said to him, "So are your seed."* (Genesis 15:3-5)

Here in Daniel 8:13, we have the Two Witnesses speaking in the same fashion as they do in Daniel 12. Notice as well in Daniel 8:13, that as they speak to each other, the time they are speaking about is when the Saints are going to be trampled, not the Sanctuary. In Daniel 12:7 we are told that "*... when they have made an end of scattering the power of the holy people, all these things shall be finished.*"

*5 Then I Dani'ĕl, looked and saw two others standing, one on this bank of the river and the other on that bank. 6 And one said to the man dressed in linen, who was above the waters of the river, "How long until the end of these wonders?" 7 And I heard the man dressed in linen, who was above the waters of the river, and he held up his right and his left hand to heavens, and swore by Him who lives forever, that it would be for a time, times, and half a time. And when they have ended scattering the power of the set-apart people, then all these shall be completed.* (Daniel 12:5-7)

Continuing on in Daniel 8 we read:

*14 And he said to me, "For two-thousand three-hundred days, then that which is set-apart shall be made right."* (Daniel 8:14)

It is not until these days have been completed, not until the saints have been trampled for 2300 days; only then are they vindicated. 2300 days is about 6 ¼ years of persecution and slaughter.

*15 And it came to be, when I, Dani'ĕl, had seen the vision, that I sought understanding, and see, before me stood one having the appearance of a mighty man. 16 And I heard a man's voice between the banks of Ulai, who called, and said, "Gab̄ri'ĕl, make this man understand the vision." 17 He then came near where I stood. And when he came, I feared and I fell on my face, but he said to me, "Understand, son of man,* **for the vision is for the time of the end.** *18 And, as he was speaking with me, I fell stunned upon my face to the ground, but he touched me, and made me stand up straight, 19 and said, "Look, I am making known to you what shall take place in the latter time of the wrath, for at the appointed time shall be the end. 20 The ram which you saw, having two horns, are the sovereigns of Media and Persia."* (Daniel 8:14-20)

Media and Persia are known as Iran at this time. And it is Iran that is stirring up all manner of unrest in the Middle East. Notice the efforts of Iran are northward, southward and westward, but *not* eastward—just as described at the beginning of this prophecy.

*21 And the male goat is the sovereign of Greece, and the large horn between its eyes is the first sovereign. 22 And that it was broken and four stood up in its place: are four*

> *rulerships arising out of that nation, but not in its power. 23 And in the latter time of their rule, when the transgressors have filled up their measure, a sovereign, fierce of face and skilled at intrigues, shall stand up.* (Daniel 8:21-23)

> *24 And his power shall be mighty, but not by his own power, and he shall destroy incredibly, and shall prosper and thrive, and destroy mighty men, and the set-apart people. 25 And through his skill, he shall make deceit prosper in his hand, and hold himself to be great in his heart, and destroy many who are at ease, and even stand against the Prince of princes—yet without hand he shall be broken.* (Daniel 8:4-25)

This king from Europe is going to destroy the set part people and many of those at ease. The U.S.A., the UK and her commonwealth nations are nations at ease and they are the descendants of Israel. They are the "Set-Apart People."

> *26 And what was said in the vision of the evenings and mornings is truth. And hide the vision, for it is after many days. 27 And I, Dani'ĕl, was stricken and became sick for days. Then I rose up and went about the sovereign's work. And I was amazed at the vision, but there was no understanding.* (Daniel 8:26-27)

I want you to notice verse 24. It says, "*...he shall destroy the mighty men and the set apart people.*" This word for mighty men is:

H6099 עצום עצום 'âtsûm 'âtsûm

*aw-tsoom', aw-tsoom'*

Passive participle of H6105; *powerful* (specifically a *paw*); by implication *numerous:* - + feeble, great, mighty, must, strong.

H6105 עצם 'âtsam *aw-tsam'*

A primitive root; to *bind* fast, that is, *close* (the eyes); intransitively to *be* (causatively *make*) *powerful* or **numerous**; denominatively (from H6106) to *crunch* the bones: - break the bones, close, be great, be increased, be (wax) mighty (-ier), be more, shut, be (-come, make) strong (-er).

H6106 עצם 'etsem *eh'-tsem*

From H6105; a *bone* (as *strong*); by extension the *body*; figuratively the *substance*, that is, (as pronoun) *selfsame:* - body, bone, X life, (self-) same, strength, X very.

Here you will also notice that the word used for "set-apart" people is the word qodesh, but instead of it being translated as "temple" this time it is correctly translated as "saints."

H6918 קדוש קדש qâdôsh qâdôsh *kaw-doshe', kaw-doshe'*

From H6942; *sacred* (ceremonially or morally); (as noun) *God* (by eminence), an *angel*, a *saint*, a *sanctuary:* - holy (One), saint.

Again, we are told this vision is for the time of the end—the Last Days of which Daniel's 70 Shavuot and Daniel's 2300 days, (Chapter 8 & 9), are all about—meaning, during this last forty-nine year period (or this last Shabua), starting in the middle of it the saints are going to be crushed, trampled and worn out by this new and powerful coming empire. Do not neglect the word *numerous* as one of the translated words for *mighty men*. Numerous numbers of saints will be killed. We are again told in verse 26 that this prophecy is about the *evening and mornings* and is about the saints not being able to keep any of the Feasts.

> *17 He then came near where I stood. And when he came, I feared and I fell on my face, but he said to me, "Understand, son of man, for the vision is for the time of the end"... 19 and said, "Look, I am making known to you what shall take place in the latter time of the wrath, for at the appointed time shall be the end."* (Daniel 8:17, 19)

The 2,300 days of Daniel 8 *cannot* be 2,300 years *if* they are meant to be seen in the light of the Last Days timeframe and therefore must be 2,300 *actual* days instead. Those who have used the seventy weeks of Daniel 9 as 70 x 7 to arrive at 490 years do so based on those years starting in 456 B.C. and ending in the year 27 C.E. Again, they do this by adding the 456 B.C. to 483 years with the last seven years to take place at some mysterious point in the future. It was the Millerites[442] who then took the same starting date of 456 B.C. and then added the 2,300 years to this, and arrived at 1844 C.E. Today this date is known as, "The Great Disappointment," and was the founding date for the Seventh Day Adventist's movement.

The telling clue as to when these 2,300 days actually come into effect is revealed to us in another verse in Chapter 8.

> *14 And he said to me, "For two-thousand three-hundred days, then that which is set-apart shall be made right."* (Daniel 8:14)

> *14 And he said to me, "For two-thousand, three-hundred evenings and mornings. Then the sanctuary shall be vindicated."* (Daniel 8:14 | MKJV)

Is it really the sanctuary that is vindicated or is it Yehovah's set-apart people who are vindicated? Again we must look to the Hebrew to learn what is actually being said. And once again the word that has been translated *"sanctuary"* is, in fact, supposed to be *"the saints"* just as it has been shown in both Daniel 8 and Daniel 9 as you have just seen. It is at the end of these 2,300 days that the saints will, at long last, be vindicated.

Take another look at the verse we just read and take special note that these events take place at the *appointed time*.

> *19 and said, "Look, I am making known to you what shall take place in the latter time of the wrath, for at the appointed time shall be the end."* (Daniel 8:19)

---

[442] http://en.wikipedia.org/wiki/Millerism

What are the appointed times? You can read about each one of them in Leviticus 23.

> *2 Speak to the sons of Israel and say to them, The feasts of Jehovah, which you shall proclaim, holy convocations, even these are **My appointed feasts**. 3 Six days shall work be done, but the seventh day is the sabbath of rest, a holy convocation. You shall not do any work. It is a sabbath to Jehovah in all your dwellings. 4 These are the appointed feasts of Jehovah, holy convocations which you shall proclaim in their appointed seasons.* (Leviticus 23:2-4)

Yehovah then goes on to explain each of the seven Appointed Feasts we are to keep in the rest of Leviticus 23. It is in understanding these appointed times that we are able to place the time when this persecution and destruction of the saints takes place, when it ends and when the vengeance or vindication begins. That vindication begins at the end of the 2300 days of hell, once that world ruling empire has made a complete destruction of the saints. Those saints are both those who keep the Torah and those who do not keep it and are the descendants of Abraham.

From *The Prophecies of Abraham* you know when the Sabbatical Cycles are and you also know when this last Shabua began in 1996. You also know that the fall Holy Days, when plotted out according to the Sabbatical Cycles, land on those years marked in blue. (To keep the cost down we have had to do this book in black and white. To see the colored charts go to The Prophecies of Abraham at the back of the book). The following is a chart of the 119th Jubilee Cycle with the Sabbatical Cycles laid out in seven year increments:

- 2045 represents the 8th Day of the Feast and is a Jubilee Year. (not shown)
- 2044 represents the Last Great Day of the Feast of Tabernacles.
- 2038 represents the 1st Day of the Feast of Tabernacles, which begins the Marriage Feast ceremonies.

- 2033 represents the Day of Atonement when Satan is locked away. It is five days before the feast of tabernacles in the fall and is here 5 years before 2038.
- 2024 represents the Feast of Trumpets. It is ten days before the Day of Atonement in the fall and is here 10 years before the year of Atonement of 2033
- Finally, 2030 is Shabbat Shuva, which takes place on the weekly Sabbath during the Ten Days of Awe between the Feast of Trumpets and the Day of Atonement. Shabbat Shuva here is represented by a Sabbatical Year.

| Sabbath | 6th Cycle | 5th Cycle | 4th Cycle | 3rd Cycle | 2nd Cycle | 1st Cycle |
| --- | --- | --- | --- | --- | --- | --- |
| 2044 | 2037 | 2030 | 2023 | 2016 | 2009 | 2002 |
| 2043 | 2036 | 2029 | 2022 | 2015 | 2008 | 2001 |
| 2042 | 2035 | 2028 | 2021 | 2014 | 2007 | 2000 |
| 2041 | 2034 | 2027 | 2020 | 2013 | 2006 | 1999 |
| 2040 | 2033 | 2026 | 2019 | 2012 | 2005 | 1998 |
| 2039 | 2032 | 2025 | 2018 | 2011 | 2004 | 1997 |
| 2038 | 2031 | 2024 | 2017 | 2010 | 2003 | 1996 |

In Daniel 8:14 that word "vindicated" is:

H6663: tsâdaq *tsaw-dak'*

A primitive root: to *be* (causatively *make*) *right* (in a moral or forensic sense): –cleanse, clear self, (be, do) just (-ice, -ify, -ify self), (be, turn to) righteous (-ness).

And the word used for "sanctuary" is:

H6944: qôdesh *ko'-desh*

From H6942: a *sacred* place or thing; rarely abstractly *sanctity*: –consecrated (thing), dedicated (thing), hallowed (thing), holiness, (X most) holy (X day, portion, thing), saint, sanctuary.

But as I explained in the last chapter, if this *was* the Holy of Holies, Daniel would have used "Miq qedosh" and not just "qedosh." And as I have also already explained in the last chapter, the word here is "saints" and *not* "sanctuary."

It is *the saints* who are going to be justified and vindicated at the end of these 2,300 days. They will be *vindicated* after having been mercilessly slaughtered for 6 ¼ years by those who hate the descendants of Abraham, Isaac and Jacob. Knowing this, now read the passage in Revelation:

> *9 And when He opened the fifth seal, I saw under the altar the beings of those having been slain for the Word of Elohim and for the witness which they held, 10 and they cried with a loud voice, saying, "How long, O Master, set-apart and true, until You judge and avenge our blood on those who dwell on the earth?"* (Revelation 6:9-10)

Again by examining the word avenge we have:

G1556 ἐκδικέω ekdikeo˜ *ek-dik-eh'-o*

From G1558; to *vindicate, retaliate, punish:* - a (re-) venge.

G1558 ἔκδικος ekdikos *ek'-dik-os*

From G1537 and G1349; carrying *justice out*, that is, a *punisher:* - a (re-) venger.

That word slain in Revelation 6:9 means butchered or slaughtered. It is Yehovah who is the avenger and the one who is going to carry out justice.

> *47 The El who avenges me, and He humbles the peoples under me.* (Psalms 18:47)

> *34 Is it not stored up with Me, sealed up among My treasures? 35 "Vengeance is Mine, and repayment. At the time their foot slips; for near is the day of their calamity. And the matters prepared are hastening to them." 36 For* יהוה

> rightly rules His people and has compassion on His servants. When He sees that their power is gone, and there is no one remaining, shut up or at large, 37 and He shall say, "Where are their mighty ones, the rock in whom they sought refuge?" (Deuteronomy 32:34-37)

> 1 O יהוה, El of vengeance; O El of vengeance, shine forth! 2 Raise Yourself up, O Judge of the earth; render punishment to the proud. 3 יהוה, how long are the wrong, how long are the wrong going to exult? 4 They pour forth words, they speak arrogantly; all the workers of wickedness boast in themselves. 5 They crush Your people, O יהוה, and they afflict Your inheritance. 6 They slay the widow and the stranger, and murder the fatherless. 7 Yet they say, "Yah does not see, and the Elohim of Ya'aqob pays no heed." (Psalms 94:1-7)

Here in Psalms 94 we read how the saints are "crushed." Is this not one of the meanings of the word "mighty men" which pertains to when the saints will be crushed, which we just looked at in Daniel 8:24?

Now the question is *when*? When does this take place and *where* does it fit chronologically into the broad scheme of things? The answer is already given to us in Daniel 9:27—the very verse we are looking closely at in this chapter of the book.

> 27 And he shall confirm a covenant with many for one week. And in the middle of the week he shall put an end to slaughtering and meal offering. And on the wing of abominations he shall lay waste, even until the complete end and that which is decreed is poured out on the one who lays waste. (Daniel 9:27)

It is in the middle of this last Jubilee Cycle that these events are going to begin to take place that will crush the anointed ones of Yehovah. The anointed ones are the descendants of all 12 Tribes whether they keep the Torah of Yehovah or not. It is these people who will stop praying to Yehovah and will be trampled underfoot for 2,300 mornings and evenings. It is during this 2,300 days that no one will be able to keep the appointed times, the Feasts of Yehovah.

Already now at the end of 2013 you can read more and more news events about Christians being killed by Muslims because they are praying.[443] Revelation 20:4 tells us that these Saints will be beheaded for their beliefs. Who is it today that beheads other faiths on the nightly news?

When you understand the Holy Days and what they mean, then you will know that Satan is going to be locked away on the Day of Atonement. This is the *meaning* of this great and very solemn day. You can learn more about this event historically in Leviticus 16 and compare it to the future reality in Revelation 20. I have already shown you in *The Prophecies of Abraham* that the Day of Atonement comes in the fall of 2033.

The significance of the year 2033 can be seen in Luke where Yehshua is speaking of the Last Days, as follows:

> *26 And as it came to be in the days of Noah, so also shall it be in the days of the Son of Adam: 27 "They were eating, they were drinking, they were marrying, they were given in marriage, until the day that Noah went into the ark, and the flood came and destroyed them all. 28 "And likewise, as it came to be in the days of Lot: They were eating, they were drinking, they were buying, they were selling, they were planting, they were building, 29 but on the day Lot went out of Sedom, it rained fire and sulphur from heaven and destroyed them all. 30 "It shall be the same in the day the Son of Adam is revealed." (Luke 17:26-30)*

The hidden meaning of this is lost in the verse itself, and does not become visible until you actually plot these events out chronologically. Only then do you understand what Yehshua was actually saying. It is in the Jubilee Cycle of the *"Days of Noah"* that we can see the actual year

---

[443] http://www.freerepublic.com/focus/f-news/1034090/posts

the Flood took place, which was the fourth year of the sixth Sabbatical Cycle; that is 1,656 years after the creation of Adam.

| Sabbath | 6th Cycle | 5th Cycle | 4th Cycle | 3rd Cycle | 2nd Cycle | 1st Cycle |
|---|---|---|---|---|---|---|
| 1666 | 1659 | 1652 | 1645 | 1638 | 1631 | 1624 |
| 1665 | 1658 | 1651 | 1644 | 1637 | 1630 | 1623 |
| 1664 | 1657 | 1650 | 1643 | 1636 | 1629 | 1622 |
| 1663 | 1656 | 1649 | 1642 | 1635 | 1628 | 1621 |
| 1662 | 1655 | 1648 | 1641 | 1634 | 1627 | 1620 |
| 1661 | 1654 | 1647 | 1640 | 1633 | 1626 | 1619 |
| 1660 | 1653 | 1646 | 1639 | 1632 | 1625 | 1618 |

Yehovah waited as long as possible for the people of the world to repent and begin to obey Him. It was not until the start of the New Year in 1656 A.C. (after the creation of Adam), that Yehovah executed His punishment on the world and sent the Great Flood.

Again, when we come to know the year Sodom and Gomorrah are destroyed, their destruction in the Jubilee Cycles comes in the year 2047 at Passover time counting from the creation of Adam.

| Sabbath | 6th Cycle | 5th Cycle | 4th Cycle | 3rd Cycle | 2nd Cycle | 1st Cycle |
|---|---|---|---|---|---|---|
| 2058 | 2051 | 2044 | 2037 | 2030 | 2023 | 2016 |
| 2057 | 2050 | 2043 | 2036 | 2029 | 2022 | 2015 |
| 2056 | 2049 | 2042 | 2035 | 2028 | 2021 | 2014 |
| 2055 | 2048 | 2041 | 2034 | 2027 | 2020 | 2013 |
| 2054 | 2047 | 2040 | 2033 | 2026 | 2019 | 2012 |
| 2053 | 2046 | 2039 | 2032 | 2025 | 2018 | 2011 |
| 2052 | 2045 | 2038 | 2031 | 2024 | 2017 | 2010 |

*3 But he urged them strongly, and they turned in to him and came into his house. And he made them a feast, and baked unleavened bread, and they ate. (Genesis 19:3)*

| Sabbath | 6th Cycle | 5th Cycle | 4th Cycle | 3rd Cycle | 2nd Cycle | 1st Cycle |
|---|---|---|---|---|---|---|
| 2044 | 2037 | 2030 | 2023 | 2016 | 2009 | 2002 |
| 2043 | 2036 | 2029 | 2022 | 2015 | 2008 | 2001 |
| 2042 | 2035 | 2028 | 2021 | 2014 | 2007 | 2000 |
| 2041 | 2034 | 2027 | 2020 | 2013 | 2006 | 1999 |
| 2040 | 2033 | 2026 | 2019 | 2012 | 2005 | 1998 |
| 2039 | 2032 | 2025 | 2018 | 2011 | 2004 | 1997 |
| 2038 | 2031 | 2024 | 2017 | 2010 | 2003 | 1996 |

This is the third year of the sixth Sabbatical Cycle. We know this is 2047 A.C. because the angels had told Abraham that Isaac would be born a year from the time they met, and we know Isaac was born in the year 2048 A.C. when Abraham was 100 years old.

Knowing the two dates mentioned by Yehshua in the Gospel of Luke, you should now be able to compare them to the Day of Atonement in our current Jubilee Cycle, which will be in 2033. Understand that at this time, when Satan is going to be locked away, *"as it was in the days of Noah and as it was in the days of Lot, so shall it be in the last days."*

The Great Tribulation is spoken of in Daniel and it is 3½ years in length. As you read the verses that follow, make note of the fact that this Beast power is going to "wear out the saints of the Most High." Over and over it is the saints who are going to be trampled and worn out. As I write this it has occurred to me that the three kings that are humbled in verse 24 are The State of Israel, The United Kingdom and the United States. The word humbled means to subdue or humiliate. This is just speculation on my part at this time.

> *19 Then I wanted to know the truth of the fourth beast, which was different from all the others, very frightening, whose teeth were of iron, and his nails of bronze; who devoured, broke in pieces, and stamped the rest with his feet; 20 and of the ten horns that were in his head, and of the other which came up, and before whom three fell; even of that horn that had eyes, and a mouth speaking very great things, whose appearance was greater than his fellows. 21 I watched, and that horn made war with the saints and overcame them 22 until the Ancient of Days came, and judgment was given to the saints of the Most High. And the time came that the saints possessed the kingdom.* **23 And he said, The fourth beast shall be the fourth kingdom on earth, which shall be different from all kingdoms and shall devour the whole earth, and shall trample it and crush it. 24 And the ten horns out of this kingdom are ten kings that shall arise. And another shall arise after them. And he shall be different from the first, and he shall humble three kings. 25 And he shall speak**

*words against the Most High, and shall wear out the saints of the Most High, and plot to change times and laws. And they shall be given into his hand until a time and times and one-half time. 26 But the judgment shall sit, and they shall take away his rulership, to cut off and to destroy until the end. 27 And the kingdom and rulership, and the greatness of the kingdom under all the heavens, shall be given to the people of the saints of the Most High, whose kingdom is an everlasting kingdom. And all kingdoms shall serve and obey Him. 28 Here is the end of the matter. As for me Daniel, my thoughts troubled me much, and my face changed on me. But I kept the matter in my heart.* (Daniel 7:19-28)

Notice once again here in Revelation where it is again speaking of the 3½ year Great Tribulation, it is the Saints who are going to be trampled and worn out.

*3 And I saw one of his heads, as having been slain to death, and his deadly wound was healed. And all the earth marveled after the beast. 4 And they worshipped the dragon who gave authority to the beast. And they worshipped the beast, saying, "Who is like the beast? Who is able to fight with him?" 5 And he was given a mouth speaking great matters and blasphemies, and he was given authority to do so forty-two months. 6 And he opened his mouth in blasphemies against Elohim, to blaspheme His name, and His Tent, and those dwelling in heaven. 7 And it was given to him to fight with the set-apart ones and to overcome them. And authority was given to him over every tribe and tongue and nation. 8 And all those dwelling on the earth, whose names have not been written in the Book of Life of the slain Lamb, from the foundation of the world shall worship him.* (Revelation 13:3-8)

We read in Daniel 7 that they are given into his hand UNTIL "... *And they shall be given into his hand until a time and times and one-half time."* The saints will be given into the hand of this world ruling empire *UNTIL* the start of the Great Tribulation.

Understanding that Satan is locked away on the Day of Atonement in 2033, at the end of the Great Tribulation, we then count back 3½ years before this date to arrive at Passover 2030.

What is it that happens in 2030 that stops this persecution of the saints? Actually this persecution stops 3½ years before 2030, which will be explained momentarily.

> *3 And another sign was seen in the heaven: and see, a great, fiery red dragon having seven heads and ten horns, and seven crowns on his heads. 4 And his tail draws a third of the stars of the heaven and throws them to the earth. And the dragon stood before the woman who was about to give birth, to devour her child as soon as it was born. 5 And she bore a male child who was to shepherd all nations with a rod of iron. And her child was caught away to Elohim and to His throne. 6 And the woman fled into the wilderness, where she has a place prepared by Elohim, to be nourished there one-thousand two-hundred and sixty days. 7 And there came to be fighting in the heaven: Mika'el and his messengers fought against the dragon. And the dragon and his messengers fought, 8 but they were not strong enough, nor was a place found for them in the heaven any longer. 9 And the great dragon was thrown out, that serpent of old, called the Devil and Satan, who leads all the world astray. He was thrown to the earth, and his messengers were thrown out with him.* (Revelation 12:3-9)

> *10 And I heard a loud voice saying in the heaven, "Now have come the deliverance and the power and the reign of our Elohim, and the authority of His Messiah, for the accuser of our brothers, who accused them before our Elohim day and night, has been thrown down. 11 And they overcame him because of the Blood of the Lamb, and because of the Word of their witness, and they did not love their lives to the death. 12 Because of this, rejoice O heavens, and you who dwell in them! Woe to the earth and the sea, because the devil has come down to you, having great wrath, knowing that he has*

*little time." 13 And when the dragon saw that he had been thrown to the earth, he persecuted the woman who gave birth to the male child. 14 And the woman was given two wings of a great eagle, to fly into the wilderness to her place, where she is nourished for a time and times and half a time, from the presence of the serpent. 15 And out of his mouth the serpent spewed water like a river after the woman, to cause her to be swept away be the river. 16 And the earth helped the woman, and the earth opened its mouth and swallowed up the river which the dragon had spewed out of his mouth. 17 And the dragon was enraged with the woman, and he went to fight with the remnant of her seed, those guarding the commands of Elohim and possessing the witness of* יהושע *Messiah.* (Revelation 12:10-17)

When Yehshua was asked about the Last Days, part of His answer was *when* they were to flee.

*16 "And you shall also be betrayed by parents and brothers and relatives and friends. And some of you shall be put to death. 17 And you shall be hated by all because of My Name. 18 But not a hair of your head shall be lost at all. 19 Possess your lives by your endurance! 20 And when you see Yerushalayim surrounded by armies, then know that its laying waste is near. 21 Then let those in Yehudah flee to the mountains, and let those who are in the midst of her go out, and let not those who are in the fields enter her. 22 Because these are the days of vengeance, to fill all that have been written.* (Luke 21:16-22)

Jerusalem is in the mountains of Judah; also known as the Judean hills, so they cannot be fleeing to these. What mountains are we to flee to then? We are to flee east—to the mountains of Moab. They are mentioned in the Book of Numbers but the confirmation comes in Isaiah.

*7 And he took up his proverb and said, "Balaq the sovereign of Mo'ab has brought me from Aram, from the mountains of*

> the east. 'Come, curse Ya'aqob for me, and come, rage at Yisra'el!'" (Numbers 23:7)

> *1 Send a lamb to the ruler of the land, from Sela to the wilderness, to the mountain of the daughter of Tsiyon. 2 And it shall be, like a wandering bird, a nest thrown out, so are the daughters of Mo'ab at the fords of Arnon. 3 "Bring counsel, execute judgment; make your shadow like the night in the middle of the day; hide the outcasts, do not betray him who escapes. 4 Let My outcasts dwell with you, O Mo'ab; be a shelter to them from the face of the ravager. For the oppressor has met his end, destruction has ceased, those trampling down have perished from the land."* (Isaiah 16:1-4)

We are also told in Daniel another clue. Yehovah is speaking to Moab here in Isaiah 16. Moab is modern day Jordan and consists of the former nations of Moab, Ammon and Edom, and it is to this nation that the woman flees to.

> *40 And at the time of the end shall the king of the South push at him, and the king of the North shall come against him like a whirlwind with chariots, and with horsemen, and with many ships, and he shall enter into the countries, and shall overflow and pass over. 41 He shall enter also into the glorious land, and many countries shall be overthrown: but these shall escape out of his hand, even Edom, and Moab, and the chief of the children of Ammon.* (Daniel 11:40-41)

The prevailing thought in modern-day prophecy teaching is that the Tribulation period is seven years long. This false understanding comes from the Daniel's 70th week teaching that we have already addressed. According to Scripture the Tribulation period is 3½ years long and not seven.

Why are the saints given into the Beast powers hand UNTIL the Great Tribulation, which begins in 2030? How are they going to be vindicated as was stated earlier in Daniel 8?

Looking at our charts once again we see that the year 2030 is colored in blue. It is not a Holy Day. The meaning of this day comes from Jewish tradition. This is Shabbat Shuva and 2030 is also a Sabbatical Year.

> Shabbat Shuvah literally means "Sabbath of Return," but it is also a play on the phrase "Shabbat Teshuvah" (Sabbath of Repentance). It is the Shabbat that occurs between Rosh Hashanah and Yom Kippur and is a time for reflection leading up to the atonement of Yom Kippur. Shabbat Shuvah has two special half Torah readings, one dealing with the importance of heartfelt repentance (Hosea 14:2-10) and one praising the Creator's mercy (Micah 7:18-20).[444]

This Shabbat Shuva or the year 2030 represents the year all 12 Tribes of Israel will be brought back to the land of Israel from their Captivity all around the world. We are working our way back in time from the end, when Satan is locked away on the Day of Atonement (Yom Kippur) in 2033, back to the start of the 2,300 days. We have to work backwards because we know for sure when the Great Tribulation ends in 2033.

It is on this special Sabbath called Shabbat Shuva that the scroll of Hosea is read. In the context of everything I've shared with you thus far, I find the words of the following first two verses to be very striking.

> *1 O Yisra'el, return to* יהוה *your Elohim, for you have stumbled by your crookedness. 2 Take words with you, and return to* יהוה. *Say to Him, "Take away all crookedness, and accept what is good, and we render the bulls of our lips."* (Hosea 14:1-2)

Once again it is the calves of our lips that Yehovah is looking for and the only thing we will have to offer at that time as we come out of the terrible captivity we will have just endured.

---

[444] http://www.jewfaq.org/special.htm

| Sabbath | 6th Cycle | 5th Cycle | 4th Cycle | 3rd Cycle | 2nd Cycle | 1st Cycle |
|---------|-----------|-----------|-----------|-----------|-----------|-----------|
| 2044 | 2037 | 2030 | 2023 | 2016 | 2009 | 2002 |
| 2043 | 2036 | 2029 | 2022 | 2015 | 2008 | 2001 |
| 2042 | 2035 | 2028 | 2021 | 2014 | 2007 | 2000 |
| 2041 | 2034 | 2027 | 2020 | 2013 | 2006 | 1999 |
| 2040 | 2033 | 2026 | 2019 | 2012 | 2005 | 1998 |
| 2039 | 2032 | 2025 | 2018 | 2011 | 2004 | 1997 |
| 2038 | 2031 | 2024 | 2017 | 2010 | 2003 | 1996 |

Examining the chart of this current and last Jubilee Cycle, we know the curses of Leviticus 26 come in a precise order. The first curse in verses 14-17 is the one called Terror and comes during the first Sabbatical Cycle from 1996-2002. The second curse in verses 18-20 is called Severe or Extreme Weather and comes during the years 2003-2009. This curse is added to the first curse so they are *both* going on at the *same* time. The third curse is found in verses 21-22 and is known as Pestilence, Earthquakes and Famine. This curse began in 2010 and will continue through 2017. This curse is now added to the first two. The fourth curse of Leviticus 26 is found in verses 23-26, and comprises the years 2017-2023. This fourth Sabbatical Cycle is then added to the first three curses. This Sabbatical Cycle is the curse of War. The fifth Sabbatical Cycle from 2024-2030 is the curse of Captivity and is found in verses 27-39 and it is added to the previous four curses.

As we go back in time from the time when Satan is locked away on the Day of Atonement in 2033, keep in mind these curses of Leviticus 26. The Great Tribulation begins 3½ years before this time at Passover in the Sabbatical Year of 2030, when all 12 Tribes will have just been brought back from Captivity to the Land of Israel. Right after they are brought back to the Land they must flee into the Wilderness to hide during this Great Tribulation period. Also, remember what I said earlier about the 2,300 days in which the prayers of the saints and the keeping of the Holy Days or appointed times, will be stopped and how this period begins in 2020, the middle of this 120th Jubilee Cycle.

The event (or events) which cause the 12 Tribes to be returned to the Land of Israel in 2030 are a result of the curses the Two Witnesses will be unleashing around the world for 3½ years leading up to the year

2030. We read of this great event known today as the Second Exodus in both Jeremiah and Isaiah.

> *14 Therefore see, the days are coming," declares יהוה "when it is no longer said יהוה lives who brought up the children of Yisra'el from the land of Mitsrayim.' 15 but, as יהוה lives who brought up the children of Yisrael from the land of the north and from all the lands where He had driven them.' For I shall bring them back into their land I gave to their fathers. 16 See, I am sending for many fishermen," declares יהוה, "and they shall fish them. And after that, I shall send for many hunters, and they shall hunt them from every mountain and every hill, and out of the holes of the rocks."* (Jeremiah 16:14-16)

> *6 "In His days Yehudah shall be saved, and Yisra'el dwell safely. And this is His Name whereby He shall be called: 'יהוה our Righteousness.' 7 Therefore, see, the days are coming," declares יהוה, "when they shall say no more, 'As יהוה lives who brought up the children of Yisra'el out of the land of Mitsrayim,' 8 but, 'As יהוה lives who brought up and led the seed of the house of Yisra'el out of the land of the north and from all the lands where I had driven them.' And they shall dwell on their own soil."* (Jeremiah 23:6-8)

> *10 And in that day there shall be a Root of Yishai, standing as a banner to the people. Unto Him the gentiles shall seek, and His rest shall be esteem. 11 And it shall be in that day that יהוה sets His hand again a second time to recover the remnant of His people who are left, from Ashshur and from Mitsrayim, from Pathros and from Kush, from Eylam and from Shin'ar, from Hamath and from the islands of the sea. 12 And He shall raise a banner for the nations, and gather the outcasts of Yisra'el, and assemble the dispersed of Yehudah from the four corners of the earth.* (Isaiah 11:10-12)

I have mentioned the Two Witnesses already in Daniel 8 and Daniel 12. In both cases one of them understood the chronology of events while the other did not. They will be turning the world upside down during the last 3½ years of their ministry. Their ministry ends as the Great Tribulation begins at Passover in 2030.

> *7 And when they have ended their witness, the beast coming up out of the pit of the deep shall fight against them, and overcome them, and kill them, 8 and their dead bodies lie in the street of the great city which spiritually is called Sedom and Mitsrayim, where also our Master was impaled, 9 and some of the peoples and tribes and tongues and nations see their dead bodies for three and a half days, and not allow their dead bodies to be placed into tombs, 10 and those dwelling on the earth rejoice over them and exult. And they shall send gifts to each other, because these two prophets tortured those dwelling on the earth. 11 And after the three and a half days a spirit of life from Elohim entered into them, and they stood upon their feet, and great fear fell on those who saw them. 12 And they heard a loud voice from the heaven saying to them, "Come up here." And they went up into the heaven in a cloud, and their enemies saw them. 13 And in that hour there came to be a great earthquake, and a tenth of the city fell. And in the earthquake seven-thousand men were killed, and the rest became afraid and gave esteem to the Elohim of the heaven.* (Revelation 11:7-13)

Moses and Aaron as well as Elijah and Elisha are examples of the ministry of the Two Witnesses in the Bible and are there for us to learn more about the nature of their ministry in the Last Days.

> *3 "And I shall give unto my two witnesses, and they shall prophesy one-thousand two-hundred and sixty days, clad in sackcloth." 4 These are the two olive trees and the two lampstands that are standing before the Elohim of the earth. 5 And if anyone wishes to harm them, fire comes out from their mouths and consumes their enemies. And if anyone wishes to harm them, he has to be killed in that way. 6 These possess authority to shut the heaven, so that no rain falls in the days of their prophecy. And they possess authority over*

> *waters to turn them to blood, and to smite the earth with all plagues, as often as they wish.* (Revelation 11:3-6)

The Book of Malachi warns us of the spirit the Two Witnesses would have before the coming Day of Yehovah. They are to turn the hearts of the people, the children of Yehovah, back to keeping the Sabbath, the Holy Days of Leviticus 23 and them only. They are not to add to those seven Holy Days in Leviticus 23 any other holi-day days, such as the world now keeps. The Two witnesses will also be telling people to keep the Sabbatical years and by doing these things they will be turning the hearts of the children back to Yehovah.

> *4 "Remember the Torah of Mosheh, My servant, which I commanded him in Horeb for all Yisra'el—laws and right-rulings. 5 See, I am sending you Eliyah the prophet before the coming of the great and awesome day of יהוה. 6 And he shall turn the hearts of the fathers to the children, and the hearts of the children to their fathers, lest I come and smite the earth with utter destruction."* (Malachi 4:4-6)

> *"Lest I come and smite the earth with utter destruction"*,

Because the world does not and will not keep those appointed times of Leviticus 23 and 25, utter destruction is going to come. First to the house of Israel, those saints who are descended from Abraham, then to the rest of the world. These curses are already happening. These are the curses of Leviticus 26, starting in verse 14.

Each of the symbols used to represent these Two Witnesses is significant and is intended to communicate to you the characteristics of Yehovah and His Two Representatives. By witnessing, they are in fact giving testimony; that is speaking by the authority of the torah. The olive trees refer to Yehovah's Spirit and by extension, Yehovah's truth. The two lamp stands give light to a darkened world.

> *23 "But the hour is coming, and now is, when the true worshippers shall worship the Father in spirit and truth, for the Father also does seek such to worship Him. 24 Elohim*

These Two Witnesses are closely connected to the two olive trees and the two lampstands of Zechariah's vision.

> *1 And the messenger who was speaking to me came back and woke me up as a man is awakened from sleep. 2 And he said to me, "What do you see?" So I said, "I have looked, and see: a lampstand all of gold with a bowl on top of it, and on the stand seven lamps with seven spouts to the seven lamps. 3 "And two olive trees are by it, one at the right of the bowl and the other at its left." 4 Then I responded and spoke to the messenger who was speaking to me, saying, "What are these, my master?" 5 And the messenger who was speaking to me answered and said to me, "Do you not know what these are?" And I said, "No, my master." 6 And he answered and said to me, "This is the word of יהוה to Zerubbabel, 'Not by might nor by power, but by My Spirit,' said יהוה of hosts.* (Zechariah 4:1-6)

The Two Witnesses of Revelation 11 will be warning this End-Time Babylonian Empire one last time and in so doing, will also be calling for the saints to *"Come out of her."*

> *4 And I heard another voice from the heaven saying, "Come out of her, my people, lest you share in her sins, and lest you receive of her plagues."* (Revelation 18:4)

Just as Malachi has indicated, these End-Time Two Witnesses will be like Moses and Elijah. In Exodus we read of Moses being like a god to Aaron, who would speak for him. Also Pharaoh thought of Moses as a god.

> *15 "And you shall speak to him and put the words in his mouth. And I am with your mouth and with his mouth, and I shall teach you what to do 16 and he shall speak for you to the people. And it shall be that he shall be a mouth for you, and*

(continued from previous: *is Spirit, and those who worship Him need to worship in spirit and truth."* (John 4:23-24))

> *you shall be an elohim for him. 17 And take this rod in your hand, with which you shall do the signs."* (Exodus 4:15-17)

> *1 So יהוה said to Mosheh, "See, I have made you an elohim to Pharaoh, and Aharon your brother is your prophet."* (Exodus 7:1)

Moses and Aaron told Pharaoh to let them go so they could keep the Feasts of Yehovah. These are the very same feasts told to us in Leviticus 23.

> *1 And afterwards Mosheh and Aharon went in and said to Pharaoh, "Thus said יהוה Elohim of Yisra'el, 'Let My people go, so that they keep a festival to Me in the wilderness.'"* (Exodus 5:1)

In the same manner, the Two Witnesses will be speaking with the then world ruling Emperor, to let the saints who are still alive go, so they can return to Jerusalem to keep the feasts. This Emperor will refuse just as Pharaoh did and the Two Witnesses will then stop the rain from falling anywhere on the earth.

> *3 And I shall give unto my two witnesses, and they shall prophesy one-thousand two-hundred and sixty days, clad in sackcloth." 4 These are the two olive trees and the two lampstands that are standing before the Elohim of the earth. 5 And if anyone wishes to harm them, fire comes out from their mouth and consumes their enemies. And if anyone wishes to harm them, he has to be killed in that way. 6 These possess authority to shut the heaven, so that no rain falls in the days of their prophecy. And they possess authority over waters to turn them to blood, and to smite the earth with all plagues, as often as they wish.* (Revelation 11:3-6)

Just like Moses, they will implement the very same kinds of plagues as was done before the First Exodus, but they will also have the power of Elijah to stop it from raining anywhere on the entire earth during this 3½ year time period of their ministry.

> *1 And Eliyahu the Tishbite, of the inhabitants of Gil'ad, said to Ahab, "As יהוה Elohim of Yisra'el lives, before whom I stand, there shall be no dew or rain these years, except at my word."* (1 Kings 17:1)
>
> *17 Eliyahu was a man with feelings like us, and he prayed earnestly that it would not rain. And it did not rain on the land for three years and six months. 18 And he prayed again, and the heaven gave rain, and the land brought forth its fruit.* (James 5:17-18)

You must now pause and consider what will be the ramifications of it not raining on the Earth for 3½ years. This event takes place *after* the 4th Sabbatical Cycle of War when the 12 Tribes find themselves in Captivity. With no rain you will have no crops and it will not take long for those foods stored away to be eaten up. We read in Revelation about the seals that are opened before the martyrdom of the saints and that ¼ of the people of the world die from sword and hunger during this 4th and 5th Sabbatical Cycle. It is my opinion that the 5th Seal takes place when the Two Witnesses are killed at Passover in 2030.

> *1 And I saw when the Lamb opened one of the seals, and I heard one of the four living creatures saying, like a sound of thunder, "Come and see." 2 And I looked and saw a white horse, and he who sat on it holding a bow. And a crown was given to him, and he went out overcoming and to overcome. 3 And when He opened the second seal, I heard the second living creature saying, "Come and see." 4 And another horse, fiery red, went out. And it was given to the one who sat on it to take peace from the earth, and that they should slay one another. And a great sword was given to him.* (Revelation 6:1-4)
>
> *5 And when He opened the third seal, I heard the third living creature say, "Come and see." And I looked and saw a black horse, and he who sat on it holding a pair of scales in his hand. 6 And I heard a voice in the midst of the four living creatures saying, "A quart of wheat for a day's wage, and three quarts*

> *of barley for a day's wage. And do not harm the oil and the wine." 7 And when He opened the fourth seal, I heard the voice of the fourth living creature saying, "Come and see." 8 And I looked and saw a pale horse. And he who sat on it had the name Death, and the grave followed with him. And authority was given to them over a fourth of the earth, to kill with sword, and with hunger, and with death, and by the beasts of the earth.* (Revelation 6:5-8)

The white horse is the religion of Islam, which is going to conquer the world by force. This word *conquer* comes from the word nike – to conquer, prevail and to get the victory over another and in this case the Islamic world will conquer and gain the victory over the 12 Tribes of Israel. This will be done by war and will result in starvation and death. ¼ of the earth's people will die because of these four curses.

When the Two Witnesses call for no rain for 3½ years it will be on top of an already suffering planet.

> G3528 νικάω nikao⁻ *nik-ah'-o*
>
> From G3529; to *subdue* (literally or figuratively): - conquer, overcome, prevail, get the victory.
>
> G3529 νίκη nike⁻ *nee'-kay*
>
> Apparently a primary word; *conquest* (abstractly), that is, (figuratively) the *means of success:* - victory.

Elijah was a no-nonsense, direct-to-the-point prophet who simply laid it all on the line. His antagonists could not kill him and when they threatened him, lightning struck them dead at his command.

> *5 And if anyone wishes to harm them, fire comes out from their mouth and consumes their enemies. And if anyone wishes to harm them, he has to be killed in that way.* (Revelation 11:5)

> *9 He then sent to him a captain of fifty with his fifty men. And he went up to him, and see, he was sitting on the top of a hill. And he spoke to him, "Man of Elohim, the sovereign has said, 'Come down!'" 10 And Eliyahu answered and said to the captain of fifty, "And if I am a man of Elohim, let fire come down from the heavens and consume you and your fifty men." And fire came down from the heavens and consumed him and his fifty. 11 He then sent another captain of fifty with his fifty men to him. And he answered and said to him, "Man of Elohim, this is what the sovereign said, 'Come down at once!'" 12 And Eliyah answered and said to them, "If I am a man of Elohim, let fire come down from the heavens and consume you and your fifty men." And a fire of Elohim came down from the heavens and consumed him and his fifty. 13 And again he sent a third captain of fifty with his fifty men. And the third captain of fifty went up, and came and fell on his knees before Eliyahu, and pleaded with him, and said to him, "Man of Elohim, please let my life and the life of these fifty servants of yours be precious in your eyes. 14 "See, fire has come down from the heavens and burned up the first two captains of fifties with their fifties. But let my life be precious in your eyes."* (2 Kings 1:9-14)

The world will be enraged with the Two Witnesses after these 3½ years. In order to appease them and avoid further calamities from them, the world will acquiesce to their demands to let the remaining Israelites return to Jerusalem for Passover in 2030 the Sabbatical Year. They will bring them in from the four corners and farthest reaches of the world and will do so in great haste in order to have it rain once again.

In the life of Jacob is another prophetic indicator you need to be very aware of. Jacob worked seven years for Laban in order to marry Rachel. At the end of those seven years, Jacob was deceived and given Leah instead. These events took place at the end of the 5th Sabbatical Cycle in the year 2191 A.C.

| Sabbath | 6th Cycle | 5th Cycle | 4th Cycle | 3rd Cycle | 2nd Cycle | 1st Cycle |
|---|---|---|---|---|---|---|
| 2205 | 2198 | 2191 | 2184 | 2177 | 2170 | 2163 |
| 2204 | 2197 | 2190 | 2183 | 2176 | 2169 | 2162 |
| 2203 | 2196 | 2189 | 2182 | 2175 | 2168 | 2161 |
| 2202 | 2195 | 2188 | 2181 | 2174 | 2167 | 2160 |
| 2201 | 2194 | 2187 | 2180 | 2173 | 2166 | 2159 |
| 2200 | 2193 | 2186 | 2179 | 2172 | 2165 | 2158 |
| 2199 | 2192 | 2185 | 2178 | 2171 | 2164 | 2157 |

When you compare our current Jubilee Cycle to that of Jacobs above, you can see the year Jacob is deceived is also the year in which those who comprise the nation of Israel (the 12 Tribes from around the world), are to be brought back to the Land. Once they arrive back in the land of Israel, they will face a life or death decision, which we explain in moment. They have been brought back for one purpose from around the world and that purpose is so the Beast power can have them all in one place where he can complete the job he has been trying to do all along and that is to completely trample the saints underfoot and slaughter them all until *not one* is left.

Pharaoh, as most of you know, after he let the Israelites go with Moses and Aaron, had yet another change of heart and set out to wipe the Israelites out and destroy them completely. This resulted in the entire Egyptian army being destroyed in the Red Sea when the waters came rushing back over the top of them.

Just like Pharaoh, the End-Time Beast power is seeking to destroy every last one of the children of Israel. But as I have already shared with you, the Scriptures warn us that when we see the armies surrounding Jerusalem, we are to flee to the mountains. When we do flee into the Wilderness, the Beast power then pursues us with a vengeance.

> *15 And out of his mouth the serpent spewed water like a river after the woman, to cause her to be swept away by the river. 16 And the earth helped the woman, and the earth opened its mouth and swallowed up the river which the dragon had spewed out of his mouth. 17 And the dragon was enraged with the woman, and he went to fight with the remnant of her seed, those guarding the commands of Elohim and possessing the witness of יהושע Messiah.* (Revelation 12:15-17)

Take special notice of the fact that, once those who pursued the woman are killed, by being swallowed by the earth, then the Beast power turns and attacks the rest of her seed who keep the Commandments. Who are these people and why did they not flee with the woman when the armies surrounded Jerusalem?

It is my personal belief that, just as there is this dispute today between those who follow the Holy Days based on the Jewish Hebrew Calendar and others who follow the Holy Days set out by the barley to begin the year and the first sliver of the Sighted Moon to start the month, there will be a conflict over when Passover is, based on the two calendar systems and they will be one month apart. When the saints are all brought back to Jerusalem in 2030, this issue will again arise. I believe those who keep the first Passover and do as they are told in Exodus: to eat it in haste with their shoes on and their staff in their hands ready to flee, will be those who run into the wilderness and do so successfully. We have been eating the Passover in haste all these years in preparation for this future flight once again.

> *11 And this is how you eat it: your loins girded, your sandals on your feet, and your staff in your hand. And you shall eat it in haste. It is the Passover of יהוה.* (Exodus 12:11)

Once this first group escapes, the armies of this Beast power will turn on those who are keeping the commandments and preparing to keep Passover in the second month.

> *17 And the dragon was enraged with the woman, and he went to fight with the remnant of her seed, those guarding the commands of Elohim and possessing the witness of יהושע Messiah.* (Revelation 12:15-17)

I have now covered the Great Tribulation, which begins at Passover 2030 and ends on the Day of Atonement in 2033. The Two Witnesses precede this tribulation and have now been at work 3½ years and are killed at Passover in 2030. It is my position that the fifth seal of Revelation takes place at this time at the second Passover when both the Two Witnesses and those who had not fled are martyred.

> *9 And when He had opened the fifth seal, I saw under the altar the souls of those who had been slain for the Word of God, and for the testimony which they held. 10 And they cried with a loud voice, saying, Until when, Master, holy and true, do You not judge and avenge our blood on those who dwell on the earth? 11 And white robes were given to each one of them. And it was said to them that they should rest yet for a little time, until both their fellow servants and their brothers (those about to be killed as they were) should have their number made complete.* (Revelation 6:9-11)

The reason we have explained about the Two Witnesses is because of the question we posed earlier. When does the vindication of the saints begin? The vindication of the saints begins when the Two Witnesses begin their calling at the Feast of Trumpets 2026, 3½ before Passover 2030.

> *14 And he said to me, "For two-thousand, three-hundred evenings and mornings. Then the sanctuary shall be vindicated."* (Daniel 8:14 | MKJV)

Again the word *sanctuary* here should be *saints*. It is the saints that are going to be vindicated and that vindication begins with the Two Witnesses calling for it not to rain anywhere on the earth and the many other curses they call upon the nations of the world.

I must also remind you that when the Two Witnesses begin their work in 2026, it is in the 5th Sabbatical Cycle, which is the cycle of captivity as we are told in Leviticus.

> *27 And if you will not for all of this listen to Me, but will walk contrary to Me, 28 then I will walk contrary to you also in fury. And I, even I, will chastise you seven times for your sins. 29 And you shall eat the flesh of your sons, and the flesh of your daughters you shall eat. 30 And I will destroy your high places and cut down your images, and throw your carcasses on the carcasses of your idols, and My soul shall despise you. 31 And I will make your cities waste and cause your sanctuaries to be deserted. And I will not smell the savor of*

> *your sweet odors. 32 And I will turn the land into wasteland. And your enemies who dwell in it shall be astonished at it. 33 And I will scatter you among the nations, and will draw out a sword after you. And your land shall be waste, and your cities waste. 34 Then shall the land enjoy its sabbaths, as long as it lies waste, and you are in your enemies' land; then shall the land rest and enjoy its sabbaths. 35 As long as it lies waste it shall rest, because it did not rest in your sabbaths when you lived on it. 36 And on those of you that are left I will send a faintness into their hearts in the lands of their enemies. And the sound of a driven leaf shall chase them, and they shall flee as if fleeing from a sword. And they shall fall when none pursues. 37 And they shall fall on one another, as if it were before a sword, when none pursues. And you shall have no power to stand before your enemies. 38 And you shall perish among the nations, and the land of your enemies shall eat you up. 39 And they that are left of you shall putrefy in their iniquity in the lands of your enemies. And also they shall putrefy with them in the iniquities of their fathers.* (Leviticus 26:27-39)

The 12 Tribes of Israel are going to be punished and punished severely for breaking the covenant of Mount Sinai. That curse of war, which is the 4th curse, (Leviticus 26:23-26) is then followed by the curse of captivity. Now that the nations of Israel have been destroyed and some of those who kept the Torah were martyred, they now ask for vengeance. (Revelation 6:9-11) This vengeance comes at the end of the 2,300 days of Daniel 8 and is executed in part by the Two Witnesses.

When you count from the Feast of Trumpets in 2026, (the time the Two Witnesses begin their 3½ years work of no rain), back in time by 2,300 days, you arrive at the Feast of Shavuot (Pentecost) in 2020. This takes you right back to the start of this chapter where you read in Daniel the following verse segment:

> *27 And in the middle of the week he shall put an end to slaughtering and meal offering. (Daniel 9:27)*

I have now helped you to identify when these 2,300 days of sheer hell on earth will begin. I say it this way because of the many examples we already have of those nations that have been invaded and taken over by Islamic forces.

In Sudan, Nigeria, Samalia and even in Syria, the news reports tell us of how those women that are captured and even young girls or those who have to go through a check point, are raped and gang raped many times over. The News reports from England, Norway and Sweden report how gangs of men go about and rape those who are not Muslim. Still other reports record how in these very countries of North Western Europe, Muslim men shout out how they are going to take the native women as war booty once they have killed the men. These things are already happening right now and it is coming to North America and the United Kingdom and Australia. And no one is telling these people of these great nations what is coming. Are you ready for this horror that is already being prepared because we will not obey Yehovah?

Counting back from the Feast of Trumpets by 2,300 days, shows us that this horror begins in 2020 at Shavuot and it is from this time forward that the saints and all 12 Tribes of Israel, will be hunted down and murdered around the world for a very long, drawn out and excruciating 6¼ years. In Daniel 8:14 the question was asked, "How long before the saints (not the Sanctuary) are vindicated?"

> 9 And when He opened the fifth seal, I saw under the altar the beings of those having been slain for the Word of Elohim and for the witness which they held, 10 and they cried with a loud voice, saying, "How long, O Master, set-apart and true, until You judge and avenge our blood on those who dwell on the earth?" 11 And there was given to each one a white robe, and they were told that they should rest a little while longer, until both the number of their fellow servants and their brothers, who would be killed as they were, was completed. (Revelation 6:9-11)

> 2 "Because true and righteous are His judgments, because He has judged the great whore who corrupted the earth with

*her whoring. And He has avenged on her the blood of His servants shed by her."* (Revelation 19:2)

Those saints will be murdered, raped and enslaved for 2,300 days from the time of Shavuot in 2020 until the Two Witnesses begin to curse the world for their sake at the Feast of Trumpets in 2026. This is when the saints will be set apart and vindicated, just as Israel was set apart in Goshen from being affected by the curses of Moses after the third plague.

This year of 2026 is also the third year in the cycle of Captivity and the third year during the 10 Days (years) of Awe (from the Feast of Trumpets to the Day of Atonement each fall are 10 days known as the 10 Days of Awe), this year of 2026 is the third year in these ten years from 2024 the year of Trumpets until 2033 the year of Atonement.

In summary then, of what I have now fully gone over with you:

Atonement 2033–Passover 2030: 3 ½ yearlong Great Tribulation

Passover 2030–Trumpets 2026: Two Witnesses for 3½ years

Trumpets 2026–Shavuot 2020: 2,300 days of hell

| Sabbath | 6th Cycle | 5th Cycle | 4th Cycle | 3rd Cycle | 2nd Cycle | 1st Cycle |
|---|---|---|---|---|---|---|
| 2254 | 2247 | 2240 | 2233 | 2226 | 2219 | 2212 |
| 2253 | 2246 | 2239 | 2232 | 2225 | 2218 | 2211 |
| 2252 | 2245 | 2238 | 2231 | 2224 | 2217 | 2210 |
| 2251 | 2244 | 2237 | 2230 | 2223 | 2216 | 2209 |
| 2250 | 2243 | 2236 | 2229 | 2222 | 2215 | 2208 |
| 2249 | 2242 | 2235 | 2228 | 2221 | 2214 | 2207 |
| 2248 | 2241 | 2234 | 2227 | 2220 | 2213 | 2206 |

The trampling underfoot can only occur once you are dead and your body is turned from ashes to dust and then walked all over.

It is during this time of the 2,300 days that all of Israel, who will not keep Yehovah's Commandments, *will* be killed. Even some of those who *do* keep His Commandments will be killed as Ezekiel shows us in his prophecy about the hairs. You will not be able to go and keep any of the Feasts as you will be killed and you will not be able to trust those who are coming. It will be the scariest *of all possible* times.

The doing away with of the daily will also entail doing away with the keeping of each of the Holy Days by those who seek to keep them.

As I considered how the Two Witnesses would be calling for the same curses as Moses and Aaron to the Egyptian nation, it occurred to me that each time the Egyptian nation interacted with Israel from the time of Abraham up to and including the nation of Babylon in 586 B.C. that they all represents different aspects of the End-Time Babylonian empire now coming on the world scene and how it was going to interact with the 12 Tribes in these last days.

These examples of this End-Time empire are throughout the Bible. But the one that perplexed me the most for some time, as I considered the Sabbatical Cycles was the story of the Seven Years of Plenty and the Seven Years of Famine.

When I plotted them out in the Sabbatical and Jubilee Year Cycles, I expected them to fall within two of the Sabbatical Cycles, starting and ending on a Sabbatical Year. But when I did Joseph's chronology, I realized they did not fit within any of the Sabbatical Cycles.

It would not be until several months later that I would come to see that the end of the Seven Years of Famine parallels the time of Noah's Flood, the time of Sodom and Gomorrah, and the time in which Satan is going to be locked away during our Jubilee Cycle in 2033.

The Seven Weeks of Plenty during Joseph's time (diagram #3 on the next page) for Egypt represents the End-Time Babylonian superpower. Once the Beast power has defeated the Israelite nations, they will have free and unlimited access to all our natural resources, and also, free labor once they have enslaved all those of us who survive. For this End-Time empire, it will be the best of times and they will prosper inordinately at our expense.

But once those Seven Years of Plenty for Babylon are over, then begins the Seven Years of Famine. This is brought on by the curses the Two Witnesses will then be administering upon whomever they so choose. Notice that the Famine years in Joseph's Jubilee Cycle (diagram #3) begin in 2237 A.C., which matches our own Jubilee Cycle (diagram #4) in the year 2027. The Two Witnesses begin at the Feast of Trumpets in 2026, just six months earlier. With no rain for 3½ years, there most certainly *will* be Famine. Furthermore, with the Wars of the Tribulation from 2030 C.E.–2033 C.E. and the ultimate defeat and destruction of the last Babylonian Empire, this falls in line precisely with the Seven Years of Famine in Joseph's day from 2237 A.C.–2243 A.C.

As we move on to the first part of the verse in Daniel 9:27 in the next chapter, you will once again see just how terrifyingly *accurate* these dates prove themselves to be. Keep in mind what I have impressed upon you thus far concerning the start of the 2,300 days at Shavuot in the middle of this last Jubilee Cycle, in the year of 2020.

In conclusion for this chapter, I am now going to show you each of the applicable Jubilee Cycles all on one page so you can see them and compare them one with the other for yourselves.

1) **The Jubilee Cycle for the Great Flood in 1656 A.C.**

| Sabbath | 6th Cycle | 5th Cycle | 4th Cycle | 3rd Cycle | 2nd Cycle | 1st Cycle |
|---|---|---|---|---|---|---|
| 1666 | 1659 | 1652 | 1645 | 1638 | 1631 | 1624 |
| 1665 | 1658 | 1651 | 1644 | 1637 | 1630 | 1623 |
| 1664 | 1657 | 1650 | 1643 | 1636 | 1629 | 1622 |
| 1663 | 1656 | 1649 | 1642 | 1635 | 1628 | 1621 |
| 1662 | 1655 | 1648 | 1641 | 1634 | 1627 | 1620 |
| 1661 | 1654 | 1647 | 1640 | 1633 | 1626 | 1619 |
| 1660 | 1653 | 1646 | 1639 | 1632 | 1625 | 1618 |

2) **The Jubilee Cycle for the destruction of Sodom & Gomorrah in 2047 A.C.**

| Sabbath | 6th Cycle | 5th Cycle | 4th Cycle | 3rd Cycle | 2nd Cycle | 1st Cycle |
|---|---|---|---|---|---|---|
| 2058 | 2051 | 2044 | 2037 | 2030 | 2023 | 2016 |
| 2057 | 2050 | 2043 | 2036 | 2029 | 2022 | 2015 |
| 2056 | 2049 | 2042 | 2035 | 2028 | 2021 | 2014 |
| 2055 | 2048 | 2041 | 2034 | 2027 | 2020 | 2013 |
| 2054 | 2047 | 2040 | 2033 | 2026 | 2019 | 2012 |
| 2053 | 2046 | 2039 | 2032 | 2025 | 2018 | 2011 |
| 2052 | 2045 | 2038 | 2031 | 2024 | 2017 | 2010 |

3) The Jubilee Cycle for the Seven Years of Plenty (2230 A.C.–2236 A.C.) & Seven Years of Famine (2237 A.C.–2243 A.C.) in Egypt during Joseph's life.

| Sabbath | 6th Cycle | 5th Cycle | 4th Cycle | 3rd Cycle | 2nd Cycle | 1st Cycle |
|---|---|---|---|---|---|---|
| 2254 | 2247 | 2240 | 2233 | 2226 | 2219 | 2212 |
| 2253 | 2246 | 2239 | 2232 | 2225 | 2218 | 2211 |
| 2252 | 2245 | 2238 | 2231 | 2224 | 2217 | 2210 |
| 2251 | 2244 | 2237 | 2230 | 2223 | 2216 | 2209 |
| 2250 | 2243 | 2236 | 2229 | 2222 | 2215 | 2208 |
| 2249 | 2242 | 2235 | 2228 | 2221 | 2214 | 2207 |
| 2248 | 2241 | 2234 | 2227 | 2220 | 2213 | 2206 |

4) The Jubilee Cycle for this the 120th cycle today. The 2,300 days begin at Shavuot 2020- Trumpets 2026 & The Two Witnesses begin their work for 3½ years from Trumpets 2026-Passover 2030 & the Great Tribulation begins at Passover 2030 & ends on the Day of Atonement 2033 C.E.

| Sabbath | 6th Cycle | 5th Cycle | 4th Cycle | 3rd Cycle | 2nd Cycle | 1st Cycle |
|---|---|---|---|---|---|---|
| 2044 | 2037 | 2030 | 2023 | 2016 | 2009 | 2002 |
| 2043 | 2036 | 2029 | 2022 | 2015 | 2008 | 2001 |
| 2042 | 2035 | 2028 | 2021 | 2014 | 2007 | 2000 |
| 2041 | 2034 | 2027 | 2020 | 2013 | 2006 | 1999 |
| 2040 | 2033 | 2026 | 2019 | 2012 | 2005 | 1998 |
| 2039 | 2032 | 2025 | 2018 | 2011 | 2004 | 1997 |
| 2038 | 2031 | 2024 | 2017 | 2010 | 2003 | 1996 |

# Chapter 11 | The Great Enlightenment of Mankind (Daniel 9:27)

*24 Seventy weeks are decreed for your people and for your set-apart city, to put an end to the transgression, and to seal up sins, and to cover crookedness, and to bring in everlasting righteousness, and to seal up vision and prophet, and to anoint the Most Set-apart. 25 Know, then, and understand: from the going forth of the command to restore and build Yerushalayim until Messiah the Prince is seven weeks and sixty-two weeks. It shall be built again, with streets and a trench, but in times of affliction. 26 And after the sixty-two weeks Messiah shall be cut off and have naught. And the people of a coming prince shall destroy the city and the set-apart place. And the end of it is with a flood. And wastes are decreed, and fighting until the end. 27 And he shall confirm a covenant with many for one week. And in the middle of the week he shall put an end to slaughtering and meal offering. And on the wing of abominations he shall lay waste, even until the complete end and that which is decreed is poured out on the one who lays waste.[1]* [Footnote: [1]Matthew 24:15 (Daniel 9:24-27)]

*27 And he shall confirm a covenant with many for one week. And in the middle of the week he shall put an end to slaughtering and meal offering. And on the wing of abominations he shall lay waste, even until the complete end and that which is decreed is poured out on the one who lays waste.* (Daniel 9:27—full)

*27 And he shall confirm a covenant with many for one week.* (Daniel 9:27—partial)

This verse was one of the most challenging for me to unravel. The first part should now be fairly self-evident as a result of having studied it as in depth as we have thus far. You now know that the word "week" is Shabua and is a 49-year period. You also know that Seventy "Weeks" is Seventy Shavuot and 70 x 49 = 3,430 years. Last, but not least, you know the last Shabua began in 1996.

I began to look for a *"covenant made with many"* that would begin around 1996, thinking it had to fall somewhere within this last Sabbatical Week from 1996-2044. The *Oslo Accord* was not it and none of the other treaties made between the State of Israel and any other nation or nations seemed to match a *"covenant made with many."* I found this to be much harder than originally expected until one day, one of the people in the group I work with shared something that blew us all away, to put it mildly—not only with regard to pinning down the *"covenant made with many,"* but also, when all the evidence was in, being struck with the realization of just how far reaching and elaborate it is and how it totally supersedes the elected governments currently in power. The more we looked at this *"covenant made with many,"* as well as the potentially far reaching implications of it, the more we kept asking ourselves "Why is this so bad? Why is this *covenant* so evil according to the *Bible*?" The more we uncovered and the deeper we looked into it, the more diabolical and sinister we found it to be.

I am now very close to the trail's end when it comes to me conclusively explaining to you the Daniel 70 Weeks Prophecy—which includes the clincher in all the proofs I have presented to you thus far. That being said, I must now present this last one to you from the beginning so that you too can see how evil this is and understand. So, please bear with me as I proceed to explain this complex subject as simply as I possibly can.

# The Enlightenment of Mankind

> *16 And יהוה Elohim commanded the man, saying, "Eat of every tree of the garden 17 but do not eat of the tree of the knowledge of good and evil, for in the day that you eat of it you shall certainly die."* (Genesis 2:16-17)

We were commanded not to eat of the Tree of the Knowledge of Good and Evil. This tree embodied both good information and bad information. It is much like how the conspiracy teachings which run rampant today include some sound facts and/or biblical knowledge and yet, are mixed in with some out and out lies or not quite the truth stories. Or, in other words:

> *12 "Do not say, 'a conspiracy,' concerning all that this people call a conspiracy, nor be afraid of their threats, nor be troubled."* (Isaiah 8:12)

Let us now read in Genesis how Eve had a conversation with the serpent:

> *1 And the serpent was more crafty than any beast of the field which יהוה Elohim had made, and he said to the woman, "Is it true that Elohim has said, 'Do not eat of every tree of the garden?'" 2 And the woman said to the serpent, "We are to eat of the fruit of the trees of the garden, 3 but of the fruit of the tree which is in the midst of the garden, Elohim has said, 'Do not eat of it, nor touch it, lest you die.'" 4 And the serpent said to the woman, "You shall certainly not die. 5 For Elohim knows that in the day you eat of it your eyes shall be opened, and you shall be like Elohim, knowing good and evil."* (Genesis 3:1-5)

The word serpent is: **H5175** nâchâsh *naw-khawsh'*

From **H517**: a *snake* (from its *hiss*): –serpent.

**H5172**: nâchash *naw-khash'*

A primitive root; properly to *hiss*, that is, *whisper* a (magic) spell; generally to *prognosticate:* –X certainly, divine, enchanter, (use) X enchantment, learn by experience, X indeed, diligently observe.

**H5174**: nᵉchâsh *nekh-awsh'*

(Chaldee); corresponding to **H5154**; *copper:* –brass.

We also read of Satan being described in 2 Corinthians.

*13 For such are false emissaries, deceptive workers, masquerading as emissaries of Messiah. 14 And no wonder! For Satan himself masquerades as a messenger of light! 15 It is not surprising, then, if his servants also masquerade as servants of righteousness,¹ whose end shall be according to their works!²* [Footnotes: ¹Matthew 7:15-23; 2 Peter 2:1-22. ²Matthew 13:41-42 (2 Corinthians 11:13-15)]

W.E. Bullinger writes of this very thing;

The Hebrew word rendered "serpent" in Genesis 3:1 is **Nachash** (from the root **Nachash, to shine**), and means **a Shining One**. Hence, in Chaldee it means **brass** or **copper**, because of its **shining**. Hence also, the word **Nehushtan**, a piece of brass, in 2 Kings 18:4.

*4 He took away the high places and broke the pillars, and cut down the Ashĕrah, and broke in pieces the bronze serpent which Mosheh had made, for until those days the children of Yisra'ĕl burned incense to it, and called it Neḥushtan.* (2 Kings 18:4)

In the same way **Saraph**, in Isaiah 6:2, 6 means **a Burning One**, and, because the serpents mentioned in Numbers 21 were burning, in the poison of their bite, they were called **Saraphim**, or **Seraphs**.

But when the LORD said unto Moses, "Make thee a fiery serpent" (Numbers 21:8), He said, "Make thee a *Saraph*," and, in obeying this command, we read in verse 9, "Moses made a *Nachash* of **brass**." *Nachash* is thus used as being interchangeable with *Saraph*.

Now, if *Saraph* is used of a serpent because its bite was *burning*, and is also used of a celestial or spirit-being (a Burning One), why should not *Nachash* be used of a serpent because its appearance was *shining*, and be also used of a celestial or spirit-being (a Shining One)?

The *Nachash*, or serpent, who beguiled Eve (2 Corinthians 11:3) is spoken of as "an Angel of Light" in verse 14. Have we not, in this, a clear intimation that it was not a snake, but a glorious shining being, apparently an angel, to whom Eve paid such great deference, acknowledging him as one who seemed to possess superior knowledge, and who was evidently a being of a superior (not of an inferior) order? Moreover, in the description of Satan as "the King of Tyre"[445] it is distinctly implied that the latter being was of a supernatural order when he is called "a cherub" (Ezekiel 28:14, 16; read from vv. 11-19). His presence "in Eden, the Garden of Elohim" (v. 13), is also clearly stated, as well as his being "perfect in beauty" (v. 12) his being "perfect" in his ways from the day he was created "until iniquity was found in him" (v. 15), and as **being "lifted up because of his beauty"** (v. 17).

We cannot conceive Eve as holding converse with a snake, but we can understand her being fascinated[446] by one, apparently

---

[445] Ezekiel 28:11-19, who is quite a different being from "the Prince of Tyre," in vv. 1-10, who is purely human.

[446] It is remarkable that the verb *nachash* always means to enchant, fascinate, bewitch; or of one having and using occult knowledge. See also: Genesis 30:27; 44:5, 15; Leviticus 19:26; Deuteronomy 18:10; 1 Kings 20:33; 2 Kings 17:17, 21:6 and 2 Chronicles 33:6. So also is the noun used in Numbers 23:23, 24:1.

"an Angel of Light" (i.e., a glorious angel), possessing superior and supernatural knowledge.[447]

Satan is an archangel and appears to us as an Angel of Light and as such had Eve's undivided attention, as he would have had with any of us. Satan came to Eve not as a snake, but as an Angel of Light and was stunning in his beauty. This is why she talked to him. Satan is not going to change his ways today, nor has he anytime in human history or will he in the future.

Inasmuch as Satan appears to us as an angel of light, so are the Egyptian and Babylonian gods, a 'type' of Satan.

The wax candle was a hieroglyphic symbol and was intended to exhibit the Babylonian god in one of the essential characters of "the Great Mediator." To learn *which god* this act of lighting candles represented, I invite you to read the following in depth excerpt by Alexander Hislop:

> Another peculiarity of the papal worship is the use of lamps and wax candles. If the Madonna and Child are set up in a niche, they must have a lamp to burn before them; if mass is to be celebrated, though in broad daylight, there must be wax candles lighted on the altar; if a grand procession is to be formed, it cannot be thorough and complete without lighted tapers to grace the goodly show. The use of these lamps and tapers comes from the same source as all the rest of the papal superstition.
>
> That which caused the "Heart," when it became an emblem of the incarnate Son, to be represented as a heart on fire, required also that burning lamps and lighted candles should form part of the worship of that Son; for so, according to the established rites of Zoroaster, was the sun-god worshiped. When every Egyptian on the same night was required to light a lamp before his house in the open air, this was an act of

---

[447] http://www.bibleunderstanding.com/serpent.htm

homage to the Sun that had veiled its glory by enshrouding itself in a human form.

When the Yezidis of Kurdistan, at this day, once a year celebrate their festival of "burning lamps," that, too, is to the honor of Sheikh Shems, or the Sun. Now, what on these high occasions was done on a grand scale was also done on a smaller scale, in the individual acts of worship to their god, by the lighting of lamps and tapers before the favorite divinity. In Babylon, this practice had been exceedingly prevalent, as we learn from the Apocryphal writer of the Book of Baruch.

"They (the Babylonians)," says he, "light up lamps to their gods,[448] and that in greater numbers, too, than they do for themselves, although the gods cannot see one of them, and are senseless as the beams of their houses."

In pagan Rome, the same practice was observed.

Thus we find Licinius, the pagan emperor, before joining battle with Constantine, his rival, calling a council of his friends in a thick wood, and there offering sacrifices to his gods, "lighting up wax tapers" before them, and at the same time, in his speech, giving his gods a hint, that if they did not give him the victory against Constantine, his enemy and theirs, he would be under the necessity of abandoning their worship, and lighting up no more "wax tapers to their honor."

In the pagan processions, also, at Rome, the wax candles largely figured. "At these solemnities," says Dr. Middleton, referring to Apuleius as his authority, "the chief magistrate used to frequently assist, in robes of ceremony, attended by the priests in surplices, with wax candles in their hands, carrying upon a pageant or thensa, the images of their gods, dressed out in their best clothes; these were usually followed by the principal youth of the place, in white linen vestments

---

[448] http://www.biblebelievers.com/babylon/sect55.htm

or surplices, singing hymns in honor of the gods whose festivals they were celebrating, accompanied by crowds of all sorts that were initiated in the same religion, all with flambeaux or wax candles in their hands."

Now, so thoroughly and exclusively pagan was this custom of lighting up lamps and candles in daylight, that we find Christian writers, such as Lactantius, in the 4th-century, exposing the absurdity of the practice, and deriding the Romans "for lighting up candles to God, as if He lived in the dark." Had such a custom at that time gained the least footing among Christians, Lactantius could never have ridiculed it as he does, as a practice peculiar to paganism. But what was unknown to the Christian church in the beginning of the 4th-century, soon thereafter began to creep in, and now forms one of the most marked peculiarities of that community that boasts that it is the "Mother and mistress of all churches."

While Rome uses both lamps and wax candles in her sacred rites, it is evident, however, that she attributes some pre-eminent virtue to the latter above all other lights. Up to the time of the Council of Trent, she thus prayed on Easter eve, at the blessing of the Easter candles:

> Calling upon thee in thy works, this holy eve of Easter, we offer most humbly unto thy Majesty this sacrifice; namely, a fire not defiled with the fat of flesh, nor polluted with unholy oil or ointment, nor attained with any profane fire; but we offer unto thee with obedience, proceeding from perfect devotion, a fire of wrought WAX and wick, kindled and made to burn in honor of thy name. This so great a MYSTERY therefore, and the marvelous sacrament of this holy eve, must needs be extolled with due and deserved praises.

That there was some occult "Mystery," as is here declared, couched under the "wax candles," in the original system of idolatry, from which Rome derived its ritual, may be well believed, when it is observed with what unanimity nations the most remote have agreed to use wax candles in their sacred rites. Among the Tungusians, near the Lake Baikal in Siberia, "wax tapers are placed before the Burchans," the gods or idols of that country.

In the Molucca Islands, wax tapers are used in the worship of Nito, or Devil, whom these islanders adore.

"Twenty or thirty persons having assembled," says Hurd, "they summon the Nito, by beating a small consecrated drum, whilst two or more of the company light up wax tapers, and pronounce several mysterious words, which they consider as able to conjure him up."

In the worship of Ceylon, the use of wax candles is an indispensable requisite. "In Ceylon," says the same author, "some devotees, who are not priests, erect chapels for themselves, but in each of them they are obliged to have an image of Buddha, and light up tapers or wax candles before it, and adorn it with flowers." A practice thus so general must have come from some primeval source, and must have originally had some mystical reason at the bottom of it. The wax candle was, in fact, a hieroglyphic, like so many other things which we have already seen, and was intended to exhibit the Babylonian god in one of the essential characters of the "Great Mediator." The classic reader may remember that one of the gods of primeval antiquity was called Ouranos, that is, "the Enlightener."

For Aor or *our*, "light," and *an*, "to act upon" or produce, the same as our English particle *en*, "to make." Ouranos, then, is "the Enlightener." This Ouranos is, by Sanchuniathon, the Phoenician, called the son of Elioun (i.e., as he himself), or Philo-Byblius, interprets the name, "the Most High." (SANCH) Ouranos, in the physical sense, is "the Shiner"; and by Hesychius it is made equivalent to Kronos, which also has the same meaning, for *Krn*, the verb from which it comes, signifies either "to put forth horns," or "to send forth rays of light"; and, therefore, while the epithet Kronos, or "the Horned One," made primary reference to the physical power of Nimrod as a "mighty" king; when that king was deified, and made "Lord of Heaven," that name, Kronos, was still applied to him in his new character as "the Shiner or Lightgiver." The distinction made by Hesiod between Ouranos and Kronos, is no argument against the real substantial identity of these divinities originally as *pagan* divinities; for Herodotus states that Hesiod had a hand in "*inventing* a theogony" for the Greeks, which implies that some at least of the details of that theogony must have come from his own fancy; and, on examination, it will be found, when the veil of allegory is removed, that Hesiod's "Ouranos," though introduced as one of the pagan gods, was really at bottom the "God of Heaven," the living and true God.

In this very character was Nimrod worshiped when he was deified. As the sun-god he was regarded not only as the Illuminator of the Material World, but as the Enlightener of the Souls of Men, for he was recognized as the Revealer of "Goodness and Truth." It is evident, from the Old Testament, not less than the New, that the proper and personal name of our Lord Jesus Christ is, "the Word of God," as the "Revealer of the Heart" and "Counsels of the Godhead."

Now, to identify the sun-god with the great "Revealer of the Godhead," while under the name of Mithra, he was exhibited in sculpture as a lion; that lion had a bee represented between his lips. The bee between the lips of the sun-god was intended to point him out as "the Word"; for Dabar, the expression which signifies in Chaldee a "bee," signifies also a "word"; and the position of that bee in the mouth leaves no doubt as to the idea intended to be conveyed. It was intended to impress the belief that Mithra (who, says Plutarch, was worshiped as

Mesites, "the Mediator"), in his character as Ouranos, "the Enlightener."[449]

All religions of the world light candles as part of their worship to their god. That god, as you have just read, is Satan! We have no text in the written Word of Yehovah, or in His *Torah* to light candles in order to worship Him, yet in many religions this is, in fact, what they do. The *Bible* does not instruct us to light candles—a Menorah yes, but not candles. You now know where it has come from. It originated from the worship of Nimrod.

Those who are readers of classic history will know that one of the gods of ancient antiquity was called Ouranos, that is, "the Enlightener." In this very same character of Ouranos was Nimrod worshiped when he was deified. As the sun-god he was regarded not only as the Illuminator of the material world, but as the Enlightener of the souls of men, for he was recognized as the Revealer of "Goodness and Truth." And if we go back to the Garden of Eden, what was Satan actually doing there with Eve?

> *4 And the serpent said to the woman, "You shall certainly not die. 5 For Elohim knows that in the day you eat of it your eyes shall be opened, and you shall be like Elohim, knowing good and evil."* (Genesis 3:4-5)

Satan was revealing information, secret information that they would become just *like* God once they partook of the Tree of the Knowledge of Good and Evil—that tree being Satan who was brilliant in appearance and was giving them new information.

The "Shining One," Ouranos, challenged the first and only *Command* Yehovah gave man. The result was death, theft and destruction. If Satan was willing to challenge Yehovah right here in the very beginning, don't you think the written *Covenant Commandments* Yehovah has given to mankind will be challenged by Satan in these Last Days *every bit as* subtly? You bet they will!

---

[449] *The Two Babylons* by Alexander Hislop
http://www.biblestudy.org/bibleref/the-two-babylons/lamps-and-wax-candles-ch5s5.html

What you're about to learn in this chapter about Daniel's 70 Weeks is, without a doubt, going to stun you right down to the very core—and to think it all started in the Garden with Eve.

Cush was "The Great Enlightener" to mankind and the instigator of the great rebellion against Yehovah. Nimrod would overthrow him to become the world's very first emperor. He was worshiped as the sun god and candles were used to show the passersby that these patrons worshiped him. This concept was further developed later and built upon by rulers who came after.

As the sun grew darker in the fall, it would reach its lowest point in the Northern Hemisphere around December 21$^{st}$, or what is now called the Winter Equinox. To encourage the Sun to return and in the name of the worship of Nimrod, a Yule log was burned at this time of year.

> Traditionally, a Yule log was burned in the fireplace on Christmas Eve and during the night, as the log's embers died, there appeared in the room, as if by magic, a Christmas tree surrounded by gifts. The Yule log represented the Sun-god Nimrod and the Christmas tree represented himself resurrected as his own son Tammuz.
>
> So our Christmas tree–and our Yule log—have tremendous meaning, but not a Christian meaning. The Yule log is the dead Nimrod, human ruler of ancient Babylon, who was eventually deified as the sun incarnate, and hence a god. The Christmas tree is mystical Tammuz, the slain god come to life again.[450]

We can only see deception by knowing the truth. We have already entered into the most deceptive time in the history of mankind! Most of the *Bible* tells us of a time that is coming known as the Last Days. I have shown you from Daniel's 70 Shavuot that we are *in* the *last* Jubilee Cycle, and just a few years away from the middle section of it when the *rest of* Daniel's prophecy is to become a reality. This is *the time* spoken

---

[450] *After Armageddon* by John A Sarkett, *Where Do We Get Our Ideas?*, Ch.4

of with regard to the Last Days when many will call evil good and good evil as prophesied by Isaiah.

> *18 Woe to those who draw crookedness with cords of falsehood, and sin as with wagon ropes, 19 who are saying, "Let Him hurry! Let Him hasten His work, so that we see it! And let the counsel of the Set-apart One of Yisra'ĕl draw near and come, so that we know." 20 Woe to those who call evil good, and good evil; who put darkness for light, and light for darkness; who put bitter for sweet, and sweet for bitter! 21 Woe to those who are wise in their own eyes,[1] and clever in their own sight!* [Footnote: [1]Proverbs 3:7 (Isaiah 5:18-21)]

Read the above passage again carefully and notice how Isaiah is also talking about the same things I have been sharing. Those who call good evil and evil good who exchange darkness for "light" and light for darkness and are "bright" as in a light unto themselves.

In Leviticus 23 we are told of a Holy Day called the Day of Atonement. On the Day of Atonement the high priest customarily had to choose lots to know which goat was to be the Azazel Goat that represented Satan and which goat would be sacrificed that represented Yehshua.

> *27 "On the tenth day of this seventh month is the Day of Atonement. It shall be a set-apart gathering for you. And you shall afflict your beings, and shall bring an offering made by fire to* יהוה*. 28 And you do no work on that same day, for it is the Day of Atonement, to make atonement for you before* יהוה *your Elohim. 29 For any being who is not afflicted on that same day, he shall be cut off from his people. 30 And any being who does any work on that same day, that being I shall destroy from the midst of his people. 31 You do no work—a law forever throughout your generations in all your dwellings. 32 'It is a Sabbath of rest to you, and you shall afflict your beings. On the ninth day of the month at evening, from evening to evening, you observe your Sabbath.'"* (Leviticus 23:27-32)

*5 And from the congregation of the children of Yisra'ěl he takes two male goats as a sin offering, and one ram as a burnt offering. 6 And Aharon shall bring the bull as a sin offering, which is for himself, and make atonement for himself and for his house. 7 And he shall take the two goats and let them stand before* יהוה *at the door of the Tent of Meeting. 8 And Aharon shall cast lots for the two goats, one lot for* יהוה *and the other lot for Azazel. 9 And Aharon shall bring the goat on which the lot for* יהוה *fell, and shall prepare it as a sin offering. 10 But the goat on which the lot for Azazel fell is caused to stand alive before* יהוה*, to make atonement upon it, to send it into the wilderness to Azazel.* (Leviticus 16:5-10)

*11 And Aharon shall bring the bull of the sin offering, which is for himself, and make atonement for himself and for his house, and shall slaughter the bull as the sin offering which is for himself, 12 and shall take a fire holder filled with burning coals of fire from the altar before* יהוה*, with his hands filled with sweet incense beaten fine, and shall bring it inside the veil. 13 And he shall put the incense on the fire before* יהוה*, and the cloud of incense shall cover the lid of atonement which is on the Witness, lest he die. 14 And he shall take some of the blood of the bull and sprinkle it with his finger on the lid of atonement on the east side, also in front of the lid of atonement he sprinkles some of the blood with his finger seven times.* (Leviticus 16:11-14)

*15 And he shall slaughter the goat of the sin offering, which is for the people, and shall bring its blood inside the veil, and shall do with that blood as he did with the blood of the bull, and sprinkle it on the lid of atonement and in front of the lid of atonement. 16 And he shall make atonement for the Set-apart Place, because of the uncleanness of the children of Yisra'ěl, and because of their transgressions in all their sins. And so he does for the Tent of Meeting which is dwelling with them in the midst of their uncleanness. 17 And no man should be in the Tent of Meeting when he goes in to make atonement in the Set-apart Place, until he comes out. And he shall make atonement for himself, and for his household, and for all the assembly of Yisra'ěl.* (Leviticus 16:15-17)

*18 And he shall go out to the altar that is before יהוה, and make atonement for it. And he shall take some of the blood of the bull and some of the blood of the goat, and put it on the horns of the altar all around. 19 And he shall sprinkle some of the blood on it with his finger seven times, and cleanse it, and set it apart from the uncleanness of the children of Yisra'ěl. 20 And when he has finished atoning for the Set-apart Place, and the Tent of Meeting, and the altar, he shall bring the live goat. 21 Then Aharon shall lay both his hands on the head of the live goat, and shall confess over it all the crookednesses of the children of Yisra'ěl, and all their transgressions in all their sins, and shall put them on the head of the goat, and shall send it away into the wilderness by the hand of a fit man. 22 And the goat shall bear on itself all their crookednesses, to a land cut off. Thus he shall send the goat away into the wilderness.* (Leviticus 16:18-22)

The Day of Atonement reflects back to Passover and it is on the Day of Atonement that the identity of the false light is revealed. At Passover you are told to take either a lamb or a goat for the sacrifice. This is telling us to look to Atonement for something.

*5 "Let the lamb be a perfect one, a year old male. Take it from the sheep or from the goats."* (Exodus 12:5)

Yehshua is the true light but Satan has counterfeited that identity. In fact, he has done such an exemplary job of it, that it is *extremely hard* to tell the difference. You can if you open your *Bible*, read it in earnest, and do what it says by not just being a hearer of the Word, but a doer also. But most will not and will choose to do their own thing and keep the holidays they are accustomed to keeping.

*12 Therefore יהושע spoke to them again, saying, "I am the light of the world. He who follows Me shall by no means walk*

> *in darkness, but possess the light of life."*[1] [Footnote: [1]See 11:9-10 (John 8:12)]

> *4 "It is necessary for Me to work the works of Him who sent Me while it is day—night is coming, when no one is able to work. 5 While I am in the world, I am the light of the world."* (John 9:4-5)

Satan has so deceived the world that the day is not at all long in coming when the world is going to mistake Satan for the Messiah. He has changed light to darkness and has most of the entire world calling good evil.

In the ceremony on the Day of Atonement the High Priest has two goats in front of him and he must:

> *"...8 cast lots for the two goats; one lot for יהוה and the other lot for Azazel. 9 And Aharon shall bring the goat on which the lot for יהוה fell, and shall prepare it as a sin offering."* (Leviticus 16:8-9)

Aaron *must* do this because he alone, leaning on his own understanding, is unable to determine (as would be the case with any of us) which one is the guilty goat upon which the sins are placed—in other words, the Azazel goat.

The reason Yehovah decides is because it is based on His *Torah*, which most of us have easy access to and can read. Satan has convinced most not to read or obey it and to keep other religious laws and/or traditions of men instead. Satan has appeared to mankind as the light when, in fact, he is the master imposter. The Azazel goat is shown to us in *Revelation* and is the very same event rehearsed each year in *Leviticus*:

> *1 And I saw a messenger coming down from the heaven, having the key to the pit of the deep and a great chain in his hand. 2 And he seized the dragon, the serpent of old, who is the Devil and Satan, and bound him for a thousand years,*

*3 and he threw him into the pit of the deep, and shut him up, and set a seal on him, so that he should lead the nations no more astray until the thousand years were ended. And after that he has to be released for a little while.* (Revelation 20:1-3)

You will notice in the next picture two seemingly opposite characters. The truth is they *both* represent the very *same* being; Satan. The one on the left is obvious and the one on the right is not so obvious. Do you remember reading earlier from Alexander Hislop's excerpt about the rays that issue forth from the head?

Let me refresh your memory:

> Ouranos, in the physical sense, is "the Shiner"; and by Hesychius it is made equivalent to Kronos, which also has the same meaning, for *Krn*, the verb from which it comes, signifies either "to put forth horns," or "to send forth rays of light"; and, therefore, while the epithet Kronos, or "the Horned One," had primarily reference to the physical power of Nimrod as a "mighty" king; when that king was deified, and made "Lord of Heaven," that name, Kronos, was still applied to him in his new character as "the Shiner or Lightgiver."[451]

---
[451] *The Two Babylons* by Alexander Hislop
http://www.biblestudy.org/bibleref/the-two-babylons/lamps-and-wax-

You can only tell the difference when you go to the *Ten Commandments* and then *do* them. These *Ten Commandments* are the standard, spoken by Yehovah and given to *all* mankind.

Below Are Yehovah's *Ten Commandments*, The Backbone To His *Covenant*.

## The *Ten Commandments* & *Covenant* of Yehovah

1. Have no other gods before me.
2. Do not make for yourself a carved image.
3. Do not bring the Name of Yehovah your Elohim to naught.
4. Remember the Sabbath Day, to set it apart.
5. Honor your father and your mother.
6. You do not murder.
7. You do not commit adultery.
8. You do not steal.
9. You do not bear false witness against your neighbor.
10. You do not covet your neighbor's house; you do not covet your neighbor's wife, nor his male servant, nor his female servant, nor his ox, nor his donkey, or whatever belongs to your neighbor.[452]

This is Yehovah's *Covenant* for all of us. It has always been inerrant, has never change, nor has it had to be amended or have any kinks worked out of it. But there is *another Covenant* already at work in the world that you will, at some point or another, be presented with. It has already been approved and has already been adopted by most of the world and you may have already been subjected to it in one way or another.

Isaiah calls it the *"Covenant with death."*

> *18 "And your covenant with death shall be annulled, and your vision with the grave not stand. When an overflowing scourge passes through, then you shall be trampled down by it. 19 As often as it passes through it shall take you, for it shall pass through every morning, and by day and by night.*

---

candles-ch5s5.html
[452] Exodus 20:3-17

> *And it shall be only trembling to understand the message."*
> (Isaiah 28:18-19)

Daniel also calls it "a *Covenant*" and this chapter is going to explain it so that you too can see it. In *Revelation* it is explained as the Mark of the Beast. Enough has been prophesied in the *Bible* on this *Covenant* of which I'm now speaking, to where we need to take this matter very seriously and to heart.

> *9 And a third messenger followed them, saying with a loud voice, "If anyone worships the beast and his image, and receives his mark upon his forehead or upon his hand, 10 he also shall drink of the wine of the wrath of Elohim, which is poured out undiluted into the cup of His wrath. And he shall be tortured with fire and sulphur before the set-apart messengers and before the Lamb. 11 And the smoke of their torture goes up forever and ever. And they have no rest day or night, those worshiping the beast and his image, also if anyone receives the mark of his name." 12 Here is the endurance of the set-apart ones,[1] here are those guarding the commands of Elohim and the belief* יהושע*.*[2] [Footnotes: [1]In Revelation 12:17 they are called "the remnant" [2]See *Sevenfold Message of Revelation* in Explanatory Notes.] *13 And I heard a voice out of the heaven saying to me, "Write, 'Blessed are the dead who die in the Master from now on.'" "Yes," says the Spirit, "in order that they rest from their labors, and their works follow with them."* (Revelation 14:9-13)

Remember the "Angel of Light" may *look* and even *sound* good, yet is anything but. He has been relentlessly hard at work throughout the history of mankind! He has slowly and subtly been about the business of amending away Yehovah's *Commandments* to the point where the Christian faith even says the *Torah* (the Law) or the *Commandments* have been done away with! He appears to us all as an Angel of Light. He comes bearing a striking resemblance to the Messiah when, in fact, he is *not*. His works will look good when in truth they are *evil*.

Here is just one example of looking like an angel and speaking as a devil. It is the following conclusion of a greater discourse on keeping the *Ten Commandments* by a "Christian" group.

> The principle when speaking of "God's Law" or "*Commandments*" is (based on) the following. No requirements from the Old Covenant—including the *Ten Commandments*—are binding on Christians except the spiritual-moral principles, which are abundantly repeated in the Scriptures of the *New Covenant* (the *New Testament*). However, keeping the Sabbath by not working is not based on any eternal, spiritual-moral principle. Nor is it mentioned in the *New Testament* as a Christian requirement. We must conclude (then) that, at its heart, Sabbath regulations were ceremonial practices and not necessary for Christians to "keep holy."[453]

This is blatantly a false teaching yet many Christian Churches and groups believe it to be true.

This shining of light or sending forth rays of light is portrayed in the shape of halos in pictures *long before* Yehshua was ever born. All of these are depictions of Nimrod worship who is represented by the Sun as it gives forth its rays of light, enlightening mankind. Halos are depicted in *both* Christian and eastern religions. The things I will be addressing in this chapter cover *both* Christian and far eastern religions; they all originate from this same *false* light, as depicted in the following additional imagery:

---

[453] Grace Communion International, http://www.gci.org/law/sabbath/doneaway

In other words, imagery referring back to Ouranos, "the Enlightener." The passage below in *2 Corinthians* gives us further insight into this:

> *13 For such are false emissaries, deceptive workers, masquerading as emissaries of Messiah. 14 And no wonder! For Satan himself masquerades as a messenger of light! 15 It is not surprising, then, if his servants also masquerade as servants of righteousness,[1] whose end shall be according to their works![2]* [Footnotes: [1]Matthew 7:15-23, 2 Peter 2:1-22. [2]Matthew 13:41-42 (2 Corinthians 11:13-15)]

I have already shown you that Ouranos was also known as Kronos and is the son of Ham but is also called Cush. I will now explain some of the names of Ham's family.

> Ham, the third son of Noah, was the father of Cush, and his name comes from the Chaldean "khem," which means the "burnt one" or the "burning one" and is in reference, not only to **Ham** as the son of Noah, the father of Cush, but also as the name of their **Sun-god**. Right after the Flood, **Ham** showed his true colors by an act of disrespect towards his father. It is evident that the **offense** was greater than merely making fun of his father by the curse given to his youngest son, Canaan. The flaw in his character was far more of a **spiritual** flaw that would go against the righteousness of his father.
>
> If the original is flawed, so shall all copies from it be flawed. So it is with Cush. Although most references to this word in the *Bible* is to the **country** of Ethiopia, the word is derived from the Hebrew "kvsh" and is Chaldean in origin. It comes from the word "khus," which in pronunciation is "**kha wos**." It is from where we get the word **chaos**. This was the **name of the first father of the gods**, "Khaos," the Confounder, he who caused the **confusion** of tongues and **scattered** the inhabitants of the once united Earth abroad. Under the name Belus, which is another Chaldean word meaning "the Confounder," he is said to be the father of **Ninus**, the first king of Babylon.

Perhaps in resentment for the harshness God had shown towards his father when He cursed Ham's youngest son Canaan, perhaps in sympathy for his youngest brother, or perhaps in the same corrupt desire to be **like God** that Satan had, by the time his son **Nimrod** was born, Cush had developed a plan by which the suffocating religion of his righteous uncle could be replaced by his own.

Nimrod was the great-grandson of Noah and a contemporary with **Eber**, the great-grandson of Shem. **Nimrod** comes from the Chaldean words "nimr": leopard, and "rad": to subdue. **Nimrod** was famous for his exploits as a mighty hunter. Most Hebrew names in the *Bible* are based on puns and the name **Nimrod** is very similar in pronunciation to a compound Hebrew word, "niyn": progeny and "marad": be rebellious, rebel. The word carries with it the meaning of breaking **covenant** with someone, whether man or God. So, **Nimrod** the Mighty Hunter (the Hunter of Men's Souls) becomes **Nimrod** the Rebellious One, or the Son of Rebellion. **Cush** would carefully nurture his **Son of Rebellion** in this new religion, and thereby rule the world through him. **Cush**, declaring himself a prophet of "the Only One," and assuming the name Hermes, became the interpreter of the gods. **Hermes** is a compound word created from the Egyptian "her," which in Chaldean means the "burnt one," therefore it is synonymous with **Ham**. This is also the derivative from which the name **Horus** originates and connects him with both the Babylonian and Egyptian **Sun-god**. The second half of the word Hermes comes from the word "Mesheh," (Moses) which means to draw forth, to extract, to give birth. Therefore, **Hermes** means the child of Ham, or the son of Ham. This can be seen in the Pharaoh names Rameses and Thothmes which mean "son of Ra" and "son of Thoth."

In direct violation to the *Commandments* of God, Cush persuaded the people to establish one place where they could all dwell together to worship their god, and there to build a great tower to better observe the messages of their god written in the stars.[454]

Kronos is also known in history as Father Time.[455] And the New Year baby is none other than Nimrod who usurped Cush as we are told in mythology. Over a period of centuries, Nimrod would also come to be known as Kronos in Greek mythology.

But also in Greek Mythology, you will find that Ouranos was known as Uranus. He was the first son of Gaia (the Earth) and he also became her husband.[456]

> Ouranos was the first ruler of the universe, created by Gaea when she emerged from Chaos. Ouranos, with Gaea, became the father of the Titans, the Cyclopes and the Hecatoncheires (hundred-handed ones).
>
> Ouranos was afraid that some of his children would rebel against him, so he imprisoned them within Gaea's Earth womb. Kronos, the youngest of the Titans, freed his siblings by castrating his father. Ouranos' blood gave birth to the Furies, and Aphrodite was born of the discarded member when it fell into the foaming sea.[457]

Notice the terminology here, as this is important to understand. Ouranos, also known as Kronos and also known as either Ham and or Cush, married his mother and had children. Gaia was the mother of Ham known as Ouranos and was also his wife. Yet this woman Gaia was said to be "the Mother of All Living." Think about that. Who exactly, *is* "the Mother of All Living?"

"The Mother of All Living" is Noah's wife. Gaea is creator of Ouranos (the Ruler of the Universe) and this Gaea emerged from chaos. The chaos was the Flood and Gaea is "the Mother of All Living." In

---

[454] http://www.angelfire.com/va/bibler/xmas1.html
[455] http://en.wikipedia.org/wiki/Chronos
[456] http://www.pantheon.org/articles/u/uranus.html
[457] http://www.ancient-mythology.com/greek/ouranos.php

other words, the *only one* to emerge from the chaos of the Flood and come forth as the mother of all that was alive and all to come thereafter was Noah's wife. Then, the Earth (Gaea) and the light (Ouranos) become both father and mother.

It is with this mythology in mind that I would now have you return to the *Bible* to understand what has actually taken place here and why we are not given the name of Noah's wife.

> *18 And the sons of Noah who went out of the ark were Shĕm and Ḥam and Yepheth. And Ham was the father of Kena'an. 19 These three were the sons of Noah, and all the earth was overspread from them. 20 And Noah, a man of the soil, began and planted a vineyard. 21 And he drank of the wine and was drunk, and became uncovered in his tent. 22 And Ham, the father of Kena'an, saw the nakedness of his father, and told his two brothers outside. 23 So Shĕm and Yepheth took a garment, laid it on both their shoulders, and went backward and covered the nakedness of their father, but their faces were turned away, and they did not see their father's nakedness. 24 And Noah awoke from his wine, and he knew what his younger son had done to him, and he said, 25 "Cursed is Kena'an, let him become a servant of servants to his brothers." 26 And he said, "Blessed be* יהוה, *the Elohim of Shĕm, and let Ken'an become his servant. 27 Let Elohim enlarge Yepheth, and let him dwell in the tents of Shĕm. And let Kena'an become his servant."* (Genesis 9:18-27)

It has always seemed to me that the curse given to Canaan was very severe just because Ham saw Noah naked and made fun of it. Later, I suspected that Ham had sodomized Noah and for that, this punishment seemed more justifiable. But it has only come to my attention recently what has taken place in light of reading over these legends of Ham, Cush and Nimrod, and then reading again the biblical account. I will now show you what I found about this word "nakedness."

**Genesis 9:22:** And Ham,[H2526] the father[H1] of Canaan,[H3667] saw[H7200 (H853)] the nakedness[H6172] of his father,[H1] and told[H5046] his two[H8147] brethren[H251] without.[H2351]

**H6172:** ערוה 'ervâh *er-vaw'*

From H6168; *nudity*, literally (especially the *pudenda*) or figuratively (*disgrace, blemish*): –nakedness, shame, unclean (-ness).

**H6168:** ערה 'ârâh *aw-raw'*

A primitive root; to *be* (causatively *make*) bare; hence to *empty, pour* out. *Demolish:* –leave destitute, discover, empty, make naked, pour (out), rase, spread self, uncover.

There are some very revealing scriptures in *Leviticus* that help us to understand what is going on here with Noah and Ham.

> *6 No one is to approach anyone of his own flesh to uncover his nakedness. I am יהוה. 7 The nakedness of your father or the nakedness of your mother you do not uncover. She is your mother, you do not uncover her nakedness. 8 The nakedness of your father's wife you do not uncover, it is your father's nakedness. 9 The nakedness of your sister, the daughter of your father, or the daughter of your mother, whether born at home or elsewhere, their nakedness you do not uncover. 10 The nakedness of your son's daughter or your daughter's daughter, their nakedness you do not uncover, for theirs is your own nakedness. 11 The nakedness of your father's wife's daughter, brought forth by your father, she is your sister, you do not uncover her nakedness. 12 The nakedness of your father's sister you do not uncover, she is your father's flesh.* (Leviticus 18:6-12)

> *13 The nakedness of your mother's sister you do not uncover, for she is your mother's flesh. 14 The nakedness of your father's brother you do not uncover, you do not approach his*

*wife, she is your aunt. 15 The nakedness of your daughter-in-law you do not uncover, she is your son's wife, you do not uncover her nakedness. 16 The nakedness of your brother's wife you do not uncover, it is your brother's nakedness. 17 The nakedness of a woman and her daughter you do not uncover, nor do you take her son's daughter or her daughter's daughter, to uncover her nakedness. They are her relatives—it is wickedness. 18 And do not take a woman as a rival to her sister, to uncover her nakedness while the other is alive. 19 And do not approach a woman to uncover her nakedness in her monthly separation of uncleanness.* (Leviticus 18:13-19)

*17 And a man who takes his sister, his father's daughter or his mother's daughter, and sees her nakedness and she sees his nakedness: it is wickedness, and they shall be cut off before the eyes of their people. He has uncovered his sister's nakedness, he bears his crookedness. 18 And a man who lies with a woman during her sickness and uncovers her nakedness: he has laid bare her flow, and she has uncovered the flow of her blood, both of them shall be cut off from the midst of their people. 19 And do not uncover the nakedness of your mother's sister nor of your father's sister, for that is laying bare one's own flesh, they bear their crookedness. 20 And a man who lies with his uncle's wife: he has uncovered his uncle's nakedness, they bear their sin, they die childless. 21 And a man who takes his brother's wife: it is uncleanness, he has uncovered his brother's nakedness, they are childless.* (Leviticus 20:17-21)

In each of these previous descriptions, when someone lies with or has sex with a next of kin they have uncovered their nakedness and this is a sin. What you are reading of in *Genesis 9* about Ham uncovering the nakedness of Noah was not about Noah so much as it was about Ham having had sexual relations with his mother, the wife of Noah, and by doing that he uncovered the nakedness of Noah.

*7 The nakedness of your father or the nakedness of your mother you do not uncover. She is your mother, you do not uncover*

> *her nakedness. 8 The nakedness of your father's wife you do not uncover, it is your father's nakedness.* (Leviticus 18:7-8)

> *11 And a man who lies with the wife of his father has uncovered the nakedness of his father, both of them shall certainly be put to death, their blood is upon them.* (Leviticus 20:11)

Ouranos (Ham) was the first ruler of the universe, created by Gaea (Noah's wife and mother of Ham) when she emerged from Chaos. (the Great Flood) Ouranos, with Gaea, became the father of the Titans.

We read of the children of Ham in Genesis 10;

> *6 And the sons of Ham: Cush and Mizraim and Phut and Canaan. (Genesis 10:6)*

Canaan is the youngest of Ham's Children. It is my opinion that Canaan was the result of Ham's impregnation of Noah's wife. Noah in legends is said to have taken the animals from the Ark and spread them around the world. This would necessitate his being gone for long periods of time giving Ham the opportunity to usurp authority. Again these are my opinions based on my research and thoughts.

What Ham was doing was usurping the power and authority that belonged to Noah by "uncovering" his mother and at the same time "uncovering" Noah. It is this very same thing, which Absalom did when he was attempting to usurp his father King David.

> *20 And Aḇshalom said to Aḥithophel, "Give your advice. What should we do?" 21 An Aḥithophel said to Aḇshalom, "Go in to your father's concubines, whom he has left to look after the house. And all Yisra'ěl shall hear that you have made yourself a stench to your father. And the hands of all who are with you shall be strong." 22 So they pitched a tent for Aḇshalom on the top of the house, and Aḇshalom went in to his father's concubines before the eyes of all Yisra'ěl.* (2 Samuel 16:20-22)

Noah's wife is the one who is the "Mother of all Living," she is the one who came out of the chaos of the Flood and landed near the Euphrates. Her name is Semiramis. She was known to the Greeks and to the Romans as the goddess:

- Of love by the name Aphrodite & Venus.
- Of hunting & birth as Artemis & Diana
- Of crafts, war & wisdom as Athena & Minerva
- Of growing things as Demeter & Ceres
- Of fertile Earth as Gaea & Terra
- Of Marriage & Women as Hera & Juno
- Of the hearth as Hestia & Vesta
- As Wife of Kronos Rhea & Ops

Today her statutes consist of the Mother and Child, as the "Mother of God," and as the Blessed Virgin Mary.

This picture is Sandro Botticelli's "Birth of Venus" as she comes ashore from the Euphrates after the Flood. She is Noah's wife and mythology records her name as Gaia. She came out of the chaos of the Flood and is the mother of all who came after her. Including Ham who had Cush, who is also known as Kronos and he begat Nimrod.

This is a picture of a Greek vase of the goddess Gaia. She is known as "the Mother of All Living" and also as Mother Earth, but she also has been given some other names we have just seen.

In Greek Mythology there is another god we need to learn about. His name is APOLLO and he is one of the most important of the Olympian gods.

He was well versed in prophecy, medicine, music, poetry, and the pastoral arts. A moral god of high civilization, he was associated with law, philosophy, and the arts. He was widely known as a "god of light," or Phoebus Apollo. After the 5th-century B.C., he was often identified with the Sun god, Helios. Apollo's oracles had great authority; his chief shrine was at Delphi, where he was primarily a "god of purification." In art he was portrayed as the "perfection of youth and beauty."

The most celebrated statue of him is the Apollo Belvedere, a marble copy of the original Greek bronze (statue), now in the Vatican in Rome.[458]

This picture is of Apollo Belvedere and can be viewed at:

http://en.wikipedia.org/wiki/Apollo_Belvedere

Did you notice what you just read? "He was widely known as a 'god of light,' or Phoebus Apollo. After the 5th-century B.C., he was often identified with the Sun-god, Helios."

In Roman tradition, Helios was simply translated by the Latin word "Sol" meaning "Sun." But this Sol was also sometimes called Phoebus, a Greek word meaning "shining," which was *also* a traditional name for

---

[458] http://deoxy.org/gaia/goddess.htm#APOLLO

Apollo ... In classic Latin verse it was customary to refer to the Sun as Phoebus in his car or chariot. But one can't always be sure, especially when ancient religious texts, which connected Apollo with the Sun, were also common knowledge. Despite this, the identification of Phoebus the sun god with Phoebus Apollo had become standard in Victorian times.[459]

Now that I've given you this piece, I strongly recommend you take all of the information you have just read and integrate it with everything else I've shared with you thus far on this subject. Apollo is known as "the God of Light." Phoebus, another name for Apollo, is known as "the Shining." And I shared with you at the beginning of this chapter that "the Hebrew word rendered 'serpent' in Genesis 3:1 is **Nachash** (from the root **Nachash**, "**to shine**,") and means a **Shining One**. Hence, in Chaldee it means **brass** or **copper**, because of its **shininess**.

Now return to your Bible and read what Yehovah tells you. We read in *Revelation* that this book is here to *show* us things—not to conceal the truth from us but to reveal to us the truth and warn us of things that are still yet to come.

> *1 Revelation of* יהושע *Messiah, which Elohim gave Him to show His servants what has to take place with speed. And He signified it by sending His messenger to His servant Yoḥanan.* (Revelation 1:1)

Summarily, you have been reading about Satan the serpent, or the "Shining One" and you have been following ancient mythology to learn who he is today and what this means to us in the context of this chapter about the "Covenant with many" he is to make for one Shabua.

> *1 And the fifth messenger sounded, and I saw a star from the heaven which had fallen to the earth. And the key to the pit of the deep was given to it. 2 And he opened the pit of the deep, and smoke went up out of the pit like the smoke*

---

[459] www.fanpop.com/spots/greek-mythology/articles/7768/title/god-sun-helios-apollo

*of a great furnace. And the sun was darkened, also the air, because of the smoke of the pit. 3 And out of the smoke locusts came upon the earth, and authority was given to them as the scorpions of the earth possess authority. 4 And it was said to them that they shall not harm the grass of the earth, or any green matter, or any tree, but only those men who do not have the seal of Elohim upon their foreheads. 5 And it was given to them that they should not kill them, but to torture them for five months. And their torture was like the torture of a scorpion when it stings a man.* (Revelation 9:1-5)

*6 And in those days men shall seek death and shall not find it. And they shall long to die, but death shall flee from them. 7 And the locusts looked like horses prepared for battle, and on their heads were crowns like gold, and their faces were like the faces of men. 8 And they had hair like women's hair, and their teeth were like lions' teeth. 9 And they had breastplates like breastplates of iron, and the sound of their wings was like the sound of chariots of many horses running into battle. 10 And they have tails like scorpions, and stings. And in their tails is their authority to harm men five months. 11 And they have over them a sovereign, the messenger of the pit of the deep, whose name in Heb̲rew is Abaddon, but in Greek he has the name Apolluon.* (Revelation 9:6-11)

His name is Apollo!

**G623**: Ἀπολλύων Apolluōn *ap-ol-loo'-ohn*

Active participle of G622; a *destroyer* (that is, *Satan*): – Apollyon. –Apollyon 1; 1 Apollyon = V Destroyer V1) the angel of the bottomless pit, the Destroyer

The True Light is Yehshua, yet the world does not want to follow Him. Masquerading as the true light is the serpent, or the "Shining One," also known as Phoebus or Apollo and is mentioned by name in the Book of Revelation. Yehovah says in His Word, that Apollyon is "the destroyer" from the bottomless pit. The imposter says Apollo is the "light" and the way in which we should all go.

We have some more to learn about Apollo as we read about his love for Daphne:

> Daphne was a nymph (a young priestess) of the Earth Goddess Gaia. She attracted Apollo's attention when he warned her about the deception of a man named Leucippus, who had dressed in women's clothing to penetrate her sacred circle. The priestess made Leucippus strip naked, confirmed the deception and killed him, but Apollo, in the meantime, had become obsessed with Daphne. She did not return his interest.
>
> Apollo's ardor was persistent, and Daphne eventually fled in terror. As Apollo gained on her, she called to her mother Gaia to save her from Apollo's rape. Gaia responded by transforming Daphne into a laurel tree. In remorse, Apollo pulled a branch from the tree and vowed he would always wear laurel leaves in remembrance of Daphne. This is why Apollo is usually pictured with a laurel crown, and why a person of high achievement in the arts or another realm of Apollo is said to "receive laurels."[460]

This story ties in with the Christmas tree, which was also a symbol of Nimrod from the Babylonian mythologies.

I have now shown you that Nimrod, who took the title of Kronos from his father Cush, who took it from his father Ham, who was also known as the Shining One; he was also called Ouranos, the Enlightener of Mankind and he was also known in Greek Mythology as Apollo and they are all representations of the *same* being—Satan. Ham, Cush and Nimrod, over the centuries, have all melded into one another and have become an amalgam, if you will, or have come to be looked upon as all one person or one in the same.

---

[460] http://hearthmoonblog.com/daphnes-appeal-to-gaia/

We have also seen that the "Mother of All Living," later became known as Gaia, and is also known as Mother Earth or Mother Nature. But she also is known by other names—one of which is Cybele, the God of Fortresses and Ishtar, the Queen of Heaven and the Blessed Virgin.

We read of this God of Fortresses again in Daniel:

> *38 But in his place he shall give esteem to a mighty one of strongholds. And to a mighty one which his fathers did not know he shall give esteem with gold and silver, with precious stones and costly gifts.* (Daniel 11:38)

Before we go too far down this ancient mythology trail, I would like to remind you again of the primary objective of this chapter.

> *27 And he shall confirm a covenant with many for one week.* (Daniel 9:27)

I have shown you that the word *week* is one Shabua or one forty-nine year period. I had presumed that period of time began in 1996, which was also the last Jubilee Year, but although this covenant is for 49 years it does not start in 1996. I will explain shortly. The "he" here is Satan who is also called in the Hebrew tongue Abaddon, but in Greek his name *is* Apollyon according to *Revelation*.

So what is "the *Covenant*" Daniel is speaking of? We are looking for a "*Covenant made with many*" which is to last forty-nine years or one Shabua.

The word "confirm" comes from **H1396**: gâbar *gaw-bar'*

> A primitive root; to *be strong*; by implication to *prevail, act insolently:* −exceed, confirm, be great, be mighty, prevail, put to more [strength], strengthen, be stronger, be valiant.

I would also have you note that the word "covenant" also means confederacy. But notice this covenant is going to be adding more and more *strength* to it.

**H1285**: bᵉrîyth *ber-eeth'*

From **H1262**: [in the sense of *cutting* (like **H1254**)]; a *compact* (because made by passing between *pieces* of flesh): –confederacy, [con-]feder[-ate], covenant, league.

Remember the phrase, *"put to more strength,"* as this is what this particular *Covenant* does year after year.

We are told to expose the false things and to reprove them so others do not fall into that same trap.

> *11 And have no fellowship with the fruitless works of darkness, but rather reprove¹ them.* [Footnote: ¹Or confute, or expose. (Ephesians 5:11)]

Brethren, this subject is HUGE and at times it overwhelms me with the amount of information that must be digested in order to understand the full extent of what is, in truth, actually going on. Even as I write more and more information comes to light. Even as review these pages, the sources have changed their names and locations. It is continuing to evolve daily and is extremely hard to keep up with.

I have explained to you the ancient mythology side of it. That will come back into play a bit later. But I will now have you look at the larger-than-life monster Satan has created. Because most do not know the history behind this behemoth organization, I will provide you with the necessary background and give you more than just a brief history of how it came to be.

> The concept of *a peaceful community of nations* had been proposed as far back as 1795, when Immanuel Kant's, *Perpetual Peace: A Philosophical Sketch*[461] outlined the idea of a **"League of Nations"** to control conflict and promote peace between states.[462] Kant argued for the establishment

---

[461] *Perpetual Peace: A Philosophical Sketch* by Immanuel Kant. Mount Holyoke College. Retrieved May 16th, 2008.
[462] Skirbekk & Gilje 2001, p. 288.

of a peaceful world community, not in a sense of a global government, but in the hope that each state would declare itself a free state that respects its citizens and welcomes foreign visitors as fellow rational beings, thus promoting peaceful society worldwide.[463] International cooperation to promote collective security originated in the Concert of Europe that developed after the Napoleonic Wars in the 19th-century in an attempt to maintain the *status quo* between European states and so avoid war. This period also saw the development of International Law, with the first Geneva Conventions establishing laws dealing with humanitarian relief during wartime, and the international Hague Conventions of 1899 and 1907 governing rules of war and the peaceful settlement of international disputes.[464]

In 1862, Henry Dunant published his book, *Memoir of the Solferino*, on the horrors of war.[465] His wartime experiences inspired Dunant to propose:

- A permanent relief agency for humanitarian aid in times of war
- A government treaty recognizing the neutrality of the agency and allowing it to provide aid in a war zone.

The former proposal led to the establishment of the Red Cross in Geneva. The latter led to the first Geneva Convention. For both of these accomplishments, Henry Dunant became co-recipient of the first Nobel Peace Prize[466] in 1901.[467]

---

[463] *Perpetual Peace: Constitution Society* by Immanuel Kant (1795). Retrieved August 30th, 2011.

[464] http://en.wikipedia.org/wiki/League_of_Nations#cite_note-FOOTNOTE Bouchet-SaulnierBravOlivier200714.E2.80.93134-10

[465] *A Memory of Solferino* by Henry Dunant. English version, full text online. http://www.icrc.org/eng/resources/documents/publication/p0361.htm

[466] The *Nobel Peace Prize and the Laureates: An Illustrated Biographical History* by Irwin Abrams (2001). 1901-2001. US: Science History Publications. Retrieved July 14th, 2009.
http://www.irwinabrams.com/books/centennial.html

[467] *The Story of An Idea*, film on the creation of the Red Cross, Red Crescent Movement & the Geneva Conventions

> The ten articles of this first treaty were initially adopted on August 22nd, 1864 by twelve nations.[468]

This initial Geneva Convention would lead to the First Hague Conference of 1899. Another Geneva Convention would take place in 1906 followed by a Second Hague Conference in 1907. The third Geneva Convention was promoted after WWI in 1929, and the fourth Geneva Convention was held after WWII in 1949. All of these conventions were convened as peace conferences to regulate how individuals were to conduct themselves during times of warfare and/or in war-torn zones.

> The **Hague Conventions** were two international treaties negotiated at international peace conferences at The Hague in the Netherlands: The **First Hague Conference** in 1899 and the **Second Hague Conference** in 1907. Along with the Geneva Conventions, the Hague Conventions were among the first formal statements of the laws of war and war crimes in the body of secular international law. A third conference was planned for 1914 and later rescheduled for 1915, but never took place due to the start of World War I.[469]

> [In] 1918, the German international law scholar and neo-Kantian pacifist Walther Schücking called the assemblies the "International Union of Hague Conferences."[470] Schücking saw the Hague Conferences as a nucleus of a future international federation that was to meet at regular intervals to administer justice and develop international law procedures for the peaceful settlement of disputes, asserting that "a definite political union of the states of the world

---

[468] *International Law: A Treatise* by Ronald Roxburgh (1920). London: Longman's, Green and Co. p. 707. Retrieved July 14th, 2009. The twelve original countries were Switzerland. Baden, Belgium, Denmark, France, Hesse, Holland, Italy, Portugal, Prussia, Spain and Württemberg. Baden, Hesse, Prussia and Württemberg were all states, which would join together to form the state of Germany.
[469] http://en.wikipedia.org/wiki/Hague_Conventions_%281899_and_1907%29
[470] *The International Union of the Hague Conferences* by Walther Schücking, Clarendon Press, 1918.

has been created with the First and Second Conferences."[471] The various agencies created by the conferences, like the Permanent Court of Arbitration, "are agents or organs of the union."[472]

A major effort in both the conferences was the creation of a binding international court for compulsory arbitration to settle international disputes, which was considered necessary to replace the institution of war. This effort, however, failed to realize success either in 1899 or in 1907; instead, [as previously mentioned] a voluntary forum for arbitration, the Permanent Court for Arbitration was established.[473]

The First Conference was generally a success and was focused on disarmament efforts. The Second Conference failed to create a binding international court for compulsory arbitration but did enlarge the machinery for voluntary arbitration, and established conventions regulating the collection of debts, rules of war, and the rights and obligations of neutrals. Along with disarmament and obligatory arbitration, both conferences included negotiations concerning the laws of war and war crimes. Many of the rules laid down at the Hague Conventions were violated during WWI.[474]

The forerunner of the League of Nations, the Inter-Parliamentary Union, was formed by peace activists, William Randal Cremer and Frédéric Passy in 1889. The organization was international in scope, with a third of the members of parliaments (in the twenty-four countries that had parliaments) serving as members of the I.P.U. by 1914. Its aims were to encourage governments to solve international disputes by peaceful means. Annual conferences were held to help governments refine the process of international

---

[471] http://en.wikipedia.org/wiki/Hague_Conventions_%281899_and_1907%29
[472] *The International Union of the Hague Conferences* by Walther Schücking, p. vi.
[473] http://en.wikipedia.org/wiki/Hague_Conventions_%281899_and_1907%29
[474] https://sites.google.com/site/bioterrorbible/treaties/hague-conventions-1899-1907

arbitration. Its structure consisted of a council headed by a president, which would later be reflected in the structure of the League.[475]

The **League of Nations** (abbreviated as **L.N.** in English, and S.D.N. in its other official languages), was an intergovernmental organization founded as a result of the Paris Peace Conference that ended World War I. It was the first international organization whose principal mission was to maintain world peace.[476] Its primary goals, as stated in its covenant, included preventing wars through collective security and disarmament, and settling international disputes through negotiation and arbitration.[477] Other issues in this and related treaties included labor conditions, just treatment of native inhabitants, human and drug trafficking, arms trade, global health, prisoners of war, and protection of minorities in Europe.[478] At its greatest extent from September 28th, 1934 to February 23rd, 1935, it had 58 members.

The diplomatic philosophy behind the League represented a fundamental shift from the preceding one-hundred years. The League lacked its own armed force and depended on the Great Powers to enforce its resolutions, keep to its economic sanctions, or provide an army when needed. However, the Great Powers were often reluctant to do so. Sanctions could hurt league members, so they were reluctant to comply with them. When, during the second Italo-Abyssinian War, the League accused Italian soldiers of targeting Red Cross medical tents, Benito Mussolini responded that "the League is very well when sparrows shout, but no good at all when eagles fall out."[479]

---

[475] http://en.wikipedia.org/wiki/League_of_Nations#cite_note-12
[476] *The United Nations at Age Fifty: A Legal Perspective* by Tomuschat Christian (1995). Martinus Nijhoff Publishers, p. 77
[477] *Covenant of the League of Nations. The Avalon Project.* Retrieved August 30th, 2011.
[478] *Covenant of the League of Nations. Treaty of Versailles. Minority Rights Treaties.* See *Article 23.*
[479] *The Elusiveness of Trust: The Experience of Security Council and Iran* by

After a number of notable successes and some early failures in the 1920's, the League ultimately proved incapable of preventing aggression by the Axis Powers in the 1930's. Germany withdrew from the League, as did Japan, Italy, Spain and others. The onset of World War II showed that the League had failed its primary purpose, which was to prevent any future world wars. The League lasted twenty-seven years. The United Nations (U.N.) replaced it after the end of the war and inherited a number of agencies and organizations founded by the League.[480]

The forerunner of the U.N. was the League of Nations, an organization conceived in similar circumstances during World War I, and established in 1919 under the *Treaty of Versailles* "to promote international cooperation and to achieve peace and security." The International Labor Organization was also created under the *Treaty of Versailles* as an affiliated agency of the League of Nations. The League of Nations ceased its activities after failing to prevent World War II.

The name "United Nations," coined by United States President, Franklin D. Roosevelt, was first used in the Declaration by United Nations of January 1st, 1942, during World War II, when representatives of twenty-six nations pledged their governments to continue fighting together against the Axis Powers.

In 1945, representatives of fifty countries met in San Francisco at the United Nations Conference on International Organization to draw up the *United Nations Charter*. Those delegates deliberated on the basis of proposals worked out by the representatives of China, the Soviet Union, the United Kingdom and the United States at Dumbarton Oaks, United States in August-October 1944.

---

Farhang Jahanpour (PDF). Transnational Foundation of Peace and Future Research, p. 2. Retrieved June 27th, 2008.

[480] http://en.wikipedia.org/wiki/League_of_Nations

The *Charter* was signed on June 26th, 1945 by the representatives of the fifty countries. Poland, which was not represented at the Conference, signed it later and became one of the original fifty-one member states.

The United Nations officially came into existence on October 24th, 1945, when the *Charter* had been ratified by China, France, the Soviet Union, the United Kingdom, the United States and by a majority of other signatories. United Nations Day is celebrated on October 24th each year.[481]

Due to its unique international character, and the powers vested in its founding *Charter*, the Organization can take action on a wide range of issues, and provide a forum for its 193 member states to express their views, through the General Assembly, the Security Council, the Economic and Social Council and other bodies and committees.

The work of the United Nations reaches *every corner* of the globe. Although best known for peacekeeping, peace building, conflict prevention and humanitarian assistance, there are many other ways the United Nations and its system (specialized agencies, funds and programs) affect our lives and make the world a better place. The organization works on a broad range of fundamental issues, from sustainable development, environment and refugees protection, disaster relief, counter-terrorism, disarmament and non-proliferation, to promoting democracy, human rights, gender equality and the advancement of women, governance, economic and social development, international health, clearing landmines, expanding food production, and more, in order to achieve its goals and coordinate efforts for a safer world for this and future generations.[482]

---

[481] http://www.un.org/en/aboutun/history/index.shtml, Signature page of *U.N. Charter*, San Francisco, 1945.
[482] http://www.un.org/en/aboutun/index.shtml

Currently, the U.N. has 97,000 military and police forces at their disposal from over 110 countries.[483] In 2011, the U.N. formed a coalition army to assist the rebels of Libya and helped to depose a leader of a U.N. member nation. Yet, with an upwards total of 115,000 civilian deaths in Syria as of October 2013,[484] the U.N. *still* refuses to step in and help.

We have clear examples in our recent history to show us that this body, the U.N., whose goal is the pursuit of "peace," is full of hypocrisy. Consequently, this makes me think about what the Bible has to say about "peace, peace" when there is no peace.

> *3 For when they say, "Peace and safety!" then suddenly destruction comes upon them, as labor pains upon a pregnant woman, and they shall not escape.* (1 Thessalonians 5:3)

> *10 Who say to the seers, "Do not see," and to the prophets, "Do not prophesy to us what is right. Speak to us what is smooth, prophesy deceits."* (Isaiah 30:10)

> *11 And they heal the breach of the daughter of My people slightly, saying, "Peace, peace!" when there is no peace.* (Jeremiah 8:11)

> *13 But I said, "Ah, Master יהוה! See, the prophets say to them, 'You are not to see a sword, nor have scarcity of food, for I give you true peace in this place.'"* (Jeremiah 14:13)

> *10 "Because, yea because they have led My people astray, saying, 'Peace!' when there is no peace. And when one is building a wall, see, they are coating it with whitewash!"* (Ezekiel 13:10)

> *16 "... the prophets of Yisra'ĕl who are prophesying concerning Yerushalayim, and who are seeing visions of peace for her when there is no peace," declares the Master יהוה.* (Ezekiel 13:16)

---

[483] http://www.un.org/en/peacekeeping/issues/military.shtml
[484] http://www.huffingtonpost.com/2013/10/01/syria-death-toll_n_4022414.html

> *9 "And if the prophet is deceived, and shall speak a word, I יהוה have deceived that prophet, and shall stretch out My hand against him and destroy him from the midst of My people Yisra'ěl."* (Ezekiel 14:9)
>
> *5 Thus said יהוה concerning the prophets who lead my people astray, who are biting with their teeth and have called out, "Peace!" They even set apart a battle against him who does not give for their mouths.* (Micah 3:5)

Sadly enough, people do not want to hear the grim realities that are about to come upon all of mankind, but just want to have their ears tickled and be told that everything is going to be O.K. Today it is called the "Peace and Prosperity" message.

I have now addressed two legs of this monstrosity of a world system—one rooted in ancient mythology, which is against Yehovah and His truths as found in His *Torah*—the other one finding its full expression in the creation of the United Nations, which already has its tentacles deeply embedded in every major facet of the power infrastructure of the world and poses as the "peacemaker" in the world of national and international politics. I am now going to show you how these two legs are joined together and although they are wrapped up to look good on the surface, once we dig down just a little, you will then see why they are in fact not good at all.

During the 1950's, 1960's, and 1970's, several events illustrated the magnitude of environmental damage caused by humans.

> On March 1st 1954, the twenty-three man crew of the Japanese fishing vessel Lucky Dragon 5[485] was exposed to and contaminated by radioactive fallout from the United States Castle Bravo thermonuclear device test at Bikini Atoll.[486] The publication of the book, *Silent Spring* (1962)[487] by Rachel Carson drew attention to the impact of chemicals

---
[485] http://en.wikipedia.org/wiki/Daigo_Fukuryū_Maru
[486] http://en.wikipedia.org/wiki/Castle_Bravo
[487] http://en.wikipedia.org/wiki/Silent_Spring

on the natural environment. In March 1967, the oil tanker, Torrey Canyon,[488] struck Pollard's Rock on Seven Stones Reef between the Cornish mainland and the Scilly Isles, off the Southwest Coast of England, and in 1969 oil spilled from an offshore well in California's Santa Barbara Channel.[489] In 1971, the conclusion of a lawsuit in Japan drew international attention to the effects of decades of mercury poisoning on the people of Minamata.[490]

At the same time, emerging scientific research drew new attention to existing and hypothetical threats to the environment and humanity. Among them (was) Paul R. Ehrlich, whose book, *The Population Bomb* (1968),[491] revived concerns about the impact of exponential population growth. Biologist Barry Commoner generated a debate about growth, affluence and "flawed technology."[492] Additionally, an association of scientists and political leaders known as the Club of Rome[493] published their report, *The Limits To Growth*[494] in 1972, and drew attention to the growing pressure on natural resources from human activities.

Meanwhile, technological accomplishments such as nuclear proliferation and photos of the Earth from outer-space provided both new insights and new reasons for concern over Earth's seemingly small and unique place in the universe.[495]

In 1972, the United Nations Conference on the Human Environment[496] was held in Stockholm, Sweden, and

---

[488] http://en.wikipedia.org/wiki/Torrey_Canyon
[489] http://en.wikipedia.org/wiki/1969_Santa_Barbara_oil_spill
[490] Most of the information in this section comes from John McCormick, *The Global Environmental Movement* by John Wiley, London: 1995.
[491] http://en.wikipedia.org/wiki/The_Population_Bomb
[492] http://en.wikipedia.org/wiki/Environmental_movement
[493] http://en.wikipedia.org/wiki/Club_of_Rome
[494] http://en.wikipedia.org/wiki/The_Limits_to_Growth
[495] http://en.wikipedia.org/wiki/Environmental_movement
[496] http://en.wikipedia.org/wiki/United_Nations_Conference_on_the_Human_Environment

for the first time, united the representatives of multiple governments in discussions relating to the state of the global environment.[497]

When the U.N. General Assembly decided to convene the Stockholm Conference, at the initiative of the Government of Sweden, U.N. Secretary-General U. Thant invited Maurice Strong[498] to lead it as Secretary-General of the Conference.[499]

The Conference was opened and addressed by the (late) Swedish Prime Minister Olof Palme and Secretary-General Kurt Waldheim to discuss the state of the global environment. Attended by the representatives of 113 countries, nineteen inter-governmental agencies, and more than 400 inter-governmental and non-governmental organizations, it is widely recognized as the beginning of modern political and public awareness of global environmental problems.[500]

I would like to point out to you that 1972 was the fifth year of the fourth Sabbatical Cycle. What this means is that forty-nine years later (or one Jubilee Cycle later) will bring us to 2020, which is right in the middle of this, the 120th Jubilee Cycle—again, the very last one for this 6th Millennial Day of man. (Just as a baby is not one until having lived for one full year, the first Jubilee Cycle did not count until having completed the first forty-nine years. 1996 was the completion of the 119th Jubilee Cycle. When we arrive at 2045, this 120th Jubilee Cycle we are currently in will have been completed and we will then begin the 7th Millennial Age.)

The current verse we are studying says that in the middle of this 70th Shabua, the anointed will be cut off. As we have shown you those *"anointed"* are the Saints, who will be cut off and killed. It also says

---

[497] http://en.wikipedia.org/wiki/Environmental_movement#cite_note-4
[498] http://en.wikipedia.org/wiki/Maurice_Strong
[499] *Where On Earth Are We Going?* by Maurice Strong; *Introduction* by Kofi Annan (2001). (Reprinted). New York, London: Texere. pp. 120–136
[500] *The Globalization of World Politics* by John Baylis and Steve Smith (2005). (3rd ed.) Oxford. Oxford University Press, pp. 454-45,

that he (the Antichrist *or* Apollyon) shall make a *"Covenant with many"* for (one week, one Shabua,) one forty-nine year period of time. I am pointing out to you here when this *Covenant* actually began. It began during the week of June 5th–16th of 1972. Out of a potential 196 countries in the world, this *Covenant* began in 1972 with 113 members and representatives from the others.

I had been looking for an agreement that involved *many* that began around 1996 to line up with this last Jubilee Cycle. But, if Satan is cut off in 2033 as I have been maintaining, then a covenant that begins in 1996 and only goes to 2033 will not be one complete forty-nine year period of time making this verse 27 of Daniel void. In order to be a complete Jubilee Cycle of forty-nine years, it must last *at least* that length of time.

The United Nations Environmental Program began at the Stockholm Conference in June of 1972 and forty-nine years later will bring us to June 2020. This is mind-blowing to come to grips with. This *is* the *Covenant* made with many spoken of in Daniel:

> 27 *And he shall confirm a covenant with many for one week.* (Daniel 9:27)

> The Stockholm Conference[501] created a new mold for how to materialize and administer a global environmental meeting. The conference was envisioned as action-oriented, and was intended to lead to positive results, not just a statement of principles.[502]

> This conference led directly to the creation of government environmental agencies and the U.N. Environmental Program (U.N.E.P.).[503] The United States also passed new legislation such as the Clean Water Act, the Clean Air Act, the Endangered Species Act, and the National Environmental

---

[501] http://www.youtube.com/watch?v=mJUk70tfELA
[502] http://www.bemonaco2011.org/index.php?option=com_content&view=article&id=47&Itemid=64
[503] http://en.wikipedia.org/wiki/UN_Environment_Program

Policy Act[504 & 505]—the foundations for current environmental standards.

By the mid-1970's anti-nuclear activism had moved beyond local protests and politics to gain a wider appeal and influence. Although it lacked a single, coordinating organization, the anti-nuclear movement's efforts gained a great deal of attention.[506] In the aftermath of the Three Mile Island "accident" in 1979, many mass demonstrations took place. The largest one was held in New York City in September, 1979 and involved 200,000 people;[507] speeches were given by Jane Fonda and Ralph Nader.[508 & 509]

Since the 1970's, public awareness, environmental sciences, ecology, and technology have advanced to include modern (focal) points like ozone depletion, global climate change, acid rain, and the potentially harmful genetically modified organisms (GMO's).[510]

The name and concept of Earth Day was pioneered by John McConnell in 1969 at a U.N.E.S.C.O.[511] Conference in San Francisco. He proposed March 21st, 1970, the first day of spring in the Northern Hemisphere. This day of nature's

---

[504] http://www.epa.gov/region2/ff/ca.htm
[505] http://en.wikipedia.org/wiki/Environmental_movement#cite_note-eleven-5
[506] *Three Mile Island: A Nuclear Crisis in Historical Perspective* by Samuel J. Walker (2004). (Berkeley: University of California Press), pp. 10-11.
[507] http://en.wikipedia.org/wiki/Anti-nuclear_protests
[508] http://en.wikipedia.org/wiki/Three_Mile_Island_accident
[509] http://en.wikipedia.org/wiki/Environmental_movement#cite_note-eleven-5
[510] http://en.wikipedia.org/wiki/Environmental_movement#cite_note-eleven-5
[511] The **United Nations Educational, Scientific and Cultural Organization U.N.E.S.C.O.**; pron.: /juːˈnɛskoʊ/) is a specialized agency of the United Nations (U.N.). Its purpose is to contribute to peace and security by promoting international collaboration through education, science, and culture in order to further universal respect for justice, the rule of law, and human rights along with fundamental freedom proclaimed in the *U.N. Charter*. [1] It is the heir of the League of Nations' International Commission On Intellectual Cooperation. U.N.E.S.C.O. has 195 member states.

equipoise[512] was later sanctioned in a proclamation signed by Secretary General U. Thant at the United Nations.[513 & 514]

A month later, a separate Earth Day, the first Earth Day, was celebrated on April 22nd, 1970. Its founder, former Wisconsin Senator, Gaylord Nelson[515] was inspired to create this day of environmental education and awareness after seeing the oil spill off the coast of Santa Barbara in 1969.[516] Greenpeace was created in 1971 as an organization that believed that political advocacy and legislation were ineffective or inefficient solutions and supported non-violent action. 1980 saw the creation of Earth First! —a group with an eco-centric view of the world believing in the preservation of every living thing being put on the same plane as human survival.[517]

Earth Day is an annual day on which events are held worldwide to increase awareness and appreciation of the Earth's natural environment. Earth Day is planned for April 22nd ... at least through 2015.[518] The April 22nd date was designated as International ***Mother Earth Day***[519] by a consensus resolution adopted by the United Nations in 2009.[520] While this April 22nd Earth Day was focused on the United States, an organization launched by Denis Hayes, who was the original national coordinator in 1970, took it international in 1990 and organized events in 141 nations.[521] Numerous communities celebrate Earth Week, an entire

---

[512] http://www.thefreedictionary.com/equipoise
[513] http://en.wikipedia.org/?title=Earth_Day
[514] http://en.wikipedia.org/wiki/Earth_Day
[515] http://en.wikipedia.org/wiki/Earth_Day
[516] http://www.earthday.org/earth-day-history-movement
[517] *Culture Wars: An Encyclopedia of Issues, Viewpoints, and Voices* by Roger Chapman (2010). M.E. Sharpe, Inc., p.162. ISBN 0-7656-1761-7.
[518] http://www.daysuntil.com/Earth-Day/index.html
[519] http://en.wikipedia.org/wiki/International_Mother_Earth_Day
[520] *General Assembly Proclaims April 22nd 'International Mother Earth Day' Adopting by Consensus Bolivia-Led Resolution*. United Nations. 2009-04-22. Retrieved 2011-04-22.
[521] http://www.earthday.org/earth-day-history-movement

week of activities focused on environmental issues. Earth Day is ... celebrated on April 22nd ... and is now coordinated globally by the Earth Day Network[522] and celebrated in more than 192 countries every year.[523]

An estimated 20,000,000 Americans participated in Earth Day the first year. In 1990 a resounding 200,000,000 citizens participated in 141 countries as Earth Day went global. In 2013, there were over a billion worldwide participating in Earth Day.[524]

Did you catch this? What began with good intentions to protect the environment and was supported by most of the world's governing bodies has now been subtly relabeled "Mother Earth Day." It has also grown from the original 113 member nations to, again, 193 of a possible 196 nations. I have now just shared with you how this movement went from an environmental one to a religious one—one that is anti-Yehovah.

**International Mother Earth Day** was established in 2009 by the General Assembly under Resolution A/RES/63/278. The resolution was introduced by the plurinational state of Bolivia and endorsed by over fifty member states.[525] It recognizes that "the Earth and its ecosystems are our home" and that "it is necessary to promote harmony with nature and the Earth." The term "Mother Earth" is used because it "reflects the interdependence that exists among human beings, other living species and the planet we all inhabit." It is decided to designate April 22nd as **International Mother Earth Day.**[526]

General Assembly President Miguel d'Escoto Brockmann welcomed the creation of International Mother Earth Day,

---

[522] http://www.earthday.org
[523] http://en.wikipedia.org/wiki/Earth_Day
[524] http://eluxemagazine.com/magazine/why-do-we-celebrate-earth-day-a-brief-history/
[525] http://www.un.org/News/Press/docs/2009/ga10823.doc.htm
[526] http://www.un.org/Docs/journal/asp/ws.asp?m=A/RES/63/278

saying: "International Mother Earth Day promotes a view of the Earth as the entity that sustains all living things found in nature. Inclusiveness is at the heart of International Mother Earth Day; fostering shared responsibilities to rebuild our troubled relationship with nature is a cause that is uniting people around the world."[527]

Having now shown you how this *covenant* became a religious act, I want to return back to the events leading up to and influencing the Stockholm conference to uncover other aspects of this stunning *"covenant made with many."*

In 1972, an association of scientists and political leaders known as the Club of Rome[528] published their report, *The Limits To Growth*,[529] and drew attention to the growing pressure on natural resources from human activities.

> The common enemy of humanity is man. In searching for a new enemy to unite us, we came up with the idea that pollution, the threat of global warming, water shortages, famine and the like would fit the bill. All these dangers are caused by human intervention, and it is only through changed attitudes and behavior that they can be overcome. The real enemy then, is humanity itself. **–Club of Rome.** ***The First Global Revolution.***

> We are facing an imminent, catastrophic, ecological collapse and our only hope is to transform humanity into a global, interdependent, sustainable society, based on respect and reverence for the Earth. **–Club of Rome.**[530]

> So, *what* exactly *is* the Club of Rome and *who* are its members? Founded in 1968 at David Rockefeller's estate in Bellagio, Italy; the C.o.R. describes itself as "a group of

---

[527] http://www.un.org/ga/president/63/statements/motherearth220409.shtml
[528] http://en.wikipedia.org/wiki/Club_of_Rome
[529] http://en.wikipedia.org/wiki/The_Limits_to_Growth
[530] http://green-agenda.com/globalrevolution.html

world citizens, sharing a common concern for the future of humanity." It consists of current and former heads of state, U.N. bureaucrats, high-level politicians and government officials, diplomats, scientists, economists, and business leaders from around the globe.

The Club of Rome subsequently founded two sibling organizations—the Club of Budapest and the Club of Madrid. The former is focused on social and cultural aspects of their agenda, while the latter concentrates on the political aspects. All three of these 'clubs' share many common members and hold joint meetings and conferences. As explained in other articles on this website it is abundantly clear that these are three heads of the *same* beast. The C.o.R. has also established a network of thirty-three National Associations. Membership in the 'main club' is limited to 100 individuals at any one time. Some members, like Al Gore and Maurice Strong, are affiliated through their respective National Associations (e.g., U.S.A.C.O.R., C.A.C.O.R., etc.).[531]

In the early 1970's, a book was published [titled], *The Limits To Growth*, a report of the Club of Rome's project on the predicament of mankind. Its conclusions were stunning. It was ultimately published in thirty languages and sold over 30,000,000 copies. According to a sophisticated M.I.T. (Massachusetts Institute of Technology) computer model, the world would ultimately run out of many key resources. These limits would become the "ultimate" predicament to mankind.[532]

What you are sure to notice as you continue reading, if you haven't already, is how these groups keep changing names and taking on new identities while continuing to promote, via the U.N., this environmental *Covenant* to "save" the Earth. The hard part about me trying to convince you this is evil is that this appears to be a very noble pursuit, a worthy

---

[531] http://green-agenda.com/globalrevolution.html
[532] http://peakenergy.blogspot.com/2005_01_01_archive.html

cause, and a lofty ideal to aspire to. Where they cross the line, however, is when they turn this into Mother Earth worship.

Again, the names of these organizations (and all they espouse) are in a constant state of flux and the various groups involved on multi-governmental levels continue to expand. They are comprised of non-elected bureaucrats acting under the auspices and directives of the U.N., a law unto itself, creating laws around the world that local governments then enforce. Understand this point, un-elected bureaucrats from other countries are making laws that you then are forced to obey in your country.

Traditional Christian thinking was that this *Covenant* was going to involve some kind of peace deal involving the State of Israel. That is based on a misunderstanding of the words of *Daniel* and it is because we had been looking for some sort of a peace agreement that we overlooked the environmental movement entirely. But the more my team and I look at it, the more convinced we are, that this is *EXACTLY* what Daniel 9:27 is prophesying about.

> In 2002, the World Summit on Sustainable Development was held in Johannesburg, South Africa, from August 26th–September 4th to take stock of achievements, challenges and new issues arising since the 1992 Earth Summit. It was an "implementation" Summit, designed to turn the goals, promises and commitments of *Agenda 21* into concrete, tangible actions.[533]
>
> To help advance the cause of **sustainable development** in a continuous fashion, the General Assembly also declared the period 2005-2014 as the United Nations Decade of Education for Sustainable Development. The Decade, for which the United Nations Educational, Scientific and Cultural Organization (U.N.E.S.C.O.) as the lead agency, aims to help people to develop the attitudes, skills and knowledge to make

---

[533] http://sightedmoon.com/the-covenant-made-with-many-for-one-week/

informed decisions for the benefit of themselves and others, now and in the future, and to act upon those decisions.[534]

The list of U.N. bodies active in support of the environment and sustainable development includes the World Bank, the United Nations Development Programme (U.N.D.P.), the International Maritime Organization (I.M.O.), the United Nations Industrial Development Organization (U.N.I.D.O.), the Food and Agriculture Organization of the United Nations (F.A.O.), the United Nations Human Settlements Programme (U.N.-HABITAT), the United Nations Educational, Scientific and Cultural Organization (U.N.E.S.C.O.), and the International Atomic Energy Agency (I.A.E.A.). The United Nations Global Compact engages the international business community in the observance of environmental principles, and the Global Environment Facility (G.E.F.), a World Bank–U.N.D.P.-U.N.E.P. initiative, helps to fund it all.[535]

In view of the crucial importance of the environmental perspective and the principle of sustainability, the General Assembly has declared a number of observances to catalyze positive action worldwide.

Among those currently in effect are the United Nations Decade of Education for Sustainable Development (2015-2014), and the International Decade for Action, "Water for Life," which began on March 22nd, 2005. In addition, the world community will observe the International Year of Natural Fibres in 2009, the International Year of Biodiversity in 2010, and the International Year of Forests in 2011.[536]

Annual environment-related observances declared by the Assembly also include World Water Day (March 22nd), the International Day for Biological Diversity May 22nd), World Environment Day (June 5th), World Day to Combat

---

[534] http://green-agenda.com/globalrevolution.html
[535] https://www.un.org/en/globalissues/environment/
[536] https://www.un.org/en/globalissues/environment/

Desertification and Drought (June 17th), International Day for the Preservation of the Ozone Layer (September 16th), International Day for Preventing the Exploitation of the Environment in War and Armed Conflict (November 6th), and International Mountain Day (December 11th).[537]

The original Covenant that began in Stockholm in 1972 has morphed into this bureaucratic monster with many different names, with its bylaws buried in mountains of paper and booklets and even still, it is not yet done. It looks so good and beneficial on the surface, but it is the principles put forth in the document itself that you begin to see why this is so revolting. Below I have listed the twenty-six principles of the original document.

## *Stockholm Declaration*[538]

> The United Nations Conference on the Human Environment, having met at Stockholm from 5 to 16 June 1972, having considered the need for a common outlook and for common principles to inspire and guide the peoples of the world in the preservation and enhancement of the human environment,
>
> Proclaims that:

Do you see what the opening paragraph is saying? This covenant is *"to inspire and guide the peoples of the world."* Just as Satan was very subtle in the garden with Eve, this covenant subtly is going to undermine the 10 Commandments given at Mount Sinai.

The meeting agreed upon a *Declaration* containing 26 principles concerning the environment and development; an *Action Plan* with 109 recommendations and a resolution.[539]

---

[537] https://www.un.org/en/globalissues/environment/

[538] http://www.unep.org/Documents.multilingual/Default.asp?DocumentID=97&ArticleID=1503

[539] *The Globalization of World Politics* by John Baylis & Steve Smith. 2005. (3rd ed). Oxford. Oxford University Press. pp. 454-455

**Principles of the *Stockholm Declaration*[540]:**

1. Human rights must be asserted, apartheid and colonialism condemned.
2. Natural resources must be safeguarded.
3. The Earth's capacity to produce renewable resources must be maintained.
4. Wildlife must be safeguarded.
5. Non-renewable resources must be shared and not exhausted.
6. Pollution must not exceed the environment's capacity to clean itself.
7. Damaging oceanic pollution must be prevented.
8. Development is needed to improve the environment.
9. Developing countries therefore need assistance.
10. Developing countries need reasonable prices for exports to carry out environmental management.
11. Environment policy must not hamper development.
12. Developing countries need money to develop environmental safeguards.
13. Integrated development planning is needed.
14. Rational planning should resolve conflicts between environment and development.
15. Human settlements must be planned to eliminate environmental problems.
16. Governments should plan their own appropriate population policies.
17. National institutions must plan development of states' natural resources.
18. Science and technology must be used to improve the environment.
19. Environmental education is essential.
20. Environmental research must be promoted, particularly in developing countries.
21. States may exploit their resources as they wish but must not endanger others.
22. Compensation is due to states thus endangered.
23. Each nation must establish its own standards.

---

[540] http://en.wikipedia.org/wiki/United_Nations_Conference_on_the_Human_Environment

24. There must be cooperation on international issues.
25. International organizations should help to improve the environment.
26. Weapons of mass destruction must be eliminated.

The *Stockholm Covenant* has human rights listed as its first and most prominent principle and declaration, and yet, the underwriters of it would have us to believe this agreement was to be all about the environment. Take a moment now to take careful note of what those "human rights" consist of.

> Human Rights are "commonly understood as inalienable fundamental rights to which a person is inherently entitled simply because she or he is a human being." Human rights are thus conceived as universal (applicable everywhere) and egalitarian (the same for everyone). These rights may exist as natural rights or as legal rights, in local, regional, national, and international law. The doctrine of human rights in international practice, within international law, global and regional institutions, in the policies of states and in the activities of non-governmental organizations, has been a cornerstone of public policy around the world. The idea of human rights states, "if the public discourse of peacetime global society can be said to have a common moral language, it is that of human rights." Despite this, the strong claims made by the doctrine of human rights continue to provoke considerable skepticism and debates about the content, nature and justifications of human rights to this day. Indeed, the question of what is meant by a "right" is itself controversial and the subject of continued philosophical debate.[541]

> Many of the basic ideas that animated the human rights movement developed in the aftermath of the WWII and the atrocities of the Holocaust, culminating in the adoption of the *Universal Declaration of Human Rights* in Paris by the United Nations General Assembly in 1948. The ancient world did not possess the concept of universal human

---

[541] http://en.wikipedia.org/wiki/Human_rights

rights. The true forerunner of human rights discourse was the concept of natural rights which appeared as part of the *Medieval Natural Law* tradition that became prominent during the Enlightenment with such philosophers as John Locke, Francis Hutcheson, and Jean-Jacques Burlamaqui, and featured prominently in the political discourse of the American Revolution and the French Revolution.[542]

From this foundation, the modern human rights arguments emerged over the latter half of the 20th-century.[543]

This *Declaration* on human rights intended to prevent another Holocaust has led to the following *Declaration* on Lesbian, Gay, Bi-Sexual and Transgendered rights.

### Sexual Orientation & Gender Identity

Sexual orientation and gender identity rights relate to the expression of sexual orientation and gender identity based on the right to respect for private life and the right not to be discriminated against on the ground of "other status" as defined in various human rights conventions, such as *Article 17* and *Article 26* in the *United Nations International Covenant on Civil and Political Rights* and *Article 8* and *Article 14* in the European Convention on Human Rights.[544]

Laws affecting **lesbian, gay, bisexual, and transgender** (L.G.B.T.) people vary greatly by country or territory—everything from legal recognition of same-sex marriage or other types of partnerships, to the death penalty as punishment for same-sex romantic/sexual activity or identity.[545]

L.G.B.T. rights are human rights and civil rights. L.G.B.T. rights laws include, but are not limited to, the following:

---

[542] http://en.wikipedia.org/wiki/Human_rights
[543] http://en.wikipedia.org/wiki/Human_rights
[544] http://en.wikipedia.org/wiki/Human_rights
[545] http://en.wikipedia.org/wiki/LGBT_rights_by_country_or_territory

government recognition of same-sex relationships (such as via same-sex marriage or civil unions), L.G.B.T. adoption, recognition of L.G.B.T. parenting, anti-bullying legislation and student non-discrimination laws to protect L.G.B.T. children and/or students, immigration equality laws, anti-discrimination laws for employment and housing, hate crime laws providing enhanced criminal penalties for prejudice-motivated violence against L.G.B.T. people, equal age of consent laws, and laws related to sexual orientation and military service.[546]

Anti-L.G.B.T. laws include, but are not limited to, the following: sodomy laws penalizing consensual same-sex sexual activity with fines, jail terms, or the death penalty, anti-'lesbianism' laws, and higher ages of consent for same-sex activity.[547]

In 2011, the United Nations Human Rights Council passed its first resolution recognizing L.G.B.T. rights, which was followed up with a report from the U.N. Human Rights Commission documenting violations of the rights of L.G.B.T. people, including hate crime, criminalization of homosexuality, and discrimination. Following up on the report, the U.N. Human Rights Commission urged all countries, which had not yet done so, to enact laws protecting basic L.G.B.T. rights.[548]

Homosexuality is illegal in seventy-six countries, and is punishable by execution in seven countries. The criminalization of private, consensual, adult sexual relations, especially in countries where corporal or capital punishment is involved, is one of the primary concerns of L.G.B.T. human rights advocates.

---

[546] http://en.wikipedia.org/wiki/LGBT_rights_by_country_or_territory
[547] http://en.wikipedia.org/wiki/LGBT_rights_by_country_or_territory
[548] http://en.wikipedia.org/wiki/LGBT_rights_by_country_or_territory

Other issues include: government recognition of same-sex relationships, L.G.B.T. adoption, sexual orientation and military service, immigration equality, anti-discrimination laws, hate crime laws regarding violence against L.G.B.T. people, sodomy laws, anti-lesbianism laws, and equal age of consent for same-sex activity.

A global charter for sexual orientation and gender identity rights has been proposed in the form of the *Yogyakarta Principles*,[549] a set of twenty-nine principles whose authors say they apply international human rights law statutes and precedents to situations relevant to L.G.B.T. people's experience. The principles were presented at a United Nations event in New York on November 7th, 2007, co-sponsored by Argentina, Brazil and Uruguay.[550]

The principles have been acknowledged with influencing the French proposed U.N. declaration on sexual orientation and gender identity, which focuses on ending violence, criminalization and capital punishment and does not include dialogue about same-sex marriage or the right to start a family. The proposal was supported by sixty-seven of the *then* 192 member countries of the United Nations, including all E.U. member states and the United States. An alternative statement opposing the proposal was initiated by Syria and signed by fifty-seven member nations, including all twenty-seven nations of the Arab League as well as Iran and North Korea.[551]

This *U.N. Covenant* has also been covered up or hidden because of the many wild and unbelievable stories that oftentimes are erroneously associated with it. These originate from the sensationalism perpetrated by conspiracy theorists who engage in elaborate conjecture and vainly speculate about the Illuminati and the Jesuit Order, just to give a couple

---

[549] http://en.wikipedia.org/wiki/Yogyakarta_Principles
[550] http://en.wikipedia.org/wiki/Human_rights
[551] http://en.wikipedia.org/wiki/Human_rights

of examples. They continually mix the truth with blatant lies. I have tried very hard to steer clear of any of these conspiratorial based lies.

This *U.N. Covenant*, forged in 1972, adopted by 113 nations initially, but now includes 192 of 196[552] nations altogether, is the very same *Covenant* that Daniel is warning us about. You are now about to read how this covenant has been reworded since that time until roughly 2010.

### Earth Charter Preamble[553]

"... we are one human family and one Earth community with a common destiny. We must join together to bring forth a sustainable global society founded on respect for nature. ... Toward this end, it is imperative that we, the peoples of (the) Earth, declare our responsibility to one another, to the greater community of life, and to future generations."[554]

According to the *Charter*, humanity must undergo a global "change of mind and heart." And the U.N.'s all-wise (in their own eyes) seers visualize themselves as the leading and key "change agents" for this global undertaking.

The *Earth Charter Initiative*,[555] however, candidly admits that it intends to recruit your children as change agents, as well[556]—as put forth in the following:

We seek to increase the participation of young people in utilizing the *Earth Charter* as a guideline in their work as active agents of change.[557 & 558]

---

[552] http://geography.about.com/cs/countries/a/numbercountries.htm
[553] http://www.earthcharterinaction.org/content/pages/Read-the-Charter.html
[554] http://www.earthcharterinaction.org/content/pages/Read-the-Charter.html
[555] http://www.earthcharterinaction.org/content/pages/The-Drafting-Process.html
[556] http://agendatwentyone.wordpress.com/2010/07/08/test-2/
[557] http://beforeitsnews.com/alternative/2010/07/the-earth-charter-companion-to-agenda-21-99141.html
[558] http://pacificfreedomfoundation.org/wp-content/uploads/2012/10/Agenda_21_NEW_7.31.pdf

They have been doing precisely that, and will be accelerating their program throughout the world—including schools in your neighborhood. The U.S. Conference of Mayors[559] is but one of hundreds of organizations along with schools, municipalities, and other entities that have signed on as supporters of this declaration of a new "global ethic" for the world.

In sharing with you the particulars of the *Earth Charter*, I am, by necessity, going to have to waffle between fact and conjecture. The problem with interpreting political data is that it always requires inferential analysis. The reasons for this are manifold, but the most obvious are simply because legislation is drafted in legal language and thus requires such interpretations; and secondly, those interpretations then have to be weighed against a body of empirical evidence that illuminates a political agenda or an overall philosophy that has been at work and in effect over an extended period of time.

Nothing is ever as simple as it appears, nor does anything ever happen without a reason. It is an arduous task to fit all the pieces together and reveal the big picture, but one thing you can be certain of is that there is a framework of thought that precedes all policy. To fully understand the far reaching implications of the *Earth Charter*, it must be interpreted within the context of the Club of Rome and *Agenda 21*. Supplemental information on this can be obtained by checking out their respective links as they appear in the following article:

> Club of Rome[560] board members **Mikhail Gorbachev** and **Maurice Strong** authored the *Earth Charter* as a project undertaken by their respective organizations, Green Cross International[561] and the Earth Council Alliance.[562] The idea for the *Earth Charter* was conceived in 1987 by another Club of Rome board-member, Gro Harlem Brundtland.[563]

---

[559] http://www.usmayors.org/climateprotection/agreement.htm
[560] http://agendatwentyone.wordpress.com/2010/06/28/the-club-of-rome-where-the-buck-stops/, A complete list of who makes up this think tank can be found at this link.
[561] http://www.gcint.org
[562] http://earthcouncilalliance.org
[563] http://en.wikipedia.org/wiki/Gro_Harlem_Brundtland

As an interesting side note, Gro Harlem Brundtland served as Prime Minister of Norway for three terms. I cannot help but wonder if it is possible that she had any influence in helping fellow Club of Rome board member **Al Gore** obtain his Nobel Peace Prize?

Gro Harlem Brundtland was invited by then United Nations Secretary-General Javier Pérez de Cuéllar[564] (and current C.o.R. board-member) to establish and chair the World Commission on Environment and Development[565] (W.C.E.D.), widely referred to as the Brundtland Commission.[566] This Commission published its report in 1987 titled, *Our Common Future*[567] and was the precursor to the Rio Earth Summit which gave rise to *Agenda 21*.[568]

If you notice, *both* documents parallel one another in their language. Excerpts below are from *Our Common Future*:

> Sustainable global development requires that those who are more affluent adopt lifestyles within the planet's ecological means.[569]

> "... sustainable development can only be pursued if population size and growth demographic developments are in harmony with the changing productive potential of the ecosystem."[570]

## Development

The Earth Charter Commission approved the final draft of the *Earth Charter* in 2000, and it has *since* been embraced

---

[564] http://en.wikipedia.org/wiki/Javier_Pérez_de_Cuéllar
[565] http://en.wikipedia.org/wiki/World_Commission_on_Environment_and_Development
[566] http://en.wikipedia.org/wiki/Brundtland_Commission
[567] http://www.un-documents.net/ocf-02.htm
[568] http://canadafreepress.com/index.php/article/25028
[569] http://www.un-documents.net/ocf-ov.htm
[570] http://www.un-documents.net/ocf-02.htm

by the United Nations, many religious leaders around the world, the majority of world governments and countless Non-Governmental Organizations (N.G.O.'s) and activist groups. Following the release of the *Charter*, a series of international forums, called *The Earth Dialogues*[571] were held at the United Nations to discuss how the general public could be convinced to adopt the **"Covenant with the Earth"** in a real and personal way.[572 & 573]

Perhaps most revealing was the Forum for Inter-Religious Groups and Spiritual Leaders. As stated in the Forum's official meeting minutes,[574] the intent was to deal with "the ethics of intolerant righteousness and the greed of short term gain, as these cannot lead us to sustainable development. **It is clear that our religious institutions have barely begun to articulate the core values of sustainable development.** In their fundamentalist-fanatical forms, religions throughout history have justified terrorism, jihads and crusades against people who hold different beliefs and against the Earth itself." So we can clearly see who they consider their enemy to be.[575]

While supporters of the *Earth Charter* consider traditional monotheistic religions to be the main obstacle to peaceful coexistence and sustainable life on Earth, they do not propose doing away with spirituality. The *Earth Charter* goes into detail about the need for faith and spirituality in human life. The *Preamble* of the *Charter* states "the spirit of human solidarity and kinship with all life is strengthened when we live with reverence for the mystery of being, gratitude for the gift of life, and humility regarding the human place in nature.[576]

---

[571] http://www.greencrossinternational.net/earth-dialogues
[572] http://green-agenda.com/earthcharter.html
[573] http://agendatwentyone.wordpress.com/2010/07/08/test-2/
[574] http://www.commongood.info/cooperation.html
[575] http://green-agenda.com/earthcharter.html
[576] http://green-agenda.com/earthcharter.html

So what exactly does this *Earth Charter* contain? Compared to most U.N. publications, it is very short, only four pages long, direct, and to the point. It clearly lays out the *Constitution for a New Green Order*:

> "The choice is ours," it states, "form a global partnership to care for Earth and one another or risk the destruction of ourselves and the diversity of life. Fundamental changes are needed in our values, institutions, and ways of living."[577]

> (The) five (shared) principles[578 & 579] of the *Earth Charter* are as follows:
>
> - Reverence for Earth & the Cosmos
> - Respect for myriad species
> - Restraint in the use of natural resources
> - Redistribution of wealth & resources
> - Responsibility for future generations & for the community of life.

I must point out the subtlety once again to make sure it does not go by without you noticing it. The first principle we are to incorporate into our values and institutions and our way of living is to *"reverence"* the Earth. This causes us to place the earth in a position of something holy, something to be revered and as you will soon see something to be worshipped. Watch for this expression as we continue, along with *sustainable development* and the redistribution of wealth.

> rev·er·ence [580] *noun*
> : honor or respect that is felt for or shown to (someone or something)
> : honor or respect felt or shown : deference deference;
>   *especially* : profound adoring awed respect
> : a gesture of respect (as a bow)
> : the state of being revered

---

[577] http://www.earthcharterinaction.org/content/pages/Read-the-Charter.html
[578] http://www.contenderministries.org/articles/earthcharter.php
[579] http://tinyurl.com/kbzeg32
[580] http://www.merriam-webster.com/dictionary/reverence

: one held in reverence —used as a title for a clergyman

In closing, the *Earth Charter* concludes:

> **As never before in history, common destiny beckons us to seek a new beginning. Such renewal is the promise of these *Earth Charter* principles.** To fulfill this promise, we must commit ourselves to adopt and promote the values and objectives of the *Charter*.[581]

> This requires a change of mind and heart. It requires a new sense of **global interdependence** and universal responsibility. We must imaginatively develop and apply the vision of a sustainable way of life locally, nationally, regionally, and globally. Our cultural diversity is a precious heritage and different cultures will find their own distinctive ways to realize the vision. We must deepen and expand the global dialogue that generated the *Earth Charter*, for we have much to learn from the ongoing collaborative search for truth and wisdom.[582]

> Life often involves tensions between important values. This can mean difficult choices. However, we must find ways to harmonize diversity with unity, the exercise of freedom with the common good, short-term objectives with long-term goals. Every individual, family, organization, and community has a vital role to play. The arts, sciences, religions, educational institutions, media, businesses, non-governmental organizations, and governments are all called to offer creative leadership. The partnership of government, civil society, and business is essential for effective governance.[583]

> In order to build a sustainable global community, **the nations of the world must renew their commitment to the United**

---

[581] http://www.earthcharterinaction.org/content/pages/Read-the-Charter.html
[582] http://www.earthcharterinaction.org/content/pages/Read-the-Charter.html
[583] http://www.earthcharterinaction.org/content/pages/Read-the-Charter.html

**Nations**, fulfill their obligations under existing international agreements, and support the implementation of *Earth Charter* principles with an international legally binding instrument on environment and development. **Let ours be a time remembered for the awakening of a new reverence for life, the firm resolve to achieve sustainability**, the quickening of the struggle for justice and peace, and the joyful celebration of life.[584]

Unlike *Agenda 21*, which is a hard law document, the *Earth Charter* lays out the principles, which laws and regulations will have to promote and enforce. The *Charter* "was drafted in coordination with a hard law treaty that is designed to provide an integrated legal framework for all environment development law and policy." This hard law treaty is called the *International Covenant on Environment and Development*[585] and is being prepared by the Commission on Environmental Law at the International Union for the Conservation of Nature (I.U.C.N.),[586] a behemoth agency, which oversees 700+ governmental agencies worldwide. Interestingly, Maurice Strong[587] (busy man!) is on the I.U.C.N.'s Board of Directors.[588]

Again, unlike *Agenda 21*, the *Earth Charter* is not being forced on local communities from above. The United Nations is quietly fostering a grassroots mainstream movement where people personally commit themselves to the *Charter*. They believe that this personal commitment will be necessary to bring about the societal transformation that the *Charter* requires. The primary tool being used to permeate society with awareness and acceptance of the *Charter* is the *Earth*

---

[584] http://www.earthcharterinaction.org/content/pages/Read-the-Charter.html
[585] http://www.i-c-e-l.org/indexen.html
[586] http://iucn.org
[587] http://en.wikipedia.org/wiki/Maurice_Strong#Changing_attitudes
[588] http://green-agenda.com/earthcharter.html

*Charter Initiative*.[589] This is another brainchild of Strong and Gorbachev.[590]

According to their own description, the *Earth Charter Initiative* is the collective name for an extraordinarily diverse, global network of people, organizations, and institutions who participate in promoting the *Earth Charter*, and in implementing its principles in practice. The *Initiative* is a broad-based, voluntary, civil society effort, but participants include leading international institutions, national governments, university associations, N.G.O.s, cities, faith groups, and many well-known leaders in sustainable development.[591]

The *Earth Charter Initiative* is located in, and managed by, the United Nations University of Peace.[592] The governing council of this university contains some very interesting names. Many of its top academics are members of the Club of Rome. In fact, the infamous Maurice Strong is the president of the university and its Rector, Martin Lees, is the Secretary General of the Club of Rome. The founder and current chancellor of the university is Robert Muller, former Assistant-Secretary of the United Nations, and its #2 ranked official.[593]

Dr. Muller is very active in the educational and spiritual aspects of the *Earth Charter* and apparently he has the power of "God" behind him to give his voice much more moral authority. From his own website, Good Morning World,[594] you can read the entire list of ideas[595] he has conjured and bounces off "God" for approval (scroll down to the bottom,

---

[589] http://en.wikipedia.org/wiki/Earth_Charter_Initiative
[590] http://green-agenda.com/earthcharter.html
[591] http://green-agenda.com/earthcharter.html
[592] http://en.wikipedia.org/wiki/United_Nations_University_of_Peace
[593] http://green-agenda.com/earthcharter.html
[594] http://goodmorningworld.org/G1/Home.html
[595] http://robertmuller.org/ideas/

and on the way down, notice that prior to his final stamp of approval from "God," he has been dialoguing with "Earth").

One of the documents designed to advance this process, the long-awaited *Earth Charter*, was formally unveiled to the world at Johannesburg. Crafted by a conclave of "Wise Persons" headed by former Soviet Dictator, Mikhail Gorbachev, it is set to become the Holy Writ of the U.N.'s new "global spirituality." Although the *Earth Charter* is not a legally binding document, its impact may prove damaging and pervasive. Its benign sounding verbiage and symbolic nature camouflage its dangerous purpose. The *Charter* is intended to become a universally adopted creed that will psychologically prepare the world's children to accept the necessity of world government to save the environment. It is also an outrageous attempt to indoctrinate your children into the U.N.'s New Age paganism.[596 & 597]

Weeks before the start of Earth Summit II, the *Earth Charter* arrived in Johannesburg for a series of rituals, celebrations, and promotions aimed at setting the spiritual tone for the global conference. The venerated *Charter* is housed and transported in the Ark of Hope, a blasphemous mimicry of the biblical Ark of the Covenant, which held the two tablets containing the *Ten Commandments* that God gave to Moses. The Ark of Hope is actually designed to look like the Ark of the Covenant and its devotees carry it around with worshipful solemnity. Accompanying the *Charter* and the Ark are the Temenos Books,[598] containing aboriginal Earth Masks and "visual prayers/affirmations for global healing, peace, and gratitude," created by 3,000 artists, teachers, students, and mystics. According to the Temenos

---

[596] http://www.thenewamerican.com/culture/faith-and-morals/item/15091-the-new-world-religion

[597] http://agendatwentyone.wordpress.com/2010/07/08/test-2/

[598] http://www.earthcharterinaction.org/invent/images/uploads/ENG-Linder.pdf. They also have a picture of this Ark here to view.

Project,[599] which launched the effort, a Temenos is "a magical sacred circle where special rules apply and extraordinary events inevitably occur."[600]

The Ark, *Charter*, and Temenos Books were placed on display at the U.N. summit site and then put to work building the new global ethic. Day after day, U.N. acolytes carried the sacred objects from school to school, where tens of thousands of children already had been prepped with *Earth Charter* propaganda. Public ceremonies with mayors and celebrities augmented the school events.[601]

The summit's opening day featured a four-hour symposium titled, "Educating For Sustainable Living With the *Earth Charter*." Steven Rockefeller, a religion professor and scion of the fabulously wealthy banking family that donated the land for the U.N. headquarters in New York, was preeminent among the presenters. Professor Rockefeller is also chairman of the Rockefeller Brothers Fund[602] and the Earth Charter International Drafting Committee.[603] According to Rockefeller, the way to go about "building peace on Earth" is through the "inclusive, integrated and spiritual approach" of the *Earth Charter*.[604]

Covering the summit for U.S.A. Radio, Cathie Adams told *The New American* that Rockefeller described the *Charter* as an effort to incorporate the "wisdom of the world's religions." Razeena Wagiet,[605] environmental adviser to South Africa's national minister of education, was one of the presenters who followed Rockefeller to the podium. According to Wagiet,

---

[599] http://sueliz1.wordpress.com/2010/05/13/ark-of-hope-the-ark-of-the-new-age-covenant/
[600] http://www.canadafreepress.com/index.php/article/25233
[601] http://www.canadafreepress.com/index.php/article/25233
[602] http://www.rbf.org
[603] http://www.earthcharterinaction.org/content/pages/The-Drafting-Process.html
[604] http://www.canadafreepress.com/index.php/article/25233
[605] http://www.sourcewatch.org/index.php?title=Razeena_Wagiet

astrologers have foreseen that the world is about to enter a "Golden Age, a New Age, an Age of Aquarius."[606]

Outlining how the *Earth Charter* is to be integrated into lifelong education for all,[607] Hans van Ginkel, chairman of the International Association of Universities (the U.N. University in Costa Rica), told the symposium:

> "We must mobilize all in education about sustainability; that's how we meet the next generation ... sixteen million teachers must be trained" and that "the only way to move forward is by integrating the *Earth Charter* into curriculum and to link all universities based on regional bases of excellence."[608]

The Strong-Gorbachev *Earth Charter* effort is already fast at work on that score. Their website declares:

> The *Earth Charter* values and principles must be taught, contemplated, applied and internalized. To this end, the *Earth Charter* needs to be incorporated into both formal and non-formal education. This process must involve various communities, continue to integrate the *Charter* into the curriculum of schools and universities, and constitute an ongoing process of lifelong learning.[609]

According to the same website, the Earth Council, U.N.E.S.C.O., and the *Earth Charter Initiative* folks already have many of the curriculum materials and programs prepared; in fact, they're already up and running in

---

[606] http://www.thenewamerican.com/culture/faith-and-morals/item/15091-the-new-world-religion
[607] http://www.canadafreepress.com/index.php/article/25233, Earth Charter Integration
[608] http://www.eagleforum.org/un/2002-Africa/02-08-29.shtml
[609] http://www.canadafreepress.com/index.php/article/25233

schools across the globe.[610] & [611] Some American schools got an advance start on the rest of humanity with *Charter* activities, coinciding with the journey last year of the Ark and its contents to the U.N. in New York. The pilgrimage began in Vermont, where Steven Rockefeller, in his role as dean of religion at Middlebury College, held a sacred Earth ceremony. Joining him and the other worshipers was Jane Goodall, the celebrity chimpanzee expert who has become a fixture at forums sponsored by Mikhail Gorbachev and the U.N. The *Charter* was carried on foot, by car, and by boat, arriving in New York City on November 8th, to be greeted by Pete Seeger, the leftist folksinger. On January 24th, the Ark and *Charter* were carried in a procession from the Interfaith Center of New York to the United Nations Church Center Chapel, a distance of about fifteen blocks.[612]

The *Charter's* authors are not shy about the importance of their handiwork. "My hope is that this *Charter* will be a kind of '*Ten Commandments*,' a '*Sermon On the Mount*,' that provides a guide for human behavior toward the environment in the next century and beyond," Gorbachev stated in a 1997 interview with the *Los Angeles Times*. Canadian billionaire socialist, Maurice Strong, who presided over the 1992 Earth Summit in Rio de Janeiro, is somewhat less tentative. "The real goal of the *Earth Charter*," said Strong, "is that it will, in fact, become like the *Ten Commandments*." Mr. Strong had high hopes that the *Charter*, conceived in 1987, would be adopted by the world at Rio. It was decided that the world was not ready for the release of a charter to invigorate the world into embracing a paradigm of sustainable consciousness. My interpretation of this hesitation is simply due to the fact that the notion of manmade global climate change had not been indoctrinated thoroughly enough to start cramming

---

[610] http://www.canadafreepress.com/index.php/article/25233
[611] http://agendatwentyone.wordpress.com/2010/07/08/test-2/
[612] http://agendatwentyone.wordpress.com/2010/07/08/test-2/

something as radical as the *Earth Charter* down everyone's throats without threat of massive resistance.[613]

I must point out to you at this juncture that *"global climate change"* that Mr. Strong is referring to, is in fact the second curse of Leviticus 26. It is this curse of severe weather that many assume to be *global warming*, when in fact it is Yehovah pouring out the second of five curses upon those who will not obey His commandments. All of these curses are found in Leviticus 26.

> *18 And if you will not yet listen to Me for all this, then I will punish you seven times more for your sins. 19 And I will break the pride of your power, and I will make your heaven like iron and your earth like bronze. 20 And your strength shall be spent in vain. For your land shall not yield its increase, neither shall the trees of the field yield their fruits.* (Leviticus 26:18-20)

Returning to the Earth Charter commentary:

> I listed some of the organizations that are committed to promulgating the spiritual/educational aspects of *Agenda 21* via the *Earth Charter*. We will never know if these people actually believe this stuff, or merely recognized how convenient it would be to have everyone else subscribe to this paganism. Whatever that case may be, it is obvious that Earth worshipers would gleefully embrace policies that serve to protect her. When the *Earth Charter* is considered in conjunction with *Agenda 21*, then the achievement of a total transformation of the world can be more fully comprehended. Global citizenship, ecological stewardship, social equity, and all these new-age terms take on meaning with much greater significance.[614] & [615]

---

[613] http://agendatwentyone.wordpress.com/2010/07/08/test-2/
[614] http://agendatwentyone.wordpress.com/2010/07/08/test-2/
[615] http://www.pvbcw.com/Pages/Agenda21.aspx

All of these environmental events led by the United Nations in a bid to head off the extinction of man and all life on this Earth, led to the gathering in 1992 known as the Rio Summit[616] or Earth Summit.[617] Again this verbiage can be read in Mathew where Yehshua is warning them of the last days:

> *20 But pray that your flight is not in the winter, nor on the sabbath day; 21 for then shall be great tribulation, such as has not been since the beginning of the world to this time; no, nor ever shall be. 22 And unless those days should be shortened, no flesh would be saved. But for the elect's sake, those days shall be shortened.* (Mathew 24:20-22)

The Earth Summit, also called the Rio Summit produced what has been called Agenda 21.

> The United Nations Conference on Environment and Development (U.N.C.E.D.), also known as the Rio Summit, Rio Conference, Earth Summit (Portuguese: Eco '92) was a major United Nations conference held in Rio de Janeiro from June 3rd to June 14th, 1992.[618]

> *Agenda 21* is a non-binding; voluntarily implemented action plan of the United Nations (U.N.) related to sustainable development and was an outcome of the U.N. Conference on Environment and Development (U.N.C.E.D.) held in Rio de Janeiro, Brazil, in 1992.[619]

*Agenda 21* was a soft law or set of suggestions in 1992 and was then codified and made into national law with penalties and fines that could be enforced in a court of law.

> It is a comprehensive blueprint of action to be taken globally, nationally, and locally by organizations of the

---

[616] http://www.publications.gc.ca/collections/Collection-R/LoPBdP/BP/bp317-e.htm
[617] http://www.un.org/geninfo/bp/enviro.html
[618] http://en.wikipedia.org/wiki/Earth_Summit
[619] http://en.wikipedia.org/wiki/Agenda_21

U.N., governments, and major groups in every area in which humans directly affect the environment.[620]

Although *Agenda 21* was originally a soft-law document, it was, from the start, intended to be the precursor of an all-encompassing *U.N. Treaty*. The most recent iteration of that treaty has now been obtained and reviewed. It is called, in its present form, *Draft International Covenant on Environment and Development*. It is organized into eleven parts, containing a total of seventy-two *Articles*. It will convert the "soft-law" recommendations of *Agenda 21*, into legally binding "hard" International Law.[621]

Before examining the document itself, it is helpful to realize that the procedure for making International Law has evolved since 1948 and is now recognized by the international community as "the norm." The *Introduction* to the *Draft Covenant* says:

> The progression of legal principles from recommendatory 'soft' to legally clear 'hard' is well-known in International Law. For example, the 1948 *Universal Declaration of Human Rights*, a 'soft law' instrument, was the precursor to the two 1966 *U.N. Covenants On Human Rights*.[622]

From the start, *Agenda 21* was intended to be a "soft law" document. Therefore, its ideas are presented initially in the form of recommendations with no discussion at all regarding compliance and enforcement. The *Draft Covenant*, however, *does address* those issues. A third meeting of the I.U.C.N. group was held shortly after U.N.C.E.D. to incorporate ideas presented in Rio into the *Draft Covenant*. Two more meetings occurred, in April and September 1993.

---

[620] http://sustainabledevelopment.un.org/index.php?page=view&nr=23&type=400
[621] http://sovereigntyonline.org/p/sd/covenant.htm
[622] http://www.sovereignty.net/p/sd/covenant.htm

> Both the chairs of the I.U.C.N.'s Ethics Commission and the I.U.C.N.'s Species Survival Commission were invited to participate. The drafting committee met again in April, and September 1994. While the I.U.C.N. is clearly the *driving force* behind the document, other organizations that participated in the development of the *Covenant* included the International Council of Environmental Law (I.C.E.L.); and the United Nations Environmental Programme's Environmental Law and Institutions Programme Activity Center (U.N.E.P./E.L.I.P.A.C.).[623]

> The current *Draft Covenant* was completed in March 1995, in Bonn, Germany.[624]

The year 1995 just so happened to be the 49th year of the 118th Jubilee Cycle, whereas 1996 was the Jubilee Year and the first year in this the last Jubilee Cycle of this Sixth Millennial Day.

> The *Kyoto Protocol* was initially adopted on December 11th, 1997 in Kyoto, Japan, and entered into force on February 16th, 2005.[625] As of September 2011, 191 states have signed and ratified the *Protocol*. The only remaining signatory not to have ratified the *Protocol* is the United States. Other United Nations member states, which did not ratify the Kyoto Protocol, *are Afghanistan, Andorra and South Sudan. Somalia ratified the protocol on July 26th, 2010.*[626]

> In December 2011, Canada became the first nation to renounce the Protocol against global warming.[627]

---

[623] http://sovereigntyonline.org/p/sd/covenant.htm
[624] http://sovereigntyonline.org/p/sd/covenant.htm
[625] http://unfccc.int/essential_background/kyoto_protocol/items/6034.php
[626] http://www.charlesayoub.com/life-style/index.php/more/1/6400
[627] http://www.dailymail.co.uk/news/article-2073520/Canada-abandons-Kyoto-Protocol-save-14bn-penalties-missing-greenhouse-gas-targets.html

**Implementation of *Agenda 21***

The Commission on Sustainable Development acts as a high-level forum on sustainable development and has acted as a preparatory committee for summits and sessions on the implementation of *Agenda 21*. The U.N. Division for Sustainable Development acts as the "secretariat" to the Commission and works "within the context of" *Agenda 21*. Implementation by member states remains essentially voluntary and its adoption has varied.[628]

**Local *Agenda 21***

The implementation of *Agenda 21* was intended to involve action at international, national, regional and local levels. Some national and state governments have legislated or advised that local authorities take steps to implement the plan locally, as recommended in *Chapter 28* of the document. These programs are often known as "Local Agenda 21" or "L.A.21." For example, in the Philippines, the plan is "Philippines Agenda 21" or "P.A.21." The group, I.C.L.E.I.– Local Governments for Sustainability, formed in 1990; today its members come from 1,200 cities, towns, and counties in seventy countries and is widely regarded as a paragon of *Agenda 21* implementation.[629 & 630]

In other countries, opposition to *Agenda 21*'s ideas has surfaced to varied extents. In some cases, opposition has been legislated into several states limiting or forbidding the participation and/or funding of local government activities that support *Agenda 21*.[631 & 632]

---

[628] http://en.wikipedia.org/wiki/Agenda_21
[629] *Activists Fight Green Projects, Seeing U.N. Plot* by Leslie Kaufman & Kate Zernike (February 3rd, 2012). *New York Times*. Retrieved August 15th, 2012.
[630] http://en.wikipedia.org/wiki/Agenda_21
[631] *Alabama Adopts First Official State Ban on U.N. Agenda 21* by Alex Newman (June 4th 2012), *The New American*. Retrieved August 15th, 2012.
[632] http://en.wikipedia.org/wiki/Agenda_21

### *Agenda 21* At A National Level

The U.N. Department of Economic and Social Affairs' Division for Sustainable Development monitors and evaluates progress, nation by nation, toward the adoption of *Agenda 21*, and makes these reports available to the public on its website.[633 & 634]

Australia, for example, is a signatory to *Agenda 21* and eighty-eight of its municipalities subscribe to I.C.L.E.I.,[635] an organization that promotes *Agenda 21* globally. Australia's membership is second only to that of the United States.[636] Opposition to *Agenda 21* in Australia is not covered in the major media outlets,[637] even though groups such as Act Australia, a "fringe" political organization, has labeled *Agenda 21* a "threat to freedom."[638] European countries generally possess well documented *Agenda 21* statuses. France, whose national government, along with fourteen other cities, is a signatory, boasts nationwide programs supporting *Agenda 21*. Like Australia, however, some opponents have expressed that they view *Agenda 21* as a "sham."[639]

In Africa, national support for *Agenda 21* is strong and most countries are signatories. But support is often closely tied to environmental challenges specific to each country; for example, in 2002, Sam Nujoma, who was then president

---

[633] *Areas of Work—National Information by Country or Organization U.N. Department of Economic and Social Affairs.* United Nations. Retrieved August 15th, 2012.
[634] http://en.wikipedia.org/wiki/Agenda_21
[635] http://en.wikipedia.org/wiki/ICLEI
[636] *I.C.L.E.I. Local Governments For Sustainability: Global Members, I.C.L.E.I.* Retrieved August 15th, 2012.
[637] http://en.wikipedia.org/wiki/Agenda_21
[638] *Threats To Freedom: Agenda 21, Act for Australia.* Retrieved August 15th, 2012.
[639] *Agenda 21: L'Opposition n'y Voit Qu'une Imposture* by Sébastien Laporte, March 12th, 2012 (in French). *L'Union: Champagne, Ardenne, Picardie.* Retrieved August 15th 2012.

of Namibia, spoke about the importance of adhering to *Agenda 21* at the 2002 Earth Summit, noting that as a semi-arid country, Namibia sets a lot of store in the United Nations Convention to Combat Desertification (U.N.C.C.D.).[640]

Furthermore, there is little mention of *Agenda 21* at the local level in indigenous media. Only major municipalities in sub-Saharan African countries are members of I.C.L.E.I. *Agenda 21* participation in North African countries mirrors that of Middle Eastern countries, with most countries being signatories but little to no adoption on the local government level. Countries in sub-Saharan Africa and North Africa generally have poorly documented *Agenda 21* status reports. By contrast, South Africa's participation in *Agenda 21* mirrors that of modern Europe, with twenty-one city members of I.C.L.E.I. and support of *Agenda 21* by national-level government.[641]

### *Agenda 21* In the United States

The United States is a signatory country to *Agenda 21*, but because *Agenda 21* is not a treaty, the U.S. Senate was unable to hold a formal debate or vote on it,[642] nor was it ratified by the Executive Branch of the United States. Several congressmen and senators, however, have spoken in Congress in support of *Agenda 21*—these include Representative Nancy Pelosi, Senator John Kerry, and Senator Harry Reid.[643]

In the United States, over 528 cities are members of I.C.L.E.I., an international sustainability organization that helps to implement the *Agenda 21* and local *Agenda 21* concepts across the world. The United States has nearly half of the I.C.L.E.I.'s global membership of 1,200 cities promoting

---

[640] *Namibian President Calls for Implementation of Agenda 21.* Xinhua News Agency. September 2nd, 2002. Retrieved August 15th, 2012.
[641] http://en.wikipedia.org/wiki/Agenda_21
[642] http://en.wikipedia.org/wiki/Agenda_21
[643] http://www.youtube.com/watch?v=9MxMifltBVk

sustainable development at a local level. The United States also has one of the most comprehensively documented *Agenda 21* status reports.[644]

**Opposition In the United States**

During the last decade, opposition to *Agenda 21* has increased within the United States at the local, state, and federal levels. The Republican National Committee has adopted a resolution opposing *Agenda 21*, and the Republican Party platform[645] stated that, "We strongly reject the U.N. *Agenda 21* as erosive of American sovereignty."[646] Several state and local governments have considered or passed motions and legislation opposing *Agenda 21*.[647] Alabama became the first state to prohibit government participation in *Agenda 21*, but Arizona rejected a similar bill.[648]

Activists, some of whom have been associated with the Tea Party Movement by the *New York Times* and the *Huffington Post*, have said that *Agenda 21* is a conspiracy by the United Nations to deprive individuals of property rights. Columnists in the *Atlantic* have linked opposition to *Agenda 21* to the property rights movement in the United States.[649] A poll of 1,300 United States voters by the American Planning Association found that 9% supported *Agenda 21*, 6% opposed

---

[644] http://www.un.org/esa/agenda21/natlinfo/countr/usa/natur.htm

[645] *Fears of Agenda 21 Go Mainstream In the Republican Party Platform* by Peter Jamison (August 30th, 2012). *Tampa Bay Times*. Retrieved October 23rd, 2012.

[646] *Republican Platform 2012*. Republican Party (United States). Retrieved October 23rd, 2012.

[647] *Activists Fight Green Projects, Seeing U.N. Plot* by Leslie Kaufman & Kate Zernike (February 3rd, 2012). *New York Times*. Retrieved August 15th, 2012; *Tennessee House Joint Resolution 587*; *Kansas Resolution HR 6032*; *Colfax City Council Resolution 12-2012*; *New Hampshire House Bill 1634*; *Tea Party Activists Fight Agenda 21, Seeing Threatening U.N. Plot*. October 15th, 2012. Retrieved October 16th, 2012.

[648] *Alabama Adopts First Official State Ban On U.N. Agenda 21* by Alex Newman (June 4th, 2012). *The New American*. Retrieved August 15th, 2012.

[649] *The Anti-Environmentalist Roots of the Agenda 21 Conspiracy Theory* by Llewellyn Hinkes-Jones (August 29th, 2012). Retrieved October 16th, 2012.

it, and 85% thought they didn't have enough information to form an opinion.[650]

## *Agenda 21* Summary

*Agenda 21* is an ambitious, action plan, which is being implemented throughout the world on national as well as local levels.

> It is a plan to inventory and control all land, all water, all minerals, all plants, all animals, all construction, all means of production, all energy, all education, all information, and all human beings in the world.[651 & 652]

*Agenda 21* consists of 115 programs designed to facilitate the transition to "Sustainable Development." These individual programs can be broken down into broader categories such as agriculture, biodiversity and ecosystem management, education, energy and housing, population, public health, resources and recycling, transportation, sustainable economic development and more. Under these programs, the government would heavily control land usage, water and electrical consumption as well as transportation and public health—among other things. Their objective is to bring about change in the current systems of independent nations to help them govern. *Agenda 21* is a 40 chapter document listing goals to be achieved globally. It is the global plan to change:

> The way we "live, eat, learn and communicate" because we must "save the Earth."[653 & 654]

The agency created to spread *Agenda 21* policies throughout the world, as referenced a little earlier in this chapter, is the International Council on Local Environmental Initiatives—also known as the "I.C.L.E.I."

---

[650] http://en.wikipedia.org/wiki/Agenda_21
[651] http://www.democratsagainstunagenda21.com/
[652] http://en.wikipedia.org/wiki/Agenda_21
[653] http://www.canadafreepress.com/index.php/article/a-brief-history-amp-description-of-agenda-21
[654] https://archive.org/details/AGENDA_21

> The I.C.L.E.I. is the world's leading association of cities and local governments dedicated to sustainable development. I.C.L.E.I. is a powerful movement of twelve mega-cities, 100 super-cities and urban regions, 450 large cities as well as 450 small and medium-sized cities and towns in eighty-four countries.[655]

Therefore, it is very obvious that I.C.L.E.I. is the agency primarily responsible for having brought *Agenda 21* to many of our cities and counties throughout the world. According to their website, they promote:

> Local action for global sustainability and supports cities to become sustainable, resilient, resource-efficient, bio diverse, low-carbon; to build a smart infrastructure; and to develop an inclusive, green, urban economy.[656]

The numbers stated above include offices in every state of the U.S. However:

> *Agenda 21* has *no power* until a government body incorporates the recommendations into a law, rule, or ordinance. Then, and only then, does the recommendation have legal enforcement authority.[657]

> But, within the states where these offices are located, the implementation of the U.N. dictated policies of *Agenda 21* are taking place without congressional or voter approval through non-governmental organizations (N.G.O.'s). These N.G.O.'s have privately appointed representatives that get their authority through *Federal Executive Order and Agency Regulations*.[658]

---

[655] http://www.iclei.org/index.php?id=about
[656] http://www.iclei.org/index.php?id=about
[657] http://www.canadafreepress.com/index.php/arHYPERLINK "http://www.canadafreepress.com/index.php/article/45325"ticle/45325
[658] http://www.teaparty911.com/issues/what_is_agenda_21.htm

Taking these facts into consideration, *Agenda 21* priorities are still being written into laws, rules and ordinances through the influence of the N.G.O.'s, therefore making them legally binding in municipalities nationwide.

> One of the primary objectives of *Agenda 21*, and the P.C.S.D. (President's Council on Sustainable Development), is to transform the policy-making procedure into what is called 'collaborative consensus building.'[659]
>
> We need a new collaborative decision process that leads to better decisions; more rapid change; and more sensible use of human, natural, and financial resources in achieving our goals.[660 & 661]
>
> The function of the new process is to bypass elected officials and put policy-making into the hands of selected individuals who agree with the objectives of *Agenda 21* and the P.C.S.D. The consensus process is used exclusively throughout the United Nations, and is rapidly becoming the process by which public policy is made in the United States.[662 & 663]

Though only an action plan, *Agenda 21* does have four treaties associated with it that are or will be legally binding. They are:

> The *Draft International Covenant on Environment and Development*, the Framework Convention on Climate Change (U.N.F.C.C.C.), the Convention on Biological Diversity (C.B.D.) and the Convention to Combat Desertification (C.C.D.).[664]

---

[659] http://disc.yourwebapps.com/discussion.cgi?disc=153941;article=38954;
[660] http://clinton2.nara.gov/PCSD/Publications/TF_Reports/amer-believe.html, *We Believe Statement* #8, P.C.S.D.
[661] http://disc.yourwebapps.com/discussion.cgi?disc=153941;article=38954;
[662] http://sovereignty.net/p/sd/sdtut.htm
[663] http://disc.yourwebapps.com/discussion.cgi?disc=153941;article=38954;
[664] http://www.thegef.org/gef/sites/thegef.org/files/documents/document/419.pdf

These different treaties were presented and/or ratified at different times since the U.N. Convention on Environmental Development and the Earth Summit, which occurred in Rio de Janeiro in 1992.

The most all-encompassing treaty that is associated with *Agenda 21* is *the Draft International Covenant on Environment and Development*. This treaty is also known as *"Agenda 21 On Steroids"*[665] as it will be its legally binding equivalent. This treaty, which was originally drafted and presented in March 1995, is using *Agenda 21*'s action plan to build collaborative consensus in an effort to have it ratified and put into force as a legally binding treaty.

> The *Draft Covenant* is a blueprint for an international framework (or umbrella) agreement consolidating and developing existing legal principles related to environment and development. The intention is that it will remain a "living document" until as is the hope and expectation of those who have been involved in the project "it is adopted as a basis for multilateral negotiations."[666]

The *Framework Convention on Climate Change* came into existence March 21st, 1994[667] and its *Kyoto Protocol* was adopted on December 11th, 1997 and opened for signature from March 16th 1998 to March 15th of 1999.[668]

---

[665] http://ppjg.me/2012/03/14/agenda-21-on-steroids/
[666] http://www.uncsd2012.org/index.php?page=viewHYPERLINK "http://www.uncsd2012.org/index.php?page=view&type=400&nr=83&menu=45"&HYPERLINK "http://www.uncsd2012.org/index.php?page=view&type=400&nr=83&menu=45"type=400HYPERLINK "http://www.uncsd2012.org/index.php?page=view&type=400&nr=83&menu=45"&HYPERLINK "http://www.uncsd2012.org/index.php?page=view&type=400&nr=83&menu=45"nr=83HYPERLINK "http://www.uncsd2012.org/index.php?page=view&type=400&nr=83&menu=45"&HYPERLINK "http://www.uncsd2012.org/index.php?page=view&type=400&nr=83&menu=45"menu=45
[667] http://en.wikipedia.org/wiki/United_Nations_Framework_Convention_on_Climate_Change
[668] http://unfccc.int/kyoto_protocol/status_of_ratification/items/2613.php

> The ultimate objective of the *Convention* is to stabilize [atmospheric] concentrations of greenhouse gases "… at a level that would prevent dangerous anthropogenic (human induced) interference with the climate system."[669] [It states that] such a level should be achieved within a timeframe sufficient to allow ecosystems to adapt naturally to climate change, to ensure that food production is not threatened, and to enable economic development to proceed in a sustainable manner.[670 & 671]

The *Convention on Biological Diversity* came to be on December 29th, 1993.[672] Its *Cartagena Protocol on Biosafety* was put into effect on September 11th, 2003[673] as featured below:

> The *Convention on Biological Diversity* was inspired by the world community's growing commitment to sustainable development. It represents a dramatic step forward in the conservation of biological diversity, the sustainable use of its components, and the fair and equitable sharing of benefits arising from the use of genetic resources.[674]

The *Convention to Combat Desertification* was implemented on December 26th, 1996. Its ten-year strategy was adopted in 2007 and is as follows:

> Desertification, along with climate change and the loss of biodiversity, were identified as the greatest challenges to sustainable development during the 1992 Rio Earth Summit. Established in 1994, U.N.C.C.D. is the sole, legally binding international agreement linking environment and development to sustainable land management.[675]

---

[669] http://unfccc.int/cop3/fccc/climate/fact19.htm
[670] http://unfccc.int/essential_background/convention/items/6036.php
[671] http://unfccc.int/essential_background/convention/background/items/1353.php
[672] http://www.cbd.int/doc/vacancies/2013/consultants/cbd-2013-consult-SCBD_functional_review-en.pdf
[673] http://en.wikipedia.org/wiki/Cartagena_Protocol_on_Biosafety
[674] http://www.cbd.int/history/
[675] http://www.unccd.int/en/about-the-convention/Pages/About-the-Convention.

These four treaties are the ones, which constitute the teeth behind Agenda 21 policies, and the ones, which are being used on a national government level to make policy decisions, and laws, which promote "sustainable development" on a worldwide basis.

One of the most disturbing facets of *Agenda 21* policy is that it infringes upon the personal property rights of individuals. The official policy of the U.N. is for government to control the use of *all* land. It is also true that *"Chapter 7* of *Agenda 21* recommends ways for government to take complete control of land use."[676]

Moreover, U.N.'s official policy on land with regard to *Agenda 21* has this to say in the *Preamble*:

> Land ... cannot be treated as an ordinary asset, controlled by individuals and subject to the pressures and inefficiencies of the market. Private land ownership is also a principal instrument of accumulation and concentration of wealth, therefore contributes to social injustice. [677 & 678] Private land use decisions are often driven by strong economic incentives that result in several ecological and aesthetic consequences ... The key to overcoming it is through public policy ..."[679]
>
> Current lifestyles and consumption patterns of the affluent middle class—involving high meat intake, use of fossil fuels, appliances, home and work air conditioning, and suburban housing are not sustainable.[680]

This is also explained in greater detail in the following quote:

---

aspx
[676] http://www.canadafreepress.com/index.php/article/45325
[677] http://waketea.com/main/issues/agenda-21-sustainable-development/, *Agenda Item #10*, Vancouver WA, May 31st-June 11th, 1976
[678] http://americanpolicy.org/agenda21/, U.N.'s report on Human Settlements (Habitat I) Conference, 1976.
[679] http://americanpolicy.org/agenda21/, President Council's Report on Sustainable Development, p. 112
[680] http://americanpolicy.org/agenda21/, Maurice Strong, Secretary General of the U.N.'s Earth Summit, 1992

7.30. Subsequently, all countries should consider developing national land-resource management plans to guide land-resource development and utilization and, to that end, should:

> (a) Establish, as appropriate, national legislation to guide the implementation of public policies for environmentally sound urban development, land utilization, housing and for the improved management of urban expansion ... (c) Develop fiscal incentives and land-use control measures, including land-use planning solutions for a more rational and environmentally sound use of limited land resources.[681]

Because of these recommendations, there are documented cases that show how:

> *Agenda 21*, where it has been adopted into local ordinances, is removing people from their land *without compensation* and is destroying private property rights.[682]

It is also interfering with the right of farmers to irrigate their land. These are just but two detrimental ways in which *Agenda 21* has *already* impacted local government land usage policy.

One of the most significant court cases involving land use is *Tokerud v. the city of Santa Rosa* where concerned citizens and businesses fought against the Santa Rosa city council for having approved a thirty-acre redevelopment project known as the Gateways Redevelopment Project. This project authorized the use of Eminent Domain over a period of twelve years. Eminent Domain is:

---

[681] http://www.canadafreepress.HYPERLINK "http://www.canadafreepress.com/index.php/article/45325"com/index.php/article/45325, Sovereignty International Chairman & Environmental Conservation Organization's (E.C.O.) Executive Vice President, Henry Lamb

[682] http://www.canadafreepress.HYPERLINK "http://www.canadafreepress.com/index.php/article/45325"com/index.php/article/45325, Sovereignty International Chairman & Environmental Conservation Organization's (E.C.O.) Executive Vice President, Henry Lamb

> "... the power to take private property for public use by a state, municipality, or private person or corporation authorized to exercise functions of public character, following the payment of just compensation to the owner of that property."[683]

This policy of Eminent Domain severely transgresses personal property rights as it forces people to give up their property for little or no financial compensation.[684]

> As rights were restricted by such regulations, an even greater threat to private property was mounted by a shadow government—a government which operated under the radar of legislative or judicial oversight, a government administered by appointed agencies created by statute and empowered to control and take private property for the 'public good.' Some of the earliest of these appointed agencies were created to implement and oversee federally funded Urban Renewal Projects. Their tragic impact on poor homeowners went largely unnoticed, precisely because the impact was mainly on the poor residents and small business owners located in the inner cities, which had been deserted by middle and upper class residents.[685 & 686]

Eminent Domain is a vehicle that is utilized by many municipalities in an effort to promote their plans to redesign the areas where people live and conduct business to conform to U.N. ideals as specified in their

---

[683] http://legal-dictionary.thefreedictionary.com/eminent+domain

[684] "...The property of subjects is under the eminent domain of the state, so that the state or he who acts for it may use and even alienate and destroy such property, not only in the case of extreme necessity, in which even private persons have a right over the property of others, but for ends of public utility, to which ends those who founded civil society must be supposed to have intended that private ends should give way. But it is to be added that when this is done the state is bound to make good the loss to those who lose their property."

[685] http://www.santarosaneighborhoodcoalition.com/rosa-koire--kay-tokerud.html

[686] http://americanstewards.us/36-march-2007/129-kelo-the-great-fighting-eminent-domain-in-santa-rosa-california

*Agenda 21* action plan. The U.S. Supreme Court legalized these abuses with the decision that they handed down in *Kelo v. city of New London*.

> The U.S. Supreme Court struck a blow against homeowners and small businesses on June 23rd, 2005, when it ruled in *Kelo v. City of New London* that Eminent Domain could be used for economic development purposes. By implication, the Court ruled that government could take land from one private owner and sell or give it to another if government officials believed that the new owner would use the land in a more productive manner to create jobs and increase tax revenues. By ruling in favor of the city, the Supreme Court greatly expanded the permissible uses of Eminent Domain beyond the traditional purpose of taking private property only for broadly used public facilities such as roads, schools, and fire stations. In the process, the Court has substantially weakened individual property rights.[687]

It was this case which more than set the precedent for others to seize privately owned property to further the goals of *Agenda 21*.

Another court case of interest is *Sackett v. the E.P.A.* where the E.P.A. declared land that the Sacketts had purchased to build a home as falling under the category and jurisdiction of being considered "Wetlands," technically speaking.

> [The] E.P.A. issued a "compliance" order, demanding that the Sacketts stop construction, remove the gravel and return the land to E.P.A.'s liking. **Moving the gravel would cost $27,000**—more than what the Sacketts paid for the land.[688]

The U.S. Supreme Court heard this case and here is the end result:

> On March 21st, with a 9-0 vote, the United State Supreme Court ruled that landowners have a right to direct, meaningful

---

[687] http://www.heritage.org/research/reports/2007/02/states-vote-to-strengthen-property-rights

[688] http://www.pacificlegal.org/Sackett

judicial review if the U.S. Environmental Protection Agency effectively seizes control of their property by declaring it to be "Wetlands."[689]

Another water usage case, which was heard in Washington State Supreme Court, was *Kittitas County v. Eastern Washington Growth Management Hearings Board*.[690] The following is a summary of that case:

> A recent Washington Supreme [Court] opinion will make it more difficult for rural housing developers to secure water rights for their projects. In *Kittitas County v. Eastern Washington Growth Management Hearings Board*, the court held that Kittitas County violated Washington's Growth Management Act (G.M.A.) by failing to protect water resources when it passed a revised comprehensive plan and growth code ... that allowed developers to develop rural land without disclosing common ownership of side-by-side subdivisions. The court affirmed a decision by the Eastern Washington Growth Management Hearings Board that connected the G.M.A.'s mandates to protect water with the Court's 2002 decision in *Department of Ecology v. Campbell & Gwinn, L.L.C.*, which held that "... the total group groundwater use in a residential development must be considered, rather than the separate use of each residential lot, for purposes of determining if use is in excess of Washington's 5,000 gallons per day ... permit exemption."
>
> As a general rule, under Washington's Ground Water Code, anyone who wishes to use underground water ("groundwater") in Washington must receive a permit from the Department of Ecology. Since the end of World War II, groundwater wells using less than 5,000 gallons of water per day for domestic use have been exempt from Washington's permit requirement. As a result of rapid growth and recent

---

[689] http://www.pacificlegal.org/Sackett
[690] http://templeofjustice.org/cases/2010/kittitas-county-central-wash-homebuilders-assoc-v-eastern-wash-growth-mgmt/

droughts, permit-exempt wells have created increasing conflict among water users and Ecology has received requests to limit or prohibit exempt wells, particularly in dry Eastern Washington. Kittitas County, situated in Central Washington's Yakima River Basin, is the area of the state with the most contentious groundwater exempt well issues because the Basin is one of the state's most water-short areas.[691]

The United States District Court for the Eastern District of California also conducted a hearing on another interesting case that placed the interests of a small fish over the sanctity of human life. The Delta Smelt is a small, inedible fish that does not have any commercial value nor benefit to the environment other than providing a food source for larger fish.

> However, using the weapon of the Endangered Species Act, environmentalist groups sued, and on December 14th, 2007, Judge Oliver Wanger of the United States District Court for the Eastern District of California issued an Interim Remedial Order. The Order remanded the U.S. Fish and Wildlife Service in conjunction with the United States Department of the Interior, to issue an opinion or permit that dramatically reduced the delivery of water from the Delta. The result has been the diversion of tens of billions of gallons of fresh water away from vital agriculture and population needs and directly into the Pacific Ocean. A precious resource essentially wasted.[692]
>
> The impact on farmers in the area has been devastating with the San Joaquin Valley unemployment rate reaching 14% and leaving thousands of previously productive farming acres scorched and unusable. In addition, water utilities in Southern California have already begun raising rates

---

[691] http://www.martenlaw.com/newsletter/20111013-wash-water-rights-restricted, Marten Law *Environmental News*, November 4th, 2009.

[692] http://www.examiner.com/article/the-delta-smelt-a-fish-more-important-than-people

and creating tiered pricing to address the 85% increase in imported water. To make matters worse, California is already under drought conditions, and in combination with the Delta pumping restrictions, local politicians are calling for Draconian reductions in water use by individuals of 40%.[693]

Many more cases like the ones discussed here exist and have the same impact of limiting our land and water usage. They have become so pervasive that many states have either outlawed or are trying to outlaw *Agenda 21* and its U.N.-sanctioned policies.

> Alabama became the first state to adopt a tough law protecting private property and due process by prohibiting any government involvement with or participation in a controversial United Nations' scheme known as *Agenda 21*. Activists from across the political spectrum celebrated the measure's approval as a significant victory against the U.N. "sustainability" plot, expressing hope that similar sovereignty-preserving measures would be adopted in other states as the nationwide battle heats up.[694]
>
> In late March, the Arizona State Senate approved anti-*Agenda 21 Bill SB 1507*, but the measure died on May 3rd, after House lawmakers failed to bring the legislation to a vote before the legislative session concluded that night.[695]
>
> In total, five states have tried and failed to pass such rules back in the year 2012, with Arizona's battle being the most well known. Efforts in Alabama, Kansas and Louisiana are still in the works.[696]

---

[693] http://www.examiner.com/article/the-delta-smelt-a-fish-more-important-than-people

[694] http://www.thenewamerican.com/tech/environment/item/11592-alabama-adopts-first-official-state-ban-on-un-agenda-21

[695] http://insideclimatenews.org/news/20120511/bill-ban-united-nations-agenda-21-sustainability-climate-change-global-warming-iclei-john-birch-society-kansas

[696] http://insideclimatenews.org/news/20120511/bill-ban-united-nations-agenda-21-sustainability-climate-change-global-warming-iclei-john-birch-society-

Tennessee passed a resolution condemning—though not abolishing—the principles [back] in May of 2012.[697 & 698]

Even more recently, other states have joined in on the action trying to ban *Agenda 21*:

> Two Republican members of the Virginia House of Delegates have introduced legislation opposing the United Nations' *Agenda 21*, the international organization's non-binding sustainability program.[699]

> State Delegate L. Scott Lingamfelter (R-Woodbridge) has put forward a resolution calling on the State Legislature to oppose the U.N. program, while State Delegate Danny Marshall (R-Danville) has filed a bill banning the implementation of *Agenda 21* in Virginia.[700]

> The battle over *Agenda 21*, the United Nation's sustainable agenda, moves back to New Hampshire as a Republican state lawmaker has signaled her intent to ban the program from the state. State Representative Lenette Peterson (R-Merrimack) has filed legislation to ban implementation of *Agenda 21* in the state, along with prohibiting local governments from receiving funding from the International Council for Local Environmental Initiatives, an international group seeking to promote *Agenda 21*. Peterson's legislation is similar to a state bill to ban *Agenda 21* that passed the State House earlier this year before failing in the Senate.[701 & 702]

---

kansas
[697] http://insideclimatenews.org/news/20120511/bill-ban-united-nations-agenda-21-sustainability-climate-change-global-warming-iclei-john-birch-society-kansas
[698] http://www.motherjones.com/mojo/2012/05/arizona-still-vulnerable-sustainabilty
[699] http://www.huffingtonpost.com/2013/01/17/virginia-agenda-21_n_2497163.html
[700] http://www.huffingtonpost.com/2013/01/17/virginia-agenda-21_n_2497163.html
[701] http://www.huffingtonpost.com/2012/11/27/agenda-21-new-hampshire_n_2198466.html
[702] http://www.infiniteunknown.net/2012/11/29/new-hampshire-lawmaker-

> A Republican state senator in Oklahoma has introduced legislation seeking to block the implementation of United Nations *Agenda 21*, the international organization's "non-binding" sustainability program. State Senator Patrick Anderson (R-Enid) is introducing legislation for next year that would block local Oklahoma governments from entering into agreements with the International Council for Local Environmental Initiatives, a European sustainability group.[703]

These court cases were *instrumental* in bringing the abuses of governmental power used to promote *Agenda 21* ideals to the forefront and, as a result, raising public awareness. They were the ones, which helped to spread the word about *Agenda 21* to American citizens resulting in current efforts by other concerned citizens and small business owners to fight against these practices. But, it is proving to still be an uphill battle, as you will soon see.

"Smart Growth" has now become a popular buzzword that we hear a lot about in the media. It is a term that has been developed by the U.N. to hide their *Agenda 21* plans. They chose this term because:

> "... participating in a U.N.-advocated planning process would, very likely, bring out many of the conspiracy-fixated groups and individuals in our society such as the National Rifle Association, citizen militias and some members of Congress. This segment of our society who fear 'one-world government' and a U.N. invasion of the United States, through which our individual freedoms would be stripped away, would actively work to defeat any elected official who joined 'the conspiracy' by undertaking *L.A.21*. So, we call our process something else, such as comprehensive planning, growth management, or **Smart Growth** [emphasis added]."[704]

---

battles-agenda-21/
[703] http://www.huffingtonpost.com/2012/12/27/oklahoma-agenda-21_n_2370123.html
[704] http://www.americanthinker.com/2009/10/un_agenda_21_coming_to_a_neigh.html

So, just what *is* "Smart Growth," exactly?

> [It] is an urban planning and transportation theory that concentrates growth in compact, walkable, urban centers to avoid sprawl. It also advocates compact, transit-oriented, walkable, bicycle-friendly, land use—including neighborhood schools, complete streets and mixed-use development with a range of housing choices.[705]

> The goal of Smart Growth is to avoid no growth or even slow growth. Rather, the overall goal is sensible growth that balances our need for jobs and economic development with our desire to save our natural environment.[706]

Many of the new ordinances and rezoning that is occurring within our towns, cities and rural areas are taking place as they adopt this *Agenda 21* strategy for concentrating the population into urban areas and making every effort to protect rural areas in an effort to preserve the environment. However:

> A new study from the Center for Immigration Studies indicates that this approach will have only limited success in saving rural land because it fails to address a key reason for sprawl—immigration-driven population growth. Based on data from the Census Bureau and from the U.S. Department of Agriculture's Natural Resources Conservation Service, the study finds that about half the loss of rural land in recent decades is attributable to increases in the U.S. population, while changes in land use account for the other half.[707]

So, if it is a *known fact* that this Smart Growth program does not actually achieve its stated goals, why is it *still being used* as a major blueprint for future development?

---

[705] http://en.wikipedia.org/wiki/Smart_gHYPERLINK "http://en.wikipedia.org/wiki/Smart_growth"rowth
[706] http://www.epa.gov/dced/pdf/whtissg4v2.pdf
[707] http://www.cis.org/node/492

> The claim of the urban Eco-city Model is that they can regulate climate change, food distribution, nutrient balance, and water securitization that provide the general masses with provisions, culture and support in ways that are not facilitated by the current living conditions... Control over life in the Eco-city will include:
>
> - Forced reduction of public water use.
> - Controlled use of energy, water & waste.
> - Regulated community food production spaces.
> - Mandated, green, high-end technology buildings.
> - Reduction of urban city temperature by 3-4 degrees.
> - Mandated reduction of travel time with intelligent transit systems.
>
> [These] Eco-cities are the global elite's answer to dense and controlled urban landscapes where human life is severely restricted.[708]

Therefore, the true goal of this Smart Growth/Eco-city movement is much more sinister and subversive than it appears on the surface.

But why do the global elite and the U.N. want to control population centers and severely restrict human life? It is because of the *perceived threat* of carbon emissions. According to Dick Morris:

> Already, thousands of localities around America have adopted *Agenda 21* as the framework for their zoning and land use decisions. In the name of carbon emission reductions, to avert the theoretical danger of climate change, we are being told to live differently, work differently, and play differently.[709]

The term "carbon footprint" has become popular in the green movement and is one of the primary driving factors of *Agenda 21*'s policy. According to TimeForChange.org:

---

[708] http://www.activistpost.com/2012/07/agenda-21-eco-cities-built-for.html
[709] http://www.dickmorris.com/agenda-21-obamasHYPERLINK "http://www.dickmorris.com/agenda-21-obamas-plans-for-america/"-plans-for-america/

> The carbon footprint is a very powerful tool to understand the impact of personal behavior on global warming. Most people are shocked when they see the amount of CO2 their activities create! If you personally want to contribute to stop global warming, the calculation and constant monitoring of your personal carbon footprint is essential.[710]

Therefore, it should come as no surprise that there are several calculators available on the Internet to determine the carbon footprint of individuals and gauge their impact on the environment. This new Eco-centric type of thinking ultimately puts the blame for climate change onto human beings and makes it every individual's responsibility to change their behavior. This is the driving philosophy behind *Agenda 21* and why they want to control *every* facet of human life and human behavior.

This begs the question as to whether or not the growth of the world population is addressed by *Agenda 21*. According to a determination of *Chapter 5* of *Agenda 21,* the International Institute for Sustainable Development (I.I.S.D.) had this to say:

> Human beings, demographic dimensions, quality of life, and other terms are vaguely defined in the *Chapter* and give rise to contradictory interpretations depending on social, political or religious contexts. In fact, religious constraints, inhibitions or dictates about population issues, family planning and contraception are barely alluded to, despite their pervasive influence on populations generally and policy-makers specifically.[711]

> While this *Chapter* recommends increased research into various aspects of demographic dynamics, it may be argued that research should also be directed at ways to reduce the growth rate of the planet's population. Indeed, terms such as 'family planning' and 'contraception' do not appear at all in *Agenda 21*. Despite this weakness, the activities suggested in

---
[710] http://timeforchange.org/what-is-a-carbon-footprint-definition
[711] http://www.iisd.org/worldsd/canada/projet/c05.htm

this chapter are nonetheless necessary to develop appropriate policies which encourage sustainable development. As such, the merit of these activities should not be diminished. What is missing, however, is some resolution on the importance of controlling growth in global population. If global population is indeed a 'crisis' as many believe it to be, then it should have been treated as such in *Agenda 21*.[712]

Therefore, population control is not a stated component of *Agenda 21*'s action plan. However, it was also stated in the I.I.S.D. determination that:

"...semantics were important: 'population control' was condemned, whereas reproductive, maternal and child health care strategies—including family planning information and services—were called for, within the wider framework of development, human rights and empowerment of women and communities."[713]

So, we must conclude that even though population control isn't specifically addressed, it still may be a part of the overall agenda and it is *indeed* a goal of the I.I.S.D.

Sustainable Development is *definitely* a part of *Agenda 21* policy.

Sustainable Development philosophy teaches that mankind is living beyond the 'carrying capacity' of the Earth and that we are in the midst of multiple crises that are converging to create conditions that are not livable unless they are halted by a rapid global transition to a sustainable development system. Some of these perceived crises include overpopulation, global poverty and wealth inequality, manmade global climate change, and rampant environmental destruction... The Sustainable Development philosophy

---

[712] http://www.iisd.org/worldsd/canada/projet/c05.htm
[713] http://www.iisd.org/worldsd/canada/projet/c05.htm

perceives the automobile and the ongoing use of fossil fuels as unsustainable.[714]

Therefore, if Sustainable Development and *Agenda 21* see human behavior as the culprit behind global warming and have implemented their policies in an effort to change it, how are they going to get human populations on board with their ideas? Their modus operandi is to subtly change how we think about the environment and therefore behave toward it. Their goal is to gradually create a shift in our own personal philosophies to a more Eco-centric view that is more in line with their agenda. This Eco-centric philosophy with which they are slowly indoctrinating us with has its origins in the *Gaia Theory*. I have taken you down a long journey in this chapter explaining to you this *covenant made with many* to bring you to this point, so you can understand why this covenant is so evil.

> Over about the last 400 years, thanks largely to scientific enquiry and technological innovation, we have, as a species, become alienated from the rest of the natural world. We think we can do whatever we like and find a techno fix if things go wrong, and so we have developed the habit of subconsciously looking at what we call 'progress' from a purely human-centered viewpoint. Climate change is the wake-up call. The big danger is that if we try to tackle the social and cultural implications of climate change with the ways of thinking that caused the problems in the first place, behaving as though we are somehow separate from and superior to nature, then we will only make things worse—'business as usual' thrives on the 'green herring effect' of such initiatives as carbon trading and light-bulb changing, and thus deepens the crisis. What we need, along with changing our light-bulbs, is a different way of thinking about ourselves and where we fit into the planetary system, a way of thinking that is based on what is really going on in the natural world—we need a Gaian-centered viewpoint.[715]

---

[714] http://northtexasagainstunagenda21.wordpress.com/
[715] http://esd.escalate.ac.uk/downloads/2015.doc

So, just what *is* the *Gaia Theory*, exactly?

> The *Gaia Theory* posits that the organic and inorganic components of Planet Earth have evolved together as a single living, self-regulating system. It suggests that this living system has automatically controlled global temperature, atmospheric content, ocean salinity, and other factors, that maintain its own habitability. In a phrase, "life maintains conditions suitable for its own survival." In this respect, the living system of Earth can be thought of [as] analogous to the workings of any individual organism that regulates body temperature, blood salinity, etc.[716, 717 & 718] So, for instance, even though the luminosity of the Sun—the Earth's heat source—has increased by about 30% since life began almost four billion years ago, the living system has reacted as a whole to maintain temperatures at levels suitable for life... The *Gaia Theory* was developed in the late 1960's by Dr. James Lovelock, a British scientist and inventor.[719 & 720]

*Gaia Theory* is goddess worship repackaged in an Eco-centric wrapping.

> Anyone who has studied the global green movement has no doubt heard of "Gaia." Believers in Gaia, or "Gaians" as they often refer to themselves, claim that the Earth is a sentient super-being, an ancient goddess spirit, deserving of worship and reverence. Sir James Lovelock, in his book, *Gaia: A New Look At Life*, states that:
>
>> "... all of the life forms on this planet are a part of Gaia—part of one spirit goddess that sustains life on Earth. Since this transformation into a living

---

[716] http://climatesanity.wordpress.com/2013/01/26/james-lovelock-says-nuclear-better-than-wind/
[717] http://www.shepherdsofgaia.com/p/shepherds-of-gaia.html
[718] http://www.gaiatheory.org/overview/
[719] http://www.gaiatheory.org/synopsis.htm
[720] http://www.shepherdsofgaia.com/p/shepherds-of-gaia.html

> system, the interventions of Gaia have brought about the evolving diversity of living creatures on planet Earth."

> Gaians teach that the "Earth Goddess," or "Mother Earth," must be protected from destructive human activity. It is this belief that fuels the environmental movement, sustainable development, and a global push for the return of industrialized nations to a more primitive way of life.[721]

It is a most ridiculous and absurd philosophy that Lovelock espouses; yet here is some more of James Lovelock's rhetoric in case you are not yet fully convinced:

> Still more important is the implication that the evolution of humans, with his technological inventiveness and his increasingly subtle communications network, has vastly increased Gaia's range of perception. She is now, through us, awake and aware of herself. She has seen the reflection of her fair face through the eyes of astronauts and the television cameras of orbiting spacecraft. Our sensations of wonder and pleasure, our capacity for conscious thought and speculation, our restless curiosity and drive are hers to share.[722 & 723]

> This new interrelationship of Gaia with man is by no means fully established; we are not yet a truly collective species, corralled and tamed as an integral part of the biosphere, as we are as individual creatures. It may be that the destiny of mankind is to become tamed, so that the fierce, destructive, and greedy forces of tribalism and nationalism are fused into a compulsive urge to belong to the commonwealth of all creatures which constitute Gaia.[724]

---

[721] http://www.green-agenda.com/gaia.html
[722] http://tinyurl.com/ol2dw6z
[723] *Gaia: A New Look At Life* by James Lovelock, 1972
[724] *Gaia: A New Look At Life* by James Lovelock, 1972

Here is yet some more philosophical rhetoric coming out of the Gaia Movement:

> All life is born of Gaia and each life has a spirit. Each new spirit is housed in a physical body. Through their experiences on Earth, each spirit matures and grows. When the physical body dies, the mature spirit enriched by its life on Earth returns to Gaia, bringing with it the experiences, enabling Gaia to live and grow.[725]
>
> The religion of Gaia is not a faith so much as a philosophy. There are no gods, no rites, no Bible. A theory for life itself, almost everyone, short of the Jenovians, subscribes to this without question.
>
> The most basic explanation is that Gaia, the planet itself, is alive. Other than being the rock in which things live and grow and die upon, the planet itself streams with energy. This is called the Lifestream. It flows in (and) throughout the entire planet and all that is alive. The Lifestream is the essence of the Planet and the memories, emotions, and knowledge of all who have lived on it. It is from the Lifestream that all life is created from. When a living being dies, it does not extinguish, but instead joins Gaia again. From it, the Lifestream is enriched from the thoughts, experiences, memories, and dreams of those that lived. This allows the planet to stay alive in a continuing and never-ending cycle.[726]

Though all this rhetoric may sound ridiculous, it is something we must take very *seriously* as it is a philosophy that has been adopted by the U.N. and many of our national and international leaders. In fact, Gaia was the main focus, believe it or not, at the opening of the last Earth Summit, Rio + 10:

> The official opening ceremony was conducted by the Dalai Lama and centered around a Viking long-ship that was

---

[725] http://www.natama-nataraja.com/blog/
[726] http://www.wasdarwinwrong.com/korthof69.htm

constructed to celebrate the Summit and sailed to Rio from Norway. The ship was appropriately named Gaia.[727] A huge mural of a beautiful woman holding the Earth within her hands adorned the entrance to the Summit. Al Gore led the U.S. delegation where he was joined by 110 Heads of State, and Representatives of more than 800 N.G.O.'s.[728]

Maurice Strong, Club of Rome member, devout Baha'i, founder and first Secretary General of U.N.E.P., has been the driving force behind the birth and imposition of *Agenda 21*. While he chaired the Earth Summit, outside, his wife Hanne, and 300 followers called the Wisdom-Keepers, continuously beat drums, chanted prayers to Gaia, and tended sacred flames in order to *"establish and hold the energy field"* for the duration of the Summit. You can view actual footage[729] of these ceremonies on YouTube.[730]

This Eco-centric philosophy has spread and is being embraced by other religions and religious leaders worldwide. As stated above, this is all being done to change our personal belief systems and make them more favorable to the restrictive environmental policies that *Agenda 21* is forcing upon us.

One earth-centric religion that has latched onto Gaia is Baha'i, which interestingly and alarmingly enough, is an outgrowth of Islam.

As many of you are aware there is an ongoing onslaught against traditional Judeo-Christian religions and values, while simultaneously seemingly embracing Islamic values. In fact, all of our usual "players" (Al Gore, Maurice Strong, Mikhail Gorbachev, et. al) claim to be devout disciples of the Baha'i faith.[731]

---

[727] http://www.youtube.com/watch?v=yvPcRkohiBM&feature=player_embedded#!
[728] http://www.green-agenda.com/agenda21.html
[729] http://www.youtube.com/watch?v=YrmQU24068I
[730] http://www.green-agenda.com/agenda21.html
[731] http://www.canadafreepress.com/index.php/article/25233, *Transformation Of the Soul*

Baha'i literature proclaims the following:

> National rivalries, hatreds, and intrigues will cease, and racial animosity and prejudice will be replaced by racial amity, understanding and cooperation. The causes of religious strife will be permanently removed, economic barriers and restrictions will be completely abolished, and the inordinate distinction between classes will be obliterated. Destitution on the one hand, and gross accumulation of ownership on the other, will disappear.[732]

Baha'i grew out of Islam, and is, in fact, a stepchild of the Islamic faith, albeit a despised one. Rather than naming Muhammad as the greatest of the prophets as the Muslims do, Baha'i adherents hold Baha'u'llah to be the greatest of the prophets while extolling the virtues of Gaia, Mother Earth.[733]

The Baha'i faith has become a popular religion in an environment of ecumenism, inclusiveness and political correctness. Embraced eagerly by the United Nations and other interfaith organizations, Baha'i is a growing humanist influence on our world.[734]

If you believe these Eco-centric, Earth-based religious precepts do not affect mainstream Christian values, you would be mistaken. The paradigm shift is nearly complete—to the extent that the New Age has, to a highly significant extent, infiltrated evangelical, protestant, mainline Christianity. Rick Warren, dubbed "America's favorite pastor," is a primary example of this. Just check out his Global P.E.A.C.E. Plan[735], which speaks for itself. But also, a handful of Berean, whistle-blowing, Apologetics authors like the late Dave Hunt, Ray Yungen,

---

[732] http://www.canadafreepress.com/index.php/article/25233, *Transformation Of the Soul*

[733] http://www.canadafreepress.com/index.php/article/25233, *Transformation Of the Soul*

[734] http://www.canadafreepress.com/index.php/article/25233, *Transformation Of the Soul*

[735] http://www.lighthousetrailsresearch.com/peaceplan.htm

Warren Smith, etc., have attested to this fact as well. The late Francis Schaeffer also predicted that the Christian church was already going in the wrong direction back in the 60's! Even the former Pope himself has gotten on board and has made statements that are in total accordance with these Gaia-based beliefs:

> I would say that the emergence of the ecological movement in German politics since the 1970's, while it has not exactly flung open the windows, nevertheless was and continues to be a cry for fresh air which must not be ignored or pushed aside, just because too much of it is seen to be irrational. Young people had come to realize that something is wrong in our relationship with nature, that matter is not just raw material for us to shape at will, but that the Earth has a dignity of its own and that we must follow its directives. In saying this, I am clearly not promoting any particular political party—nothing could be further from my mind. If something is wrong in our relationship with reality, then we must all reflect seriously on the whole situation and we are all prompted to question the very foundations of our culture. *Allow me to dwell a little longer on this point. The importance of ecology is no longer disputed. We must listen to the language of nature and we must answer accordingly.*[736] [Emphasis mine]

> My dear friends, God's creation is one and it is good. The concerns for non-violence, sustainable development, justice and peace, and care for our environment are of vital importance for humanity.[737]

Not only has Pope Benedict XVI made these statements, he is also known for promoting sustainable development and integrating it into the Catholic worldview.

---

[736] http://catholicclimatecovenant.org/catholic-teachings/vatican-messages/
[737] http://catholicclimatecovenant.org/catholic-teachings/vatican-messages/, Pope Benedict XVI, World Youth Day, June 2008

> Rumor has it that Pope Benedict may address climate change during his visit to the United Nations this week. Whether he does or not, his young papacy can claim to be the "greenest" ever. Benedict has identified extensive common ground between sustainability concerns and a Catholic worldview—adding weight to the argument that the world's religions could be instrumental in nudging policymakers and the public to embrace sustainability. Now, the Pope has the opportunity to further develop the links between sustainability and religious values, markedly advancing thinking in both arenas. Benedict's predecessor, John Paul II, made important environmental statements during his long papacy, but Benedict is the first "green pope."[738]

Therefore, it is very evident that *Agenda 21*'s sustainable development and environmental policies are not only being embodied in new Eco-centric religions, but in Islam as well as Christianity. As stated earlier, this is all being done in an effort to change our personal philosophies (or worldviews) and religious (or spiritual) beliefs to make us all the more receptive to the U.N.'s plan. This is how they are achieving collaborative consensus building on a grand scale.

I am sure you can clearly see by now, from this chapter alone even, just how incredibly BIG and how truly *massive* a movement this U.N. *Agenda 21* truly is—also known as the *Kyoto Accord* or *Kyoto Protocol*. The U.S.A., being the only one not to sign on to it yet (as a nation), and Canada, having signed on to it only to later withdraw from it; and yet, far too many of the *individual* states, provinces, cities and municipalities have already signed on to *Agenda 21*.

It is not the *protection of the environment* that is the evil unfolding here. It is the *worship of the Earth* or Mother Earth. This can be seen in most major government ceremonies where you have native indigenous peoples doing the opening prayers and dances to nature or Mother Nature.

---

[738] http://www.worldwatch.org/node/5707

Speaking of which, I have already explained who Gaia is as the god of nature and Mother Earth. Notice what else James Lovelock writes concerning the Earth:

> We have inherited a planet of exquisite beauty. It is the gift of four billion years of evolution. We need to regain our ancient feeling for Earth as an organism and revere it again. Gaia has been the guardian of life for all of its existence; we reject her care at our peril. We can use technology to buy us time while we reform, but we remain accountable for the damage we do.[739]

He is saying we must *revere* the Earth. I pointed this point out to your earlier in this chapter. To "revere" is synonymous with the "worship" of the Earth. It is worshiping the creation and not the Creator! And Lovelock repeatedly and consistently subscribes to the notion that the Earth *is* Gaia in each and every one of his books. These books also take on a great deal of significance due to his high ranking status in the scientific world.

## Further Information: *Gaia Hypothesis*

> First formulated by Lovelock during the 1960's as a result of work for N.A.S.A. concerned with detecting life on Mars, the *Gaia Hypothesis* proposes that living and non-living parts of the Earth form a complex interacting system that can be thought of as a single organism. Named after the Greek goddess Gaia at the suggestion of novelist William Golding, the *Hypothesis* postulates that the biosphere has a regulatory effect on the Earth's environment that acts to sustain life. While the *Gaia Hypothesis* was readily accepted by many in the environmentalist community, it has not been widely accepted within the scientific community ... In Lovelock's 2006 book, *The Revenge of Gaia*, he argues that the lack of respect humans have had for Gaia, through the damage done to rainforests and the reduction in planetary biodiversity, is

---

[739] http://www.gaia-movement.org/TextPage.asp?SubMenuItemID=106&MenuItemID=47

> testing Gaia's capacity to minimize the effects of the addition of greenhouse gases in the atmosphere.[740]
>
> In his most recent book, *The Vanishing Face of Gaia*, he rejects scientific modeling that disagrees with the scientific findings that sea levels are rising faster, and Arctic ice is melting faster than the models predict and he suggests that we may already be beyond the tipping point of terrestrial climate into a permanently hot state. Given these conditions, Lovelock expects human civilization will be hard-pressed to survive.[741]

James Lovelock's influence has not gone unnoticed—to the contrary! The Apollo-Gaia Project coordinated by David Wasdell as part of the Meridian Programme[742] & [743] also has brought those things Lovelock writes of to the attention of the G8 Summit, the Club of Rome[744] and the U.N.

> Drawing on three decades of consultancy-research focused on the psychodynamics of social systems facing rapid change in conditions of low resources and high stress, I began to explore how best to consult to the process. A three-part paper titled *Global Warning* was prepared in order to begin to raise awareness of this agenda of social psychology.[745]
>
> *Global Warning* was produced as a background resource document for the G8 Summit at Gleneagles under the Presidency of U.K. Prime Minister, Tony Blair. Climate change was high on the agenda. It was published as an Internet cascade by the Meridian Programme at the beginning of June 2005 and launched on the eve of the United Nations World

---

[740] http://en.wikipedia.org/wiki/James_Lovelock
[741] http://en.wikipedia.org/wiki/James_Lovelock
[742] http://tinyurl.com/nd75usa, *Antichrist & the Green Prince* by John D. Christian, p. 70
[743] http://www.apollo-gaia.org/ClubofRome.html
[744] http://www.apollo-gaia.org/ClubofRome.html,
[745] http://www.apollo-gaia.org/A-GProjectDevelopment.pdf, *The Apollo Gaia Project: Global Warming & It's Aftermath*, p. 3

Environment Day during a Symposium on Climate Change held in University College London.[746]

As the G8 Summit at Gleneagles came to an end, I was putting the finishing touches to the first draft of the conceptual analysis of the feedback dynamic system.[747]

At this point, I received an unexpected e-mail from Prince El Hassan bin Talal, President of the Club of Rome, to say that he was interested in what I was doing and wanted to support the work of the Meridian Programme. All members of the Club of Rome had received e-copy of *Global Warning* and it was to this that the Prince was responding. I talked over our present work with his executive assistant, and agreed to airmail half a dozen copies of the initial draft of *The Feedback Crisis In Climate Change* to the Palace in Amman. Two months later, I received an invitation to attend (as the President's guest) the next Annual Conference of the Club of Rome to be held in Norfolk, Virginia, at the beginning of October.[748]

The concluding comments spelled out the agenda for an action-research programme at a global level. It is that initiative which led to the proposal for the Feedback Dynamics Research Project[749 & 750] which then merged with John Schellnhüber's call for a Manhattan Project of Climate Science, and has now evolved into the Apollo-Gaia Project.[751]

---

[746] http://www.apollo-gaia.org/A-GProjectDevelopment.pdf, *The Apollo Gaia Project: Global Warming & It's Aftermath*, p. 3

[747] http://www.apollo-gaia.org/A-GProjectDevelopment.pdf, *The Apollo Gaia Project: The Feedback Crisis in Climate Change*, p. 6

[748] http://www.apollo-gaia.org/A-GProjectDevelopment.pdf, *The Apollo Gaia Project: The Feedback Crisis in Climate Change*, p. 6

[749] http://www.docstoc.com/docs/96814166/Feedback-Dynamics-and-the-Acceleration-of-Climate-Change

[750] http://www.apollo-gaia.org/A-GProjectDevelopment.pdf, *The Apollo Gaia Project: Convergent Ideas in Parallel Worlds,* pp. 19-20

[751] http://www.apollo-gaia.org/A-GProjectDevelopment.pdf, *The Apollo Gaia Project : The Club of Rome,* p. 8

In mid-June, an inter-directorate initiative within the E.U. Commission led to the convening of a workshop to explore the possible contribution of emergent fields of complexity science to the task of decision-making. I was asked to act as one of the rapporteurs for the event. John Schellnhüber, the Director of P.I.K. Potsdam was one of the participants. The night before the workshop we were able to arrange a small seminar in the Royal Academy of Brussels in order to explore the analysis of Feedback Dynamics in climate change.[752]

A few days after returning from Potsdam, I traveled down to visit James Lovelock in his West-country hideaway. Jim is the father of the *Gaia Hypothesis*, the understanding of the whole Earth system as an interactive, co-evolutionary web of complex-adaptive, bio-geo-chemical subsystems that cohere in a life-supporting dance.[753]

"Gaia" is a pre-Copernican anachronism. On her own, the Earth is barren. Gaia did not give birth to the heavens, the Moon, the Sun and the stars. There is no father for her children without the Sun. The Earth system is devoid of life in the absence of solar gravity and radiation, the regular stirring of the lunar tides and the stream of emitted energy returning to the cold void of space. To be sure, living systems emerged in a co-evolutionary dance within this negentropic pocket of interstellar debris. But Gaia, on its own, is an inadequate and misleading symbol for the whole Earth system on which we depend, whose complex environment we have put at risk, and for whose future sustainability we are now responsible. In contrast to geocentric mythology, Gaia depends on Apollo for her life.[754]

---

[752] http://www.apollo-gaia.org/A-GProjectDevelopment.pdf, *The Apollo Gaia Project: EU Commission Workshop: Sustainability & the Science of Complexity*, p. 10

[753] http://www.apollo-gaia.org/A-GProjectDevelopment.pdf, *The Apollo Gaia Project: From "Manhattan" to "Apollo-Gaia"* p. 14

[754] http://www.apollo-gaia.org/A-GProjectDevelopment.pdf, *The Apollo Gaia Project: From "Manhattan" to "Apollo-Gaia,"* p. 16

So "Manhattan," the symbol of war, was replaced by "Apollo-Gaia" as a symbol of life.[755]

Gaea the Greek god is also known as Tellus or Terra-Mater in Roman mythology and was an ancient Earth goddess. Tellus was later identified with the Greek Gaea and the Phrygian Cybele.[756]

Cybele is also known as the mother goddess. Cybele (Kybele) was a Phrygian mother goddess, who was worshiped in Greece and Rome. She had often been equated with the two other Greek mother goddesses—Rhea and Demeter (Ceres) ... Cybele was so revered that she was often called the "Mother of All" or the "Great Mother of the Gods."[757]

We are seeing the world today worshiping nature—as in, Mother Nature, Earth Day, the Virgin Mary, Easter (Ishtar, the Queen of Heaven), Mother Earth Day and the like. We are witnessing in real-time the U.N., operating under the guise of environmentalism, seeking to control our every move under the dictates of a pseudo-religious umbrella that is to cover all mankind and, at the same time, ignore the Creator Yehovah in all that they do. This is spiritual *idolatry*.

> *18 For the wrath of Elohim is revealed from heaven against all wickedness and unrighteousness of men, who suppress the truth in unrighteousness, 19 because that which is known of Elohim is manifest among them, for Elohim has manifested it to them. 20 For since the creation of the world His invisible qualities have been clearly seen, being understood from what has been made, both His everlasting power and Mightiness, for them to be without excuse, 21 because, although they knew Elohim, they did not esteem Him as Elohim, nor gave thanks, but became vain in their reasonings, and their undiscerning heart was darkened. 22 Claiming to be wise, they became fools, 23 and changed the esteem of the incorruptible Elohim*

---

[755] http://www.apollo-gaia.org/A-GProjectDevelopment.pdf, *The Apollo Gaia Project: From "Manhattan" to "Apollo-Gaia,"* p. 17

[756] http://www.timelessmyths.com/classical/roman.html, Timeless *Myths | Classical Mythology: Genealogy: Roman Pantheon: Tellus (Terra-Mater)*

[757] http://www.carnaval.com/cybele/

*into the likeness of an image of corruptible man, and of birds and of four-footed beasts and of reptiles.* (Romans 1:18-23)

*24 Therefore Elohim gave them up to uncleanness in the lust of their hearts, to disrespect their bodies among themselves, 25 who changed the truth of Elohim into the falsehood, and worshiped and served what was created rather than the Creator, who is blessed forever. Amĕn. 26 Because of this Elohim gave them over to degrading passions. For even their women exchanged natural relations for what is against nature, 27 and likewise, the men also, having left natural relations with woman, burned in their lust for one another, men with men committing indecency, and receiving back the reward which was due for their straying.* (Romans 1:24-27)

*28 And even as they did not think it worthwhile to possess the knowledge of Elohim, Elohim gave them over to a worthless mind, to do what is improper, 29 having been filled with all unrighteousness, whoring, wickedness, greed, evil; filled with envy, murder, fighting, deceit, evil habits; whisperers, 30 slanderers, haters of Elohim, insolent, proud, boasters, devisers of evils, disobedient to parents, 31 without discernment, covenant breakers, unloving, unforgiving, ruthless; 32 who, though they know the righteousness of Elohim, that those who practice such deserve death, not only do the same but also approve of those who practice them.* (Romans 1:28-32)

*Agenda 21* is not at all the well-intentioned save the Earth doctrine the U.N. would have you believe it is. Agenda 21 has told us the extreme weather events around the world are caused by *Global Warming*, when in truth they are being sent as one of the curses of Leviticus 26 for not obeying Yehovah. But instead of repenting from our sins and returning to Yehovah's way of life, Satan has subtlety seduced and enticed us all, for the most part, to worship the Earth as Mother Earth—also known as the Mother of all living (Noah's wife), Cybele, the Queen of Heaven or Mother Mary worship. At the same time he is through the U.N. bringing the whole world under the leadership of a non-elected bureaucracy that is not answerable to anyone and that will be according to your bible, led by one future dictator.

At the beginning of this chapter I demonstrated to you how in Greek mythology Apollo chased Daphne and just as he was about to catch her and rape her, she cried out to Mother Earth to save her. She was then turned into a tree and Apollo took and made a wreath of her branches. At each of the Earth Summits you see all sorts of people wearing wreaths, which they believe represent the U.N. banner, which are two laurel wreaths wrapping around the Earth featured on the U.N. symbol.

The wreaths represent Apollo and the Earth represents Gaia.

We read a very sobering statement in *Revelation* in light of all that you have been shown here in this chapter.

> *11 And they have over them a sovereign, the messenger of the pit of the deep, whose name in Hebrew is Abaddon, but in Greek he has the name Apolluon.* (Revelation 9:11)

Apollo and Mother Earth, alongside of Satan and Mary worship, have already manifested right in front of us all, right before our very eyes, and yet, very few have been discerning enough to earnestly take heed of this. How involved in this are you and your family?[758] How

---

[758] You can look up what the I.C.L.E.I. is doing in your respective state at the

many times have you voted on environmentally based ballots without realizing or taking the time to research what the driving force behind those ballots were or are? I admonish you to remain mindful *from here on out* of what *Agenda 21* is promoting. It is promoting the worship of nature and of one non-elected government for every nation. It ignores the fact that Yehovah has sent these severe weather events and blames man for the troubled environment.

> *24 Therefore, Elohim gave them up to uncleanness ... 25 who changed the truth of Elohim into the falsehood, and worshipped and served what was created rather than the Creator, who is blessed forever. Aměn.* (Romans 1:24, 25)

Even in *Revelation* as we read about Armageddon, there are some strange things being told to us. The angels are told not to hurt the grass or the trees until the saints have been sealed. But then, in *Chapter 9*, the followers of the Antichrist are told not to harm the trees or grass or any green thing. They are the environmentalists in those very Last Days—in the exact same context, manner and spirit as the world is bending the knee to the U.N.-inspired environmental programs today.

> *1 And after this I saw four messengers standing at the four corners of the earth, holding the four winds of the earth, that the wind should not blow on the earth, nor on the sea, nor on any tree. 2 And I saw another messenger coming up from the rising of the sun, holding the seal of the living Elohim. And he cried with a loud voice to the four messengers to whom it was given to harm the earth and the sea, 3 saying, "Do not harm the earth, nor the sea, nor the trees until we have sealed the servants of our Elohim upon their foreheads."*[1]
> [Footnote: [1] See 9:4, 14:1, 22:4. (Revelation 7:1-3)]

---

following link in the U.S.A.: http://www.icleiusa.org/main-page/about-iclei/members/member-list
If you are in Canada, here is the link for your communities that have signed up with them: http://www.iclei.org/index.php?id=611
And here is the link to the international community that are joining this union where they give up their freedoms to this group in the E.U. (European Union) who are turning this voluntary laws or soft laws into hard laws with penalties and the loss of freedoms: http://www.iclei.org/

> *1 And the fifth messenger sounded, and I saw a star from the heaven which had fallen to the earth. And the key to the pit of the deep was given to it. 2 And he opened the pit of the deep, and smoke went up out of the pit like the smoke of a great furnace. And the sun was darkened, also the air, because of the smoke of the pit. 3 And out of the smoke locusts came upon the earth, and authority was given to them as the scorpions of the earth possess authority. 4 And it was said to them that they shall not harm the grass of the earth, or any green matter, or any tree, but only those men who do not have the seal of Elohim upon their foreheads. 5 And it was given to them that they should not kill them, but to torture them for five months. And their torture was like the torture of a scorpion when it stings a man. 6 And in those days men shall seek death and shall not find it. And they shall long to die, but death shall flee from them.* (Revelation 9:1-6)

Will *Agenda 21* be brought to bear upon those of us who are still left standing in wartime? The *Book of Revelation* seems to be telling us it surely will.

Each time we attribute anything to "Mother Nature," we take away the glory that belongs to Yehovah. When a storm comes and we say Mother Nature must be very angry today, we discredit Yehovah who has sent the storm to chasten us. Yehovah *alone* is the One who creates physical evil in the form of calamities and natural disasters when He sees fit:

> *5 "I am יהוה, and there is none else—there is no Elohim besides Me. I gird you, though you have not known Me, 6 so that they know from the rising of the sun to its setting that there is none but Me. I am יהוה, and there is none else, 7 forming light and creating darkness, making peace and* **creating evil***. I, יהוה, do all these."* (Isaiah 45:5-7)

Each time we ascribe to Mother Nature what we should be giving Yehovah full credit for, we promote the worship of Gaia, the Blessed Virgin Mary, the Queen of Heaven (Ishtar), and the Mother of all living

(Noah's wife) while ignoring the actual One who spoke creation into existence in the first place—Yehovah.

Are you ready for the fight of your life? Are you ready to use the gifts Yehovah has given you to fight on His behalf, and to put your faith in Yehovah *no matter what?*

In 2005, I was standing in the riverbed of the Valley of Elah where David had selected the five stones for his slingshot. It was my last day of my very first trip to Israel and I was very emotional.

The guide asked us, "Who is going to **stand up** for Israel like David did?! Who is going to **stand in the gap** and do *whatever it takes* to defend the Torah and to stop the evil that is coming *no matter what it costs?!*"

And I said "I will."

*Agenda 21* is a colossal, hydra-headed monster, having charters and laws that affect every aspect of our lives—laws that are forcing us to break with the Torah of Yehovah. It is both a Goliath and a Leviathan by nature. Leviathan is HUGE! This *Covenant with death* is *also* huge. *Agenda 21* is a behemoth of a plan that involves the entire world and has its tentacles in nearly every expression of human government imaginable—whether it be directly or indirectly and whether it be soft law or hard law. This is the *Covenant* of *Daniel 9:27* made with many for one 49-year period.

> *21 For look, יהוה is coming out of His place to punish the inhabitants of the earth for their crookedness. And the earth shall disclose her blood, and no longer cover her slain.* (Isaiah 26:21)
>
> *1 In that day, יהוה with His severe sword, great and strong, punishes Liwiathan the fleeing serpent, Liwiathan that twisted serpent. And He shall slay the monster that is in the sea.* (Isaiah 27:1)

The United Nation's *Agenda 21* is a sprawling giant upon the face of the Earth and involves nearly every country of the Earth. Who is going to stand with Yehovah and who is going to shrink back?

> *8 And I heard the voice of* יהוה *saying, "Whom do I send, and who would go for us?" And I said, "Here am I! Send me!" 9 And He said, "Go, and you shall say to this people, 'Hearing, you hear, but do not understand; and seeing, you see, but do not know.' 10 Make the heart of this people fat, and their ears heavy, and shut their eyes; lest they see with their eyes, and hear with their ears, and understand with their heart, and shall turn and be healed." 11 Then I said "*יהוה *until when?" And He answered, "Until the cities are laid waste and without inhabitant, and the houses are without a man, and the land is laid waste, a ruin."* (Isaiah 6:8-11)

We are all called as *Ezekiel* watchmen to speak out and warn the people Yehovah would have us warn, but although they hear the message, they will not heed it and we are to do this until the land is utterly wasted.

> *27 And he shall confirm a covenant with many for one week. And in the middle of the week he shall put an end to slaughtering and meal offering. And on the wing of abominations he shall lay waste, even until the complete end and that which is decreed is poured out on the one who lays waste."*[1] [Footnote: [1]Matthew 24:15 (Daniel 9:27)]

This is the *Covenant made with many* as prophesied in Daniel:

> *27 And he shall confirm a covenant with many for one week.* (Daniel 9:27)

The many began with 113 signing on to save the environment. As it evolved, more was added to it; such as the human rights resolutions and still later the promotion of the gay agenda. Today, there are 193 of 196 nations that have signed up teaching the youth to love "Mother Nature" and to embrace L.B.G.T. lifestyles now being taught in elementary schools.

*Agenda 21* has now spilled over into nearly all the states, provinces, cities and municipalities around the world. Again, it is beyond huge and is monstrous in size.

That *"one week"* began on June 5th-16th, 1972. When you tack forty-nine years on to this, you arrive at the year 2020. Actually you must count them starting with the year 1972.

As you can see, this *Agreement* goes against the *Torah Commandments* about homosexuality and the gay life style. This U.N.-inspired *Declaration* condemns those of the Christian, Jewish and Muslim faiths and supports those who practice earth and nature worship—the indigenous people of the Earth. This is why when you attend a large government ceremony, it is always begun with native dancing and prayers offered to "Mother Nature."

This *Covenant*, which involves worshiping nature and false gods, is an abomination to Yehovah. What's more, those behind this Covenant mistakenly blame man for the extreme and severe weather that is wreaking havoc on nations around the Earth. Yet, the truth of the matter being, these severe weather calamities are sent by Yehovah to chastise an unrepentant, global human populace, as evidenced in the following passage in Isaiah:

> Behold, יהוה *is a mighty and strong one, like a hailstorm, a destroying storm; like a flood of mighty waters overflowing, He casts down to the earth with the hand.* (Isaiah 28:2)

The U.N. however, with this *Covenant*, will use these destructive storms to claim more and more power over the lives of the peoples of the Earth.

## DISCLAIMER

Please be aware that this Chapter was not only difficult to write because of its scope and sequence, but also because the SOURCE MATERIAL for this Chapter is always in a constant state of flux on the Internet. Both myself and my editor have found that in the researching of this chapter; the writing of and the proofreading/editing of this Chapter, we BOTH had to go back and retrace our steps to find alternate SOURCE MATERIAL because SOURCE MATERIAL that was available to us at the time we were gathering information for this chapter of this book, was no longer available for cross referencing or corroborating in the editing and proofing of this book.

My concern then is obvious. I worry that by the time this book goes to print, the information that was available in the final proofing of this book, may no longer be easily corroborated (or might have been scrubbed from the Internet altogether) once this book becomes available to my readership and/or anyone else who might be interested in reading this book. So please keep this in mind, for if either my editor or I were to continue to try to stay on top of the endless and ever changing information, this book would NEVER end up going to print.

# Chapter 12 | Conclusion

> *24 Seventy weeks are decreed for your people and for your set-apart city, to put an end to the transgression, and to seal up sins, and to cover crookedness, and to bring in everlasting righteousness, and to seal up vision and prophet, and to anoint the Most Set-apart. 25 Know, then, and understand: from the going forth of the command to restore and build Yerushalayim until Messiah the Prince is seven weeks and sixty-two weeks. It shall be built again, with streets and a trench, but in times of affliction. 26 And after the sixty-two weeks Messiah shall be cut off and have naught. And the people of a coming prince shall destroy the city and the set-apart place. And the end of it is with a flood. And wastes are decreed, and fighting until the end. 27 And he shall confirm a covenant with many for one week. And in the middle of the week he shall put an end to slaughtering and meal offering. And on the wing of abominations he shall lay waste, even until the complete end and that which is decreed is poured out on the one who lays waste.[1]* [Footnote: [1]Matthew 24:15 (Daniel 9:24-27)]

I have now shared with you eleven chapters and a thorough introduction to the life of Daniel, in order to show you what the Scripture above actually means. None of what I've shared thus far either foreshadows or predicts the arrival of the Messiah in 27 C.E. If the Magi or wise men had come bearing gifts because of the Daniel 9:24-27 prophecy, then why did they come in 1 B.C. when Yehshua was two years of age and not in 27 C.E., which is when most scholars claim this prophecy applies to?

If what is presented in the Prophecy of Daniel all pointed toward the arrival of the Messiah at any age, then why didn't Yehshua and any of the disciples cite this passage as evidence of His Messiah-ship? The reason was because it *did not* apply to that time, or to Yehshua and everyone knew it.

Is this prophecy to be broken up with a 2,000 Year Gap Theory devised by Africanus after the year 232 C.E.? No, it is not, and yet, as I write this in 2013-2014, many eagerly wait and watch for the "last" 3½ years to get underway. Unfortunately, they watch and wait in vain, for they mistakenly believe the last 3½ years began on Purim or Passover 2013 and will draw to a close at some point during what they believe to be the Jubilee Year in 2017, which it clearly is not. They will all be disappointed and have already become very upset with me as I speak out against this widely accepted false teaching and try to explain to them and educate them as to when the Jubilee Years actually *are,* which can be easily proven from history.

The reason none of prevalent interpretations of the past or the present have any merit is because Scripture makes it very clear that these things are for the *Last Days.* More specifically, these words are *sealed* until "the time of the end."

> *3 And those who have insight shall shine like the brightness of the expanse, and those who lead many to righteousness like the stars forever and ever. 4 But you, Dani'ĕl, hide the words, and seal the book until the time of the end. Many shall diligently search and knowledge shall increase.* (Daniel 12:3-4)

And no one has been able to accurately establish where we are in relation to the time of the end—at least not with any degree of absolute certainty and especially not in relation to the biblical calendar. This is why I am so humbled by the fact that Yehovah revealed to someone such as myself not only the significance of the Sabbatical and Jubilee

Cycles, but also, when they were in times past—including the dynamics which were at work then, where they will fall in the future, and most importantly, exactly where we are now with regard to those cycles. I am of the conviction that if Yehovah can do this in and through me, He can do this in and through anyone, if only they have ears to hear and eyes to see. Many have suspected they were in the time of the end ever since the days of the Apostle Paul—not to mention those who currently believe we are in the last 3½ years now. Countless numbers of people who have come and gone have guessed and speculated but have never truly known.

Knowing the truth about the Sabbatical and Jubilee Year Cycles, when they have come and gone throughout history, and acquiring the historical proofs to authenticate these Sabbatical and Jubilee years, one can, with a surprising level of accuracy, know when the 120th Jubilee Year will come and where we are precisely in this last Jubilee Cycle. We cannot know the hour or the day, for Scripture even tells us as much, speaking of The Feast of Trumpets, (a feast that comes on a day and at an hour no one can know until the crescent moon is first seen in the 7th month) but we can know the year.

This is not a matter of me being arrogant or cocky in my understanding of things. Rather, it is the end product of biblical revelation, of which I have every reason to be absolutely confident of, especially when confirmed with historical fact—all of which was based on and corroborated by exhaustive and thorough research both biblically and historically. Yehovah showed me the Sabbatical and Jubilee Cycles, and at the same time, He showed me the curses, which have already happened, still are happening and have yet to happen.

After that, Yehovah showed me how *The Prophecies of Abraham* reveal to us how the events of Abraham's, Noah's, Isaac's, Jacob's and Joseph's life during each of the respective Jubilee Cycles, are a prophetic message to us in these Last Days. It was again Yehovah who showed me the truth about this Prophecy of Daniel 9:24-27, which no one can understand or unravel unless they actually *keep* the Sabbatical and Jubilee Years, as this was what Daniel *himself* had been shown. The revelation of the Scriptures, I believe, comes only by and through obedience. If we do not walk in obedience in accordance to what Yehovah has already shown us and currently is showing us, we will not be given more revelation. But the more we walk in obedience, the more revelation we will be given. Obedience is not just keeping *part of* Torah, but ALL of Torah—the most rewarding part being, the more Torah we keep, the closer we come to seeing in full and not just in part. But we will never totally see in full until we see Yehshua face to face and are made just like Him.

It is a sad, true but little known fact that the Sabbatical and Jubilee Years have not been kept since *before* the days of the Simon Bar Kochba Revolt. As I explained in my previous book, *Remembering the Sabbatical Years of 2016*, the last known and recorded Sabbatical Year stopped after that revolt due to the faulty information the leading Jewish authorities began to circulate and adopted as truth from that point on. From that moment in history and for the next 1,900 years to this day, the truth of the Sabbatical Years became (and has become) lost.

Just as I was nearing the publishing date of this book, two new references to two Sabbatical Years were brought to my attention indicating that some Jewish communities did indeed keep a record of the Sabbatical Years in relationship to the destruction of the Temple.[759] Those records just so happened to match my own records and served to add still more proof and credibility to our already growing list of proofs.

I kept my first Sabbatical Year, from Aviv (March) 2009 to Aviv 2010. And it was *while* I was keeping this Sabbatical Year that Yehovah showed me *The Prophecies of Abraham* in 2009, which I wrote of and circulated in my newsletters[760] that year before writing a book based on the very same information contained in my newsletters.

> *17 So also belief, if it does not have works, is in itself dead. 18 But someone might say, "You have belief, and I have works." Show me your belief without your works, and I shall show you my belief by my works. 19 You believe that Elohim is one. You do well. The demons also believe—and shudder! 20 But*

---

[759] http://sightedmoon.com/tombstones-of-hannah-and-hasadiah-the-priest/
[760] http://www.sightedmoonnl.com/?page_id=483

*do you wish to know, O foolish man, that the belief without the works is dead? (James 2:17-20)*

What James is telling us is that you must **DO** the *Commandments*. These revelations were given to me only once I *began* to *keep* them. You will have one more chance to **DO** a Sabbatical Year in 2016, before the cycle of war comes. The question is *will you*?

Having now explained as thoroughly as I know how to do all that I have come to understand about these four verses in great detail, let me now summarize the following passage in Daniel and my book as a whole by reading each verse and what it actually means *in full*…

I will put one line above and the meaning below it. Those who have skipped to the end and have failed to read the facts that have led to these conclusions are free to continue to guess and chances are, guess *amiss*.

*24 "Seventy weeks are decreed for your people and for your set-apart city, to put an end…"*

Seventy Jubilee Cycles of forty-nine years each (3,430 years in total) are decreed for the Tribes of Israel who became a nation in one day. They became a nation the day they crossed the Red Sea and consist of those whom, in the Last Days, will be made up of the United States of America, Britain, Scotland, Ireland and Wales, Canada, Australia and New Zealand, South Africa, Holland, Denmark, Norway, Sweden, Finland, Switzerland, parts of France, the State of Israel, and for your set-apart city of Jerusalem to put an end…

*24 "…to the transgression, and to seal up sins, and to cover crookedness, and to bring in…"*

3,430 years are decreed to put an end to those who are breaking the Torah, to put an end to sin which is the transgression of Torah and to make atonement for those sins by placing the blame on the one who brought sin into the world, Satan, and locking him away. All of this will take place at the end of the 70th Jubilee Cycle before the year of 2045 C.E. when the 7th Millennium begins. And to bring in…

> "...everlasting righteousness, and to seal up vision and prophet, and to anoint the Most Set-apart."

...the Kingdom of Yehovah which begins in the 7th Millennium or 5881 A.C. (after the Creation of Adam), which is 2045 C.E. at Aviv. At this time we will anoint our King, the Most Set-Apart. There will be no need for visions or prophets after this time.

> 25 "Know, then, and understand: from the going forth of the command to restore and..."

You who KEEP Yehovah's Torah, DO Yehovah's weekly Sabbaths, DO Yehovah's annual Holy Days and DO Yehovah's Sabbatical and Jubilee Years will KNOW and will UNDERSTAND because you keep these signs that will *mark* you as Yehovah's people: that from the time Yehovah commanded Moses at the burning bush to bring the Israelites out of Egypt and to bring them back to the land that Shem was in charge of as King Melchizedek...

> "...build Yerushalayim until Messiah the Prince is seven weeks and sixty-two weeks. It shall..."

...to rebuild Jerusalem. From the time when Yehovah first told Moses at the Burning Bush, to go and get the Israelites until the time when Yehovah anointed King David through Samuel comprised seven Jubilee Cycles or the equivalent of 343 years. The next time when Yehovah anoints King David again will be after another sixty-two Jubilee Cycles or 3,038 years—that is, after 1996 C.E.

King David was anointed by Samuel as a child and then anointed king over Judah in 1010 B.C. This was the seventh year of the fifth Sabbatical Cycle. When we compare that same seventh year of the 5th Sabbatical Cycle in David's time to this the 70th and last Jubilee Cycle, the one we are in right now, that 7th year of the 5th Sabbatical Cycle will be 2030 C.E. just a few years from now.

> "...be built again, with streets and a trench, but in times of affliction. 26 And after the..."

Jerusalem will be rebuilt by King David with a moat and a rampart to protect the city in times of war. This is the Akra, a citadel or strong tower with a moat or what we now call the Millo which was in between the Akra and the Ophel in the City of David. This is exactly what King David did during his reign after the first seven Jubilee Cycles had passed counting forward from when Moses spoke with Yehovah at the Burning Bush.

> "...sixty-two weeks Messiah shall be cut off and have naught. And the people of a coming..."

Then after the sixty-two Jubilee Cycles, or after 1996 C.E., the anointed people, also known as the Israelites, in the countries by which they will be known by, will be defeated so badly in battle that the cities they once inhabited will be thoroughly devastated. No one will have any way of knowing they had even existed before. One-third will die by war, one-third will die by disease, and one-third will go into captivity with nothing, where they will continue to be killed and die until there are only 10% left standing.

> "...prince shall destroy the city and the set-apart place. And the end of it is with a flood. And..."

Again, after the 69th Jubilee Cycle, from the time of Moses being told to go and free Israel, until after 1996 C.E., (sixty-nine Jubilee Cycles) Satan shall destroy Jerusalem and the SAINTS. Just as Ezekiel had prophesied when he reached into his tallit and pulled out those hairs that were protected and tossed some into the fire, Satan will destroy the people of all 12 Tribes of Israel and some of the obedient saints also. And before the 70th Jubilee Cycle ends, which is from the time Moses was told to go and get Israel out of Egypt right up until the year 2045 C.E. Jerusalem will be overrun with Gentiles who will overpower even the surviving 10% remnant of Israel in this last Jubilee Cycle for a brief amount of time.

> "...wastes are decreed, and fighting until the end. 27 And he shall confirm a covenant with..."

The destruction and wars, which will dominate and define the end of this Jubilee Cycle, will come to an end by the year 2033 C.E. when Satan is locked away. Before that time, however, he will succeed in finalizing an environmental agreement [known today as Agenda 21 or the United Nations Conference on the Human Environment, created in Stockholm, Sweden June 5th-16th, 1972. It is also called the United Nations Conference on Environment and Development (U.N.C.E.D.) in Rio de Janeiro, June 3rd-14th, 1992] which will eventually give him full and absolute control over the entire world. This Covenant with many began in 1972 under the United Nations banner and will come a complete end in 2020 C.E., forty-nine years later, one prophetic week also known as one shabua.

> "...many for one week. And in the middle of the week, he shall put an end to slaughtering and..."

And this environmental agreement with the entire world will be for one forty-nine year block of time, from 1972 C.E. until 2020 C.E. The year 2020 C.E. is in the middle of the 120th Jubilee Cycle, and this is when he will destroy those tribes of Israel and kill them so they no longer will be able to pray morning, noon and evening, nor be able to assemble to keep the three *hags* each at the Feasts of Passover, Pentecost and Tabernacles.

> "...meal offering. And on the wing of abominations he shall lay waste, even until the..."

And from that time forward, from 2020 C.E. onward, Satan will destroy all who oppose him around the world as he seeks to utterly destroy those remaining Israelites.

> "...complete end and that which is decreed is poured out on the one who lays waste."

Satan will do this until the Messiah comes and stops him in 2033 C.E. on the Day of Atonement. Then and only then will it be finished.

We are living in that very last shabua (week), or the very last Jubilee Cycle of which Daniel spoke and prophesied about. In the midst of this last Jubilee Cycle, which began in 1996, making the *midst* point, or middle of this current Jubilee Cycle if you will, the year 2020 C.E. Those nations, which have descended from the Twelve Tribes of Israel, will be destroyed and *once again* one third of them will go into captivity. This year of 2020 C.E. is also the end of the forty-nine years of the *Covenant* made by the United Nations, which began back in 1972. This *Covenant* not only promotes the worship of the Earth and nature, but has also added to it the *Declaration of Human Rights*, which again, goes against and is in direct opposition to the eternal, immutable and unchanging Laws of Yehovah.

To be counted amongst the 10% who survive, you must be a *doer* of the Law as spoken of in the *Book of James* and not *just* a hearer. "I will show you my faith by my works." NOW is the time to begin to keep the weekly Sabbath and immerse your whole self in the deep study of Yehovah's Word. NOW is the time to begin keeping the annual Holy Days of Leviticus 23 and to do so by taking special care to not add any unbiblical *holidays* to Yehovah's appointed times. NOW is the time to begin to adequately prepare for and to keep the Sabbatical Year of 2016.

In other words, TODAY, right here, right now, is the time to *repent* from *not* keeping the Torah and to begin thoroughly keeping it. NOW is the time to stop putting off until tomorrow what we all should have done yesterday, and if not yesterday, well then TODAY!

In just a few years' time, in the year 2020 C.E., war will come to North America. North America will be utterly destroyed and its inhabitants, captured. By the year 2023 C.E., three years later, this war in North America will come to fruition. Will you *now* begin to *obey*? Will you tell your loved ones and those of your assembly, synagogue, fellowship or congregation about the understanding of this prophecy that you now know very much about? Will you and will they get right with Yehovah *now*? I can only hope and pray the answer to this question for all who read this is a resounding "Yes!" Not just for your sake and the sake of those of your household, but also for the sake of *anyone* Yehovah puts in your path who has ears to hear.

I am now going to list the proofs I have accumulated which repeatedly, as well as most clearly and pointedly illustrate the things we need to know about this time that is soon going to be upon us. Not all of the following proofs have been covered by me in this book. You can learn more about these proofs by reading The Prophecies of Abraham[761] and by being subscribed to my weekly News Letter.

1) In 2014 during Passover, April 15th, and again in the fall during the Feast of Tabernacles, on October 8th, there will be Blood Moons. Then, when the New Year begins in March 2015, there will be a solar eclipse followed by another Blood Moon again on Passover April 4th, 2015. This phenomenon will then be followed by another solar eclipse on September 13th, 2015 just before the Feast of Trumpets and yet another Blood Moon on the Feast of Tabernacles on September 28th, 2015.

In Jewish mythology, when there have been Blood Moons they were normally thought to be harbingers of coming wars. It is a fact that these four Blood Moons coming on the High Holy Days of Passover and Sukkot two years in a row are a very rare event and as such, something to most definitely be carefully considered and closely examined.

In 2016 those following the conjunction calendar will have a forced leap year. If the barley in Israel is ready, we could have the calendar start one month before the conjunction as in other years. If it is indeed one month early then, on Passover that year and again on Sukkot in 2016 there will be a "dark moon." A dark moon is one that is almost in eclipse like the blood moon is.

In Jewish mythology, when there have been Dark Moons they were normally thought to be harbingers of coming famines. In Lev 26 when the curse speaks of the coming sword that Yehovah would send, it also tells us that there will also be shortage of food and that you would have to eat your food by weight.

> 23 And if you will not be reformed by Me by these things, but will still walk contrary to Me, 24 then I will walk contrary

---

[761] http://sightedmoon.com/store/products/

*to you and will punish you seven times more for your sins. 25 And I will bring a sword on you that shall execute the vengeance of the covenant. And when you are gathered inside your cities, I will send the plague among you. And you shall be delivered into the hand of the enemy. 26 When I have broken the staff of your bread, ten women shall bake your bread in one oven, and they shall deliver you your bread again by weight. And you shall eat and not be satisfied.* (Leviticus 26:23-26)

When you plot the Blood Moons out during the course of our current Jubilee Cycle, you can see they occur just before the 4th Curse of War, which is expected to come during the 4th Sabbatical Cycle between 2017 C.E. and 2023 C.E.

| Sabbath | 6th Cycle | 5th Cycle | 4th Cycle | 3rd Cycle | 2nd Cycle | 1st Cycle |
|---|---|---|---|---|---|---|
| 2044 | 2037 | 2030 | 2023 | 2016 | 2009 | 2002 |
| 2043 | 2036 | 2029 | 2022 | 2015 | 2008 | 2001 |
| 2042 | 2035 | 2028 | 2021 | 2014 | 2007 | 2000 |
| 2041 | 2034 | 2027 | 2020 | 2013 | 2006 | 1999 |
| 2040 | 2033 | 2026 | 2019 | 2012 | 2005 | 1998 |
| 2039 | 2032 | 2025 | 2018 | 2011 | 2004 | 1997 |
| 2038 | 2031 | 2024 | 2017 | 2010 | 2003 | 1996 |

2) The destruction of the world during the Great Flood of Noah in 1656 A.C., coupled with how that parallels the subsequent destruction of Sodom and Gomorrah in 2047 A.C. and correlates directly with our current Jubilee Cycle of 2033 C.E.—all of this was told to us by Yehshua in the *Gospel of Luke*. See the following three charts to gain a deeper understanding of this.

| Sabbath | 6th Cycle | 5th Cycle | 4th Cycle | 3rd Cycle | 2nd Cycle | 1st Cycle |
|---|---|---|---|---|---|---|
| 1666 | 1659 | 1652 | 1645 | 1638 | 1631 | 1624 |
| 1665 | 1658 | 1651 | 1644 | 1637 | 1630 | 1623 |
| 1664 | 1657 | 1650 | 1643 | 1636 | 1629 | 1622 |
| 1663 | 1656 | 1649 | 1642 | 1635 | 1628 | 1621 |
| 1662 | 1655 | 1648 | 1641 | 1634 | 1627 | 1620 |
| 1661 | 1654 | 1647 | 1640 | 1633 | 1626 | 1619 |
| 1660 | 1653 | 1646 | 1639 | 1632 | 1625 | 1618 |

| Sabbath | 6th Cycle | 5th Cycle | 4th Cycle | 3rd Cycle | 2nd Cycle | 1st Cycle |
|---|---|---|---|---|---|---|
| 2058 | 2051 | 2044 | 2037 | 2030 | 2023 | 2016 |
| 2057 | 2050 | 2043 | 2036 | 2029 | 2022 | 2015 |
| 2056 | 2049 | 2042 | 2035 | 2028 | 2021 | 2014 |
| 2055 | 2048 | 2041 | 2034 | 2027 | 2020 | 2013 |
| 2054 | 2047 | 2040 | 2033 | 2026 | 2019 | 2012 |
| 2053 | 2046 | 2039 | 2032 | 2025 | 2018 | 2011 |
| 2052 | 2045 | 2038 | 2031 | 2024 | 2017 | 2010 |

| Sabbath | 6th Cycle | 5th Cycle | 4th Cycle | 3rd Cycle | 2nd Cycle | 1st Cycle |
|---|---|---|---|---|---|---|
| 2044 | 2037 | 2030 | 2023 | 2016 | 2009 | 2002 |
| 2043 | 2036 | 2029 | 2022 | 2015 | 2008 | 2001 |
| 2042 | 2035 | 2028 | 2021 | 2014 | 2007 | 2000 |
| 2041 | 2034 | 2027 | 2020 | 2013 | 2006 | 1999 |
| 2040 | 2033 | 2026 | 2019 | 2012 | 2005 | 1998 |
| 2039 | 2032 | 2025 | 2018 | 2011 | 2004 | 1997 |
| 2038 | 2031 | 2024 | 2017 | 2010 | 2003 | 1996 |

3) The ending year of the 7 Years of Famine for Egypt and the world—again, the Beast Power during the life of Joseph's Jubilee Cycle of 2243 A.C. matches the year 2033 C.E. with regard to our current Jubilee Cycle when the Beast Power and Satan are to be locked away. Again, the following chart below adding more weight to the proof of the #2 chart up above of Sodom and Gomorrah and of the Flood as Yehshua tells us in the *Gospel of Luke*.

| Sabbath | 6th Cycle | 5th Cycle | 4th Cycle | 3rd Cycle | 2nd Cycle | 1st Cycle |
|---|---|---|---|---|---|---|
| 2254 | 2247 | 2240 | 2233 | 2226 | 2219 | 2212 |
| 2253 | 2246 | 2239 | 2232 | 2225 | 2218 | 2211 |
| 2252 | 2245 | 2238 | 2231 | 2224 | 2217 | 2210 |
| 2251 | 2244 | 2237 | 2230 | 2223 | 2216 | 2209 |
| 2250 | 2243 | 2236 | 2229 | 2222 | 2215 | 2208 |
| 2249 | 2242 | 2235 | 2228 | 2221 | 2214 | 2207 |
| 2248 | 2241 | 2234 | 2227 | 2220 | 2213 | 2206 |

4) The starting year of the 7 Years of Plenty for Egypt in 2230 A.C., the Beast Power during Joseph's Jubilee Cycle, matches the year 2020 C.E. in our current Jubilee Cycle when once again the Beast Power is going to prosper, having destroyed the 12 Tribes of Israel during the coming Sabbatical Cycle of war.

5) The starting year of the Famine during Joseph's Jubilee Cycle of 2237 A.C., comes just six months after the expected time when

the Two Witnesses will stop the rain for 3½ years at the Feast of Trumpets in 2026.

| Sabbath | 6th Cycle | 5th Cycle | 4th Cycle | 3rd Cycle | 2nd Cycle | 1st Cycle |
|---|---|---|---|---|---|---|
| 2254 | 2247 | 2240 | 2233 | 2226 | 2219 | 2212 |
| 2253 | 2246 | 2239 | 2232 | 2225 | 2218 | 2211 |
| 2252 | 2245 | 2238 | 2231 | 2224 | 2217 | 2210 |
| 2251 | 2244 | 2237 | 2230 | 2223 | 2216 | 2209 |
| 2250 | 2243 | 2236 | 2229 | 2222 | 2215 | 2208 |
| 2249 | 2242 | 2235 | 2228 | 2221 | 2214 | 2207 |
| 2248 | 2241 | 2234 | 2227 | 2220 | 2213 | 2206 |

| Sabbath | 6th Cycle | 5th Cycle | 4th Cycle | 3rd Cycle | 2nd Cycle | 1st Cycle |
|---|---|---|---|---|---|---|
| 2044 | 2037 | 2030 | 2023 | 2016 | 2009 | 2002 |
| 2043 | 2036 | 2029 | 2022 | 2015 | 2008 | 2001 |
| 2042 | 2035 | 2028 | 2021 | 2014 | 2007 | 2000 |
| 2041 | 2034 | 2027 | 2020 | 2013 | 2006 | 1999 |
| 2040 | 2033 | 2026 | 2019 | 2012 | 2005 | 1998 |
| 2039 | 2032 | 2025 | 2018 | 2011 | 2004 | 1997 |
| 2038 | 2031 | 2024 | 2017 | 2010 | 2003 | 1996 |

6) The year Ishmael was born in 2034 A.C., from whom the Muslim religion has hailed, matches the year 2020 C.E. and the prophecy Isaac gave Esau. The word "dominion" means "to tramp" as in trample the entire Earth.

| Sabbath | 6th Cycle | 5th Cycle | 4th Cycle | 3rd Cycle | 2nd Cycle | 1st Cycle |
|---|---|---|---|---|---|---|
| 2058 | 2051 | 2044 | 2037 | 2030 | 2023 | 2016 |
| 2057 | 2050 | 2043 | 2036 | 2029 | 2022 | 2015 |
| 2056 | 2049 | 2042 | 2035 | 2028 | 2021 | 2014 |
| 2055 | 2048 | 2041 | 2034 | 2027 | 2020 | 2013 |
| 2054 | 2047 | 2040 | 2033 | 2026 | 2019 | 2012 |
| 2053 | 2046 | 2039 | 2032 | 2025 | 2018 | 2011 |
| 2052 | 2045 | 2038 | 2031 | 2024 | 2017 | 2010 |

| Sabbath | 6th Cycle | 5th Cycle | 4th Cycle | 3rd Cycle | 2nd Cycle | 1st Cycle |
|---|---|---|---|---|---|---|
| 2044 | 2037 | 2030 | 2023 | 2016 | 2009 | 2002 |
| 2043 | 2036 | 2029 | 2022 | 2015 | 2008 | 2001 |
| 2042 | 2035 | 2028 | 2021 | 2014 | 2007 | 2000 |
| 2041 | 2034 | 2027 | 2020 | 2013 | 2006 | 1999 |
| 2040 | 2033 | 2026 | 2019 | 2012 | 2005 | 1998 |
| 2039 | 2032 | 2025 | 2018 | 2011 | 2004 | 1997 |
| 2038 | 2031 | 2024 | 2017 | 2010 | 2003 | 1996 |

*38 And Esau said to his father, "Have you only one blessing, my father? Bless me, me too, O my father!" And Esau lifted up his voice and wept. 39 And Yitshaq his father answered and said to him, "See, your dwelling is of the fatness of the earth, and of the dew of the heavens from above. 40 And by your sword you are to live, and serve your brother. And it shall be, when you grow restless, that you shall break his yoke from your neck.* (Genesis 27:38-40)

H7300 rûd rood

A primitive root: to *tramp* about, that is, *ramble* (free or disconsolate): –have the dominion, be lord, mourn, rule.

7) The Temple built by Solomon in 967 B.C. near the beginning of the 4th Millennial Day (This was seventy years before the 4th Millennium began in 896 B.C.) was destroyed at the end of the 4th Millennial Day back in 70 C.E. (This was fourteen years before the 4th Millennial Day ended in the year 84 C.E.) When you take the seven millenniums as a week, this 4th Millennium matches our 4th Sabbatical Cycle. This is the 4th Sabbatical Cycle that Israel was destroyed in 723 B.C and it is the next Sabbatical Cycle for us.

| Sabbath | 6th Cycle | 5th Cycle | 4th Cycle | 3rd Cycle | 2nd Cycle | 1st Cycle |
|---|---|---|---|---|---|---|
| -701 | -708 | -715 | -722 | -729 | -736 | -743 |
| -702 | -709 | -716 | -723 | -730 | -737 | -744 |
| -703 | -710 | -717 | -724 | -731 | -738 | -745 |
| -704 | -711 | -718 | -725 | -732 | -739 | -746 |
| -705 | -712 | -719 | -726 | -733 | -740 | -747 |
| -706 | -713 | -720 | -727 | -734 | -741 | -748 |
| -707 | -714 | -721 | -728 | -735 | -742 | -749 |

| Sabbath | 6th Cycle | 5th Cycle | 4th Cycle | 3rd Cycle | 2nd Cycle | 1st Cycle |
|---|---|---|---|---|---|---|
| 2044 | 2037 | 2030 | 2023 | 2016 | 2009 | 2002 |
| 2043 | 2036 | 2029 | 2022 | 2015 | 2008 | 2001 |
| 2042 | 2035 | 2028 | 2021 | 2014 | 2007 | 2000 |
| 2041 | 2034 | 2027 | 2020 | 2013 | 2006 | 1999 |
| 2040 | 2033 | 2026 | 2019 | 2012 | 2005 | 1998 |
| 2039 | 2032 | 2025 | 2018 | 2011 | 2004 | 1997 |
| 2038 | 2031 | 2024 | 2017 | 2010 | 2003 | 1996 |

| Jubilee Cycle | 1st Millennial Day | 2nd Millennial Day | 3rd Millennial Day | 4th Millennial Day | 5th Millennial Day | 6th Millennial Day | 7th Millennial Day |
|---|---|---|---|---|---|---|---|
| | | | | | | | Sabbath |
| 1 | -3788 | -2808 | -1828 | -848 | 133 | 1113 | 2093 |
| 2 | -3739 | -2759 | -1779 | -799 | 182 | 1162 | 2142 |
| 3 | -3690 | -2710 | -1730 | -750 | 231 | 1211 | 2191 |
| 4 | -3641 | -2661 | -1681 | -701 | 280 | 1260 | 2240 |
| 5 | -3592 | -2612 | -1632 | -652 | 329 | 1309 | 2289 |
| 6 | -3543 | -2563 | -1583 | -603 | 378 | 1358 | 2338 |
| 7 | -3494 | -2514 | -1534 | -554 | 427 | 1407 | 2387 |
| 8 | -3445 | -2465 | -1485 | -505 | 476 | 1456 | 2436 |
| 9 | -3396 | -2416 | -1436 | -456 | 525 | 1505 | 2485 |
| 10 | -3347 | -2367 | -1387 | -407 | 574 | 1554 | 2534 |
| 11 | -3298 | -2318 | -1338 | -358 | 623 | 1603 | 2583 |
| 12 | -3249 | -2269 | -1289 | -309 | 672 | 1652 | 2632 |
| 13 | -3200 | -2220 | -1240 | -260 | 721 | 1701 | 2681 |
| 14 | -3251 | -2171 | -1191 | -211 | 770 | 1750 | 2730 |
| 15 | -3102 | -2122 | -1142 | -162 | 819 | 1799 | 2779 |
| 16 | -3053 | -2073 | -1093 | -113 | 868 | 1848 | 2828 |
| 17 | -3004 | -2024 | -1044 | -64 | 917 | 1897 | 2877 |
| 18 | -2955 | -1975 | -995 | -15 | 966 | 1946 | 2926 |
| 19 | -2906 | -1926 | -946 | 35 | 1015 | 1995 | 2975 |
| 20 | -2857 | -1877 | -897 | 84 | 1064 | 2044 | 3024 |
| | 20 | 40 | 60 | 80 | 100 | 120 | |

8) Yehovah spoke to Abraham and told him that after four generations then Yehovah would bring Abraham's children back to the Land. The word generation is:

**H1755 dôr dôr** *dore, dore*

From **H1752**; properly a *revolution* of time, that is, an *age* or generation; also a *dwelling:* –age, X evermore, generation, [n-]ever, posterity.

*16 Then, in the fourth generation they shall return here, for the crookedness of the Amorites is not yet complete.* (Genesis 15:16)

After "four periods of time" can also mean after "four millennial days." Yehovah spoke this promise to Abraham in 1809 B.C., which, as you can see on the chart above, is at the beginning of the 3rd Millennial Day. Four millennial days later, including the 3rd one, will bring you to the end of the 6th Millennial Day. As you can see, we are in the year 2014 C.E. now. This 6th Millennial Day ends in 2044 C.E. This promise of

Yehovah is about to happen to *all of* Israel. This means *us* and we will be brought back to the Land of Israel very soon and must be brought, at the time of this promise's fulfillment, back *from captivity.*

| Jubilee Cycle | 1st Millennial Day | 2nd Millennial Day | 3rd Millennial Day | 4th Millennial Day | 5th Millennial Day | 6th Millennial Day | 7th Millennial Day Sabbath |
|---|---|---|---|---|---|---|---|
| 1 | -3788 | -2808 | -1828 | -848 | 133 | 1113 | 2093 |
| 2 | -3739 | -2759 | -1779 | -799 | 182 | 1162 | 2142 |
| 3 | -3690 | -2710 | -1730 | -750 | 231 | 1211 | 2191 |
| 4 | -3641 | -2661 | -1681 | -701 | 280 | 1260 | 2240 |
| 5 | -3592 | -2612 | -1632 | -652 | 329 | 1309 | 2289 |
| 6 | -3543 | -2563 | -1583 | -603 | 378 | 1358 | 2338 |
| 7 | -3494 | -2514 | -1534 | -554 | 427 | 1407 | 2387 |
| 8 | -3445 | -2465 | -1485 | -505 | 476 | 1456 | 2436 |
| 9 | -3396 | -2416 | -1436 | -456 | 525 | 1505 | 2485 |
| 10 | -3347 | -2367 | -1387 | -407 | 574 | 1554 | 2534 |
| 11 | -3298 | -2318 | -1338 | -358 | 623 | 1603 | 2583 |
| 12 | -3249 | -2269 | -1289 | -309 | 672 | 1652 | 2632 |
| 13 | -3200 | -2220 | -1240 | -260 | 721 | 1701 | 2681 |
| 14 | -3251 | -2171 | -1191 | -211 | 770 | 1750 | 2730 |
| 15 | -3102 | -2122 | -1142 | -162 | 819 | 1799 | 2779 |
| 16 | -3053 | -2073 | -1093 | -113 | 868 | 1848 | 2828 |
| 17 | -3004 | -2024 | -1044 | -64 | 917 | 1897 | 2877 |
| 18 | -2955 | -1975 | -995 | -15 | 966 | 1946 | 2926 |
| 19 | -2906 | -1926 | -946 | 35 | 1015 | 1995 | 2975 |
| 20 | -2857 | -1877 | -897 | 84 | 1064 | 2044 | 3024 |
|  | 20 | 40 | 60 | 80 | 100 | 120 |  |

9) Yehshua the Messiah was killed on Wednesday, the fourth day of the week, again giving us a clue as to when we, the Temple of Yehovah, will also be destroyed in the 4th Sabbatical Cycle.

> *16 Do you not know that you are a Dwelling Place of Elohim, and that the Spirit of God dwells in you? 17 If anyone destroys the Dwelling Place of Elohim, Elohim shall destroy him. For the Dwelling Place of Elohim is set-apart, which you are.* (1 Corinthians 3:16-17)

| Sabbath | 6th Cycle | 5th Cycle | 4th Cycle | 3rd Cycle | 2nd Cycle | 1st Cycle |
|---------|-----------|-----------|-----------|-----------|-----------|-----------|
| 2044 | 2037 | 2030 | 2023 | 2016 | 2009 | 2002 |
| 2043 | 2036 | 2029 | 2022 | 2015 | 2008 | 2001 |
| 2042 | 2035 | 2028 | 2021 | 2014 | 2007 | 2000 |
| 2041 | 2034 | 2027 | 2020 | 2013 | 2006 | 1999 |
| 2040 | 2033 | 2026 | 2019 | 2012 | 2005 | 1998 |
| 2039 | 2032 | 2025 | 2018 | 2011 | 2004 | 1997 |
| 2038 | 2031 | 2024 | 2017 | 2010 | 2003 | 1996 |

10) Israel, the 10 Northern Tribes were defeated and destroyed by 723 B.C., which matches the 4th Sabbatical Cycle when Israel is again expected to be defeated.

| Sabbath | 6th Cycle | 5th Cycle | 4th Cycle | 3rd Cycle | 2nd Cycle | 1st Cycle |
|---------|-----------|-----------|-----------|-----------|-----------|-----------|
| -701 | -708 | -715 | -722 | -729 | -736 | -743 |
| -702 | -709 | -716 | -723 | -730 | -737 | -744 |
| -703 | -710 | -717 | -724 | -731 | -738 | -745 |
| -704 | -711 | -718 | -725 | -732 | -739 | -746 |
| -705 | -712 | -719 | -726 | -733 | -740 | -747 |
| -706 | -713 | -720 | -727 | -734 | -741 | -748 |
| -707 | -714 | -721 | -728 | -735 | -742 | -749 |

The 4th Sabbatical Cycle is the time period of the 4th Curse of Leviticus 26. From 2017 C.E.–2023 C.E.

> *23 And if you are not instructed by Me by these, but walk contrary to Me, 24 then I also shall walk contrary to you, and I Myself shall smite you seven times for your sins. 25 And I shall bring against you a sword executing the vengeance of My covenant, and you shall gather together in your cities, and I shall send pestilence among you, and you shall be given into the hand of the enemy. 26 When I have cut off your supply of bread, ten women shall bake your bread in one oven, and they shall bring back to you your bread by weight, and you shall eat and not be satisfied.* (Leviticus 26:23-26)

11) Yehovah spoke to Moses at the Burning Bush after the 50th Jubilee Year 1387 B.C. had finished and the 51st Jubilee Cycle of 1386 B.C. had begun. Seventy Jubilee Cycles later (70 x 49) brings you to 2045 C.E. when all these things must be completed.

This gives us a total of 120 Jubilee Cycles—fifty up to the Exodus and seventy from the Exodus to the end of this current Jubilee Cycle. In Genesis the word "years" is "shanah" (**H8141**) and means *periods of time* or 120 ***Jubilee Cycles***.

> *3 And said, "My spirit shall not strive with man forever in his going astray. He is flesh, and his days shall be a hundred and twenty years."* (Genesis 6:3)

| | | | | | | -1337 | 51 |
|---|---|---|---|---|---|---|---|
| Sabbath | 6th Cycle | 5th Cycle | 4th Cycle | 3rd Cycle | 2nd Cycle | 1st Cycle | |
| -1338 | -1345 | -1352 | -1359 | -1366 | -1373 | -1380 | |
| -1339 | -1346 | -1353 | -1360 | -1367 | -1374 | -1381 | |
| -1340 | -1347 | -1354 | -1361 | -1368 | -1375 | -1382 | |
| -1341 | -1348 | -1355 | -1362 | -1369 | -1376 | -1383 | |
| -1342 | -1349 | -1356 | -1363 | -1370 | -1377 | -1384 | |
| -1343 | -1350 | -1357 | -1364 | -1371 | -1378 | -1385 | |
| -1344 | -1351 | -1358 | -1365 | -1372 | -1379 | -1386 | |
| | | | | | | -1386 | 50 |

| | | | | | | Jubilee | |
|---|---|---|---|---|---|---|---|
| | | | | | | 2045 | 120 |
| Sabbath | 6th Cycle | 5th Cycle | 4th Cycle | 3rd Cycle | 2nd Cycle | 1st Cycle | 6th |
| 2044 | 2037 | 2030 | 2023 | 2016 | 2009 | 2002 | Millennial |
| 2043 | 2036 | 2029 | 2022 | 2015 | 2008 | 2001 | Day |
| 2042 | 2035 | 2028 | 2021 | 2014 | 2007 | 2000 | Ended |
| 2041 | 2034 | 2027 | 2020 | 2013 | 2006 | 1999 | |
| 2040 | 2033 | 2026 | 2019 | 2012 | 2005 | 1998 | |
| 2039 | 2032 | 2025 | 2018 | 2011 | 2004 | 1997 | |
| 2038 | 2031 | 2024 | 2017 | 2010 | 2003 | 1996 | |
| | | | | | | 1996 | 119 |

| Jubilee Cycle | 1st Millenial Day | 2nd Millenial Day | 3rd Millenial Day | 4th Millenial Day | 5th Millenial Day | 6th Millenial Day | 7th Millenial Day Sabbath |
|---|---|---|---|---|---|---|---|
| 1 | -3788 | -2808 | -1828 | -848 | 133 | 1113 | 2093 |
| 2 | -3739 | -2759 | -1779 | -799 | 182 | 1162 | 2142 |
| 3 | -3690 | -2710 | -1730 | -750 | 231 | 1211 | 2191 |
| 4 | -3641 | -2661 | -1681 | -701 | 280 | 1260 | 2240 |
| 5 | -3592 | -2612 | -1632 | -652 | 329 | 1309 | 2289 |
| 6 | -3543 | -2563 | -1583 | -603 | 378 | 1358 | 2338 |
| 7 | -3494 | -2514 | -1534 | -554 | 427 | 1407 | 2387 |
| 8 | -3445 | -2465 | -1485 | -505 | 476 | 1456 | 2436 |
| 9 | -3396 | -2416 | -1436 | -456 | 525 | 1505 | 2485 |
| 10 | -3347 | -2367 | -1387 | -407 | 574 | 1554 | 2534 |
| 11 | -3298 | -2318 | -1338 | -358 | 623 | 1603 | 2583 |
| 12 | -3249 | -2269 | -1289 | -309 | 672 | 1652 | 2632 |
| 13 | -3200 | -2220 | -1240 | -260 | 721 | 1701 | 2681 |
| 14 | -3251 | -2171 | -1191 | -211 | 770 | 1750 | 2730 |
| 15 | -3102 | -2122 | -1142 | -162 | 819 | 1799 | 2779 |
| 16 | -3053 | -2073 | -1093 | -113 | 868 | 1848 | 2828 |
| 17 | -3004 | -2024 | -1044 | -64 | 917 | 1897 | 2877 |
| 18 | -2955 | -1975 | -995 | -15 | 966 | 1946 | 2926 |
| 19 | -2906 | -1926 | -946 | 35 | 1015 | 1995 | 2975 |
| 20 | -2857 | -1877 | -897 | 84 | 1064 | 2044 | 3024 |
| | 20 | 40 | 60 | 80 | 100 | 120 | |

12) Joseph and his brothers reunited in 2238 A.C. All Twelve Tribes are predicted to be reunited between 2028 C.E. and 2030 C.E. when they are returned to the Land of Israel.

| Sabbath | 6th Cycle | 5th Cycle | 4th Cycle | 3rd Cycle | 2nd Cycle | 1st Cycle |
|---------|-----------|-----------|-----------|-----------|-----------|-----------|
| 2254 | 2247 | 2240 | 2233 | 2226 | 2219 | 2212 |
| 2253 | 2246 | 2239 | 2232 | 2225 | 2218 | 2211 |
| 2252 | 2245 | 2238 | 2231 | 2224 | 2217 | 2210 |
| 2251 | 2244 | 2237 | 2230 | 2223 | 2216 | 2209 |
| 2250 | 2243 | 2236 | 2229 | 2222 | 2215 | 2208 |
| 2249 | 2242 | 2235 | 2228 | 2221 | 2214 | 2207 |
| 2248 | 2241 | 2234 | 2227 | 2220 | 2213 | 2206 |

| Sabbath | 6th Cycle | 5th Cycle | 4th Cycle | 3rd Cycle | 2nd Cycle | 1st Cycle |
|---------|-----------|-----------|-----------|-----------|-----------|-----------|
| 2044 | 2037 | 2030 | 2023 | 2016 | 2009 | 2002 |
| 2043 | 2036 | 2029 | 2022 | 2015 | 2008 | 2001 |
| 2042 | 2035 | 2028 | 2021 | 2014 | 2007 | 2000 |
| 2041 | 2034 | 2027 | 2020 | 2013 | 2006 | 1999 |
| 2040 | 2033 | 2026 | 2019 | 2012 | 2005 | 1998 |
| 2039 | 2032 | 2025 | 2018 | 2011 | 2004 | 1997 |
| 2038 | 2031 | 2024 | 2017 | 2010 | 2003 | 1996 |

13) In 1859 C.E., Henry Durant saw many wounded in the battlefield and no one tending to their wounds. This would lead to the founding of the First Geneva Convention in 1863 C.E. When you count from 1863 C.E., 3½ Jubilee Cycles later, you end up at 2033 C.E. when Satan is going to be locked away. The Geneva Conventions, in turn, would eventually lead to the United Nations, as we know it, which is part of this End-Time Beast Power. The U.N., League of Nations, the Hague Conventions and the Geneva Conventions are all about waging war in a *civilized* manner.

| Sabbath | 6th Cycle | 5th Cycle | 4th Cycle | 3rd Cycle | 2nd Cycle | 1st Cycle |
|---------|-----------|-----------|-----------|-----------|-----------|-----------|
| 2044 | 2037 | 2030 | 2023 | 2016 | 2009 | 2002 |
| 2043 | 2036 | 2029 | 2022 | 2015 | 2008 | 2001 |
| 2042 | 2035 | 2028 | 2021 | 2014 | 2007 | 2000 |
| 2041 | 2034 | 2027 | 2020 | 2013 | 2006 | 1999 |
| 2040 | 2033 | 2026 | 2019 | 2012 | 2005 | 1998 |
| 2039 | 2032 | 2025 | 2018 | 2011 | 2004 | 1997 |
| 2038 | 2031 | 2024 | 2017 | 2010 | 2003 | 1996 |

| Sabbath | 6th Cycle | 5th Cycle | 4th Cycle | 3rd Cycle | 2nd Cycle | 1st Cycle |
|---------|-----------|-----------|-----------|-----------|-----------|-----------|
| 1995 | 1988 | 1981 | 1974 | 1967 | 1960 | 1953 |
| 1994 | 1987 | 1980 | 1973 | 1966 | 1959 | 1952 |
| 1993 | 1986 | 1979 | 1972 | 1965 | 1958 | 1951 |
| 1992 | 1985 | 1978 | 1971 | 1964 | 1957 | 1950 |
| 1991 | 1984 | 1977 | 1970 | 1963 | 1956 | 1949 |
| 1990 | 1983 | 1976 | 1969 | 1962 | 1955 | 1948 |
| 1989 | 1982 | 1975 | 1968 | 1961 | 1954 | 1947 |

| Sabbath | 6th Cycle | 5th Cycle | 4th Cycle | 3rd Cycle | 2nd Cycle | 1st Cycle |
|---------|-----------|-----------|-----------|-----------|-----------|-----------|
| 1946 | 1939 | 1932 | 1925 | 1918 | 1911 | 1904 |
| 1945 | 1938 | 1931 | 1924 | 1917 | 1910 | 1903 |
| 1944 | 1937 | 1930 | 1923 | 1916 | 1909 | 1902 |
| 1943 | 1936 | 1929 | 1922 | 1915 | 1908 | 1901 |
| 1942 | 1935 | 1928 | 1921 | 1914 | 1907 | 1900 |
| 1941 | 1934 | 1927 | 1920 | 1913 | 1906 | 1899 |
| 1940 | 1933 | 1926 | 1919 | 1912 | 1905 | 1898 |

| Sabbath | 6th Cycle | 5th Cycle | 4th Cycle | 3rd Cycle | 2nd Cycle | 1st Cycle |
|---------|-----------|-----------|-----------|-----------|-----------|-----------|
| 1897 | 1890 | 1883 | 1876 | 1869 | 1862 | 1855 |
| 1896 | 1889 | 1882 | 1875 | 1868 | 1861 | 1854 |
| 1895 | 1888 | 1881 | 1874 | 1867 | 1860 | 1853 |
| 1894 | 1887 | 1880 | 1873 | 1866 | 1859 | 1852 |
| 1893 | 1886 | 1879 | 1872 | 1865 | 1858 | 1851 |
| 1892 | 1885 | 1878 | 1871 | 1864 | 1857 | 1850 |
| 1891 | 1884 | 1877 | 1870 | 1863 | 1856 | 1849 |

14) The *Covenant Made With Many* spoken of in Daniel 9:27 began with the convening of the United Nations in Stockholm, Sweden in 1972. For the very first time in human history, this conference on the Human Environment united the representatives of multiple governments in discussions pertaining to the state of the global environment. This conference directly resulted in the creation of government-based environmental agencies and the U.N. Environmental Program (U.N.E.P.). This original *Covenant* made in Stockholm back in 1972 has now turned into the bureaucratic monster we know it to be today.

This *Declaration* originally contained twenty-six principles concerning the environment and development—an *Action Plan* with *109 Recommendations*, and a *Resolution*. The *Stockholm Covenant* has, as its first principle and as the most prominent *Declaration*, a *Declaration on "Human Rights."* This *Declaration on Human Rights*, allegedly intended to prevent another Holocaust, has led to the *Declaration on Lesbian, Gay, Bi-Sexual and Transgendered Rights*.

In 2011, the United Nations Human Rights Council passed its first *Resolution* recognizing L.G.B.T. rights, which was followed up with a report from the U.N. Human Rights Commission documenting violations of the rights of L.G.B.T people—including hate crimes, criminalization of homosexuality, and discrimination. Following closely on the heels of the report, the U.N. Human Rights Commission urged all countries, which had not yet done so, to enact laws protecting basic L.G.B.T. rights. The practice of homosexuality is still illegal in seventy-six countries, and is punishable by execution in seven of those countries— most of which are Islamic nations.

| Sabbath | 6th Cycle | 5th Cycle | 4th Cycle | 3rd Cycle | 2nd Cycle | 1st Cycle |
|---------|-----------|-----------|-----------|-----------|-----------|-----------|
| 2044 | 2037 | 2030 | 2023 | 2016 | 2009 | 2002 |
| 2043 | 2036 | 2029 | 2022 | 2015 | 2008 | 2001 |
| 2042 | 2035 | 2028 | 2021 | 2014 | 2007 | 2000 |
| 2041 | 2034 | 2027 | 2020 | 2013 | 2006 | 1999 |
| 2040 | 2033 | 2026 | 2019 | 2012 | 2005 | 1998 |
| 2039 | 2032 | 2025 | 2018 | 2011 | 2004 | 1997 |
| 2038 | 2031 | 2024 | 2017 | 2010 | 2003 | 1996 |

| Sabbath | 6th Cycle | 5th Cycle | 4th Cycle | 3rd Cycle | 2nd Cycle | 1st Cycle |
|---------|-----------|-----------|-----------|-----------|-----------|-----------|
| 1995 | 1988 | 1981 | 1974 | 1967 | 1960 | 1953 |
| 1994 | 1987 | 1980 | 1973 | 1966 | 1959 | 1952 |
| 1993 | 1986 | 1979 | 1972 | 1965 | 1958 | 1951 |
| 1992 | 1985 | 1978 | 1971 | 1964 | 1957 | 1950 |
| 1991 | 1984 | 1977 | 1970 | 1963 | 1956 | 1949 |
| 1990 | 1983 | 1976 | 1969 | 1962 | 1955 | 1948 |
| 1989 | 1982 | 1975 | 1968 | 1961 | 1954 | 1947 |

This is not the first time this sort of thing has happened. It is recorded and, surprisingly, has played a very prominent role in the history of the Twelve Tribes of Israel.

The Curse of Balaam[762] was to have Israel sin by committing fornication with the Moabite women who either sought to entice them to forsake Yehovah and His Commandments and worship other gods or to incorporate the worship of other gods with Israel's worship of Yehovah.

---

[762] http://sightedmoon.com/the-doctrine-of-balaam/

I must now explain this in more detail for those who may not understand how significant this actually was and now is in light of current events for us now living in the Last Days and the time of Jacob's Trouble.

But first let me share some scriptures with you that attest to the true nature of the worship of Balaam.

> 9 "... then יהוה knows how to rescue the reverent ones from trial and to keep the unrighteous unto the day of judgment, to be punished, 10 and most of all those walking after the flesh in filthy lust and despising authority—bold, headstrong, speaking evil of esteemed ones, 11 whereas messengers who are greater in strength and power do not bring a slanderous accusation against them before the Master." (2 Peter 2:9-11)

> 12 "But these, like natural unreasoning beasts, having been born to be caught and destroyed, blaspheme that which they do not know, shall be destroyed in their destruction, 13 being about to receive the wages of unrighteousness, deeming indulgence in the day of pleasure, spots and blemishes, reveling in their own deceptions while they feast with you, 14 having eyes filled with an adulteress, and unable to cease from sin, enticing unstable beings, having a heart trained in greed, children of a curse, 15 having left the right way they went astray, having followed the way of Bil'am the son of Be'or, who loved the wages of unrighteousness, 16 but he was rebuked for his transgression: a dumb donkey speaking with the voice of a man restrained the madness of the prophet."(2 Peter 2:12-16)

> 17 "These are fountains without water, clouds driven by a storm, to whom the blackest darkness is kept forever. 18 For speaking arrogant nonsense, they entice—through the lusts of the flesh, through indecencies—the ones who have indeed escaped from those living in delusion." (2 Peter 2:17-18)

I am about to explain the *way of Balaam* so there is no misunderstanding or mistaking exactly what it entails. Allow me to continue to lay the foundation by providing you with a few more scriptures:

*10 But these blaspheme that which they do not know. And that which they know naturally, like unreasoning beasts, in these they corrupt themselves. 11 Woe to them! Because they have gone in the way of Qayin, and gave themselves to the delusion of Bil'am for a reward, and perished in the rebellion of Qoraḥ. 12 These are rocky reefs in your love feasts, feasting with you, feeding themselves without fear, waterless clouds borne about by the winds, late autumn trees without fruit, twice dead, pulled up by the roots, 13 wild waves of the sea foaming up their own shame, straying stars for whom blackness of darkness is kept forever. 14 And Ḥanok̠, the seventh from Adam, also prophesied of these, saying, "See, יהוה comes with His myriads of set-apart ones, 15 to execute judgment on all, to punish all who are wicked among them concerning all their wicked works which they have committed in a wicked way, and concerning all the harsh words which wicked sinners have spoken against Him." 16 These are grumblers, complainers, who walk according to their own lusts, and their mouth speaks proudly, admiring faces of others for the sake of gain.* (Jude 1:10-16)

*14 "But I hold a few matters against you, because you have there those who adhere to the teaching of Bil'am, who taught Balaq to put a stumbling-block before the children of Yisra'ěl, to eat food offered to idols, and to commit whoring."* (Revelation 2:14)

This *Doctrine of Balaam* is not something we can afford to be ignorant of, especially when we are told to be aware of it in the *Book of Revelation*.

In *Numbers* 22-25 and *Numbers* 31:1-16, we are told the story of Balaam but we are never really told what Balaam or the Moabite and Midianite women did specifically, that led Israel to commit harlotry and spiritual idolatry with them. Balaam could not effectually curse Israel, but he successfully conspired with Balak about how to cause Israel to curse themselves by sinning against Yehovah.

To better understand, one must start with the rape of Dinah, the daughter of Jacob (Israel), by comparing it to the rape of Tamar, the daughter of King David.

The unifying word in both stories is the word *afflict*–H6031. Dinah and Tamar both represent the Twelve Tribes of Israel in the Last Days. That being said, keep this word *afflict* and its meaning in mind as I continue in my explanation.

> *1 And Dinah, the daughter of Lĕ'ah, whom she had borne to Ya'aqoḇ, went out to see the daughters of the land. 2 And Sheḵem, son of Ḥamor the Ḥiwwite, prince of the land, saw her and took her and lay with her, and humbled her. 3 And his being clung to Dinah the daughter of Ya'aqoḇ, and he loved the girl and spoke kindly to the girl. 4 And Sheḵem spoke to his father Ḥamor, saying, "Take this girl for me for a wife." 5 And Ya'aqoḇ heard that he had defiled Dinah his daughter. Now his sons were with his livestock in the field, so Ya'aqoḇ kept silent until they came. 6 And Ḥamor, the father of Sheḵem, went out to Ya'aqoḇ to speak with him. 7 And the sons of Ya'aqoḇ came in from the field when they heard it. And the men were grieved and very wroth, because he had done a senseless deed in Yisra'ĕl by lying with Ya'aqoḇ's daughter, which should not be done.* (Genesis 34:1-7)

> *8 But Ḥamor spoke with them, saying, "My son Sheḵem's being longs for your daughter. Please give her to him for a wife. 9 And intermarry with us, give us your daughters and take our daughters for yourselves, 10 and dwell with us, and let the land be before you. Dwell and move about in it, and have possessions in it." 11 And Sheḵem said to her father and her brothers, "Let me find favor in your eyes, and whatever you say to me I give. 12 Ask of me a bride price and gift ever so high, and I give according to what you say to me, but give me the girl for a wife."* (Genesis 34:8-12)

Now compare the rape of Dinah's account in *Genesis* with the rape of Tamar's account in *2 Samuel*:

*1 And after this it came to be that Aḇshalom son of Dawiḏ had a lovely sister, whose name was Tamar, and Amnon son of Dawiḏ loved her. 2 And Amnon was distressed, even to become sick, because of his sister Tamar—for she was a maiden—and it was hard in the eyes of Amnon to do whatever to her. 3 And Amnon had a friend whose name was Yonaḏaḇ son of Shim'ah, Dawiḏ's brother. Now Yonaḏaḇ was a very wise man. 4 And he said to him, "Why are you, the sovereign's son, becoming thinner day after day? Explain it to me." And Amnon said to him, "I love Tamar, my brother Aḇshalom's sister." 5 And Yonaḏaḇ said to him, "Lie down on your bed and pretend to be sick. And when your father comes to see you, say to him, 'Please let my sister Tamar come and give me food, and make the food before my eyes so that I see it, and eat it from her hand.'"* (2 Samuel 13:1-5)

*6 So Amnon lay down and pretended to be sick. And when the sovereign came to see him, Amnon said to the sovereign, "Please let Tamar my sister come and make a couple of cakes for me before my eyes, so that I eat from her hand." 7 And Dawiḏ sent to Tamar, to the house, saying, "Please go to the house of your brother Amnon, and make food for him." 8 So Tamar went to her brother Amnon's house, while he was lying down. And she took dough and kneaded it, and made cakes before his eyes, and baked the cakes. 9 And she took the pan and turned them out before him, but he refused to eat. And Amnon said, "Make everyone go away from me." And they all went out from him. 10 And Amnon said to Tamar, "Bring the food into the bedroom, that I eat from your hand." And Tamar took the cakes which she had made, and brought them to Amnon her brother in the bedroom.* (2 Samuel 13:6-10)

*11 And she brought them to him to eat, and he took hold of her and said to her, "Come, lie with me, my sister." 12 And she answered him, "No, my brother, do not humble me, for it is not done so in Yisra'ěl. Do not do this wickedness! 13 And I, where could I take my shame? And you—you would be like one of the fools in Yisra'ěl. And now, please speak to the sovereign, for he would not withhold me from you." 14 But he would not listen to her voice, and being stronger than she, he humbled her and lay with her. 15 Amnon then hated her exceedingly, so that the hatred with which he hated her was greater than the love with which he had loved her. And Amnon said to her, "Arise, go!" 16 And she said to him, "No, for this evil of sending me away is worse than the other you have done to me." But he would not listen to her. 17 And he called his young man serving him, and said, "Now put this one out, away from me, and bolt the door behind her."* (2 Samuel 13:11-17)

*18 And she had on a long coat, for the sovereign's maiden daughters wore such garments. And his servant put her out and bolted the door behind her. 19 And Tamar put ashes on her head, and tore her long coat that was on her, and put her hand on her head and went away crying bitterly. 20 And Aḇshalom her brother said to her, "Has Amnon your brother been with you? But now, keep silent, my sister. He is your brother, do not take this matter to heart." So Tamar remained in the house of her brother Aḇshalom, but was ruined.* (2 Samuel 13:18-20)

When we examine the word "violated" in *Genesis* 34:2 we see it is H6031, which in Hebrew is *anah*. This is the same word used in *2 Samuel* 13:14 but is translated as "forced."

> And when Shechem[H7928] the son[H1121] of Hamor[H2544] the Hivite,[H2340] prince[H5387] of the country,[H776] saw[H7200] her, he took[H3947] her, and lay with[H7901] her, and defiled[H6031] her. (Genesis 34:2)

> Howbeit he would[H14] not[H3808] hearken[H8085] unto her voice:[H6963] but, being stronger[H2388] than she, forced[H6031] her, and lay with[H7901] her. (2 Samuel 13:14)

> H6031  ענה  ʻânâh  aw-naw'

> A primitive root (possibly rather identical with H6030 through the idea of *looking* down or *browbeating*); to *depress* literally

or figuratively, transitively or intransitively (in various applications). (*sing* is by mistake for H6030):–abase self, afflict (-ion, self), answer [by mistake for H6030], chasten self, deal hardly with, defile, exercise, force, gentleness, humble (self), hurt, ravish, sing [by mistake for H6030], speak [by mistake for H6030], submit self, weaken, X in any wise.

H6030 ענה 'ânâh *aw-naw'*

A primitive root; properly to *eye* or (generally) to *heed*, that is, *pay attention*; by implication to *respond*; by extension to *begin* to speak; specifically to *sing, shout, testify, announce*: – give account, afflict [by mistake for H6031], (cause to, give) answer, bring low [by mistake for H6031], cry, hear, Leannoth, lift up, say, X scholar, (give a) shout, sing (together by course), speak, testify, utter, (bear) witness. See also, H1042, H1043.

Another thing you should notice is how the expression in *Genesis* 34:7 **'such a thing is not done in Israel'** is remarkably similar to *2 Samuel* 13:12 **'for no such thing should be done in Israel.'** This too is one of the primary connections between the two stories.

Shechem lusted for Dinah and forced himself upon her in very much the same way Amnon lusted after Tamar and forced himself upon her. In the story of Shechem, you are told that Hamor the Hivite is Shechem's father and because Shechem is a prince, it means that Hamor is the king of that land. Hamor proceeds to do all the talking on behalf of Shechem.

In *2 Samuel*, you are told that the one advising Amnon was Jonadab the son of Shimeah, David's brother. Jo-nadab means Jehovah-spontaneously.

H5068 נדב nâdab *naw-dab'*

A primitive root; to *impel*; hence to *volunteer* (as a soldier), to *present* spontaneously: –offer freely, be (give, make, offer self) willing (-ly).

Jonadab is going to voluntarily offer free advice to Amnon, without giving any thought or care to what he is saying or the consequences of it. We are also told that Jonadab is a very crafty man.

> *3 But Amnon had a friend whose name was Jonadab the son of Shimeah, David's brother.* **Now Jonadab was a very crafty man.** (2 Samuel 13:3)

> But Amnon[H550] had a friend,[H7453] whose name[H8034] *was* Jonadab,[H3122] the son[H1121] of Shimeah[H8093] David's[H1732] brother:[H251] and Jonadab[H3122] *was* a very[H3966] subtle[H2450] man.[H376] (2 Samuel 13:3)

> H2450    חכם    châkâm    khaw-kawm'

> From H2449; *wise,* (that is, intelligent, skilful or artful): – cunning (man), subtle, ([un-]), wise ([hearted], man).

> H2449    חכם    châkam    khaw-kam'

> A primitive root, to *be wise* (in mind, word or act): –X exceeding, teach wisdom, be (make self, shew self) wise, deal (never so) wisely, make wiser.

This word 'subtle' leads us right back to the incident in the Garden of Eden.

> *1 And the serpent was more crafty than any beast of the field which* יהוה *Elohim had made, and he said to the woman, "Is it true that Elohim has said, 'Do not eat of every tree of the garden?'"* (Genesis 3:1)

> Now the serpent[H5175] was[H1961] more subtle[H6175] than any[H4480 & H3605] beast[H2416] of the field[H7704] which[H834] the LORD[H3068] God[H430] had made.[H6213] And he said[H559] unto[H413] the woman,[H802] Yea,[H637 & H3588] hath God[H430] said,[H559] Ye shall not[H3808] eat[H398] of every[H4480 & H3605] tree[H6086] of the garden?[H1588] (Genesis 3:1)

H6175     ערום     'ârûm     *aw-room'*

Passive participle of H6191; *cunning* (usually in a bad sense): —crafty, prudent, subtle.

H6191     ערם     'âram     *aw-ram'*

A primitive root; properly to *be* (or *make*) *bare*; but used only in the derived sense (through the idea perhaps of *smoothness*) to *be cunning* (usually in a bad sense): —X very, beware, take crafty [counsel], be prudent, deal subtly.

This source of Jonadab's advice to Amnon was satanic advice, the same as it was in the Garden of Eden. Satan volunteered the advice. Eve did not solicit it. The same dynamics were also at work when Hamor advised Jacob to let his sons intermarry with the daughters of Shechem. It was Satan inspired. The key thematic expressions positively identify a common origin from which both stories hail from and illustrate how, in both cases, the counsel given was unsolicited. It was Satan inspired.

Balaam used divination in order to prophesy, which means he used Satan as his undisclosed source.

> *7 And the elders of Mo'aḇ and the elders of Miḏyan left with the fees for divination in their hand, and they came to Bil'am and spoke the words of Balaq to him.* (Numbers 22:7)

> *22 And the sons of Yisra'ěl killed with the sword Bil'am son of Be'or, the diviner, among those who were killed by them.* (Joshua 13:22)

Balaam was hired by Balak (which means "devastator") to come and curse Israel. Yehovah prevented Balaam from cursing Israel, and only allowed him to bless Israel. But Balaam did volunteer some advice to Balak and this is what we are being shown here. The advice, again, is actually coming from Satan.

Examining the meaning of the name of Shechem, the son of Hamor the Hivite, who was an Amorite, brings new information to bear in mind to the surface. "Hivi" is an Aramaic word meaning "serpentine." It describes the character of both Shechem and his father, Hamor. Both of them acted in a serpentine-like and treacherous manner.

> *8 He who digs a pit falls into it, and whoever breaks through a wall is bitten by a snake.* (Ecclesiastes 10:8)

Is this not *exactly* what Dinah did by leaving the safe confines of her hedge or encampment, so that she might see the daughters of the land—after which a serpent found her?

> *1 And Dinah, the daughter of Lĕ'ah, whom she had borne to Ya'aqob̠, went out to see the daughters of the land.* (Genesis 34:1)

And when Shechem[H7928] the son[H1121] of Hamor[H2544] the Hivite,[H2340] prince[H5387] of the country,[H776] saw[H7200] her, he took[H3947] her, and lay with[H7901] her, and defiled[H6031] her. (Genesis 34:2)

Hamor means:

H2544    חמור    chămôr    *kham-ore'*

The same as H2543; *ass*; *Chamor*, a Canaanite: –Hamor.

H2543    חמר    חמור    chămôr    chămôr    *kham-ore', kham-ore'*

From H2560; a male *ass* (from its dun *red*): –(he) ass.

H2560    חמר    châmar    *khaw-mar'*

A primitive root; properly to *boil* up; hence to *ferment* (with scum); to *glow* (with redness); as denominative (from H2564) to *smear* with pitch: –daub, foul, be red, trouble.

H2564    חָמָר    chêmâr    *khay-mawr'*

From H2560; *bitumen* (as *rising* to the surface): –slime (-pit).

Hamor was an ass, and based on the description above, would turn red whenever his temper "boiled up" or flared. He could also be described as "scum" or "slime."

Once again, this links us to the story of Balaam. In *both* cases it is an ass that is speaking. Who says Yehovah does not have a sense of humor?!

> *21 And Bil'am rose in the morning and saddled his donkey, and went with the heads of Mo'ab. 22 But the displeasure of Elohim burned because he went, and the Messenger of יהוה stationed Himself in the way as an adversary against him. And he was riding on his donkey, and his two servants were with him. 23 And the donkey saw the Messenger of יהוה standing in the way with His drawn sword in His hand, and the donkey turned aside out of the way and went into the field. So Bil'am beat the donkey to turn her back onto the way. 24 Then the Messenger of יהוה stood in a narrow passage between the vineyards, with a wall on this side and a wall on that side. 25 And when the donkey saw the Messenger of יהוה, she pushed herself against the wall and crushed Bil'am's foot against the wall, so he beat her again. 26 And the Messenger of יהוה went further, and stood in a narrow place where there was no way to turn aside, right or left.* (Numbers 22:21-26)

> *27 And when the donkey saw the Messenger of יהוה, she lay down under Bil'am. So Bil'am's displeasure burned, and he beat the donkey with his staff. 28 Then יהוה opened the mouth of the donkey, and she said to Bil'am, "What have I done to you, that you have beaten me these three times?" 29 And Bil'am said to the donkey, "Because you have mocked me. I wish there were a sword in my hand, for I would have killed you by now!" 30 And the donkey said to Bil'am, "Am I not*

*your donkey on which you have ridden, ever since I became yours, to this day? Was I ever known to do so to you?" And he said, "No." 31 Then* יהוה *opened Bil'am's eyes, and he saw the Messenger of* יהוה *standing in the way with His drawn sword in His hand. And he bowed his head and fell on his face.* (Numbers 22:27-31)

There is more information to be gleaned from reading the rest of story in *Genesis*.

*13 But the sons of Ya'aqob answered Shekem and Ḥamor his father, and spoke with deceit, because he had defiled Dinah their sister. 14 And they said to them, "We are not able to do this matter, to give our sister to one who is uncircumcised, for that would be a reproach to us. 15 Only on this condition would we agree to you: If you become as we are, to have every male of you circumcised, 16 then we shall give our daughters to you, and take your daughters to us. And we shall dwell with you, and shall become one people. 17 But if you do not listen to us and be circumcised, we shall take our daughter and go." 18 And their words pleased Ḥamor and Shekem, Ḥamor's son. 19 And the young man did not delay to do this because he delighted in Ya'aqob's daughter. Now he was more respected than all the household of his father.* (Genesis 34:13-19)

*20 And Ḥamor and Shekem his son came to the gate of their city, and spoke with the men of their city, saying, 21 "These men are at peace with us, so let them dwell in the land and move about in it. And see, the land is large enough for them. Let us take their daughters for us for wives, and let us give them our daughters. 22 Only on this condition would the men agree to dwell with us, to be one people: if every male among us is circumcised as they are circumcised. 23 Their herds and their possessions, and all their beasts, should they not be ours? Only let us agree with them, and let them dwell with us." 24 And all who went out of the gate of his city listened to Ḥamor and Shekem his son; every male was circumcised, all who went out of the gate of his city.* (Genesis 34:20-24)

In verse 19 it says Shechem was also more honorable than all his brothers, yet he had just raped Dinah. This should speak volumes to his character (or more like, lack thereof) and that of the rest of his sordid clan.

These people were scoundrels, greedy for gain. Shechem not only lusted after Dinah, but the entire clan lusted after all that Jacob had. They wanted to intermarry with Israel so that all that Israel possessed would become their possession too. They coveted the wealth of Israel, would do anything to procure it and little else would suffice.

> *23 Their herds and their possessions, and all their beasts, should they not be ours? Only let us agree with them, and let them dwell with us.* (Genesis 34:23)

Hamor, Jonadab and Balaam all gave unsolicited advice in the very *same* way Satan did. Satan caused Eve to lust after the forbidden fruit of the Tree of Knowledge of Good and Evil. Hamor gave advice in order to cover up the rape and take all that Jacob had for himself. Jonadab gave advice on how to rape Tamar. Balaam, in an effort to earn the wages being offered to him, gave advice on how to defeat Israel, by causing them to lust after sexual perversions. He offered this advice because Yehovah would not allow him to curse Israel. In each and every case, the advice was unsolicited, and had to do with encouraging the lusting after something forbidden sexually.

The event between Shechem and Hamor, who both represent Satan here, and Dinah and Jacob, both of whom are representative of the whole house of Israel, followed right on the heels of Jacob entering the land after his exile with Laban and his encounter with Esau.

> *17 And Ya'aqob set out to Sukkoth, and built himself a house, and made booths for his livestock. That is why the name of the place is called Sukkoth. 18 And Ya'aqob came safely to the city of Shekem, which is in the land of Kena'an, when he came from Paddan Aram. And he pitched his tent before the city. 19 And he bought the portion of the field where he had pitched his tent, from the children of Ḥamor, Shekem's father, for one hundred qesitah.* (Genesis 33:17-19)

Joshua would later set up an altar[763] at this same place once they crossed over the Jordan River.

Thirty-eight years after the Exodus and just before the Twelve Tribes of Israel enter the land, when they are still on the other side of the Jordan, the incident of Baal-Peor ensues and Balaam's proposal to Balak, to use the Moabite and the Midianite women in a sexually deviant manner is now being applied.

> *1 And the children of Yisra'ĕl set out and camped in the desert plains of Mo'aḇ beyond the Yardĕn of Yeriḥo. 2 And Balaq son of Tsippor saw all that Yisra'ĕl had done to the Amorites. 3 And Mo'aḇ was exceedingly afraid of the people because they were many, and Mo'aḇ was in dread because of the children of Yisra'ĕl. 4 And Mo'aḇ said to the elders of Miḏyan, "Now this company is licking up all that is around us, as an ox licks up the grass of the field." Now Balaq son of Tsippor was sovereign of the Mo'aḇites at that time, 5 and he sent messengers to Bil'am son of Be'or at Pethor, which is near the River in the land of the sons of his people, to call him, saying, "See, a people has come from Mitsrayim. See, they have covered the surface of the land, and are settling next to me! 6 And now, please come at once, curse this people for me, for they are too strong for me. It might be that I smite them and drive them out of the land, for I know that he whom you bless is blessed, and he whom you curse is cursed." 7 And the elders of Mo'aḇ and the elders of Miḏyan left with the fees for divination in their hand, and they came to Bil'am and spoke the words of Balaq to him.* (Numbers 22:1-7)

Israel has now come to the close of their forty years of wandering in the wilderness. All those who sinned and were cursed due to their lack of faith when the ten spies brought back an evil report had already died in fulfillment of the curse placed upon them by Yehovah.

---

[763] http://www.setapartpeople.com/joshua-altar-found-on-mount-ebal

Balaam even tells us how pure Israel was at that time.

> 21 He has not looked upon wickedness in Ya'aqoḇ, nor has He seen trouble in Yisra'ěl. יהוה his Elohim is with him, and the shout of a Sovereign is in him. (Numbers 23:21)

But then we come to *Numbers* 25 and something of a clearly disturbing nature has happened, but we are not told specifically what it is. This is precisely why I have gone through this thematic analogy of interrelated scriptures with you. The Israelites, along with the Moabite and Midianite women, have committed abominations that are revolting in Yehovah's sight.

> 1 And Yisra'ěl dwelt in Shittim, and the people began to whore with the daughters of Mo'aḇ, 2 and they invited the people to the slaughterings of their mighty ones, and the people ate and bowed down to their mighty ones. 3 Thus Yisra'ěl was joined to Ba'al Pe'or, and the displeasure of יהוה burned against Yisra'ěl. 4 And יהוה said to Mosheh, "Take all the leaders of the people and hang them up before יהוה, before the sun, so that the burning displeasure of יהוה turns away from Yisra'ěl." 5 And Mosheh said to the judges of Yisra'ěl, "Each one of you slay his men who were joined to Ba'al Pe'or." (Numbers 25:1-5)

> 6 And see, one of the children of Yisra'ěl came and brought to his brothers a Miḏyanite woman before the eyes of Mosheh and before the eyes of all the congregation of the children of Yisra'ěl, who were weeping at the door of the Tent of Meeting. 7 And when Pineḥas, son of El'azar, son of Aharon the priest, saw it, he rose up from among the congregation and took a spear in his hand, 8 and he went after the man of Yisra'ěl into the tent and thrust both of them through, the man of Yisra'ěl, and the woman through her belly. Thus the plague among the children of Yisra'ěl came to a stop. 9 And those who died in the plague were twenty-four thousand. (Numbers 25:6-9)

The rape of Dinah by Shechem just after Jacob entered the Promised Land was a prophetic event foretelling of the time when Israel was going to be returning to the land approximately three hundred years later. The sexual perversion was now at a *national* level! We are now nearing that same critical juncture when we are about to return to the land, as I have shown you in points #8 and #11 of this same chapter and now some 3400 years later, all the Israelite nations are involved in this same sexual perversion.

But what was it that was so evil? Moses gives us a clue a few verses later in *Numbers* 25 after Phineas took action.

> *14 And the name of the Yisra'ĕlite who was killed, who was killed with the Miḏyanite woman, was Zimri, son of Salu, a leader of a father's house among the Shim'onites. 15 And the name of the Miḏyanite woman who was killed was Kozbi the daughter of Tsur. He was head of the people of a father's house in Miḏyan. 16 And* יהוה *spoke to Mosheh, saying, 17 "Distress the Miḏyanites! And you shall smite them, 18 for they distressed you with their tricks with which they deceived you in the matter of Pe'or and in the matter of Kozbi, the daughter of a leader of Miḏyan, their sister, who was killed in the day of the plague because of Pe'or."* (Numbers 25:14-18)

It has something to do with Baal-Peor, but *what*?

When we look at Hamor and Jonadab, we can also see parallels to Pharaoh of Egypt. He is similar to Laban who pursued Israel after Jacob fled his country. These are all thematic correlations, which help us to understand what will take place in these Last Days.

Pharaoh is pronounced *Pa Rah*. Pa means *Mouth* and Rah means *Bad*. Pharaoh can then be read as *bad mouth*. Pharaoh and Laban as well as Hamor and Jonadab represent Satan speaking evil in the sight of the God of heaven.

> *6 And he opened his mouth in blasphemies against Elohim, to blaspheme His Name, and His Tent, and those dwelling in the heaven.* (Revelation 13:6)

Each of these events from the past represents in part, what will be just before the final Shuva (aka, the Second Exodus) or the final return to the land of Israel. Satan and the false prophet will be speaking blasphemies against Yehovah. They will encourage the Israelites with false teachings and by whatever other ways and means necessary to cause them to stumble.

But I still have not yet adequately explained to you what this *Doctrine of Balaam* is exactly and what Baal-Peor exemplifies. But before proceeding, we are reminded of the seriousness of this in *Numbers:*

> 13 And Mosheh, and El'azar the priest, and all the leaders of the congregation, went to meet them outside the camp. 14 But Mosheh was wroth with the officers of the army, with the commanders of thousands and commanders of hundreds, who had come from the campaign. 15 And Mosheh said to them, "Have you kept all the women alive? 16 Look, they are the ones who caused the children of Yisra'ĕl, through the word of Bil'am, to trespass against יהוה in the matter of Pe'or, and there was a plague among the congregation of יהוה. 17 And now, slay every male among the little ones. And every woman who has known a man by lying with a man you shall slay. 18 But keep alive for yourselves all the female children who have not known a man by lying with a man." (Numbers 31:13-18)

The *Doctrine of Balaam*—and the inherent conspiracy found therein—is serious business. It was meant to be a stumbling block to Israel back then and it is to us again today. But what is it? This is no longer speaking to a future event. It is speaking to us, *today,* in our lives *now*.

Consider the following:

> 18 Look at Yisra'ĕl after the flesh: Are not those who eat of the offerings sharers in the altar? 19 What then do I say? That an idol is of any value? Or that which is offered to idols is of any value? 20 No, but what the gentiles offer they offer to demons[1] and not to Elohim, and I do not wish you to become sharers with demons. [Footnote: [1]*Leviticus 17:7*] 21

> *You are not able to drink the cup of the Master and the cup of demons, you are not able to partake of the table of the Master and of the table of demons. 22 Do we provoke the Master to jealousy? Are we stronger than He?* (I Corinthians 10:18-22)

> *3 Any man from the house of Yisra'ĕl who slaughters a bull or a lamb or a goat in the camp, or who slaughters it outside the camp, 4 and does not bring it to the door of the Tent of Meeting, to bring an offering to* יהוה *before the Dwelling Place of* יהוה, *blood-guilt is reckoned to that man. He has shed blood, and that man shall be cut off from among his people, 5 in order that the children of Yisra'ĕl bring their slaughterings which they slaughter in the open field. And they shall bring them to* יהוה *at the door of the Tent of meeting, to the priest, and slaughter them as peace offerings to* יהוה. *6 And the priest shall sprinkle the blood on the altar of* יהוה *at the door of the Tent of Meeting, and shall burn the fat for a sweet fragrance to* יהוה. *7 And let them no longer slaughter their slaughterings to demons, after whom they whored. This is a law forever for them throughout their generations.* (Leviticus 17:3-7)

> *1 And Bil'am said to Balaq, "Build seven altars for me here, and prepare seven bulls and seven rams for me here." 2 And Balaq did as Bil'am had spoken, and Balaq and Bil'am offered a bull and a ram on each altar.* (Numbers 23:1-2)

The sacrifice of Baal-Peor was to demons because it was false worship and not according to Yehovah's instructions—instructions of which Moses had just taught to Aaron at Mount Sinai. Those who do not sacrifice according to the commands of Yehovah do it as unto demons and are guilty of spiritual idolatry, harlotry and the shedding of innocent blood.

> *1 Cry aloud, do not spare. Lift up your voice like a ram's horn. Declare to My people their transgression, and the house of Ya'aqoḇ their sins.* (Isaiah 58:1)

Because Israel was upright before the Lord, Balaam's attempts to curse the nation had failed. They had been to the high places of Satan. Now King Balak takes Balaam to yet another high place called Peor (meaning "open"). Here, Balak again repeats the sacrifices and Balaam again petitions to Yehovah. Once again, Yehovah blesses Israel and does not curse them.

When we look up the word Peor, we learn the following:

> H6465   פעור   pᵉʽôr   peh-ore'

From H6473; a *gap*; *Peor*, a mountain East of Jordan; also (for H1187) a deity worshipped there: –Peor. See also, H1047.

> H6473   פער   pâʽar   paw-ar'

A primitive root; to *yawn*, that is, *open* wide (literally or figuratively): –gape, open (wide).

It was here that Balaam counseled Balak on how to defeat Israel. This is recounted in the following Scripture:

> *14 "But I hold a few matters against you, because you have there those who adhere to the teaching of Bil'am, who taught Balaq to put a stumbling-block before the children of Yisra'ĕl, to eat food offered to idols, and to commit whoring."* (Revelation 2:14)

What exactly was the stumbling block Balaam offered to King Balak? It was the worship of Baal-Peor! After Balaam departs from Moab, we see the ramifications of this instruction as Israel joins itself to Baal-Peor.

> *1 And Yisra'ĕl dwelt in Shittim, and the people began to whore with the daughters of Mo'aḇ, 2 and they invited the people to the slaughterings of their mighty ones, and the people ate and bowed down to their mighty ones. 3 Thus*

> *Yisra'ĕl was joined to Ba'al Pe'or, and the displeasure of* יהוה *burned against Yisra'ĕl.* (Numbers 25:1-3)

Baal-Peor is a Moabite god who was worshiped with obscene rituals. The name means *"Lord of the Opening"* from "Baal" meaning owner/husband and "Peor" coming from pa'ar meaning *"open wide."*

> *10 "I found Yisra'ĕl like grapes in the wilderness. I saw your fathers as the first-fruits on the fig tree in its beginning. They themselves have gone to Ba'al Pe'or, and separated themselves to shame, and became as abominable as that which they loved."* (Hosea 9:10)

The worship of Baal-Peor ***IS*** an abomination. Notice that those who join themselves to Baal-Peor also "become" an abomination before Yehovah.

Another name for Baal-Peor is Belphegor, who was depicted either as a beautiful naked woman or a bearded demon with open mouth, horns, and sharply pointed nails (the open mouth being an indicator of the sexual rites used to worship him). St. Jerome reported that statues of Baal-Peor he encountered in Syria depicted the god with a phallus in his mouth.

The worship of Baal-Peor is the worship of the "god of holes." It is the sexual act of either anal or oral sex. Any hole will do, whether it be the mouth or the anus of a man, woman or child—just so long as the man is gratified sexually.

In condemnation of those who abused Israel in the Last Days, Yehovah declares through the prophet Joel:

> *3 "And they have cast lots for My people, and have given a young man for a whore, and sold a girl for wine, and drank it."* (Joel 3:3)

Young boys and young girls are used for anal or oral sex. This can be nothing else other than the worship of Baal-Peor.

Now in these, the Last Days of this age, what do we see all around us? We see the promotion of L.G.B.T. rights around the world and the unnatural relationships between men and men as well as women and women being legalized. But most disturbingly of all, the pedophilic act against children is also being legalized in many countries around the world.

Just like Israel, a few years before they were to enter the Promised Land, when they fell for the Moabite and Midianite women, being initiated into the worship of the "god of holes," and were led astray from the purity that had kept them safe before that time, modern day Israel and nations of Israelite heritage such as the U.S., the British Commonwealth—now known as the Commonwealth of Nations,[764] etc., have also taken up the L.G.B.T. "Human Rights" cause.

Every kind of TV show imaginable, features sexual innuendo and/or explicit, illicit sexual content. Comedy shows making light of sexual improprieties as well as the "gay" lifestyle cause it to be more and more readily acceptable. This is the "new normal."

To get higher ratings, each show has to become raunchier than the one that went before it. Musicians and actors are expected to engage in this kind of depravity on TV to ensure higher ratings. All porn is depicted as anal and oral sex scenes making it part of the normal lovemaking. What are you watching and what are you being attracted to?

Amsterdam is the undisputed sex capital of Europe. Holland is the Tribe of Zebulon— one of the Twelve Tribes of Israel. Amsterdam is also one the best places to be gay, as is Los Angeles, New York, San Francisco, Copenhagen, Toronto, Sydney, Barcelona, Paris, London and Tel Aviv—all of which are heavily populated with people who are descendants of Israelite nations.

Just as the inhabitants of the land of Israel suffered as a result of a severe pestilence that claimed 24,000, the scattered nations of Israel today are about to suffer from similar plagues. As many of you know, I have been warning you of the 4th Curse coming in the 4th Sabbatical

---

[764] http://en.wikipedia.org/wiki/Member_states_of_the_Commonwealth_of_Nations

Cycle. It is the Curse of War which begins in 2017 C.E. and persists for seven years before coming to an end in 2023 C.E. Read again what this verse also has to say about the diseases that will be accompanying it:

> *23 "And if you are not instructed by Me by these, but walk contrary to Me, 24 then I also shall walk contrary to you, and I Myself shall smite you seven times for your sins. 25 And I shall bring against you a sword executing the vengeance of My covenant, and you shall gather together in your cities, and I shall send pestilence among you, and you shall be given into the hand of the enemy. 26 When I have cut off your supply of bread, ten women shall bake your bread in one oven, and they shall bring back to you your bread by weight, and you shall eat and not be satisfied."* (Leviticus 26:23-26)

Having posted this article[765] on Baal-Peor on my website, I have been asked many times if sodomy and oral sex in the context of being married is sin?

The answer is, YES it *is* a sin—even in the context of marriage. There are several reasons why.

Sodomy[766] /ˈsɒdəmi/ is generally anal sex, oral sex or sexual activity between a person and a non-human animal (bestiality), but may also include any non-procreative sexual activity. Originally, the term *sodomy* was primarily restricted to anal sex, and is derived from the story of Sodom and Gomorrah in Chapters 18 and 19 of the *Book of Genesis* in the Bible. Sodomy laws in many countries criminalized not only these behaviors, but other disfavored sexual activities as well. In the Western world, however, many of these laws have been overturned or are not routinely enforced.

1. Sodomy[767] is a sin. Similar to the meaning of Beor (Balaam's father), the Hebrew word for Sodom literally means "burning." Sodomy is defined as "anal or oral copulation with a member of

---

[765] http://sightedmoon.com/lgbt-human-rights-baal-peor/
[766] http://en.wikipedia.org/wiki/Sodomy#cite_note-Edsall-1
[767] http://thelatterdays.blogspot.ca/2009/03/worship-of-baal-peor.html

the opposite sex; copulation with a member of the same sex; or bestiality." The act is considered sodomy *even when* it pertains to the opposite sex. Heterosexuals who participate in this act are sodomites by the very definition of the word. It wouldn't take long in reviewing the Scriptures to understand how God feels about sodomy. The Bible is *not silent* on this topic.

2. It is idolatry. The word "sodomite" in the Old Testament is the word "*qadesh*" which means "male temple prostitute." The female counterpart to that (the word "*qĕdeshah*") is often translated as "harlot" or "whore." Some say that God only disapproved of this act as it related to temple prostitution. Yet, the act *itself, by its very nature,* is an act of idolatry no matter who performs it. One does not have to be a temple whore of Baal for the act to be sinful. On the contrary, one becomes a temple whore of Baal simply by giving oneself over to performing an act or engaging in any kind of ritual that is Baal-inspired. Holding true to the definition of the word sodomy, these temple prostitutes would perform homosexual acts on anyone, regardless of gender. The act itself was the *means by which* the participants were joined to or became one with Baal. The act itself was the means of worship by which Baal was sought to cross over and indwell the participants.

3. The marriage bed should be kept in honor (Hebrews 13:4). Some assert that there is an "anything goes" mentality to intimacy in marriage because "the marriage bed is undefiled." However the Bible prefaces that text by saying that marriage is first honorable. The text also states that fornication and adultery defiles the marriage bed. The word for fornication is the Greek word *porneia,* which means illicit sexual intercourse. So, sex acts that God deems as illicit are not acceptable just because they are practiced well within the confines of a marriage. These acts defile the marriage bed, which should be held in honor. The question then becomes: are acts of sodomy illicit?

4. God only gives us GOOD gifts (James 1:17). God does not give us gifts that would cause us harm. Therefore, we can look at the function, purpose, and design of certain acts to determine

whether or not these would be considered *natural* in God's eyes. If a sexual act is ordained by God (i.e. it is natural), then it would have certain inherent protections for the participants in the act.

**Design**: The woman and man are given sexual organs that physically correlate to and fit each other. They are designed to meet and come together naturally, without forced manipulation.

**Protection:** God built in special protection within the human body for this kind of interaction. The lining of the uterus is specially designed to prevent the semen from entering into the bloodstream of the woman, just to give an example. God does not provide the same protection for acts of sodomy. These acts can disrupt normal bodily functions and cause damage to bodily systems. There is also an element of danger involved in the act of oral sex performed on women that can lead to death. It is not a protected act (in terms of the body's design) the way that sexual intercourse is.

**Union:** Man and woman being joined together sexually and becoming "one flesh" occurs only during sexual intercourse.

**Procreation:** Children can only result after sexual intercourse. We can see by its design, function, and purpose that sexual intercourse between a man and woman is a natural use of sex. All of these elements work together to provide a safe, enjoyable, and purposeful interaction. The same cannot be said for acts of sodomy.

5. It is uncleanness. Apart from the physical uncleanness of the act, there is also a spiritual component. Romans, Chapter 1 describes mans degradation into becoming reprobate. Man doesn't just wake up one-day reprobate, but there are a series of steps man takes further and further into sin. The sin immediately preceding homosexuality is men and women dishonoring their bodies between themselves with uncleanness. The word for dishonor in that text is a derivative of the word honorable in the Hebrews 13:4 passage about marriage. This refers to *all* heterosexual

sexual sin, which includes oral and anal copulation, as well as bestiality, etc.

6. It is an "unnatural use." Romans 1:26 states, *"For this cause God gave them up unto vile affections: for even their women did change the natural use into that which is against nature."* The word "use" is the Greek word *"chrēsis"* which refers to use of the sexual parts of the woman. Note that there is a "natural" use and an "unnatural" use. What the women were doing with each other sexually was an unnatural use of that part of their bodies.

   Similarly, we are told in Romans 1:27 that the acts performed between the men were likewise unnatural. *"And likewise also the men, leaving the natural use of the woman, burned in their lust one toward another; men with men working that which is unseemly, and receiving in themselves that recompense of their error which was meet."* Romans 1:26-27 therefore not only condemns the affections that draw men and women to the same gender (vile affections), it also condemns the acts they performed as a result of these desires (against nature).

7. It programs the mind to be asexual. The act itself is not gender-specific. In an attempt to validate homosexuality as a norm, Jamake Highwater's book, *The Mythology of Transgression: Homosexuality as Metaphor,*[768] states how the masculine and feminine depiction of Baal-Peor represents a bi-gender nature. He goes on to say, "during the worship of Baal-Peor, priests dressed as women and priestesses dressed as men." The transgender cross-dressing is entirely consistent with the asexual nature of the act. Since it can be performed by anyone who has a mouth, gender becomes irrelevant. It is an intentional blurring of the sexes. **That makes participation in this act a critical step for Satan to use in preparing man's mind for the acceptance of homosexuality.**

---

[768] http://books.google.com/books/about/The_Mythology_of_Transgression.html?id=ECwbAAAAYAAJ

The Moabite and Midianite women performed both oral and anal sex upon the Israelites, which was and is, even today, the worship of Baal-Peor. Satan was able to lead the entire nation of Israel into sin just before they were to enter into the Land of Milk and Honey. He is doing the exact same thing now in these Last Days. Are you part of the problem or part of the solution?

As the time quickly encroaches when we will, once again, be returning to the land of Israel, there can be no mistaking how Satan has thrown the *Doctrine of Balaam* at us yet again without the majority of us even so much as realizing it.

James Dobson maintains that **80% of all the men in all churches** are involved in sexual pornography to some degree.[769] Some are extreme and some are mild in their level of involvement. Some view porn online, whereas others prefer the kind found in magazines, on TV or on videos. It is so easy to get porn today. Sexual advertising is all around us all the time. A recent study has revealed that 80% of the men in your own church or synagogue are, more than likely, into sexual pornography. Think about it.

Again, read what was said by the Apostle Peter, only now with a better understanding of what he was actually getting at. He was referring especially to those worshiping Baal-Peor.

> 10 "... and most of all those walking after the flesh in filthy lust and despising authority—bold, headstrong, speaking evil of esteemed ones, 11 whereas messengers who are greater in strength and power do not bring a slanderous accusation against them before the Master. 12 But these, like natural unreasoning beasts, having been born to be caught and destroyed, blaspheme that which they do not know, shall be destroyed in their destruction, 13 being about to receive the wages of unrighteousness, deeming indulgence in the day of pleasure, spots and blemishes, reveling in their own deceptions while they feast with you, 14 having eyes filled with an adulteress, and unable to cease from sin, enticing

---

[769] http://allnationsfamily.wordpress.com/2007/03/16/is-mary-so-contrary/

> *unstable beings, having a heart trained in greed, children of a curse, 15 having left the right way they went astray, having followed the way of Bil'am the son of Be'or, who loved the wages of unrighteousness, 16 but he was rebuked for his transgression: a dumb donkey speaking with the voice of a man restrained the madness of the prophet."* (2 Peter 2:10-16)

> *17 "These are fountains without water, clouds driven by a storm, to whom the blackest darkness is kept forever. 18 For speaking arrogant nonsense, they entice—through the lusts of the flesh, through indecencies—the ones who have indeed escaped from those living in delusion, 19 promising them freedom, though themselves being slaves of corruption—for one is a slave to whatever overcomes him. 20 For if, after they have escaped the defilements of the world through the knowledge of the Master and Saviour* יהושע *Messiah, they are again entangled in them and overcome, the latter end is worse for them than the first. 21 For it would have been better for them not to have known the way of righteousness, than having known it, to turn from the set-apart command[1] delivered unto them." [Footnote: [1]The singular "command" often means "commands"—see 1 Timothy 6:14, Deuteronomy 17:20, Psalm 19:8] 22 "For them the proverb has proved true, 'A dog returns to his own vomit,' and, 'A washed sow returns to her rolling in the mud.'"* (2 Peter 2:17-22)

Sexual immorality is spiritual harlotry. This is the doctrine of Balaam: elicit sex and greed or lust and coveting.

Our sins drive Yehovah away from us. Consider in earnest what it will take on our part for Him to return to us. I don't know about you, but I find this to be terrifying. For when His face is turned toward us, He is for us and not against us, but when He returns to His abode, His face is turned away from us and He is against us and no longer for us.

> *15 "I shall go, I shall return to My place, until they confess their guilt and seek My face, in their distress diligently search for Me."* (Hosea 5:15)

I will go[H1980] *and* return[H7725] to[H413] my place,[H4725] 'til[H5704 & H834] they acknowledge their offense,[H816] and seek[H1245] my face:[H6440] in their affliction[H6862] they will seek me early.[H7836] (Hosea 5:15)

H6862  צר  צר  tsar tsâr  *tsar, tsawr*

From H6887; *narrow*; (as a noun) a *tight* place (usually figuratively, that is, *trouble*); also a *pebble* (as in H6864); (transitively) an *opponent* (as *crowding*): –adversary, afflicted (-tion), anguish, close, distress, enemy, flint, foe, narrow, small, sorrow, strait, tribulation, trouble.

H6887  צרר  tsârar  *tsaw-rar'*

A primitive root; to *cramp*, literally or figuratively, transitively or intransitively: –adversary, (be in) afflict (-ion), besiege, bind (up), (be in, bring) distress, enemy, narrower, oppress, pangs, shut up, be in a strait (trouble), vex.

Yehovah is telling us that the same type of affliction that occurred with Dinah and Tamar is going to happen to *all* of Israel. It is only when we are in the middle of being raped as a nation, which will be thrust upon us, will we *then* seek Yehovah. Only then when we are abjectly afflicted and humbled beyond all recompense will we finally and at long last seek Him.

You only need to watch the nightly news and see how I.S.I.S. is slaughtering all men and taking the women and all the possessions from the Christian community as booty. The women and children are then turned into sex slaves. It has already begun.

I have shown you the Sabbatical Cycle in points #3, #4 and #5 (of this concluding chapter) when Israel is going to be afflicted. The ruling empire at that time will have Satan's power and authority. They will force themselves upon us, raping us both materially and physically as a nation. The king of the South's kingdom is Islam and extends across the Middle East and Africa. The king of the North's kingdom is Assyria (known as

Germany today) and involves all of Europe. When they join forces, as Daniel warns us they soon will, then they will unleash the harsh realities of war. The very same tenets I.S.I.S. is already demonstrating on other religions of Syria and Iraq, raping and pillaging those they conquer. These are the realities of war that we are witnessing in the Middle East now. Soon they will be upon the Twelve Tribes of Israel, US!

This begins in 2020 C.E.—just a few years from now.

The Holy Days of Leviticus 23 reveal to us another important point we should be aware of. The Feast of Trumpets is represented by the year 2024 C.E. This is the beginning of the 5th Curse of Captivity, which like the Curse of War, also endures for seven years, from 2024 C.E. to 2030 C.E. At the end of this period all Twelve Tribes of Israel are then brought back to the land of Israel from their captivity.

It is during this captivity that all of Israel is humbled to the point of death. They are greatly decimated by this time and in great *affliction*. Again, take note of this word *afflict*.

The end of these ten years comes in 2033 C.E. (2024-2033 is ten years). It is the same as the Ten Days of Awe that we keep in the fall during the Holy Day season. From the Feast of Trumpets to the Day of Atonement or Yom Kippur that represents the locking away of Satan, are these Ten Days of Awe.

Going back to the story of Dinah, we read what Levi and Simeon do to rectify the sin against Dinah.

> *24 And all who went out of the gate of his city listened to Ḥamor and Shekem his son; every male was circumcised, all who went out of the gate of his city. 25 And it came to be on the third day, when they were in pain, that two of the sons of Ya'aqob, Shim'on and Lĕwi, Dinah's brothers, each took his sword and came boldly upon the city and killed all the males. 26 And they killed Ḥamor and Shekem his son with the edge of the sword, and took Dinah from Shekem's house, and went out. 27 The sons of Ya'aqob came upon the*

> slain, and plundered the city, because they had defiled their sister. 28 They took their flocks and their herds, and their donkeys, and that which was in the city and that which was in the field, 29 and all their wealth. And all their little ones and their wives they took captive, and they plundered all that was in the houses. (Genesis 34:24-29)
>
> 30 And Ya'aqob said to Shim'on and Lĕwi, "You have troubled me by making me a stench among the inhabitants of the land, among the Kena'anites and the Perizzites. And I am few in number, they shall gather themselves against me and shall smite me, and I shall be destroyed, my household and I." 31 But they said, "Should he treat our sister like a whore?" (Genesis 34:30-31)

Levi and Simeon kill Shechem and Hamor. Levi is the father of Kohath, the father of Amran, the father of Moses and Aaron. Aaron is the father of Eleazar who was the father of Phineas who later stopped the plague of Moabite women. Phineas took action just as Levi and Simeon did.

The Aaronic line is the line from which all High Priests hail from.[770]

Now consider the events on the Day of Atonement:

> 26 And יהוה spoke to Mosheh, saying, 27 "On the tenth day of this seventh month is the Day of Atonement. It shall be a set-apart gathering for you. And you shall afflict your beings, and shall bring an offering made by fire to יהוה. 28 And you do no work on that same day, for it is the Day of Atonement, to make atonement for you before יהוה your Elohim. 29 For any being who is not afflicted on that same day, he shall be cut off from his people. 30 And any being who does any work on that same day, that being I shall destroy from the midst of his people. 31 You do no work—a law forever throughout your generations in all your dwellings. 32 It is a Sabbath of rest to you, and you shall afflict your beings. On the ninth

---

[770] http://en.wikipedia.org/wiki/List_of_High_Priests_of_Israel

> *day of the month at evening, from evening to evening, you observe your Sabbath."* (Leviticus 23:26-32)

At the end of these Ten Days of Awe is the Day of Atonement. It is on this day that Satan is taken out of the camp. It is upon the Azazel Goat that all the sins of Israel are placed and then a strong man is to come and lead it away from the camp. And even here, at this juncture, Satan has deceived us again by claiming to be the scapegoat. That is, the one who is blamed, but is not guilty. Satan, without a doubt, is most assuredly guilty.

When you read the procedures for the Day of Atonement in *Leviticus* 16, you will do well to compare them to the revelation found in *Revelation* 20.

> *1 And I saw a messenger coming down from the heaven, having the key to the pit of the deep and a great chain in his hand. 2 And he seized the dragon, the serpent of old, who is the Devil and Satan, and bound him for a thousand years, 3 and he threw him into the pit of the deep, and shut him up, and set a seal on him, so that he should lead the nations no more astray until the thousand years were ended. And after that he has to be released for a little while.* (Revelation 20:1-3)

Pay attention to this teaching on this Day of Atonement and consider what is being said and what is happening around us. We are to afflict our souls. We are to be so humbled that we earnestly seek Yehovah's mercy for our sins and His provision. Just as Dinah was raped and humbled by Shechem, and just as Tamar was raped and humbled by Amnon, so is Satan going to rape Israel and humble all Twelve Tribes of Israel who are now nations in these Last Days.

Satan, like Hamor, who was an ass of a man and burned with lust—even as those of Sodom burned with lust, offers free, unsolicited advice in the same form, as does the United Nations today. Just as we near the end of the 120th Jubilee Cycle, we find ourselves in a Covenant *Made With Many* on June 5th-16th, 1972 in Stockholm, Sweden—a *Covenant* that was originally suggested by the U.N. and is now accepted as law by 193 nations out of 196.

This *Covenant,* made with 193 nations, is causing the Israelite nations to allow immoral sexual activity in the form of the worship of Baal-Peor, but disguised under the *Human Rights* law as L.G.B.T. rights, which is against the *Torah.* The powers that are behind this environmental movement and *Human Rights* law are now worshiping, and having us worship, Mother Earth and/or Mother Nature and every sexual abomination imaginable, including the worship of Baal-Peor. Balaam's curse was to get Israel to sin so that Yehovah *Himself* would punish them. History is now repeating itself as our societies embrace the L.G.B.T. parades around the world and now treat those who practice Baal-Peor worship as just an alternative lifestyle and nothing more—the worst part being, it is even being taught to kindergarten children as such.

Daniel 9:27 says this: The *Covenant Made With Many* or the *Covenant Made With Death*[771] would last one week or one "shabua"—a forty-nine year period of time. Just days after the Feast of Pentecost in 1972, on June 16th, this *Covenant* was made with many and signed by 113 of a possible 196 nations and many N.G.O.'s. Forty-nine years later brings us to Pentecost 2020 C.E. As of this writing, in 2014 C.E., 193 of the 196 world's nations are now signed on to this *Covenant!*

Daniel 9:27 says that the saints will be cut off in the middle of this final 70th week, which is the 120th Jubilee Cycle of this, the 6th Millennial Day. The middle of this 120th Jubilee Cycle is 2020 C.E.

Yehovah is going to send His armies to destroy the twelve nations of Israel just as Balaam said He would once they began to sin with Baal-Peor. We are about to be so afflicted and so humbled words cannot begin to describe what is about to come. Consider these things as you afflict

---

[771] *18 And your covenant with death shall be wiped out, and your vision with hell shall not stand; when the overwhelming rod shall pass through, then you shall be beaten down by it. 19 From the time that it goes out it shall take you; for morning by morning it shall pass over, by day and by night; and it shall be only a terror to understand the message.* (Isaiah 28:18-19)

your souls during the Ten Days of Awe and on the Day of Atonement from this day forward. Mourn for your sins now.

15) The Prophecy in the *Law of Niddah* shows us that every twenty-eight years, Israel has the potential to lose a war and have her soldiers bleeding out as a filthy rag or as a menstrual rag. You can watch my teaching on this subject at: www.sightedmoon.com under the media center. I began with the creation of Adam and began noticing a pattern that kept reoccurring in twenty-eight year increments. Each Niddah Cycle lasts for seven years at a time, once every twenty-eight years the same as monthly menstrual cycles last for seven days once every twenty-eight days. With each cycle lasting seven years in our experiment I learned that when Adam died, it was during a Niddah Cycle as was the Great Flood in Noah's day. Notice below just how many patriarchs died during a given Niddah Cycle:

Adam died in 930 A.C.—a Niddah Cycle.

| Sabbath | 6th Cycle | 5th Cycle | 4th Cycle | 3rd Cycle | 2nd Cycle | 1st Cycle |
|---|---|---|---|---|---|---|
| 931 | 924 | 917 | 910 | 903 | 896 | 889 |
| 930 | 923 | 916 | 909 | 902 | 895 | 888 |
| 929 | 922 | 915 | 908 | 901 | 894 | 887 |
| 928 | 921 | 914 | 907 | 900 | 893 | 886 |
| 927 | 920 | 913 | 906 | 899 | 892 | 885 |
| 926 | 919 | 912 | 905 | 898 | 891 | 884 |
| 925 | 918 | 911 | 904 | 897 | 890 | 883 |

Enoch died in 987 A.C.—a Niddah Cycle.

| Sabbath | 6th Cycle | 5th Cycle | 4th Cycle | 3rd Cycle | 2nd Cycle | 1st Cycle |
|---|---|---|---|---|---|---|
| 1029 | 1022 | 1015 | 1008 | 1001 | 994 | 987 |
| 1028 | 1021 | 1014 | 1007 | 1000 | 993 | 986 |
| 1027 | 1020 | 1013 | 1006 | 999 | 992 | 985 |
| 1026 | 1019 | 1012 | 1005 | 998 | 991 | 984 |
| 1025 | 1018 | 1011 | 1004 | 997 | 990 | 983 |
| 1024 | 1017 | 1010 | 1003 | 996 | 989 | 982 |
| 1023 | 1016 | 1009 | 1002 | 995 | 988 | 981 |

Seth died in 1042 A.C.—a Niddah Cycle.

| Sabbath | 6th Cycle | 5th Cycle | 4th Cycle | 3rd Cycle | 2nd Cycle | 1st Cycle |
|---|---|---|---|---|---|---|
| 1078 | 1071 | 1064 | 1057 | 1050 | 1043 | 1036 |
| 1077 | 1070 | 1063 | 1056 | 1049 | 1042 | 1035 |
| 1076 | 1069 | 1062 | 1055 | 1048 | 1041 | 1034 |
| 1075 | 1068 | 1061 | 1054 | 1047 | 1040 | 1033 |
| 1074 | 1067 | 1060 | 1053 | 1046 | 1039 | 1032 |
| 1073 | 1066 | 1059 | 1052 | 1045 | 1038 | 1031 |
| 1072 | 1065 | 1058 | 1051 | 1044 | 1037 | 1030 |

Kenan died in 1235 A.C.—a Niddah Cycle

| Sabbath | 6th Cycle | 5th Cycle | 4th Cycle | 3rd Cycle | 2nd Cycle | 1st Cycle |
|---|---|---|---|---|---|---|
| 1274 | 1267 | 1260 | 1253 | 1246 | 1239 | 1232 |
| 1273 | 1266 | 1259 | 1252 | 1245 | 1238 | 1231 |
| 1272 | 1265 | 1258 | 1251 | 1244 | 1237 | 1230 |
| 1271 | 1264 | 1257 | 1250 | 1243 | 1236 | 1229 |
| 1270 | 1263 | 1256 | 1249 | 1242 | 1235 | 1228 |
| 1269 | 1262 | 1255 | 1248 | 1241 | 1234 | 1227 |
| 1268 | 1261 | 1254 | 1247 | 1240 | 1233 | 1226 |

Mahalalel died in 1290 A.C.—a Niddah Cycle.

| Sabbath | 6th Cycle | 5th Cycle | 4th Cycle | 3rd Cycle | 2nd Cycle | 1st Cycle |
|---|---|---|---|---|---|---|
| 1323 | 1316 | 1309 | 1302 | 1295 | 1288 | 1281 |
| 1322 | 1315 | 1308 | 1301 | 1294 | 1287 | 1280 |
| 1321 | 1314 | 1307 | 1300 | 1293 | 1286 | 1279 |
| 1320 | 1313 | 1306 | 1299 | 1292 | 1285 | 1278 |
| 1319 | 1312 | 1305 | 1298 | 1291 | 1284 | 1277 |
| 1318 | 1311 | 1304 | 1297 | 1290 | 1283 | 1276 |
| 1317 | 1310 | 1303 | 1296 | 1289 | 1282 | 1275 |

The Flood took place in 1656 A.C.—a Niddah Cycle.

| Sabbath | 6th Cycle | 5th Cycle | 4th Cycle | 3rd Cycle | 2nd Cycle | 1st Cycle |
|---|---|---|---|---|---|---|
| 1666 | 1659 | 1652 | 1645 | 1638 | 1631 | 1624 |
| 1665 | 1658 | 1651 | 1644 | 1637 | 1630 | 1623 |
| 1664 | 1657 | 1650 | 1643 | 1636 | 1629 | 1622 |
| 1663 | 1656 | 1649 | 1642 | 1635 | 1628 | 1621 |
| 1662 | 1655 | 1648 | 1641 | 1634 | 1627 | 1620 |
| 1661 | 1654 | 1647 | 1640 | 1633 | 1626 | 1619 |
| 1660 | 1653 | 1646 | 1639 | 1632 | 1625 | 1618 |

Sodom and Gomorrah was destroyed in 2047 A.C.—a Niddah Cycle.

| Sabbath | 6th Cycle | 5th Cycle | 4th Cycle | 3rd Cycle | 2nd Cycle | 1st Cycle |
|---|---|---|---|---|---|---|
| 2058 | 2051 | 2044 | 2037 | 2030 | 2023 | 2016 |
| 2057 | 2050 | 2043 | 2036 | 2029 | 2022 | 2015 |
| 2056 | 2049 | 2042 | 2035 | 2028 | 2021 | 2014 |
| 2055 | 2048 | 2041 | 2034 | 2027 | 2020 | 2013 |
| 2054 | 2047 | 2040 | 2033 | 2026 | 2019 | 2012 |
| 2053 | 2046 | 2039 | 2032 | 2025 | 2018 | 2011 |
| 2052 | 2045 | 2038 | 2031 | 2024 | 2017 | 2010 |

Melchizedek—also known as Shem—died in 2158 A.C.—a Niddah Cycle. In 2187 A.C., Eber died. Esau threatened Jacob who fled to Laban and began his seven years of servitude lasting from 2185 A.C.–2191 A.C., in return for Rachel's hand and is deceived in the end and marries Leah in 2191 A.C.—also a Niddah Cycle.

| Sabbath | 6th Cycle | 5th Cycle | 4th Cycle | 3rd Cycle | 2nd Cycle | 1st Cycle |
|---|---|---|---|---|---|---|
| 2205 | 2198 | 2191 | 2184 | 2177 | 2170 | 2163 |
| 2204 | 2197 | 2190 | 2183 | 2176 | 2169 | 2162 |
| 2203 | 2196 | 2189 | 2182 | 2175 | 2168 | 2161 |
| 2202 | 2195 | 2188 | 2181 | 2174 | 2167 | 2160 |
| 2201 | 2194 | 2187 | 2180 | 2173 | 2166 | 2159 |
| 2200 | 2193 | 2186 | 2179 | 2172 | 2165 | 2158 |
| 2199 | 2192 | 2185 | 2178 | 2171 | 2164 | 2157 |

Joseph is sold into slavery in 2216 A.C.—a Niddah Cycle.

| Sabbath | 6th Cycle | 5th Cycle | 4th Cycle | 3rd Cycle | 2nd Cycle | 1st Cycle |
|---|---|---|---|---|---|---|
| 2254 | 2247 | 2240 | 2233 | 2226 | 2219 | 2212 |
| 2253 | 2246 | 2239 | 2232 | 2225 | 2218 | 2211 |
| 2252 | 2245 | 2238 | 2231 | 2224 | 2217 | 2210 |
| 2251 | 2244 | 2237 | 2230 | 2223 | 2216 | 2209 |
| 2250 | 2243 | 2236 | 2229 | 2222 | 2215 | 2208 |
| 2249 | 2242 | 2235 | 2228 | 2221 | 2214 | 2207 |
| 2248 | 2241 | 2234 | 2227 | 2220 | 2213 | 2206 |

The 10 Northern Tribes of Israel fall to Assyria in 723 B.C.—a Niddah Cycle.

| Sabbath | 6th Cycle | 5th Cycle | 4th Cycle | 3rd Cycle | 2nd Cycle | 1st Cycle |
|---|---|---|---|---|---|---|
| -701 | -708 | -715 | -722 | -729 | -736 | -743 |
| -702 | -709 | -716 | -723 | -730 | -737 | -744 |
| -703 | -710 | -717 | -724 | -731 | -738 | -745 |
| -704 | -711 | -718 | -725 | -732 | -739 | -746 |
| -705 | -712 | -719 | -726 | -733 | -740 | -747 |
| -706 | -713 | -720 | -727 | -734 | -741 | -748 |
| -707 | -714 | -721 | -728 | -735 | -742 | -749 |

The Tribe of Judah falls to Babylon in 586 B.C.—a Niddah Cycle.

| Sabbath | 6th Cycle | 5th Cycle | 4th Cycle | 3rd Cycle | 2nd Cycle | 1st Cycle |
|---|---|---|---|---|---|---|
| -554 | -561 | -568 | -575 | -582 | -589 | -596 |
| -555 | -562 | -569 | -576 | -583 | -590 | -597 |
| -556 | -563 | -570 | -577 | -584 | -591 | -598 |
| -557 | -564 | -571 | -578 | -585 | -592 | -599 |
| -558 | -565 | -572 | -579 | -586 | -593 | -600 |
| -559 | -566 | -573 | -580 | -587 | -594 | -601 |
| -560 | -567 | -574 | -581 | -588 | -595 | -602 |

Yehshua was born in 3 B.C.—the year the Word became flesh and King Herod had all male children and infants two years of age and younger killed. Yehshua was crucified on Passover in 31 C.E.- a Niddah Cycle

| Sabbath | 6th Cycle | 5th Cycle | 4th Cycle | 3rd Cycle | 2nd Cycle | 1st Cycle |
|---|---|---|---|---|---|---|
| 35 | 28 | 21 | 14 | 7 | -1 | -8 |
| 34 | 27 | 20 | 13 | 6 | -2 | -9 |
| 33 | 26 | 19 | 12 | 5 | -3 | -10 |
| 32 | 25 | 18 | 11 | 4 | -4 | -11 |
| 31 | 24 | 17 | 10 | 3 | -5 | -12 |
| 30 | 23 | 16 | 9 | 2 | -6 | -13 |
| 29 | 22 | 15 | 8 | 1 | -7 | -14 |

I also noticed that the Vietnam War, which the U.S.A. did not win, was during a Niddah Cycle.

| Sabbath | 6th Cycle | 5th Cycle | 4th Cycle | 3rd Cycle | 2nd Cycle | 1st Cycle |
|---|---|---|---|---|---|---|
| 1995 | 1988 | 1981 | 1974 | 1967 | 1960 | 1953 |
| 1994 | 1987 | 1980 | 1973 | 1966 | 1959 | 1952 |
| 1993 | 1986 | 1979 | 1972 | 1965 | 1958 | 1951 |
| 1992 | 1985 | 1978 | 1971 | 1964 | 1957 | 1950 |
| 1991 | 1984 | 1977 | 1970 | 1963 | 1956 | 1949 |
| 1990 | 1983 | 1976 | 1969 | 1962 | 1955 | 1948 |
| 1989 | 1982 | 1975 | 1968 | 1961 | 1954 | 1947 |

And, as we follow human history down through the ages up to our time now, we see that the 4th Sabbatical Cycle from 2017 C.E.–2023 C.E. is a Niddah Cycle when we can also expect our soldiers to die and bleed out once again on the battlefield.

| Sabbath | 6th Cycle | 5th Cycle | 4th Cycle | 3rd Cycle | 2nd Cycle | 1st Cycle |
|---|---|---|---|---|---|---|
| 2044 | 2037 | 2030 | 2023 | 2016 | 2009 | 2002 |
| 2043 | 2036 | 2029 | 2022 | 2015 | 2008 | 2001 |
| 2042 | 2035 | 2028 | 2021 | 2014 | 2007 | 2000 |
| 2041 | 2034 | 2027 | 2020 | 2013 | 2006 | 1999 |
| 2040 | 2033 | 2026 | 2019 | 2012 | 2005 | 1998 |
| 2039 | 2032 | 2025 | 2018 | 2011 | 2004 | 1997 |
| 2038 | 2031 | 2024 | 2017 | 2010 | 2003 | 1996 |

16) In the Bible is another woman known as the "Great Whore" and "Babylon." The first time we encounter her is when Abraham defeats the four kings who kidnapped Lot. This was the year 2027 A.C.

| Sabbath | 6th Cycle | 5th Cycle | 4th Cycle | 3rd Cycle | 2nd Cycle | 1st Cycle |
|---|---|---|---|---|---|---|
| 2058 | 2051 | 2044 | 2037 | 2030 | 2023 | 2016 |
| 2057 | 2050 | 2043 | 2036 | 2029 | 2022 | 2015 |
| 2056 | 2049 | 2042 | 2035 | 2028 | 2021 | 2014 |
| 2055 | 2048 | 2041 | 2034 | 2027 | 2020 | 2013 |
| 2054 | 2047 | 2040 | 2033 | 2026 | 2019 | 2012 |
| 2053 | 2046 | 2039 | 2032 | 2025 | 2018 | 2011 |
| 2052 | 2045 | 2038 | 2031 | 2024 | 2017 | 2010 |

When we count each Niddah Cycle for this "whore" from this date forward, we have many interesting periods we can look at. I will leave this part of it up to you, to do your own digging and inquiry. But, to help get you off to a good start, you are to look for those wars which this "whore" has lost and for her soldiers who are bleeding out. This whore is Egypt, Babylon, Rome and the European Empire (now known as the European Union).

Although I could show you many that match, I will only show you three for the sake of brevity.

609 B.C.—the year Assyria fell to the Babylonians.

| Sabbath | 6th Cycle | 5th Cycle | 4th Cycle | 3rd Cycle | 2nd Cycle | 1st Cycle |
|---|---|---|---|---|---|---|
| -603 | -610 | -617 | -624 | -631 | -638 | -645 |
| -604 | -611 | -618 | -625 | -632 | -639 | -646 |
| -605 | -612 | -619 | -626 | -633 | -640 | -647 |
| -606 | -613 | -620 | -627 | -634 | -641 | -648 |
| -607 | -614 | -621 | -628 | -635 | -642 | -649 |
| -608 | -615 | -622 | -629 | -636 | -643 | -650 |
| -609 | -616 | -623 | -630 | -637 | -644 | -651 |

When I first did this, I expected World Wars I and II to match the cycle I had just shown you concerning Israel. But they did not. The reason they did not line up was because I was looking at Israel's menstrual cycles. The whore has a different menstrual cycle altogether and once I traced it out, I then realized the year Assyria was defeated in 609 B.C., as well as World War I from 1914 C.E.–1918 C.E., were both a part of the European whore's menstrual cycle. And as I counted four more weeks of years after World War I, I could also plainly see how World War II, which lasted from 1939 C.E.–1945 C.E., was also part and parcel of the whore's menstrual cycle as well.

| Sabbath | 6th Cycle | 5th Cycle | 4th Cycle | 3rd Cycle | 2nd Cycle | 1st Cycle |
|---------|-----------|-----------|-----------|-----------|-----------|-----------|
| 1946 | 1939 | 1932 | 1925 | 1918 | 1911 | 1904 |
| 1945 | 1938 | 1931 | 1924 | 1917 | 1910 | 1903 |
| 1944 | 1937 | 1930 | 1923 | 1916 | 1909 | 1902 |
| 1943 | 1936 | 1929 | 1922 | 1915 | 1908 | 1901 |
| 1942 | 1935 | 1928 | 1921 | 1914 | 1907 | 1900 |
| 1941 | 1934 | 1927 | 1920 | 1913 | 1906 | 1899 |
| 1940 | 1933 | 1926 | 1919 | 1912 | 1905 | 1898 |

As I continue to follow this natural progression right up to this last Jubilee Cycle, I also have come to see how the European Whore is going to have a Niddah Cycle from 2024 C.E.–2030 C.E., the exact same timeframe in which the Two Witnesses begin carrying out their orders to shut up the heavens, ensuring there will be no rain for 3½ years during this same time.

| Sabbath | 6th Cycle | 5th Cycle | 4th Cycle | 3rd Cycle | 2nd Cycle | 1st Cycle |
|---------|-----------|-----------|-----------|-----------|-----------|-----------|
| 2044 | 2037 | 2030 | 2023 | 2016 | 2009 | 2002 |
| 2043 | 2036 | 2029 | 2022 | 2015 | 2008 | 2001 |
| 2042 | 2035 | 2028 | 2021 | 2014 | 2007 | 2000 |
| 2041 | 2034 | 2027 | 2020 | 2013 | 2006 | 1999 |
| 2040 | 2033 | 2026 | 2019 | 2012 | 2005 | 1998 |
| 2039 | 2032 | 2025 | 2018 | 2011 | 2004 | 1997 |
| 2038 | 2031 | 2024 | 2017 | 2010 | 2003 | 1996 |

17) In this book I have shown you how the 2300 days begins at Shavuot (Pentecost) in 2020 C.E. and goes to the Feast of Trumpets in 2026 C.E. The 3½ years the Two Witnesses work commences at the Feast of Trumpets in 2026 C.E. and goes until Passover 2030 C.E. This is when the woman, Israel, flees into the wilderness for the 1260 days from Passover 2030 C.E. until Satan is locked away in 2033 C.E.

18) The 1335 days begins at the Feast of Trumpets in 2030 C.E. I say this because the 144,000 of Revelation who must go through the Great Tribulation.

> *13 And one of the elders answered, saying to me, Who are these who are arrayed in white robes, and from where do they come? 14 And I said to him, Sir, you know. And he said to me, These are the ones who came out of the great tribulation and have washed their robes, and have whitened them in the blood of the Lamb.* (Revelation 7:13-14)

They cannot be changed until the dead rise up first and this takes place after the Feast of Trumpets in 2030, 1335 days later is Shavuot (Pentecost) 2033.

> *51 Behold, I speak a mystery to you; we shall not all fall asleep, but we shall all be changed; 52 in a moment, in a glance of an eye, at the last trumpet. For a trumpet shall sound, and the dead shall be raised incorruptible, and we shall all be changed. 53 For this corruptible must put on incorruption, and this mortal must put on immortality.* (1Corinthians 15:51-53)

The resurrection of the saints takes place at Shavuot (Pentecost) 2033 C.E. This is our current opinion and we may change as more information is revealed.

> *12 Blessed is he who waits and comes to the thousand three hundred and thirty-five days.* (Daniel 12:12)

19) It is also my belief at this time that the 1290 days of Daniel 12 begins at the same time as the 2300 days of Daniel 8. From Shavuot (Pentecost) 2020 C.E. when the 2300 days of *hell* begin until the abomination is set up 1290 days later brings us to Christmas 2024 C.E.

> *11 And from the time that the daily sacrifice shall be taken away, and the desolating abomination set up, a thousand two hundred and ninety days shall occur.* (Daniel 12:11)

Ladies and Gentlemen, Brethren and family alike, we are just a few short years away from this terrible, terrible time when our soldiers and military will be utterly destroyed. Our defenses unable to protect us from the German led military machine and those Islamic suicidal hoards that are about to come against us in this epic battle. This is the King of the North, Europe, united with the King of South Islam.

Because, we Israelites, have broken the Covenant that our ancestors agreed to at Mount Sinai, we now must pay for having done so with our very own lives. Yes Yehshua did pay this price for us "IF" we would repent and turn back and begin to keep the Covenant once again. But for those who refuse to do so, there is no sacrificial bloodshed. There is no atoning sacrifice. It is only shed for those who repent.

Your own bible tells you many times that if you will not repent, then, you will go into captivity. You will eat the flesh of your own sons and your own daughters. You will die by the sword and by famine. Your wives and your daughters will be used as sex slaves. Your sons will be sold for sex for a bottle of wine.

You only need to watch the news of the atrocities that come out of Syria, or Somalia, or Sudan or any other North African nation that is gripped in the battle between Islamic forces and Christians. You can read of the many rapes already taking place in Norway and Sweden and England by Islamic gangs of men as they exercise their rights. According to the Koran they can legally rape any woman who is not of the same Islamic faith. And they do this to girls as young as twelve.

Your bible tells you that 90% of Israel is about to be destroyed. Think about this fact. Think about just how many 90% of the USA's population of 300 + million actually is. What this is telling us is that only 30 million will survive. For Canada this is about 3 million survivors, Britain, about 5.4 million and Australia about 2 million.

10% of the current populations of each of the 12 Israelite nations will be left and multiple millions will be destroyed.

You have only one choice and that is to repent and begin to keep the 7th day Sabbath from sunset Friday to Sunset Saturday. You will also need to begin to keep the Holy Days of Lev 23 and not add any others to the 7 that are there. No exceptions. And you need to keep the next Sabbatical year from Aviv 2016 to Aviv 2017. You need to do this in order to show Yehovah you will be obedient and then He will protect you and keep you safe and feed you. No amount of food stored up or ammo and guns you have or any secret hiding place is going to save you. Yehovah has said that every single one of you will be removed from your place. But the rebellious ones who will not obey will die along the road and will not come into the Promised Land.

*40 If they shall confess their wilfulness and the wilfulness of their fathers, with their sin which they sinned against Me, and that also they have walked contrary to Me, 41 I also will walk contrary to them and will bring them into the land of their enemies. If then their uncircumcised hearts are humbled, and they then pay for their iniquity, 42 then I will remember My covenant with Jacob, and also My covenant with Isaac, and also My covenant with Abraham I will remember. And I will remember the land. 43 The land also shall be forsaken by them, and shall enjoy its sabbaths, while it lies waste without them. And they shall accept the punishment of their iniquities; because, even because they despised My judgments, and because their soul hated My statutes. 44 And yet for all that, when they are in the land of their enemies, I will not cast them away, neither will I hate them, to destroy them utterly and to break My covenant with them. For I am Yehovah their God. 45 But for their sakes, I will remember the covenant of their ancestors, whom I brought forth out of the land of Egypt in the sight of the heathen, so that I might be their God. I am Jehovah. 46 These are the statutes and judgments and laws, which Jehovah made between Him and the sons of Israel in Mount Sinai by the hand of Moses.* (Leviticus 26:40-46)

# Epilogue

My first book, *The Prophecies of Abraham*,[772] was written in the form of a series of newsletters from my web site sightedmoon.com. These News Letters were edited into a book at the request of the brethren, and *The Prophecies of Abraham* was published by Authorhouse[773] in March of 2010. Many people struggled with understanding *The Prophecies of Abraham* due to the fact that the Sabbatical and Jubilee Year Cycles were all so new to them. However, those who did read it, did so as many as four times, learning more and more each time, as they read it from cover to cover.

I had no intention of ever writing another book, but I received an onslaught of emails and letters comprised primarily of the same questions being asked over and over again in an effort to better understand the Sabbatical and Jubilee Cycles. In response to these questions, I had to write my second book, *Remembering the Sabbatical Years of 2016*, which was published by Xlibris[774] in 2013. In this book I made a special point to take every question I had ever been asked about the Sabbatical Years—including the objections, how to prove when they are, and how things became twisted over time. I set forth to answer every question put to me by my readership by providing my readers with the simplest and easiest of all possible explanations with regard to their questions so that anyone could understand. *Remembering the Sabbatical Years*

---

[772] http://www.authorhouse.co.uk/Bookstore/BookSearchResults.aspx?Search=The%20Prophecies%20of%20Abraham
[773] http://www.authorhouse.co.uk/
[774] http://www.xlibris.com/

*of 2016* has proven to be instrumental in helping people to understand when the Sabbatical Years are and how to keep them. It continues to educate people *to this day*.

The publishing of my third and current book, *The 2,300 Days of Hell* has singularly been one of the most exhaustive endeavors I have ever undertaken. It first began as *The 70 Shabua of Daniel* but few people understood what the word "shabua" meant, so late in 2013, the title was changed to the current one. By understanding the word "shabua" and how it relates to the forty-nine days of Shavuot or Pentecost is actually the key to understanding Daniel's prophecy in Daniel 9.

I wrote this book in the fall and winter of 2012-2013. It just flowed out of me and onto the virtual pages of my Word program. I began to write *The 2,300 Days of Hell* and had it finished for the most part before I had published *Remembering the Sabbatical Years of 2016* in February of 2013. All of these books are interrelated and provide the reader with an ever deepening understanding of the many things that are revealed and made manifest just by coming into an accurate and complete understanding of the Sabbatical and Jubilee Year Cycles.

Shortly thereafter, a number of things happened which made it very apparent to me that I needed to do more research and explain precisely who the Ten Lost Tribes of Israel are and incorporate this critical information into *The 2,300 Days of Hell*. I had to prove this beyond all reasonable doubt in order to explain whom Daniel's people are, in order for everyone to understand to whom this particular Bible prophecy is being applied to. It is not just for the Jews in the State of Israel.

The rewriting of certain chapters and the research that went into other chapters lasted the entirety of that winter. It went to the editor that winter as well. At the same time, I had it proofed by some trusted friends. Along with the edits and the rewrites that went on during that time, I also incorporated any suggestions or corrections the proofreaders came up with.

That winter of 2013 I was invited to speak for all eight days of Sukkot to a mixed group of people hailing from all over the country and around the world about the very things I was currently writing about. It would be the first time I had ever been given the opportunity to share it all, in chronological order in one series of presentations. The people researching and working on the book with me were highly motivated to have me be the keynote speaker at that particular Sukkot celebration because they recognized the truths and could now see them coming to life on the nightly news.

As The *2,300 Days of Hell* was being edited and rewritten during the winter of 2013, I had to develop teachings about each chapter of the book to present to the brethren. Each teaching would take about a month to put together using Power Point and I had eleven teachings to prepare for all eight days of the Feast. (two teachings on both High Holy Days, two on Shabbat and one teaching for each of the other days). In addition to the rewrite, edits, further research, and of course, the weekly newsletter, I was also able to present some of the completed presentations to a local assembly a few hours away. It was a very busy year for me.

By the time Sukkot came in the fall of 2013 I had just made the final edits to the Power Point presentation. The edits to the book, however, were ongoing. This work in progress was now becoming a huge project that I just wanted to finally be finished with. World events were proving the book true and those who had read it were yelling out the warnings to others. I.S.I.S. was inflicting their reign of terror across Syria and Iraq and making threats to the rest of the world. Right now, as I prepare to publish this book, it is September 11, otherwise known as 9/11 and the U.S.A. has just announced they are going after I.S.I.S. If they succeed, then another group will rise up and take their place after this, using a different name.

I presented my teachings at Sukkot in 2013 and we were able to videotape them and have them edited by a professional. Each day as I walked around the camp, after presenting the teaching for that day, I would come upon people who had their Bible open and were studying the very things I had just taught on. Some were alone and others were in groups openly discussing these things. It was new to them and although they had heard it all before in bits and pieces, no one had ever presented it to them using the Sabbatical and Jubilee Cycles as the basis by which to fully understand biblical prophecy.

I proceeded with a considerable degree of trepidation when I first began to present what Yehovah had shown me, but soon realized and became cognizant of just how much people wanted to hear all of what I had come to understand. By the time I reached the final presentation mark toward the week's end, I had the entire audience in tears as they could see these truths I was presenting in relation to the nightly news. They got it, the very same way those who had been reading the e-book were also understanding and amazed by these very same and now obvious truths.

As I struggled to get this message out, there was another dynamic in the works that I had noticed earlier but did not realize the full extent of until a number of things blew up in my face. Each time someone would come to assist me in this work involving any or all aspects of sharing my message—whether it involved videotaping, research, editing, the website or anything involving technology, something would happen to each of those people that would eventually take them away from helping me do whatever it was that needed to be done and slow down the presentation of this work.

The more we did and the more work that needed to get done, the more these people were attacked and restrained from doing more. It would visit us in every way imaginable—from deaths in the family to spouses fighting and breaking up. Others got so sick they would end up in I.C.U. This trend has continued to be the case right up to this very moment in time when I am about to publish this book. The problems continue to insurmountably pile up preventing this book from being published. Delays and more delays, but also, publishing problems or a lack of time afforded me to finish a task. I am still struggling intensely to make this book available for public consumption along with all the other things myself and those helping me are trying to get done.

One day as I discussed this with some friends, I realized what was going on. We are told in Daniel how the message he had seen made him sick for weeks and that the angel who was dispatched to him to explain the message was held up by one of Satan's demons for twenty-*one days*. How any demon could hold back an angel sent by Yehovah is far beyond my capacity to comprehend and yet, that is what the Scriptures say.

Satan does not want this message to be presented. He wants it stopped because the message in this book all too clearly conveys that his time is almost up. This book, coupled with an accurate and complete understanding of the Sabbatical Cycles, shows the reader precisely when Satan is going to be locked away and also provides a timeframe for when all twelve tribes of Israel are going to be attacked, destroyed and wind up in captivity. It is my firm belief that Satan is going out of his way to hinder and thwart this message as much as he can in order to keep this information hidden. Satan would rather we all remained in the dark, but this book explains Daniel's Prophecy unlike any other teaching and its true meaning is both stunning and shocking to all who read it.

This brings me to 2014. I hired the publisher in late spring of 2014 when I thought I had completed the book and it was ready to go to print. One of the main issues the publisher began having with this book being published, however, was that it has too many scriptural quotes in it. As shocking to me as this was, I was not about to remove any of the biblical quotes I had and take away from the message I was sharing. I have wanted to throw in the towel on many a day after dealing with people who do not understand how to engage in any type of exegetic study on biblical subjects. The unsuccessful, yet altogether exasperating, back and forth during the spring and summer of 2014 has really taken its toll on me and drained me dry.

In the summer of 2014, I began to present another teaching on the Four Blood Moons and the Two Dark Moons and explain the elephant in the room that no one else was addressing. After presenting this subject, those in the audience were dumbfounded at the obvious answer to the problems posed by those now presenting this subject. Because of the audience's reactions to the presentation, I have now organized this information into what will be our fourth book, but it is only going to be around fifty pages in length. Considering I never wanted to write in the first place, and yet to now have four books to my credit, or more ultimately, Yehovah's credit, is nothing short of amazing to me. Each of them is revolving around some aspect of the Sabbatical and Jubilee Cycles.

Everything I am learning, ranging from the curses of Leviticus 26 for not keeping the Sabbatical Years to the 70 weeks of Daniel 9:24-27 and the Four Blood Moons, as well as the geo-political events that continue to draw us into wars in the Middle East—all point to the defeat and destruction of the U.S.A., the U.K. and her commonwealth nations.

These things all must come to pass in order for prophecy to be fulfilled. We are also told in Amos that Yehovah does nothing unless He first warns us through His prophets. In Ezekiel we are told that if we see war coming, we are to warn others. It is time to get ready for that time that is directly in front of us. It is time to obey Yehovah and to keep His Commandments. Most people will not keep the fourth one, which includes the weekly seventh day Sabbath, the Holy Days of Leviticus 23 and the Sabbatical and Jubilee Years of Leviticus 25. It is time to get off your high horse and humble yourself before your Creator and do as He tells you to do.

You no longer have years to continue doing your own thing your own way. Things will not carry on as they always have. At some point in history, some group of people had to be that last generation who would live through all of these terrible times. That time is now. That generation is you and your family. You have been put here for such a time as this. It is time to return to obeying Yehovah and to stop with all excuses. NOW is the time.

I would now like for you to read some of the comments I have collected about the three books I've written thus far, the presentations I have done about this book and the next one to come. These are the comments from those who have read or heard me teach. If you want me to come to your group, go to my web site and write me. admin@sightedmoon.com

*Shalom,*

*I have been reading Joe's newsletters for years, and for years he has been defending his stance that we are to follow the Torah even if not in the Land. The use of pictures was actually a wise teaching tool in order to "shock and awe" some people who just don't get it into finally understanding. It was his way of trying to finally get some hard-hearted people to see, hear, and understand. Joe is not a professor at Cambridge (although he's certainly smarter than one!), but a Canadian ditch-digger. Sometimes his speech/ways reflect that. And actually, it's a part of him I actually love.*

*I have learned more from Joe's newsletters in the past few years than I did for a decade in church! His (Yehovah's) message is so important, it could mean the difference between getting raised in the first or second resurrection. Yes, his message has such eternal significance. You see, most believers keep the weekly Sabbath, but not the yearly Sabbath. "Guard my Sabbaths..." (Lev. 26:2). The next Sabbatical year is approaching quickly and the message must get out. Please let those who want to come, come. "Warn" them in advance if you have to, but please don't be a "stumbling block to the blind." I guarantee you will not be disappointed.*

*Sincere thanks,*

*E.E., Colorado*

*The 2,300 Days of Hell and The 70 Shabua of Daniel.*

*This book is an amazing expression that follows the thread of the House of Israel from YHVH's making of the Covenant with Abraham, concerning Abraham's seed through Isaac, all the way to the present day. For those who are first descendants of the House of Israel, but most importantly, the Children of YHWH, who are the obedient ones of that Covenant in this present day.*

*Joseph has repeatedly stated that all this information is in the history books and that it is a mystery to him that it is not being taught in all the schools today. Joseph is a man of the earth, a ditch digger; whose fingernails, like mine, (I am a Soil Scientist) get dirt under them every day. I give him credit that he persevered in this search and expression like no one else has done. YHWH has blessed him in giving him understanding through which these conclusions, until these books, have not been given expression. Daniel is "sealed up until the end" for the specific reason that it is an end-time prophecy that is unlocked by what is written in The 2,300 Days of Hell and the 70 Shabua of Daniel and Joseph's other books as well.*

*This thread, most certainly, can only be understood when Joseph Dumond's three books, The Prophecies of Abraham, Remembering the Sabbatical Years of 2016 and The 2,300 Days of Hell and the 70 Shabua of Daniel are understood from beginning to end. Understanding comes from the knowledge of the Jubilee Cycles and Shabua (sevens) Cycles, which are the manner in which YHWH's "periods of time" (Gen 6:3) are measured.*

*Once we are armed with this simple fact, that Jubilees are cycles that are paralleled by the Feast of Weeks manner of counting seven "sevens" plus one; the "plus one" being the first day of the next cycle of days (or the next week). It is then that the 7 Shabua or cycles of weeks/years becomes clearly understood as the completed Jubilee. The Jubilee year is simply the first year of the following Jubilee cycle. Within this definition, all known Shabbats; whether weekly, yearly (7 Feasts), seven year land rests or Jubilee (double land rests) those Commanded of YHWH, fall into place. I spent 3 months proving to myself that the Prophecies of Abraham was, in fact, true.*

*With this as my personal testimony, my understanding of The 2,300 Days of Hell and the 70 Shabua of Daniel was easily discernible; even for me. I confess I have nowhere near the appetite nor endurance for history that Joseph has. However, through his well documented and referenced publications, even I was able to gain understanding of who I am, where I am and what it will take for me to become a participant in the greatest event this earth will ever experience: the return of Yeshua our Bridegroom! Who, by shedding His blood and gaining power over death, returns as a new man. He will overcome the divorce required by Deuteronomy 24 of his unclean wife (Israel) who was and still is unclean, by whoring after all the other mighty ones—the false gods of HaSatan. Yeshua, being a new "man" by being resurrected, can retake His bride; those who voluntarily return to the Sinai Covenant and do as Yeshua stated in John 14:15 which states: If ye love me, keep my commandments.*

*The 2,300 Days of Hell and the 70 Shabua of Daniel reveals when the Jubilees occurred as well as at what point within the Jubilees the curses fell on disobedient Israel. It also explains when these curses are most likely to fall on us, disobedient Israel. YHWH's cycles appear to be highly repetitive and that means it can be predicted with some degree of certainty when curses will affect us.*

*Brothers and sisters, time is short and knowledge of just how short has given me added strength to prepare to face what is coming. I no longer have to guess where we are in this last Jubilee, Yah's cycles reveal it!*

*The House of Israel is YHWH's chosen people. Being part of Israel is your choice since it is a matter of adoption by entering the Covenant and obeying His commands. His plan for us is right on schedule. The clock is ticking and if you are still unaware of the impending 2,300 Days of HELL that are approaching, you need to read these books.*

*In my opinion, without following the thread described above, you cannot understand one of the most definitive keys to the Daniel prophecies of the Bible! That includes its Covenants, both its promises as well as curses; which means you may very well miss your destiny of being part of the Marriage with the resurrected new man who is YHWH thru His right Arm, Yeshua our Messiah.*

*J.F., Ohio*

*I first heard Joseph Dumond speaking at the Petra Hostel in Jerusalem during Sukkot 2010. He had just started teaching his understanding of the chronological patterns of biblical events during sabbatical and jubilee years. I found this absolutely interesting and decided to look into it farther. Since then I have read and studied both his books, The Prophecies of Abraham and Sabbatical Years 2016 and have listened to many of his videos. I also attended Sukkot at Falls Creek Falls Park in Tennessee in 2013 where he spoke for 8 days straight. Everyone who attended was awestruck with the slam dunk truth and power of his messages and they left that place a different person and with a very different outlook on life and their relationship with their Creator. I look forward to the release of his latest book, 2,300 Days of Hell, because I know it will be as profound and as biblically provable as all his other work.*

*I cannot put into words how much my understanding of prophecy and of the urgency and seriousness of the times we are living in has increased since I have come into contact with Joseph's tireless teachings. I was never so aware of the awesomeness of our Creator and of His immense love for all mankind and the incredible Master Plan he has for each and every one of us as I am now. I am humbled beyond words and my only desire now is to serve Him with all my being because now I understand what it is all about and why we are living in such frightening times as we are right now... it is because of our choices which have resulted in either the blessings or the cursings of Leviticus 26. I know these apply to us today because I have learned the identity of the Lost 10 tribes of Israel. I am one of them. I challenge everyone to study, prove and learn these truths and to return to the ancient paths that we have all been called to follow. There is nothing more important in these very scary times into which the world is very rapidly spiraling.*

*B.H. Alberta*

*Review for the 2,300 Days of Hell and The Two Witnesses*

*(1) Scripture begins with 'In the beginning.' Our Creator created time with man in mind for His purpose. His promised blessings and curses will be delivered in His time. Understanding how His plan for mankind on earth will finally climax before His Kingdom comes is available in this book. These prophecies in particular are a message for these end days. Here a little, there a little. Joseph Dumond has put the line upon line all together and made it comprehendible. This is why you should buy this book because it's all in one place. After reading this book and proving it for yourself, you too will finally be able to see and share what will befall anyone not living in accordance to His expressed will now and in the final days. Sadly, many will not even try and therefore will not make it into His Kingdom. The 2,300 Days of Hell and the Two Witnesses is a message that is timely and urgent.*

*(2) The 2,300 Days of Hell and the Two Witnesses is an urgent message for you today. These scriptural topics not only tie together, they provide a hard hitting warning for everyone choosing the curses versus the blessings as shown in His Word! By reading this message you can prove His warnings for yourself. If not for your own preparation for your last days, then for those whom you love. Yes, the world as we know it is getting more and more difficult to be a part of as a professing Christian. Take hold of the simplicity*

*which is in Christ. He who was in the beginning wants you to be aware of what is coming. The sifting is happening. Since having heard Joseph Dumond's explanation of these prophecies, I have seen the proverbial hedge about me and my family as a result of this understanding. Being in His covenant brings this blessing. It comes from the same promise that speaks of the curses of choosing otherwise. The understanding you gain from this reference book provides what the Patriarchs longed to gain from what was given to them so long ago. It wasn't for their day but it is for yours. It's real and it's current. Terrifying, yet awesome. Before life sinks your hope, reach out and grab hold of this book to help your perspective of what is happening and why. With this understanding comes great peace.*

*M.H., Texas*

*Prior to Sukkot of 2013, I had never heard of Joseph Dumond, nor of his writings. He was the main speaker at our Sukkot gathering, so I was able to hear him every day and was absolutely floored at what he presented. I was already familiar with some of the information, but much of it was new to me.*

*I do not trust teachings that are based on single verses pulled out of context, so the fact that Joe backed everything up with large amounts of Scripture, whole chapters at times, helped me to accept many of the new ideas he presented. Those ideas filled gaps in my understanding of things ranging from how the Jubilee Years were figured, who and where the "lost" ten tribes of Israel are, and why it is so very important to ALL those who love the Messiah to keep ALL the commands that He gave to us. That includes ALL the Sabbaths, from the weekly 7th day thru the Holy Days and the Sabbatical Years.*

*The last few years it has been frustrating and confusing to see how believers worldwide are suffering in Yeshua's name—I now understand that these things are happening in part because so much of the Bible has been taught incorrectly and the people have been misled. Scripture is filled with conditional words..."IF this, THEN that"..."If you DON'T, then I WILL..." Blessings and curses aren't detailed just to fill up space. Our Almighty Elohim had them put there for a reason and we have suffered greatly by not knowing and understanding about them.*

*The presentations that Joe gave during Sukkot have been made into wonderful videos, available on Facebook and YouTube so that anyone can learn what they need. We need to study to show ourselves approved—not just accept what Joe or any other teacher tells us to believe. Because this is such an important message, I encourage everyone to start their study NOW—the time is short... you NEED to understand WHY you should prepare to keep the next Sabbatical Year, starting Aviv 2016!*

*P.P. Tennessee*

*I, too, like most of the "Believers" in our present world, was asleep; asleep to much of the Truth—and most definitely asleep to the Truth contained within this book! It is time to awaken from our sleep and put on Strength! We will need it as we close out this final chapter in the History of this world as we know it.*

*Joseph Dumond has written an excellent study on the Sabbatical and Jubilee Cycles as they are contained in Scripture—uncovering many mysteries that have been hidden from YHVH's people for centuries. This book has opened my understanding of Scripture and the world around us like no other book than perhaps Scripture itself. The detail and charts within this book are stunning to say the least— they completely remove any and all doubts of where we are in our Father's Timeline. The details are stunning to see when they are laid out so plainly. I have never read a book as succinct at explaining a Biblical Truth as this one. The charts are many—and they are necessary for your understanding. There is so much Scriptural documentation to back up the premise of this teaching!*

*It is beyond time to Wake Up! It is time to see what is staring back at us through the pages of Scripture and know that this very Divine plan that YHVH has orchestrated on our behalf is proceeding just as He saw it would. We must begin at Genesis 1:1 all over again with this knowledge and apply it to all Scripture to uncover this mystery of 120 Jubilee Cycles that our Father implemented long ago after the Great Flood of Noah.*

*We must come to understand the importance NOW of observing His Cycles of time which will include the next Sabbath Year of 2016. There is no time left to assume, to play church games or to trust that our "leaders" will lead us into all Truth. They have not done so, nor can they. It is YOUR responsibility to seek out the Truth! It is then your responsibility to ask the Holy One to send you His Spirit TO lead you into that Truth, just as Scripture promises us He will! Once you read this book and grasp it's content, you will then, in fact, be able to "prove all things, hold fast to that which is good." (1 Thess. 5:21) This book? This book is GOOD!*

*My life has been changed by 3 books so far. The first, being Scripture itself. The second, being one in which I learned my identity as a Hebrew woman. But this one—it shows me why and what to do about it like no other! It has forever changed my life!*

*I will forever be thankful for Mr. Dumond's many endless sacrifices in bringing The Prophecies of Abraham to us; to those who hunger and thirst after Righteousness. For those who needed more than what had been offered thru the rituals of all the current "movements" be they the* "church" or within "messianic-ism." The Truth presented in this book has been there all along—waiting for someone with the right heart, strength and perseverance to uncover it. That person has been found and he has done a most excellent job in presenting that Truth thru' The Prophecies of Abraham.

Few things in life change your perspective—this book has changed my perspective. I will never view Scripture the same way—nor our responsibility to our Father's Loving Commands ever again.

Truly, you never know you've been asleep till you wake up—it's time to wake up, folks. NOW is the time to know and understand these things. Now may be your last opportunity to do so. Don't wait—order this book now!

Don't wait—order this book now.

This review is from: Remembering The Sabbatical Years of 2016: Breaking The Curses By Obedience (Paperback)

This book is by far the best resource on the topic of the Sabbatical and Jubilee Years as recorded in Scripture. The Author has done an excellent job of breaking down each and every previous argument—proving beyond a doubt his point like no one else has done thus far. Once you read it, you, too, will understand their importance and relevance to our history and our future better than most scholars! Read and study this book to understand this topic—you will then understand your evening news and the newspaper like never before. Be prepared—what is coming is not being taught anywhere else and it is information that you NEED to know; the sooner the better for you and your family!

J.D. South Carolina

How Joseph's presentation on Aug 2nd-3rd, 2014 has impacted my life:

*I would like to share my thoughts about the recent meeting I attended in which Joseph Dumond shared his teachings. He gave a somewhat detailed overview of the Land Sabbatical and Jubilee years; the curses of Leviticus 26 and how they are impacting us today; our ancestral heritage; the blood moons and eclipses of this and next year; an overview of the timeline of this current Jubilee cycle; and last but not least, question and answer sessions throughout our two day gathering.*

*Our gathering was attended mostly by folks who are pretty well acquainted with Joseph's teachings, but also some who were new to these teachings. Overall, the room was filled with a positive energy and expectation of information. This was not going to be one of the ho-hum messages we get in our local churches... and it certainly was not.*

*The history of the wanderings of the northern ten tribes of ancient Israel was once a mainstay teaching of my church culture. It showed us where we, the Anglo-Americans, came from and why our nation had the tremendous blessings we have enjoyed for 200 years, as well as what God's overall plan for the whole house of Israel was from the beginning. Sadly, over the decades that teaching has been put aside. It is still believed, but not overtly taught. That Joseph has rekindled this teaching in his presentation is refreshing.*

*Our church also used to teach all that they understood about the land Sabbath, which was minutely basic, and the timing of its observance was based upon when that person was baptized, because no one knew when the Jubilees were in times past; and only those who had farms or backyard gardens were encouraged to keep it. That was the bulk of the teaching we received in our area. In the past 42 years I have been in my church, and having listened to more than a dozen pastors who have been in the areas I have lived in, and add to that all the speaking elders, deacons, and sermons at the various Feast sites I've been to in all those years,*

*I have probably heard a message about the land Sabbath only twice. Joseph's understanding of all the facets of the Sabbatical and Jubilee cycles goes in-depth.*

*How has Joseph's teaching of this very important subject affected my life... TREMENDOUSLY! First of all, it is part of the fourth commandment—the test command. We have never been taught that it is just as important, just as expected to be observed as the 7th day Sabbath and the Holy Days. Granted, what is not understood cannot be taught in its fullness, until now. Understanding of this vital scriptural point has been opened up and it is time for all who call themselves followers of Christ our Savior to wake-up, pay attention, learn, and do.*

*Joseph's presentation of the seven year Land Sabbaths and the Jubilees is so eye-opening that it will humble you to repentance of our negligence, though through ignorance. When we came to the understanding of the need to change from Sunday-keeping to 7th day Sabbath keeping, and from the world's holidays to God's specific Holy Days we did the same thing... we repented of our negligence out of our ignorance and thanked Him for showing us the truth of how He wants us to live within His 10 instructions, judgments and statutes. The same is true today... He has opened the understanding of the Sabbatical and Jubilee years, and it is awesome.*

*On top of this, if you read your Bible, Leviticus 26 lists Blessings and Cursings. Now, our ministry taught us that by virtue of the fact that we were members of our church we would receive all the blessings because we keep the Sabbath and Holy Days. The curses were relegated to those nations in conflict with ancient Israel and/or people/nations in the Tribulation and Day of the Lord sometime in the future whenever the end-times come. That's what I got out of what they taught, and that was decades ago.*

*Our God has said that if we observe to do His commandments, judgments and statutes, then we can expect to live with these blessings upon us; but if we are rebellious and do not keep all the parts of that Covenant ratified at Mt. Sinai (Ex. 19:1-Ex. 24:11)... which Covenant our Savior kept to the letter, and then told His disciples (extending to all who are baptized into the New Covenant) keep the Commandments (John 14:15, 21; 15:10), which includes the judgments and statutes... if you will NOT keep them, then expect the curses to come upon you—individually and nationally. The LORD God of the Old Testament plainly expressed that these curses would become compounded until there was repentance. If we say we are in covenant with Him, He then expects us to follow the terms of the Covenant. This happened to ancient Israel... first the northern 10 tribes; and later the southern tribes. Only the southern tribes were made to understand that the length of the 70-year sentence of captivity was itself due to the fact that the nation of Israel as a whole had not kept the Sabbatical years for 70 times. God intended that the land have a rest. We never understood that before.*

*Which brings us to the timeline of the Jubilees. Joseph has been able to show that God has given mankind a period of time of stewardship over the earth... 120 Jubilee cycles, of which we are nearly in the middle of the last cycle before the 120th Jubilee. This 120th Jubilee is when all humanity will be released from the clutches of the evil one who has been against God and His creation and plan of salvation since his own rebellion. It is the time of entering into the REST of the LORD. The Jubilee's were periods of release of indenture—freedom. How does that impact me? I have been jubilant to realize that there is so much more order in God's plan than I ever realized or was taught before. Now there is no question mark hanging over me as to when is this all going to end, and when is the Kingdom finally going to come.*

*Joseph has been able to lay out the Leviticus 26 curses overtop the timeline of these last 7 year Sabbatical cycles within the current Jubilee cycle, and show how those curses line up with events of our time from the last Jubilee to our present day.*

*This is astounding to understand. This information has always been in our Bibles, there for us to read, and we did read it but did not see it as though a veil was still over our eyes. Now that veil is being lifted for those who will see.*

*Lastly, Joseph's teaching of the blood moons and eclipses during these years of 2014-2015 were amazing to see. Not only does he explain what the red and dark moons represent by Hebrew beliefs of ages past, carried down to today, but when you lay these astronomical moon days upon both the Hebrew calculated calendar, which the Jews and the majority of the 7th day Sabbath-keepers use, next to the new crescent sighted moon that is being revived and in fact the correct calendar to observe—wow, it was awesome and nearly everyone in the room sucked in their breath at the same time because it plainly showed which calendar is the correct one.*

*How has this teaching affected my life? Once again I say... tremendously! I am awed; I am humbled; I am repentant; I am thankful; I am exuberant and filled with passion for it as when I began my journey with my Savior well over 40 years ago. Now I have a light shining on the rest of the path of my walk toward the Kingdom. I am grateful... grateful to our Savior for revealing this information at this time just prior to the opening of the seals of Revelation 6, and grateful to Joseph for persevering in sharing what he has learned over these years.*

*Since stumbling into Joseph's website accidently two years ago, I have been stirred to much deeper personal Bible study and have come to understand things I never saw before.*

*The major and minor prophets nearly jump off the page now, whereas it was difficult and tedious reading because I had never been shown how those things were written for today and how they would impact my life and my family because of our ignorant disobedience.*

*It is God who reveals knowledge, and for those who are willing to look at it honestly in seeking His will in their lives, He will open their eyes so they may see. With that He gives a space of time to make choices of repentance and a turning around to follow His way. The whole house of Israel has been given way more than 2,000 years to repent of their wrongdoings and turn around. Is God patient? I would say so. Are these issues relevant for today? Absolutely.*

*If Joseph is correct, and I think he is, that we are almost in the middle of this last Jubilee cycle, and that this coming Sabbatical year beginning Abib 2016 is the last opportunity we, as a set-apart people, have to finally get it right concerning being obedient to the test command... may the veil be lifted off our eyes so we can see it and do it.*

C. S. Ohio

http://www.asis.com/users/stag/royalty.html

SOURCE: "Royal Lines from Zarah and Pharez Judah," (1937). http://www.angelfire.com/alt2/antichrist/royalgene.html.

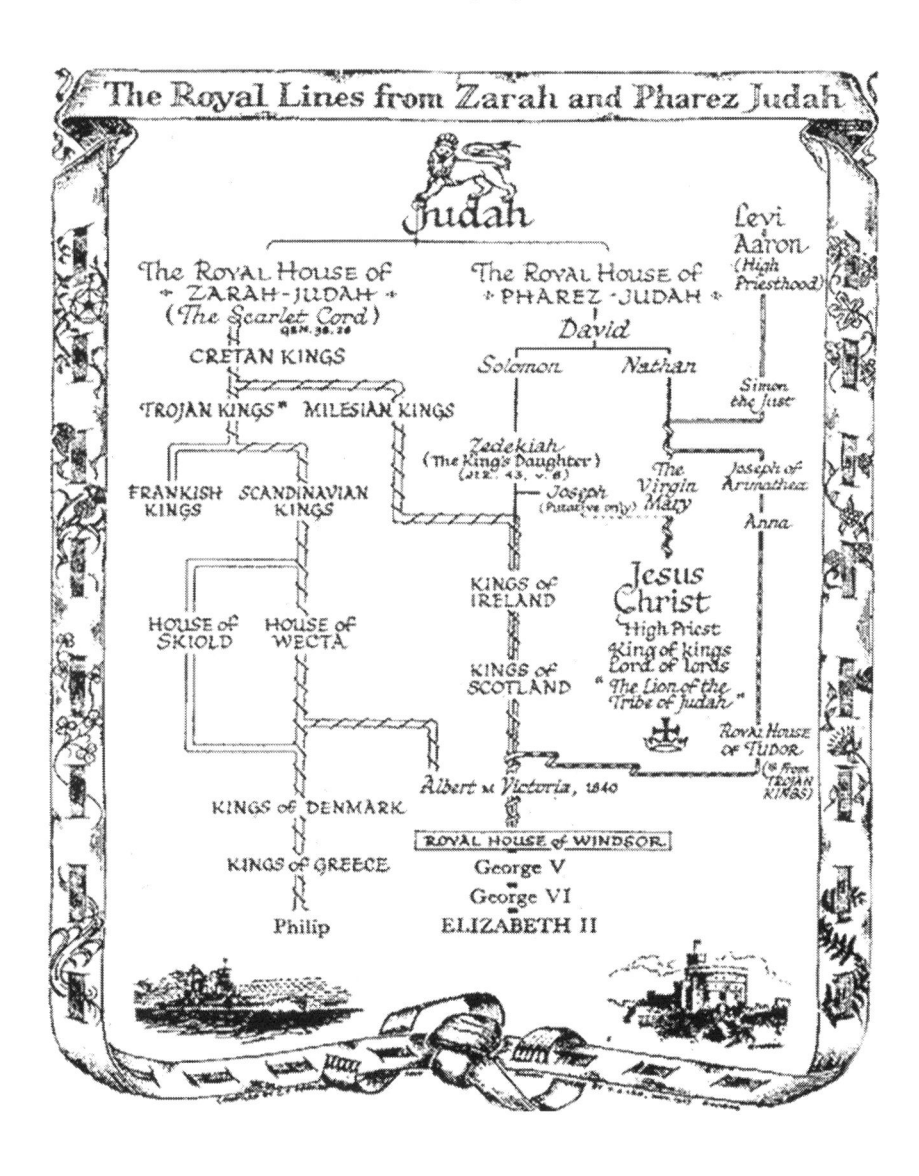

# GOD BLESS OUR GRACIOUS QUEEN
### And Blessed Be The Lord Our God, Which Delighted In Her To Set Her On His Throne

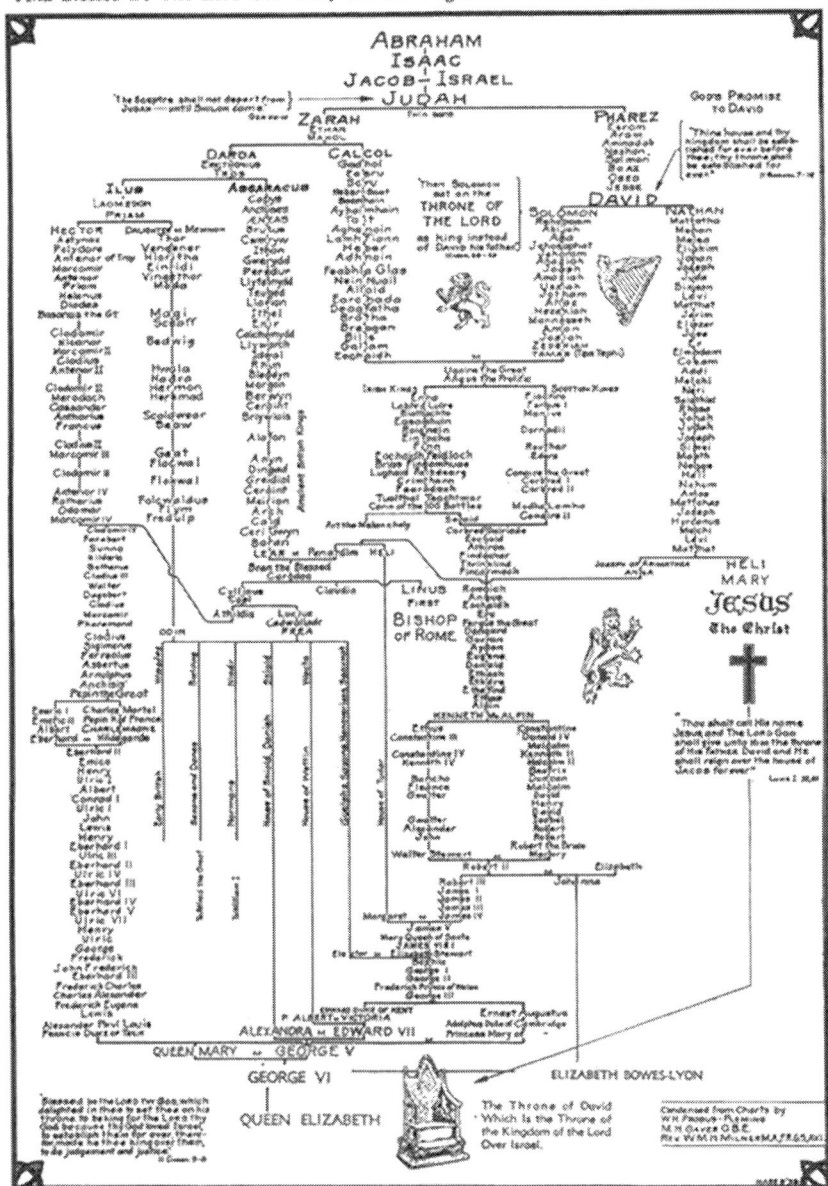

## THE GENEALOGY OF QUEEN ELIZABETH II

# Adam to the Queen of England

Source: *Judah's Sceptre and Joseph's Birthright* by J.H. Allen Edited, corrected by Joseph F Dumond according to the Sabbatical cycles.

1. Adam, Eve
2. Seth
3. Enos
4. Cainan
5. Mahalaleel
6. Jared
7. Enoch
8. Methusaleh
9. Lamech
10. Noah, Naamah
11. Shem
12. Arphaxad
13. alah
14. Heber
15. Peleg
16. Reu
17. Serug
18. Nahor
19. Terah, Amtheta
20. Abraham, Sarah
21. Isaac, Rebekah
22. Jacob, Leah
23. Judah, Tamar
24. Perez 24 Zerah
25. Hezron 25 Dardanus (Darda) 25 Calchol (Cercrops)
26. Aram 26 Erictanus
27. Aminadab 27 Tros (Troy)
28. Naasson 28 Laomedon
29. Salmon 29 Priamus (Priam)
30. Boaz, Ruth 30 Aeneas
31. Obed
32. Jesse

## Kings in Palestine *

(Dates are years person served as King)

33  K. David (B.C. 1010 - 970), Bathsheba
32  K. Solomon (B.C. 970 - 930), Naamah

## Kings of Judah *

33  K. Rehoboam (B.C. 930 - 913), Maacah
34  K. Abijah (B.C. 913 - 910)
35  K. Asa (B.C. 910 - 869), Azubah
36  K. Jehoshaphat (B.C. 872 - 848**)
37  K. Jehoram (B.C. 853 - 841**), Athaliah
38  K. Ahaziah (B.C. 841), Zibiah
39  K. Joash (Jehoash) (B.C. 835 - 796), Jehoaddan
40  K. Amaziah (B.C. 796 - 767), Jecholiah
41  K. Azariah (Uzziah) (B.C. 792 - 740**), Jerusha
42  K. Jotham (B.C. 750 - 732**)
43  K. Ahaz (B.C. 735 - 715**), Abi
44  K. Hezekiah (B.C. 715 - 686), Hephzibah
45  K. Manasseh (B.C. 696 - 642**), Meshullemeth
46  K. Amon (B.C. 642 - 640), Jedidiah
47  K. Josiah (B.C. 640 - 609), Mamutah
48  K. Jehoahaz (Shallum) (B.C. 609)
49  K. Jehoiakim (B.C. 609 - 598)
50  K. Jehoiachin (B.C. 598 - 597)
51  K. Zedekiah (B.C. 597 - 586).

## Irish Kings

51  Q. Tea Tephi (b. B.C. 565), marries Herremon, a Prince of the scarlet thread
52  K. Irial Faidh (reigned 10 years)
53  K. Eithriall (reigned 20 years)
54  Follain
55  K. Tighernmas (reigned 50 years)
56  Eanbotha

57   Smiorguil
58   K. Fiachadh Labhriane (reigned 24 years)
59   K. Aongus Ollmuchaidh (reigned 21 years)
60   Maoin
61   K. Rotheachta (reigned 25 years)
62   Dein
63   K. Siorna Saoghalach (reigned 21 years)
64   Oholla Olchaoin.
65   K. Giallchadh (reigned 9 years)
66   K. Aodhain Glas (reigned 20 years)
67   K. Simeon Breac (reigned 7 years)
68   K. Muirteadach Bolgrach (reigned 4 years)
69   K. Fiachadh Toigrach (reigned 7 years)
70   K. Duach Laidhrach (reigned 10 years)
71   Eochaidh Buailgllerg.
72   K. Ugaine More the Great (reigned 30 years)
73   K. Cobhthach Coalbreag (reigned 30 years)
74   Meilage
75   K. Jaran Gleofathach (reigned 7 years)
76   K. Coula Cruaidh Cealgach (reigned 25 years)
77   K. Oiliolla Caisfhiachach (reigned 28 years)
78   K. Eochaidh Foltleathan (reigned 11 years)
79   K. Aongns Tuirmheach Teamharch (reigned 30 years)
80   K. Eana Aighneach (reigned 28 years)
81   Labhra Suire.
82   Blathucha
83   Easamhuin Famhua.
84   Roighnein Ruadh
85   Finlogha
86   Fian
87   K. Eodchaidh Feidhlioch (reigned 12 years)
88   Fineamhuas
89   K. Lughaidh Raidhdearg.
90   K. Criomhthan Niadhnar (reigned 16 years)
91   Fearaidhach Fion Feachtnuigh.
92   K. Fiachadh Fionoluidh (reigned 20 years)
93   K. Tuathal Teachtmar (reigned 40 years)
94   K. Coun Ceadchathach (reigned 20 years)

95   K. Arb Aonflier (reigned 30 years)
96   K. Cormae Usada (reigned 40 years)
97   K. Caibre Liffeachair (reigned 27 years)
98   K. Fiachadh Sreabthuine (reigned 30 years.)
99   K. Muireadhach Tireach (reigned 30 years)
100  K. Eochaidh Moigmeodhin (reigned 7 years.)
101  K. Nail of the Nine Hostages.
102  Eogan
103  K. Murireadhach
104  Earca.

## Kings of Argyleshire

105  K. Fergus More (A.D. 487)
106  K. Dongard (d. 457)
107  K. Conran (d. 535)
108  K. Aidan (d. 604)
109  K. Eugene IV. (d. 622)
110  K. Donald IV. (d. 650)
111  Dongard
112  K. Eugene. V. (d. 692)
113  Findan
114  K. Eugene VII. (d. A.D. 721), Spondan
115  K. Etfinus (d. A.D. 761), Fergina
116  K. Achaius (d. A.D. 819), Fergusia
117  K. Alpin (d. A.D. 834)

## Sovereigns of Scotland

118  K. Kenneth I. (842 - 858)
119  K. Constantin I. (862 - 876)
120  K. Donald II. (889 - 900)
121  K. Malcolm I. (943 - 954)
122  K. Kenneth II. (971 - 995, d. A.D. 995)
123  K. Malcolm II. (1005 - 1034, d. A.D. 1034)
124  Bethoc, married to Crinan, Mormaer of Atholl and lay abott of Dunkeld
125  K. Duncan I. (1034 - 1040, d. A.D. 1040), Sybil

126  K. Malcolm III. Canmore (A.D. 1058 - 1093), Margaret of England
127  K. David I. (1124 - 1153, d. A.D. 1153), Matilda of Huntingdon
128  Prince Henry (d. A.D. 1152), Ada of Surrey
129  Earl David of Huntingdon (d. A.D. 1219), Matilda of Chester
130  Isobel m. Robert Bruce III
131  Robert Bruce IV. m. Isobel of Gloucester
132  Robert Bruce V. m. Martha of Carrick
133  K. Robert I. (The Bruce) (A.D. 1306 - 1329), Isobel, daughter of Earl of Mar
134  Marjorie Bruce m. Walter Stewart III
135  K. Robert II. (b. 1317, 1371 - 1390, d. A.D. 1390), Euphemia of Ross (d. A.D. 1376)
136  K. Robert III. (b. 1337, 1390 - 1406, d. A.D. 1406), Arabella Drummond (d. A.D. 1401)
137  K. James I. (A.D. 1406 - 1437), Joan Beaufort
138  K. James II. (b. 1430, 1437 - 1460, d. A.D. 1460), Margaret of Gueldres (d. A.D. 1463)
139  K. James III. (b. 1451, 1460 - 1488, d. A.D. 1488), Margaret of Denmark (d. A.D. 1486)
140  K. James IV. (b. 1473, 1488 - 1513, d. A.D. 1543), Margaret of England (d. A.D. 1539)
141  K. James V. (b. 1513, 1513 - 1542, d. A.D. 1542), Mary of Lorraine (d. A.D. 1560)
142  Q. Mary (also known as *Mary, Queen of Scots*) (b. 1542, 1542 - 1567, d. A.D. 1587), Lord Henry Darnley (d. 1567). (Mary became Queen when she was just six days old. She was deposed as Queen in 1567 and was executed in 1587).

## Sovereigns of Great Britain

143  K. James VI. and I. (A.D. 1603 - 1625), Ann of Denmark. This King James was known as *King James VI of Scotland* when he reigned over that country from 1567 to 1625. He was known in England as *King James I* when he also ruled that country from 1603 to 1625. He was the first King over both Scotland and England.
144  Princess Elizabeth (d. 1662), Frederick V, Elector Palatine.
145  Princess Sophia, (d. 1714), m. Duke Ernest of Brunswick (d. 1698).
146  K. George I. (1714 - 1727), Sophia Dorothea of Zelle (1667 - 1726).

147 K. George II. (b. 1683, 1727 - 1760), Princess Caroline of Brandenburg - Anspach (1683 - 1737).
148 Prince Frederick Lewis of Wales (1707 - 1751), Princess Augusta of Saxe - Gotha - Altenberg.
149 K. George III. (b. 1738, 1760 - 1820), Princess Sophia of Mecklenburgh - Strelitz (1744 - 1818).
150 Duke Edward of Kent (1767 - 1820), Princess Victoria of Saxe - Coburg (d. 1861)
151 Q. Victoria (b. 1819, 1837 - 1901), Prince Albert of Saxe - Coburg & Gotha.
152 K. Edward VII. (b. 1841, 1901 - 1910), Princess Alexandra
153 K. George V. (b. 1865, 1910 - 1936), Princess Mary
154 K. George VI. (b. 1895, 1936 - 1952), Lady Elizabeth Bowes - Lyon (Queen Elizabeth, The Queen Mother) (b. 1900, d. 2002)
155 Q. Elizabeth II (b. 1926, 1952 to Present), Philip Duke of Edinburgh

Printed in Great Britain
by Amazon